no
started only
5·6 pages

swordfish

Sword

A TRUE STORY OF AMBITION,

DAVID McCLINTICK

PANTHEON BOOKS • NEW YORK

Library of Congress Cataloging-in-Publication Data

McClintick, David.
Swordfish : a true story of ambition, savagery, and betrayal / David McClintick.
p. cm.
Includes index.
ISBN 0-679-42019-3
1. Narcotics, Control of—United States. 2. Narcotic enforcement agents—United States. 3. United States. Drug Enforcement Administration. 4. Drug traffic—United States. I. Title.
HV5825.M358 1993
363.4'5'0973—dc20   92-50777
CIP

Manufactured in the United States of America

First Edition
9 8 7 6 5 4 3 2 1

TO JOANNA AND JUDY

CONTENTS

AUTHOR'S NOTE TO READER

This is a work of nonfiction. Every character, episode, scene, weather reference, conversation, and name is real (except for pseudonyms assigned to two minor characters for security reasons). None of the dialogue is invented. Most conversations, in fact, were secretly recorded as they occurred, an unusual circumstance that allows me to tell the story of Swordfish and its people with special intensity and intimacy. People are the heart of *Swordfish*—people living under life-threatening pressure, people grappling with the psychological quagmire of espionage, people pursuing ambitions both grand and petty in occasionally destructive ways.

"I have never heard such a tale in my life. This poor jury—their minds are going to be boggled."

The Honorable Lenore C. Nesbitt
United States District Judge
Southern District of Florida
Miami, Florida

Comment to lawyers about Operation
Swordfish and Robert Darias out of the
presence of the jury.

CAST

Principal Characters

Robert Darias—a spy for the United States Government

Carol Cooper—Darias's control; a Special Agent of the Federal Drug Enforcement Administration (undercover Carol Collins)

Marlene Navarro—Darias's target; the chief of North American operations and finance for a large syndicate of the Colombian narcotics mafia.

Carlos Jader Alvarez—Navarro's boss; a godfather of the Colombian mafia

Thomas J. Clifford—the DEA's chief of intelligence in Miami and the founder of Operation Swordfish (undercover Thomas Belise)

Frank Chellino—DEA Special Agent (undercover Frank Dean)

Paul Sennett—DEA Special Agent (undercover Paul Shafer)

Supporting Characters

Amelia Darias—Robert's wife

Robert Russo—a DEA intelligence analyst (undercover Robert Caruso)

Felipe Calderon—a Colombian banker and spy for the United States Government

The family of Carlos Jader Alvarez—*Wives:* Marina Murrillo and Maria Lilia Rojas; *Children:* Zuleika, Yidid, Xouix, and Wilkander

Other Key Characters

DEA Special Agents

Edwin Hernandez (undercover Manolo Ramos)
Nick Zapata (undercover Nicolas Sandoval)
José Hinojosa (undercover Juan Carlos Stabile)
David Wilson
Steven Gibbs
Robert Candelaria

DEA Group Supervisors and Managers—Miami Field Division

Peter F. Gruden—Special Agent in Charge
Sylvester B. "Sam" Billbrough—Associate Special Agent in Charge
Jack Lloyd—Assistant Special Agent in Charge
Dan Hoerner
Jeff Scharlatt

DEA Executives—Washington, D.C.

John C. Lawn—Deputy Administrator
Ronald J. Caffrey—Chief of Cocaine Investigations

Department of Justice—Washington, D.C.

William French Smith—the Attorney General of the United States
Charles W. Blau—Deputy Associate Attorney General (formerly
    chief of the Narcotics and Dangerous Drug Section and supervisor
    of Operation Greenback)
Edward S.G. Dennis, Jr.—Chief of the Narcotics and Dangerous
    Drug Section and later Assistant Attorney General in charge of the
    Criminal Division

Department of State—Caracas, Venezuela

Ludlow "Kim" Flower—Acting United States Ambassador

The White House

President Ronald Reagan
Vice President George Bush
Admiral Daniel Murphy—Chief of Staff for the Vice President

Prosecutors

Stanley Marcus—the United States Attorney for the Southern District
    of Florida
Myles H. Malman
Susan Tarbe
Gregory Bruce English
Michael S. Pasano
Mark P. Schnapp

Defense Attorneys

Raymond J. Takiff
Michael Brodsky
Roy Black

U.S. District Judges

Alcee L. Hastings
William M. Hoeveler
Lenore C. Nesbitt

Targets of Operation Swordfish

The Bankers:
Lionel Paytubi—Great American Bank of Dade County
Manuel Sanchez—Bank of Miami and Intercontinental Bank

The Colombian Drug Syndicates:
José Antonio "Pepe" Cabrera Sarmiento (also known as Juan
    Molina)
Juan Mata Ballesteros
Santiago Ocampo
Isaac Kattan
José Estupinan
Jaime Murcia
Luis Antonio Rodriguez (also known as Luis Fabio Rodriguez)
Carlos Alvarado (also known as Tocayo)
Oscar Garcia (also known as "El Barrigoncito")
Teodoro Terselich (also known as "Baltazar" and "Ivan")
Bertha Paez
Nelson Batista
Ricardo Pavon
Said Pavon
Carmenza Valenzuela
Barbara Mouzin
Dorothy Hackett

The Humberto Garcia Group:
Humberto Garcia Rivero
Antonio Uribe Calle
"The Colombian Kids"

Lawyers for Marlene Navarro

> Lester M. Rogers
> Harvey Rogers

Lawyer for José Antonio Cabrera

> S. David Jaffe

The Government of Colombia

> Belisario Betancur—the President
> Juvenal Betancur—his brother
> Rodrigo Lara Bonilla—the Minister of Justice

The Government of Venezuela

> Rene de Sola—the President of the Supreme Court
> José Manzo Gonzalez—the Minister of Justice

The M-19 Guerrillas

> Edgar Helmut Garcia Villamizar
> Orlando Garcia Villamizar
> Pedro Pablo Silva

The People of Gachalá

> Bernardo Acosta
> Guillermo Alvarado
> Ana Elvira Zarate de Alvarado
> Victor Manuel Reyes Pena
> Efrain Cortes

The Bail Bondsman

> Arthur J. "Artie" Balletti

The Interior Designers/Decorators

> Gustavo Delgado
> Dick Lawrence

part one

THE SPY

Red and black—friend of Jack
Red and yellow—kill a fellow.

Rhyme taught to Miami schoolchildren to
distinguish the king snake, which is harmless,
from the coral snake, which is lethal.

1

ROBERT DARIAS DROVE east into a white haze that muted the green of the majestic Australian pines along the Tamiami Trail. It was the late morning of Monday, December 22, 1980, and Darias was desperate. He had spent the last several days in bed, adrift in the fitful sleep of depression, deepened by the Christmas blues.

Darias had been despondent for much of the past two years, ever since a federal judge in Miami sentenced him to prison rather than probation for evading taxes on real estate profits. Although he had served only seventy-six days at a minimum security facility, the experience had left him—as well as his proud Cuban family—profoundly ashamed.

The tax case was only part of a larger nightmare. While Darias was in federal prison, the Florida state attorney's office had charged him with "grand theft" in some of his real estate deals. Demoralized, and lacking good legal counsel, he decided that he had no choice but to plead guilty. At age forty-six, after half a lifetime of decent living, he had been marked as a felon, twice over.

As a Cuban exile doing business in the United States, Darias had been undeniably negligent, and more than a bit cavalier, about American business practices and tax obligations, which were much stricter than those in Cuba. He had cut corners, and he was not proud of his conduct. But Darias's intent had not been criminal. And the judge in the theft case, sensing as much, had deferred formal determination of guilt while giving him an opportunity to repay the $7,000 that he allegedly had misapplied.

In recent months, however, Darias had found it difficult to make the $259 monthly payments he'd agreed to. He had run out of money. He had run out of credit. In addition to his real estate debts, he owed the IRS more than $200,000. His most recent business venture— selling American electronic equipment to rich businessmen along the Caribbean coast of Colombia—had failed. He was living on loans from his in-laws, who were paying for everything, including his Christmas gifts to his wife and six-year-old daughter. His self-respect was nearly gone.

Darias had risen on this balmy December morning determined to attack his problems before Christmas. He was prepared to do just about anything to avoid wallowing in despair through the long holiday period. Christmas was an even bigger event for Cubans than for Americans, a two-week extravaganza of conviviality, celebrated day and night, extending through the Festival of the Three Kings on January 6.

He drove in silence, the radio off, as shoppers swelled the traffic. The Tamiami Trail, a busy, four-lane boulevard divided by a strip of ratty tropical grass, passed beneath the Florida Turnpike at 116th Avenue and then formed a border between the sparse campus of the new Florida International University to the south, and the community of Sweetwater, which was fast becoming a haven for refugees from the deposed Somoza regime in Nicaragua. The word "Tamiami" dominated this part of suburban Miami, ten miles due west of Little Havana and downtown. In addition to the Tamiami Trail, there was the Tamiami Park, the Tamiami Mall, the Tamiami Airport, and dozens of stores and churches that bore the name. "Tamiami" wasn't a Seminole word, as some people assumed, but only an abbreviation of "Tampa-to-Miami," the name given to the road after it had been blasted through the Everglades and opened to traffic in the 1920s. Despite considerable real estate development of the swampy marshland, the area still was splotched by unclaimed stands of jungle that supplied the spongy lawns of nearby homes with profuse quantities of fire ants and the occasional coral snake.

Darias's prolonged melancholy baffled him. It had no precedent in his life. He had always been a dynamic and versatile man, an optimist, confident that he could weather any crisis. And as humiliating as his prison term for tax fraud had been, it had not been his first experience with imprisonment, or with humiliation. That had come nearly two decades earlier, in Cuba, at the Bay of Pigs. Darias had been the second-in-command of one of the six CIA-trained battalions that had gone ashore at Playa Giron in April of 1961. In his blackest moments of recent years, he had always taken some solace from the conviction that nothing he would ever experience could match the horror of the Bay of Pigs debacle.

Abandoned by the Americans, members of the decimated brigade slogged through the swamps of southern Cuba seeking a means of escape. After three days without food or water, Darias and about 150 of his comrades were captured and jammed into a large truck that the

Cuban army had commandeered for transporting POWs to Havana. It was a refrigeration truck, sealable and airtight, and its refrigeration and ventilation units had been turned off. As the men were being loaded aboard, Darias and several other prisoners warned that with the doors of the truck closed the men would soon consume all available oxygen and be unable to breathe.

"Let them die, it will save us from shooting them!" yelled the Castro military supervisor, Osmani Cienfuegos, ordering the driver to seal the truck and depart.

The sounds of screaming, gagging, and retching inside the truck reached a crescendo about halfway through the eight-hour journey to Havana and then subsided to a low cacophony of cries and groans. When the truck arrived and the doors were opened, chilly evening air met the broiling filth of the van's stifling interior, and condensation set in. The moisture—a warm rain, actually—congealed with large quantities of vomit, feces, urine, and sweat, coating the prisoners and the inside of the vehicle with a hideous muck.

By the time Darias and the others were removed from the truck, nine of the men had died of suffocation and most of the others were ill and delirious from lack of oxygen.

As one of the ranking officers of the brigade, Darias was held that night in isolation at Castro's intelligence headquarters. He was told repeatedly that he would be executed if he did not give evidence against his comrades and go on television to denounce the United States. He refused. At dawn the next morning, he was taken from his cell, purportedly to be shot. Instead, he was questioned further. This routine was repeated on subsequent mornings. He still refused to talk. Eventually Darias and most of the others were transferred to a prison on the remote Isle of Pines, off the south coast of Cuba. Many of them feared they would never leave alive. The U.S. Government ransomed them 20 months later for $53 million in farm equipment and medical supplies.

The Bay of Pigs had been the most searing experience of Darias's life. It still haunted him. But it had never depressed him as much as his recent calamities.

He eased into the left-turn lane and headed north on 87th Avenue, a two-lane, undivided street through open pasture a mile outside the Palmetto Expressway and two miles west of the huge Miami International Airport. A friend of Darias had owned some of this land in years past and grazed cattle on it. Now it was checkered by tracts of new low-priced garden apartments, acre after acre of beige stucco with brown trim extending to the perfectly flat horizon. Coming from the mountainous island of Cuba, Darias had always been struck by the unrelenting flatness of Florida. The peninsula seemed stretched taut— the flattest place in North America.

Three miles north, 87th Avenue bisected the Doral County Club, one of the few islands of immaculately groomed opulence in the scruffy suburban sprawl. Just beyond the Doral, Darias turned into the Koger Executive Center, an enclave of contemporary two- and three-story office buildings in stark black and white, set in a quarter-square-mile of lawn, shade trees, and flower beds. Drivers instinctively slowed upon entering the Koger Center's parklike atmosphere, a sudden calm after the bustle of the bordering thoroughfares. The center's buildings were all named after middle-sized American cities (Albany, Richmond, Billings) and for aesthetic reasons bore only a few discreet signs identifying some of their occupants—insurance and real estate firms, high-technology companies, and federal government offices.

Darias parked next to the Phoenix Building, whose roof bore a large cluster of radio antennas. Wearing a jacket and tie for the first time in weeks, he was buzzed through a security door and spoke to a receptionist behind a bulletproof window festooned with blinking Christmas lights.

"I would like to talk to someone in charge of hiring for investigations," he said.

After about fifteen minutes, a husky, blond man in a navy blazer appeared, introduced himself as "Paul," and ushered Darias into a small, windowless room with two chairs and a table. Before asking Darias to be seated, the man searched him for concealed weapons.

"You understand we have to do this," he said with a smile.

"Of course," Darias said. "You must be careful."

There were no concealed weapons, except for the Walther PPK that the blond man carried in an ankle holster.

Darias was inside the Miami field headquarters of the Federal Drug Enforcement Administration. He had come to offer his services as a narcotics spy for the United States Government. He was entering a world far more treacherous than any he had ever known.

2

HE MAN IN THE BLAZER was Special Agent Paul Sennett of Group Three, the duty group for the month of December. Group Three was one of seven DEA Enforcement Groups—the agency's basic, all-purpose operating teams—based in Miami. With a dozen agents each, the groups were configured a bit like squads in a military combat battalion. In addition to their other responsibilities, they shared the "duty"—rotating it monthly—of screening unsolicited visits, calls, inquiries, and proffers of intelligence from people outside the agency.

Robert Darias was a "walk-in," a person unknown to the DEA who simply arrived on its doorstep offering information or services. A number of such people wandered into DEA field offices around the world each year, and most of them proved useless; either the individual or his information was faulty. They were screened carefully, however, in hopes of finding the rare walk-in who would become valuable.

At the table in the interview room, Darias summoned his usual poise, masking for the moment the depression that gripped him. He told Paul Sennett that in the course of doing business in Colombia over the past two years, he had learned a great deal about the burgeoning commerce in illegal narcotics between Latin America and the United States and thought perhaps the DEA could use his information.

Before detailing what he had seen, Darias sketched his own background. Born in Havana in 1934, he had lived in various cities in Cuba as a child, studied at the University of Havana for a few years and been enrolled in the law curriculum when Batista closed the university. His father had been a member of the Cuban legislature and a subcabinet minister in the Batista regime. The family had migrated to Miami shortly after Castro seized power in 1959.

Darias had married twice into families even more prominent than his own. His first wife was the daughter of the dean of medicine at the University of Havana. His second wife was the granddaughter and grandniece, respectively, of an architect and engineer who in the early part of the century had participated in the design and construction of some of the most distinguished buildings in Havana—the Capitol and the Presidential Palace—as well as the Central Highway, the main automobile route through Cuba.

Prior to the Bay of Pigs invasion, Darias had been trained by the CIA in espionage, sabotage, infiltration, weaponry, and guerrilla warfare and had participated in several secret incursions into Cuba as far back as ten months before the invasion. Although two decades had passed, he felt he still had an aptitude for intelligence work and perhaps could employ his experience in helping the DEA, specifically in investigating the drug traffickers that he had encountered recently.

"How did you meet these drug people?" Sennett asked.

"Some of them I met when I sold them air conditioners for their homes," Darias said, "big ten-ton air conditioners that I installed in their mansions along the coast of Colombia. I also sold them short-wave radios and remote-control electronic car starters, so they could start a car from fifty yards away if they were afraid somebody had put a bomb in it."

"How did you know they were in drugs?" Sennett asked.

"They talked very freely about drugs," Darias said. "I became friendly with some of them. I went to their parties. I was a guest on their yachts in Cartagena and Barranquilla."

"Did you get involved in the drug business yourself?" Sennett asked.

"No, never, I couldn't," Darias replied. "I'm against it." He paused, then added, "I know people in Miami, too, who are in this business, or who at least know a lot about it."

Sennett asked for names, and Darias made a list. Prominent on it was a Miami private detective, José Miguel Carvajal, a Cuban whom Darias had met in Colombia. They had introduced themselves to each other in a restaurant after overhearing each other's Cuban accents. José Carvajal later had introduced Darias to several people both in Miami and Colombia who turned out to be major drug dealers. There was an American pilot who flew large quantities of cocaine from Colombia to the United States. There was a Colombian lawyer who had business relationships with drug smugglers. There was a Miami bank vice president who laundered money for traffickers. And Darias had met a number of other drug people with no connection to José Carvajal.

Sennett was impressed. A few of the names were familiar to him as DEA targets, and he was confident that he would find most of them identified in the DEA's computer as having narcotics connections.

Sennett asked Darias why he was volunteering to help the DEA. "I am concerned as a citizen that drugs are ravaging this community and

this country," Darias said. "I would like to do what I can to help."
Not wanting to appear overly altruistic, he stopped short of telling
Sennett that he hated drugs perhaps more than the average person
because one of his daughters from his first marriage had nearly died
of narcotics addiction.

Darias added that he expected to be paid for his services and that
he was experiencing severe financial problems. "That's okay, everybody works for money," Sennett said, assuring Darias that if hired he
would be paid. The agent explained that before proceeding the DEA
would have to run a computerized background check on Darias.

"Fine, please do that," Darias said. "You will reassure us both."

"Do you have a criminal record?" Sennett asked, mentioning that
a lot of DEA informants did.

"I don't know if you would call it 'criminal,' " Darias replied with
a smile, and revealed that he had a "big problem with Internal Revenue." Shame overcame candor, however, and he did not volunteer
details of his prison sentence or the State of Florida "grand theft"
case. Sennett did not press, preferring to see what the background
check showed.

For use in the computers, Sennett photographed and fingerprinted
Darias and recorded his date of birth, social security number, and
other information. Sennett asked Darias to return on Monday, January 5, the first full business day after the holidays. By then, the
background check would be complete and they could discuss more
specifically how Darias might work for the DEA.

On his way home Darias felt better. Christmas was far from joyous,
but it was not as bleak as it might have been.

Paul Sennett ran Darias's name and other pertinent data through
four computer systems: the FBI's National Crime Information Center, or NCIC, which is the world's leading repository of identifying
data on people with criminal records of all types; the DEA's Narcotics
and Dangerous Drugs Information System, or NADDIS, the leading
data bank specializing in narcotics criminals; and the Dade County
and State of Florida criminal computers. None of the computers
contained any information on Robert Darias, despite his tax conviction and Florida prosecution.

Sennett was pleased. He had been impressed not only by the apparent quality of Darias's information but by Darias himself, his dyna-
mism and his obvious intelligence. Darias was different from most
Latins whom Sennett had met as a federal agent. He looked like a
Castilian gentleman, with a perfect Roman nose thrown in. Though

their exchange had been brief, Sennett and Darias had liked each other instinctively. They both had an easy laugh. They were both in their forties, a little older than most DEA agents. They both were big men. Like Darias, Sennett was a burly six-footer with a pronounced physical presence, a way of carrying himself that bespoke fitness and likely familiarity with contact sports or hard physical labor. And though neither was a braggart, it was clear that they had war stories to exchange. They both had heard shots fired in anger. In Churchill's phrase, they both had experienced the exhilaration of being "shot at without result." And they knew the dark side of violence as well.

Though Paul Sennett had played football in school and run marathons as an adult, he was best known within the Drug Enforcement Administration for physical dexterity and bravery in the line of duty. Sennett's first experience under fire was a shoot-out just two weeks after he graduated from the agents' academy and was assigned to the DEA field office in New York City. At about ten o'clock one evening, two Latin drug dealers surprised and shot two DEA undercover agents in a suite at the Sheraton Midtown Motor Inn on 42nd Street. As the gunmen rushed from the suite, leaving one agent dead and the other paralyzed from the armpits down, they encountered Paul Sennett and a fourth agent running along the hallway toward them. The agents and the gunmen opened fire on each other instantaneously. The gunmen missed, and both were mortally wounded by Sennett's bullets. It wasn't like the movies, however. Instead of collapsing when hit, one of the traffickers remained on his feet, frozen in shock, his gun still extended. In the frenzy of the moment, Sennett clubbed him to the floor, where he died within seconds.

After he was transferred to Miami a few years later, Paul Sennett, along with his colleagues in Group Three, was involved in other shootings in the course of arresting heavily armed drug dealers. For a period in the late 1970s and early 1980s, Miami's Group Three arrested more major narcotics smugglers than any other squad of agents in the entire DEA. The Group Three agents were a team of unusual competence and street savvy.

Among the twelve members of Group Three was one woman, Carol Cooper, who was Paul Sennett's partner. Cooper came from the small town of Dixon, Illinois—Ronald Reagan's boyhood home—and looked enough like Paul Sennett to be his sister—blonde with a ruddy complexion. Although by 1980 Cooper had been a DEA agent for less than three years, she already shared the Group Three reputation for poise under fire. Cooper also was known for a more unusual episode. She had been on the ground floor of the DEA building one

morning photocopying a stack of currency to be used in an undercover drug purchase. It was early, before the DEA receptionists came
on duty, and an unemployed convict just out of jail managed to slip
into the locked building. He surprised Cooper, knocked her to the
floor, and grabbed a bundle of hundred-dollar bills. Unarmed (her
gun was upstairs in her office), Cooper grabbed the thief's leg and
hung on as he made for the door. Big and muscular, the man lurched
along the corridor, beating her savagely to try to free himself. She
hung on. Other agents finally heard the commotion, and subdued the
man. Carol Cooper was hospitalized with a concussion and cracked
ribs.

She and Paul Sennett had become partners when they found that
they both liked to work lab cases. The DEA was discovering in those
years that the destruction of a single cocaine processing laboratory
could have a greater impact than the seizure of multiple cocaine
shipments. Sennett had studied chemistry in college and worked in the
chemical industry in his native New Jersey for a decade before joining
the DEA. Carol Cooper liked the challenge of lab investigations,
which were more complex than the usual drug case.

Lab cases arose only occasionally, however. There weren't many
narcotics labs in the United States, so Sennett and Cooper spent much
of their time on other investigations. Now their task was breaking in
a promising new spy.

3

OVERNMENT BUREAUCRACIES that collect intelligence and enforce criminal laws could not function without spies.

The Drug Enforcement Administration and the Federal Bureau of Investigation in particular, as well as big urban police departments, need spies to accomplish their most formidable task—infiltrating the massive criminal enterprises responsible for much major crime. Only if these criminal enterprises are penetrated in secrecy can they be prosecuted successfully. Since the enterprises are organized to prevent infiltration, the task thwarts ordinary investigative techniques. It demands the irregular qualities—the guile and subterfuge—of a spy, a spy classically defined: *a person employed by a government to obtain information secretly on a hostile entity, often through the use of false pretenses and other secret methods of infiltration.*

Spies have a spotty reputation in America. Only failed espionage is regularly publicized; successful spying by definition usually remains secret. And the core ingredient in spying, the calculated deception and betrayal of one person by another, is troubling if not repugnant to many people, even if the target is a criminal or a genuine enemy and the spy is an altruist risking his life. At best, spying is dirty.

Government bureaucracies are uncomfortable with their spies, whose security is a constant worry. The bureaucracy is embarrassed by its inability to function without spies and prefers to avoid publicly acknowledging their existence, much less their crucial role. The bureaucracy doesn't even use the word "spy." It prefers "informant," a somewhat demeaning term (only slightly less pejorative than "informer"), implying incorrectly that the spy's function is limited to "informing." In the spy's presence, to avoid offense, the bureaucracy calls him a "confidential informant" or the euphemistic "cooperating individual," abbreviated "CI," a term some spies like because it reminds them of "CIA."

Skilled spies are rare. People who are willing to work as spies often are not competent for the task. Those who are competent often are unwilling. Those who are both willing and competent often have ulterior motives or are impossible to control. For the few who qualify, the work is solitary, frustrating, and dangerous. The risks of failure, and of violent death, are high.

Three types of people generally function as government spies.

First are those whom the law enforcement agency attempts to recruit from its own ranks and train for prolonged undercover work. The agency usually finds that few of its people can succeed in this role. A spy must have imagination, flexibility, and ingenuity—an ability to improvise under pressure. Most law enforcement agents lack those qualities. They tend to be cautious, conservative, by-the-book survivors in bureaucracies that discourage originality.

The second category (for whom the labels "informant," "informer," and even "snitch" sometimes are appropriate) are people whom law enforcement agencies quietly catch in a crime and then induce to spy on their cohorts in exchange for lenient treatment. "Turning," or "flipping," the practice is called. This type presents a host of problems. While he may have excellent access to the criminal organization, his motives in cooperating with the government—determination to please his captors at all costs in order to avoid jail—may prompt him to lie, embellish, and be otherwise unreliable, or, equally important, *appear* unreliable to a jury if a case goes to court and the spy is required to testify.

The third group are the unusual people who become spies in a quirk of circumstance. They are in the right place at the right time. They have the right temperament and skills. And they are willing to exploit the opportunity. These people are not criminals themselves but know criminals or are in a position to get to know them without arousing suspicion. Some of these people are motivated by the large sums of money that the government pays its successful spies. Some of them want something other than money in exchange for their help. Some of them are repulsed by the particular criminal activity under investigation to such an extent that they feel compelled to help. Whatever their motives, and the motives usually are complex, these are the most effective spies of all—and the rarest.*

When Robert Darias returned to the DEA on Monday, January 5, 1981, Paul Sennett introduced him to Carol Cooper, who liked Darias

---

*Spies for law enforcement bodies such as the DEA and FBI beg comparison with CIA spies. While there are many similarities, particularly in modus operandi, they differ in purpose. DEA and FBI spies serve the ends of infiltrating, apprehending, and prosecuting criminals. CIA spies are concerned mainly with gathering political, military, and economic intelligence.

as much as Sennett did. "We feel we can use you, Bob, and we'd like to try," Sennett told Darias, "but we'll have to take it one case at a time. You'll have to prove yourself by making an actual case. If that works out, we'll go on from there."

"That's good," Darias said. "I'm ready."

Sennett and Cooper explained their goal: to have Darias infiltrate a narcotics smuggling organization and help them gather enough evidence to arrest and prosecute its members. Aware that the job was far easier described than done, Darias agreed to try. He proposed to start by contacting José Miguel Carvajal, the private detective through whom he had met drug dealers in Colombia and Miami. Sennett and Cooper agreed, and before the end of the day Darias was sitting in Carvajal's office in Coral Gables renewing their acquaintance and mentioning that he was now representing some people interested in purchasing a large quantity of narcotics for resale in New York.

If José Carvajal was surprised that Robert Darias had switched from the electronics business to narcotics trafficking, he did not show it. Drug smuggling had become ubiquitous in Miami, particularly in Latin circles. The staggering amounts of money that narcotics generated had seduced a large number of otherwise law-abiding people.

Carvajal sent Darias to see a man who operated a hair salon on Bird Road. The hairdresser sent him to a musician across town. The musician sent him to a photographer with a studio on Flagler Street. The photographer, Francisco Navia, turned out to be the man who had photographed Robert and Amelia Darias's wedding nine years earlier. Navia knew Amelia's parents. It was a quintessential Miami small world story, circa 1981, and Robert easily ingratiated himself with Navia. They chatted, and Navia indicated that he could supply Robert's clients with unlimited quantities of his product of the moment—Quaaludes. That seemed promising to Robert, who said he would be back in touch.

Robert didn't know precisely what Quaaludes were, but they sounded illegal and he hadn't revealed his ignorance to Navia. An hour later, inside the DEA office, Paul Sennett and Carol Cooper explained that selling Quaaludes—a dangerous, highly addictive hypnotic sedative in pill form—was just as serious a crime under the narcotics laws of the United States as selling cocaine or heroin. Quaaludes were smuggled into the United States from Latin America—Colombia in particular—and many of the same people trafficked in all three drugs. The agents were eager for Darias to proceed, so he arranged for a member of Francisco Navia's group to confer later that week with his "clients," Sennett and Cooper, whom Robert planned to introduce only as "Paul and Carol from New York." The meeting was to take place where many drug negotiations occurred—in an expansive parking lot, this time at the Midway Mall, a huge shopping center at the junction of the Palmetto and Dolphin expressways near the Miami International Airport. The participants rendezvoused just after dark on Friday, January 9, 1981. After extensive haggling, it was agreed that "Paul and Carol from New York" would purchase half a million Quaaludes at 85 cents each, or $425,000 cash. The suppliers wanted to conclude the deal that evening, but Paul demurred, saying that he and Carol were on their way out of town for the weekend. Actually, Sennett and Cooper wanted to give Group Three time to investigate Francisco Navia and his associates.

Darias kept everyone in touch by telephone until the talks climaxed the following Wednesday, January 14. One of Navia's men, using a van supplied by Paul Sennett, drove to a warehouse in southwest Miami, picked up a load of Quaaludes—a popular type known as Lemon 714s, and returned to a parking lot in front of Midway Ford, adjacent to the Midway Mall. Again, it was just after dark. As Francisco Navia looked on from his car in the shadows across the street, Paul and Carol spot-checked the half-million pills, which were in packages in the rear of the van, and the Navia driver inspected the buyers' money, $425,000 in U.S. currency packed neatly in a suitcase. At Paul's signal, removal of his jacket, ten agents from Group Three, who had concealed themselves in the vicinity, moved in quickly with drawn guns. One of Navia's men bolted and was subdued as he ran through the brightly lit showroom of Midway Ford, terrifying several salesmen and customers. Staying in character, Robert Darias also fled and the agents let him go after making a pretense of chasing him. In the shock of the moment, Francisco Navia and his men did not notice that Darias was getting special treatment. The DEA arrested six people in all, including Navia.

Later that evening Group Three agents executed a search warrant at Navia's warehouse and found a stash of about three million freshly manufactured Quaaludes. It was the largest confiscation of Quaaludes in history.

The Navia arrests dazzled the hierarchy of the DEA. The case attracted attention throughout the agency worldwide and got a lot of publicity. ("Pill Seizure Is World Record," headlined the *Miami Herald*.) And it was the most significant case thus far in the careers of Paul Sennett and Carol Cooper.

Although Robert Darias was given no public credit, the DEA privately embraced him. The agency paid Darias $15,000 cash for his pivotal role in the case, and Cooper and Sennett invited him to work with them permanently. They made him welcome in the inner sanctum of Group Three, the suite of offices upstairs in the Phoenix Building headquarters at the Koger Center where only trusted insiders were permitted to go. Darias became friendly with the other Group Three agents, who called him a hero. "You're fantastic," he was told. "You're a gold mine."

When he was alone Robert had to laugh at the irony. Here he was working again for the United States Government, the same government that had betrayed him and his comrades on the beaches of Cuba in 1961, the same government that had put him in prison for tax evasion in 1978, the same government that was still dunning him for more than $200,000 in back taxes. That government was now calling him a hero and handing him envelopes bulging with crisp hundred-dollar bills.

Spies often are paid in cash. The CIA had paid Robert in cash during the Bay of Pigs period. It reduced the risk that either the money or the spy might be traced to the government. And though it also reduced the likelihood that the spy would pay taxes on the money, the CIA and DEA considered that the IRS's concern.

From his Navia windfall, Darias took $2,348 to the Dade County Courthouse and paid the remainder of the money he owed in settlement of the State of Florida "grand theft" real estate case. A judge terminated Darias's probation, formally declared the matter closed, and later expunged the theft case from the court record.

Robert had refrained from telling his wife, Amelia, the details of his newfound work, knowing she would be opposed. Spying for the U.S. Government had been abhorrent to most Cubans in Miami since the Bay of Pigs. But Amelia knew something was up. There was new money in the house. Robert was getting calls from a strange American woman named Carol who always asked for "Bob." (Amelia called him Roberto.) And Robert's mood had improved dramatically. Amelia asked him if he was working again for the CIA. He assured her that he wasn't, that what he was doing was legal, and that it might solve all their financial and tax problems.

Several days after the arrest of Francisco Navia, Robert finally confided in Amelia. He asked Carol Cooper and Paul Sennett to come to the Dariases' home in the Tamiami neighborhood and help him explain his new job to her.

"Bob is the best CI we've ever had in Miami," Carol told Amelia.

"He's the greatest." The agents recounted details of the world-record Quaalude seizure. "Bob can do very well with us," Paul said. "We'll take care of him."

Amelia was dubious. She knew something about governments and bureaucrats. Her family, one of the most prominent in pre–Castro Cuba, had done business with governments since the turn of the century. She had been conditioned since childhood to believe that governments in general, and the United States Government in particular, were often unreliable.

"Are you sure you're not being gullible?" she asked Robert after Cooper and Sennett left. "This may be a song and dance. They may use you and let you go."

Robert pointed out that the DEA was offering him an opportunity to earn more money than he had seen in a long time. And he felt that at some point the agency might be willing to intercede on his behalf with the Internal Revenue Service. While he hadn't yet taken up that issue with the DEA, he at least was building goodwill toward such a goal.

On a deeper level, which he did not articulate, even to Amelia, Robert also hoped that productive work for the U.S. Government in its anti-drug efforts might somehow redeem him of the shame he still felt at having gone to prison for tax evasion.

"Remember, Inspector Javert is still after me," Robert said of the IRS. His allusion to the dogged police agent who pursues Jean Valjean in Victor Hugo's novel *Les Misérables* was a small running joke he had with Amelia. Robert had long identified with Jean Valjean and other beleaguered characters in nineteenth-century French literature such as Edmond Dantès in *The Count of Monte-Cristo*.

Amelia smiled. She wasn't convinced, but she conceded that it would be unwise to forgo the opportunities that Robert's work with the DEA seemed to present.

Robert Darias quickly proved that his infiltration of Francisco Navia's smuggling organization had not been a fluke. Over the next two months, Darias found himself hurtling through a maze of horrors in the netherworld of narcotics reminiscent of Grade B films noir and, for that matter, of Jean Valjean in the sewers of Paris.

In late January, Darias and an undercover Group Three agent, Barry Carew, flew to the Colombian city of Cali where they posed as Philadelphia gangsters and briefly pierced the inner sanctum of one of the most exalted drug godfathers in the world, Santiago Ocampo, whose empire stretched from Peru through Colombia to the United

States. Though Ocampo normally hid behind layers of aides and dummy corporations, Darias had managed to contact him through a lawyer he had gotten to know the previous year in Colombia. After being screened by Ocampo's men for two days, the Americans finally met with the godfather and tentatively negotiated a multimillion-dollar cocaine shipment to their "organization" in the U.S. Just hours after Darias and Carew returned to Miami, however, Santiago Ocampo learned Carew's true identity, perhaps from a mafia spy in the Colombian police who had known of the Americans' visit. Had the breach occurred before Carew and Darias departed, they surely would have been detained, tortured, and killed. Their narrow escape became fabled in the annals of U.S. Government undercover work as a *"very* near miss." Despite the failure of the mission, the DEA was astounded by Darias's "coup" in infiltrating the highest levels of the Colombian mafia.

In the middle of February, through an American pilot named Bertram Mark Schwartz whom he had known in Colombia, Darias penetrated a smuggling group led by another Colombian lawyer, Juan Crump-Perez, also known as Johnny Crump, a man of "extremely broad, very delicate criminal activities on a worldwide basis," as he was later called in court. After extensive negotiations, including a round of drinks at his home, Darias lured Crump, Schwartz, and their confederates to a shopping mall in northwest Miami to sell 11 kilo-grams of cocaine to Darias's "buyers" for $660,000. There, at noon on a Wednesday, the Crump group was arrested by the agents of Group Three.

On a hunch that Darias had been secretly working for the government, Bert Schwartz, after being released on bail, appeared outside the Dariases' Tamiami home with a henchman who was wielding a MAC-10 machine pistol. Darias escaped death only after a harrowing car chase through the quiet neighborhood. Schwartz was rearrested and his bail revoked.

In March, Darias infiltrated still another big smuggling group and learned that its ring leader was a Cuban who had been in his battalion at the Bay of Pigs, Eric Arias. Although they had not met for years, Darias and Arias recognized each other immediately and had a warm reunion. It was another "small world" experience for Darias. Eric Arias told his people to cooperate with his "old friend Roberto." After the requisite negotiations, the DEA arrested Arias and several other smugglers late one evening at five locations around Miami, including a farm in the Everglades where access was so difficult that the arrests required the assistance of helicopters with floodlights and loudspeakers. The scene reminded some participants of night missions in the Vietnam War.

"Normally when someone comes to us and promises the world, nothing happens," Paul Sennett remarked to his Group Three colleagues. "When Bob promises the world, a lot happens."

In less than three months of working for the DEA, Robert Darias had been directly responsible for the arrest of seventeen drug dealers—many of whom the DEA considered important figures—as well as the seizure of more than $3 million worth of narcotics, numerous luxury automobiles, significant quantities of cash, and a dozen firearms. For his efforts he had been paid a total of $30,700, a bargain for the DEA and a relief from financial emergency for Darias, who was both exhilarated and perplexed by his experiences.

Having been chased near his home by a man wielding a machine gun, and having barely escaped from Colombia after an unprecedented meeting with a shadowy narcotics lord, Darias was acutely aware of the perils of the drug world. And yet the physical danger bothered him less than it did some of the younger DEA agents, who had never heard shots fired in anger.

Guns, danger, and purposeful violence had been part of the fabric of Robert's life from his earliest days in Cuba. In the 1930s his father had been a member of the secret society known as ABC Radical,* which used terror and violence to help rid Cuba of President Gerardo Machado, a dictator of exceptional brutality and corruption. Robert's uncle, also a member of ABC Radical, had been blown to bits in a terrorist bombing. Robert had learned to use guns as a youngster in the rugged Sierra Maestra in southeastern Cuba, where his father had worked as a collector of coffee taxes, often using a Colt .45 revolver with a six-inch barrel to encourage payment.

As a CIA-trained commando, Robert had slipped into Cuba secretly three times in the months leading to the Bay of Pigs invasion. He had been fired on by guards atop a cliff overlooking the port of Santiago de Cuba on the south coast of the island a few minutes after he and four other commandos had shot up two gasoline storage tanks. He had been fired on by a Castro militia patrol that his incursion team had encountered a mile inland from Cuba's north coast as they were

---

*The name apparently was adapted from the fictional radical group "Friends of the ABC" in *Les Misérables,* so called because the letters ABC were pronounced in French like *abaisse,* the word for "oppressed." Thus, Robert Darias's introduction to nineteenth-century French literature came at an early age.

attempting to deliver explosives to the anti-Castro underground. He had been fired on by harbor guards on the north coast a day after he and a CIA team had parachuted into sparsely populated ranch land and secured a supply of detonators for the underground. Each time he had managed to escape to U.S. vessels waiting offshore.

Two decades later, Darias found he still could handle the stress of physical danger. But now he was troubled by another kind of danger—the psychic danger of spying on people he knew personally in the insular world of Cuban Miami.

It had bothered him when his first infiltration in January had turned up the man who had photographed his and Amelia's wedding. It had bothered him when another investigative trail a few weeks later had led to a man who had been in his battalion at the Bay of Pigs. Darias had not been entirely surprised. If one was a Cuban of middle age like Robert and Amelia Darias, if one was socially prominent as their families had been for decades, first in Havana and again after the exodus to Miami, if one had fought at the Bay of Pigs and survived, one knew—either personally or through relatives or friends—just about everyone of importance or notoriety in Cuban Miami, whether banker, lawyer, businessman, drug smuggler, or CIA operative. Sometimes these people were one and the same person. By 1981, it was not terribly unusual to discover that a previously reputable Cuban businessman, perhaps a Bay of Pigs veteran, had been seduced by the extraordinary money that could be made smuggling illegal drugs. The photographer Navia and the brigade veteran Arias had not started out in the narcotics business. They had come to it in recent years as a lucrative sideline.

Though Navia and Arias were criminals, and Robert felt they deserved what he had done to them, he still was troubled by the calculated betrayal of people he knew.

After the Arias arrests, Robert suggested to Carol Cooper and Paul Sennett that he lie low for a while. They agreed. Cooper and Sennett understood the discomfort Darias felt in spying on people in his own community. And though he was handling the physical danger well, the agents believed that Darias, because he was working in his hometown, was in greater peril than a stranger would be. A hiatus seemed prudent. Perhaps he could return in a month or two in a different role.

part two

THE TARGET

Ambition must be made to counteract ambition.

—Federalist No. 51

4

THERE WAS A SENSE of warp, of siege, of dread, of losing control, as the United States Government began to struggle with the nation's narcotics epidemic in the late 1970s. America was awash in drugs. Americans in frightening numbers were snorting, smoking, swallowing, and injecting all the narcotics they could get their hands on.

It wasn't the country's first drug epidemic. That all but forgotten scourge had lasted from roughly 1885 to 1920. Cocaine and opiates, having been used in the mid-1800s for limited medicinal purposes, were circulating freely and with devastating effect by the end of the century. Following the lead of several states, the federal government finally outlawed drugs in 1914, and by the twenties the problem was ebbing, partly because of vigorous law enforcement and partly because of growing public antagonism toward narcotics.

By the 1960s two generations had passed and the nation's memory had faded. Though still illegal, drugs were back, in alarming and unprecedented variety. Marijuana alone would have been manageable, but marijuana was only the least of a proliferation of lethal substances. The number of heroin addicts in the United States rose ten-fold between 1960 and 1970. In the seventies the abuse of cocaine, Quaaludes, and other drugs exploded, blighting every sector of American society from the poorest ghetto, to the vast suburban middle class, to the highest reaches of Wall Street and the corporate world, to the most eminent families in the country. Between 1976 and 1980 deaths associated with cocaine and PCP (an extraordinarily dangerous hallucinogen) more than tripled and the overall indicia of drug abuse—addiction levels, overdoses, emergency room admissions—soared. Clinics and treatment centers were overwhelmed. Most of the abuse festered unattended.

Many people, moreover, were experiencing the principal by product of the drug epidemic—crime. The new drug epidemic spawned a crime wave that became the most formidable challenge ever to confront American police and law enforcement agents. The murders, robberies, and burglaries that drug users committed were only part of the problem. The complexity and sophistication of the organized criminal groups in control of international narcotics trafficking made traditional organized crime seem primitive by comparison. And since most of the criminal organizations were based abroad, they were uniquely difficult for American law enforcement agents to penetrate.

Government and police efforts to combat drugs and drug crime had been as chaotic historically as the drug scene itself. Federal narcotics agents in the U.S. had carried a total of thirty different badges since the federal government had outlawed drugs in 1914. The first federal antinarcotics law was a tax law and was enforced by a small group of agents from the Department of the Treasury. In the late 1920s there was a scandal—drug agents were found to be in business with drug dealers—and in 1930 the enforcement responsibility became the sole function of a newly created Treasury agency called the Federal Bureau of Narcotics, or FBN, which was semiautonomous and presumably easier to monitor. Another Treasury unit, the Customs Service, also had a role in drug enforcement—trying to stop illegal drugs at the borders of the U.S.—and Customs and FBN agents frequently engaged in bitter competition for arrest headlines. Occasionally the White House would ask J. Edgar Hoover's FBI to assume responsibility for drug law enforcement, but Hoover always declined, fearing corruption like that which already had infected the Treasury's drug agents.

Other cabinet departments and agencies entered the fray, however. Fighting drugs became glamorous. By the late 1960s the bureaucracies responsible for the various facets of the drug issue had metastasized. Drug "agencies," drug "bureaus," and drug "offices" popped up across the government—even within the White House—often working at cross-purposes.

BNDD. FBN. BDAC. FDA. HEW. ODALE. ONNI. IRS. ATF.

Customs, the only agency without initials, vied with BNDD, the Bureau of Narcotics and Dangerous Drugs, which had been formed in the Justice Department by a merger of the Treasury's FBN with BDAC, the Bureau of Drug Abuse Control, an appendage of the Food and Drug Administration in the Department of Health, Education and Welfare. ONNI, the Office of National Narcotics Intelligence, and ODALE, the Office of Drug Abuse Law Enforcement, also were parts of the Justice Department, though they were being run out of the White House. ODALE, in turn, was authorized to borrow agents from BNDD and three Treasury agencies—Customs, IRS, and ATF (Alcohol, Tobacco and Firearms)—as well as former or detached agents of the CIA.

In 1973 a frustrated Nixon administration decreed the grafting of

BNDD, ODALE, and ONNI together with 500 Customs agents to form a "superagency" called the Drug Enforcement Administration. The DEA was placed under the aegis of the Justice Department. "We have turned the corner on drug addiction in America," Richard Nixon declared.

There were grim chuckles in the ranks at Nixon's remarkable statement, and more chaos ensued. The DEA had three heads in its first three years, as factions vied for control. There were charges of scandal and malfeasance. It took years, and the new, younger blood that came with attrition, to begin to heal the old animosities and allow the DEA to function with any degree of institutional stability and effectiveness. Even then, turf wars flared anew. The Internal Revenue Service was increasingly interested in the huge revenues that flowed from drug trafficking. The Customs Service still patrolled parts of the narcotics arena, fueling its ancient feud with what had once been the Treasury Department's narcotics bureau and was now the Justice Department's DEA. The Justice Department, meanwhile, reversed the course of J. Edgar Hoover, who had died in 1972, and pushed the FBI into narcotics investigations, sparking additional conflicts with the other agencies.

Despite its shaky start and the competitive bureaucratic environment, the DEA emerged by 1980 as the dominant federal agency in the slowly evolving effort against the drug criminals. It was developing a unique identity and style. DEA agents as a group were innovative, aggressive, adept at undercover work, steeled to the constant threat of violence, accustomed to making arrests at the most dangerous moment—during the commission of the crime (the only opportunity in many drug cases). The typical FBI agent, in contrast, was aloof, austere, relentlessly bureaucratic, earnestly well-behaved in a suit and tie, uncomfortable in the quagmire of spying and undercover work, unused to violence, and accustomed to investigating most crimes in the FBI's purview (extortions and bank robberies, for example) in a relatively leisurely fashion, after the fact.

DEA agents called FBI agents "Fucking Blithering Idiots," "Famous But Incompetent," "fibbies," and "feebs" for "feebleminded." FBI agents called DEA agents "Drunk Every Afternoon" "Don't Expect Anything," and "cowboys."

Stylistic differences aside, the DEA had two distinct advantages over the FBI and other agencies in the federal police establishment as the government groped for a handle on the drug problem. First, the DEA was comfortable in foreign environs, the source of most of the drugs. It stationed more than twice as many of its agents overseas (about 200 out of 2,000) as all other U.S. law enforcement agencies combined deployed abroad. Working intimately with the CIA and the State Department, as well as with foreign intelligence and police agencies, the DEA gained a quiet reputation for conducting an array of foreign undercover operations that were effective in disrupting drug traffic.

The second advantage: The DEA knew how to handle spies. It was an intelligence agency as much as it was a law enforcement agency. Unlike their counterparts in the FBI, Customs, and the IRS, most DEA agents worked undercover much of the time. Running spies was central to their task. It was routine—if the volatile netherworld of betrayers with whom one had to deal in the drug business could ever be considered routine.

"We didn't know how the criminals were doing things. We didn't know how they were handling and moving their money, how they were managing to transact such a huge amount of illegal business without our finding out. By the late 1970s it had reached crisis proportions. . . . And no one in Washington or anywhere else in the government knew the answers to those questions. *Literally no one knew.* There was a real sense of futility, even panic."

That was a Justice Department official describing the government's desperation. And yet the enemy had to be engaged somewhere. And the more the authorities in Washington looked—the more the assistant attorneys general Federal Reserve economists, and deputy Treasury secretaries peered at their computer runs—the more they focused on one place.

Florida. The Sunshine State. Especially southern Florida. The nation's sandbox. The Sun and Fun Capital of the World. Miami.

The federal authorities didn't need computers to tell them that Florida had changed radically from what it once had been. In 1950, when Arthur Godfrey was making it his winter headquarters, the population of metropolitan Miami was about 750,000. A majority was white, mostly middle class. A minority was black, mostly poor. And there were few Latins. It was a leisurely city, typical in many ways of the American South at mid-century, a few years before air-conditioning and commercial jet aircraft.

By 1960 the population had doubled to 1.5 million and the Latin migration had begun. By the late 1970s, the population of South Florida had soared past 3 million, and of the 1.7 million residents of Dade County, nearly half were Latin, mostly Cubans, but also Colombians, Venezuelans, Peruvians, Bolivians, Chileans, Argentinians, Hondurans, Nicaraguans, Mexicans, Panamanians, and Puerto Ricans. The mayor of Miami was Puerto Rican–born Maurice Ferre, and many other municipal offices were held by Latins.

In important sociological and psychological ways, Miami had ceased to be a U.S. city. It had become the de facto capital of Latin America and the city that linked South and Central America with North America and the rest of the world. At least 100 multinational corporations had established their Latin American headquarters in South Florida. All the big U.S. banks, all the big European banks, all the big Japanese banks—Citibank, Lloyds, Credit Suisse, the Bank of Tokyo—had opened branches in Miami to serve Latin clients. Department stores stocked furs in the steamy Florida summer for customers from south of the equator who were returning to winter. The stores carried Oxford cloth shirts whose labels read "SAVILE ROW" in big letters and "Made in Nicaragua" in small print.

It was inevitable that when the drug business exploded, the international drug mafia, which needed a U.S. headquarters, would look to Miami. Even without its Latin connections and financial resources, Florida was the most natural of entry points for illegal narcotics. With thousands of miles of tidal coastline, much of it uninhabited and unguarded, and with more than 250 airports ranging from the giant Miami International to small rural strips on uniquely flat topography, the state could not have been more inviting to smugglers. By the late 1970s federal authorities were estimating that more than half of all the drugs arriving in the United States were coming through Florida.

The drug *money*—burgeoning billions of dollars—added a new and ominous dimension to the problem. The computers of the Federal Reserve System in Washington were generating numbers that at first seemed curious, then strange, then sinister. Nationwide, the normal flow of money into and out of the Federal Reserve System over time averaged a slight deficit. That is, a bit more money went out than came in, as the Fed went about its business of priming the nation's banking system and controlling the supply of money. In 1978, of the thirty-six Fed branches across the country, thirty-five were running an aggregate deficit of $3.5 billion, an average of $100 million per branch, a tiny amount for a system that turns over hundreds of billions of dollars a year. In the thirty-sixth branch, however, the computers were detecting bizarre distortions. That branch alone was showing a *surplus* of $3.3 billion, a warp that was already huge and growing rapidly. The surplus had been $89 million in 1971, $924 million in 1974. By 1980 it would be $6 billion on its way to $10 billion. The thirty-sixth Fed jurisdiction was Miami. And as experts at the Federal Reserve, the

Treasury, and the IRS began to peer behind the aggregate numbers, they grew even more concerned. Of the $68 million in cash that a single Miami bank had deposited with the Federal Reserve, 63 percent of it, $42 million, was in $20 bills, and another 16 percent, $10.5 million, was in $100 bills. At another bank, a customer from Colombia had walked in one day with several aides and deposited $13 million in cash from an assortment of suitcases, boxes, satchels, and shopping bags.

The Washington experts made three inferences from the numbers. First, Florida's banking system, the financial center of the entire Caribbean and much of Central and South America, was awash in the revenues of illegal narcotics. Most of Miami's 250 banks, whether wittingly or unwittingly, were handling this dirty money as a part of their normal business and were accomplices in the often complicated process of "laundering" it, that is, engaging in various artifices to hide the money's origins and make it appear clean and legitimate. The second inference Washington drew was that the flood of drug money in Florida was distorting the economy and the entire social fabric of the region. "Drug funds are part of a kaleidoscopic cancer," said *Washington Post* writer Joel Garreau. "The drug money is shredding the institutions theoretically committed to other economic and social goals and standards of morality. Professions founded on trust, such as banking, accounting, and the law are thoroughly compromised."

It was clear, for one thing, that drugs were at least as big a business as real estate and tourism, Florida's two leading legitimate businesses, and actually much bigger when one considered that a great deal of drug money apparently was being invested in real estate and tourism.

The third Washington inference was that the billions of drug dollars, as profits of an illegal business, were subject to seizure and taxation by the U.S. Government—if it could get its hands on the money.

These observations, however, were insufficient grounds for summary action. U.S. authorities couldn't simply walk in and, based on inference, seize billions of dollars. The law required hard evidence against specific individuals, specific corporations, specific banks. And the authorities' knowledge of such details, firm knowledge usable in a court of law, was primitive. Only careful, intensive investigation would tell them what they needed to know.

There was another dimension to the crisis. The drugs and money that were swamping Florida had brought with them an unprecedented wave of violence. Violent crime in South Florida nearly tripled in the decade of the seventies. Hundreds of thousands of guns were being sold in Dade County, where it was easier bureaucratically to buy a pistol than an automobile. Of the most crime-ridden cities in the United States, Miami was well on its way to being number one, and nearby Fort Lauderdale and West Palm Beach, as well as four other major Florida cities, were in the top eleven nationwide. Seven of the eleven most dangerous cities in America were in a single state. The statistic was unprecedented.

Miami's murder rate was the nation's highest, but that raw number only began to tell the story. A quarter of the homicides were committed with machine guns. And an extraordinary number of the murders were multiple, that is, two, three, four, or more people were being killed at one moment and place.

The period that got everyone's attention was the spring and summer of 1979. There were so many killings that the Dade County Medical Examiner had to rent a refrigeration van to handle the overflow of bodies from the morgue. One episode in particular was so shocking that it inspired a television series and entered the lore of American crime alongside the exploits of Bonnie and Clyde and Al Capone.

On a Tuesday afternoon in July, three men in a delivery van labeled "Happy Time Complete Party Supply" on one side and "Happy Time Complete Supply Party" on the other drove into the parking lot of the Dadeland Mall in Miami, the largest shopping center in the region. The van stopped in front of a liquor store near the mall's southwest corner. As two customers stood at the counter buying a bottle of Chivas Regal Scotch, the occupants of the van entered the store and opened fire, one with a MAC-10, the other with a .380 Beretta automatic, killing the two shoppers. Then the gunmen sprayed the store, wounding the clerk in the chest and shoulder and shattering dozens of bottles of liquor. A stock boy tried to slip out unnoticed, but the gunmen pursued him into the crowded parking lot, again unleashing a spray of fire. The stock boy was hit in both feet, and bullets shattered plate-glass windows and punctured automobile gasoline tanks, covering the pavement with broken glass and flowing gasoline. Amidst screams and commotion, the gunmen escaped on foot. Searching the abandoned van a few minutes later, the police found that it was armor-plated and contained several automatic weapons and bulletproof vests. The gunmen's motive was unclear.

The "Dadeland massacre" and other such carnage spawned an atmosphere heavy with fear. Many of the killings lingered unsolved. And even though a disproportionate number of the shootings were drug-related and a disproportionate number of both assailants and victims were Latin, no one in South Florida—Anglo, Latin, or black, lawyer, teacher, businessman, or suburban housewife—felt immune. People who lived through those years there, including people originally from crime-plagued northern cities like New York and Chicago, had never experienced anything like the shudder of menace in the soft air of Miami.

5

LIKE POLICE BUREAUCRACIES everywhere, the Drug Enforcement Administration lived by statistics. From junior street agents in small jurisdictions, to experienced supervisors in large cities, to high-level Washington managers, one's promotions, one's time in a civil-service grade, one's very career, depended on statistics. How many arrests did you, or your group, or your field office, or your division, make last month or last year? How many pounds, or kilograms, or tons of drugs did you seize? "Powder on the table" was the criterion of success. The FBI and the IRS used similar standards. How many bank robbers did you arrest? How much stolen property did you recover? How many taxpayers did you audit? How much additional tax revenue did you extract? Those with rising statistics got promoted from GS-12 to GS-13. Those with flat statistics found their careers stagnating. Agency heads with impressive numbers got warmer receptions at congressional budget hearings than those with what were perceived as bad numbers.

It had always been like that in law enforcement. And it remained like that until a few of the smarter people in the Departments of Justice and Treasury, and in the DEA and FBI, began to discern that law enforcement agencies had become mired in statistics—statistics that could be manipulated, statistics that measured quantity of law enforcement but ignored quality. It became clear to the smarter people that the old approach to drug law enforcement—arresting the street dealer and confiscating whatever drugs and cash he had with him—was having little effect on the drug scourge, no matter how astronomical the statistics of arrest and seizure. The street dealer's bosses replaced him within days at most, and business proceeded as usual. While local police might usefully continue to harass traffickers at the street level, the smarter strategists proposed that the federal government shift its efforts away from the street dealer to his boss, and not just his immediate boss waiting in some hotel room across town, but the higher boss ensconced on an estate in Miami Beach, and even *his* ultimate boss—the godfather, *el padrino*—on his *finca* near Bogotá. The federal government should forfeit the single kilogram of cocaine in the dealer's car and focus instead on the hundred kilograms that arrived at Miami International Airport from Latin America concealed behind the wall of the first-class rest room in the Avianca or Pan Am wide-body. Federal attention should turn from the $25,000 in cash in the trunk of the dealer's BMW to the $5 million that had been deposited in the Miami bank account under the phony corporate name and later transferred by wire to the secret numbered account at the Credit Suisse in Zurich or the Banque Nationale de Paris branch in Panama City.

Such a fundamental change of approach would require much more time, effort, and investigative persistence, and would produce far fewer arrests in a given statistical period. But it was clear to these strategists that only if U.S. authorities could get at the big people, the big organizations, and the big assets of the drug world did they stand any chance at all of "getting their arms around the problem," as they put it.[1]

As they reached these conclusions in the late seventies, the smarter people in Washington focused on three laws that had been passed by Congress and signed by Richard Nixon in 1970. They were the Racketeer Influenced and Corrupt Organization law, or RICO; the Continuing Criminal Enterprise law, or CCE; and the Bank Secrecy Act.

The RICO and CCE laws reflected the notion that the most successful criminals operated not as individuals but as groups—groups that were as tightly organized as well-run corporations and deployed huge amounts of money and assets in pursuit of their illegal ends. The recognition that major crime was *organized* was not new. What was new was the determination to attack these criminal enterprises as organizations, rather than prosecute their members only for individual actions.

The statutes (RICO's jurisdiction was general, while CCE applied strictly to drug syndicates) made it a crime simply to supervise or operate a criminal organization. Anyone convicted of doing so could be imprisoned for many years, in some cases for life. The laws also made it easier for the government to confiscate the criminal organization's ill-gotten gains. And in an attempt to facilitate the tracing of

---

[1]The efforts by U.S. officials toward "getting their arms around the problem," of course, included not only trying to stop drugs from being smuggled into the U.S. but trying to stop Americans from using the drugs once they arrived. This latter aspect of the problem, vital though it was and is, is beyond the narrative scope of this book. However, the relationship between the supply and demand sides of the drug problem is discussed briefly in the epilogue.

illegal assets, the Bank Secrecy Act required banks to report to the IRS any cash deposit of more than $10,000, fully identifying the depositor, and required anyone leaving or entering the United States with more than $5,000 in cash to report the amount to U.S. Customs.

The three laws were complex, and several years passed before the lawyers in the Justice Department, the Treasury Department, and the criminal divisions of the ninety-four United States Attorneys offices around the country, as well as the thousands of agents in the DEA, the FBI, and the IRS, learned how to use them effectively.

In 1977, the Department of Justice deployed the DEA and FBI, despite their mutual animosity, in a joint undercover investigation in Miami called Operation Banco. The ambitious mission was to prosecute the leaders and seize the assets of the Latin American narcotics mafia. The Justice Department hoped the FBI agents' training in accounting and bank fraud would complement the DEA agents' training in drug smuggling conspiracies. The agents began with information already contained in the DEA's worldwide intelligence computer, NADDIS, a clearinghouse for all information, unsubstantiated as well as verified, that the agency had collected over the years about international narcotics trafficking—millions of names, descriptions, events, agent debriefings, communications intercepts, and myriad other data.

From the NADDIS base, a young DEA intelligence analyst in Miami named Jonathan Stockstill constructed a picture—sketchy, blank in spots—of the major South American groups that were suspected of importing narcotics into Florida. Then Stockstill began the laborious task of examining thousands of reports that U.S. banks were required to file with the IRS on all cash deposits of more than $10,000. While many banks had been slow to comply with the law, and some banks weren't filing the reports at all (the penalties were negligible), Stockstill was able to derive a number of correlations between the names in his computer picture of the reputed Latin drug mafia and the names on IRS forms of people who had made large cash deposits in Miami banks.

The DEA-FBI team then issued more than 500 grand jury subpoenas for bank account records, corporate records, and witness testimony. Some 120 bank employees were interrogated and shown photo spreads of suspected narcotics dealers.

Though the investigators learned a great deal about the narcotics mafia from the subpoenaed information, they were unable to develop many prosecutable cases. Two problems proved insoluable. One was the investigators' inability to *infiltrate* the targeted crime families and

the banks that were servicing them. The DEA and FBI did not have
in their ranks, and were unable to recruit, a single person—a spy—
who could insinuate himself or herself into the tightly knit groups
under investigation and gather specific evidence usable in court.

The other dilemma was the differing bureaucratic cultures of the
DEA and FBI, which clashed repeatedly and overcame the logic of
pairing them. There were bitter disagreements both important and
petty. A DEA supervisor enraged the FBI agents by sending them on
routine drug arrests to inflate the group's statistics, reducing the time
they could devote to their primary mission. Some agents asked to be
reassigned. One filed a grievance with a federal judge. Eventually the
supervisor ordered the FBI agents to return the keys and badges that
admitted them to the DEA offices.

Amidst anger and recrimination, Operation Banco quietly with-
ered, with little to show for the more than $1 million the venture had
cost.

Charles Blau had never heard of Operation Banco. An amiable thirty-
three-year-old assistant United States Attorney in Indianapolis, Blau
had made an excellent record prosecuting drug smugglers and bank
embezzlers in southern Indiana. He was aggressive and worked exceptionally hard. "If there was a case on the moon, you'd want to try it,"
his first wife once told him—before they were divorced. In late 1979
Blau received a call from the Department of Justice in Washington
asking him to move to Miami and join a major investigation of the
financial infrastructure of the drug mafia—the same targets Operation
Banco had failed to infiltrate. The probe was being planned by the
Treasury and Justice departments. Blau's assignment was to coordinate the investigation and prosecute any cases that evolved from it.
The venture was to be called Operation Greenback.

Charlie Blau reported to Miami on New Year's Day, 1980, and
over the next several months encountered a situation even more alien
than his ex-wife's notion of trying a case on the moon. Miami was
surreal. At first glance the place was lovely—the beaches were beautiful, the breezes balmy. But drugs were being sold with impunity, and
millions of dollars in drug cash was being carried openly into banks
in suitcases and shopping bags. Bullet-riddled bodies seemed to be
everywhere—on the streets, in canals, in trunks of cars. After a meeting one afternoon on ways to combat violence, participants emerged
from a building in downtown Miami to find a freshly shot body
sprawled on the sidewalk.

The Office of the United States Attorney, where Operation Greenback was billeted, resembled a beleaguered fort in hostile territory. It was the year of the Mariel boatlift from Cuba—125,000 new immigrants were arriving in Miami, including a remarkable number of hardened criminals. The U.S. Attorney's building was surrounded by hundreds of sweltering Marielitos impatiently awaiting processing by immigration authorities whose offices were in the same building. Federal attorneys were sometimes mugged as they were entering or leaving the premises. The lawyers were required to carry guns and undergo firearms training, and were issued electronic devices with which to sweep their cars for bombs. The woman who was to become Charles Blau's second wife refused to date him for a time because she felt she was in danger when she was with him.

All of this was dramatically foreign to Blau's experience in southern Indiana. And there was another difference. In southern Indiana the local offices of federal agencies cooperated with each other. In Miami, it seemed, they fought like spoiled children. Blau had been told that Operation Greenback would involve all four of the U.S. Government's principal drug-fighting agencies—the Customs Service and the IRS, which were parts of the Treasury Department, as well as the DEA and FBI, which were parts of the Justice Department. In fact, only Customs and the IRS were full participants. Operation Greenback had been launched at the initiative of Customs. The IRS had joined, and the Treasury Department had then invited its "colleagues" at the Justice Department to participate.

The Justice Department itself had agreed; its lawyers would have to prosecute Operation Greenback's cases. But its subsidiary agencies, the DEA and FBI, declined to join. The FBI, arrogantly independent under the best of circumstances, was determined to work alone after its bad experience with the DEA in Operation Banco. In fact, Charles Blau learned to his dismay, the FBI had already begun its own undercover probe of some of the same drug financiers that Customs and the IRS were after, and had not invited the participation of any other agency. The FBI's investigation was called Operation Bancoshares.

The DEA for its part refused to join any activity that involved the Customs Service. DEA and Customs were still feuding after decades of conflict over which agency would have primacy in drug law enforcement. On both an institutional and personal level, the two agencies hated each other.

Instead of spending full-time coordinating a four-agency operation, therefore, Charlie Blau found himself spending only part of his time on a two-agency operation while devoting the rest to a largely futile attempt to coax the DEA and FBI into participating. The FBI was adamant in its refusal. The DEA, under pressure from the Justice Department in Washington, grudgingly assigned a few agents to work with Operation Greenback as "liaison only," and those agents and their Customs counterparts spent most of their time trying to undermine each other.

Blau was horrified. "There was a great deal of conflict, a great lack of trust, a great deal of misunderstanding, a total lack of communication, *and all of it was intentional,"* he said years later. "South Florida is the most difficult place I've ever worked anywhere, anytime."

In Washington, some of the more thoughtful officials at the top of the Justice Department grew exceedingly concerned about the deteriorating situation in Miami. With competing federal agencies conducting separate undercover operations against some of the same targets, there arose the ludicrous prospect that Operation Greenback and Operation Bancoshares might wind up inadvertently infiltrating each other. The assistant attorney general in charge of the criminal division, former Harvard Law School professor Philip B. Heymann, told his boss in an internal memorandum that it was "essential that the FBI share in intelligence produced by the Customs-IRS investigation so that the FBI's own investigation is not inadvertently compromised." As for the DEA, its attitude is "completely repugnant to any spirit of cooperation."

Assailing all investigations to that time—early 1980—as ineffectual, Heymann concluded: "A full scale investigation into the financial aspects of narcotics trafficking in Florida has not yet taken place."

part three

OPERATION SWORDFISH

I saw him extend his short flipper of an arm for a gesture that took in the forest, the creek, the mud, the river—seemed to beckon with a dishonouring flourish before the sunlit face of the land a treacherous appeal to the lurking death, to the hidden evil, to the profound darkness of its heart.

—*Joseph Conrad*, Heart of Darkness

6

ONE OF THE SMARTER PEOPLE that Washington sent to Miami to work on the drug problem in the late seventies was Special Agent Thomas Clifford of the DEA. Tom Clifford grew up in the Woodlawn section of the north Bronx, a stable neighborhood of Irish, Italian, and German working people. His grandparents had been born in Ireland and his father was a longshoreman-union boss from Hell's Kitchen who worked the docks of Manhattan's West Side. ("Think of Lee J. Cobb in *On the Waterfront,*" Tom would say in describing his father.) Clifford attended small Catholic schools, Mount St. Michael Academy in the Bronx and Iona College in New Rochelle. His hero as a teenager was John F. Kennedy and two decades later he still kept photographs of Kennedy in his DEA offices and in his study at home.

Attracted by public service, Clifford began graduate studies in psychology at Fordham while working part-time for a psychiatrist on cases of disturbed children. Although he loved the work, he found he became too involved personally in his cases. Both his wife, Carol, and his boss counseled him to be more detached, but he found he couldn't do that, and eventually decided to switch careers.

Clifford joined the DEA (then still called the Bureau of Narcotics and Dangerous Drugs) in 1971 at the age of twenty-six. The aura of adventure surrounding federal lawmen was part of the lure, and Clifford had become specifically aware of the drug problem as an adolescent in the Bronx where his peers generally were of two types—the kids who drank beer and were energetic at parties (Clifford was one of those) and the kids who got high on pills and nodded off at parties. Some of the latter group had quickly graduated to heroin and a few years later were either dead or in prison.

As a young drug agent in New York, Clifford worked on the fabled Jaguar case, an offshoot of the French Connection. After a delicate undercover investigation, U.S. agents in 1971 broke up a ring of French and Cuban smugglers and seized 200 pounds of heroin hidden under the floorboards of a Jaguar that arrived in New York aboard the *Queen Elizabeth 2*. The more complicated the case, the more Clifford enjoyed it. A bright man with an inquisitive mind, a quick, aggressive wit, and a mischievous smile, Clifford loved to diagram international conspiracies. "Clifford's spaghetti bowls," his charts were called.

The DEA promoted Tom Clifford to Washington and then Miami, where in 1979 he was named chief of intelligence for the Miami region, a crucial post as the government struggled to expand its meager knowledge of the Latin narcotics mafia.* Still only thirty-four years old, Clifford was one of the youngest agents ever to hold so sensitive a position in the DEA. A few of Clifford's contemporaries envied his rapid rise, and his garrulous Irish banter was a bit much for some people. But he pleased his superiors and thus thrived.

Shortly after arriving in Miami, Tom Clifford was assigned to conceive and plan an operation which the DEA could mount on its own against the upper ranks of the Latin drug mafia. Loath to collaborate with its archrival Customs in Operation Greenback, and estranged from the FBI after Operation Banco, DEA headquarters was eager to prove that it could surpass the other agencies. The DEA wanted to try a new tool—a 1979 amendment to the 1970 laws—facilitating the confiscation of drug traffickers' assets.

Tom Clifford recognized that the first requirement of infiltrating the Latin mafia was recruiting spies (or "informants" in the bureaucracy's misleading parlance) capable of deep penetration. Clifford also knew that such work could not be done by most Americans. While Americans surely were in the narcotics business, some at high levels, Jonathan Stockstill's analysis had shown that the godfathers behind the influx of drugs through Florida were virtually all Latins, some Cubans, but mainly Colombians—an ethnic and cultural miasma that posed a dilemma for the largely Anglo intelligence and law-enforcement agencies of the U.S. Government.

The cultures of Latin America for the most part had been inscrutable to North America since Europeans settled the New World centuries earlier. From a North American perspective, the Spanish had all but disappeared into the jungles and mountains of Latin America behind stereotypes of sombreros, coffee beans, and mystical religious rites. After centuries of alternately ignoring, patronizing, betraying, and misunderstanding Latin America, the United States possessed virtually no capacity for espionage against the Latin narcotics mafia.

The modern Latin mafia had been born in Chile in the early 1970s, where traffickers had processed coca leaf from Bolivia and Peru and

---

*Unlike comparable groups elsewhere, who take umbrage at the term "mafia," organized crime groups in South America call *themselves* mafia.

smuggled it into the United States. But after General Augusto Pinochet had seized power in a coup in 1973, he had arrested virtually the entire drug industry, jailing most and sending some to the U.S. for prosecution. With the Chilean mafia gutted, the entrepreneurial criminals of Colombia, whose networks were already in place after decades of smuggling emeralds, had promptly seized control of the growing cocaine trade. And the Colombians posed an even greater mystery to U.S. intelligence than the Chileans had.

More than most Latin criminals, the Colombians were extremely distrustful not only of North Americans as a group but of other Latin nationalities as well. Thus it was very difficult either for an American or for a Latin of the "wrong" nationality, a Mexican, for instance, to infiltrate their ranks. Tom Clifford needed to find Colombians or perhaps Cubans to serve as his spies. And since his targets were the money magnates of the drug world, people who maintained luxury condominiums on Brickell Avenue and read the *Wall Street Journal,* his spies couldn't be street thugs. They had to be capable of posing as professionals in the world of business and finance.

It appeared to Clifford, moreover, that to attract and gain the confidence of the targets, the spies would have to provide a service that the criminals required—the laundering of their huge drug profits. *Money-laundering.* The term sounded so prosaic that it numbed the minds of many DEA agents. In Tom Clifford's view, however, money-laundering was the most stimulating challenge that contemporary narcotics agents faced. For it was only by fathoming how the narcotics mafia concealed its vast profits that the DEA could get at that money and, ultimately, prosecute the hierarchy of the mafia.

To offer the money-laundering services that Clifford envisioned, the DEA's spies would need a structure within which to function, perhaps an investment firm. The firm would be entirely bogus—a government undercover operation—but it would have to appear entirely credible to its criminal targets.

Before he thought further about spies, Clifford focused on his bogus corporation and how it would function. He knew little of finance, investments, and banking, and nothing of how to start a corporation. He needed help.

While few Anglos in Miami numbered Latins among their intimate friends, one of the people to whom Tom Clifford had become close since moving to South Florida was Angel Santiago, a Puerto Rican who had grown up in a blue-collar neighborhood of Staten Island and worked nights while obtaining a degree in finance from New York University. Santiago had worked for several international banks and securities firms, specializing in South American clients. The Cliffords and the Santiagos had been neighbors since both families had moved to Florida. Tom Clifford had been hesitant at first; an Irish kid from the Bronx and a Puerto Rican kid from Staten Island didn't seem a natural match. But the families had grown fond of each other and spent lots of time together.

Angel Santiago, Tom Clifford decided, could be the private guide he needed to the intricacies of banking and finance. Clifford organized a family excursion to Orlando on Easter weekend of 1980. After dispatching their wives and children to Disney World, the two men settled in lounge chairs on the shore of a lake with a pitcher of rum coolers. Although he trusted Angel implicitly, Tom kept his questions general and hypothetical, not wanting to invest Angel with sensitive knowledge that might later slip out, even in total innocence. He told Angel only that the DEA was thinking of trying something new and he needed Angel's expertise.

"If I wanted to start an investment management company, what are the mechanics?" Clifford began. "How do I start, what papers do I have to file, and what happens after that? How would I establish credit? How would I open a corporate bank account? How would I open a brokerage account?"

Angel responded at length, and Tom asked more questions. "How much information do I have to give the bank and the brokerage firm? How do offshore accounts work? What will happen at a bank or brokerage firm if I want to deposit a million dollars in cash from a suitcase? What kinds of questions will be asked?"

On it went for three days. Tom filled several legal pads with notes and diagrams. Angel was delighted to help—he was something of a police and spy buff and enjoyed talking to Tom about his work—but he was "amazed, absolutely amazed" that the United States Government found it necessary to use him, an outsider without a security clearance, for such a purpose. Why couldn't Tom Clifford have gone to the Securities and Exchange Commission or the Federal Reserve for answers to these questions? Tom was amused by Angel's naïveté about the federal bureaucracy. Government agencies are not predisposed to help each other. They are predisposed to compete with each other. It was so much easier and more pleasant, Tom observed, to sit with a trusted friend on the shore of a lake sipping rum coolers, without memos, authorizations, or interagency suspicion.

Back in Miami, Tom Clifford composed a classified eleven-page memorandum to his DEA bosses. Observing the unwritten rules of bureaucracy, Clifford crafted a bold new approach without its seeming particularly bold or new. The document sounded important but not threatening to vested interests. It sounded grand but bland at the same time. The memo wasn't even couched as a proposal. It was a "position paper" with a perfect grand but bland title: *Expansion of the Miami District Office's Financial Investigative and Intelligence Program: Redirection of Resources to Maximize Priorities.*

Reviewing the history of intelligence gathering in Miami since 1977, culminating with Operation Banco, Clifford noted that there continued to be a "lack of informants" (i.e., spies) to penetrate the narcotics mafia and its financial infrastructure. He proposed that the DEA try to recruit such people and, if successful, that the agency open a "proprietary"—an undercover business that would pose as an investment management company and provide a vehicle for the spies. The company would offer services to drug smugglers wishing to conceal their assets, including such things as the creation of shell corporations overseas, the opening of numbered foreign bank accounts for those corporations, and the movement of clients' money to those bank accounts. The company would accept only word-of-mouth referrals and only from clients it had reason to believe were in the narcotics business. When clients came to the company to do business, the conversations would be secretly videotaped. The DEA would use the evidence it gathered to build cases against the targets and develop information on other targets. The spies and control agents would take their time. Such work could not be rushed. In the end, if everything worked, the DEA would arrest and prosecute as many drug financiers as it could implicate and would confiscate as much of their money and property as it could identify.

"The successful handling of one or two groups' money should spread by word of mouth among the smuggling community, bringing new customers," Clifford predicted in the memorandum. He sketched a monthly budget for rental of office space, furniture, equipment, telephones, and the like, as well as for travel. He named the enterprise Operation Barracuda and submitted his proposal on June 17, 1980.

There were many naysayers. There were people in the Miami field office and people in Washington who said the plan would not work— who told Tom Clifford that the cautious Latin mafia would never be attracted to the corporation he was proposing to form. "You're wasting time and resources," he was told. Clifford's memorandum was shunted among offices at headquarters for months. On December 16, 1980, in an effort to spur the bureaucracy, Clifford submitted a twenty-one-page "operational plan" for Operation Barracuda that was more elaborate than the initial memorandum. Headquarters responded with two nitpicking teletypes in early 1981, asking Clifford to delineate his intentions for the "experimental" operation further. He submitted another revision, which Washington finally approved formally on April 1. Along the way Clifford learned that the word "barracuda" had been used once before in the title of a DEA operation. He renamed his venture Operation Swordfish, which he hoped someday would symbolize "spearing the big ones."

In advance of formal approval, Clifford's bosses in Miami had authorized him to begin considering agents from within the ranks of the DEA for Operation Swordfish. While he intended to run the operation personally, he couldn't devote all his time to it because of other responsibilities as head of intelligence.

The first person Clifford assigned to the operation was not a DEA special agent but an intelligence analyst, Robert Russo. There was a major difference between intelligence analysts and special agents, at least to the agents. Although analysts performed vital functions, agents tended to look down on them. "He's an 'intel type,'" was a pejorative reference, like a high school jock's reference to "nerds" who get straight A's but no girls. Intelligence analysts sat at desks and analyzed data. They tended to be less physically adept than agents. They did not carry guns. They were not in danger of being wounded or killed. Nor did they have the authority to wound or kill, or to arrest—the life and death responsibilities that created a special bond among agents and set them apart, in their own minds at least.

Bob Russo was different, in Tom Clifford's opinion. Russo had been a special agent for several years and switched to intelligence analysis only so that he could avoid the frequent transfers that agents faced. To Clifford, Russo had the moxie of an agent—he came from the streets of Detroit—to go with his years of intelligence experience. Clifford trusted him completely and looked to him as a wise sounding board. Russo would keep track of the intelligence generated by Operation Swordfish, and would manage the budget and the files. He would be the treasurer of the undercover business. And he would be Tom Clifford's eyes and ears inside the operation.

But intelligence analysts couldn't actually conduct Operation Swordfish. Only special agents could be given that authority, mainly because the risk of violence and the potential for arrests would always be present. So Clifford turned next to the selection of special agents to go undercover full-time, play the roles of the top officers of the bogus investment company, and supervise the spies. Clifford wanted agents

who looked and acted like stereotypical businessmen, "bullshit art-
ists" who could carry off their roles after some intensive orientation
in the rudiments of banking and finance.

Tom Clifford studied the organization chart of the Miami field
headquarters, topped by the special-agent-in-charge, or SAC. Reporting to the SAC were two assistant special-agents-in-charge, or
ASACs. Clifford reported to one of the ASACs. Each ASAC supervised, among other things, several "enforcement groups" of a dozen
special agents each. In all, some ninety agents were stationed in
Miami.

Clifford found that the best candidates for his undercover operation—a very short list of only three or four agents—were committed
to other assignments. Finally he settled on an agent he had first met
years earlier in New York but had never known well, Frank Chellino.
A native of a small town in Pennsylvania, and a member of Miami's
Group Three until recently, Chellino was the same age as Clifford,
thirty-five, and looked more like a stockbroker or an accountant (his
former occupation) than a cop. Gray around the temples and a bit
pudgy, he was well-groomed, and preferred a jacket and tie to the polo
shirts and jeans that agents were permitted to wear to the office
because they were appropriate for many undercover situations. Chellino's complexion was Mediterranean swarthy, his hair and eyes were
dark, and he wore a mustache. Clifford hoped that Chellino (along
with the equally swarthy Bob Russo) would lend at least a faint
Sicilian Mafia cast to the undercover operation. (Latin drug traffickers
were known to be intrigued by their Sicilian counterparts.) Frank
Chellino also had the advantage of being unusually short, under five
feet six, and therefore was unlikely in physical terms to evoke a
cautious criminal's suspicion that he might be a cop.

Chellino was smart, glib, and a bit cocky. Perhaps as partial compensation for his short stature, he was a needler. He liked controlling
his surroundings and keeping people off balance. And he was reputed
to be adept at handling money. "Frank would steal the gold out of
your teeth," one of Clifford's friends said.

Although they had joined the DEA within a year of each other,
Chellino's career was not moving as fast as Clifford's. In 1979 and
1980, as Tom Clifford was settling in as chief of intelligence with a civil
service grade of GS-14, Frank Chellino remained a street agent, having difficulty getting promoted above GS-12. He accepted the job in
Clifford's undercover operation. It sounded challenging. And if it
succeeded it would be a sure ticket to GS-13.

Clifford sent Frank Chellino to a two-day University of Miami seminar on foreign investments in U.S. assets. Held at the Sheraton Bal Harbor, the courses sounded like just what the drug mafia needed: "Expectations and Motivations of Foreign Investors," "U.S. Taxes on Foreign Investors," "Asset Acquisitions by Foreign Investors," and "Anonymity and Discretion for Foreign Investors."

As he screened possible recruits for Operation Swordfish, Clifford also began the process of choosing undercover names, obtaining fake identification and credentials, and establishing false personal and financial histories for his agents. Even though Clifford was to supervise rather than participate in the operation, he established credentials for himself in case his presence ever was required. He would be known undercover as Thomas Belise, a name he had used years earlier in New York and the Caribbean. Bob Russo would be Bob Caruso. Frank Chellino would be Frank Dean. And since Clifford had decided that Chellino/Dean would be the president of the undercover investment business, its name would be Dean International Investments Incorporated. The name "Dean" was conceived by Chellino's wife, Sally, who thought it would be clever to use a short, one-syllable word incorporating the initials *D. E. A.* Tom Clifford wondered if that might be a bit provocative but Frank Chellino liked "Dean" and no one thought of anything better, so Dean it was. There were more important things to worry about.

Creating a bogus history for Dean International Investments and its principals was an exacting task. Sophisticated criminal groups were reputed to be meticulous in checking the background of people they did not know. But keeping Dean's true colors a secret from its targets wouldn't be enough. Much of the business and financial community of South Florida had been corrupted by the narcotics trade. Since Dean's credit history would be investigated when it applied to lease offices, rent cars, and order phones, companies like Southern Bell, Florida Power & Light, and local real estate brokerages would have to be misled into believing that Dean was a genuine company.

The DEA needed to take at least one bank into its confidence; without a bank account Dean International could not establish even a first echelon of credibility. And yet the Miami banking community was under suspicion and potentially a target of the DEA's investigation. Dean would have to sink its first banking roots outside of South Florida. Tom Clifford chose Chicago, and one of that city's biggest banks, the La Salle National, where the DEA's Chicago office did its banking. A ranking DEA official in Miami had formerly headed the agency's Chicago field division and had a warm relationship with the La Salle officer who handled the DEA's banking.

Tom Clifford and Bob Russo flew to Chicago to brief the La Salle assistant vice president, Robert Force. Force agreed to handle deposits, withdrawals, and wire transfers between La Salle and other banks in the U.S. and abroad. Force also was coached to say, in response to any outside inquiry, that Dean International Investments had funds in the middle six figures on deposit at La Salle and that its principal officer, Frank Dean, had banked there for many years. In addition to Robert Force, only three employees of La Salle knew that the bank was participating in an international undercover operation.

Since La Salle was to be Dean International's primary bank, Chicago became Frank Dean's hometown. The DEA's Chicago office arranged with a contact in the Illinois Department of Motor Vehicles to implant false information in the department's computer so that if inquiries were made the computer would say that a Mr. and Mrs. Frank Dean had held valid Illinois driver's licenses and had lived at an address in Arlington Heights, a Chicago suburb, until moving to Florida.

Through a contact in the Florida state police in Tallahassee, Tom Clifford got Florida driver's licenses for himself and Frank Chellino in their undercover names. As their addresses on the Florida licenses the agents used the street numbers of two large luxury condominium apartment buildings on Biscayne Bay where a number of South American narcotics traffickers were known to maintain residences. The same contact in the state police arranged with the director of corporations for the State of Florida to issue a false certificate of incorporation for Dean International Investments and to place Dean in the state's corporation file and computer. The security branch of American Express arranged for the undercover agents to get Gold Cards. And a discreet and sympathetic Florida state judge with a drug problem in his family arranged informally for the agents to obtain false voter registration cards.

In a small room on the second floor of the Phoenix Building DEA headquarters, adjacent to Tom Clifford's office in the Intelligence Group, technicians installed a telephone that was to be answered only "Dean International"—an arrangement that would last until Clifford and Chellino had rented a suite of offices for their new company. The office had to meet several requirements. It had to comprise four or five rooms and accommodate hidden video cameras and recorders. It had to have a prosperous appearance in an affluent neighborhood. It had to be within a few minutes' drive of the DEA (so that help would be near in an emergency) and the Federal Reserve Bank (which the agents planned to use a lot). It had to be in a quiet location, without a lot of traffic, in order to minimize any discomfort that the operation's targets might feel visiting the office.

Clifford and Chellino decided to locate in Miami Lakes, a distinctly affluent residential and commercial area just inside the "big bend" of the Palmetto Expressway where it framed the northwest corner of Miami. Graced by lakes and curving, tree-lined avenues, Miami Lakes had been developed in the early sixties by the renowned Graham family. (Bob Graham was later governor of Florida and a U.S. senator; his sister-in-law, Katharine Graham, was chairman of the Washington Post Company.) By the 1980s, Miami Lakes was vying with Coral Gables and Key Biscayne as a community of choice. Don Shula, the coach of the Miami Dolphins, lived there. Half an hour from downtown Miami, it was only ten minutes from the DEA and the Federal Reserve and fifteen minutes from Miami International Airport.

Chellino, in the guise of Frank Dean, the investment counselor from Chicago, approached a real estate broker in Miami Lakes and arranged to lease a suite of offices in Windmill Gate, a small shopping center on Ludlam Road not far from the Miami Lakes Inn & Country Club. A one-story structure in the shape of a square, Windmill Gate housed a variety of concerns, including a bank, a medical office, a real estate brokerage, a travel agency, and a French restaurant. Protected by large trees and a heavy tile roof with a wide overhang, the entrances to the establishments in Windmill Gate were shaded most of the day. The suite that Chellino and Clifford selected was on the quietest side of the square, the side farthest from busy Ludlam Road. The suite consisted of three offices, a conference room, a reception area, two rest rooms, and a storage room. There was plenty of parking near the entrance. The monthly rent was $1,330.

On the lease application, Chellino listed Dean International as the tenant, with Frank Dean and Thomas Belise as Dean's officers. Robert Force of the La Salle National Bank in Chicago was given as the primary financial reference and Thomas Belise was listed as Frank Dean's personal reference. A few days later, the real estate broker called the Dean International telephone number (the undercover phone in the DEA intelligence office) and said that Mr. Dean would need an additional local reference. Chellino/Dean claimed that he hadn't been in Miami long and knew very few people. He promised to get back to the broker.

Clifford and Chellino knew that security could never be absolute. To establish the credentials of Dean International they had already been forced to confide in a few carefully selected people outside the DEA's ranks. Now Frank Chellino had to expand that outer circle by one. Even though he had lived in South Florida for five years, his selection was limited. Most DEA agents' social lives were confined to other agents; their work was so secret and stressful that they found it difficult to risk letting their hair down with anyone else. And Chellino couldn't list a DEA agent on his lease application.

He approached a neighbor who had been with Eastern Airlines for a number of years, had his own real estate business, and knew Chellino was a DEA agent. "I can't tell you what we're doing," Chellino told the man, "but I need some outside help. We've got a long-term undercover operation that we're going to be running, and we need somebody in the outside business community to vouch for the fact that you've known me for a certain amount of years; that you know what type of business I do, which is investments, and most of all, that you know my name, which is Frank Dean, and that I recently moved here from Chicago. In effect, I need you to lie for us to help us establish our cover."

The neighbor rose to the occasion. He told the Miami Lakes real estate broker that he had known Frank Dean and his family in Chicago for many years, both personally and professionally. "Mr. Dean is completely reliable," the neighbor said.

Before furniture and equipment were moved into the offices of Dean International, additional partitions were built and configured to hide cameras and recorders. The agents, with help from the DEA technical staff, did all of the work themselves to ensure security. They also painted the office, and Frank Chellino decorated it with some inexpensive lithographs. When Tom Clifford inspected the premises he chuckled.

"Who the hell lives here, a bunch of dwarfs?" Clifford said.

"What do you mean?" Chellino asked.

"They're too low," Clifford said, "The pictures are too low."

"What do you mean, too low," Chellino said, taken aback.

"They're too low—anybody can see that."

"They look all right to me."

"Of course they look all right to you," Clifford retorted with a laugh. "You're too short to notice. You should never hang pictures."

Chellino seethed. "Shit," he muttered, and grudgingly agreed to raise them.

Tom Clifford was learning that his bluster occasionally rankled Frank Chellino, who was very sensitive about his height. He wore boots with two-inch heels but was still considerably shorter than most men. When he had been an agent in Group Three his buddies had ragged him mercilessly and given him a string of nicknames: "Louie" (for the Danny DeVito character on *Taxi*), "Levitt" (for the short cop on *Barney Miller*), "Tattoo" (for the dwarf on *Fantasy Island*), and, when he was bossy, "The Führer," "Little Hitler," "Little Napoleon," or "Little Caesar." Chellino had had little choice but to tolerate such banter in the give-no-quarter atmosphere of the Group Three squad room, but it seemed undignified now that he was Frank Dean, chief executive officer, with his own office and a Cadillac.

Dean International needed someone to pose as a secretary and receptionist, and Tom Clifford decided it had to be a woman. He anticipated that the typical Latin narcotics tycoon would be put off, however slightly, by a male secretary. Clifford did not have the option of bringing a stenographer from the DEA to Dean International. Regulations required that all undercover roles be filled by trained special agents because of the constant risk of violence and possible need to use firearms. Clifford's first choice was a strikingly attractive agent named Joan Marin but she was unavailable. Frank Chellino recommended another agent, Carol Cooper, whom he had known in Group Three. Tom Clifford interviewed Cooper and accepted her as Dean International's secretary. She was issued undercover credentials in the name of Carol Collins.

Clifford added one more special agent to the Dean International staff, José "Pepe" Hinojosa, a Mexican-American from Texas. Although Pepe Hinojosa was a skilled agent who was respected by his peers and Justice Department lawyers, Clifford's main motive in recruiting him for Operation Swordfish was his native fluency in Spanish. Since neither Frank Chellino nor Carol Cooper spoke Spanish, Clifford hoped that Hinojosa, who had worked for the DEA in Latin America, could aid the communication between Dean International and its target clientele, some of whom might not speak English. In his undercover role, Pepe Hinojosa would be known as Juan Carlos Stabile.

With the roster of undercover agents complete, at least for the moment, Tom Clifford turned at last to the delicate matter of recruiting spies. The DEA knew a good deal about the reliability of its own special agents, who underwent extensive background investigations, psychological testing, and intensive training—and were given security clearances—before being hired. The agency often knew little, however, about the outsiders it employed as spies or "informants." There was an institutional presumption that these people were potentially unreliable and could be used only under strict supervision. Clifford and Chellino discreetly interviewed a number of candidates in March and April—most of them at a secluded corner table at the Miami Lakes Inn & Country Club—but did not get lucky until May.

A DEA agent who had just returned to the United States after a tour in Bogotá introduced Clifford to Felipe Calderon, a thirty-five-year-old international banker from one of the richest and most prominent families in Colombia. Calderon's father had headed the Liberal Party of Colombia, one of the two major parties, and Calderon himself was either a relative or friend of every recent president of the country. Calderon had been educated at the London School of Economics and the University of Madrid and had been a dual U.S.-Colombian citizen since he was thirteen. He had worked in Europe, America, and Colombia, and had recently returned to the U.S. after resigning from a bank in Colombia because he disagreed with its policy of loaning money to narcotics traffickers. Well connected in diplomatic circles in Bogotá, Calderon had friends at the American Embassy and had been secretly passing information on his bank's drug clients to the DEA.

Although his colleagues in the bank had not known of his contacts with American agents, they had been angered by his opposition to their drug loans. The depth of their anger had become graphic when Calderon began finding plastique bombs in his office. The bombs had not been fused, and clearly had been only warnings. After finding a bomb in his car, however, Calderon had conferred briefly with his DEA control and caught the next plane to Miami. His wife and two sons had joined him later.

After a lengthy meeting in a room at a Marriott hotel near the Dadeland Mall, Tom Clifford decided that Felipe Calderon would make an ideal addition to Operation Swordfish. As a genuine banker, Calderon would bring credibility to an operation which at that point had no genuine banking or investment expertise, only the limited knowledge that Clifford had picked up from Angel Santiago, and that Chellino had gleaned from the University of Miami seminar at the Sheraton Bal Harbor. Felipe Calderon could educate and advise the agents on technical aspects of finance and banking, as well as sit in on meetings with prospective clients to consult on their needs. Calderon moreover had an encyclopedic knowledge of the upper echelon of the narcotics mafia of Latin America.

Clifford also was impressed with Calderon personally. Although he stood six feet tall and weighed over 200 pounds, he looked more like a well-fed aristocrat than an athlete. He wore conservative suits, button-down collars, quiet ties, and loafers, and had a soft baritone speaking voice and a soothing manner, the nonchalant mien of the well-born and secure.

There was one false note, however. Felipe Calderon's hands trembled. The tremor was slight but nevertheless constant, and was noticeable to any observant person who was around him for more than a few minutes. Tom Clifford inquired, and learned that the tremor resulted from a minor palsy condition, brought on by too much nicotine and caffeine over many years. (Calderon chain-smoked Merits.) Clifford suggested that Calderon take the initiative in mentioning the condition to new clients in the undercover operation so that they wouldn't think he was nervous.

As reassuring a presence as Felipe Calderon would be inside Dean International, Clifford considered him insufficiently dynamic to move comfortably and credibly in the financial circles of Miami—an essential asset for penetrating the narcotics mafia. Clifford felt he needed another Latin with more flair as well as more local grounding to serve as the principal spy.

Dean International's new secretary, Carol Cooper, had a suggestion. Along with other agents, including her Group Three partner, Paul Sennett, she had worked for three months earlier that year with one of the most effective spies in the annals of the DEA in Miami, a Cuban named Robert Darias.

7

WHEN THE DEA recruited a spy with Robert Darias's talent, agents fought over him. A skilled spy could make an agent's career. In Group Three, Carol Cooper and Paul Sennett had vied for Darias's allegiance with Barry Carew, the agent with whom he had barely escaped from the Colombian city of Cali in late January after the abortive negotiation with the godfather Santiago Ocampo.

In the spring Carew had approached Darias about working undercover as the chief of security for a Miami corporation that the DEA suspected of being a center of drug trafficking. Darias had been inclined to take the job, but when Carol Cooper learned of the offer, she promised that she and Sennett would have something better for him soon.

A few weeks later Carol summoned Robert, and asked whether he knew any bankers in Miami and was familiar with the laundering of narcotics money. Robert smiled. "I know a few bankers and I have a few ideas," he said, thinking to himself that he probably knew more about the banking system, having borrowed a lot of money and then experienced the revocation of his credit, than Cooper did. "I can certainly learn," he said.

Carol explained that she had just been assigned to a top secret operation which the DEA was going to mount against the financial hierarchy of the narcotics mafia. "We think if we can grab their money, we can put them out of business," Carol said. The operation would be far more ambitious and delicate than anything Darias had worked on so far. It would last a long time—perhaps three years. It would be dangerous.

Robert assured her he would like to participate, and Carol said that she and Paul Sennett would introduce Robert to the agent who was going to run it. Sennett, who was restless in Group Three, had been promised a transfer to Operation Swordfish in a few months. In the meantime, as a confidant of Cooper's, he was conferring with her about the directions the operation might take.

Frank Chellino invited Cooper and Sennett to bring Darias to lunch on Wednesday, June 24, at the Miami Lakes Inn & Country

Club. They met at their usual corner table overlooking the putting green. Chellino enjoyed Darias, who was charming and witty. He was sure of himself, an important attribute for undercover work. And he seemed to have an intimate knowledge of the large and diverse Miami banking community. Impressed, too, by Cooper and Sennett's strong recommendation, Chellino approved Darias for Operation Swordfish.

Tom Clifford, who met Darias later that day, also approved him and immediately gave him the title of senior vice president of Dean International Investments, the same title he had given to Felipe Calderon, the Colombian banker.

That afternoon Cooper began consulting Darias about how to proceed. In considering which Miami bankers might be involved in the narcotics business, Darias thought again of José Miguel Carvajal, the private detective who had introduced him to several drug traffickers. A few months before he had begun working for the DEA, Robert recalled, he had been with Carvajal when the detective stopped at the downtown headquarters of the Bank of Miami to see one of its officers, a Cuban named Manuel Sanchez. It had appeared to Darias that Carvajal was a valued client of Sanchez's. Carvajal had asked Sanchez, in front of Darias, if the bank could exchange large-denomination currency—hundred-dollar bills and fifty-dollar bills—for several hundred thousand dollars in small bills that a friend of Carvajal's wanted to get rid of. It was important that the transaction not be traceable to the friend. Sanchez had responded that while the Bank of Miami's official policy barred such exchanges (unless the client was in a legitimate cash business), he knew a ranking officer at another bank who could accommodate the transaction for a "fee." While Darias didn't know whether the exchange had ever occurred, he had inferred that the money was drug money. Narcotics dealers had a perpetual need to exchange their voluminous small bills—the raw revenues of drug trafficking—for more compact large bills, or perhaps a cashier's check, for easier concealment. Darias had also inferred that Manuel Sanchez knew the money was drug proceeds, and that he was prepared to launder it for a bribe which he would have shared with the other banker. Cooper and Sennett confirmed Darias's notion that Sanchez's actions constituted criminal conduct. They suggested that Darias discreetly determine whether Sanchez would be interested in the services offered by Dean International Investments. If he was, he might lead the DEA to high-level drug people who used major Miami banks.

Darias wondered whether Manuel Sanchez might check up on him by contacting José Carvajal, but Cooper and Sennett assured him

Carvajal posed no risk. He had become an informant for the DEA in the months since Darias had last been in touch with him.

Manuel Sanchez was a short man in his middle forties with a medium build, hazel eyes, and salt-and-pepper hair. With his horn-rimmed glasses, he looked like a conservative banker, correct and cordial, fluent in English as well as Spanish. Sanchez had been born in Havana just before Christmas of 1935. That made him a little less than two years younger than Robert Darias. Sanchez had come to Miami in the early sixties and had worked his way through a succession of banking jobs to the position of vice president and operations manager of the Bank of Miami, an eleven-branch institution that catered to the growing number of small, profitable Latin-owned businesses in South Florida.

Greeting Darias warmly, Sanchez recalled meeting him when he had come to the bank with José Carvajal, whom Sanchez said he had not seen in some time. The banker listened as Darias explained that his new company, Dean International Investments, not only could exchange large bills for small bills but also could deposit currency of any denomination in its own bank accounts, wire the money out of the country, wire it back to the U.S. in the Dean name, perhaps disguise it as a loan from an offshore corporation, and present it to the depositer in the form of a cashier's check or interest-bearing certificate of deposit. Dean also could invest the money in real estate, stocks, or any other security. And whatever the form of the money, its origin would be concealed from the Internal Revenue Service.

Sanchez was impressed. "This sounds promising," he said. "As you can understand, things are hot in all the banks now because of the Kattan episode."

"I can imagine," Darias said, recalling the arrest four months earlier of a Miami-based Colombian businessman named Isaac Kattan, whom federal authorities alleged had been the leading money manager for the South American drug mafia and had laundered more than $100 million in drug money through a worldwide network of bank accounts. When Kattan was arrested standing in front of a bank on Biscayne Boulevard, federal agents had found $16,000 cash under the front seat of his car, $385,000 in cashier's checks in his briefcase, and a $1.2 million wire transfer to a Swiss bank in a satchel. In an associate's car that Kattan had just dispatched across town, the agents found 44 pounds of cocaine in an orange-red suitcase. The next day federal agents (the Customs and IRS agents of Operation Greenback) had raided the two principal banks that Kattan had used, the Bank of

Miami, where Manuel Sanchez worked, and another South Florida institution called the Great American Bank. The agents had trucked away thousands of subpoenaed documents, and a federal affidavit unsealed in court had alleged that Isaac Kattan had $4 million in drug money on deposit at the Bank of Miami and had laundered many millions more through both banks. One federal official dubbed him the "Al Capone of South Florida."

The affidavit also alleged that the Great American Bank's senior vice president in charge of commercial loans, a man named Lionel Paytubi, had helped Kattan exchange millions of dollars in drug cash for cashier's checks without filing the required reports with the IRS. Although the Great American Bank had summarily fired Paytubi, a Cuban of Spanish-Moroccan origin, he had not been indicted or arrested yet, and four months later, neither Manuel Sanchez nor any other official of the Bank of Miami had been implicated in that bank's alleged participation in Kattan's crimes.

The Kattan episode had badly frightened Manuel Sanchez, however. "There are ways to handle millions of dollars," he was saying now to Robert Darias. "But it must be done in a nice way, not carried into a bank in bags. That's no way for gentlemen to transact business." Sanchez said he had a number of clients who might be interested in Dean International's services. He would contact them and get back to Darias.

Once a spy had ingratiated himself with a target, he was expected to introduce the target as soon as possible to DEA undercover agents who would then attempt to establish their own relationship with the suspect. That way, the agents themselves would witness the suspect's crimes, and they, instead of the spy, could testify about the crimes in court. The spy's security could be protected. And since most spies had checkered reputations, their testimony was assumed to be less credible to a jury than the agents' testimony.

Darias immediately arranged to introduce Manual Sanchez to Frank Chellino. The first day on which all three men were available was just after the long Fourth of July weekend, Monday, July 6. Darias and Chellino, in the role of Frank Dean, picked up Sanchez at the Bank of Miami and took him to lunch nearby in the semiprivate dining room of Floridita's, a small, pleasant Cuban restaurant on Flagler Street in downtown Miami.

Chellino explained the array of services that Dean International Investments offered to customers with large amounts of cash that needed laundering, and told Sanchez that he was looking not only for customers but also for banks in which to deposit cash. Would it be possible for Dean to open a corporate account at the Bank of Miami?

Sanchez reiterated his comment to Darias several days earlier that the bank was "hot" as a result of the ongoing investigation of Isaac Kattan. "Shortly after the Kattan episode, I could have sent you a lot of clients," Sanchez said. "I would have to see whether I can still get in touch with them and whether they have made other plans in the meantime. I would also have to look into the question of an account for you."

"I don't expect you to do all of that for nothing," Chellino said with a smile. "Dean International will take care of you."

"Thank you," Sanchez replied.

A few days later Manuel Sanchez told Robert Darias that he had a client who was interested in exchanging small denomination bills for large bills at the rate of about $1 million a week, more than $50 million a year. Darias drove to the Bank of Miami and picked up Sanchez, who directed him to the parking lot of the Westland Mall, a large shopping center in Hialeah. There, Sanchez introduced Darias to his "client," a bulky man in his forties with receding dark hair, who was none other than Lionel Paytubi, the fired officer of the Great American Bank who had been implicated in the Kattan scandal. Although Robert had seen the prominently displayed newspaper accounts in February of the arrest of Isaac Kattan and the raids on the two banks, he had forgotten Paytubi's name. And there was a great deal more that Robert did not yet know about the relationship of Manuel Sanchez and Lionel Paytubi. They had been close friends for twenty years. Paytubi had trained Sanchez in banking procedures shortly after they had arrived from Cuba as young men. Some of the drug financiers for whom Paytubi had laundered money at the Great American Bank were clients of Sanchez, who had sent them to Paytubi because of the Bank of Miami's tightened policy on deposits of large amounts of cash. Sanchez and Paytubi had charged a "fee" for the illegal service and split the proceeds. Each had made over $100,000 since they had begun laundering money in the late 1970s. When Operation Greenback agents had raided the two banks, and Lionel Paytubi's name had been in the *Miami Herald,* Manny Sanchez had rushed to Paytubi's home one evening agitated about whether his name, too, had come up in the investigation. It had not, and over the subsequent months investigators had tentatively concluded that none of the officers of the Bank of Miami had knowingly violated the law. Manny Sanchez was enormously relieved. Still, with Lionel Paytubi fired from the Great American Bank, and with the Bank of Miami barring large cash deposits, Sanchez's and Paytubi's drug clients were left without a ready outlet for laundering their money.

Darias drove Sanchez and Paytubi to Miami Lakes and the Dean International offices, where they settled in upholstered chairs across the desk from Frank Dean. Darias and Felipe Calderon sat in on the meeting. From a credenza behind Dean a camera lens the size of a pinhead transmitted the scene into a Sony V-220 videotape recorder in the next room.

"I don't know whether I'll be able to help you or not," Chellino said, his tenor voice squeaking a little. "We're an investment company, primarily. We have customers who bring us a lot of cash and we handle it for them. We put it in banks here in Miami. I have offices in New York, Denver, and Houston where I also bring money into. Then I can wire it anywhere in the world that you would like it, overseas, South America. I don't know exactly what your objectives are."

"I don't know what their system has been for depositing money," Paytubi said of his clients. "They run into quite a bit of cash a week. They're talking about a million dollars a week, and they want a swap."

"What denominations are you talking about?" Chellino asked.

"Twenties, tens, and fives, and they want hundreds and fifties in return," Paytubi said. "I guess they want to be able to go through the airport more easily—hand-carrying it, you know."

"I have the facilities to do anything with cash, in or out of the United States, any place in the world," Chellino said. "Is the money ultimately leaving the country?"

Paytubi said he didn't know in detail what the clients wanted. He hadn't yet met them, only their lawyer, whom he had known for many years. "I think they're in a state of panic at the moment because of the federal investigation, you know, with Operation Greenback going on," Paytubi said, toying with his sunglasses in his left hand. "They may be hand-carrying the cash out of the country."

"That's a risky business," Chellino said.

"Yeah, it's a helluva risky business."

"Let me tell you, I'm not particularly interested in swaps now," Chellino said, his voice calmer and more authoritative. "All I would be doing is providing a money-laundering service. That's not my primary purpose. I want to take that money and invest it for them someplace, in real estate, stocks, money market funds. That's how I make my money."

"Very good," Paytubi said.

"However," Chellino continued, "I guess there's no reason why I couldn't swap large-denomination bills the first time. Initially these people are gonna wanta see whether or not we can do it."

"Right," Paytubi said.

"Is there any particular reason why these people should be going through you with this?" Chellino asked, trying to get Paytubi to elaborate on his "clients."

"No, no, it's just that the lawyer asked me if I knew anyone that could make a swap for large bills."

Manuel Sanchez interjected. "This lawyer is a very close friend of ours."

"Twenty-six years I've known him," Paytubi said. "Twenty-six years."

"I'm very cautious about who I meet with," Chellino said. "I don't want to be meeting with a lot of people."

"Absolutely, I don't blame you," Paytubi said. "You've got to be careful nowadays. The only thing that will save the day would be if the government doesn't fund any more money for Operation Greenback."

"We're losing money, we're losing deposits," Sanchez said, referring to Greenback's impact on the Bank of Miami.

"What is happening with that?" Chellino asked. "Greenback. Is that Kattan?"

"The Kattan deal," Paytubi said. "He's in jail."

"Business has never been greater for me since that thing happened," Chellino said.

After the meeting Robert Darias took Paytubi and Sanchez to lunch at the Miami Lakes Inn & Country Club so that he could talk to them again Cuban-to-Cuban, without having to speak English for the benefit of the gringo Frank Dean. They were even more candid than they had been in the office. "Paytubi said that he works with people in cocaine instead of marijuana because the people handling cocaine are more sophisticated and educated," Darias reported later that day, dictating a report to Carol Cooper. "He said he was under investigation by Operation Greenback and may be indicted. Isaac Kattan was one of his main clients at the Great American Bank."

Darias stayed in touch with Paytubi and Sanchez, and a few days later Paytubi reported that the lawyer who had asked him about money-exchange services had introduced him to the client who needed the services. It was not a man, as Paytubi had assumed, but a woman, who claimed to have a million dollars in small bills that she wanted exchanged for large bills. Paytubi asked for another meeting with Frank Dean. On Tuesday, July 21, Darias again picked up Paytubi at the Westland Mall and drove him to Dean International. Manuel Sanchez did not attend the meeting, knowing Paytubi would represent his interests.

The agents were amused with Lionel Paytubi—his loquacity, and his wardrobe. Today he wore a brightly striped polo shirt and a garish, violently clashing baseball cap that he kept on during the meeting. The agents also were amused that Paytubi, while oblivious to Operation Swordfish, was obsessed with Operation Greenback. He handed Frank Chellino a sheet of paper that he said listed all the IRS and Customs agents who were working on Greenback. A Customs agent had inadvertently dropped the list in Paytubi's office when the bank had been raided, and Paytubi had recovered it.

"I put it in my pocket," Paytubi said, gesturing with his sunglasses. "That shows you how unprofessional they are. Charlie Blau, see the name down there? Charles Blau. He's a prosecutor, and the people I got circled are the agents in charge of my case . . . Mike Hammer, Lydia Pulez, she's a Spanish girl, speaks perfect Spanish. A real bitch, too. You could tell she was unprofessional. Just out of school. A dumb cunt."

"Boy, oh, boy, I appreciate this," Chellino said, inwardly savoring the moment when the DEA could rag the Justice Department's Charles Blau about the carelessness of his Greenback agents.

"It was a wild deal," Paytubi went on, recalling the raid on the bank. "You've never seen anything like it in your life. Thirty agents with walkie-talkies all over the bank, kicking the customers out of the bank. There were old people that almost fainted."

"That must have been a scene," Chellino said.

"It had an effect on the banking community in Miami. I've been in the banking business twenty-one years, and I know a lot of bankers in town that are running scared. I'd like to take a bazooka to Operation Greenback. I'd like to fire a rocket right into the U.S. Attorney's office where they work."

"There had to be a lot of drug money coming in that bank," Chellino said. "There had to be a shit load of money."

"Maybe forty-five million dollars in one year. That's nothing. I heard other banks do that much in a couple of months."

Paytubi went on to recount a meeting he had had the previous day with the woman who wanted to launder a million dollars in cash.

"She has an account in Panama, with numbers, no names."

"What is her name?" Chellino asked.

" 'Marlene' is all that I could find out," Paytubi said, spelling the name and pronouncing it "Mar LEEN." "That's her first name. She wouldn't give me her phone number. She wouldn't give me her last name."

"Is she American?" Chellino asked.

"She looks Spanish to me, but she speaks English, very good English."

According to Paytubi, the woman called Marlene had been paying "commissions" to various illegal money-launderers equal to seven and eight percent of the cash she was laundering. Chellino and Paytubi agreed that Dean International would exchange the money for six percent. Dean would keep half the commission, and Paytubi would take the other half, keeping some for himself and paying Manny Sanchez and the lawyer, who actually had turned out to be two lawyers, whatever they negotiated.

"This woman Marlene, is she an old lady?" Chellino asked.

"She's not an old lady, no. Pretty nice-looking girl. Thirty-five, thirty-six, thirty-seven."

"Don't have her bring the money here in shopping bags and that kind of thing," Chellino said. "Make it suitcases or something professional-looking. Briefcases."

Frank Chellino was pleased by his first two encounters with Lionel Paytubi and Manuel Sanchez and looked forward to cultivating the relationship with them. First, however, he had to deal with the imperative that Operation Swordfish had just collided head-on with Operation Greenback. Chellino recalled that although the raids on the Bank of Miami and the Great American Bank had been carried out by Customs and IRS agents assigned to Greenback, the information leading to the raids had come from the DEA. And it had been DEA agents who had arrested Isaac Kattan, against the wishes of the Greenback agents, who thought the arrest was premature. The Greenback staff had quarreled with the DEA about every aspect of those actions, heightening the animosity between the agencies. And now, a prime target of Operation Greenback, Lionel Paytubi, had wandered into the DEA's Operation Swordfish. Another interagency clash seemed inevitable.

Chellino drove from Miami Lakes down the Palmetto Expressway to the Phoenix Building to brief Tom Clifford and show him the videotapes of Lionel Paytubi and Manuel Sanchez. After hearing Paytubi's remarks about Operation Greenback, Clifford called Charles Blau, the Justice Department's attorney in charge of Greenback. Clifford and Blau had gotten to know each other well in the year and a half that Blau had been in Miami coordinating Greenback and trying to convince the DEA to support it. Despite the rancor between

the DEA and Customs, Blau and Clifford had developed a cordial
relationship, an off-the-record, back-channel of communication
about the problems both had had launching their operations. Blau's
fantasy was to bring Operation Swordfish under the aegis of Operation Greenback, but Clifford had convinced him that the DEA would
never agree to such an arrangement.

"Ever hear of Lionel Paytubi?" Clifford asked Blau.

"He's my guy," said Blau.

"He's *my* guy, now," said Clifford.

The following day Clifford drove downtown and met with Blau,
who, it turned out, had already begun preparing an indictment of
Lionel Paytubi for his criminal activities at the Great American Bank.
Blau had been under considerable pressure from Customs and the IRS
to present the Paytubi indictment promptly to a grand jury. And Blau
was eager to arrest Paytubi because he anticipated that the banker
would implicate his bosses at Great American in its laundering of drug
money. The bank's chairman was Marvin L. Warner, who was a
major Democratic Party fund-raiser and had been President Jimmy
Carter's ambassador to Switzerland.

"If Paytubi rolls over, it's golden, those guys are dead ducks," Blau
said of the Great American officers. "He's my smoking gun to get to
the higher management of the bank. I've got to nail him."

Clifford showed Blau the videotapes that the Swordfish agents had
made of Lionel Paytubi as the banker was railing at Charles Blau and
several Greenback agents by name and musing about firing a rocket
into their offices. While it appeared that Paytubi had been joking, it
wasn't clear, and Blau was both amused and horrified.

Tom Clifford argued vehemently that if Blau's agents arrested
Lionel Paytubi, Operation Swordfish would be destroyed. In any
prosecution the government is required to disclose all its evidence
from all sources to the defendant's attorney. In the case of Paytubi
that would have included not only Blau's evidence but also the DEA's
evidence, most notably the videotapes and the circumstances under
which they had been made, i.e., that the DEA was running an undercover operation known as Dean International Investments in Miami
Lakes. The DEA would have to terminate Operation Swordfish just
as it was getting started after many months of meticulous preparation.

"If they get our videotape, we're dead," Clifford told Blau.

It was a heated meeting, but Clifford persuaded Blau to defer
indicting Lionel Paytubi until the DEA had an opportunity to see
where he would lead Operation Swordfish.

The delivery of $1 million cash to Dean International by the woman called Marlene was postponed, and the delay riled Frank Chellino, who was an impatient man under the best of circumstances. Robert Darias suggested that possibly Frank and his colleagues were experiencing nothing more than the phenomenon of "Latin time." Some Latins, Darias explained, pay less attention to the passage of time than Anglos do. They can be quite casual about being late and skipping appointments. Perhaps Marlene was like that. One needed to be patient. Meanwhile Darias urged Paytubi to introduce him to Marlene so that he could present Dean's services to her personally.

On Tuesday, August 4, 1981, the FBI ended its own undercover investigation of the drug mafia, the venture that it had undertaken unilaterally and called Operation Bancoshares, with the indictment of some sixty-one people and the seizure of thirty-five vehicles, five parcels of land, 23 pounds of cocaine, and $12 million in cash, most of it on deposit in twenty-one Miami banks. At the obligatory press conference, the United States Attorney for Miami, Atlee Wampler III, said that Operation Bancoshares had been "one of the most aggressive, imaginative probes ever conducted by the FBI" and asserted that the arrests and seizures would disrupt established patterns of laundering narcotics proceeds in South Florida. (The U.S. Attorney did not mention that none of those indicted was a major figure. And only twenty-eight of the sixty-one were arrested; many of the thirty-three others were either in Colombia or at large elsewhere.)

Across town within the DEA there were two suppositions about the impact of Operation Bancoshares. The optimists felt that the arrests and indictment would drive the narcotics mafia directly into the arms of Operation Swordfish, that need would overcome caution and that Dean International's business would pick up. The pessimists predicted that the publicity surrounding Bancoshares would frighten major drug financiers out of Miami to New York or Los Angeles, and that Dean's business would wither.

Lionel Paytubi phoned Robert Darias shortly after noon the next day.

"This lady wants to meet you."

"Where and when?"

"She said she would be at the Steak and Egg Kitchen near Coconut Grove, the one on Coral Way, two o'clock."

The Steak and Egg Kitchen was a large, comfortable coffee shop, and Marlene was waiting in a corner booth by the window when Darias and Paytubi arrived. Her full name was Marlene Navarro, and she pronounced her first name "Mar LAY nay," not "Mar LEEN." She appeared to be in her middle thirties. She was a slender woman, very small, barely five feet, but her figure was stunning, her grooming exquisite, and her manner engaging, all of which diverted attention from her height. She had bright brown eyes, moderately short, expertly coiffed brown hair, and wore designer clothes.

Navarro said she was sorry she had been difficult to reach but she had just flown in from Bogotá. She wanted to deliver $1.2 million to Dean International within a few days, and another $2 million within two weeks. Some of the money was coming from Los Angeles and Houston. She said she generally handled between $4 million and $6 million in cash monthly. Her need for Dean's services had increased because of "the problem yesterday," which Darias took to mean the indictment stemming from the FBI's Operation Bancoshares. She promised to telephone Paytubi or Darias when the first delivery was ready.

The new delay further angered Frank Chellino. But shortly after noon on Friday, August 14, Lionel Paytubi phoned Darias and said that Marlene Navarro wanted them to come immediately to her lawyer's office to pick up a delivery of money. The offices of Navarro's attorney, Lester Martin Rogers, were in a shabby two-story beige stucco building just off the Dolphin Expressway near the Orange Bowl. As Darias drove into the parking lot, Paytubi emerged from the building, and a few minutes later Marlene Navarro arrived in her black Mustang.

"The money's in the trunk," she told Darias.

"It's dangerous handling money in parking lots," Darias said. "We should make other arrangements next time." Navarro agreed, and opened her trunk to reveal a large brown suitcase.

"It's about five hundred thousand," she said. "I didn't have time to count it all." The suitcase was too heavy for her to lift, so Paytubi moved it to Darias's trunk and Navarro went inside the building to Lester Rogers's office. Darias and Paytubi left for Dean International in their separate cars. When they arrived, Paytubi seemed nervous and accepted the offer of a Scotch. Darias and Chellino joined him.

"How much is it? Five hundred thousand?" Chellino asked.

"Over," said Paytubi. "That's what she said, around or over."

"She doesn't really give a shit, does she," Chellino said.

"As long as it's close," Paytubi replied.

There was excitement as the suitcase was opened. "Oh, God," Chellino exclaimed, his voice rising, and then falling when he saw the money. "Shit, twenties. I thought it was going to be all hundreds." In the anxiety of the moment Chellino forgot he was expecting small bills.

He asked Paytubi to help him carry the suitcase into the conference room. "Any cameras?" Paytubi murmured, glancing about the walls with a nervous chuckle, as he grasped one end of the suitcase. Everyone laughed.

Instead of exchanging the cash for large-denomination currency, Marlene Navarro had decided she wanted it deposited in a Dean International bank account and then wired to Panama. Paytubi gave Chellino the name of the bank in Panama and the number of the account to which the money was to be wired. It was the Banco Nacional de Paris in Panama City.

Carol Cooper and Felipe Calderon joined Chellino, Darias, and Paytubi for the counting, which took four hours. Pepe Hinojosa, the third DEA special agent in Operation Swordfish, also pitched in, as did Robert Russo, the intelligence analyst who was acting as Dean International's treasurer. There was $484,800 in fives, tens, twenties, and fifties. After setting aside six percent in commissions for Dean, Paytubi, Manuel Sanchez, and their lawyers, Chellino gave Paytubi a receipt for the balance—approximately $455,800—and Paytubi left.

Cooper had been quietly updating Tom Clifford by phone through the afternoon and now was able to report that Dean International had finally completed its first major deposit of narcotics money. The agents deposited the money in two banks—Capital Bank's North Bay Village branch and Republic National's Hialeah office—where Dean had opened accounts after establishing credit in Chicago. Then they took Darias and Calderon for celebratory drinks to the Le Sabre Club, a dark, wood-paneled bar near the Dean International offices. The group was exhilarated. They had implicated two officers of major Miami banks, as well as an intriguing, designer-clothed woman from Bogotá, in serious drug crimes. Two Miami attorneys apparently were involved as well. These were not street pushers. They obviously were people of substance, who probably were connected to the elite of the Latin American drug mafia.

Operation Swordfish was under way.

Dean International was closed part of the following week as Tropical Storm Diana drenched South Florida with nearly ten inches of rain, felling trees and cutting power. Still, Frank Chellino managed to wire Marlene Navarro's $455,800 to the Banco Nacional de Paris in Panama for the account that carried no name but was numbered 698–B. Navarro had stressed the dash between 698 and B; without it, the money might go astray, she had cautioned.

The agents hoped that Dean International's clients eventually would agree to have their money invested in U.S. real estate, securities, or other financial instruments that could be seized by the government at the end of Operation Swordfish. Processing drug cash, however, was at least a start toward infiltrating their targets.

Manuel Sanchez telephoned Darias to say that he was delighted with his commission and hoped soon to refer more business to Dean International. At the DEA's instruction, Darias spent the week trying to meet the lawyers, Lester Rogers and Arthur Karlick, through whom he and Paytubi had met Marlene Navarro. Since lawyers in general hold themselves out as rectitudinous, the DEA loved the irony of implicating them in crimes. On Thursday, Darias took photocopies of Marlene Navarro's bank wire transfer documents to Rogers's office and the lawyer received him cordially. Rogers said that he was pleased with Dean's handling of the first transaction; that he agreed with Darias's feeling that in the future Navarro should bring money directly to Dean International for security purposes rather than transfer it in parking lots; that the organization for which Marlene Navarro worked owned "chemical plants" in Cali, Colombia; and that the organization handled between $300 million and $500 million annually.

By the last week of August, it was clear that Marlene Navarro was starting to trust Robert Darias. She gave him her telephone number and they began talking directly, without Lionel Paytubi as a go-between. She began to confide in Darias. On Monday afternoon, August 24, she asked him to meet her at Tony Roma's restaurant in Coral Gables. Settling back with a glass of iced tea, she complained that she was swamped with the details of moving into a new home near the Doral Country Club.

"Where is it from the Doral?" Darias asked.

"Two blocks west. It's called the Costa del Sol, condominium town houses."

"Oh, yes, I've seen them. Very nice."

Marlene complained that she hadn't heard from her son in a long time. "I'm afraid he's turning into a bum," she said.

"Where does he live?" Robert asked.

"In Europe, the Netherlands. He's eighteen and living with a girl. He was going to school but he dropped out. And he doesn't have a job. I support him."

"I can't believe you are old enough to have a child eighteen."

"He was born when *I* was very young," Marlene said with a smile.

"My child is only seven," Robert said. "I have a few years before I have to worry about all those problems."

"I'm still a schoolgirl myself—law school, that is," Marlene said. "Really?"

"Yes, I take classes at the University of Miami law school."

"That's very interesting. I studied law in Cuba."

"Well, between the two of us, we should be able to avoid doing anything illegal," Navarro replied with a little laugh.

"Yes."

"I love studying," she added. "I'm also taking flying lessons."

"That's extraordinary," Darias said. "You'll be ready for anything."

Getting down to business, Marlene said she was upset because one of her couriers from the West Coast had been stopped by the police while driving east through Texas en route to Miami with $500,000 in cash. The money had been seized. She had another half-million dollars in Miami that she had intended to deposit with Dean International, but now she would need to keep that money for "expenses." Could Dean International, she asked, take delivery of money in San Francisco? If so, her "big people" in California wouldn't need to transport cash across the country by automobile. Darias assured her that Dean could help, and he and Navarro made tentative plans to fly to San Francisco within the next two weeks.

Navarro said that she would like to give Dean International all of her business but that her people around the U.S. and overseas were being very careful about sending money to or through Miami or investing in South Florida. They were frightened, she said, by Operation Greenback and Operation Bancoshares, which had gotten national publicity. Almost parenthetically, she mentioned that her people in Colombia were "powder people" (which Darias took as a reference to cocaine) and dealt in "big money." One of Navarro's "groups" had actually considered purchasing the Bank of Miami but had decided against it because it had been implicated in the Isaac Kattan case.

Navarro gave Darias her travel schedule. She was flying to New York on Friday for a long weekend (staying at the Plaza Hotel), returning to Miami on Tuesday, flying to Bogotá on Wednesday (staying with friends), and returning to Miami on Labor Day, September 7.

Robert liked Marlene. He liked women in general more than men. And after the reserved Manuel Sanchez and the buffoonish Lionel Paytubi, he enjoyed Marlene's spunk and spark, and her mystery.

Though lively and informal, she spoke some of the most erudite Spanish he had ever heard. Clearly she was very intelligent and well educated. Since he knew virtually nothing about her, she would be a challenge. It was good for a change to be spying on someone he had not known before Operation Swordfish.

8

ROBERT DARIAS GOT to know Humberto Garcia in the fifties when Garcia headed the Batista youth organization in Cuba. Garcia, who was three years older than Darias, had a law degree from the University of Havana and worked in politics for Darias's father. Garcia had become the youngest member of the Cuban legislature before emigrating to Miami in the wake of the Castro revolution. Starting as a truck driver, he worked his way to a high executive position in an air-conditioning and refrigeration company, Refricenter of Miami,* which had annual sales of $30 million and branches in Puerto Rico, the Dominican Republic, and Colombia.

In 1979, when Robert Darias was mired in financial difficulties, Humberto Garcia hired him to head Refricenter's office in Colombia. Darias had just begun work when he was unexpectedly sentenced to three months in prison for tax evasion. Although Garcia had known about Darias's legal problems, he refused to hold the job open, and also refused to make any restitution when Darias's furniture and belongings were lost in transit back to Miami. Garcia paid up only when Darias threatened him. The two men stopped speaking.

Two years later, as Darias was solidifying his relationships with Marlene Navarro, Lionel Paytubi, and Manuel Sanchez, it occurred to him that Humberto Garcia might be involved in narcotics trafficking. Darias knew that Garcia was active daily in business transactions between Miami and Colombia and thus it seemed likely he was at least acquainted with people who were smuggling drugs. Robert agonized over whether to approach Humberto. Investigating friends and acquaintances still smacked of snitching. It had bothered him when Francisco Navia, the man who had photographed his wedding, had turned out to be a drug dealer. It had bothered him when Eric Arias, who had been with him at the Bay of Pigs, turned out to be a drug dealer. But Humberto Garcia had never been a close friend. And Robert felt that Humberto had betrayed him over the job in Colombia and the missing furniture.

*Garcia has no connection to the Refricenter of Miami doing business in 1993.

Robert telephoned Humberto in September, expressed regret over their estrangement, and invited him to lunch. They met at Centro Vasco in Little Havana, the quintessential Spanish restaurant in Miami, a transplant of a restaurant that had been popular in Havana in the fifties. In a suit, tie, and horn-rimmed glasses, with gray streaking his dark hair, Humberto Garcia, at age fifty, looked the part of a successful Miami businessman of the early eighties. Over generous servings of Johnnie Walker Black Label Scotch, Humberto and Robert chatted about how much they both regretted the incidents that led to their parting two years earlier. Then Robert told Humberto about Dean International Investments and the services it offered to people with large amounts of cash on their hands.

"Are you sure you're not with the DEA or the FBI?" Humberto asked.

Robert smiled. "If I were a *federal* I would not have had to go to prison. I would have made a deal with them."

That explanation made sense to Humberto, who proceeded to confirm Robert's suspicions: Not only did he know people in the drug business, he was in the business himself and was having particular difficulty handling quantities of cash. "Just last week," Humberto confided, "somebody gave me five hundred thousand in small bills and asked me to 'find a place for it.' " Humberto had decided that the "heat" the government was putting on Miami banks made it too risky to handle the money and he had returned it to the client. Humberto told Robert that he knew people in Medellín, Colombia, who handled more than a million dollars a month in cocaine proceeds and wanted him to launder the money for them; he had reluctantly said he wasn't able to.

Robert explained a specific money-laundering technique that he felt Humberto might be able to use. (Although he didn't tell Humberto, the method had been used often by Isaac Kattan.) "It's simple," Robert said. "Let's say your client has U.S. dollars here, wants to get rid of them, and is willing to exchange them for Colombian pesos."

"Yes."

"I know someone [Robert was thinking of Marlene Navarro] who *needs* U.S. dollars here, and would be willing to deposit the equivalent of those dollars in Colombian pesos in your client's bank account in Colombia, in exchange for the dollars in Miami."

"Yes, sounds good," Humberto said.

Calling the technique a "peso exchange," Robert mentioned that it in some ways resembled the common banking practice known as compensating balances. For clients interested in secrecy, it had the advantage of being more anonymous than an international wire transfer. No money crossed international boundaries, or even left its country of origin. Only Darias's company, Dean International Investments, would know the identities of both parties to the transaction.

Humberto Garcia promised to call Robert the next time he or a cash-laden client needed help.

Marlene Navarro returned from Bogotá with a bad cold. She had a bronchial condition and had difficulty adjusting to the sudden changes between sweltering, sea-level Miami and cool, mountainous Bogotá. Arriving after the Labor Day weekend, she drove directly from the airport to her Miami doctor and then spent the next few days in bed.

During the last half of September, Navarro and Darias met for drinks or meals at Tony Roma's in Coral Gables, Steak and Egg on Southwest 8th Street, Neighbors Restaurant close to her new home adjacent to the Doral Country Club, and the Marshall Majors delicatessen in the fashionable Sunset district of South Miami. Although Marlene initiated each contact, none led to additional deposits of money at Dean International Investments. The trip to San Francisco she had discussed with Darias was postponed indefinitely. To Robert, this was typical foreplay in the Latin business world—obligatory schmoozing before getting down to the business of moving drug money. To the tense DEA agents, it was another irritating waste of time.

"You pretty well know we want to get this thing rolling," Carol Cooper said to Robert. "If she's waiting for some enormous amount, or if she's talking about waiting for an extensive period of time, why don't you tell her, hey, why don't we at least get the ball rolling with a smaller amount."

"I will find out what the story is and what the problem is," Robert said. "At least we know she's there."

"I'd like to know what she does all day."

"Well, for one thing, she goes to the University of Miami law school. Then she also mentioned that she was taking flying lessons."

"That's incredible," Cooper exclaimed.

Darias began to lobby Navarro. "Marlene, you haven't delivered any more money to me," he said one morning at Steak and Egg. "I need to know more or less how much you think we are going to be handling."

"It's hard to say," she replied. "It depends on the deliveries and collections, and any problems we might have. The heat is really on.

Two of my California people are in jail now on ten-million-dollar bond. We'll see what happens when they get out. I have four hundred [$400,000] now, but they've ordered me not to deliver to you until I have at least a million." Navarro asked again how Darias could be sure that Dean International was immune from "all the heat" that the *"federales"* (U.S. Government agents) were applying to Miami. He explained that Dean International had relationships with banks and corporations in other cities "where there is less heat." Darias indicated that his partner, Frank Dean, was part of a major Italian Mafia group in the Northeast and ran his money through some of the same bank accounts that service the big gambling casinos in Atlantic City and Las Vegas. "There is no way anyone can identify it as narcotics proceeds from Florida," Darias claimed.

While Navarro did not promise any immediate new cash deposits at Dean International, she did agree to exchange pesos in Colombia for dollars in Miami in accord with the "peso exchange" mechanism that Darias had outlined for Humberto Garcia.

Although Darias shared some of Carol Cooper's frustration with Navarro's seeming inertia, he was optimistic that Marlene would use Dean International again. Darias also continued to cultivate Humberto Garcia, who proved to be as cautious as Navarro. Over drinks at Victoria Station, a restaurant near the airport, Humberto told Robert of a client in the copper tubing business in Medellín, Colombia, who needed to launder a minimum of $600,000 to $800,000 a month in cocaine money. Garcia said the man was coming to Miami soon and wanted to meet Darias. However, the introduction had not been made by the end of September.

In addition to meeting with his targets in bars and restaurants, Darias also was expected to hang out with the DEA agents in their favorite haunts. When Operation Swordfish began, the agents' habit of drinking at bars near the DEA offices changed. They were expected to minimize their contacts with other agents. Even within the DEA, information about Operation Swordfish was disseminated only on a need-to-know basis, and rather than risk uncomfortable barroom encounters with curious friends, the Swordfish agents kept to themselves at bars near Dean International in Miami Lakes, usually the Le Sabre Club, where they had celebrated Marlene Navarro's delivery of nearly $500,000.

Darias didn't mind a quick one after work, but he soon tired of the DEA agents' protracted drinking sessions. The liquor didn't bother him as much as the smoke from Cooper and Chellino's cigarettes. But Darias went along because it was clear to him that there was an almost ritualistic quality about the agents' bar time. It was part of the work-day.

At Le Sabre one evening, Tom Clifford chatted with Robert Darias about his cases, specifically the manner in which he was pursuing Marlene Navarro and Humberto Garcia. Did Darias feel that he would be able soon to introduce Navarro and Garcia to Frank Chellino or another DEA agent, as he had Paytubi and Sanchez? Yes, Darias said, he was confident it wouldn't be long. Clifford stressed that Chellino needn't replace Darias in his relationship with the targets. Perhaps Chellino (or preferably another agent, since Chellino was so short) could pose as a bodyguard and simply observe what the target does or says for purposes of later corroboration.

Darias and Clifford also talked about how Darias was to be compensated for his work, an issue that had been left unsettled when Darias joined the group in June. Spies typically were paid each time they made a case, according to the quantity of the narcotics or money that they were responsible for confiscating, and the importance of the traffickers who were arrested. That was how Darias had been paid early in the year when he had fostered the arrests of Francisco Navia and the others. In Operation Swordfish, however, arrests and seizures were unlikely until the end of the operation, perhaps two years or more in the future. Thus it seemed more appropriate to pay Darias a monthly salary, as the CIA had during the Bay of Pigs period.

Darias and Clifford discussed a salary of $5,000 a month and the use of a government-financed automobile. Clifford said he thought that arrangement was reasonable and would talk it over with Frank Chellino. Darias was surprised a few days later, therefore, when Chellino informed him that he would be paid only $4,000 a month and would have to use his own car.

"Tom made me believe it would be five thousand and a car," Darias said.

"Tom and I discussed it and this is the final decision," Chellino replied.

"It is not fair," Darias replied. "I'm spending a lot of money just on my car."

"Well, if you're unhappy, Bob, you are under no obligation to us," the blunt Chellino retorted. "No one is forcing you to stay here."

Darias got angry. "Don't insult my intelligence, Frank! I don't work for you. I work for the United States Government. First of all, I work for Carol and Paul." Paul Sennett's transfer to Operation Swordfish from Group Three was expected soon, and Darias still felt a strong allegiance to Sennett as well as Cooper. "They were the ones who brought me here," he told Chellino. "When Carol and Paul tell me that I have to get out of this office, then I get out of this office. But you cannot give me that order. You are only an agent, the same as Carol and Paul. You are not the president here or anything like that. I walked into DEA to work for the government, not for you."

"All I'm saying is that you aren't obligated to us."

"Would you say that to an agent?"

"You are not an agent, Bob. And if you don't like the way we do things you can leave the operation. You are not obligated to us to stay."

"If I leave this operation because of you, Frank, you are going to get in trouble. Because you don't have anything else going on in this operation. If I had not brought that first delivery from Marlene, the operation would be closed today. So I am not trying to paint myself as a hero, but don't tell me to leave. You cannot fire me!"

Darias and Chellino also quarreled about when and under what circumstances Darias would introduce Chellino or other undercover agents to his targets. Darias said he would make the introductions when he felt it was appropriate. Chellino retorted that it had better be soon.

Livid, Darias strode out of the office and drove home.

Carol Cooper, who had heard the end of the conversation as the voices were raised, told Chellino, "You just said the wrong thing to the wrong person."

It fell to Carol to calm Robert later on the telephone. "Honest to God, Bob, if you ever left, Frank would be crushed—we both would," Carol said. "We enjoy working with you. I don't think Frank ever had it in his mind that you would walk out. He just wanted you to understand that you are not obligated to us."

"I am a different type of animal from Frank."

"You are totally different, so we have to think differently from the normal routine of what we're used to. Paul and I both think of you as a friend and we totally trust you on anything. Frank hasn't seen all that yet. We want you to think that you're part of us. You're not a CI. I don't think of you as a CI. I know Paul doesn't. I want you to give us ideas and tell us what you think. We need to be flexible, all of us. The point is, you're doing the job and we all know it."

"This is a very complicated business, Carol. And very soon it is going to be difficult and dangerous both."

"Which is the main reason why we want to get someone else with you to be your bodyguard."

Darias agreed that on at least some future deliveries of cash outside of Dean International's offices a DEA agent would be designated to accompany him, posing as a driver or bodyguard.

The DEA's welshing on its original compensation commitments deeply angered Robert Darias—even more than he had let on to Frank Chellino and Carol Cooper. If Darias couldn't trust the agents' commitments on how much to pay him, how could he trust anything else they said, particularly about Operation Swordfish? He had embarked on a top-secret mission for the United States Government that promised to be more dangerous than anything he had ever done with the possible exception of his incursions into Cuba. The U.S. Government had betrayed him and his colleagues then. Why should he trust it now? Protecting himself against detection and retribution by the narcotics mafia would be challenge enough. What could he do to protect himself against betrayal by his control agents in the DEA? He had heard stories about how intelligence agencies sometimes mistreated spies—how agents made commitments and then cast the spy adrift when he was no longer needed, how they disclaimed all knowledge of him and his activities if something went wrong. He had heard stories about corrupt DEA agents. And even in situations short of corruption or conscious betrayal, how could Darias be sure the agents wouldn't tell him one thing after a few drinks in a bar, and something else later after they had sobered up?

At the very least, Darias decided, he should keep an unchallengeable record of everything the agents said to him in the future about his mission, about his compensation, about every aspect of his work for the government. They had recently equipped him with a small, gray Sony tape recorder for use in surreptitiously recording his telephone conversations with Marlene Navarro and his other targets. The agents had not barred him from using it for other purposes. Perhaps it would be wise for him to quietly record his conversations with the DEA agents as well.

Amelia Darias, who remained deeply skeptical of the government, enthusiastically endorsed Robert's decision.

The money drought ended two days later. On Friday, October 2, Humberto Garcia summoned Darias to Refricenter of Miami and introduced him to two Colombian drug traffickers named Alvaro and Aurelio. They were young and scrawny, and Garcia called them "the Kids." The Kids gave Darias a plastic bag containing $67,250 and asked that the equivalent in Colombian pesos be deposited in a bank account in Colombia, whose number they supplied. The following

Tuesday, Manuel Sanchez of the Bank of Miami asked Darias to pick up $395,000 in small bills from one of his clients and exchange them for hundreds. The next afternoon Darias received a beeper message to call Humberto Garcia. The Colombian Kids had another $325,000 for laundering by Dean International. Darias and Paul Sennett, who was now informally working for Operation Swordfish even though his transfer was not yet official, picked up the money at Refricenter.

Darias and the agents were ecstatic. In its first four months Operation Swordfish had taken in just $484,800, in a single transaction with Marlene Navarro. Now, in just four business days, it had received an additional $787,250 in three deposits.

"This is going to get to the point where we have to have a line outside the door," Darias said to Carol Cooper on the phone that evening, his tape recorder running.

"Take a number, guys, stand in line," Cooper said. "Nobody can believe this."

The prickly Frank Chellino shared the joy only momentarily. After complaining for weeks about the lack of cash deposits, Chellino now passed the word that he didn't want to receive any more money for a few days because the three new deposits had created more paperwork than Dean International could handle. Meanwhile, there was still nothing more from Marlene Navarro, and Navarro's organization in Colombia had been slow to handle the deposit of pesos in exchange for the Kids' dollars in Miami, and in the end had deposited only part of the required amount. Marlene had been out of town and unreachable. Dean International had to issue cashier's checks to the Kids to cover the difference. Chellino got angry, and concluded that Navarro perhaps was more trouble than she was worth. He instructed Darias to stop pursuing her for the time being.

"Let her come to you," Chellino said.

The paperwork at Dean International indeed was onerous, and dominated the daily routine. Each deposit of drug money at Dean, each deposit and withdrawal at a bank, each transfer of money between banks, each transfer of funds overseas, each debriefing of Robert Darias and other sources of intelligence had to be elaborately documented and then typed on official DEA forms requiring the signatures of an agent and a supervisor.

The paperwork, plus the growing enmity between Frank Chellino and Robert Darias, prompted Chellino to assign the day-to-day handling of Darias to Carol Cooper. Robert was pleased. In much the way he preferred Marlene Navarro to Lionel Paytubi, he liked Carol much more than Frank. Robert liked women. They intrigued him.

Most men he knew talked about nothing but sports, which bored him, or conquests in business or sex. While not uninterested in business and sex, Robert had always shared what in his experience were the more eclectic, less competitive interests of women in such things as books and art.

Robert and Carol got along well. She had a sense of humor, and they kidded each other in a way that Robert could never kid Frank Chellino. Unlike Chellino, she seemed to care about Robert's personal welfare and that of his family. She was always available and encouraged Robert to call her at home. Chellino had given Robert his home phone number only grudgingly and warned him "not to abuse it."

Carol had even seemed appreciative when Robert made a suggestion to her, which might have offended someone less secure. Since Dean International's target clientele consisted largely of Latin males who considered themselves macho, Robert gently suggested to Carol on the phone one evening that she wear more makeup and more feminine clothing than she was inclined to—nothing flamboyant or provocative, just a heightened nuance—so that the first person that Dean's new clients encountered, at the secretary's desk inside the company's offices, would be an attractive, well-groomed woman, which Carol was capable of being with a little effort, rather than a ruddy tomboy in pants, which was her natural state.

Robert looked forward to getting better acquainted with Carol, who appeared to live a life of isolation. She seemed to have little curiosity about the wider world. Although she had lived most of her life an hour's drive from Chicago, she had spent little time in the city, and had never been to New York, the West Coast, or abroad. Now that she lived in South Florida, her only trips out of town were back to Illinois to see her parents. Like many Anglos, she had had few contacts with—and showed no interest in—Miami's huge and diverse Latin community.

Trained for a career in education, Carol had soured on high school teaching, scored well on the federal civil service examination, and was offered a choice between selling savings bonds for the Treasury Department and investigating errant doctors for the DEA. She chose the DEA, was accepted by the agents' academy after a few years, and was assigned to Miami, one of only a few female special agents in the DEA.

Carol lived alone with her calico cat, Mateus, in a small, sparsely furnished town house north of Miami in the Broward County suburb of Pembroke Pines. She seemed to have little social life outside of DEA circles. "It's impossible to imagine Carol drunk on some guy's lap at a party," someone had once commented. Her friends considered her laughably frugal. "She comparison-shops laundromats," one of them had jested. She spent many Sundays ironing and watching football on television, with the air-conditioning off to save money.

As the autumn of 1981 progressed, Robert and Carol fell into a daily pattern. They became telephone buddies—the spy and the spy's control, the resonant Cuban accent and the light Midwestern twang, back and forth across the phone wires for at least an hour each evening. Robert would report on his activities from an easy chair in a small bedroom converted to an office in his home in Tamiami. Carol would ask questions, take notes, and give suggestions and instructions from her den in Pembroke Pines.

Despite Frank Chellino's rantings, Carol and Robert knew that infiltrating the narcotics smuggling organizations of Colombia would require great patience.

9

THE ECCENTRIC COLOMBIAN industrialist, who hailed from the violent and primitive province of Caquetá on the edge of the Amazon, gave names to his children that were so odd and obscure that they baffled just about everyone who heard them. What was even odder was the delight the father took in refusing to explain the names, even to his wives and friends. His seven-year-old daughter was Zuleika. Had he gotten the name from Kipling, Max Beerbohm, or Persian poetry? He wasn't saying. Zuleika's six-year-old sister was Yidid, which sounded Middle Eastern. So far as anyone knew, the father had never been to the Middle East. The five-year-old boy was Xouix, pronounced like Soyuz, the Soviet spacecraft. The father seemed to know little of space exploration. The two-year-old boy was Wilkander, which sounded vaguely Eastern European. But the father had no apparent connection to Europe.

Zuleika. Yidid. Xouix. Wilkander.

Z. Y. X. W.

It was clear—the father admitted it—that he liked to work backward from the end of the alphabet.

Wilkander, known as Willy, normally accompanied the older Alvarez children on their ride to school each morning on the northern outskirts of Bogotá. The chauffeur, Carlos, and the security guard, Jaime, would secure Willy in the burgundy Chevrolet Malibu station wagon for the twenty-minute drive and then return him to his nanny. But Willy had a cold on Tuesday, October 6, 1981, and because of the damp chill that cloaked Bogotá most mornings in the rainy season, he was kept at home.

At 7:00 A.M., Yidid and Xouix scampered down the steps of the soaring, angular, five-story, glass-faced house known as *La Iglesia* (the church) where the Alvarez family lived in El Chico Alto, one of the city's richest neighborhoods, overlooking the Colombian capital from the slopes of the Andean foothills. Jaime and Carlos, both armed as usual, loaded the children into the station wagon, drove out of the cul-de-sac past the security guard's booth, and headed down the steep, twisting street through the pines and eucalyptus, past the high stone gates of neighboring mansions.

Half a mile below *La Iglesia,* the Malibu turned left into the southbound flow of Carrera 7, the principal north-south avenue through Bogotá along the base of the hills. The chauffeur was half an hour ahead of the heaviest morning traffic and was able to average forty miles per hour along the six-lane thoroughfare, past the shaded confines of El Chico Children's Park, where the Alvarez children sometimes played, and past the campus of the Louis Pasteur French School, one of the city's most prestigous private academies.

The chauffeur turned west at a big Esso station down Calle 85, a residential artery divided by a grassy median and flanked by twin rows of giant Japanese *urapan* trees, whose roots made a shambles of the sidewalks. After descending past a brick English colonial mansion housing the Doctors' Club of Bogotá, the Malibu eased into the driveway of a luxury ten-story glass and beige stucco apartment building. Seven-year-old Zuleika Alvarez, who had spent the night with relatives, emerged from the building and climbed into the station wagon, which continued west down Calle 85.

After passing through several blocks of contemporary bank offices, pricey boutiques, and travel agencies, the chauffeur headed north on the six-lane divided *Autopista del Norte,* the Northern Highway. This was a more industrial area of the city—dusty and unkempt—with service stations, body shops, hardware stores, lumber yards, small factories, and big billboards advertising Bavaria beer, Esso gasoline, Chivas Regal, and the local soft drink Colombiana.

The Malibu took only a few more minutes to get to Calle 170, a two-lane street through cattle and horse country where the campuses of some of Bogotá's most expensive private schools were situated. Xouix and Yidid Alvarez attended the Abraham Lincoln School just west of the *autopista;* Zuleika went to the Colombian-British School a mile up Calle 170 toward the mountains.

As the Malibu slowed along the exit road from the *autopista,* a young man in the white helmet and blue uniform of the traffic police stepped into the station wagon's path and waved it over. The uniformed man asked to see the chauffeur's license and registration. As Jaime and Carlos were producing their credentials, three young men in plain clothes appeared and announced that they were agents of the Colombian National Police F-2 branch, a unit roughly comparable to the FBI and DEA in the United States. One of the plainclothesmen had curly blond hair and bloodshot eyes. Another had short dark hair with a thin mustache and black horn-rimmed glasses. The third had long dark hair and a thick, droopy mustache.

The blond man, who appeared to be their spokesman, said they needed to search the station wagon. Such searches were routine in Bogotá, and the chauffeur and guard were not particularly concerned, even as the four men set about frisking and disarming them. But then the blond man asked the chauffeur where his boss, "Señor Alvarez," was and said the police suspected that narcotics were hidden in the station wagon. The four men then forced Jaime and Carlos into the backseat of the vehicle. The long-haired man got behind the wheel, and his cohorts also climbed in. Jaime reassured the children, who were becoming frightened.

The blond man ordered the chauffeur and guard to keep their eyes to the floor. The station wagon made a sharp left on to Calle 170, passing over the *autopista,* and another left into the southbound lanes of the highway, back toward the center of Bogotá.

The blond man again asked the chauffeur, "Where is Señor Alvarez?"

"I don't know where he is."

"Don't lie to us," the blond man said.

The chauffeur and guard said nothing but were no longer in doubt about what was happening: The four men were not traffic policemen or F-2 agents. They were kidnappers, probably guerrillas from the movement known as the M-19. Their targets were the Alvarez children. Had two-year-old Willy not been kept at home, he would have been taken as well. It seemed likely that the kidnappers had been tracking the regular route of the Malibu station wagon from El Chico Alto to Calle 170.

If there had been witnesses to the episode, they probably would not report it. Bogotános were accustomed to seeing men dressed as policemen detaining people at roadsides. Often the men actually were policemen. Still, to guard against the possibility that someone had seen the incident and followed them, the kidnappers left the *autopista* after a few miles and meandered briefly through side streets. Detecting no pursuit, they proceeded south on Avenida 68, another six-lane thoroughfare across Bogotá. It was past seven-thirty and the chaotic traffic had thickened. There were rivers of Toyotas, Fiats, Renaults; vintage DeSotos, Studebakers, and Oldsmobiles; Chevrolet taxies; and brightly striped mini-buses—different designs, sizes, and fares for different classes of rider.

Just before reaching the Bogotá headquarters of the International

Red Cross, the station wagon headed west into an inner city *barrio* called Bellavista Occidental and stopped adjacent to a small park enclosing two basketball and mini-soccer courts and the Banda Sinfonica, the quaint, two-story, tile-roofed brick headquarters of the Police Band of Bogotá. The kidnappers ordered the Alvarez chauffeur and guard out of the station wagon. The guard complied, but the chauffeur resisted until the blond man brandished a gun and pushed him out. The man with the droopy mustache who had been driving and the man in the police uniform departed in the station wagon with the children. The other two kidnappers escorted the chauffeur and guard across the park, and into a small coffee shop where they ordered *tinto*—black coffee. The blond man looked at his watch and remarked that it was eight o'clock. The same time showed on a big Timex wall clock bearing likenesses of the infant and adult Jesus Christ.

After finishing their coffee, the group strolled briefly through the quiet residential neighborhood. The blond man handed the chauffeur a letter and a map, and told him to give them to Señor Alvarez.

"Don't make a mistake," he said. "We are watching you constantly."

The chauffeur and guard hurried the five blocks back to Avenida 68, where they flagged a taxi and directed it to El Chico Alto and the mansion called *La Iglesia.*

The other two kidnappers had continued south in the station wagon with the children through the heavy traffic on Avenida 68. After skirting the two largest of Bogotá's many parks, the Parque el Salitre, with its vast green spaces, soccer and baseball fields, and carnival rides, and the Parque Simón Bolívar, where the Pope had greeted hundreds of thousands of Bogotános in 1968, the thoroughfare passed into the industrial south of Bogotá, past cement factories and steel assembly plants, and past the headquarters of the second-largest daily newspaper in Colombia, the esteemed *El Espectador.*

Twenty miles across the city from where they had seized the children, the kidnappers turned off Avenida 68 into a dusty industrial *barrio* called Talavera. They parked the Malibu on a secluded back street across from a scruffy sandlot soccer field and a big shoe factory. Reassuring the children that they would soon see their parents, the strangers escorted them to a nearly treeless enclave of small, two-story brick town houses and into a house numbered 54-A-70 Diagonal 42-B South, Interior 6. A young woman and two men were waiting inside. The house had a combination living-dining room, a kitchen, pantry, three bedrooms, two bathrooms, and a brick-enclosed patio at the rear with clotheslines. All of the rooms and the patio were tiny, however. The bedrooms were only eight feet square with seven-foot ceilings, which were common in that section of Bogotá but alien to the experience of the three Alvarez children at *La Iglesia,* with its cathedral ceilings, huge crystal and stainless-steel chandeliers, and walk-in doll house.

The woman locked the children in a second-floor bedroom whose curtains had been closed and lone light bulb removed. She instructed the children to keep quiet if they wanted to see their parents.

One of the kidnappers then drove the station wagon several miles east toward the mountains and abandoned it on a side street in a busy commercial sector of the city. A confederate in an unmarked black taxi picked him up, and they rejoined their colleagues in the town house in Talavera.

It was 9:00 A.M. The young men and the woman could relax, at least for the moment. They were pleased with themselves. Calmly and efficiently, without being detected, a group of M-19 guerrillas had just kidnapped the children of one of the biggest narcotics godfathers in Latin America.

With a population of four million in 1981, Bogotá was slightly larger than San Francisco and somewhat smaller than Detroit. Situated on a lush plateau in the eastern Andes more than 8,700 feet above sea level, Bogotá is one of the loftiest cities in the world, causing many visitors to feel a bit dizzy until they grow used to the thin air. The Nobel laureate Gabriel García Márquez, who comes from Colombia's sultry Caribbean coast, hates Bogotá's cool climate, calling it "glacial." In fact, because of the altitude, Bogotá's climate the year-round—the average temperature is 60 degrees Fahrenheit—resembles summer in the Montana Rockies with afternoon drizzle.

Despite gibes from its beloved García Márquez, Bogotá is proud of its climate, its majestic mountains, its world-class golf courses, and its renowned cyclists. It is proud of Colombia's leadership in the production of emeralds, gold, and coffee. And Bogotá is prouder still of its reputation as the cultural mecca of South America. "The Athens of South America" or "The Athens of the Andes," the city is often called. The Nicaraguan poet Ruben Dario, a favorite in Colombia, called Bogotá "a paradise of the spirit, a city which cared about literature, a place long famous for its cultivation of intellectual disciplines, a city of Greek and Latin." Bogotá's several renowned universities draw students from all over South America, especially for the study of law. The city is noted for its vigorous newspapers and fine bookstores. It is said that more poets than soldiers have occupied the presidency of Colombia. Bogotános speak the purest Spanish outside of Spain. Even illiterate peasants speak well. Miguel de Cervantes, the novelist laureate of Spain, is a hero in Colombia; he may have used the original *conquistador* of Colombia, Gonzalo Jiménez de Quesada, as a model for Don Quixote. Cervantes' statue stands in front of the magisterial marble headquarters of the Colombian Academy of Language in downtown Bogotá. The 110-year-old academy decrees strict standards in Colombians' use of Spanish and wields linguistic influence in the Hispanic world second only to its counterpart in Madrid.

A formal yet convivial city, Bogotá also is a family city, a city of children. There are more children per adult in Bogotá than in almost any other city in the world, and they are by no means all from the poor *barrios.* Children are everywhere in prosperous north Bogotá as well. Parents with children are more numerous in the parks than lovers or joggers.

It was the ubiquity of children that made the dark side of Bogotá especially chilling. Bogotá and much of Colombia in the early 1980s were being overwhelmed by a reign of violence—murder, torture, kidnapping—that in some ways was unique in the world of the twentieth century. Colombia historically has been an exceptionally violent country. Civil wars have ravaged the nation periodically since the beginning of the Spanish conquest in the sixteenth century. In the twentieth century the violence has increased. At least 200,000 people died between 1946 and 1966, a period so wracked by political mayhem that it was known simply as *La Violencia.* A formal "state of siege" has been in effect continually ever since. The leading cause of death among Colombian males aged fifteen to forty-four by the early 1980s was homicide. The murder rate was several times that of the urban United States, a violent country in its own right.

So pervasive was the violence in Colombia, and so complex were its origins, that a group of young professors at the Institute of Political Studies of Bogotá's esteemed National University created an academic speciality—"violentology." The professors became known as "violentologists." But even they had difficulty explaining the roots of the violence. Treatises were written about how violence was fostered by Colombia's fragmented geography, by the atrocities of the *conquistadors,* by the Catholic Church's intimate involvement in politics, by the centuries-long struggle over land, by the guerrillas, by the drug traffickers.

Whatever its origins, there was little debate about one of the reasons for the increase in violence in recent decades. Colombians had lost faith in the ability of their government to administer justice. The government seemed unable to apprehend and punish any significant number of violent criminals. The judiciary was impotent. And this paralysis spawned more violence, as the criminals, knowing punishment was unlikely, killed with abandon.

Some of the violence was random. A man with razor blades attached to his fingertips clawed the throat of a woman in the lobby of the chic Hotel Tequendama Inter-Continental in downtown Bogotá as he was grabbing her necklace. She bled to death. He escaped.

Some of the violence was directed against "social undesirables." Reputed homosexuals, prostitutes, beggars, drug addicts, and the mentally ill were gunned down in the streets.

Much of the violence was organized. The military threw its weight around, killing a lot of people deemed to be "security risks." The drug mafia, which contributed to the government's impotence by routinely killing policemen and judges, accounted for many of the murders and added a new element to the climate of violence: financial greed. Where some past savagery had been perpetrated for social, religious, or political ideals, enabling its perpetrators to claim a degree of extenuation, however twisted, the drug mafia killed solely for money. The traffickers solved every problem—from law enforcement, to press exposure, to competition for territory or markets, to the pettiest personal disputes—with murder, most of it murder for hire. With no mitigating moral pretensions, the rampant drug murders degraded life in Colombia still further. The guerrillas, seeing the drug mafia make money with murder, began killing for money, too, cheapening their ideals.

Guerrillas had been active in Colombia since *La Violencia.* The most flamboyant of the guerrilla groups was the *Movimiento de 19 Abril,* the April 19 movement, usually called the M-19. Radical, nationalistic, and non-Marxist, the M-19 was master of the grand gesture. In 1974 it stole Simón Bolívar's sword, one of Colombia's most potent national symbols, from a Bogotá museum. In 1979 it stole 5,000 weapons from a military arsenal in north Bogotá, humiliating the army. In 1980 it seized the embassy of the Dominican Republic on Carrera 30 during a cocktail party and held fifteen diplomats hostage for two months, including the ambassador from the United States.

With the government seemingly paralyzed by such barbarism, other segments of society responded with "private justice," combatting murder with murder. Settling scores with violence—with a private system of vendetta, judgment, and punishment—became commonplace. Private armies were formed—"death squads" with names like Black Hand and Rambo. There were schools for assassins, known as *sicarios.* Life became extraordinarily cheap for such a civilized country. An assassination could be arranged for twenty dollars. The general population, particularly the affluent, armed itself. There were nearly 400 private security companies registered to do business in Bogotá, employing between 40,000 and 200,000 armed guards, vastly outnumbering the police.

By the early 1980s, the violence had grown into what the violentologists at the National University called an "infrastructure of death" with kidnapping at its core. The guerrillas and others had found that they could raise more money by kidnapping people for ransom than by robbing banks. In Bogotá, the city of children, children as well as fathers and mothers were being kidnapped. Although families fortified themselves with guns and security guards, they lived in constant fear, especially the rich families in the big homes in the northeast neighborhoods of the city like El Chico Alto, spread along the foothills with the panoramic views. Everybody had a kidnapping story. If one had not lost a child, one knew somebody who had: a son's classmate, the banker's daughter, the dentist's nephew. Sometimes the children were ransomed. Sometimes they disappeared indefinitely. Sometimes they turned up dead, shot through the back of the head.

By the early 1980s, the cosmopolitan family city of Bogotá, the city of children, had become the city of children and blood.

"From today on, your children are in our custody," the ransom letter declared. "They are KIDNAPPED! For their freedom, you must do as we say. Your children are going to be all right, but only if you comply with what we are asking you. If you do not, your children will PAY WITH THEIR LIVES! If you make any attempt to tell the police, or capture us, they will PAY WITH THEIR LIVES! We are going to be watching you constantly for any suspicious movements, so be very careful what you do."

Carlos Alvarez and his wife, Marina, stared at the letter which their distraught chauffeur and security guard had brought from their frightening encounter that morning. Just two months earlier, Carlos Alvarez had sent Marina and the children to the United States because he was concerned about kidnapping in Bogotá. They had returned at the beginning of September for the start of the school year.

The ransom letter, typewritten and single-spaced, demanded 5 million U.S. dollars or the equivalent in Colombian pesos (280 million) for the children's return. "We know about the land you have taken from us, and about the cocaine, and that has given you a lot of money." The letter suggested that if the family did not have the money in liquid form it could mortgage one or more of its many properties in Bogotá and Cartagena. It warned against trying to use a presumed connection to the incumbent government of Colombia. "That would take a long time and make the business long and tedious. We would give your children back to you CUT INTO LITTLE PIECES in a wooden coffin which we already have ready."

The letter instructed the Alvarez family to place a coded classified advertisement in the pets-for-sale section of *El Tiempo,* the largest daily newspaper in Colombia, indicating how much they were prepared to pay. The ad was to read: "Real cute, [number] basset hound puppies, pure blood," with a telephone number. The number of puppies was to be the number of millions of dollars the Alvarez family was offering for the children, e.g., "five basset-hound puppies" would indicate $5 million. The letter also gave instructions for encoding the telephone number.

"WE REPEAT THAT IF YOU DO NOT COMPLY IMMEDI-ATELY WITH WHAT WE ARE TELLING YOU, WE WILL KILL YOUR BEAUTIFUL CHILDREN. . . . You must pay within 15 days. If you do not pay within 15 days, we will send you Xouix's ear. If 20 days pass, we will kill Yidid. If one month passes, we will finish off Xouix and send him to you in the condition we described above. . . ." (The note did not mention the older daughter Zuleika. It appeared that the kidnappers might not have expected her to be in the station wagon that morning.)

"THE LIVES OF YOUR CHILDREN WILL BE RESPECTED ONLY IF YOU MEET OUR DEMANDS. NO DIRTY TRICKS."

The tone of fanaticism and rage in the letter was especially chilling. The reference to "land you have taken from us" sounded to the Alvarezes like a notion concocted by a guerrilla organization.

The letter instructed the family to wait for a call late the next afternoon.

Using the map provided by the kidnappers, the Alvarez's chauffeur took one of the family's other vehicles and easily located the Chevrolet Malibu station wagon where it had been left in south Bogotá that morning. It was clear that the kidnappers had wanted the Alvarezes to find the car quickly so that it would not attract the attention of the police.

Carlos Alvarez did not call the police about the kidnapping, not because of the kidnappers' warning but because, as an organized-crime boss, he tried to avoid dealing with the police under any circumstances. He had a formidable organization of his own that was capable of dealing with guerrillas. However, Alvarez did call the chief financial officer of his international drug network: Marlene Navarro in Miami. He asked her to prepare to move large quantities of U.S. dollars to Bogotá.

Her boss's identity still unknown to the DEA, Navarro immediately called Robert Darias late that Tuesday to report that her "main guy" needed to transfer as much money to Bogotá as possible: his three children had been kidnapped. Marlene was in tears. She was close to the children. They called her *tía,* or "auntie." She had spent time with them in Colombia only two weeks earlier and had promised to bring them toys from New York.

"It is an emergency," she told Darias. Navarro planned to have $2 million cash delivered to her home by the next morning and asked how quickly Dean International could move it to Colombia. Darias said he would inquire and get back to her. Carol Cooper was unable to give Darias an immediate answer. She had to check with Frank Chellino, who had to check with Tom Clifford. By morning, with the DEA waffling, Navarro told Darias that she had decided to transfer the money another way. She also said she was canceling a trip to New York and was leaving instead for "where the snow is." Darias was unable to clarify what she meant.

10

MIAMI HAD ITS godfathers, too. They tended to be more self-conscious than those in Bogotá, perhaps because of their slightly lower rank in the hierarchy of the international drug mafia. The most notorious was José Medardo Alvero-Cruz, who was actually called The Godfather—*El Padrino*—around Little Havana, and relished both the title and the role. Alvero-Cruz moved about Miami accompanied by two armed bodyguards and kept Frank Sinatra's "My Way" and the theme from *The Godfather* on the tape deck in his car. He was once arrested for threatening to kill a newspaper editor who published unflattering articles about him.

Alvero-Cruz was known to be very rich but acknowledged only that he owned a hair salon and a discotheque, both located on Coral Way. The DEA believed, however, that Alvero-Cruz derived most of his wealth from narcotics smuggling, and that at age forty-two he headed perhaps the largest drug organization in South Florida.

The DEA was obsessed with José Alvero-Cruz. The agency had investigated him for more than a decade without success. It had been forced to drop a drug conspiracy case against him in 1978 when its chief witness refused to testify—"out of fear," the government alleged, that Alvero-Cruz would kill him.

A native of Cuba and a Bay of Pigs veteran, Alvero-Cruz had obtained a fresh Cuban passport in Madrid in 1976 and the DEA believed he was using Cuba as a conduit for drugs bound from Colombia to the United States. The NADDIS computer contained reports that he had met at least four times in recent years with Raul Castro, Fidel's brother and the second-in-command of the Cuban government.

After the DEA failed to make a significant drug case against Alvero-Cruz, the IRS finally got him for tax evasion, and in 1980, he was sentenced to ten years in prison. However, he remained free on bond, pending an appeal, and the frustrated DEA still yearned to prosecute him for drug trafficking.

In October 1981, a small-time, self-styled gangster of Italian-Cuban lineage known as Angie, who had worked occasionally as a snitch for the DEA and the Coral Gables police, quietly announced to his handlers that he was close to José Alvero-Cruz and his organization. Angie claimed that in addition to proving drug allegations against Alvero-Cruz he could provide access to his vast fortune. Since tracing money was one of the missions of Operation Swordfish, the agents who had been handling Angie turned him over to Tom Clifford and Frank Chellino.

Over coffee at the Miami Lakes Inn & Country Club, Angie told the Swordfish agents that José Alvero-Cruz planned to flee the country before he was ordered to report to prison on his tax conviction, and wanted to secure his fortune, which Angie estimated at $60 million. If Alvero-Cruz could be convinced that Dean International's investment management services were reliable, perhaps he could be convinced to do business.

Clifford, Chellino, and Intelligence Analyst Robert Russo found Angie repulsive. He was loud, cocky, and numbingly crude. Bob Russo, an expert on the Italian Mafia, found his claim of membership in the Mafia implausible. It also seemed farfetched that the immensely wealthy *padrino* José Alvero-Cruz, who was known for expensive tastes, would associate with this threadbare thug. Chellino and Russo doubted his entire story.

Tom Clifford, however, decided that Operation Swordfish had to cultivate Angie. José Alvero-Cruz was a "hot item" for the DEA, and they should not overlook a chance to infiltrate his organization, Clifford felt. With DEA headquarters pressing for progress, and with other investigations moving slowly, Alvero-Cruz might turn out to be the only truly prominent target of Operation Swordfish. Clifford ordered Chellino to proceed with the first steps of Angie's proposal to infiltrate *el padrino*.

When Robert Darias learned that the DEA was interested in Alvero-Cruz, whom he had known slightly in the Bay of Pigs brigade, he suggested that he meet with Angie and try to help. Darias again wrestled with doubts about spying on people he knew in the Cuban community, particularly alumni of the brigade and related ventures with whom he shared such a strong bond. They had not only fought together, they had been betrayed together, imprisoned together, ransomed together, and returned to Miami together to proceed with their often haunted lives. Darias felt affection for all of them, even those who had subsequently involved themselves in crime. He knew Rolando Otero, the youngest man to fight at the Bay of Pigs, who was later prosecuted for smuggling drugs, for exploding a bomb at Miami airport, and for trying to assassinate the nephew of Chilean president

Allende. He knew Antonio Veciana, who served time in prison for cocaine trafficking, and who claimed to have seen his CIA case officer with Lee Harvey Oswald in Dallas two months before the assassination of John F. Kennedy. He knew Bernard "Macho" Barker and Eugenio "Musculito" Martinez, who had been arrested at the Watergate in Washington in 1972 while inside the headquarters of the Democratic National Committee.

But the sentiments that Darias felt were outweighed, in the case of José Alvero-Cruz, by the nature of his crimes. The huge quantities of drugs that Alvero-Cruz had been responsible for selling in the United States made him more lethal than any terrorist.

The DEA, however, decided to isolate the Alvero-Cruz investigation from the rest of Operation Swordfish for the time being. Frank Chellino wanted to test Angie's credibility before exposing him to Darias or anyone else.

As Robert Darias continued to ingratiate himself with Marlene Navarro, the DEA's intelligence group in Miami launched an investigation of Navarro's long-distance telephone calls. In response to a secret subpoena, Southern Bell disclosed to the DEA that in recent months Navarro had dialed fourteen numbers in Bogotá, three in Israel, two in the Netherlands, one in Madrid, seven in Curaçao, and three in Aruba. She had dialed some of the numbers repeatedly, especially those in Bogotá. Tom Clifford via telex asked DEA offices in Colombia, Europe, and the Caribbean to obtain and report the names of the subscribers to the numbers. (The government could only subpoena the records of outgoing long-distance calls and incoming collect calls, the same detailed listing that appeared on a monthly phone bill. To get local calls and regular incoming long-distance—and to listen to telephone conversations on a wiretap—a separate order from a federal judge was required.)

"Real cute. Basset-hound puppies. Pure bred."

As instructed by the kidnappers, the Alvarez family placed a classified advertisement in the pets-for-sale section of *El Tiempo* on Saturday, Sunday, and Monday, October 10, 11, and 12. Alvarez omitted the number of puppies as an added lure for the kidnappers to call. He also gave an encoded telephone number, as they had asked.

The children had been missing since Tuesday.

As Operation Swordfish crept along its secret path, the philosophy underlying the operation received a ringing public endorsement from the *Miami Herald,* which that Sunday began publishing a seven-part series entitled "U.S. Drug Enforcement: The Billion-Dollar Bust." Six reporters and two editors had worked on the project for four months. The first article, bannered across the top of page one, was headlined: "Why the U.S. is losing the war on drugs."

"Eight years after Richard Nixon launched a global narcotics police force called the Drug Enforcement Administration," the *Herald* asserted, "the war on drugs is a rout—a lopsided romp for the bad guys. . . . Despite notable successes in several major cases, the DEA has singularly failed its mission, failed at all levels to stanch the distribution of illegal drugs, . . . The scope of the government's failure to enact a successful drug policy is sweeping, numbing—and disputed by almost no one."

The *Herald's* central recommendation: "The answer is going after money and assets" of the biggest traffickers, not amassing arrest statistics by pursuing street-level dealers.

One of the articles, by *Herald* reporter Carl Hiaasen, profiled the agents and activities of the DEA's Group Three, the enforcement group in which Carol Cooper, Paul Sennett, and Frank Chellino had worked prior to joining Operation Swordfish. It was clear that the agents agreed with the negative thrust of the *Herald* findings. "Street agents as a group are cynical," Hiaasen wrote, "because they are so frequently outspent, outmanned, and outmaneuvered by the criminals they pursue."

The *Herald* published photographs with the articles but was careful to keep the faces of undercover agents undistinguishable.

Regardless of considerations raised by the *Herald,* the DEA bureaucracy was breaking its promise to be patient with Operation Swordfish. Although headquarters ostensibly had agreed with Tom Clifford's view that it could take years to penetrate the targeted narcotics organizations, the bureaucracy, after only four months, was pressuring Clifford for results. Operation Swordfish was being criticized for failing thus far to induce criminal clients to invest their money in sizable assets as distinct from merely "laundering" it. Although Clifford rebutted the criticism, he also passed it along to Frank Chellino, who relayed it to Carol Cooper, who conveyed it that same week to Robert Darias.

"Right now we're just playing around with their money," Carol told Robert. "If that's all we're doing, Washington'll put a kabosh on it real quick. We've gotta have some results—be it investments or whatever. We've got to have something tangible at the end that we can latch onto."

"We might be getting intelligence in different areas," Darias suggested.

"Well, the thing is, the intelligence has to pay off somewhere along the line," Cooper said. "How do you feel about Humberto, Bob, you're the only one who's talking to him, none of us have met him. Do you think he'll definitely turn around and invest this money he's getting in?"

"Well, I have a feeling that we will be able to convince him," Robert said.

"The problem we're having, Bob, is that people keep comparing us to the FBI and what they did in Operation Bancoshares," Cooper said. "What everyone is telling us is we don't want to do what the FBI did. All they did was launder money—they didn't seize anything." (Actually, the FBI had said it seized $12 million and assorted other assets.)

"It takes *time,* Carol," Robert emphasized. "We are changing our minds continuously, and that's what I don't like. We *were* talking about doing business with people for *months* before we really can have their confidence to start investing their money. And now you are talking about when the guy does his first business, he is going to be presented with something that is not in his mind at all. And he is going to be meeting Frank, and the first day Frank expects him to say he is going to invest his money with Frank. That is completely ridiculous. If the guy for any reason reacts in the wrong way, we will be closing a door."

Darias was scheduled to have lunch with Humberto Garcia's young Colombian cohorts "the Colombian Kids" on Monday and give them cashier's checks for the $300,000 in cash they had deposited a few days earlier.

"Couldn't Frank go with you at that point?" Cooper asked.

"No, I don't think it's a good idea to mix Frank in this lunch. Not this time."

"We've got to get Frank in at some point soon."

"If somebody sits with me at that lunch we are going to blow the whole thing. Because these people are not expecting anybody." Robert was getting angry again. "I have the relationships and the contact that I have because I have been able to carry on in my own way, not Frank's way, *my own way,* and that's the only way I can infiltrate these people. I am trying to convince these guys to do something that is against their own interest."

"Yeah, I understand."

"We agreed at the beginning that I was going to be able to have some latitude to work with these people. But now Frank wants to talk about investments the second time that I talk to them. If the government really believes that these people are going to invest with us the second time I talk to them, it is completely nuts. Frank cannot gear these people's minds to do things that fast, even though he thinks he can. He is not in the street talking to these people every single day like I am."

The Kids had asked Robert for cashier's checks in $25,000 denominations to cover their $300,000. That meant twelve times the paperwork for Dean International that a single check would have involved, and Frank Chellino refused. "I'm not gonna do these scumbags any favors," he declared.

"You certainly are," Cooper said. "These people don't want large checks."

"I'm not gonna do these scumbags any favors," Chellino snarled.

"We have to give them what they want," Cooper said. "They're our customers."

Felipe Calderon, the Colombian banker who was advising the DEA on banking techniques, backed Cooper. "The request is reasonable," Calderon said. "We're supposed to be providing banking services for these people."

Chellino stormed off to the bank and got the twelve checks.

At about one-thirty that afternoon, Darias met the Colombian Kids—who still were known only as Aurelio and Alvaro—at the dining room of the Marriott Hotel on the east edge of the airport. After they had ordered lunch, Darias gave them a sealed Dean International envelope containing the cashier's checks. The two Colombians inspected the checks and pronounced them satisfactory. In a bag at their feet they had an additional $100,000.

As they were discussing options for laundering the new cash, Frank Chellino suddenly appeared at the table. Darias looked surprised for only a second before recovering his composure.

"This is Mr. Dean, Frank Dean, my partner," Darias said in both English and Spanish. The Kids spoke no English.

"I was in the neighborhood and thought I'd drop by and say hello," Chellino said to the Kids as Darias translated. "I hope everything is satisfactory. We're glad to have your business and hope you'll continue to come to us when the need arises."

Aurelio and Alvaro were nonplussed at the arrival of the short gringo with the mustache. Although they made awkward bilingual small talk, Alvaro told Darias after Chellino left that he had made them nervous. At the end of the meal the Kids held onto their bag of fresh cash.

Darias, who was furious, went home and called Cooper, who clearly had known of Chellino's intention to surprise Darias at the lunch.

"What was the point in going into a lunch when that is exactly what we had discussed last night, that it wasn't a good idea?" Darias said. "For no reason at all, he shows up at a place where nothing is happening. Those are the changes that I have to be aware of. Because it proves to me, Carol, it proves just one thing. *Frank doesn't trust me.* He looks at me like a regular informant."

"No, no, no, Bob. It's not that we don't trust you."

"It's a difficult situation, Carol. You have to give me leeway with these people. It might take three days. It might take three months with each one of them. I need that time in order to really prepare them for meeting you people. Look, Carol, when they see Americans in this business they go crazy! I cannot have this type of treatment."

"I want the situation resolved," said Cooper. "I don't want anymore misunderstanding."

"My mind is working twenty-four hours a day, cued into this operation," Robert said. "There is nothing else."

"You and all the rest of us."

"But that is exactly how I want *Frank* to say it. That I am as concerned as he is. That he's not more honest than I am. That he's not working for this more than I am. I don't mind supervision. It just has to be my way. It shook me like crazy when Frank came in there. I am a very good actor, but believe me it was very hard."

"We were just checkin' to see if you deserve an Academy Award this year," Carol said.

"If I can live through this I am going to deserve it," replied Robert, switching off his tape recorder.

11

HE DEA NEEDN'T have worried that José Alvero-Cruz would be its only prominent target. The agency's field office in Bogotá identified the subscribers to the telephone numbers that Marlene Navarro had been calling.

"She's been calling some very, very important people," Cooper reported to Darias. "They're all in our computer, every single one of them. It's looking very good."

Robert knew better than to ask the names of these people. Cooper hoped that eventually Navarro would tell Robert directly, and didn't want to risk his inadvertently dropping a name to her that he had been given by the DEA. The agency had not yet been able to identify conclusively the father of the kidnap victims, about whom Navarro had spoken to Darias without giving the name, or even confirm that a kidnapping had occurred. None had been reported to the Colombian police.

The DEA had determined through telephone records that Marlene Navarro had received five collect calls from a Marriott hotel in Houston, Texas, in August around the time she reported to Darias that the police had stopped one of her couriers in Texas and seized $500,000.

"As soon as I saw those telephone calls, I said to Frank, man, she's not giving us a story," Carol told Robert. "She's doing exactly what she says she's doing."

Frank Chellino met again with the gangster Angie, who said that the José Alvero-Cruz organization wanted to deposit $250,000 with Dean International as a test of the firm's capacity to launder money, and would deposit an additional $3 million when the company had demonstrated its competence. Alvero-Cruz was about to close the sale of a thousand kilograms of cocaine for about $60 million, Angie reported, and would want to invest that money. Angie asked for the address and phone number of Dean International; he said Alvero-Cruz wanted to check the company's background and credit record.

Although Chellino was reluctant, Tom Clifford felt they had to give

Angie the information in order to nurture Dean's credibility with Alvero-Cruz.

That same afternoon, the Dean office received several calls in which the caller either hung up or said he had the wrong number. A few days later the Swordfish group noticed a man with a camera standing across the parking lot from Dean snapping pictures of the premises and the cars parked in front. They assumed he had been sent by Alvero-Cruz to record license plate numbers.

Operation Swordfish needed a lawyer.

Although the Swordfish agents had only begun to form relationships with their targets, legal guidance was needed to ensure that the operation was building the tightest possible cases for prosecution at the end. In choosing a lawyer, a federal law enforcement agency normally would look to the United States Attorney in the district where the operation was centered. One of the tasks of the ninety-four U.S. Attorneys' offices around the country is prosecuting federal criminal cases originated by investigative agencies in their jurisdictions. In the autumn of 1981, however, the United States Attorney's office in Miami was in disarray. The U.S. Attorney himself, Atlee Wampler III, was a lame duck, awaiting selection of a replacement by the Reagan Justice Department. And his staff, overwhelmed by the explosion of crime in South Florida, lacked expertise in the complex prosecutions that the DEA hoped Operation Swordfish would spawn. The DEA decided to use an option available to any federal investigative agency in such circumstances: it requested a lawyer from the Department of Justice in Washington, the same choice that Operation Greenback had made the previous year in bringing Charles Blau to Miami.

The DEA was pleased to learn that one of the drug agency's favorite lawyers was available for Operation Swordfish. Gregory Bruce English, a husky, thirty-five-year-old graduate of the University of Virginia's excellent law school, was a senior trial attorney in the narcotics section of the criminal division. English was known in the Drug Enforcement Administration for using a "linebacker's approach to prosecution—very aggressive." English also was noted for liking the DEA and loathing the FBI, which he found arrogant and frequently unwilling to cooperate with other law enforcement agencies. "In a joint operation with the FBI, it's always the other guy's joint that gets operated on," English was fond of saying.

Greg English flew to Miami and spent the week of Monday, October 19, conferring with Tom Clifford and his agents, viewing the secret videotapes they had made at Dean International, and reading their reports.

English, a bit of a hail-fellow-well-met, thought that the agents of Operation Swordfish were "absolutely remarkable people, the new breed of DEA agent, a joy to work with." The agents were delighted with English, as well, and hoped he would become their advocate not only against their criminal targets but also against their adversaries in the law enforcement bureaucracy such as Operation Greenback and its lead attorney Blau, who still yearned to absorb Operation Swordfish and was determined to indict Lionel Paytubi soon.

"Greg's super energetic and super aggressive, and he's just super, *super* impressed with the operation," Carol Cooper told Darias. "He is about as top notch as we're gonna get. If anybody like Greenback wants to jeopardize our cases, Greg goes straight to Washington and puts the kabosh on it."

While the agents made sure English was briefed on their battles with Operation Greenback, they did not choose to enlighten English on equally serious problems that were growing in their own ranks. The rancor between Robert Darias and Frank Chellino was poisoning the atmosphere in the office. Darias found Chellino dictatorial and arbitrary, and Chellino found Darias headstrong and insubordinate. Darias was still furious at Chellino for having appeared without warning at the luncheon with the Colombian Kids. And he remained angry about the ham-handed way that Chellino had decreed his monthly salary at a lower figure than had been discussed with Tom Clifford.

Darias was not the only person at odds with Frank Chellino. Pepe Hinojosa, the DEA agent whose undercover pose was Juan Carlos Stabile, executive vice president of Dean International, concluded in the late summer that he could not work with Chellino and Carol Cooper. Hinojosa complained to Tom Clifford that Chellino and Cooper had "shut him out" and "partitioned" him from much of Operation Swordfish, especially the activities of Robert Darias. When Clifford inquired about the matter, Chellino was vague, saying, "Pepe does things his way—we do things our way." Hinojosa finally sought and received a transfer to the DEA field office in Bolivia. He left Operation Swordfish in October.

Chellino's rifts with Darias and Hinojosa, however, were less serious than the tension that was building between Chellino and Tom Clifford. The main problem, as Chellino saw it, was that Clifford wasn't around enough to supervise Swordfish effectively. There was a continual need to make investigative decisions and get Clifford's signatures on documents. But Chellino always had difficulty finding

Clifford, who had an array of other responsibilities as chief of intelligence, and also had been sitting in for his own boss, one of the two assistant special-agents-in-charge of the Miami field office. Frank Chellino felt, however, that the true explanation for Clifford's frequent absences lay elsewhere.

Tom Clifford was a drinking man, a bar man, a Budweiser man, to an extent that Chellino disapproved of. Clifford routinely had two or three Buds with lunch and more after work. As a garrulous Irishman, he loved to hold court at Ma Grundy's, a dark, loud bar near the Phoenix Building with a coterie of similarly inclined DEA managers and agents. Frank Chellino drank, too. He liked his Johnnie Walker Red Label at Le Sabre in the evening and had an occasional drink with the other agents from the liquor cabinet at Dean International. But he didn't feel that liquor had ever affected his work the way he believed it was interfering with Clifford's.

At first Chellino shared his frustrations only with Carol Cooper. But as the weeks wore on he began complaining to Bob Russo, the veteran intelligence analyst who was Tom Clifford's closest friend within Operation Swordfish.

"Fucking Clifford," Chellino said. "You can never find him. He's always out drinking."

Russo was taken aback. "The amazing thing about Tom," Russo replied, "is that he can come in in the morning, do a day's work before lunch, go out to lunch and have a few beers, come back to the office and do another day's work, and then go out and have a few more beers, and it never affects him."

"But it does affect him," Chellino said. "He's never available."

"He can have three beers with lunch like you have a glass of water."

"But we can never find him when we need him."

"He's available if you need him," Russo insisted. "He thought up and started this operation, after all. But he's just got a lot of responsibilities." And then Russo added, "And he's a personal friend of mine, so stop bad-mouthing him."

Chellino strode angrily out of the office.

It seemed to Bob Russo that Tom Clifford's drinking and alleged absences weren't the problem between Clifford and Chellino. The real issue was clashing personalities. Clifford, the loose, loquacious, innovative entrepreneur of narcotics espionage, and Chellino, the prickly, exacting, memo-writing bureaucrat, just did not like each other. And it seemed to Russo, who observed him daily, that Chellino's undercover role as Frank Dean, the president of Dean International Investments Inc., had gone to his head. Chellino appeared to have forgotten that he was just a DEA agent with a civil service ranking of GS-12. He was putting on the airs of a rich investment tycoon. That was fine when he was negotiating with targeted drug financiers like Lionel Paytubi or Marlene Navarro. But Chellino was retaining his exalted pose when dealing with his fellow agents. He even treated Tom Clifford as an employee, or at best an equal, rather than as what Clifford was in fact, the boss of Operation Swordfish.

"Are you getting any readback business-wise of what Marlene might be doing?" Carol Cooper asked Robert Darias in mid-October.

"No, and this is why I'm still mad," he said. Darias's anger at Chellino's treatment of him had been building for days and he warmed to his theme. "I was ordered, directly by Frank, not to meet with her again until she came through with some business. So now we are not getting any information at all. It was my meetings that brought us a lot of information and were getting me closer and closer to her. I don't see why I can't be meeting with everybody as much as I feel. As much as *I* feel. You are reading me wrong if you think that the problem we had the other day has been erased from my mind."

"I know it's still there," Carol said.

"If you are talking about two years for this operation, why am I being rushed into things that I don't feel comfortable with? We have rushed this thing because you apparently need some clout with somebody in your own agency or you have some political problems inside your organization. I don't like the way I'm being pushed."

"Well, I just want you to know, and Frank would probably kill me for telling you this, but he does definitely want you in this operation. Frank wants *me* to work with you because I have more patience than he does. He really doesn't have much patience with people. Don't ever tell him I told you this. But let me handle him."

"Well, that's what I'm trying to do. But the only way I am going to bring this lady in is by keeping on top of her. Otherwise, she is going to cool down and go somewhere else."

"I think she's okay. She'll come around. Just give her time."

Actually Darias had ignored Chellino's order to stop cultivating Marlene Navarro. He had continued to telephone her and, as a gesture of goodwill to Chellino, scheduled a meeting with Navarro for Wednesday afternoon, October 21, and invited Chellino to accompany him. Darias knew that Chellino, who fancied himself a ladies' man, would enjoy the sensuous and vivacious Marlene. They met in the lobby of One Biscayne Tower, an office building on the bay downtown, and went to the cocktail lounge of the Columbus Hotel around the corner.

Chellino, posing as Frank Dean, presented Navarro with a cashier's check for $67,250, the amount that Dean International owed her from the most recent peso exchange in Colombia that Darias had arranged with Humberto Garcia and the Kids. Frank also gave Marlene her commission, $1,075 in cash. She apologized for being less active than she had anticipated, and mentioned that she had been confined to bed for the last several days because of the extraction of a wisdom tooth. She said she still wanted Dean International to handle transfers of cash to Colombia that were needed to make up the balance of the kidnap ransom for her boss's children, which still was set at $5 million.

"That's a terrible thing," Chellino said. "What's the latest?"

"There is nothing new," Navarro replied. "It's awful, a tragedy."

Frank and Marlene seemed to enjoy each other, and Darias paid a leisurely visit to the men's room so that Frank could not claim that Robert's presence had been oppressive.

"You're awfully young to have accomplished so much, gotten so much education," said Chellino. Navarro had mentioned to Darias that she had degrees from both Paris and Miami.

"Ah, I don't feel young with all these stitches in my mouth," she said with a little laugh.

Frank asked Marlene about the law school classes she was taking. He told her that he would like to take her to lunch or dinner sometime and introduce her to Felipe Calderon, the Colombian banker on the staff of Dean International. She said she would be delighted.

As much as he loathed Chellino, Darias had to admit that Frank had been effective in his undercover role. He seemed to have shaken off the nerves that were evident during the first conversation in the office with Lionel Paytubi and Manuel Sanchez.

In Bogotá, at 8:20 P.M. on Friday, October 23, the telephone rang in the big house called *La Iglesia*. A man with a Medellín accent said that he was interested in the "puppies" that had been advertised in *El Tiempo* more than a week earlier. It was the first contact from the kidnappers since the children had disappeared on October 6. Marina Alvarez asked the man to call back in half an hour when her husband would be home. The phone rang again ten minutes later. A different man shouted into the phone that he had to talk to "Señor Alvarez" immediately. Alvarez had not yet arrived home.

A third call did not come until the next night, when a voice demanded $5 million. Alvarez said he did not have $5 million. "It is impossible to get that kind of money," he said. "Not even the richest man in Colombia has it." Alvarez suggested to the caller that they could negotiate "more calmly" if they met in person. The caller hung up.

Though he could easily have gathered $5 million, Alvarez was playing for time. He believed his organization could find the kidnappers. He wanted his children back, but he also wanted vengeance.

Having failed in Operation Bancoshares, the FBI now was trying to horn in on Operation Swordfish. They wanted to be briefed on it. They wanted to monitor it. It was clear that they would like to control it.

"We've been trying to keep the FBI out," Cooper told Darias. "We've been arguing with them for weeks. They've been trying to force themselves in and take over. We've been fighting them like crazy. They totally messed up their operation."

"I guess most of those guys are out of jail," Darias said.

"You got it. And they dismissed on the cases. They made a big splash in the newspapers and then they had to dismiss the charges. And all the people are footloose and fancy-free. And that's because they didn't do their operation right. When we put *these* guys down, I want them to go to jail. I'm not putting in all my time and effort, and I'm sure you're not either, just to create a big splash in the newspapers. It's not worth it."

Back in Washington after a full week in Miami, Gregory English sent a confidential fourteen-page report under a cover sheet "Sensitive Investigative Matter" to his boss, Edward S. G. Dennis, Jr., the chief of the narcotics section of the Justice Department's criminal division. To protect security, English omitted from the memorandum the names Dean International, Frank Dean, and the other undercover names. English described the potential of Operation Swordfish as "awesome."

"I believe that Operation Swordfish has the potential to immobilize many of the major traffickers in South Florida by stripping them of their assets after causing their conviction on multiple counts," English wrote. "Because this investigation has been successful in identifying major violators who control operations and earn huge illicit profits without touching the drugs themselves, I submit that they constitute precisely the type of target the federal government should concentrate upon. . . . "

English praised the agents assigned to Swordfish. "I found Tom Clifford to be an extremely capable and dedicated supervisor, and I believe his professional judgment can be relied upon. However, he also is responsible for supervising the intelligence functions of the Miami office, and I do not think that it will be possible for any one person to accomplish those missions simultaneously."

English also doubted that the operation could proceed much longer without additional agents. "Lack of adequate staffing," he wrote, "is this investigation's largest problem."

English expressed concern about potential damage from "competing governmental interests," noting specifically that Operation Greenback could destory Operation Swordfish by indicting Lionel Paytubi before the Swordfish investigation was completed. "I am not satisfied with the arrangements for coordination between federal investigative agencies."

English's concern about interagency warfare echoed a similar warning sounded at the highest levels of the Justice Department a year and a half earlier by Assistant Attorney General Philip Heymann.

As the only professional banker at Dean, and the only Colombian, Felipe Calderon had brought technical expertise and, along with Robert Darias, a genuine Latin sensibility to an undercover operation that otherwise would have been dominated by gringo amateurs. But Calderon had found it difficult to initiate as many significant cases as Darias had. With few contacts in Miami, he had worked the phones to Colombia, trying to convince his former colleagues, the bankers who were getting rich loaning money to drug dealers, that he had come over to their side and could help them handle the burgeoning assets of the traffickers. In particular, Calderon had been soliciting business from a man named Victor Covo, who was laundering huge amounts of money for the Colombian drug mafia in Panama.

In October 1981, when Covo and two companions traveled to Miami on business, Calderon met them at the airport. The DEA insisted that Calderon carry a small tape recorder inside his jacket. When the two men hugged, Covo felt the recorder.

"What's that?" Covo asked.

"A tape recorder," Calderon replied.

"What are you doing with a tape recorder?" Covo demanded.

"I didn't know who your friends were," Calderon replied with a nervous laugh.

"Take your jacket off," Covo said, quietly but firmly moving Calderon to the side of the exit from customs.

"Well, Victor, you recall I'm a lousy note taker."

"Take it off," Covo said.

After examining the tape recorder, Covo fortunately remembered that Calderon had always carried a portable Dictaphone wherever he went on business. The uncomfortable moment passed with no permanent damage to Calderon's new image as a crooked Miami investment counselor.

Still, it became clear during Covo's visit that he was cautious and in no hurry to deposit any money with Dean International.

On Tuesday, October 27, Humberto Garcia told Darias that a man whom Garcia didn't identify would deliver $475,000 the next day and wanted to exchange the money for pesos in Colombia. Darias agreed—it was an opportunity to meet still another major drug dealer—and decided to use Marlene Navarro again to accommodate the other side of the transaction, even though her organization in Colombia had partially botched the last peso exchange. Frank Chellino, however, instead of welcoming the deal with the positive attitude of an innovative businessman determined to solve problems, reacted like the prickly government bureaucrat that he was in real life.

"Absolutely not," Chellino told Cooper, who was supporting Darias's plan to pair Garcia and Navarro again.

"Frank, these people are gonna want this done periodically," Carol said.

"Absolutely not."

"Frank, you can't play games with Marlene because she screwed up on one!"

"She was responsible!"

"Yeah, but she was also out of town. And when she came back she was on the case right away. And if you're gonna sit here and play games with her and wait for her to bring something else in first, forget it. Because in the meantime you're gonna lose Humberto and all of his people."

After a loud argument, Cooper finally convinced Chellino at least to let Darias talk to Marlene about the proposed deal. Chellino set "ground rules," however. He insisted that Humberto Garcia deliver the entire amount or Dean would accept nothing, that Marlene take the entire amount or nothing, and that in talking to Marlene, Darias must make it appear that Dean International was "giving her another chance since she fucked up the first one."

Navarro accepted immediately and assured Darias she could handle the full amount. Humberto Garcia, too, reassured Darias.

When Garcia's client appeared at Refricenter the next morning, however, he had only $100,000 instead of $475,000. Based on Chellino's all-or-nothing insistence, Darias refused to take delivery and Humberto got angry.

"What's the matter with you people?" Garcia said. "The guy just wants to see how it goes with this initial deposit. Then he'll give you larger amounts."

Cooper told Darias he was right to reject the delivery. "That's okay, they changed the rules," she said. "He didn't do what he said he was gonna do."

Darias, who was home with a rotten cold, was furious and again resented being forced into the role of the hot-headed Latin. *"They* don't change things, Carol. *We* are playing games with these people. *We* are the ones that are changing continuously what we say. Pretty soon, I'm not going to have anybody to talk to. I lost the Kids, now I lost this. I might have lost Humberto also. Humberto was pissed off. A hundred thousand dollars is a hundred thousand dollars. The guy wanted to see how it was going to go."

Cooper asked Darias to come to the office to discuss the matter in person, but he refused, so she had Paul Sennett call him. Sennett was on the verge of being formally assigned to Operation Swordfish.

"Frank is playing games with this whole operation, Paul," Robert said. "He thinks he's a big executive type. The way I see it they will have to close this office. I am the only thing they have going, and they are closing my doors, one by one, by acting the way they are." (Darias knew that Felipe Calderon had not yet initiated a significant case.)

"Humberto's guy was supposed to deliver, what? Five hundred thousand?" Sennett asked.

"They were not *supposed* to deliver anything, Paul. This is not a drug bust. This is a business. *You* are supposed to be in this business. *I* am supposed to be in this business and take care of my clients. When someone new comes in and wants to start with a hundred, that's a lot of money to lose if something goes wrong. I told him no, and he told me to go fly a kite. Frank and Carol are not doing anything in the office. They are just talking all day about how they are going to do things when the millions arrive. But if they don't start *infiltrating* all these guys, the millions are never going to come. When I tell Frank that I am going to do something, he *immediately* opposes my idea because he feels that that is the only way to treat informants or bad guys."

"I think Frank trusts you," Paul said. "I think the problem is that Frank likes to exercise his authority, and he can rub people the wrong way."

"I think at this point I have a better sense of how to handle things than Frank does, and he doesn't want to believe it," Robert said. "He keeps trying to prove to me that he is the boss. He doesn't have to prove it to me. He *is* the boss. I am not an agent."

"That's just words—Frank's an agent, you're not an agent," Paul replied. "Because what you're doing now is probably harder than what an agent has to do. You're *making* that operation. There are no two ways about it."

"They have to understand, Paul, that when I go out to talk to somebody, I have to *sound, look,* and *think* like a bad guy, or I am not going to get anywhere. This is a regular business for these drug people. They don't consider themselves drug dealers. I know they are, and that is why I am working against them, but they consider themselves gentlemen."

"You're right."

"This operation is as much my life as it is Frank's. I am not getting any money outside. This is all I am getting. I had a lot of debts when I met you that day last December, Paul. I was desperate. I still have a lot of problems with the IRS."

"How bad is your problem with the IRS?"

"It's not bad at this point. It's only a debt. They cannot collect because I don't have any money."

"Were you ever arrested by the IRS?"

"Yeah."

"You were?"

"Yeah, I had a criminal case with them. Years ago." Robert explained that he had served seventy-six days for filing a false income tax return. Paul, who had known from the beginning that Robert had a "big IRS problem," was hearing about the prison sentence for the first time.

Sennett immediately thought ahead to how Darias's background might affect his credibility on a witness stand. "What the defense lawyers will do, you know, they will say you were working for the government so that you would have access to money to pay your debts to the Internal Revenue."

Later that day Sennett and Cooper ran another computer check on Darias. The search the previous December had turned up no criminal record. Now, although the computer systems were still missing the federal tax sentence, they turned up Darias's grand theft case in the State of Florida. After questioning Robert, Cooper and Sennett surmised that the Florida case might be less damaging to Darias's credibility as a trial witness than the tax case. In the theft case, the judge had given Darias the opportunity to repay the money in question to avoid a formal conviction. Now that he had completed the repayment, the law allowed him to ask the court to remove the case from the record. It was possible that the lawyers defending Swordfish targets would be barred from raising the theft case before a jury.

The tax case was different. It was on the public record. And it involved lying—a false income tax return. The defense lawyers would argue that if Darias had lied on his tax return he would lie to a jury. They would also argue that Darias was working for the DEA just to raise money to pay his taxes. These certainly weren't fatal flaws in the government's case, since the DEA expected to present a lot of evidence that would stand independently of Robert Darias. But the black marks on Darias's record underscored the necessity for corroboration in the cases that Robert was developing.

"It's gonna get straightened out before we get to the end of this," Carol told Robert. "I don't want you going into court owing the IRS three hundred thousand dollars. The defense attorneys'll crucify you."

Paul Sennett was less concerned. "It will be taken care of," he said. "There's no problem."

The new attention to Darias's IRS problems served to highlight the delicate matter of whether spies for the United States Government pay taxes, or should be taxed, on the money the government pays them.

"Normally," Carol told Robert, "the people that work for us, even though we're required to tell them they've got to file income taxes, I'm sure they don't. I talked to Tom and I said, hey, how can Bob possibly file income tax? They're going to ask him where he got the money. How's he going to tell them? *He can't tell them what he's doing!*"

That evening in Bogotá, a caller instructed Carlos Alvarez to go immediately to the intersection of the Northern Highway and Calle 170 where the children had been kidnapped and wait for a meeting. Several members of his organization followed him discreetly in five automobiles. Alvarez and his men waited all night without result.

The next day a note arrived at the Alvarez home. Following directions in the note, Alvarez and his driver set out on a zigzag pattern from El Chico Alto south toward downtown Bogotá, then east and back north through the Parque Nacional on the slope of the mountains. The directions took Alvarez to the campus of a private school. "In the soccer field, under the north goal, you will find a letter underneath a rock," the note said. "The envelope will be dirty. FOLLOW ALL INSTRUCTIONS."

Alvarez and the driver found nothing under either of the soccer goals. Three young people who were jogging around the rim of the soccer field appeared oblivious.

Over the next few weeks, the kidnappers sent Alvarez on a sequence of wild-goose chases:

—To a small restaurant a few blocks north of the Parque el Salitre ("sit with your back to the door; wait 10 minutes; drink a black coffee; come out and go to a post with an arrow indicating 'photocopies.' Next to the post is a dirty envelope. Follow the instructions.").

—To a park bench next to a branch of the Banco de Commercial just above the main campus of the National University. ("Under the bench, attached with a tack, is an envelope. Read it and follow the instructions.")

—To a candy and soft-drink stand 200 meters inside the main entrance of the National University. ("On top of the booth, the number 102 is painted. Below that, on the floor, there is an envelope. Follow these instructions.")

—To a second small restaurant north of the Parque el Salitre. ("Tip the maître d' and tell him you are expecting a phone call. Follow the instructions.")

—To two more restaurants in the industrial south of Bogotá to await phone calls.

—To the end of an unpaved road farther south near a sewer ditch for written instructions inside a broken aqueduct pipe.

—To the glove compartment of an orange Fiat parked on a side street in a poor neighborhood on the opposite side of the sewer ditch.

Alvarez found some of the written instructions but none led to a meeting with the kidnappers. The godfather concluded he was being toyed with and became enraged. Now he was determined to recover his children without paying ransom.

12

DEAN INTERNATIONAL INVESTMENTS could not succeed as an undercover operation infiltrating the drug mafia until it succeeded as a business attracting customers. Robert Darias had said as much to Frank Chellino and the other agents repeatedly, suggesting that they needed to "act more like bad guys." While Chellino had rebuffed Darias ("I'm not gonna do these scumbags any favors"), he could not ignore the market in which Dean International was attempting to function.

The word on the streets by early November was that the banks—at least some of them—were easing back into the business of laundering drug money. Nine months had passed since Operation Greenback had raided the Great American Bank and the Bank of Miami. There had been no indictments, and Lionel Paytubi's lawyer was saying he doubted there would be. The FBI's Operation Bancoshares had indicted a banker and several other people but some of the indictments had been dismissed and the cases generally appeared weak.

Crooked bankers were emboldened. It was getting easier again for narcotics traffickers, who were testing the marketplace every day, to exchange suitcases full of cash for whatever form of currency or security they might want.

Marlene Navarro and Humberto Garcia both had mentioned the banks' renewed activity to Robert Darias and indicated that Dean International would have to lower its commissions to get more of their business. Frank Chellino and Carol Cooper, whose DEA bosses were pressing for "results," finally agreed.

"Your gut feeling, Bob, if we come down to one and a half—do you think that'll solve the problem?" Carol asked Robert, referring to the lower commission that Dean was considering, 1 ½ percent of the amount of cash that was laundered.

"Let's put it this way: it will be a lot simpler, a lot easier, to convince them," he replied.

"Okay, run with it, kiddo. Run with it as soon as you can. I don't know how you want to approach the people. I want to make sure we appear legitimate. It would be nice if somebody brought something this week," Carol said, yearning for another deposit to include in the latest monthly report due at DEA headquarters in a few days.

Marlene called Robert to ask him to recommend a good Cuban restaurant. She had just been freed of the last of the thirty-five stitches from removal of her wisdom teeth and wanted to savor a good meal. He mentioned La Rosa, a small place in Little Havana. Robert then took the occasion to press Marlene about Dean International's seeming failure to win her business.

"We have been talking and talking for the last two months and nothing happens," Robert said. "I realize that you have special problems and that we have competitors, but if I can be of any help at all, we're prepared to be competitive. I'm prepared to do anything I can to get some business from you."

"The main problem, Roberto, is that things have gotten a little messy with the children—this kidnapping thing," Navarro said. "My people are in a bind because the kidnappers keep changing the ways they want the money, and how they want it, and when they want it and where they want it." However, she went on to say that she happened to have $400,000 in small bills that she needed to exchange for hundreds. If Robert could handle the swap by late the next afternoon, Friday, November 6, she would give it to him. Robert said he was confident he could.

Having been pressed by the DEA to elicit more business from Marlene, Robert was shocked when Carol Cooper raised the usual bureaucratic hesitation.

"There's no way we can put it off till Monday?" she asked. "I can't get a definite absolute answer whether or not we can do it. Simply because I can't get hold of Tom." (Frank Chellino was spending a long weekend at his condominium in Naples, a resort community on the west coast of Florida.)

"Do you think it's that important that we do this with her tomorrow?"

"Yes, yes, very, very important. If I don't pull her away from whoever she is doing business with, we are not going to do anything with her."

Cooper finally reached Clifford, who gave permission to do the deal. At eleven the next morning, Darias and Paul Sennett, again in the role of a bodyguard, met Navarro in the parking lot of a Holiday Inn on Brickell Avenue near the causeway to Key Biscayne. She handed Darias a leather overnight bag that she said contained about $270,000. (By this time the DEA had grown used to the Colombians'

predicting they would have a particular amount of money and showing up with less.) Sennett and Darias rushed the money to the Federal
Reserve Bank, whose count came to $285,700. The Fed exchanged the
bills for hundreds, and Darias and Sennett took the streamlined package to Navarro.

"Is Tom happy?" Robert asked Carol.

"Oh, yeah. He was very pleased. He called *his* boss and they were
very happy, too."

The financial condition of Dean International Investments undoubt-
edly was the frailest of any multinational investment firm in Miami.
DEA headquarters had insisted on funding Operation Swordfish a
month at a time, and only after reviewing its progress. Funds often
were not approved until well after the first of the month. That meant
Dean International's bills were paid late. Dun notices were frequent.
Robert Darias's $4,000 monthly salary for October had been paid
late, and during the first week of November he was paid only $1,500
and told he would have to wait for the rest. The shortage of funds
fueled the tension both inside and outside the office. Amelia Darias
urged Robert to look for another job.

"These people are Keystone Kops," Amelia said. "They're not
serious." She had observed the machinations at Dean International
with growing impatience, and questioned whether the financial bene-
fits of Robert's job were worth the disruption it had brought to their
lives. In the five months since the beginning of Operation Swordfish,
the Dariases saw less and less of their friends in the clannish and
intensely social Cuban community of Miami. They had told some
people that they were spending a lot of time in Orlando because
Robert had accepted a new job there. Though their families knew
generally that Robert was involved in sensitive work for the government, he and Amelia had not confided the details. Living with secrecy
had become a psychological burden that only the promise of long-
term financial security made bearable.

Robert wasn't as pessimistic as Amelia. Despite headquarters's
niggardly attitude, the Miami field division signaled a willingness to
support Operation Swordfish by finally assigning Special Agent Paul
Sennett full-time to the operation in mid-November. He was issued
credentials in the name of Paul Shafer, vice president, customer relations, of Dean International. Sennett's initial task was reassuring
Darias of his value and the importance of the operation itself.

Sennett took Darias to lunch at the Chalet Gourmet on LeJeune
Road near the airport.

"I'm happy to get out of there," Paul told Robert, referring to the daily grind of Group Three on the streets of Miami.

"I can imagine," Robert said.

"Y'know what this agency wants?" Sennett mused. "This agency wants somebody to go out, introduce a guy to them, knock off a kilo, and put the guy in jail for a couple of years. That's their whole philosophy. That's why we've got such a bad drug problem. They are not trying to get into the major guys that are handling the money. They are going for statistics. I guess the FBI is like that, too. 'How many people did you arrest?' If I don't go out there and have some arrests or put some powder on the table, then I get a bad evaluation."

"I know, I know."

"And now the agency's got this budget problem. They're cutting back to where we'll all be riding four to a goddamned car, from what I understand. Carol says we're gonna do our best to get you some money. But, hey, dealing with the United States Government and their shit, y'know—"

"It takes a little while," Robert said.

"And this operation is so *new,*" Paul said. "It's got a lot of problems. But it's going to go. I'm happy to start doing something I think is going to be halfway worthwhile."

Robert looked up and noticed that Humberto Garcia had just entered the restaurant and was standing at the bar. Robert summoned Humberto to the table and introduced him to Paul ("Paul Shafer, my associate") before Humberto went off to meet his luncheon companions.

"I wanted to say hello to him so that he didn't think that I was trying to avoid him," Robert said. He wasn't particularly surprised to run into Humberto. People whose offices were within the orbit of the Miami International Airport—whether they were businessmen, narcotics dealers, or federal agents—tended to frequent a handful of restaurants, and one never knew who would show up at the next table.

"My main problem with this operation," Robert said to Paul, "is that unless I have a free hand, these people I'm going after are not going to be buttered up. In order to believe all that I'm telling them, these people have to believe first of all in *me,* and then I have to be able to prove to them that I can do whatever I say I can do. Instead of every time I say I am going to do something I have to call Carol. When she calls me back ten minutes later somebody has changed her mind and given her a lot of flack on the idea. Frank has convinced her that I'm not completely useful for this operation."

"Frank lives in his own world," Paul said. "But you know and I know and other people know exactly how important you are to this whole thing. Your information is going to make it go. We'll sit down and get this thing straightened out once and for all. I won't give you any bullshit or any lies."

"I'm glad you are there," Robert said.

Robert was pleased to have Paul Sennett's candid opinions of the DEA, Operation Swordfish, and Frank Chellino on tape on the microrecorder in his pocket.

The gangster Angie asked the DEA for "some kind of investment document" that he could show to José Alvero-Cruz and his lawyers as proof that Angie had enough confidence in Dean International to have invested a significant amount of his own money with the firm. The Swordfish agents asked the help of the FBI, which supplied a bogus $125,000 certificate of deposit from its inventory of such things. The DEA put Angie's name on the CD and Frank Chellino gave him a copy to use as he saw fit. A few days later Angie frantically informed the DEA that José Alvero-Cruz's lawyers had identified his CD as precisely what it was—bogus, one of a batch that the FBI had seized a year earlier from a syndicate that was counterfeiting CDs. Apparently the FBI had circulated identifying data from the CDs to the banking and legal communities asking them to be alert for other counterfeits, and was now trapped by its own warning. Alvero-Cruz's lawyers told Angie that Dean International either had unwittingly purchased a false CD for him or was somehow affiliated with the FBI.

The Swordfish agents immediately demanded $130,000 in cash from the embarrassed FBI to purchase a genuine Dean International CD for Angie, who was sent back to Alvero-Cruz's lawyers with the story that Dean had been swindled when it bought the first CD but had immediately replaced it with a valid one in an amount that included lost interest. The lawyers confirmed the authenticity of the new CD with Dean International's bank and then proclaimed themselves impressed that Dean was reputable enough to reimburse Angie so promptly. The DEA also arranged for FBI agents to question Alvero-Cruz's lawyers about the matter and leave the impression that the FBI felt that Dean International might be a shady company.

Marlene Navarro flew back from Bogotá on the Tuesday after Thanksgiving and immediately called Robert. The kidnappers, she reported, were increasing the pressure for payment of ransom. They had sent locks of the children's hair and clippings of their fingernails, and had threatened to start amputating ears and fingers. Marlene also told Robert of another kidnapping in Colombia in recent weeks. A young woman named Marta Ochoa had been kidnapped from a university campus in Medellín by M-19 guerrillas. Marlene indicated that the Ochoa woman was a friend of hers—that she was the sister of Jorge Ochoa. Although Marlene did not further identify the Ochoa family, the name was familiar enough to Robert that he made a point of mentioning it to Carol Cooper.

"I heard that name somewhere," Robert said.

"Yeah. That's a good name," Carol replied.

"Do you know the person?" Robert asked.

"Yeah." Carol again was reluctant to prompt Robert, so she stopped short of telling him that Jorge Ochoa was a major drug lord in Colombia. Marlene Navarro's claiming to be a friend was further indication that she was affiliated with the upper echelon of the narcotics mafia.

"Is there a deadline on the kidnapping or what?" Cooper asked.

"They must be arguing back and forth, I guess. She said they had killed ten ex-secret police people in Bogotá because they were part of a gang that was kidnapping people. The army caught up with them and killed ten of them."

Navarro had given no further details. Indeed there was a great deal of information about the events of the weekend in Colombia that she had not told Robert.

In the wake of the kidnapping of Marlene's boss's children and Jorge Ochoa's sister, the high command of the mafia had convened a council of war the weekend of November 20 and 21 in the city of Cali, where Robert and Barry Carew had met Santiago Ocampo. Jorge Ochoa had called the meeting, and more than 200 top traffickers had attended, including Marlene and her boss. The group decided to take an aggressive stance against kidnappings of family members by guerrilla organizations. Each of the conferees agreed to contribute 2 million pesos ($33,000) to a common defense fund and ten men to a "vigilante" force.

"The basic objective will be the public and immediate execution of all those involved in kidnappings," the group stated in a manifesto issued a few days later. "Kidnappers will be hanged from the trees in public parks or shot. . . . Retribution will fall on their comrades in jail and on their closest family members."

A reward of 20 million pesos ($330,000) was offered for information leading to the capture of a kidnapper.

The drug lords named their vigilante group "Muerte a Secuestradores," or MAS, "Death to Kidnappers." Santiago Ocampo was elected president.

Referring to themselves only as "businessmen," the members of MAS distributed their manifesto throughout Colombia. Thousands of copies were dropped from a plane over a packed soccer stadium in Cali during a Sunday game.

At the town house in the Talavera section of Bogotá, the kidnappers of the Alvarez children had settled into a routine. It appeared to the neighbors that two of the men were taxi drivers; they came and went in the black Ford taxi that had been parked near the cluster of town houses since early October. On one occasion, a neighbor hired one of the men to drive him and his wife to a doctor's appointment. But mainly the "taxi people" kept to themselves.

The heavy white curtains on the upstairs front bedroom window of the house were always closed, and the three children were rarely seen. However, they once cried in the second-floor bathroom so loudly that a neighbor heard them, and also heard a woman he presumed to be their mother yelling: "You little motherfuckers, get out of there!" The children continued to cry. The neighbor did nothing.

But the formation of MAS and the attendant publicity in the Colombian press had an immediate effect. The guerrilla command in charge of the Alvarez children decided to move the hostages out of Bogotá. The M-19 cadre who had been guarding the children in the house in the Talavera district was instructed to tell the owner of the house that they were moving to the Amazon, hundreds of miles south of Bogotá.

Actually the guerrilla command had another destination in mind for the Alvarez children.

13

THE ROAD NORTHEAST from Bogotá, a road used frequently for international bicycle races, snaked about twenty miles through the mountains past seventeenth-century *haciendas* and then wound east and south through hamlets with Chibcha Indian names—Guásca, Gachetá, Ubalá, Gachalá. The directions of the compass meant little in such an equatorial region, where the only meaningful directions were up (chilly and blustery) and down (sultry and still).

Beyond Guásca, where the pavement ended, the rough dirt road climbed out of the pine and eucalyptus forest past the tree line, well over 10,000 feet above sea level, to the climatic zone known as *el páramo,* a high, bleak wilderness. No one lived in *el páramo,* and nothing grew except heath and scrub. The terrain resembled remote areas of the continental divide through the Rocky Mountains in the United States, except that equatorial Colombia got more moisture, producing an abundance of waterfalls, mist, fog, and, on most days, a low ceiling of thick clouds by noon. A cold, damp wind blew constantly.

The Alvarez children, now in the hands of a different M-19 cell, had never been anywhere as forbidding as *el páramo.* There was barely room on the narrow road for the kidnappers' Nissan van to pass the few other vehicles that it met.

Thirty miles above Guásca the road spiraled downward again, dropping several thousand feet through some of the severest switchbacks in the world, out of the cold, to sultry, lush fields of bananas, bamboo, and sugarcane. The air was fragrant with jasmine. The buildings in the semitropical town of Gachetá were painted hot colors—bright yellow, orange, red, and blue. Many people used umbrellas against the relentless sun.

Between Gachetá and Ubalá the kidnappers and the children endured the roller coaster effect once more. The ever narrower road climbed again toward *el páramo* through more switchbacks and then descended past ramshackle *campesino* houses back into the heat and humidity of banana groves. Beyond Ubalá a sign warned *"Peligro—transite bajo su propio riesgo. . . . "* (Danger—travel at your own risk.)

The road clung to the side of a mountain, a dramatic geologic thrust, rising straight up on the left, plunging straight down on the right. A white-water river rushed by. There were more switchbacks, rising yet again toward the cold winds, before the road descended, and the temperate hamlet of Gachalá came into view, a glimmer of white clinging to the shoulder of a mountain amidst a hundred shades of green.

Gachalá (pronounced *gah-cha-LAH*), with a population of a few hundred, was the hub of mining country—copper, uranium, limestone, and, most lucrative of all, emeralds. The mountain people around Gachalá, like many Colombians, were obsessed with emeralds. The peasant farmers, known as *campesinos,* called themselves hunchbacks because "we spend our lives hunched over looking down at the ground for emeralds." They rarely found them. Most of the gems were extracted by the big mining corporations and shipped out of the area to be cut and sold at retail in Bogotá, Madrid, Paris, New York, and Tokyo.

The *campesinos* of Gachalá for centuries had resented their exclusion from the emerald riches. In November 1981, a more contemporary resentment was building over a different kind of perceived exploitation. The Electrical Energy Company of Bogotá, one of the principal power utilities of Colombia, was in the early stages of building a massive hydroelectric dam on the Guavio River a few miles from Gachalá. Like the emeralds, most of the electricity from the new dam would not stay in the area to light the huts of the *campesinos;* instead, it would be sent over the mountains to run satellite TV dishes and microwave ovens in Bogotá. And there was a more tangible problem: the Guavio dam would flood many thousands of acres of *campesino* land, depriving the residents of their homes and livelihood. The Electrical Energy Company of Bogotá seemed indifferent to the *campesinos'* concerns.

Some of the *campesinos* had formed an organization—the Guavio Victims Committee—to confront the company. By late 1981, the committee had grown to more than 500 members and there was talk of strikes to halt work on the dam. A union organizer had been summoned to confer with the Victims Committee. Antimanagement graffiti were beginning to appear along the road to Bogotá. In addition to strikes, however, the chairman of the Guavio Victims Committee was secretly organizing activities that were far more radical.

The chairman, Bernardo Acosta, a dynamic man in his early thirties, was a popular figure around Gachalá. Acosta was one of the few local people to have gone to high school. He worked as a tailor, but also engaged in other businesses, and was one of the few Gachalunos who traveled frequently to Bogotá, where he had relatives. He was considered a wheeler-dealer, a man of action, a man who could be effective against the Electrical Energy Company of Bogotá.

Bernardo Acosta also was a man of secrets. Doubtful that strikes would be effective against the energy company, Acosta was quietly forming a guerrilla group—separate from the Victims Committee—to challenge the company with violence. Even more quietly, in the course of forming the guerrilla group, Acosta had developed a relationship with elements of the M-19 movement.

And Bernardo Acosta had an even darker secret: he had recently agreed to a request by M-19 guerrillas that he take custody of the kidnapped children of Carlos Alvarez. Acosta had not been told the identity of the children, their family, or the guerrillas who had kidnapped the children on October 6. He had not been told that the money to ransom the children was being assembled from illegal drug sales in North America. Acosta had been told only that the children had to be sequestered in strictest secrecy, perhaps for a long period of time, and that he would be paid handsomely if the scheme could be concealed and the children's family paid the ransom.

Knowing he could not hide the presence of three young Bogotáno children for long in the small town of Gachalá, Bernardo Acosta decided to take them to a remote spot high in the mountains where he had obtained the use of a deserted shanty.

In the middle of November, Acosta had enlisted the help of a man from the Guavio Victims Committee, a *campesino* named Guillermo Alvarado who was familiar with the treacherous mountain trails around Gachalá—especially a trail, used centuries earlier by the *conquistadors,* across the mountains to a town called Medina on the edge of the plains. Acosta asked Alvarado to transport a mule-load of supplies to a location on the Medina trail. Confiding nothing about kidnapping or children, Acosta said only that the supplies were for use by a new chapter of the Guavio Victims Committee. And the job had to be done at night.

"Why at night?" Alvarado asked.

"The group is being organized secretly," Acosta replied. "The energy company doesn't know about it."

Guillermo Alvarado agreed to do the job for 500 pesos.

The van carrying the Alvarez children and a man and a woman posing as their parents arrived in Gachalá at dusk on Sunday, November 29. Like many small towns, Gachalá was built around a central square.

On one side stood the steepled Catholic church. Opposite the church, past a huge, old eucalyptus tree in the square, were the rudimentary quarters of the police department and city hall. Around the square was an assortment of small sundry shops and general stores housed in two-story Spanish colonial buildings painted soft shades—pink, beige, salmon, and white, with dark doors of blue, green, and brown.

Gachalá that Sunday evening was sleeping off Market Day, a weekly ritual when the *campesinos* gathered in town to trade their wares and drink large quantities of beer and *aguardiente,* the Colombian anise-based liqueur. It was a good night for strangers to slip through town unobtrusively. The kidnappers had been told to go to a small restaurant called *El Portón* (The Big Door) two blocks off the square. The restaurant was owned by Victor Reyes, a confidant of Bernardo Acosta in the top ranks of the Guavio Victims Committee and one of the few local people Acosta had told of the kidnapping plot. The restaurant was closed that night and the children were taken to Reyes's private quarters in the back. The group planned to leave immediately for their destination in the mountains.

It was rare for visitors to set out on the Medina trail at night. The trail wound through mountains so forbidding that they were called cliffs—the *Farallones de Medina,* the Rocky Cliffs of Medina, rising above 11,000 feet into clouds and mist. And the *campesinos* feared more than the treacherous terrain. According to legend, at the time of the *conquistadors* in the sixteenth century, an Indian chief near what became the city of Bogotá had ordered 100 Indians to take 100 bags of gold to a lake high in the *Farallones de Medina* in order to keep the gold from the Spanish conquerers. To encourage security, the chief had then sent another 100 Indians to the lake to kill the first 100. In the centuries since, whenever anyone had approached the mist-shrouded lake, they had heard moans and screams, and quickly fled.

But the young urban guerrillas disdained such fears. Equipped with flashlights, together with a local guide hired by Acosta, they began the journey. The two Alvarez girls, seven-year-old Zuleika and six-year-old Yidid, were tied aboard one of the mules. Supplies were secured to a second mule. The five-year-old boy Xouix rode on the back of the guide, who walked, along with the couple posing as the children's parents.

The Medina trail twisted sharply down from Gachalá past the stone gates of small *fincas* toward the Moncobita Creek, whose rush could be heard well before the travelers reached it. The narrow, rocky trail again climbed and then eased along the side of a mountain before dropping to the banks of the Murka River. The bed of the Murka was so rocky that the riders had to dismount and allow the mules to make their way across with minimum weight. Beyond the Murka, the trail rose again, zigzagging up the side of another mountain.

Less steep now, the trail meandered through open meadow and arrived at a barbed-wire fence just below the *finca* of Guillermo Alvarado. It had taken the kidnappers and children more than three hours to cover the seven miles from Gachalá in the dark. It was after 9:00 P.M.

Guillermo Alvarado, a small, wiry man in his fifties, lived with his family in a two-room adobe shack with a tin roof in a grove of banana trees. Deeply weathered and missing several teeth, he was not much over five feet tall and his wide-set gray eyes were clouded by cataracts.

Alvarado's mule had been killed in a fall from a mountain trail, so he had borrowed a mule from a friend to transport Bernardo Acosta's supplies. As he loaded the mule, the other travelers sipped sweetened coffee to fortify themselves against the damp cold. A neighbor of Alvarado's, Efrain Cortes, joined them for the rest of the journey. Like all *campesinos* in the area, Alvarado and Cortes wore rubber knee boots to keep from slipping on the steep mountain trails muddied by the frequent rains, and to protect themselves from the deadly poisonous *talla equis* snakes, marked with a distinctive "X" pattern, which inhabited the forest below 7,000 feet or so. The guerrillas from Bogotá wore leather work shoes that were no match for the mud.

The group left the Alvarado *finca* around midnight. The mountainside above the house was so steep that the travelers had to retrace their steps through the meadow below and then follow a winding trail up along the side of the Alvarado property. Above the house the trail leveled, then climbed to another summit, Mount Minas, and proceeded into heavy jungle which blocked the intermittent moon. The trail then twisted down to the Batatas River, a yard deep and twenty yards wide, babbling over rocks. The group forded the river, followed it for a while, crossed back to the other side, followed it for another few miles, then headed up again, twisting and turning, into dense, pitch-black jungle. After passing under a natural bridge, they emerged onto the ridge line of Mount Chochos, where they found themselves above the tree line in the terrain known as *el páramo,* similar to the forbidding area in the mountains between Bogotá and Gachalá.

By this time, Guillermo Alvarado, a seasoned mountain man, had outpaced the exhausted city people and arrived alone at a branch trail which led through a wooden gate and a barbed-wire fence. It was five A.M. Alvarado removed the supplies from his mule and, in accord with Bernardo Acosta's instructions, deposited them at the gate and immediately began his return trip. He passed the group with the children struggling along the trail.

On reaching the gate where Alvarado had left the supplies, the group followed the branch trail, which twisted sharply down the side of Mount Chochos before crossing a creek and rising again to a meadow on the side of another mountain. There they found a weathered gray wooden shack marked by a solitary towering pine tree. Bernardo Acosta was waiting. It was dawn.

The ordeal of the children of Carlos Jader Alvarez, which had begun seven weeks earlier in the early morning traffic on Calle 170 in north Bogotá, and continued in the tense confines of the town house in Talavera, was beginning anew in an isolated mountain meadow high in the Andes. Although the meadow was unmapped, it had a name. The *campesinos* called it *Las Brisas,* the Breezes.

Back at his home later that morning, Guillermo Alvarado mused to his wife why people from the city, with small children, were involved in a "new branch" of the Guavio Victims Committee which Bernardo Acosta had said he was forming high in the mountains a long way from the site of the proposed Guavio dam.

"Why would they take children up there at night?" Alvarado asked.

14

OPERATION GREENBACK again brought pressure on Operation Swordfish. At Tom Clifford's request in August, Greenback had deferred its planned indictment of Lionel Paytubi and the Great American Bank to allow Swordfish to see whether Paytubi would implicate himself in significant new crimes. By December it appeared to Greenback lawyer Charles Blau that Paytubi was dormant, and Blau told Clifford he intended to proceed. In an urgent effort to spur Paytubi, Frank Chellino telephoned the deposed banker to tell him that Dean International had lowered its commissions and hoped to attract additional clients from Paytubi.

"I'm selling cars for a living now," Paytubi informed Chellino.

"You can make a lot more money working for Dean International than you can selling cars," Chellino said.

Paytubi said that in fact he hoped to attract money from a man who had been his largest depositor at the Great American Bank. The man was currently in Brazil and Paytubi would meet with him when he returned.

Tom Clifford relayed this information to Charles Blau, who reluctantly agreed to extend his deadline again.

Gangster Angie reported that the José Alvero-Cruz organization wanted a written proposal from Dean International for placing between $5 million and $10 million in various investments in Europe, the Caribbean, and the United States. Dean asked for a retainer of $10,000 for the proposal, and Angie indicated that Alvero-Cruz probably would pay. Frank Chellino set to work drafting the document.

Marlene Navarro called Darias on a Monday in the middle of December to ask if Dean International could wire $20,000 to Lima, Peru, as a favor to one of her associates. Darias got Chellino on the phone at Dean.

"Marlene wants us to wire twenty thousand to Lima, Peru, for her."

"Uhhhh! Shit! I don't like it," Chellino ranted. "I don't even want to be bothered. I don't even want to touch twenty thousand with her. Give me some time. I'll get back to you."

While Dean International equivocated, Marlene decided to send the $20,000 another way, just as she had in October when the people at Dean had failed to decide promptly whether to send $2 million to Bogotá to be used for kidnap ransom.

Marlene called Robert again the next morning. A client of hers had $285,000 in cash, she said, and wanted to purchase a 90-day certificate of deposit. Could Robert determine the best available interest rate? He conferred with Chellino, who called several banks and was given a rate of 12 percent on a CD backed by government-guaranteed securities. Darias called Manuel Sanchez who had recently left the Bank of Miami to take a new job at Intercontinental Bank. Sanchez quoted Darias 12 1/4 percent for the regular bank CD. Still not satisfied, Darias called Sanchez's boss, the president of Intercontinental Bank and an old high school friend of Robert's from Cuba. The friend gave Darias a rate of 12 1/2 percent.

"Okay, I've made my calls," Robert told Carol. "I have half a point better than Frank." Cooper laughed and put Chellino on the phone. In addition to the higher interest rate, Robert pointed out the advantage of purchasing the CD at Intercontinental; Manuel Sanchez would be drawing himself further into the DEA's net. (Darias had carefully avoided telling his high school friend the source of the money.)

Marlene invited Robert and "Mr. Dean" to meet her client over lunch at the country club of the Costa del Sol. They assembled at twelve-thirty at a round table in the center of the dimly lit carpeted dining room looking out through large picture windows at the golf course.

Marlene introduced Frank and Robert to two thirtyish Latin men whom she called Luis and Francisco. Most of the conversation was in Spanish, with Robert translating for Frank. Luis said that the $285,-000 in cash would be turned over to Marlene that evening and could be picked up by Dean International the next morning. The certificate of deposit, he said, should be put in the name of Marlene's corporation, Marlene Import and Export Inc. Luis added that there would be a lot more money arriving in January and that he wanted to invest in a new shopping center in Pompano Beach.

Back at the Dean office, which had been decorated for Christmas, the agents introduced Robert for the first time to Gregory English, the Justice Department lawyer who had been assigned to guide the Swordfish cases.

"In less than six months you guys have done what the FBI couldn't do in two years," said English, who had cast himself in a cheer-leading role. They discussed Chellino's objection to accepting relatively small amounts of money, and English explained: "If a guy wants to deliver twenty thousand, take it, because it's just as incriminating as the larger deliveries, and each delivery adds a potential five-year count to the indictment." Chellino shot a hostile look at Cooper and Sennett but said nothing.

Darias and Sennett drove to Marlene's home in Costa del Sol just west of the Doral Country Club on Wednesday morning. As Paul waited in the car, Robert for the first time saw the inside of the two-story, three-bedroom beige stucco town house where Marlene had moved in September. The place was still sparsely furnished, but Marlene had two Coral Gables decorators designing the interior and ordering furniture. Marlene handed Robert a blue and tan nylon backpack that she said contained about $245,000. Luis had brought $285,000, she explained, but had removed $40,000 in order to pay some "expenses." Darias also noted Luis's full name, Luis Fabio Rodriguez, and the number from his passport, which turned out to be Venezuelan.

Marlene said she expected Luis to deliver another $2 million in January.

On Thursday afternoon, December 17, Marlene asked Robert to meet her in the coffee shop of the Costa del Sol country club for a farewell chat before the Christmas holidays. The coffee shop was intimate and quiet, just a half-dozen tables, looking out through floor-to-ceiling picture windows onto a patio and a tranquil lake surrounded by palm and oak trees.

On his way to Costa del Sol, Robert had purchased a one-ounce bottle of Flora Danica perfume for $65, had it gift-wrapped, and presented it to Marlene as a Christmas gift. The gesture touched her, and her mood was more relaxed than Robert had ever seen it. Marlene planned to leave the next day for Bogotá and would not return until early January. Sipping a cup of tea, she told Robert that Luis Fabio Rodriguez worked for her boss, a man called Carlos in Bogotá, and would be making some shipments of cocaine over the next several days. Most of her business, she said, as well as that of Carlos, was from cocaine. (She did not use the word "cocaine" but drew her first two fingers under her nose and sniffed.)

Hearing Marlene refer to her boss by name for the first time, Robert gently asked about him. She replied that very few people knew his full name. "He is usually called Carlos Alvarez or Carlos Alvarez Moreno or Carlos Jader Alvarez," she said. "He is known as one of the godfathers in Colombia."

"Yes."

"You might recall that there was a plane that was seized at Opa-Locka Airport about a year ago with over a million dollars aboard."

"Yes, it was in the newspapers," Darias said, searching his memory.

"That was his plane and his money. Carlos was not arrested but his name came up in the investigation. That's the reason he does not want to come to Miami. One of the men who was arrested, a man called Murcia, owes *me* a hundred thousand. He jumped bail and forfeited his bail money."

"Hmmm."

"And a relative of the man Murcia was shot at the Miami airport last year. That was in the newspapers, too."

"I remember."

"And you might also recall the woman who was arrested at the airport last year with over a million dollars hidden in Monopoly boxes? That, too, was Carlos's money and the woman was his first wife, Maria Lilia."

Darias managed to conceal the excitement he felt over these long-awaited revelations. Marlene Navarro had just placed her boss—and herself—at the center of one of the most notorious drug-smuggling syndicates in Latin America. This was not information that an undercover agent gleaned in his first or second conversation with a target. This was information that came only after the gradual nurturing of trust over a long period of time.

"Dean International."

"I have thirty-five million to invest," Darias said when he heard Carol Cooper's voice.

She laughed. "You do? Good, good. What have you been up to?"

"Start writing. I have a little bit of information for you."

Midway through Robert's report about the man called Carlos, Carol said, "I think we know who he is."

"Do you remember the case with the Monopoly boxes in the airport with a million bucks or so?" Robert asked.

"Yeah."

"That girl, Maria Lilia, was Marlene Navarro's associate, and part of that money belongs to Marlene. Maria Lilia was one year in jail and is back in Colombia."

"Right," said Cooper quietly, "that is true."

"Okay, you know now I give you good information," Darias said with a laugh.

"It's all accurate so far. We thought Marlene was connected with all that stuff but we weren't positive. It's all connecting, Bob."

"Of course. She tells me the truth."

"Obviously."

"And then she said that almost all her business is from, and she put her hand to her nose, sniff, sniff. So tell Frank not to worry anymore about whether this is drug money?"

"Sounds very good. I got a file right here on my desk. Alvarez Moreno, also known as Carlos Jader Alvarez. Three pages. He's not much older than Marlene is, about three years older. We have him in our system as José but he has numerous aliases using the first name Carlos. One of them being Carlos Jader Alvarez Moreno. That's going to tie in a lot of things for us, Bob. It's all very, *very* important. This will raise a few eyebrows up in Washington. I love it. Holy cow!"

The definitive link between Marlene Navarro and the high command of the Latin American drug mafia finally was in place. In five months of cultivating Navarro, Robert Darias at last had made the crucial connection between the suppositions in the three-page NAD-DIS computer printout on Carol Cooper's desk and the reality that Navarro was the chief financial officer of one of the largest narcotics syndicates in South America, reporting directly to the godfather himself.

15

THE GODFATHERS of the narcotics mafia in Bogotá were younger than those in Miami. Carlos Jader Alvarez was only thirty-five. Born in a primitive ranching community on the edge of the Amazon 500 miles south of Bogotá, he was the son of a wealthy cattle baron who had been kidnapped by the M-19, just as his grandchildren would be years later. The elder Alvarez eventually was executed by the guerrillas.

By the middle 1970s Carlos Jader Alvarez, who had inherited upward of $1 million from his father, had gotten rich in his own right from cattle, chemicals, and emeralds, as well as cocaine.

The emerald industry in Colombia, supplier of most of the world's emeralds, was as violent as the cocaine trade. Thousands of people had died over the years as companies and individuals battled over mining claims. The black market in emeralds was estimated to be four times the size of the legal market. Smuggling was rampant. When people like Carlos Jader Alvarez expanded into cocaine, they utilized some of the same smuggling routes to North America. By the late 1970s Alvarez was considered one of the top drug lords of Colombia, operating an international smuggling network of "enormous proportions" employing upward of 300 people, according to an official U.S. intelligence estimate.

Carlos Jader Alvarez was often called simply Jader (hah-dare), though the DEA computer showed ten aliases and a nickname, *el muñeco,* "the doll," prompted by his baby face and small, compact build. Although he was living with a twenty-year-old woman who would become his third wife, he was still close to his first two wives, Maria Lilia Rojas and Marina Murrillo, who were both in their thirties. With his wives and several paramours Alvarez had sired several children, some of them born to different mothers within a few months of each other. Maria Lilia was the mother of Zuleika, Marina of Yidid, Xouix, and Wilkander. All three women were beneficiaries on separate $1 million insurance policies on Alvarez's life purchased in Panama City and issued by the Citizens Insurance Company of America in Austin, Texas.

Although the cocaine business was growing much faster than the capacity of the police to inhibit it, occasionally diligent efforts by law enforcement agents in Colombia, aided by American agents, could disrupt the activities of godfathers like Jader Alvarez, if only momentarily. Alvarez was arrested in 1974 when Colombian police seized a cocaine laboratory that he operated in Cali. The case was dismissed by a friendly judge. A few years later the Colombian authorities began tapping some of Alvarez's telephones. He was arrested again in 1979 when 580 kilograms of cocaine (worth $34.8 million on the U.S. wholesale market) were seized in Bogotá. Jader Alvarez owned the cache jointly with two other godfathers, Juan Mata Ballesteros and Bernardo Londono Quintero, who were also detained. Those charges, too, were dropped. But a few months later, in April 1980, authorities at Miami International Airport seized 138 kilograms of Jader Alvarez's cocaine, with a wholesale value of $8.3 million.

According to fragments of intelligence gathered by the DEA, Jader Alvarez began taking steps at that point to improve the security of his cocaine distribution network. Within days of the seizure in Miami, Alvarez sent one of his top aides, Jaime Murcia, a scion of a wealthy and violent Colombian emerald family, to Miami to investigate.

Although the DEA managed to monitor a few of Jaime Murcia's activities in Miami, it was unable to glean much substance. Murcia stayed at the Four Ambassadors Hotel on Biscayne Bay and drove around town in a Mercedes 450-SL. He made a down payment on a new plane for the Jader Alvarez organization, a twin-engine jetprop Beechcraft Super King Air seating eight to fifteen passengers. The full price was $1.6 million.

Also traveling to Miami in the spring of 1980 was a woman called Marlene Orejuela Sanchez, a rich Colombian landowner who was in charge of the intricate process of shipping Jader Alvarez's cocaine from Colombia to the U.S. A DEA surveillance team observed Orejuela in early May in the same Mercedes that Murcia was using.

Just after midnight on Thursday, May 8, Jaime Murcia's nephew, Carlos Murcia, flew into Miami International from Bogotá with his wife and sister. The sister was in a wheelchair, bound for a Miami hospital for treatment of more than thirty bullet wounds she had suffered two months earlier when gunmen had invaded her home in north Bogotá and machine-gunned her husband to death. It was unclear whether the assassination was related to the cocaine business or the emerald business.

As Carlos Murcia was wheeling his sister out of the airport, a young man in a three-piece suit got off a blue Honda motorcycle, strode toward the Murcia party, drew a chrome-plated revolver, shoved the sister's wheelchair aside, and shot Carlos Murcia three times in the head. He died instantly, and the gunman escaped, unidentified.

Marlene Orejuela Sanchez, who had come to the airport to meet the Murcias, arrived on the scene shortly after the shooting, and was detained and questioned by Dade County homicide detectives. (A team of DEA agents that had been shadowing Marlene Orejuela earlier in the evening had stopped for the night.)

Unable to establish a connection between Marlene Orejuela Sanchez and the assassination of Carlos Murcia, the police released her and she returned to Bogotá. A week later she was arrested in connection with the seizure there of another 137 kilograms of Carlos Jader Alvarez's cocaine.

Jader Alvarez could absorb the loss of a few cocaine shipments, even large ones; the DEA believed that he shipped several hundred kilograms a month to the U.S., more than $500 million worth annually. The arrest of his transportation chief Marlene Orejuela Sanchez, however, was more difficult to accommodate, and in the coming months there were signs that Jader Alvarez was intensifying his trouble-shooting effort. He enlisted the help of another major godfather in the Latin mafia, José Antonio "Pepe" Cabrera, who was more familiar with Miami and the technicalities of the U.S. cocaine market than was Alvarez.

Fifteen years older than Alvarez, Pepe Cabrera was one of the founders of the drug industry in Colombia. Although he traded in racehorses and owned the largest gambling casino in the picturesque Colombian coastal city of Cartagena, Cabrera made most of his money smuggling cocaine. He was believed to have smuggled more cocaine into the New York City area than anyone else, and was associated with several New York–based members of the Sicilian Mafia.

Carlos Jader Alvarez and Pepe Cabrera had done a lot of business together. And the previous year Alvarez had bought a house from Cabrera—the mansion called *La Iglesia* in north Bogotá.

During the third week of August 1980, the wiretaps in Bogotá indicated that Pepe Cabrera was about to fly to Miami in a private aircraft via the Bahamas, and would be delivering "a large sum of U.S. currency," the proceeds of a cocaine transaction, to an "unidentified female" in Miami. At the same time, DEA agents learned that Carlos Jader Alvarez was sending one of his most trusted aides, his first wife Maria Lilia Rojas, to Miami.

On Friday, August 22, Maria Lilia Rojas drove to a luxury apartment building on Biscayne Bay in Coconut Grove where Pepe Cabrera maintained an apartment. Rojas's destination turned out to be the apartment of another major drug smuggler, José Estupinan, a ranking officer of the Jader Alvarez organization and Alvarez's principal liaison in Miami with the syndicate's U.S. money launderer Isaac Kattan. Maria Lilia Rojas emerged from the apartment building with an obese man who was carrying a large blue vinyl suitcase—obviously very heavy—which he put in the trunk of the car. It was later learned that he was Teodoro "Teo" Terselich, alias Baltazar and Ivan, a Yugoslavian-born money and drug broker for Carlos Alvarez Jader and Pepe Cabrera.

The next afternoon Maria Rojas checked in at Miami International Airport for a Braniff flight that was scheduled to leave for Bogotá at 6:25 P.M. A Customs inspector, primed for the occasion, announced in both English and Spanish over the public address system in the boarding area that anyone carrying more than $5,000 cash out of the United States was required by law to declare it. No one reacted to the announcement. When the flight was called, Maria Rojas entered the runway to the plane where Customs agents stopped her and asked if she was carrying more than $5,000. She said no. The agents asked if she would consent to a search of her purse and belongings. She agreed.

In a Customs examination room, an agent opened one of her suitcases and found play money from Monopoly games scattered among the clothes. Then he found several Monopoly boxes and discovered that they were packed with real hundred-dollar bills. The total in the Monopoly boxes was $1.5 million.

Under questioning, Rojas claimed that a man she did not know had paid her $200 to transport the boxes to Bogotá. Then she burst into tears. She was arrested and taken to jail where she was held in lieu of $2 million cash bond.

A few weeks earlier, in an office in north Bogotá, Carlos Jader Alvarez had hired a vibrant, well-educated young Colombian woman to help shore up his fragile organization in the United States. The woman, who lived in Miami and traveled extensively in Europe and the Middle East, was Marlene Navarro Sanchez, whom Alvarez had met through mutual friends and business acquaintances. Although her name was sometimes confused with that of Alvarez's distribution aide, Marlene Orejuela Sanchez, they were very different in appearance and personality.

Alvarez had investigated Navarro carefully before hiring her. She had been born out of wedlock in a small town between Cartagena and Barranquilla in 1943. She had been raised there by her grandparents until she was a teenager and then was sent to Paris to live with relatives in the Colombian diplomatic service. She attended the École des Beaux Arts, the Sorbonne, and the Collège des Sciences Sociales et Économiques where she studied art and communications. She also spent time in Israel, and converted to Judaism before settling in Miami in the 1970s. There she obtained a degree from the University of Miami, concentrating in economics and business. Along the way she became fluent in English and French and gained a good deal of proficiency in Italian and Hebrew. She had worked in a number of sales and management jobs in the U.S., Colombia, and Europe. She owned an apartment in Paris. She had been married twice—to an Israeli in Tel Aviv and to an American in Miami—and had a son who lived in Europe. By the time she settled in Miami she had reduced her age on her passport by five years. Instead of her real age of thirty-seven, she claimed she was thirty-two when Carlos Jader Alvarez hired her.

A small, vibrant woman, barely five feet tall, Marlene Navarro was nicknamed "hummingbird" and "butterfly" by her friends, labels that captured her size and personality but belied her intelligence, toughness, and guile.

Navarro maintained an office in Miami with the lawyer Lester Martin Rogers.

On the August weekend in 1980 when Maria Lilia Rojas was arrested, Marlene Navarro immediately took command of her case. Navarro obtained Rojas's power of attorney and hired lawyers to represent her. She visited her in jail each day, making sure Rojas understood that Carlos Jader Alvarez wanted her to say nothing to the American authorities. If she maintained her silence, Navarro told her, Jader would reward her with $300,000. If she talked, it was implied that she would be executed, along with her family. Maria Lilia Rojas did not talk.

The Alvarez organization's troubles in Miami escalated with the Rojas arrest.

An hour after midnight the following Wednesday, August 27, a police officer spotted a man with a pistol stuck in his belt standing in the parking lot of a discotheque in the affluent community of North Miami Beach. The man was standing next to a Datsun sports car chatting with a woman in the passenger seat. When the man was unable to produce a weapon permit, the officer placed him under arrest and called for reinforcements.

Searching the car, the police found cocaine, $5,000 in cash, several uncut diamonds and emeralds, and a gold cigarette case with the name "Pepe" inscribed in emeralds. The man was wearing a bracelet with "Pepe" spelled out in diamonds. His passport identified him as Juan Antonio Molina. But on the back of his watch was yet another diamond inscription: the name José Antonio Cabrera. And in his briefcase was a copy of the criminal complaint that had been filed against Maria Lilia Rojas after her arrest at the airport on Saturday.

None of this meant much to the men on the graveyard shift at the North Miami Beach Police Department. However, since drugs had been found in the car, the police notified the DEA, which recognized the arrested man's name and alias. He was turned over to the DEA and held in jail under $5 million bond.

Pepe Cabrera had been a fugitive from U.S. authorities for six years. He was wanted on homicide and drug charges in New York as well as drug charges in Florida. After being arraigned in Miami, Cabrera was ordered sent to New York to stand trial for narcotics conspiracy and murder. There his bail was reduced to $1 million, which he posted immediately by turning over $1 million worth of Colombian emeralds. Soon after his release he fled the U.S., forfeiting the emeralds. And Carlos Jader Alvarez had lost the on-scene help of an important ally in his North American drug operations.

Several weeks later, the wiretaps on Jader Alvarez's phones in Bogotá revealed that Jader had 450 kilograms of cocaine (wholesale value in Miami $27 million) ready to ship but was reluctant to use his established smuggling routes because of the arrests of Maria Lilia Rojas and José Antonio Cabrera. Jader Alvarez decided that he must travel to the U.S. himself to repair his organization. In late October, again prompted by wiretap intercepts in Bogotá, DEA agents spotted Jader Alvarez and his associate Jaime Murcia as they prepared to fly to Miami from the Bahamas with two pilots aboard a white twin-engine Beechcraft Queen Air. The plane landed at the Opa-Locka Airport, a private airport in northwest Miami best known as a staging area for the Bay of Pigs invasion. After the four men secured the plane, surveillance agents lost track of them until a few weeks later when they were seen attending to another aircraft, a Piper Navajo, parked next to the Queen Air. Teams of agents secretly watched the two planes for several days and nights. Just after midnight on Saturday, November 22, Carlos Jader Alvarez, Jaime Murcia, and two pilots drove up to the Piper Navajo and began transferring luggage from their vehicle into the plane. Alvarez then drove away, and the three others boarded the plane, which soon began taxiing. Armed federal agents, who had been deployed around the airport in the dark, quickly flicked on the flashing blue lights on their cars and converged on the plane. The agents discovered $1.6 million in U.S. currency concealed in shoe boxes in Jamie Murcia's luggage.

Murcia denied that the shoe boxes were his and denied knowing they contained money. An agent asked if Murcia knew Carlos Jader Alvarez. Murcia said no. The agent produced a photograph of Murcia and Jader Alvarez together that had been taken surreptitiously by the DEA in the Bahamas a few weeks earlier.

"Do you know this man?" the agent asked again, pointing to Alvarez's picture.

"Yes," Murcia acknowledged.

"Doesn't the money in these shoe boxes belong to Jader Alvarez?" the agent asked.

Jaime Murcia paused and then began to cry. "You don't understand," he told the agent. "I have a wife and two daughters in Bogotá." Then he began sobbing uncontrollably, and declined to answer further questions.

Jaime Murcia and his pilots were arrested and held in jail on $3 million bond each. Having let Jader Alvarez slip away earlier that night, the agents were unable to locate him. However, the Alvarez organization again mobilized Marlene Navarro to see to the needs of the Murcia group.

Navarro made the final payment on the new Beechcraft Super King Air that Murcia had bought for Jader, and hired a pilot to fly the plane to the Bahamas. Navarro, who had taken flying lessons and knew her way around the Opa-Locka Airport, rode along as the plane took off just minutes ahead of federal agents seeking to serve a subpoena and seize the plane.

In the same way that the Alvarez organization was providing the best legal defense for Maria Lilia Rojas, it spared no expense in the lawyers Marlene Navarro hired to represent Jaime Murcia and his pilots. Navarro's lawyer Lester Rogers appeared on behalf of one of the pilots, and Rogers's cousin, Harvey Rogers, represented Jaime Murcia. The Rojas and Murcia legal proceedings moved along for a time on parallel tracks in Miami federal court in the fall of 1980.

Maria Lilia Rojas was convicted of violating currency declaration regulations and sentenced to a year in prison. The prosecutor in the Jaime Murcia case then immediately subpoenaed Rojas for testimony about the Jader Alvarez organization. She refused to testify, and was given an additional year in prison for contempt of court.

Jaime Murcia's lawyer managed to get his bail reduced from $3 million to $250,000, which he made. After he was released, Marlene Navarro bought Murcia an airline ticket to Bogotá under a false name, provided him with a disguise—a wig and glasses—and put him on the plane. He forfeited his $250,000 cash, just as Pepe Cabrera had forfeited his $1 million in emeralds.

Marlene Navarro flew from Miami to Lexington, Kentucky, to visit Maria Lilia Rojas in the federal prison there, to buoy her spirits and remind her that $300,000 would be hers if she kept her mouth shut about the Alvarez organization.

On Thursday, February 26, 1981, ten days after Navarro visited Rojas, DEA agents in Miami arrested Isaac Kattan, the principal money manager for the Alvarez and Cabrera organizations and a good deal of the rest of the South American drug mafia. In Kattan's car were 44 pounds of Jader's cocaine.

The arrest of Isaac Kattan was another blow to Carlos Jader Alvarez, but it occurred to him that he had the perfect person in place in Miami to inherit Kattan's mantle—Marlene Navarro. Navarro had already begun working with Kattan; only three weeks before Kattan was arrested, she had wired $400,000 of Alvarez's drug money to Panama from a Kattan account at the Bank of Miami. Shortly after his arrest, she had flown to Switzerland to try to block seizure of his secret numbered bank accounts there. In six months on the job for Alvarez, Navarro had displayed intelligence, skill, and imagination. Even Alvarez, however, didn't know just how good a choice Navarro was. In all that Navarro had done for the Alvarez syndicate—hiring criminal lawyers, passing bribe messages inside prisons, escorting a plane to the Bahamas just ahead of a federal subpoena, ferreting Jaime Murcia out of Miami in disguise, wiring drug money for Isaac Kattan and flying to Switzerland on Kattan's behalf—she had totally avoided detection by any U.S. law enforcement or intelligence agency. Neither her name nor any other identifying data had made its way into any federal crime computer.

With Carlos Jader Alvarez, Pepe Cabrera, and Jaime Murcia free and back in Bogotá, and with Marlene Navarro on the job in Miami, the business of the Alvarez and Cabrera organizations went on. Massive cocaine shipments continued to flow into the United States from Colombia, millions of dollars in U.S. currency continued to flow out of the U.S. to Colombia, and there were no more seizures or arrests. Although the DEA had assembled a lot of intelligence on Alvarez and his organization, it had little hope of arresting the principals and little evidence of serious drug crimes by Alvarez personally that was usable in court. The agency was starting from scratch and floundered for several months, until the summer of 1981 when Robert Darias introduced Marlene Navarro to Operation Swordfish and linked her by December to the organization of Carlos Jader Alvarez.

On Tuesday, December 22, Frank Chellino and Robert Darias purchased a $250,000 certificate of deposit for Marlene Navarro's associate Luis Fabio Rodriguez at Manuel Sanchez's bank. The drinks at Le Sabre that evening were extra festive, celebrating the new money and Darias's link of Navarro to Alvarez. Paul Sennett, who normally stuck to Lite beer, got blind drunk on mixed drinks and had to be driven home. On Wednesday, Humberto Garcia and his girlfriend invited Darias to lunch; they started with drinks at the Marriott and then ate roast pork and black beans at La Rosa. On Thursday, Christmas Eve, Humberto invited Robert to a party at Refricenter; Humberto gave Robert a bag containing $30,450 belonging to the Colombian Kids and asked for a cashier's check. On Christmas Day, Luis Fabio Rodriguez phoned Darias at home to say that he would be depositing millions of dollars after January 1.

Robert had told Marlene, Humberto, and other targets that he and his family were going skiing in Vermont between Christmas and New Year's. That was a cover story. In fact, they flew to London where they spent the next ten days touring Great Britain. Robert felt better than he had in a long time. The holiday season stood in particular contrast to the previous Christmas when Darias had been nearly destitute and had been forced to borrow money from his in-laws in order to purchase Christmas gifts for Amelia and Laura.

Christmas was very different, too, for the children of Carlos Jader Alvarez. They had spent the previous Christmas at their home, the mansion called *La Iglesia* with the walk-in doll house, overlooking Bogotá. Now, at the shanty in the meadow above the village of Gachalá, supplies were running low. The guerrilla Bernardo Acosta again hired the *campesino* Guillermo Alvarado to purchase sardines, flashlight batteries, and other items, and take them up the trail in the dead of night.

The younger Alvarez girl, Yidid, had just turned seven years old. Her birthday was December 17. Presents for her, as well as Christmas presents for all three children, lay unopened in their rooms in Bogotá.

16

ROBERT DARIAS'S success in identifying Marlene Navarro's boss as Carlos Jader Alvarez galvanized the high command of the Drug Enforcement Administration and changed its attitude toward Operation Swordfish. Before the link had been established, the DEA hierarchy had come to view Operation Swordfish as an experimental enterprise that was moving too slowly. Despite lip service to notions such as "long term" and "gradual," Washington had put constant pressure on Tom Clifford and his agents to accelerate the investigation. There had also been the exasperating battle for funds every month to keep operating and pay bills.

Now, everything changed. The DEA had never been able successfully to infiltrate the top levels of a narcotics syndicate as important as Alvarez's and the agency was determined to take advantage of the new opportunity that Robert Darias had provided. As of January 1, 1982, the budget for Operation Swordfish was approved for three months in advance instead of the usual one month. Dean International could pay its bills on time; there were no more dun notices from Florida Power & Light and Southern Bell. Darias's salary was paid promptly. Washington disseminated a classified agency-wide teletype, cleansed of sensitive information, holding up Operation Swordfish as a model for the entire DEA. And headquarters also let the Miami field office know that it would have the time and support required to properly exploit the new intelligence about Carlos Jader Alvarez.

Carol Cooper was on the phone to Darias immediately. "We can get anything we want right now," Cooper said. "Jader is bigger than Alvero-Cruz."

"Oh, yeah, you're talking about two different animals, I have no doubt about that," Darias said.

Although Jader Alvarez indeed was bigger than Alvero-Cruz, the Miami-based Cuban drug lord remained important to the DEA and the agency proceeded with its efforts to infiltrate his organization. According to the gangster Angie, Alvero-Cruz intended to pay a $10,000 retainer to Dean International on Friday, January 8, and wanted a meeting with Dean representatives on the island of Aruba

the following Tuesday. Frank Chellino and Angie planned to fly to
Aruba over the weekend along with several undercover DEA surveillance agents to prepare for the meeting. According to Angie, Alvero-
Cruz would arrive in Aruba from either Caracas or nearby Curaçao
and would have between $850,000 and $900,000 in cash that he might
turn over to Dean International. The DEA had tentative plans to
deposit the money in a bank on Aruba and then wire it to Dean's
corporate account in Miami for investment in real estate that could
later be seized by the government.

Robert Darias remained willing to participate in the effort to infiltrate Alvero-Cruz. Cooper and Chellino, however, opposed using
Darias until the role of Angie had been clarified. Although Tom
Clifford had insisted that he be exploited, Chellino and Cooper had
never trusted Angie, and their differences with Clifford over the issue
had become a growing source of tension. In contrast to Robert
Darias's extensive secret recordings of his conversations with Marlene
Navarro, Angie had yet to record even a single telephone conversation
with Alvero-Cruz or anyone else, despite having been pressed repeatedly to do so. He always had an excuse, usually that his tape recorder
had malfunctioned.

"He's talking up a big story," Carol told Robert, "but nobody's
seen anything yet. We don't know how much credibility to put into
him as far as this thing even happening Friday and next week. We'll
play it by ear, but everybody's all excited about it if it does go."

The next morning, Thursday, January 7, a Western Union Mailgram arrived at Dean International Investments addressed to Frank
Dean. Dispatched from a telegraph office in Little Havana, it read:

*We are aware of your operations. Please recall your representative.
A termination contract will be issued. We wish no business with you.
Thank you. (Signed) José Perez.*

Cooper and Chellino stared at the Mailgram, rereading it several
times. The more they studied it, the more anxious they became. Who
was José Perez? Dean International had never done business with
anyone of that name. *A termination contract will be issued.* Dean did
not have "contracts" with clients. Could it be a threat? *We are aware
of your operations.* Did the sender know or suspect that Dean was a
federal undercover operation?

Only two things were clear. First, whoever sent the telegram knew
the name and address of Dean International and its president. Even
after six months of operation, relatively few people had that information. Second, since the agents knew no one named José Perez, the
signature likely was an assumed name. The sender had a reason to

conceal his identity. And that was ominous to Cooper and Chellino.

Chellino called Tom Clifford, who decided immediately that the telegram had to be treated as a threat. Acutely aware that if he reacted too aggressively he might compromise the undercover operation, Clifford dispatched two heavily armed DEA agents to Miami Lakes with instructions to sit in their car a discreet distance from the Dean International office and be alert for any suspicious activity. Cooper and Chellino had their sidearms in the office, as well as a shotgun that had been kept in the storeroom safe since the office had opened. The main worry was the floor-to-ceiling plate-glass windows across the front of the suite—a tempting target for a bomb or a spray of machine-gun fire. Everyone thought of the Dadeland Massacre and other mayhem the Colombian mafia had brought to Miami.

One of the first people Carol Cooper called, both to warn and consult, was Darias.

"We have to sit tight and not make too many moves or talk to too many people," Robert advised Carol. "Whoever sent that telegram is not sure, he just wants to test and see what kind of moves we make."

"I don't know what he wants us to do."

"Well, either close the office or start running."

"We haven't done anything yet, Bob. We're just checking on all the possibilities."

"I'm going to be careful, but I'm pretty confident it's not coming from my side." Darias could hear the relentless ringing of the other phones in the Dean office.

"We think you're okay but we wanted you to be aware of it," Carol said.

"I have an idea that whoever it is is going to be calling or checking the office in a day or two to see what reaction we have," Darias said. "If it's business as usual, they will figure we must be investment people like we say we are."

Eventually the agents narrowed the plausible possibilities to one targeted individual—the Cuban drug lord José Alvero-Cruz. Gangster Angie had said from the outset that Alvero-Cruz intended to investigate the background of Dean International and its principal employees. There had been a spate of odd phone calls to the office—wrong numbers and hang-ups. There had been the people in the parking lot taking photographs of license plates back in November. Had Alvero-Cruz's inquiries aroused his suspicions? Had there been a leak? Had he had second thoughts after the snafu with the bogus certificate of deposit in November?

The Swordfish agents, particularly Cooper and Sennett, focused their scorn on Angie and confided their suspicions to Darias, who became a sort of telephonic crisis consultant. "Nothing that this guy has done has ever been corroborated," Paul told Robert. "We don't have any recordings, we don't have anything. They made a big mistake with him. God knows who he is really. He still says we're supposed to get money from them tomorrow. I think it's bullshit. And this isn't Frank's fault either." Sennett blamed Tom Clifford for foisting Angie on the operation.

"He's a strange guy, Bob, which is why we keep you totally away from him," Carol added. "I don't trust this guy at all. We're all going to be surprised if anything comes through tomorrow. He hasn't shown us anything. You can't tell me he's talked to these people for two months and can't even get a phone conversation taped. We've got nothing to corroborate what he's doing."

Robert and the others were instructed to be careful, but to continue with their work as usual. As Thursday ended, a sense of lurking danger infected the atmosphere at Dean International for the first time since Operation Swordfish began.

On Friday, Gangster Angie reported to the DEA that his "contact" in the Alvero-Cruz organization had not yet returned from "a trip out of town" and thus the scheduled delivery of the $10,000 retainer to Dean International that day, and the meeting on Aruba the following Tuesday, would be delayed. The agents took that as an ominous sign in the wake of the telegram. Carol Cooper asked Darias to bring a gun—he collected guns—and stay with her that afternoon because for a few hours she would be the only agent in the Dean offices. As a convicted felon, Darias was prohibited by law from owning or using firearms, but the DEA was prepared to overlook such restrictions under the circumstances.

Marlene Navarro phoned Darias the following Monday. It was their first conversation since December 17 when she had revealed the identity of her boss. After spending Christmas in Bogotá, she had gone to Puerto Rico and the Dominican Republic for several days. At a resort near Santo Domingo she had met a Scottish engineer who lived in Toronto. Alexander McIntosh had become Marlene's latest lover.

Marlene reported that the last shipment of currency she had flown from Miami to Bogotá had turned out to contain about $20,000 in counterfeit bills. Carlos Jader Alvarez, whom she called only "Carlos" on the telephone, had instructed her to deposit future deliveries of currency with Dean International and have Dean wire the money to "the Land of Omar," a telephone code Marlene used for Panama, referring to the late dictator Omar Torrijos.

There was no news about Alvarez's kidnapped children.

Luis Fabio Rodriguez, the Alvarez operative who had purchased the $250,000 certificate of deposit in December, invited Robert and Amelia Darias to dinner. Robert declined politely after Marlene Navarro advised him against it. "He is not at your (social) level," Marlene said. *El no está al su altura.* Although she didn't let on to Luis, Marlene loathed him because he often made suggestive remarks to her and called her *biscocho* ("delectable"), a purely sexual come-on. Rodriguez later asked Robert to lunch at the Playboy Club; it would be a business meeting, just the two of them, and presumably they would discuss Rodriguez's plan to deposit $2 million of drug proceeds with Dean International. Rodriguez did not show up for the lunch, however, and did not call to apologize. Darias and Carol Cooper wondered briefly if the broken date was related to the threatening telegram to the Dean office on January 7, but they concluded that it was more likely just a display of bad manners.

On Tuesday, January 12, a new special agent joined Operation Swordfish, Edwin Hernandez, a thirty-five-year-old native of Puerto Rico. Tom Clifford felt the operation had been hampered by a linguistic and cultural gap in the months since one of the original Swordfish agents, Pepe Hinojosa, had departed in a huff. The remaining agents—Chellino, Cooper, and Sennett—were Anglo, while the two spies, Robert Darias and Felipe Calderon, and their main targets, were Latin. It was hard to gauge the significance of the gap, but Clifford felt that a Latin agent in a supervisory role might pick up nuances in communications with the spies and the criminals that the Anglos were missing.

At five-foot-four, Eddie Hernandez could compete with Frank Chellino for being the shortest agent in Operation Swordfish. Hernandez had been with the DEA less than two years and had worked both in Miami and New York. (He had been one of the agents shadowing Jader Alvarez's distribution aide Marlene Orejuela Sanchez on the night of May 8, 1980, when Carlos Murcia was assassinated at Miami International Airport.) Previously Hernandez had worked for the CIA.

Eddie Hernandez was issued undercover credentials in the name of Manolo Ramos. Carol Cooper was careful to clarify Hernandez's role privately for Robert Darias, who had just met him. "Until we decide who's who, he's not gonna meet any of your people," Carol said. "The main reason he's here, Bob, is that after Pepe Hinojosa left we needed another Spanish-speaker, agent-wise. And someone who can handle Felipe. Eddie's got to get his feet wet. He knows absolutely nothing. He's very young. He's very, very aggressive. But I think he'll be very good for us. We're not going to have the personality problems we had with Pepe. He's not coming in acting like he knows everything. He's willing to learn."

"He was very nice to me."

"Oh, yeah. He likes you. He thinks you're dynamite. I basically told him what has been going on case-wise—that you have brought in basically all the business. He will leave you alone. He will go through Paul or I to get to you."

After five days, the telegram that Dean International had received remained an unsettling mystery. Western Union had been unable to identify the sender beyond the apparently false name on the telegram, José Perez, and a vague description of a Latin male who had dispatched the telegram from a Western Union office in Little Havana. Tom Clifford was frustrated. The DEA couldn't probe aggressively without compromising Operation Swordfish. And yet Clifford felt compelled to do something. The words of the telegram haunted him. *We are aware of your operations. . . . A termination contract will be issued. . . .*

He and the other agents remained convinced that someone in the Alvero-Cruz organization had sent the wire. The deposit of the $10,-000 retainer and the rendezvous with Alvero-Cruz in Aruba had been postponed without explanation. Gangster Angie was maintaining that he knew nothing about the telegram, but since his credibility had been in question even before its receipt, Clifford ordered that Angie take a lie detector test.

Like most intelligence and law enforcement bodies, the DEA relied heavily on polygraphs for internal use. Although it recognized the split in scientific opinion over whether polygraphs were reliable (they were not admissable in court), the DEA and other agencies believed they were far better than nothing for testing the veracity of their own agents and spies when other means of investigation were unavailable.

Angie agreed to the examination. He had taken at least two polygraphs before that the DEA knew about, failing one and passing the other. The test he had passed was suspect, however. The word was that he might have taken a Valium or a Quaalude to dull his reactions.

Cooper kept Darias informed. "We've about had it with this guy,"

Carol told Robert. "If he flunks this thing, we will have an extremely big security problem."

The next morning, Gangster Angie informed Tom Clifford's office that he couldn't take the polygraph test. He had been "unable to get a baby-sitter," he said, and would have to take the test another day. Dismayed, Clifford recalled Angie's checkered history with DEA polygraphs. But at least he had *taken* the previous tests. Clifford decided he had to infer the worst—that Angie was afraid to take the test because he had guilty knowledge of the telegram the previous Thursday. Could Angie be a double agent? Taking money from the DEA to penetrate Alvero-Cruz, and taking money from Alvero-Cruz to betray a federal undercover operation?

The DEA's alternatives, Clifford concluded, no longer included business as usual. The agency now had to confront the possibility that Operation Swordfish had been compromised, and that the telegram represented a genuine threat against Dean International and its people by the Alvero-Cruz organization, which was notorious for using violence. The options were unattractive: the DEA couldn't summarily arrest Alvero-Cruz; it didn't have enough evidence to make a case against him. Nor could it ignore him; if he had figured out that Dean International was a government set-up, he might quietly spread the word through the clubby drug mafia, causing Dean's targets to, at the very least, quietly slip away, or, at worst, take violent action against the DEA agents. Clifford kept thinking how the Colombian mafia slaughtered not only enemies but families of enemies. Agents and informants had been murdered just on whim.

Tom Clifford found himself thinking the unthinkable. Operation Swordfish, the enterprise that he had conceived, founded and nurtured, might have to be terminated. Actually, such a notion wasn't entirely daunting to Clifford. The principle behind the operation—infiltrating the Latin drug mafia through an undercover investment company—was valid, but Clifford had to acknowledge that there was nothing sacred about this particular operation. Surely it would be a shame to waste all the effort that had gone into it. But the narcotics war to which the U.S. Government had committed itself was longterm. If Dean International were quietly closed and the operation terminated, the DEA could wait a few months and then start another operation with a different undercover corporation, different location, and different agents.

And yet Clifford also had to acknowledge that closing Swordfish would have devastating ramifications. The DEA might have to sacrifice the now distinct possibility of penetrating the vast criminal network of Carlos Jader Alvarez. But as much as Clifford would hate giving up that opportunity, it wasn't worth the lives of his agents. And for all he knew, José Alvero-Cruz might even now be spreading the word about Dean International to the Jader Alvarez organization.

Second thoughts, inchoate thoughts, half-baked notions, flooded Clifford. Was he being too soft-hearted? He was, after all, the man who once had given up a career working with disturbed children because he became too personally involved in his cases.

Perhaps there was an alternative to terminating Operation Swordfish immediately. Maybe it would be possible to close it gradually, over a month or two or even three, focus only on targets like Navarro, Paytubi, Sanchez, and Humberto Garcia against whom they already had solid cases, and prepare those cases for indictment ahead of schedule. It could be risky to stay open that long, but maybe they could redouble the armaments in and around the office and sweat it out.

Still undecided, Clifford summoned Chellino, Cooper, and Sennett early that afternoon and told them that while he hated to do it he was inclined to order the termination of Operation Swordfish. "I can't afford to risk it any longer," he said. "What if we stay open, and tomorrow or the first of next week, Alvero-Cruz's people throw a bomb through the window or spray the place with an Uzi and you people are all killed? We can't afford to take the chance. We can always open up again a few months down the line with a different name and different covers."

The agents were shocked and furious that Clifford would even consider closing the operation. It had been Tom Clifford who had insisted on cultivating Gangster Angie against Chellino's advice, and now that Angie's man Alvero-Cruz presumably had cast a cloud over the operation, Clifford was proposing to cut and run, at great cost not only to pending investigations but also potentially to the careers of Frank Chellino, Carol Cooper, Paul Sennett, and the other agents, who clearly could not be used again in a similar operation in Miami in the near future.

"You can't do this!" Chellino yelled at Clifford.

"Hey, we'll do what we have to do," Clifford shot back. "Nobody wants this operation to continue more than I do. I started it and I may have to end it. But the decision will be made by management. It's none of your concern."

"What do you mean it's none of our concern," Carol Cooper

shouted. The usually calm Cooper rarely lost her temper. "We deserve to be the *first* to know! It's gonna affect Paul's career, Frank's, mine, everybody's! All of us have a personal interest in the operation!"

"I'm sorry," Clifford replied. "We'll let you know what we decide."

"Plus the fact of Bob and Felipe," Cooper added. "You can't leave them hanging out there."

"They'll be taken care of," Clifford said, adding that there would be a decision by the next day. "I'll discuss it with higher management. You'll have your input."

It had occurred to Clifford that if he closed Operation Swordfish he would no longer have to put up with Frank Chellino.

Preoccupied with advancing his relationship with Marlene Navarro, Robert Darias was unaware of the agents' clash with Tom Clifford that day. He had sensed the rising tension in the office, however, and when he called Carol for their usual evening chat, he had never heard her so exhausted and depressed. Robert wasn't in such good shape, either, having taken an extra Sinutab for his lingering sinus cold, and tried to calm his nerves with a third Black Label and water.

"Marlene will give me a lot of information in the morning," Robert said. "She was waiting for a call from Bogotá about the developments with the kids. And she said she was expecting Luis Fabio to call tonight. That's why I want to have coffee with her."

"Paul and I, as soon as we can tomorrow morning, are going down to the main office," Carol reported. "We've got to take care of a couple of things, and they affect you, which is why I want to get it taken care of real quick. I don't want to get you nervous about it yet."

"I guess it's one of the trials?" Robert asked, thinking of Bert Schwartz and Johnny Crump, whose arrests he had fostered the year before and who were about to go to trial.

"No, nothing at all with that," Carol said. "There's no problem with you personally. Some decisions are being made that are going to affect a lot of people including you. We all want to get it taken care of real quick."

"Okay."

"If I get an indication that it is for real, and something is in the wind, Paul and I will sit down and talk to you."

"Well, I don't know what you are telling me. But I read in the newspapers a little while ago about the budget—"

"It has nothing to do with the budget. Our budget went through. I know you don't know what I'm talking about and I don't want to get you excited."

"It's not that the operation is going to end?"

"I don't know," Cooper replied quietly. "I really don't know."

"But that's what it is, then?"

"It's a strong rumor. And I don't know what is going on. When we asked somebody about it we were told it's not important to us. No need for us to know. And I hit the ceiling. I really don't care. I told Frank they can fire me."

"Well, it might just be a rumor."

"Yeah, but the fact that somebody told me that it's not any of my concern. That irritated me. It *is* my concern."

"I think it would be stupid to close it now when things are beginning to really—"

"I agree. Paul, Frank, and I are all screaming. Eddie's not involved in this and he won't be. He doesn't know anything about it." Bob Russo was backing Clifford.

"Keep in mind, Carol, I have worked for big companies, and the government is nothing more than a big company. There are a lot of jealousies and petty everything."

"I know. And that's part of what's going on here. I wish they'd just leave us alone. We shouldn't have to put up with all this garbage from the hierarchy. It's amazing when your bosses run away from you."

Robert's other phone line rang.

"I'll talk to you tomorrow, Carol. And don't worry. I am pretty sure everything will be resolved."

Despite Robert's soothing words to Carol, he and Amelia were distraught that night. It seemed apparent to Darias that if the operation were terminated abruptly, he and his family would have to move just as abruptly, not just to another house in Miami this time, but out of South Florida. They would probably be forced into the Federal Witness Security Program. That would mean a sudden uprooting from their families and cultural ties in Miami's Cuban community where Robert and Amelia had lived for more than two decades and wanted Laura to grow up. It also was clear that the government would not have enough evidence to indict its two primary targets thus far, Carlos Jader Alvarez or José Alvero-Cruz. Even if Marlene Navarro and a few others were indicted, Robert would not be eligible for nearly as big a bonus as he would get if the higher-ranking targets were prosecuted. He also doubted that he would get any help resolving his dispute with the IRS. And future employment prospects would be uncertain at best.

Although Carol had not told Robert why Operation Swordfish might be terminated, he had alluded to rivalry within big organizations, and, without fully realizing it, touched on what had become one of the most significant problems in the operation, the poisonous enmity between Frank Chellino and Tom Clifford. Chellino felt that Clifford's drinking rendered him incompetent to supervise the operation, and that his judgment in the face of the ominous telegram had been atrocious. Clifford, for his part, considered the diminutive Chellino a miniature malcontent who perfectly fit the classic definition of the word "cockalorum," a "strutting, self-important, boastful, pretentious little man." In Clifford's opinion, Chellino was nothing more than a GS-12 street agent with delusions of grandeur, a minor bureaucrat who had convinced himself that he actually was the president of a multinational investment house. The real supervisory problem in the operation, as Tom Clifford saw it, was Frank Chellino's refusal to accept supervision.

The difficulty of deciding whether to close Operation Swordfish was compounded by the presence of a new management team in the Miami field division of the DEA. Tom Clifford's mentors, the DEA executives who had made him the youngest chief of intelligence ever in Miami, had retired the previous year.

The new special-agent-in-charge was Peter Gruden, who was just turning forty years old. A bulky native New Yorker with a somewhat severe personality, Gruden had served the DEA most recently in the inspection division, the agency's internal police.

The new second-in-command was Sylvester B. "Sam" Billbrough, a former captain in the Metro-Dade Police Department, who had joined the DEA in mid-career. Tall, amiable, gray-haired, and several years older than Gruden, Billbrough had a law degree and was considered an expert in police administration and personnel management. His DEA title was associate special-agent-in-charge, differentiating him from two assistant special-agents-in-charge who ranked immediately beneath him.

Late the second week of January, Gruden assigned Billbrough to resolve the question of whether to close Operation Swordfish. Billbrough called a meeting of Tom Clifford and the Swordfish agents for the morning of Thursday, January 14. After listening to considerable shouting, the quiet-spoken Billbrough overruled Tom Clifford and decreed that Operation Swordfish would continue. Billbrough observed that barely two weeks earlier DEA headquarters had disseminated a classified teletype holding up Operation Swordfish as a model for the agency worldwide. The possibility of infiltrating the Carlos Jader Alvarez organization was too important to be sacrificed for a security problem whose dimensions were murky and, in Billbrough's opinion, could be managed without seriously disrupting, much less terminating, the operation. The agents would continue to be extra careful and make sure the offices of Dean International were fully armed.

Billbrough, however, did endorse a suggestion by Tom Clifford that he begin looking for new office space for Dean International Investments. Any questionable clients would not be given the new address.

Gangster Angie was to be summarily eliminated from any further role in Operation Swordfish. The DEA, for the time being at least, would give up trying to infiltrate the Alvero-Cruz syndicate.

Carol Cooper immediately reported the results of the meeting to Robert Darias. "The bosses want to break Angie's legs," she said. "He will be advised legally by an attorney of the criminal liability that is going to be on his shoulders if anything happens to us. He is a blithering idiot if he even thinks about doing anything. He's going to get killed and we're not going to protect him."

Billbrough's decision was a great relief to the agents and their spies. It did nothing, however, to ease the festering bitterness between Frank Chellino and Tom Clifford.

17

AFTER A PERIOD of optimism, Carlos Jader Alvarez had grown pessimistic about the fate of his children. The vigilante group known as Death to Kidnappers, abbreviated MAS in Spanish, had by the middle of January killed or captured several dozen guerrillas whom it accused of various kidnappings. The Colombian police looked inept by comparison. In one notable episode, MAS had captured a provincial chieftain of the M-19 whom the police had been seeking for years.

The offensive by MAS at first seemed to have spurred the negotiations for the release of the Alvarez children. One arrangement called for their return one by one for piecemeal ransom payments totalling $5 million. While agreeing to the terms, Jader Alvarez formulated plans for capturing and executing the kidnappers once the children were freed. But hopes were dashed when the kidnappers did not show up at a scheduled rendezvous in late January in Bogotá where they were to release one child and pick up a payment of $1.8 million.

On Monday, January 18, Special Agent Rafael "Ralph" Aguirre of the DEA met with a Mexican informant in Room 303 of the Hotel Cristal, which was on a busy side street in downtown Bogotá. The Cristal was a rudimentary hotel—ten stories but only twenty-eight rooms—that catered to businessmen from the Colombian provinces. Room 303 was much like the Cristal's other rooms—the television set was black-and-white, the bedspread threadbare, the telephone at least two decades old.

Ralph Aguirre, a native of Cuba, had been a DEA agent for ten years—the last five in Bogotá, where he had been involved in efforts to infiltrate the Jader Alvarez narcotics syndicate. His informant had been negotiating by telephone from Mexico to purchase three kilograms of pure cocaine from a woman in Bogotá named Aida Espinosa, with whom he was having an affair. Aida Espinosa was important to the DEA because she had a relationship to the Jader Alvarez organization: her brother's business partner was married to Alvarez's sister. Unaware that her boyfriend was a paid informant for the DEA, Aida Espinosa had agreed to sell him three kilograms of cocaine for $100,000 in U.S. currency. Ralph Aguirre and his DEA colleagues hoped that in the course of the transaction they might learn more about how the Alvarez syndicate functioned.

As Aguirre listened in Room 303, the informant telephoned Espinosa, who seemed excited to hear from him. They agreed to meet later that day on the street in front of the Hotel Dann, two blocks north of the Cristal on the Avenida Ciudad de Lima, a fashionable thoroughfare in the heart of downtown Bogotá. With the arrangements proceeding, Ralph Aguirre brought in the F-2 branch of the Colombian National Police. This was classic DEA procedure in foreign countries, where the agency was prohibited from participating in actual police work such as arrests. The DEA overseas was solely an intelligence agency, and its intelligence was usually superior to that of its local counterparts. In such a setting, the DEA typically was an orchestrator, providing a completed score for the local police to play. At Ralph Aguirre's instigation, agents of the F-2 branch secretly observed the informant's meeting with Aida Espinosa in front of the Hotel Dann. Espinosa invited the informant to come to her home that evening, and then offered a startling bit of information: her brother and his business partner (Jader Alvarez's brother-in-law) were unavailable, and Jader Alvarez likely would be there to handle the cocaine transaction personally.

Though Alvarez was a major target, Ralph Aguirre realized that neither Colombian nor U.S. authorities were prepared to prosecute him on short notice. Aguirre knew that Operation Swordfish was at an early stage. Should they try nonetheless to arrest Alvarez now? He agreed with his F-2 counterparts to proceed to the next step.

The informant took a taxi just after eight that evening to Aida Espinosa's residence, a small two-story brick-and-stucco house in a middle-class neighborhood about ten miles west of the mountains not far from the Bavaria Brewery and the General Electric plant. With F-2 agents observing as best they could in the dark, and with Ralph Aguirre in radio contact with the surveillance team from his hotel room, the informant waited in the house with Aida Espinosa for nearly three hours.

Just before eleven o'clock the agents noticed a white Mercedes cruising back and forth through the neighborhood. The car finally stopped and the driver entered the Espinosa house. It unmistakably was Carlos Jader Alvarez, whose photograph was familiar to every F-2 and DEA agent in Bogotá. Alvarez told the informant that he did not normally bother with such small transactions and was doing so in this case only as a favor to Aida Espinosa. After a brief chat, the informant asked that the cocaine transaction be postponed until morning: he was hesitant to transfer $100,000 in either cash or merchandise at such a late hour. Alvarez agreed.

Ralph Aguirre arranged to have an F-2 car disguised as a taxi take the informant back to the woman's house the next morning. Surveillance agents again covered the area, and Aguirre waited two blocks away with the F-2's commanding officer, who had decided to preside personally because of the unexpected contact with Carlos Jader Alvarez. The F-2 had decided it wanted to arrest the godfather if possible.

Jader Alvarez entered the Espinosa house carrying a supermarket shopping bag. At the informant's signal, the F-2 agents, their commander, and Ralph Aguirre converged on the house and found Alvarez and Aida Espinosa standing at the dining room table. On the table was the shopping bag, which contained three kilograms of pure cocaine. Alvarez was carrying a loaded Smith & Wesson Model 59 pistol with a round in the chamber.

While Aida Espinosa was being taken to F-2 headquarters, Ralph Aguirre and two F-2 agents drove Jader Alvarez to his home in El Chico Alto. It took more than an hour to search the lavishly furnished five-story house. In Alvarez's desk the agents found several business cards, including one that read "Marlene Import and Export Inc." with an address on Brickell Avenue in Miami. They also found a note that seemed to concern ransom and kidnapping. Alvarez was vague about Marlene Import and Export, but when confronted with the ransom note, he broke down in tears, and acknowledged that three of his children had been missing for more than three months. Although the DEA in Miami had known of the kidnapping through Marlene Navarro and Robert Darias, it came as news to the Colombian National Police. Alvarez implored the agents to keep the kidnapping confidential; the kidnappers had threatened to kill his children if he reported it to the police. Alvarez did not state his even more pressing concern that a full investigation of the kidnapping would jeopardize the security of his narcotics empire.

From the house in El Chico Alto, Carlos Jader Alvarez was taken to jail where he was held, pending a hearing, for selling 3 kilograms of cocaine, an occurrence that seemed quaint in comparison to his last arrest in Bogotá in 1979 at which 580 kilograms of cocaine were found. Ralph Aguirre suspected that Alvarez would not be held for long and thus that his arrest would not disrupt Operation Swordfish.

He sealed the business card from Marlene Import and Export in an evidence envelope to be sent to Miami.

The F-2 did not pursue the kidnapping case. It had no interest in helping a godfather of the drug mafia under any circumstances. Alvarez's friend, the godfather José Antonio Cabrera, took over the negotiations with the kidnappers while Alvarez was in jail.

An unmarked van eased along North Miami Avenue across from the United States Court House and stopped beside a gray-haired man wearing sunglasses and a dark suit. The van belonged to the DEA, and Carol Cooper and a lawyer from the criminal division of the U.S. Attorney's Office, Caroline Heck, were sitting in the rear. The man who joined them from the street was U.S. District Court Magistrate Herbert Shapiro.

It was heightened concern for the security of Operation Swordfish that prompted the DEA to huddle secretly with a federal magistrate. Whenever federal agents had occasion to be at the court house, there was always the risk they would be recognized by curious defense lawyers with contacts in the criminal community or, worse, their presence noted by a targeted individual whom the agents might have met in an undercover role. The threatening telegram and the rupture of the DEA's relationship with Gangster Angie had strengthened the agency's determination to avoid any breach of secrecy.

As the van cruised through the streets, Carol Cooper handed the magistrate three documents for his signature. The first document was headed:

IN THE MATTER OF THE APPLICATION OF THE UNITED STATES OF AMERICA FOR AN ORDER AUTHORIZING THE INSTALLATION AND USE OF A DEVICE TO REGISTER TELEPHONE NUMBERS

Before installing a full wiretap on the telephone of Marlene Navarro, the DEA wanted to monitor her phones with an espionage apparatus known as a pen register. When connected to a teleprinter in a locked room at the DEA, the pen register would print out instantaneously all the telephone numbers that Marlene Navarro dialed— local and long-distance—with the date and time of each call. The numbers would enable the agents not only to determine to whom Navarro was talking but also discern potentially criminal patterns in her calls. The information would expand the knowledge the agents had gleaned by subpoenaing some of Navarro's long-distance records from Southern Bell, and by having Robert Darias secretly tape-record Navarro when they spoke by phone or in person. If the anticipated calling patterns emerged, the DEA would ask the court to authorize a full wiretap, an elaborate undertaking involving teams of agents actually listening to all of Navarro's telephone conversations around the clock.

Crouched in the van, Magistrate Shapiro signed the authorization for the pen register. The judge further ordered that the government's application be sealed and that Southern Bell Telephone "shall not disclose to the listed subscriber, nor to any other person, the existence of this investigation. . . ."

The White House announced in late January that President Reagan had appointed Vice President George Bush to head a cabinet-level task force to combat South Florida's crime, refugee, and drug-smuggling problems. "Massive immigration, rampant crime, and epidemic drug smuggling have created a serious problem," the announcement said. "The current situation in South Florida is unique. With hundreds and hundreds of miles of coastline, and as the southernmost point of our country located in the Caribbean, it has experienced difficulties that no other community could ever anticipate."

"FBI Assumes Leading Role in Drug War," said a page-one headline in the *Miami Herald* the same week. The Department of Justice announced a long-awaited plan committing the resources of the FBI to enforcement of the narcotics laws. Although the FBI had increased its drug role in recent years, its precise responsibilities and its relationship to the DEA had never been defined. With its superior resources (there were about 8,000 FBI agents and only 2,000 DEA agents), the FBI supposedly was to become the DEA's senior partner in the drug effort. Henceforth the DEA would report to the Justice Department through the director of the FBI.

"Drug enforcement will have the resources, the expertise and the support to bring this vast problem under our control and to improve the quality of our lives accordingly," said Attorney General William French Smith. The Justice Department announced that the number of DEA agents in Miami would be increased in the coming months from 90 to 120, and that the FBI would add more than 40 new agents to the 175 currently stationed in Miami. "South Florida is one of the most challenging areas in law enforcement today," FBI Director William Webster said. "We're going to experiment, but I don't foresee an effort to duplicate what the DEA is doing."

The new relationship between the FBI and the DEA was evolving on the ground in Miami differently from the platitudes being voiced in Washington. The FBI agents who had worked on the failed Operation Bancoshares had been asked to meet with the DEA's Swordfish agents to discuss the lessons the FBI had learned. A few days before the meeting, an unusually candid FBI liaison agent confided to Carol Cooper that the meeting would be a waste of time for the DEA.

"It's not worth your while—we can offer you absolutely nothing," Cooper quoted the agent as saying when she reported to Robert Darias. "Politics and the U.S. Attorney's Office and everybody wants us to get together with them, so we're just doing it out of courtesy," Cooper said, indicating that the DEA would tell the FBI nothing but generalities about Operation Swordfish. "We do not want them to know where we're at, or who we are, or anything about us. Needless to say, I do not want them to know who *you* are."

The morning after the arrest of Carlos Jader Alvarez in Bogotá, Marlene Navarro called Robert Darias in tears. Down with a sore throat and fever, she asked him to pick up the Bogotá newspapers, *El Tiempo* and *El Espectador,* which were available in Miami the day after they were published in Bogotá.

The *El Tiempo* article was headlined "Head of International Drug Traffickers Nabbed" and called Alvarez "one of the most wanted drug traffickers in Colombia and the United States." The investigation culminating in the arrest, the article said, was "one of the most important operations against drug traffickers in recent years." Warrants for Jader Alvarez's arrest "have been issued eleven times but most arraignment judges have inexplicably canceled them." The article was accompanied by a photograph of Jader, the three kilograms of cocaine, several boxes of ammunition, and the Smith & Wesson pistol. There was no mention of the role of the DEA in the arrest.

Examining the article and photograph, Navarro again began to cry. Jader had been caught, she said, because Interpol in Bogotá had been following his partner, José Antonio Cabrera, and had found Jader instead. She recalled Pepe Cabrera's arrest in Miami in August 1980, and his fleeing the country after forfeiting $1 million in emeralds that he had posted as bond.

Navarro asked Darias to call her the following morning. "I really need you now," she said. "You're the only friend I have in Miami that I can rely on."

Still sitting in a Bogotá jail, Carlos Jader Alvarez was again hit by a family tragedy. His seventeen-year-old son, a product of a liaison with a woman when he was eighteen years old, committed suicide.

Apparently distraught over his father's arrest for drug running and the attendant publicity in Bogotá, the boy shot himself in the head. Bright and studious, the boy was Alvarez's firstborn son and they were very close. When Alvarez was told of the death in his jail cell, he wept and banged his head against the wall. He was allowed out of jail to attend the funeral, and then another amenable judge dismissed the most recent drug charges against him.

The DEA in Miami learned of these events from Robert Darias. Carol Cooper resolved to ask the DEA office in Bogotá for more details.

The guard at the gate of Costa del Sol released the electronic bar and waved a van with Southern Bell markings into the compound. It took the driver several minutes to find his way along the winding central avenue and around a corner to the cluster of town houses where Marlene Navarro lived.

The van did not belong to Southern Bell, nor was the driver a Southern Bell employee. He was Richard Vasquez, a technical specialist on the staff of the DEA, and his assignment was to install an eavesdropping device on Marlene Navarro's two telephone lines. After receiving the court order that U.S. Magistrate Shapiro had signed the previous Thursday, Rick Vasquez had placed an order with the security office of Southern Bell for Marlene Navarro's "appearance information"—data that identified Navarro's "appearance point," the exact location amidst the millions of telephone cables in South Florida (other than in Navarro's home) where her telephone lines "appeared" and could be tapped. Southern Bell also provided Vasquez with data enabling him to locate a second telephone line at Navarro's appearance point that he could use to route her calls to the DEA offices in the Phoenix Building where they could be monitored.

Wearing a telephone technician's equipment belt, Vasquez located the phone lines in a Southern Bell "can"—a four-foot gray-green rectangular metal box—at the rear of the second town house north of Navarro's. It took only a few minutes for him to attach her line to the monitoring line. It appeared to Vasquez that Navarro was at home but there was no indication she was aware of his presence.

Before leaving the DEA office for Costa del Sol, Vasquez had installed small devices called DNRs, or Dialed Number Recorders (a Mitel Model 8104 and a Hekimiam Model 109), on two black teleprinters—one for each of Navarro's phone lines. For as long as the tap was in place the teleprinters would record the date, time, and number of all of Navarro's outgoing calls. The DEA would be prohibited from actually listening to the conversations or registering incoming calls without a further court order.

No one from Dean International had talked to Lionel Paytubi or Manuel Sanchez since before the first of the year when Operation Greenback had last pressured Operation Swordfish. "We definitely want to get them geared up again," Carol Cooper told Darias. "If it takes going out to lunch and just chit-chatting and renewing acquaintances, then fine, that's what we'll do. I'd like to get Paytubi in solid before anything else happens to him. The more we get on him the better chance we've got to prolong the Greenback people from doing anything. Greg's not gonna let them play around with him as long as he's actively doing something."

Greg English was finding it more difficult to deal with Operation Greenback. Its lawyers summarily canceled and rescheduled three meetings with English before he again convinced Charles Blau to postpone the indictment of Lionel Paytubi. Experience had taught English that such victories were transitory: momentum toward an indictment could build again in only a few weeks.

Robert Darias arranged to meet Paytubi for breakfast at a Denny's near Dean International. It turned out that Paytubi, who had given up his job selling cars and was now employed as an office manager at a hospital, was offended that no one had called him since Chellino spoke to him in December. He was convinced that Dean International had been doing business with Marlene Navarro and Manuel Sanchez behind his back without paying him commissions. Darias promised to arrange for Paytubi to meet again with Frank Dean.

Darias also called Manuel Sanchez and made a tentative lunch date for Friday, January 29, which Sanchez canceled at the last minute.

The Dariases' social and cultural life, normally quite active, had deteriorated since Robert had been working undercover for the government and he and Amelia had told many of their friends that they were moving to Orlando. The Dariases felt adrift. The Cuban exile community served as an important psychological haven for its members. The social elites of old Havana had been transplanted to Miami virtually intact. The five most prestigious clubs in Cuba in the fifties—the Biltmore Yacht and Country Club, the Havana Yacht Club (which had rejected Batista for membership), the Miramar Yacht Club, the Casino Español, and the Vedado Tennis Club—lived on in Miami as the Big Five Club, a secluded ten-acre enclave that was a social center of the Cuban upper crust. More than two decades after fleeing Castro, most of Miami's Cubans still considered themselves foreigners in the United States, and felt genuinely at home only among their fellow exiles. The DEA agents were no substitute for the Dariases' real friends. Still, Robert and Amelia were naturally gregarious people, and tried to make the best of the artificial situation in which they found themselves.

On Saturday evening, January 30, the Dariases gave a dinner party at their Tamiami home for the staff of Dean International. It had been four months since the group had been together socially, aside from after-work drinks at the Le Sabre Club. The last occasion involving the agents' spouses had been a lasagna dinner at Frank Chellino's home in Pembroke Pines around October 1. The agents had their own reasons for discomfort when socializing with the Dariases. DEA rules of conduct for special agents, codified in the official DEA Manual, prohibited fraternizing with people the agents were employing as spies. It was deemed unwise to become too friendly; case studies had shown that the agents' objectivity in supervising the spies could be compromised. But the rules were occasionally overlooked, and most of the Swordfish agents genuinely liked the Dariases and enjoyed their company. "As far as we're concerned, Bob's one of us," Carol Cooper had told Amelia. "He's one of the family."

Tom Clifford and Bob Russo, however, did not attend the Dariases' party, and they had not attended the Chellino gathering in October. In addition to being concerned about the fraternization rule, Clifford felt there was now too much enmity between him and Chellino for them to be comfortable together socially. There was increasing tension, as well, between Bob Russo and the rest of the Dean International staff, who felt Russo automatically sided with Clifford in any disagreement.

But everyone else was at the Dariases'—Carol Cooper, Frank and Sally Chellino, Paul and Marion Sennett, Felipe and Inez Calderon, and Eddie Hernandez, the new member of the team.

"What a beautiful house you have!" one of the Americans exclaimed, as if surprised. It appeared to the Dariases that some of the agents had never before been in a "Cuban house" and were amazed to find it much like their own. The guests seemed surprised that the Dariases had so many books—and so many in English as well as Spanish. They also examined Robert's gun collection with considerable interest.

After a few drinks Darias and Chellino began needling each other, and the others were a bit uncomfortable until it became clear that the banter was good-natured.

"Heil, Hitler," Darias said.

"You've got a big mouth, Darias," Chellino said.

"Just remember, you were nothing before I arrived in this operation and saved you," Robert retorted. "In your forty-nine-dollar Sears Roebuck suit and your fifteen-dollar Mickey Mouse wristwatch, you looked exactly like a cop and not at all like a big-time drug tycoon. You were lucky I came along and taught you how to live."

"You son of a bitch," Chellino replied, laughing and turning to Amelia. "Why are you with this guy?"

"At least he's tall," Amelia retorted, with a withering look at Chellino's short stature. Cooper and the others roared with laughter. "Keep jabbing him," Carol said. "He loves it."

Amelia and Robert served chicken cordon bleu with vegetables and salad, and *oeufs à la neige* for dessert, a recipe Amelia had gotten from the chef of the Laurent Restaurant in New York. The guests got another surprise after dinner when Amelia played the piano and serenaded them for more than an hour with songs of composers ranging from Antonio Carlos Jobim and Luis Bonfa to Cole Porter and Rodgers and Hart. Amelia was a big fan of Frank Sinatra, and she and Robert enjoyed telling guests the story of the first night Robert spent in her bedroom. As he closed the door, Robert was startled to find a life-size cutout of Frank Sinatra hanging on the back of the door. "Oh, how I wish I was the only man in this room," he had said. Amelia had laughed and stashed the poster in a closet.

Robert obviously was very proud of Amelia, and no one who observed them together could believe a rumor—circulated by others in the DEA—that he had been sleeping with Marlene Navarro.

The party did not break up until after midnight. By that time, the group was behaving like the harmonious staff of a small investment company, carefree on a Saturday night, rather than a team of spies and federal agents, suffering the stress of a dangerous undercover operation where there had been little recent action except a threatening telegram and a blown lie-detector test.

18

HE ALVAREZ CHILDREN— Zuleika, Yidid, and Xouix—looked remarkably healthy and little the worse for the wear of their captivity. Their parents were heartened as they stared at a photograph that had arrived by mail in a plain envelope, postmarked in Bogotá. They were pleased as well to see that the children were posing with a newspaper dated in early February, a common technique used by kidnappers to prove that their victims remained alive as of the date of the newspaper.

In addition to sending the photograph, the kidnappers drastically reduced their ransom demand to 25 million pesos, or about $420,000. In accord with the kidnappers' instructions, Alvarez and some of his men drove with the money in a brown duffle bag to a scheduled rendezvous. As the Alvarez party was proceeding through west Bogotá, several agents of the Colombian army's intelligence arm, or B-2, pulled them over and searched their car. It was a routine search, common in the weeks leading to a national election, which was scheduled for early March. When the agents found the cash, Alvarez told them it was kidnap ransom and explained the circumstances. Since kidnapping was so common in Bogotá, the agents allowed him to proceed with the money to the meeting. Once again the kidnappers failed to show up. But the B-2 had become the second intelligence agency of the Colombian government to learn of the Alvarez kidnapping.

In Gachalá, the guerrilla Bernardo Acosta tried to convince his friend Victor Reyes, the owner of the restaurant where the children had been taken on the way to the hideout in late November, to come to *Las Brisas* meadow and help take care of them. "You will make a lot of money when the family pays the ransom," Acosta said.

"What will happen to the children if there is no ransom?" Reyes asked.

"Infirmar," said Acosta, using a Spanish word meaning "to invalidate, make null and void."

Victor Reyes was horrified, and declined to get further involved.

He was a father himself. He had been to the crude camp at *Las Brisas*. He had heard the voices of the children coming from within the shanty. He had seen the modern firearms with which Acosta had equipped the guards. Acosta had threatened Reyes and the guards with death if they told anyone what they knew.

Acosta began to worry about the security of the camp. Though the meadow was remote and Acosta had threatened his men, he could not rule out a compromise of the location. Victor Reyes had visited the camp more than once. Guillermo Alvarado, who presumably did not know about the kidnapping, had seen the children and had brought two more loads of supplies to the trail below the hideout. *Campesinos* in the mountains might from afar have noticed the unusual activity at the normally deserted shack.

Acosta decided to move the hideout into the jungle a few miles up the mountain. There, next to a streambed, he crafted a hut from tree branches, tarpaulin, and plastic sheeting, offering considerably less protection from the elements than the wooden shack had.

"She's been calling the world this afternoon," Carol Cooper reported to Robert Darias on Tuesday, February 2, referring to data derived from the pen register on Marlene Navarro's telephones. "She's calling everybody. She's calling people on beepers all over the place. She's calling Colombia, she's calling the attorney, she's calling the Netherlands, Fort Lauderdale, all within the last hour. She's calling somebody at the Holiday Inn in Miami Springs. This is the most activity we've seen from her. She's been calling banks up in New York and the Bank of Miami here, too. She was going bananas—it was like she walked into the house and hit the phones. I wanna spend a little more time with these machines because we really don't have a pattern on her yet. Super, super important—I want to know if she's involved in any actual deliveries [of drugs] or if there's any indication people are talking to her specifically about deliveries of the merchandise itself. That's gonna make a major, major difference if we're gonna go the next step and listen to the conversations."

"Don't underestimate her," Darias said. "She is the right arm for Jader's organization here. She has been involved with all these people and yet she has been able to hide herself so that you people had no idea of what she was doing. She is very wise."

"She was calling the lawyer, Lester Rogers, this afternoon, too."

"He has a lot to do with this whole thing," Darias said.

"We had somewhat of a shaky case on him before, just because we haven't seen him yet. Now we've got the proof that she's calling him constantly. She makes all these phone calls and then all of a sudden, kaboom, here comes the attorney. We'll be able to fit him in with the machines. The machines'll put him down right in the middle."

One of Navarro's calls that afternoon was to Darias, asking him to meet her for breakfast the next morning at the Costa del Sol country club. Although Robert and Carol were hopeful that the intense telephone activity would mean new money for Dean International, Navarro made no deposits. All of the Alvarez organization's cash, she told Robert, was still being smuggled straight out of the U.S. to Bogotá in private planes to be held for the kidnappers. The shipments were arranged by a young Colombian named Carlos Alvarado, who worked for Carlos Jader Alvarez in Miami and Bogotá. Carlos Alvarez called Carlos Alvarado the "chauffeur" or "mailman." Navarro called him "Tocayo" (namesake) to avoid confusing him in conversation with Carlos Alvarez.

Tocayo bribed cargo pilots to conceal Alvarez's money in their aircraft. When it arrived in Bogotá, Tocayo would deposit it with a foreign exchange broker who had a close relationship with Jader Alvarez. In recent weeks Alvarez had decided that the cargo system was the fastest means of funneling U.S. currency to Colombia so it could be stockpiled for the kidnappers. It was very risky, however. Marlene told Robert that the money sometimes was seized by Customs inspectors or stolen. She disliked the arrangement, too, because so many people had to be paid off along the route that her commission was lower. She said Jader Alvarez had promised to deposit his money with Dean International as soon as the kidnapping was resolved.

After breakfast Marlene invited Robert back to her town house to see the new furnishings she had purchased under the guidance of two Coral Gables interior designers. It was obvious to Robert, who had an educated eye for furnishings, that Marlene had a lot of money and eclectic taste.

In the living-dining area, which was covered with deep butterscotch carpeting, there were two small white flair sofas facing each other across an ornate Persian rug and a glass-and-steel coffee table. On the coffee table was a vase of artificial white orchids made by a Japanese artisan in Coconut Grove. At right angles to the sofas on one side of the Persian rug were two gold French Empire occasional chairs with white upholstery.

The interior wall at the dining end of the room was covered with floor-to-ceiling mirrors reflecting a rectangular glass dining table mounted on a brass base formed from two rams heads whose horns supported the table. Six Queen Anne chairs around the table were black with white upholstery. The dining ensemble rested on a Bokhara rug. Over the table hung an Italian Murano clear glass chandelier.

Along an opposite wall was a wall system displaying Lalique glasses, Chinese soapstone urns, Dresden porcelain clowns, English porcelain urns, Lladró Spanish porcelain pieces, English crystal cordial decanters, and a set of English bone china.

In the corners were decorative plants and trees.

Marlene kept a ten-speed bicycle in the kitchen, where there was a Mr. Coffee and a GE food processor but little other evidence of cooking. On the wall of the staircase to the second floor hung several posters from galleries and museums in Paris (Paul Paree, Women's Resources) and a large color photograph of Marlene in a black hat and red blouse taken in Paris near the apartment she owned. There were erotic touches—including a representation of a woman tasting what appeared at first to be a pear and on second glance turned out to be a golden phallus.

The master bedroom suite had a brass four-poster double bed with a polished cotton peach-pink bedspread, a pink chiffon canopy and curtains, and a brass trunk at the foot. Draperies of the same shade of pink covered floor-to-ceiling glass doors leading to a terrace, which overlooked a lake and the Costa del Sol golf course. The closet doors were floor-to-ceiling mirrors. In the corner was a French Empire love seat, and another Persian rug ran from the love seat to the bed. Several tapestries and French posters hung on the walls. On the nightstand was an art nouveau lamp and two telephones, a beige Princess phone and a black standard phone. (Carol Cooper had spoken of having to tap two phone lines.)

Marlene's study was dominated by a dark oak desk and several bookcases containing a number of international monetary and economics books. On her desk was a report from the International Monetary Fund entitled "The Role of Exchange Rates in the Adjustment of International Payments." The bookcases contained several worn dictionaries and a stack of _Economist_ magazines. There was a large Star of David on the wall, as well as a Leon Bosch poster and a number of mounted and framed photographs, including one of Marlene in black cap and gown on the day she was awarded her degree from the University of Miami, and two more in a double-frame of Marlene nude astride a horse and standing nude on a beach in Israel.

In the guest room the only memorable item was a Peruvian alpaca rug that had been given to her by Luis Fabio Rodriguez, whose responsibilities in the Jader Alvarez organization included handling the transportation of cocaine base from Peru to processing plants in the plains of eastern Colombia.

"This is one sexy lady," Robert told Amelia later in describing the house.

"Oh?"

"As you go up the stairs, there is this small poster. When you first look at it, it looks like a woman about to eat the top part of a pear. When you look closer, you see that the pear is a penis."

"Goodness."

"And then in her den, she has a double-frame with two photographs. In one she is naked on horseback. In the other she is standing there completely nude. She said they were taken on a beach in Israel."

"You'd better watch your step," Amelia said with a smile.

"Don't worry, she's too exotic for me," Robert replied.

The next afternoon, Thursday, February 4, a federal court jury acquitted ten of fourteen people who had been indicted at the conclusion of the FBI's Operation Bancoshares the previous August. The verdict was a major defeat for the FBI. It was clear that the jury had found the evidence insufficient because the Bancoshares agents had limited themselves to laundering money for the suspected drug financiers, without proving that the money came from narcotics transactions. The verdict chilled the DEA, strengthening the hand of skeptics who had been denigrating Operation Swordfish and now suggested that it was headed toward a fate in court similar to that of Bancoshares.

Tom Clifford was ordered to draft a memorandum justifying the strategy of Operation Swordfish in the light of the FBI acquittals, and explaining why Swordfish had received no deposits since December and had induced only one actual investment from its targets—Luis Fabio Rodriguez's $250,000 certificate of deposit—in eight months of operation. Clifford called Carol Cooper at home and turned the assignment over to her. She began working immediately.

As Marlene Navarro was arriving home late that night, she suddenly realized that someone was lurking in the darkness inside her town house. She screamed and ran back outside through the front door as the intruder escaped through the sliding glass door at the back. Navarro called the police, who arrived just after eleven.

The thief had forced the sliding door with a screw driver and ransacked the house. He had tossed the contents of closets and drawers onto the floor and ripped open the fabric on the bottom of the box springs in the master bedroom upstairs. He had also found Navarro's safe, which was hidden under a carpet in a small utility closet under the stairs. Although he had beaten the handle and combination dial completely off of the safe, and had tried to chip the concrete away from its rim, he had failed to open it.

He had stolen four necklaces—a pearl-and-diamond necklace, a gold-and-diamond necklace, a plain diamond necklace, and a plain gold necklace with a gold David and Goliath pendant. He had left behind a Cartier gold watch, a Piaget gold watch, and two Nikon cameras. Navarro estimated the value of the missing necklaces at $25,000.

She telephoned Robert Darias at eight-fifteen the next morning. "Please help me," she said through tears. "You are the only real friend I have in Miami. Maybe you don't believe that, but I don't have anybody here." When Robert arrived, his concealed microcassette recorder running as usual, two police detectives were with Marlene. The detectives left after a few minutes, and for the second time in two days Robert got a good look at the inside of the house.

"The detectives said the clearest fingerprints were on these," Marlene said, pointing to the nude photographs in the study.

On the first floor, in the closet under the stairs, Robert inspected the safe, which was hidden under a flap of carpet next to a red plaid picnic hamper, a fishing rod, a collection of brooms, and the Greater Miami Yellow Pages.

While Darias was in the house, Navarro took calls from a man in Santo Domingo, from her contact at the Bank of Miami, and from Luis Fabio Rodriguez, who was in Lima, Peru, on business for Jader Alvarez. The call from Rodriguez came on the black telephone next to Marlene's bed.

Darias returned that afternoon with several burglar alarms, which he installed around Marlene's windows and doors. Then the two of them settled on the white sofas across from each other in the living room, sipping soft drinks.

"Actually, I was very lucky," she said. "I would have had to kill myself if they had stolen the documents in the safe."

"You will have to have the safe replaced," Darias said. "There's no way it can be repaired after what they did to it."

"And you will never believe what else they missed. The day before yesterday there was $650,000 cash in this house, in bags, right there in that same closet. It was too bulky to get in the safe. I gave two-fifty to somebody on Wednesday to take to Bogotá. I gave four hundred to two guys yesterday to take to Santo Domingo. Can you believe it?

If the burglar had gotten that money I would have had to kill myself!
I probably won't even tell Jader about the burglary. He might cut me
off."

"You should not keep that kind of money here. You should give
it to me."

"I know. But Jader needs it fast for the ransom. He hasn't been
himself since the kidnapping and especially since his son killed himself."

"But that's exactly why he should use me. I can get it there fast *and*
safe, at the same time."

"As soon as he gets his life under control you will handle all the
money."

Before Robert left, Marlene took him again to the study and
showed him a certified check for $500,000 that Jader had given her to
use in case of emergencies.

The past two days had drawn Robert and Marlene closer than ever.
By giving Robert a tour of her house, including the erotic accents,
Marlene had shown that she was comfortable revealing intimate dimensions of her personality and tastes. His sensitive response to her
furnishings and art, followed by his calm handling of the burglary,
had solidified his place as an empathetic friend and adviser. In temperament, though not in age, he reminded her of her late grandfather in
Colombia who had raised her as a father.

Pondering ways he might induce Navarro to deposit more money
with Dean International, Darias suggested to Chellino and Cooper
that federal agents—perhaps IRS or Customs agents from Operation
Greenback—be sent to Marlene's bank, the Bank of Miami on Brickell Avenue. The agents would make a pretense of examining a range
of bank accounts, but in fact would gradually single out Marlene
Navarro's account and feign a thorough examination of it. Navarro's
banker surely would alert her immediately, and it seemed logical that
when that happened she would be so frightened of using the bank that
she would transfer all her business to Dean International. Cooper
thought it was a good idea.

"The only thing holding me back is the problems we're having with
Greenback," she explained to Robert. "Specifically, I don't want them
to know anything about Marlene, since they're messing around with
us. They zinged the FBI. As soon as Greenback would find out a name
the FBI was working on, they started doing their own case and would
go ahead and indict them before the FBI could do anything. They
want all the credit, so as soon as they find out something they're gonna
jump in."

"That's completely ridiculous."

"I know."

Operation Swordfish could not seem to shake the specter of the Cuban godfather José Alvero-Cruz, the would-be infiltrator Gangster Angie, and the mysterious telegram. In the middle of February Tom Clifford's critics in the DEA hierarchy again used Alvero-Cruz to attack Operation Swordfish. Why, since December, they asked, had there been no deposits of narcotics money at Dean International? Why, since December, had the agents been unable to attract a single targeted individual to the Dean offices so they could be videotaped making incriminating statements? Wasn't it likely, or at least possible, that the lack of activity indicated that the operation had indeed been compromised by Alvero-Cruz, and that he had somehow spread the word among the drug mafia of Miami, as some people had suspected after receipt of the telegram?

Clifford was receptive to such questions; he had raised similar ones a few weeks earlier. And as these questions pelted him, he also confronted another issue born of the DEA's frustration with failing to prosecute Alvero-Cruz successfully on drug charges, while watching enviously as the Internal Revenue Service convicted him for tax evasion. Since Angie had told the DEA that Alvero-Cruz planned to forfeit his bail and flee rather than go to prison on the tax charge, some DEA supervisors concocted the notion of putting Angie before a grand jury and forcing him to testify about Alvero-Cruz's impending flight. Such testimony, according to this reasoning, could be used as the basis for revoking Alvero-Cruz's bail and jailing him immediately, a maneuver for which the DEA could claim credit.

The danger that such testimony would pose was that Alvero-Cruz's lawyers could then force Angie to testify about the circumstances in which he happened to be spying on Alvero-Cruz. And that inevitably would lead to disclosure of the existence and true purpose of the company in Miami Lakes called Dean International Investments. Operation Swordfish would be compromised. But Clifford's critics were now contending that Alvero-Cruz apparently had compromised the operation anyway, and that it was as good as dead.

Thoroughly frustrated, Clifford again found himself seduced by the notion that even if Operation Swordfish were terminated he could open another similarly constituted operation after a few months. He tentatively concluded that jailing Alvero-Cruz, one of the DEA's most coveted targets, was worth the cost. It would prevent Alvero-Cruz from thumbing his nose at the U.S. from a sanctuary in Spain or, worse, Cuba. And as a bonus Clifford could shed a lot of frustrations, including his cockalorum nemesis Frank Chellino.

The move would have to be made quickly. There was a rumor that Alvero-Cruz was going to flee within a few days. Clifford arrived unannounced at Dean International late Tuesday afternoon and confronted Carol Cooper. "We're going to put Angie in front of the grand jury," he declared.

"But you'll blow us sky-high," she said, getting angry.

"It may be necessary. Alvero-Cruz is about to skip out."

"But what about our cases on Jader, on Marlene?"

"Alvero-Cruz is very important."

"Fine, if you're going to court with this guy Angie, then forget it," Cooper shouted. "I'm going home right now and pack my suitcase!"

"You can't do that!"

"Hey, you're throwing the whole operation up! You're playing around with my life and everybody else's, and I'm going to have some say in it!"

Hearing the raised voices, Chellino appeared, and he and Cooper assaulted Clifford with the argument that, however slowly they were moving, they had an unprecedented opportunity to build a case against one of the most significant narcotics lords in Latin America, Carlos Jader Alvarez, and his chief North American manager, Marlene Navarro. "Marlene will eventually come around," Chellino asserted. "We just have to be patient."

Clifford left Dean without another word and drove back to the Phoenix Building. Cooper signaled Greg English in Washington, who called Clifford and argued vigorously against the move on Alvero-Cruz. Robert Darias's progress in infiltrating the Jader Alvarez syndicate was too important to sacrifice, English stated.

The next day Clifford reversed his decision and stood up to his bosses. Angie would not be hauled into court. Alvero-Cruz was free to flee if that was his intention. Perhaps someone could tip off Customs to intercept him at the airport, but there would be no compromise of Operation Swordfish. Clifford, however, conveyed two blunt messages to Frank Chellino: first, the Swordfish agents *must* induce their targets to visit the Dean International offices so they could be captured on videotape. That was essential if Clifford was to demonstrate tangible progress to his impatient superiors. Second, Gangster Angie was still deemed a security risk. Dean International would move to another location as soon as possible.

Cooper was greatly relieved. "Between you and I, and I definitely don't want this to go any further—Frank doesn't know I'm telling you this," Cooper told Darias, "Tom's the one that made the decision to bring Angie in and give him the address and the name of this place. I think Tom realized he made a mistake and was trying to save himself and make himself look good and go after the guy's bond. It was serious enough that the operation would be blown and everybody's lives would be in danger. It's a bunch of politics and it's ridiculous. You just don't question your boss normally. But that was threatening to blow the operation so we gave it the best argument we got."

Cooper again admonished Darias never to reveal that she had told him of the fighting inside the agency. She also mentioned that if she could choose one target to videotape for a team of DEA officials from Washington who were visiting Miami the following week, it would be Marlene Navarro.

"The thing with her is that everybody in the agency knows about her by now," Cooper said. "We've got to play the politics. If you can pull her in I think that's going to keep everybody happy and get everybody off our backs."

"Okay, I will try to bring Marlene in," Robert said.

In addition to laying plans to move the office, other precautions were taken, even against security breaches within the DEA. Robert Darias's name was removed from the DEA computer and case files, leaving only his number, SG1-81-0020. Henceforth his name was carried in only one file in one location in the Phoenix Building, and anyone seeking access had to get Carol Cooper's permission.

Deeper under cover than ever, Robert spent his forty-eighth birthday, Tuesday, February 16, 1982, cold-ridden and frustrated over the seeming inertia of Marlene Navarro, Humberto Garcia, and Lionel Paytubi. There was a Spanish term for his persistent head and chest cold, *la cariñosa,* "the loving one," because it seemed never to want to leave him.

19

FLYING THROUGH TREACHEROUS mountains in rain and fog less than half an hour from Bogotá, the pilot of the DC-6 radioed that he was switching from instruments to visual flight. It was his last report. The cargo plane, bound for Bogotá from Miami, slammed into a mountain at an elevation of 10,500 feet, killing the pilot and three others aboard. The weather and rough terrain kept rescuers from the crash site for three days.

Among the first to be notified of the crash, in middle-of-the-night phone calls on Saturday, February 20, were Marlene Navarro and the money "chauffeur" Tocayo. The dead pilot was a close friend of Tocayo, who flew to Bogotá immediately to help recover the bodies. It fell to Navarro to tell the pilot's wife and six-year-old son in Miami of his death. Navarro and Tocayo were motivated by more than friendship. Hidden behind the wall panels in the plane's rest room were packages containing more than $1 million of Jader Alvarez's cocaine revenues.

Navarro told Darias of the crash the next morning over coffee at the Costa del Sol country club. Marlene said she would now try to convince Jader Alvarez to let Dean International handle all his money; flying large amounts of cash in cargo planes clearly was too risky. However, she told Robert, Jader likely would raise new objections to using Dean International.

"The main problem is that he doesn't want anybody working for his organization who is not Colombian," she said.

"But by now so many of my friends and clients are Colombian that I feel Colombian," Robert replied with a smile.

"He is hesitant to bring a Cuban into the organization."

"I have clients who are bigger than he is who are Colombian."

"It's also a matter of price," Marlene said. "He will feel your prices are still too high."

Darias wrote out a list of what he felt would be competitive commissions for each of Dean International's services such as wire transfers and cashier's checks, and suggested that Marlene show it to Jader Alvarez. Marlene said she was going to Bogotá on Saturday and would speak not only to Jader but also to his associate, José Antonio "Pepe" Cabrera, whose money Navarro was soon to begin handling.

The sprawling National University two miles northwest of downtown Bogotá was the most renowned institution of higher learning in Colombia. The "National," as it was called, attracted gifted students from throughout the country. The university was a caldron of political activity. The M-19 and other guerrilla groups thrived among the idealistic students. The contemporary white and gray buildings on the tree-shaded campus were covered with angry political graffiti. There were frequent violent confrontations between students and police, both on and off campus.

Early on the morning of Thursday, March 4, a bank on the university campus was held up and damaged by gunfire. The M-19 was the prime suspect and, not for the first time, authorities closed the university temporarily. With time on their hands, a group of students lingered over coffee late that morning at the Bakery Verona a few blocks above the campus. As the students ambled out of the bakery, several men with guns suddenly emerged from a green van on the street and began shouting and shooting in the air. The students ran down the street. More vehicles and armed men appeared, and it became evident that they were interested in only two of the fleeing young people— Orlando Garcia Villamizar, a twenty-three-year-old law student, and his friend Pedro Pablo Silva, a medical student. Garcia and Silva were forced into the green van, which sped away. The armed men identified themselves as agents of the F-2 branch of the Colombian National Police. In fact, they were agents of Carlos Jader Alvarez and the vigilante group known as Death to Kidnappers, or MAS.

Intimidated by MAS, whose bloody offensive had killed a number of guerrillas, the M-19 had recently released Marta Ochoa, the sister of drug lord Jorge Ochoa, after extensive negotiations conducted in Panama under the aegis of General Manuel Antonio Noriega.* The young woman had been kidnapped from a university campus in Medellín in early November, only a few weeks after the Alvarez children were taken. The Ochoas paid $1.3 million in ransom, far less than originally demanded. Much of the money went to General Noriega. In Miami, Marlene Navarro reported to Robert Darias that "my friend is safe."

Encouraged by the release of Marta Ochoa, Carlos Jader Alvarez

*The extent of Noriega's role as a corrupt protector of the Colombian narcotics mafia would not be known to the U.S. Government for several more years.

and his MAS associates stepped up their efforts to locate those responsible for the kidnapping of Alvarez's children. There had been no further contact with the kidnappers after they had failed to show up at a planned rendezvous in early February. From the beginning, in fact, negotiations for the release of the Alvarez children had proved more difficult than for the Ochoa girl. The leaders of the M-19 apparently knew where Marta Ochoa was and could speak for the kidnappers. It seemed that they did not know where the Alvarez children were being held and could not negotiate on behalf of their kidnappers, who appeared to be a splinter group with its own agenda.

The investigation by Alvarez and MAS, however, had begun to focus on M-19 members at the National University. It had not gone unnoticed that many of the rendezvous points in the ransom notes received by Alvarez had been in the orbit of the university campus and reflected an intimate knowledge of that part of Bogotá. MAS and Alvarez operatives had kidnapped and interrogated a number of M-19 members with ties to the university. But Orlando Garcia and Pedro Silva were the first students they seized, and MAS and the Alvarez syndicate were just getting started.

On Sunday, March 7, a mechanic at an auto body shop not far from the university campus spotted two men in civilian clothes, carrying guns and walkie-talkies, who appeared to be watching an apartment building. The armed men, noticing that they were attracting attention, approached the mechanic and identified themselves as "detectives." They said they were looking for a young man named Sanjuan, who they claimed was a National University student and a member of a "very dangerous delinquent group." They warned the mechanic to say nothing of what he had seen.

The next day, Alfredo Sanjuan, who was a business student at another university in Bogotá, left the apartment building that had been under surveillance on Sunday, walked a block to the Avenida Caracas, and caught a bus to his school. He did not arrive. That afternoon, his brother Samuel Sanjuan, an anthropology student at the National University, left from the same bus stop for a meeting at a bank. He did not arrive.

Over the next several days, the families of the Sanjuan brothers, and the families of Orlando Garcia and Pedro Silva, reported their disappearances to various police agencies and to the Office of the Attorney General, as well as to hospitals and the morgue. The families learned nothing about the whereabouts of their sons.

Even though the Swordfish group in Miami had met socially only four weeks earlier at the Dariases, Carol Cooper invited everyone (again excluding Tom Clifford and Bob Russo) to her town house in Pembroke Pines for dinner Saturday evening so they could meet her parents, who were visiting from Illinois.

Again the evening's banter centered on Chellino and Darias.

"We know why you won't bring Marlene to the office," Frank said. "You don't want to introduce her to any other men. You want to keep her for yourself."

"No, all I'm doing is keeping her away from you," Robert replied. "I know how much you like her, and I don't want you to get in trouble with Sally."

"You son of a bitch," Chellino said.

A little later Paul Sennett's wife, Marion, pointedly asked Robert why he would want to work for the DEA, since it involved considerable exposure to danger. "You shouldn't be doing these dangerous things," she said. "You have a lovely wife and daughter. I wouldn't do it. Why do you do it?"

"I enjoy doing it, and I feel the government can protect me."

"The government can't protect you all the time. You're really taking a lot of risks."

Amelia Darias was taken aback. On their way home she said to Robert, "Are you sure those people aren't a bunch of amateurs?"

"Whatever you may think of them personally, they know what they're doing when it comes to protecting themselves and the people they work with. Paul and Carol have killed people."

Amelia shuddered. "The day Bert Schwartz came after you with that machine gun, Carol told me she would protect you with her life."

"I know, and I believe she would."

"These people are so one-dimensional," Amelia said. "All they talk about is their exploits at work."

"Paul and Marion aren't like that," Robert countered. "She knows a lot about art."

"You're right, they are the exceptions," Amelia said. "They even read books." Few books had been evident in Carol Cooper's house.

"I wonder if Carol has ever read *Les Misérables,*" Robert said.

"I doubt it," Amelia replied. "Or *The Three Musketeers.* But that's what she and Frank and Paul act like."

"Or *Crime and Punishment,*" Robert said.

"*What Every Woman Should Know About Men,*" Amelia offered with a laugh. "She needs that in the DEA."

"She's probably never read *All You Need to Know About the IRS*. She doesn't need that. We do."

"Prisoner Without a Name, Cell Without a Number."

"That's me," Robert said, with a grim smile.

"Marlene's probably read all of those and more," Amelia suggested.

"Yes, but I think she mainly sticks to Keynes and Adam Smith," Robert said.

"Frank just doesn't let up about you and Marlene, does he?" Amelia said with a smile.

"He's the one who has the hots for her," Robert laughed.

It had been nearly three months since anyone had deposited narcotics money with Dean International. Marlene Navarro hadn't deposited anything. Lionel Paytubi hadn't deposited anything. Nor had Manuel Sanchez, the Colombian Kids, or Humberto Garcia. Garcia in particular had become notorious for crying wolf. On countless occasions, it seemed to Darias, Garcia had called and announced that a client named Antonio Uribe, a copper tubing and cocaine tycoon from Medellín, Colombia, would deliver $1 million in cocaine proceeds "within a few days," "very soon," "tomorrow for sure," "later today perhaps." Darias was weary and frustrated from the near misses.

And then suddenly, on Friday morning, March 5, Humberto Garcia, who had been hospitalized following an auto accident, sent word that Antonio Uribe had about $130,000 to deposit immediately. Darias and Sennett picked up the money and returned to Dean, only to be summoned back later for another $100,000 of Uribe's money. An additional $400,000 arrived from Uribe a few days later, for a total of $630,000, which Dean transferred to Uribe's bank account. Meanwhile, Lionel Paytubi and Manuel Sanchez informed Darias that they had a deposit from a client of Sanchez, a toy dealer trafficking in drugs who had made a deposit at Dean the previous October. This time the man had $190,000 to exchange for cashier's checks.

"This is unbelievable," Frank Chellino said, savoring the fresh deposits. "I could have used twelve more people today."

Lionel Paytubi brought the toy dealer's cash to Dean International and Chellino was able to play the role of Frank Dean before the hidden cameras for the first time in 1982. "I like your jacket," Chellino said. Paytubi was wearing a yellow Big Bird raincoat.

"It's my kid's." Paytubi accepted a Chivas on the rocks.

Chellino took the occasion to broach a notion, which thus far had been discussed only internally, of how Dean International might further exploit Lionel Paytubi and thus keep Operation Greenback at bay. He suggested that Dean might purchase a bank of its own, and asked if Paytubi would be interested in managing such a bank as an employee of Dean.

"I could use you full-time—I really could," Chellino said. "Are you working?"

"It's just a bullshit job. If you need me I'll come down. I've been out of action for a year. Those assholes—Operation Greenback."

"Could you manage a bank if we were to place you in one? Are you that experienced?"

"I can go into a bank. That's my life. That's what I love. It's in my blood."

"One of my concerns is how it can be handled so stuff doesn't have to be reported," Chellino said.

"I've got people I'd trust with my soul scattered all over the continent," Paytubi said. "Tellers, officers I contact for this or that, and they'd come back with me. They shit in their drawers when I tell them to shit in their drawers."

"I've been toying with the idea. I'm seriously contemplating buying the controlling interest in a bank to handle my money and/or shelter it."

"I've been the head teller of a bank. I've been the auditor of a bank. And loans are the things I found the most attractive. But I'd never give the bank away. They made money with me, and those guys knew it. That's why I got bonuses every Christmas and a raise at the end of the year."

"But can the funds that I would want to run through it not be reported, and be taken care of so Uncle doesn't find out about it?" Chellino asked.

Paytubi avoided the question. "Maybe I should become personnel manager. I do the hiring. A lot of people are scared of Miami, you know that."

"If the price is right, they'll come back."

Chellino said he would get back to Paytubi as soon as he located a specific bank for sale.

Felipe Calderon, the Colombian banker turned DEA spy, was not fulfilling Tom Clifford's expectations. Although Calderon had been effective as an adviser on banking procedures at Dean International, he had failed to initiate a single major investigation of his own. In contrast to Robert Darias, who had been cultivating several promising targets since his first weeks on the job the previous summer,

Calderon, by March 1982, had made substantial contact with only one—his former banking colleague in Colombia, Victor Covo. This was partly because of Calderon's retiring personality, and partly because he knew what Robert Darias knew—that an undercover overture of this kind could not be hurried.

Under mounting pressure from his own superiors, Tom Clifford assigned the newest member of the Swordfish team, Special Agent Eddie Hernandez, to spur Calderon. "I want you to turn Felipe around," Clifford told Hernandez over drinks at Le Sabre. "He's been here a year. We've made a hell of an investment. We've got to get this guy to produce." Clifford hoped that Hernandez could manage Calderon better than the gringos could.

At Eddie Hernandez's urging, Calderon stepped up his courtship of Victor Covo, who had become one of the Colombian mafia's main drug bankers in Panama City. On Friday, March 5, the day of the new cash deliveries, Covo paid his first visit to Dean International and said he needed to convert between $1 million and $2 million worth of small bills each month into cashier's checks. It was made clear that the cash, which supposedly would start flowing "soon," was narcotics proceeds and was not to be reported to the IRS. Within a few days Covo appeared again with $123,000 in a tan briefcase and deposited it with Dean.

After the initial encounters with Covo, it became evident to Chellino and Cooper that their problems with Felipe Calderon were not limited to inertia. Calderon was afraid. He confided to Cooper that he was "petrified" of the consequences of spying on Victor Covo. "They will put out five hundred contracts on me when this is over," he told Cooper. "They will come after me and my family in a second."

Cooper tried to be understanding. "You're making a commitment now and you're going to have to live with it," she said. "I think once you're over this hurdle you'll be okay. Bringing this guy in was a big hurdle."

They all lived with fear. Federal statistics showed that DEA agents were more than four times as likely to experience a violent episode as other federal law enforcement agents, including FBI agents. The casualty rate among spies was even higher. But most were able to come to terms with fear—experienced agents tended to develop a fatalistic attitude and a blasé veneer—and the Swordfish agents could only hope that Calderon would as well. He was smoking more than his usual three packs of Merits a day and his hands seemed to shake even worse.

On the evening of Tuesday, March 9, U.S. Customs agents, acting on intelligence provided by the DEA, searched a cargo shipment that had just arrived at Miami International Airport from Medellín aboard a Boeing 707 belonging to Transportes Aéreos Mercantiles Panamericanos, or TAMPA, a Colombian-owned freight carrier. In several boxes labeled "jeans," the agents found cocaine—more cocaine than they had ever seen. First they estimated it might be as much as 500 pounds, which would have been among the largest shipments ever found in air cargo. As they searched further the estimate rose to 1,000 pounds, then 2,000, numbers that high-ranking DEA and Customs officials scoffed at as they sped from their offices to the scene of the seizure. In the end the agents found they had seized 3,906 pounds of pure cocaine, worth more than $100 million on the Miami wholesale market. It was the largest seizure ever in the United States by more than a multiple of four.

The seizure shocked the DEA, the FBI, the Customs Service, the State Department, and others whose job it was to keep illegal drugs out of the U.S. While the seizure was a victory of sorts—the agents could claim that this particular shipment would never reach the streets of America—the TAMPA seizure in a larger sense represented a major defeat in America's young drug war. It was a defeat of long-held assumptions about the dimensions of the drug crisis. Like the Tet offensive in Vietnam fourteen years earlier, the seizure indicated that the dimensions of the crisis were far greater than even the direst of previous analyses had envisioned. It seemed reasonable to assume that the TAMPA shipment was only one among many big shipments coming in. Therefore, it seemed likely that far more cocaine was being smuggled into the United States, by far more traffickers and mafia families, in a far more coordinated manner, than had been estimated. And yet the market clearly was not glutted—the wholesale price of cocaine was holding steady. The demand for the drug in America must be incalculably greater than even the epidemic proportions previously calculated.

The agents who intercepted the TAMPA shipment detained a few airport workers briefly but were unable to identify anyone of significance who could be linked to the shipment. The DEA surmised, however, that the cargo was far too large to have come from a single trafficking organization. It must be a coordinated effort of several syndicates. And the agents of Operation Swordfish did not doubt that Carlos Jader Alvarez, Pepe Cabrera, and their colleagues were among those responsible.

Marlene Navarro's telephones were even more active than usual late on the night of the seizure and for the next two days.

"She was talking like crazy last night," Cooper told Darias after reviewing the pen register. "She was on the phone all night long, once at midnight, once at two o'clock in the morning, once at three o'clock in the morning. She called somebody at three o'clock in the morning. I'm going bananas with phone numbers here. Holy Cow!"

The pen register revealed that in one thirty-four-minute period the morning after the seizure, Navarro had dialed one of Jader Alvarez's numbers in Bogotá forty-seven times. The following day she dialed numbers registered to both Jader and Pepe Cabrera twenty-two times. Most of the calls appeared to be brief; it was unclear how many of them even had been completed. Since the DEA was not yet authorized to listen there was little they could glean.

"These are times when the ability to listen to her would have really been fantastic," Robert said.

"I agree. It's going to take us some time. But, Bob, if she calls you, tape it, okay? If she's calling you I definitely want it taped."

Marlene did not call Robert, so Cooper finally instructed him to call her and gently ask some leading questions about the TAMPA seizure. The results were negative. "I taped Marlene and Tocayo, and no dice," Robert reported. "I don't think they have anything to do with it, the way they reacted. They're very calm, like always. I couldn't find one little slip when I talked to her."

Chellino and Cooper felt like celebrating the new deposits at Dean International but Tom Clifford wasn't impressed. All Clifford could talk about was why Robert Darias couldn't seem to entice Marlene Navarro to the Dean office so the agents could capture incriminating conversation on videotape. The Alvarez investigation had become the central thrust of Operation Swordfish, and Marlene Navarro was the DEA's favorite target—far more intriguing than the average drug dealer. She was an alluring, sexy female. She was smart and mysterious. The agents—especially Chellino—were smitten by her. And yet to Clifford she seemed dead in the water as a target, elusive, impenetrable.

The tension mounted at Dean International. The agency managers pressed Clifford, who pressed Chellino and Cooper, who pressed Darias, who got angry. "Well, Carol, you want to talk to her? You have her number," Darias snapped. "I mean, don't pressure me like that! I asked her twice to meet with Frank or to come to the office and she flatly said she didn't feel that she had anything to talk to him about right now."

Frank Chellino thought he discerned more evidence of Tom Clifford's drinking—more frequent absences, more seeming hangovers, more beer on his breath. Clifford had become so hard to reach, in fact, that Chellino had taken to calling Clifford's boss, the new associate special-agent-in-charge, Sam Billbrough, when Chellino needed a decision on some issue and couldn't reach Clifford. The calls to Billbrough infuriated Clifford, who felt they were a transparent attempt by Chellino to discredit Clifford and curry favor with Billbrough.

"Don't you ever tell anybody that I'm not available!" Clifford railed at Chellino. "I've been available twenty-four hours a day since I joined this agency. If you call and I'm not in the office, you beep me, and I'll be back to you in two minutes. My beeper is always on. But don't you ever call Billbrough and say 'I can't get Tom.' Is that so hard for you to grasp?"

Clifford blamed the Navarro dilemma not on Darias personally but on what Clifford considered the ineffectual manner in which Cooper and Chellino were running Darias. Although he didn't tell anyone, Clifford had begun to consider transferring control of Darias to Eddie Hernandez. He encouraged Hernandez to begin cultivating Darias.

Eddie Hernandez leapt at the challenge. He was frustrated supervising Felipe Calderon, far from a full-time job. Clifford originally had led Hernandez to believe that he was badly needed in Operation Swordfish, that he would be the control agent in some of the major cases, that he would be busier than he had ever been in his life. It hadn't worked out that way thus far. Hernandez sensed that he was being isolated from the cases of Robert Darias, who clearly was the central force in the operation. Hernandez, who was bouncy and eager to please, yearned to become involved in Darias's cases. He yearned to meet Marlene Navarro.

Hernandez began to work at winning Darias's confidence, engaging him in conversation at every opportunity. But gaining Darias's trust was not the only challenge Hernandez faced. Carol Cooper and Paul Sennett had supervised Robert Darias since the day he had arrived on the DEA's doorstep more than a year earlier. Cooper and Sennett had a proprietary interest in Darias, an extraordinarily able spy in whose glow they had basked. They weren't about to allow another DEA agent to interfere with that relationship. And Darias, who had been carefully nurturing his relationships with Marlene Navarro, Humberto Garcia, Lionel Paytubi, and Manuel Sanchez for eight months, did not want anyone—least of all the inexperienced

Eddie Hernandez, whom Darias considered too aggressive—interfering, especially since those relationships seemed about to bear more fruit.

"Eddie is very interested in working with me," Darias told Cooper, "and I keep telling him that it's up to you, Carol. I don't approach him, he approaches me."

"Everything you do has to go through either me or Paul," Carol stressed. "We've got to be able to keep track of what you're doing."

"I know. If it doesn't go through you, Carol, it doesn't go."

Hernandez confided his frustrations to Tom Clifford. "They won't let me in the door," Hernandez said, referring to Cooper, Sennett, and Chellino.

"What do you mean?"

"They close the door. They keep talking about cases as being *their* cases, not *our* cases or the DEA's cases."

Eddie Hernandez's report infuriated Tom Clifford. He had heard similar complaints about Chellino and Cooper from Special Agent Pepe Hinojosa months earlier.

By the middle of March, Operation Swordfish was seething with anger, frustration, and fear. The agents had split into hostile camps. Frank Chellino, Carol Cooper, and Paul Sennett were pitted against Tom Clifford and Bob Russo on nearly every issue. The disillusioned Eddie Hernandez was siding with Clifford. Felipe Calderon felt as if he were about to be sucked into a maelstrom, and was consumed by fear that he and his family were destined to die violently at the hands of the Colombian mafia. Robert Darias was irritated and confused; he just wanted to get on with his work, but was having difficulty staying clear of "the petty fights of these crazy gringos," as he put it to Amelia.

2 0

GREG ENGLISH, who was completing his fifth visit to Miami as the Justice Department's legal adviser to Operation Swordfish, bought St. Patrick's Day drinks for his DEA friends—those he was able to round up on Wednesday evening, March 17—Frank Chellino, Carol Cooper, Bob Russo, and Eddie Hernandez. Tom Clifford joined the group in a large U-shaped booth at the Le Sabre Club about seven o'clock.

By eight, when English left, Clifford's Budweisers and Chellino's Red Labels were still flowing. The music from the juke box was infectious, and Eddie Hernandez got up to dance.

With Hernandez away from the table, Clifford remarked to Chellino, "You're not handling Eddie right."

"What do you mean?" Chellino asked, nonplussed.

"You're not handling him right. You people are cutting him out, just like you did Pepe."

"Pepe? I don't know what you're talking about. Pepe Hinojosa? Pepe was transferred to Bolivia."

"You know, and I know, that Pepe was angry, and felt that you and Carol were shutting him out of your cases. Eddie feels the same way."

"We're not shutting Eddie out of anything."

"Well, I know for a fact that he's upset. He doesn't feel he's being included."

"The first thing you should know about Eddie," Chellino said, "is that he's wrong for this operation. He's way too aggressive, he talks too much, he has no experience, and he isn't very bright."

"That's ridiculous. He's worked for me. He's capable of doing a lot."

"He can't cut it. He's not right."

"Well, you're wrong, and you're going to have to try harder to work with him, because he's staying in the operation, and he's going to work more with Bob Darias."

"Bob won't work with Eddie."

"Bob *will* work with Eddie because I'm going to *instruct* Bob that he's going to work with Eddie," Clifford said, his ire rising. "We've got to get a Spanish-speaking agent closer to Bob. He's running wild. You've got no corroboration of anything Bob's doing. You've got no handle on Marlene."

Carol Cooper, who had been listening, interjected: "That's not true. Bob's not running wild. I know where he is twenty-four hours a day."

"Where is he right now?" Clifford asked.

"At home."

"How do you know?"

"Because he told me, I just talked to him there, and he's never lied to me."

"How do you know he's never lied?"

"Because he's been working for me more than a year, in lots of cases, and I've never caught him in a lie," Cooper said.

"I think he's got you under his spell."

"What's that supposed to mean?"

"You're supposed to be his control. *You* don't control Bob. Bob controls *you*. He's a very charming guy. He's manipulating you. He's sweet-talking you. He's pulling the wool over your eyes." Clifford was revved up, saying things he had felt but withheld for months.

"That's not true—you have no right to say that!" Cooper retorted, her face flushed with rage. She started to rise from the table and then sat back down. Bob Russo sat in stunned silence. Eddie Hernandez was still dancing, oblivious to the raging argument.

"I'm putting Eddie to work with Bob," Clifford said.

"You can't do that," Chellino said.

"Wanna bet? I just did. I've heard enough of your excuses about Marlene this and Marlene that. We've got to have somebody on Bob who can *control* him, and not be controlled *by* him, and who can get Marlene under control and bring her in."

"You put Eddie on Bob and you'll fuck up this operation," Chellino said.

"You've already fucked up this operation," Clifford shot back. "You're not getting these people into that office and on tape. You're not getting investments. Nothing's happening, and something's got to happen or management's going to shut us down."

"*I've* fucked up this operation?" Chellino said, incredulous. "*You're* the one who brought in Felipe, who hasn't done anything, who's scared shitless of his own shadow. *You're* the one who brought in Angie, who wasn't worth shit, and then wanted to put him into the grand jury and blow this whole fucking operation."

"We've got to get these people in and get 'em on tape," Clifford responded.

"Who hasn't been brought in? Marlene and Humberto Garcia. Humberto's been in the hospital and Marlene's been commuting to Bogotá, trying to help her boss ransom his kids. She'll come around. We've got to be patient."

"Starting tomorrow, Eddie is working with Bob."

"You can't do that."

"I just did. I'm the supervisor of this operation."

"The organization of the office and the company is my responsibility," Chellino declared.

"What company?" Clifford retorted. "You think you're the president of something? You're nothing but the president of the cockalorum club!"

Chellino was dumbstruck.

"I could close this operation tomorrow and open up again in six months with different people," Clifford continued. "You're nothing but a fucking street agent, and I'm your supervisor."

"Some supervisor," Chellino said. "You're never around, you're never available when you're needed, always out drinking. You've been neglecting this operation."

"You should talk about drinking. And for you to keep saying I'm not available is ridiculous, it's bullshit, and I won't stand for it anymore. That's just an excuse for you to call Billbrough and stick your nose further up his ass."

"I'm not going to take this any longer," Chellino said. "I'm resigning from this operation."

"You can't resign. You'll do whatever your supervisor tells you to do. You're fired."

Cooper, sputtering with anger, said, "If Frank's gone, I'm gone. And Darias is gone, too. *Bob is mine."*

"We'll see," Clifford said, rising from the table to go to the men's room.

Chellino and Cooper left the bar and drove home. When Clifford returned to the table, he said to Russo: "I'm not concerned about whether they're in or out. I could get Larry, Moe, and Curly to do their jobs. Darias is the one I'm concerned about. If Darias leaves with them, it's all over."

Eddie Hernandez was still dancing.

"You're not really doing this, are you?" Cooper asked Chellino as he dropped her off at her town house in Pembroke Pines. Chellino had

ranted about Clifford throughout the twenty-minute drive from
Miami Lakes.

"That's it," he said. "I'm going down there tomorrow and walking
out."

Frank Chellino felt devastated through the evening at home. "Oh
shit, my whole career is down the drain," he said to Sally.

"Do what you think you have to do," she advised.

He thought of calling Greg English for advice or intervention. But
English was not in the DEA chain of command. Appealing to him
would have made the situation worse.

Chellino's ego would not let him retreat and he did not report to
Dean International the next day. At home he began a letter requesting
a transfer out of Operation Swordfish.

With Pete Gruden out of town, Sam Billbrough was the acting
special agent-in-charge, and it was in Billbrough's spacious first-floor
office that Tom Clifford tried to explain what had happened at the Le
Sabre Club.

"We had an altercation at a bar, an argument, a flareup," Clifford
reported. "But it was an oral argument, not a fight, nothing like that,
but some things came out where Chellino and Cooper feel they can't
work in the operation anymore, and I agree. I want them out."

Billbrough was noncommittal.

"They're out," Clifford continued. "I don't care what you say,
they're not working in that operation again. Otherwise, you can put
them back in and remove me."

From his meeting with Billbrough, Clifford, in his capacity as chief
of intelligence, had to rush downtown to meet with a congressional
delegation that was being briefed on Vice President George Bush's
Florida Anti-Drug Task Force.

"Go sit on it," Billbrough said to Frank Chellino, who appeared at the
Phoenix Building late in the morning. "Get out of here and go relax.
Calm down. Let us talk about it." Chellino, having already left his
resignation letter in Clifford's office, drove to the bar of the Marriott
Hotel in Fort Lauderdale, where he began drinking Red Label and
water.

Carol Cooper and Paul Sennett were waiting in Tom Clifford's
office when he returned. Though Sennett had not witnessed the confrontation the night before, Cooper had briefed him, and he had
decided to leave Operation Swordfish with her and Chellino.

"You have five minutes," Clifford said, waving the envelope containing Chellino's resignation letter. Clifford had not spoken again with Sam Billbrough, and did not know of Billbrough's effort to defuse Chellino.

"Tom, please, don't even open that letter," Sennett pleaded. "Just rip it up, and let's talk."

"You have five minutes," Clifford repeated.

"I'm leaving," Cooper said, furious at Clifford's belligerence. "I'll be in Group Three Monday morning."

Clifford lost his temper. "You can't do that!" he shouted. "You can't tell me you're leaving! You have to *ask* to leave!"

"Okay, Tom," Sennett said, "we are both asking to be out of the operation."

"As it happens, the decision has already been made that you are out," Clifford said. He looked at Cooper and shook his finger at her. "I'll get you for this," he said.

The agents left.

Clifford picked up the phone and dialed Dean International, which no longer had a president, a vice president for customer relations, or a secretary.

Robert Darias, having spoken to Cooper before the argument early Wednesday evening and then gone out, knew nothing of the crisis engulfing Operation Swordfish until he arrived at Dean around noon Thursday. Eddie Hernandez and Bob Russo intercepted him at the front door. "Tom wants us to join him for lunch," Russo told Darias, and the three of them drove to a small, quiet restaurant just off the Palmetto Expressway.

It occurred to Darias that the founder of Operation Swordfish had never before invited him to lunch or anything else. As soon as they were seated in the restaurant, Clifford explained to Darias that a "problem had arisen" between him and Frank Chellino and that Frank might leave the operation. "Carol and Paul might go, too," Clifford said. "How would you feel if those people left?"

"I would be sorry to see them go," Robert replied, "but I don't feel that I work for Frank or Carol specifically, or for you. I feel that I work for the government. I will work with anyone, because we have an important thing going here."

"That's right. That's the right attitude," Clifford said.

"You know, Tom," Robert said, "it's hard to know how to react to you in a situation like this, because you are a person that I don't know at all, and I am a person that you don't know at all."

"That's absolutely right, and that's my fault," Clifford said. "We should be meeting, just the two of us, at least once a week just to talk, so that I can get your views on how this operation is going."

"That's fine with me," Darias said, and he took the opportunity to make a specific suggestion. He had always felt that he would be better able to entice his targets into the Dean offices if they knew they would be meeting with him alone rather than with an unfamiliar figure such as Frank Dean. They could still be videotaped.

"Some of these bad guys," he said to Clifford, "if you really want them to talk freely the way they talk to me in *their* offices, if you want them videotaped talking like that, let me handle them by myself in the Dean office and I make them talk like that."

"I have nothing against that."

It appeared to Darias that Clifford was hearing only some of what he was saying. He seemed exhausted and distracted, perhaps hung over.

Clifford declared that Operation Swordfish would continue in all events and that he was counting on Darias to keep playing his crucial role. Darias left the lunch confused and worried. Were the three agents really leaving? Clifford had not seemed hopeful that the "problem" would be resolved.

Carol Cooper and Paul Sennett paced Cooper's living room in Pembroke Pines sipping large cans of Miller Lite. They still felt part of Operation Swordfish. Even though they had left a few hours earlier, they convinced themselves that it hadn't really happened. In particular, they still felt a strong proprietary interest in Robert Darias, and were enraged by what they had learned from the tight DEA grapevine: that Tom Clifford had taken Darias to lunch and conferred with him "behind our backs." They felt Clifford had "back-doored" them, that he still had an obligation to consult with them before meeting with *their* spy, even though he already had banished them from the operation. There is a rule in the intelligence and law enforcement communities of the U.S. Government, unwritten but strictly observed, that no one communicates with a spy except through his control agent. Cooper and Sennett felt they still controlled Darias.

Carol got Robert on the phone, with Paul listening on an extension.

"Got a question for you, kid," Carol asked. "What exactly happened at that lunch today?"

"Well, first of all, Eddie and Bob Russo told me to go and have a sandwich with them, that Tom was going to be there and that he wanted to talk to me."

"Who was the one that was telling you, Russo or Eddie?"

"Actually, both of them. So we got there and sat down, and Tom started telling me that there had been a problem, that he had had a problem with Frank, and maybe Frank wasn't going to be in the office anymore, and this and that."

Cooper questioned Darias closely about precisely what Clifford had said, and whether there had been talk of Eddie Hernandez's becoming Darias's control agent. Darias dismissed Cooper's concern about Hernandez.

"I hate to see this happening, Carol. I really do."

"So do I. We've enjoyed working with you, we really have. But Tom's not being honest with us, and we're not gonna play his games."

Darias wondered whether Cooper and Sennett expected him to resign from Operation Swordfish, too, as a maneuver to strengthen their position. They hadn't asked, but he had heard from Russo that Carol and Paul had threatened to "take Bob with us." Darias was in turmoil. Although he felt a strong loyalty to Carol and Paul, he knew little of the controversy that had led to their departures and was not inclined to destroy his own position with the government—a job he was enjoying and was very good at. And he knew enough of bureaucracy to know that large disputes often grew from petty issues.

Darias had never felt more justified in secretly tape-recording his conversations with the agents.

The departure of Chellino, Cooper, and Sennett was not the only emergency threatening Operation Swordfish that Thursday, March 18. After agreeing in February to postpone its indictment of Lionel Paytubi, Operation Greenback suddenly made known that it planned to proceed with the indictment around April 15, less than a month away. Greg English had been unable to sway Charles Blau any longer. Tom Clifford hurriedly drafted, and Sam Billbrough signed, a teletype to DEA headquarters.

A MAJOR ISSUE HAS DEVELOPED BETWEEN OPERATION SWORDFISH AND OPERATION GREENBACK WHICH COULD CAUSE THE PREMATURE END OF OPERATION SWORDFISH.

OPERATION SWORDFISH HAS NEGOTIATED WITH LIONEL PAYTUBI FOR THE PAST SIX MONTHS. THESE CONTACTS HAVE LAID THE FOUNDA-

TION OF SWORDFISH'S PENETRATION INTO THE FINANCIAL DEALINGS OF
SEVERAL GROUPS, WITH THE OBJECTIVE OF MAJOR PROSECUTIONS.

OPERATION GREENBACK TENTATIVELY PLANS TO INDICT THE GREAT
AMERICAN BANK WITH LIONEL PAYTUBI ON APRIL 15, 1982. THE IN-
DICTMENT WILL RESULT IN THE EXPOSURE OF SWORDFISH. . . . THERE
ARE OTHER CASES SEPARATE FROM PAYTUBI THAT WILL BE COMPRO-
MISED.

SWORDFISH'S ACTIVITIES HAVE DRAMATICALLY INCREASED IN THE
LAST MONTH. IN OUR OPINION SWORDFISH NOW HAS THE CREDIBILITY
TO SECURE SIGNIFICANT RESULTS IN 1982, BUT THIS INDICTMENT WILL
COMPROMISE THESE INVESTIGATIONS.

Unsupervised, Robert Darias continued his undercover work. On
Friday afternoon he concealed his microcassette recorder in his jacket
and dropped by Refricenter of Miami, where he had a long talk with
Humberto Garcia. Humberto said he was going to Medellín to meet
with the syndicate whose huge load of cocaine, 3,906 pounds, had
been seized at Miami International Airport the previous week. Humberto said he wanted Darias to handle the money for the group.

"Right now, everybody is trafficking in coke," Humberto said.

It was one of the most revealing and incriminating conversations
that Darias had ever had with Garcia and it was all on tape.

From the phone in her den that evening, Carol Cooper further
confided her frustrations to Robert Darias. "They're crucifying me,"
she said. "They're spreading the word that I told them if I left I was
taking you with me. I never told them that. They were *afraid* we were
gonna take you with us if we left, so it was our gut feeling that they
were trying to get you on their side so you would stay. They back-
doored us and went into a meeting with you."

"That's right."

"They're playing stupid games, Bob. We just have a very, very
difficult time working with Tom."

"Other issues that have nothing to do with me, you mean?" Robert
asked.

"Right. He made serious mistakes, and now he's lying to us. Paul,
Frank, and I want to be in the operation. We think it's a good
operation. But Tom *yelled* at us. He threatened me. He told me to get
out of his office."

"I feel that without you they are setting this thing back easily three
or four months," Darias said.

"I would love to come back and so would Frank. All of us would.

We didn't want to do what we had to do. But Tom threatened me. In the last three days, three threats. No boss threatens me!"

Paul Sennett also called Robert and encouraged him to assert himself and exploit the fluid situation. "You will do very well out of this whole thing," Paul said. *"You can run that operation. You're going to have to."*

"Tom has to realize," Robert replied, "that things have to be done my way because I am the only one that knows how things have to go. And if he feels that he is going to bring in new people to start manipulating that office, he's completely wrong. Because they're going to mess the whole thing up. It's going to look like another FBI operation."

"Whatever happens, we still want you to know that you can depend on us if we can do anything for you," Paul said. "Whatever I can do, I'd go to the wall for you and so will Carol," Sennett said, his high, reedy voice revealing great stress.

In an effort to salvage Operation Swordfish in the face of the defections, Tom Clifford convened a strategy conference at Dean International on Monday morning. The group met in what had been Frank Chellino's office. Someone had flicked on Chellino's FM radio, so the meeting was bathed in the soft "easy listening" music of LIFE-FM, Chellino's favorite station.

Clifford began by introducing a new face—Special Agent Nick Zapata, whom he had just assigned to Operation Swordfish to further bridge what he still perceived as a "Latin gap"—gringo agents supervising Latin spies. Zapata was a close friend of Eddie Hernandez, whose advice Clifford had sought in choosing a new member of the team. Zapata was Mexican by birth but had grown up in San Antonio, Texas. Big, thick-chested, and mustachioed, he had been a Marine and a close-combat instructor for the CIA before joining the DEA.

As Zapata, Hernandez, Bob Russo, and Felipe Calderon sat listening, Clifford turned to Robert Darias.

"I got into a big problem after I met you and Eddie at the restaurant," Clifford said. "They said I back-doored them."

"They were a little unhappy with me, too," Darias said.

"That meeting wasn't prearranged like they said, but they think that's bullshit. And I told them, 'Hey, I'm sick and tired of these innuendoes. I'm telling you the straight facts of what happened. There's no back-dooring anybody. You're just allowing your emotions to overcome you.' I said, give it the weekend, give it a little thought, and cut the emotions out. They said, bullshit, we withdraw."

"After thinking about it the whole weekend," Darias said, "I feel somebody misunderstood my words or my mental attitude somehow. I thought *they* were going to be here today. I wanted to talk to everybody at the same time so I could express myself and get rid of all these things. I feel I have been working for the *government*. So nobody should turn around and say 'If I leave, *he* leaves.' I haven't been doing all this because I like Carol, because I like Paul. That's beside the point. I would love to keep working with them and I am very sorry this happened. But whoever made this mess, that's his problem. I only hope we will be able to continue this operation toward the end we thought we were going to reach. I am really beginning to convince these targets to do whatever I want. They are going to come here to this office. They are going to talk about everything—drugs, deliveries, the whole thing. Marlene will come in eventually. We will put her on tape. We just have to be patient. Now as for Carol and Paul, when I walked into the DEA the first time the first person I talked to was Paul, and I am happy to have met him, to have met Carol, and I will keep being their friend. But I didn't walk in there to belong to *anybody*. And I don't want to get involved in their petty disputes because it looks like a kindergarten type of thing."

"It does," Clifford said. "It's bullshit."

Intelligence Analyst Bob Russo spoke up. His role in Operation Swordfish had always been significant because of his close association with Tom Clifford, who privately relied on him for advice on all aspects of the experimental enterprise.

"We feel very badly," he said to Darias, "that you were brought into our internal problems. Basically, what happened was, Tom gave these people the leeway to operate this business as they saw fit. But they then forgot who was the boss, Tom Clifford. And they began to argue about the decisions that were being made, refusing to follow the decisions. They used you as their wedge. In effect, they said we don't like that, and if you do it, we're taking Darias and we're leaving. Now, they knew that *you are* the operation, that you were the guy who was bringing the money in. *And they put you right in the middle of this* with that claim that they would take you and leave. They don't *own* you. We don't *own* you. You are your own person."

"Yes, but that doesn't mean that I don't follow the rules," Darias said. "If there is any problem, we argue the point. I'm not a hot-head. You convince me or I convince you. I am always willing to come to the center of an argument to work it out."

The eager Eddie Hernandez told Darias, "Whenever you need me, I'm available, nights, Saturdays, Sundays. If you want me to go with you to help you in any way, you name it. I'm sure Nick feels the same way. I think we could have a helluva team."

Darias underscored that he wanted to meet alone at the Dean offices with his targets as long as the conversations were taped. "When these guys first come here, I want them to sit down with me by myself—to let them understand that now I'm taking over the responsibility of the business from Frank."

Tom Clifford approved. "If he feels that with a particular person he has to be alone, no problem. It'll be on tape. That's confirmed."

It was decided that clients would be told that Frank Dean had returned to Chicago temporarily and his "partner" Robert Darias was in charge of the company. Eddie Hernandez would take Darias's daily reports as Carol Cooper had been doing.

As Bob Russo observed the dynamics of the meeting, it seemed to him that something extraordinary had just happened.

For all practical purposes, Robert Darias was now in charge of Operation Swordfish.

The spy was running his handlers.

21

ACTING SPECIAL-AGENT-IN-CHARGE Sam Billbrough scheduled private forty-five-minute meetings that Monday afternoon March 22, with Frank Chellino, Carol Cooper, and Paul Sennett. Chellino was told to be at the Phoenix Building at 3:30, Cooper at 4:15, Sennett at 5:00. The tall, gray-haired administrator conducted the interviews around a coffee table across from his massive mahogony desk, which was flanked by the flags of the United States and the Department of Justice and large color photographs of Ronald Reagan and William French Smith.

As Billbrough quietly asked questions and took notes on a legal pad, each agent separately recounted the disagreements with Tom Clifford that had burst into open warfare on Wednesday evening at the Le Sabre Club and resulted in what the Phoenix Building grapevine had quickly dubbed "The St. Patrick's Day Massacre." Over two and a half hours, Billbrough distilled the agents' allegations to four basic charges:

—Tom Clifford had "neglected" Operation Swordfish. He was unavailable to the Swordfish agents much of the time, perhaps because of drinking.

—Clifford was needlessly assigning more Latin agents to Operation Swordfish, *solely because* they were Latin, in the unwarranted belief that Anglo agents were incapable of properly supervising Robert Darias and Felipe Calderon.

—Clifford had favored putting the gangster Angie before a grand jury to testify about the planned escape of the godfather José Alvero-Cruz, a move that likely would have compromised Operation Swordfish.

—Clifford was allowing his friend Intelligence Analyst Bob Russo to wield far too much influence in the operation, giving Russo responsibilities normally reserved for special agents.

"We all prefer to stay with the operation," Carol Cooper told Billbrough. "It was a major decision that we made to back out. We're sorry it happened."

Billbrough told the agents that he would look into their charges and get back to them promptly. He held out the possibility that all three of them would be transferred out of Miami. It was clear to him that each of the issues they had raised was complex and in most cases ambiguous. It was also clear to Billbrough that there was a great deal of deep-seated personal animosity between Chellino, Cooper, and Sennett on the one side, and Clifford and Russo on the other.

Chellino, Cooper, and Sennett compared notes on their meetings with Billbrough, and that evening Cooper gave Robert Darias a report that was less decorous than her comments to Billbrough.

"It's getting down to push comes to shove, and either Tom's going to be out or we're going to be out," Carol said.

"You have to be kidding," Robert replied. He had never heard Carol sound so depressed.

"It's boiled down to the decision, Bob, either they get rid of Tom or they get rid of all three of us. Our gut feeling is they're gonna have to support their supervisor, so they're going to get rid of us. If that's the case, there's absolutely nothing we're going to be able to do to help you."

"Yeah, well, I realize that, if you are not here."

"How did your thing turn out this morning?" Carol asked, referring to the meeting Clifford had held at Dean International.

"I told Tom exactly the same thing I always tell you—that I have to handle my people like Marlene by myself. Tom agreed with me and said, 'You do whatever you have to do.' "

"He did?" Cooper felt it was hypocritical for Clifford to give Darias that degree of freedom after proclaiming that she and Chellino were handling him too loosely.

"Of course, right now he doesn't want to have an argument with me," Darias said.

"You're in a controlling position right now," Carol agreed. "You can demand whatever you want."

"By the same token I don't want to push, because that would go against me later. I just wanted to set a line I would be able to hold, and it has to be a fair line for everybody."

Carol confided in Robert the specifics of the agents' conferences with Sam Billbrough. "We told him we had disagreements with Tom and Russo regarding policy issues, which is the main crux of the whole thing. Just to give you some indication, and *don't you dare tell anyone we told you this,* about a month ago Bob Russo went on record and said we should arrest Lionel Paytubi and flip him, get him to work for us."

"Oh, my God!" Darias said. "What is he talking about? That's completely nuts! He better not say that in front of me!"

"That's the kind of stuff we've been protecting you from. We've been arguing about it with Tom and as a result this is where we're at. Another big issue was the Alvero-Cruz deal. We fought with Tom all the way through that and he kept pursuing it."

"What were they going to do with Alvero-Cruz?"

"What they wanted to do was put the informant, Angie, into the grand jury—now this was the same informant that was supposed to take all these lie detector tests but would never take them—the guy had absolutely no credibility. And they would have asked him how do you know about Alvero-Cruz? Why were you talking to the guy? He would've had to tell them about us. Which would bring down our whole operation. So I got mad at Tom and I told him, Tom, go ahead and do whatever you're doing. I'm packing my bags and leaving. He didn't like that. And he has jammed me every time he could on it."

"Doesn't Russo realize that if we arrest Paytubi, we blow the whole operation?"

"Good question, Bob. Big question."

"There's a great risk that he will go and tell some of his close friends to prevent them from falling. Remember, I know the guy much better than you do. I have talked to the guy in a personal way many times. And he has expressed to me the way he thinks about the government and Greenback and all that."

"We will fight Tom on that issue. *I will not let them arrest Paytubi.*"

"I agree."

"Tom basically threatened all of us. That was the final straw. He told Frank and I he was going to terrorize us for the rest of our lives, and then when we got up to walk out, he waved his finger at me and said, 'I'll get you for this.' "

Carol Cooper then came the closest she had ventured since the crisis erupted to asking Robert Darias directly to intercede on the agents' behalf with Clifford and Billbrough—to threaten to resign from Operation Swordfish.

"Unless you tell them differently, we're probably all leaving," Carol said. "I personally would like management to talk to you. If they talk with you, Bob, you might be able to reverse their decision—if you want us back there. Obviously you're the primary guy up there and if you say you need us, that might influence them a little."

Robert was amused. "Now, everybody, *everybody*—Tom, Eddie, Russo, you, everybody—tells me that whatever *I say* is going to be done."

"What they're doing right now, Bob, is trying to keep you happy. I think they're letting you do anything you want to do. If we leave, they know the whole thing's going to rest on your shoulders. You're the one that's the most knowledgeable. You know everything that's going on. You know your clients, which are ninety-nine percent of the people coming in. What they're trying to do—and *don't you ever let them know I talked to you*—is keep you happy. They'll give you anything you want right now."

In effect, Cooper was crying out for help, acknowledging that Robert had more influence over events than she, Chellino, or Sennett did. The spy had the power to control his control.

Carol continued, "Frank said tonight, if anybody is a stand-up guy, Bob is. He'll stand up for what he believes in. You're pretty much like us. We did what we had to do, now you have to do what you have to do."

Robert sighed. "Couldn't Greg English help?"

"No. He has no jurisdiction on an internal thing like this. I wish we could call him. But I can't even call *you!* They would *crucify* me if they ever found out I called you. If Tom *ever* found out we did, God, heaven forbid! He's out to get us now. All of our careers, man, have just been shot down the drain."

"It's a real pity," Robert said.

But he remained hesitant himself to resign.

Sam Billbrough sent for Robert Darias the next day. It was unusual for a bureaucrat of Billbrough's rank to interview a spy. Billbrough knew Darias's importance to Operation Swordfish and greeted him warmly.

"I know it has come to your attention that there are some problems with this operation," Billbrough began.

"Yes, and I feel badly about it," Darias said, "because I like and respect all of the people involved."

"Well, we're sorry you've been caught up in it. We shouldn't be burdening you with our internal problems."

"Don't worry about that. They have always treated me with respect, and I'm happy to do whatever I can to help."

Billbrough asked Darias if he thought Dean International Investments should be staffed entirely by Latins. "No, not necessarily," Robert replied, "the supervisors certainly don't have to be Latin, although the direct, ongoing contacts with the targets probably should be handled by Latins. I have a close relationship now with Marlene Navarro, Humberto Garcia, and others that has taken months to develop. If suddenly now an American shows up and starts talking to them, they are going to run away. But that doesn't mean that Frank or Carol or Paul cannot *meet* these people. It simply means that it must be done carefully, and I must remain the main contact."

"If Frank Chellino, Carol Cooper, and Paul Sennett left the operation, what effect do you feel it would have on the operation?" Billbrough asked.

"It would set us back months, maybe two or three months," Darias replied.

Billbrough mentioned that Marlene Navarro hadn't laundered any narcotics money for quite some time—since December, as he understood it. Did Darias have any reason to believe that she would ever make another deposit, and that Swordfish would penetrate all the way to Carlos Jader Alvarez, the main objective?

"Yes, I talk to her just about every day, and she is getting ready to deliver. We have to be patient. And Humberto Garcia made some big deposits just last week."

"The original concept of this operation was to get these people to invest their money in real estate or other assets that we could confiscate," Billbrough said. "That doesn't seem to be happening."

"Again, you have to be patient. These Colombians don't trust anybody. It takes a long time before they begin to trust you. And a lot of them are not very sophisticated about investments. For the most part, they want to have their money readily available, in liquid form, in cash or in a bank account where they can get at it quickly and move it back and forth. But that doesn't mean that they will never invest, or that they aren't worth pursuing. Marlene's boss, Carlos Jader Alvarez, is one of the biggest drug dealers in Colombia."

"Okay, now, Bob, I need to ask you some questions about Tom Clifford and Frank Chellino personally," Billbrough said. "These are sensitive matters that are off the record. No one will know that I've asked you, and you should not tell anyone I've asked you these questions or discuss these matters with anyone outside this room."

"Okay."

"Have you ever seen Tom drink?"

"Maybe a beer with lunch. Or sometimes he will meet us for drinks in the evening after the office closes. Nothing excessive."

"Have you ever seen him drunk, where he was having trouble functioning or his judgment was impaired?"

"No, not that I can think of. You know, everybody drinks a fair amount. Usually everybody goes out for drinks in the evening. And you know there's liquor in the office—Scotch and things for clients when they come in. So sometimes we have a drink in the office. But nobody ever gets drunk."

"So you've never seen Tom drunk, or drinking to excess?"

"No."

"What about Frank?"

"No, never."

Billbrough and Darias discussed Robert's modus operandi in the operation, and Robert stressed his desire to be consulted on any policy changes. He mentioned the possible arrest of Lionel Paytubi and its dangerous and unpredictable ramifications.

"You're right, you should be consulted, and you will be," Billbrough said. He agreed that Darias could handle his targets "essentially by yourself, as you see fit, except in situations where an agent is required."

Sam Billbrough also met that day with Felipe Calderon, and with Bob Russo, who minimized the importance of Tom Clifford's drinking.

"There is no drinking problem," Russo said. "Tom has a Dean Martin reputation when it comes to drinking. It's a put-on. The real problem isn't drinking. Frank and Carol aren't exactly teetotalers. The real problem is that Frank believes he's actually the president of a company. It's no longer a role he's playing. He actually believes he's in private industry and the head of a company. He and Tom have a bad personality conflict over who's the boss."

Billbrough listened and took notes, but was noncommittal.

Still fearing that the DEA might arrest Lionel Paytubi or make some other rash move without consulting him, Darias sought and got a meeting with Tom Clifford later in the day and reiterated his concerns about the management of the operation, especially his targets.

"Any important decisions, policy changes or whatever, anything that pertains to my people, should go through me," Robert said. "I am not telling you that I am not going to accept what you say. I am trying to tell you I want to be aware of what is going on. I can follow orders, but they have to be the proper orders, and once in a while, anybody who is giving orders will have to take some orders from me, because I know how my people have to be handled."

"You've got it," Clifford said. "You won't have any trouble from me." Clifford took the occasion to solicit Robert's advice on the configuration of new offices that the DEA was leasing for Dean International on Red Road about a mile east of its Miami Lakes location. He also promised Darias the use of a government-owned automobile.

Despite Clifford's assurances, Darias felt uncomfortable and confused. How could he know whether Clifford was leveling with him, or whether Clifford even had the authority to level with him?

In Robert's evening talk with Carol he was irritable and depressed. "There's no way you will stay with me in the operation?" Robert asked.

"You didn't tell them anything I told you last night, did you?"

"No. But there's no way you will stay?"

"It's up to them, Bob."

"Don't give me that story now, Carol. It's up to *you.* You tell me yes, and I can fight for you somehow."

"We'd love to stay—Paul, Frank, and me."

"No, no, I'm talking about *you,* Carol. Everybody created his own problem."

"I would go back but I cannot work with Tom. That is the problem."

"No? Then you cannot go back. That's it. I don't believe Tom is going to be taken out of the operation."

"My gut feeling is that the operation is going to suffer drastically if Tom stays in charge of it," Carol said. "None of us can work with the man. I don't trust his opinions and I don't trust *him. He lies to me, Bob.* He tells me eighty thousand different stories. I can't work like that. But I would love to come back, and so would Frank and Paul."

"I don't think there's the slightest possibility for Frank to come back," Darias said, drawing upon various hints he had picked up during the day. "Frank made a real mess out of the whole thing. He sent that resignation letter and gave everybody ammunition to shoot him down. Frank has a bunch of enemies in there."

"I know, and we don't like to go against a supervisor. But he pushed us all to the ultimate. To tell you the truth, Bob, I don't know any way that I could go back there."

While everyone awaited Billbrough's decision on the future of Operation Swordfish, Robert Darias did his best to continue presenting a normal face to the targets. He had lunch on Wednesday with Humberto Garcia at the Airport Holiday Inn. Garcia said he had been warned by an officer of the Republic National Bank that Dean International's bank accounts there (actually they were Antonio Uribe's accounts in Dean's name) were "under observation" by the U.S. Government. Darias reassured Garcia. "If the government is examining bank accounts," he said, "it would look first at accounts of corporations with Latin names listed as officers. Dean's top officers are

American." Furthermore, Darias pointed out, Dean didn't make huge cash deposits in Miami banks that would attract attention.

Though Humberto seemed mollified, he said that Antonio Uribe would be more comfortable at another bank. Darias promised to make the change immediately. Humberto said Uribe was ready to move $3 million and might want part of it wired to Switzerland. Humberto also said he hoped soon to be arranging cocaine deliveries personally in thousand-kilogram amounts through Uribe. "If I could bring my business to that level for six months," he said, "I could then retire."

Back at the Dean office Darias telephoned instructions to close the Antonio Uribe accounts at Republic and to open an account at Intercontinental Bank, where Manuel Sanchez now worked. It turned out, however, that Sanchez's boss prohibited large cash accounts. So Darias moved Uribe's account to the Consolidated Bank near the Dean office in Miami Lakes.

Later, Robert spoke to Marlene Navarro. The 90-day certificate of deposit that Luis Fabio Rodriguez had purchased in December was coming due, and Marlene said she would determine whether Rodriguez wanted to renew it.

Sam Billbrough, with the approval of Special Agent-in-Charge Peter Gruden, resolved the management crisis in Operation Swordfish with a tangle of compromises that satisfied no one and, in order to make sense, had to be interpreted on two levels, one that was official, and was announced to the concerned parties, and the other unofficial— whispered only to those with a need to know.

Officially, Tom Clifford remained in charge of Operation Swordfish.

Frank Chellino was withdrawn from the operation and reassigned to the DEA office in Fort Lauderdale.

Paul Sennett was withdrawn from the operation and reassigned to Group Three in Miami.

Carol Cooper was returned to the operation and assigned to continue to play the role of the secretary at Dean International.

Bob Russo would remain with the operation but was withdrawn from Dean International and reassigned to the Phoenix Building.

Robert Darias and Felipe Calderon would continue pursuing their targets as usual.

The new agents, Eddie Hernandez and Nick Zapata, would continue to work undercover at Dean International and their duties would expand as they became more familiar with the operation.

The official resolution of the crisis was communicated to Tom Clifford and the agents on Wednesday, March 24. The outlines of the unofficial resolution took longer to emerge, in part because it was being improvised on a day-to-day basis.

"Oh, God, what a day," Cooper told Darias on the phone that evening. "I got thrown back into the lion's den."

"What happened?"

"I'm coming back to the operation—back into the mess," she said.

"You've got to be kidding," Darias said.

"No, I'm coming back. It was decided this afternoon."

Darias was surprised, and said nothing, as Cooper went on.

"They said they needed either Frank or I there, and because of the *big, big* conflict between Frank and Tom, they felt it would be better to get Frank out and leave me there. Frank is being transferred to Fort Lauderdale. And Paul will be gone from the operation, too, but he'll be around and available if I need him. And I mainly want you to stay on the same course we've always been on, the same routine."

"You realize some things are going to change with me," Darias said.

"As far as your cases are developing?"

"No, there is no problem with my cases."

"I hear there's a problem with Uribe's bank account."

"No, no problem. I took care of it."

"Did anyone go with you on any of this today? I didn't know if you were taking Nick around with you."

"I'm not taking anybody anywhere," Darias said, growing irritated. "I am taking somebody when I am doing something that requires an agent. Otherwise it was understood, and I told Billbrough and I told Tom, and everybody knows, I am going to be handling these people myself."

"Don't read me wrong," Carol said. "You didn't have to take anybody with you. I was just asking."

"Well, I told them that whatever it took to make my clients happy and to bring them in and make good cases, that is what I was going to do. But that any major policy changes that affect my clients, they had to discuss it with me and convince me that was the best way to go. Everybody accepted that, and Billbrough told me that he realized I was right."

"Nothing will happen policy-wise without you being told," Cooper said. "But I still don't want you involved in the internal problems that we have."

"Carol, you cannot keep me out now. I am *in*."

"I'm not trying to keep you out."

"What I am trying to tell you is I am already inside the problem. There is no way—"

"You're not inside all of them yet, Bob. You and I have to stick together on this thing. I can still support you, but I'm gonna end up in run-ins with these folks again, I can see it coming already. I had Billbrough telling me one thing this morning, and less than an hour later Tom's telling me something else. I'm not in charge. Nobody's in charge."

"Tom told everybody that I was completely free to handle my cases my own way, and not to meddle with me," Robert said.

"That's exactly what I want you to do. They're your people and you're gonna handle them the way you feel is best. You know the guidelines, the parameters we have to work in."

"Okay."

Having just gotten used to increased autonomy, Darias was confused again. The resolution of the crisis sounded jerry-built, with lines of authority unclear. As Carol had said, "Nobody's in charge." But it sounded as if he would be working directly with Carol again. At least she was a known quantity—not difficult to work with—and perhaps with the dictatorial Chellino no longer in the operation, she, too, would be permitted more flexibility.

As if certain aspects of the "reorganization" needed underscoring, Paul Sennett called Darias from Carol's town house a few minutes later. "It's been solved," Paul said. "Frank is no longer president. I am no longer around. Carol will be there. I'm gonna be back on the street knockin' off people and doing what I gotta do—put dope dealers in jail."

"But you are going to be here in Miami?" Darias asked.

"I'll be around," Paul said, "and I got one favor to ask of you. I don't know what they told you or if they leveled with you. Carol's going to be back at that operation trying to put this whole thing together. Just don't give her a hard time. I'm going to be around, and if she feels she needs to get some help from me, I'll be around doing what has to be done to help you and to help her. They're putting a lot of weight on Carol. They're going to put a lot of pressure on her. You're going to have to really listen to her. I don't know if you want to or not, but you're going to have to listen to her. She's going to be in touch with Frank and me, and we're going to try to work it out. You can work with Carol. No problem with that. But *no matter who they say is in charge, she's in charge.* You know what I'm saying?"

"I have been given quite a lot of latitude to work with right now," Robert said.

"You've been given a lot."

"I will be bringing in my own people and talking to them myself in the office and more or less calling the shots with my own people."

"I understand that, but remember this: *Listen to Carol.*"

"I don't have any problems with Carol. I never did."

"As long as nobody screws with her, and I know you're not going to do that. I told Tom and I told Russo: They screw with her, I'll get 'em. I'll rip their noses off. They're a little bit scared of me because they know I'll beat the shit out of them."

"I don't think that's going to be the situation," Darias said, recognizing that he had just been threatened.

"I'm going to be there somewhere in the background," Sennett said. "If you have any sort of problem and you can't get Carol or anybody else, you give me a call and I'll be there."

"She has to go in with an open mind, Paul. Please try to tell her."

"Just give her a chance to calm down and get her act together," Paul said. "There's been a lot of pressure the last couple of days."

"I know. She should take a couple of days anyway. I am making notes on everything so I can tell her exactly what is going on."

Darias was even more puzzled after the conversation with Sennett. Although he recognized a threat when he heard one—Paul in effect had threatened to beat up Robert, as well as Clifford and Russo, if they "screwed with" Carol—it was now even less clear who was in charge of Operation Swordfish. *No matter who they say is in charge, she's in charge.* What did that mean? At the beginning of the conversation Paul had said, "I am no longer around." Later he had said, "I'll be around" and "I'm going to be there somewhere in the background" and "She's going to be in touch with Frank and me." What did that mean? Had Sam Billbrough set up a back-channel of communication through which Carol Cooper would report secretly to him, keeping Paul and Frank on call, while Tom Clifford, without knowing it, would be only in titular charge of the operation? Darias sensed that Sennett was in no mood for interpretive questioning, so he didn't press. And the threats were probably just macho blustering, like Clifford's reputed threat to "destroy the careers" of Chellino, Cooper, and Sennett.

Still, the words "solution" and "resolution" did not seem appropriate to describe what had been done to ease the crisis inside the U.S. Government's most ambitious effort to date to penetrate the drug mafia of Latin America.

After taking Laura to the Youth Fair at Tamiami Park, and taking Amelia to dinner in celebration of their wedding anniversary on Saturday, March 27, Robert had another disturbing conversation with Carol—the kind of conversation that two people have when they sense their relationship has changed but they are unsure how.

Carol said that Dean International Investments no longer had an authority structure. "Until they tell me I'm the one to give the orders, or until they tell Eddie he's the one, he's going to do his own thing and I'm going to do my own thing," she said.

Carol was paranoid about whether Eddie Hernandez or Nick Zapata would try to take over the supervision of Robert, the very thing that Tom had threatened on St. Patrick's Day, ten days earlier. Although Carol seemed to think that Robert remained her responsibility, she grilled him on the evolving relationships within the office while she had been away.

"I just want to make sure nobody else there butts into your business," Carol said.

"Don't worry about that."

"Was Nick working with you last week before I came back?"

"Nobody was working with me." Actually, both Eddie and Nick had made overtures to Robert.

"If somebody tries to make a move on you or your people, I'll step on 'em and scrunch 'em right in the ground," Carol said.

"Don't worry about that. They don't want any problems with you, Carol, and Tom knows now he better not touch me either."

Carol said, "I have other avenues that are open to me that I don't even have to go through Tom." Was this the secret back-channel to Billbrough? Robert wondered. "They know Tom and I cannot get along and they know they threw me back into a very bad situation. But I still got Paul there when I need him, and they've got Frank in the background."

Robert said, "We cannot let anybody outside see what we *really* are, *inside.*"

At the end of more than a week embroiled in internal intrigues, Robert found it a relief to get back to the business at hand. He and Marlene Navarro met late Sunday morning for the first time since she had briefed him on the crash of the plane containing a Jader Alvarez money shipment in the mountains near Bogotá a few weeks earlier. They had breakfast at the Neighbors Restaurant just east of the Doral Country Club. Navarro said that Carlos Jader Alvarez had now accumulated enough cash in U.S. currency to negotiate with the kidnappers, and, based on the most recent Dean International price schedule, would resume using Dean to move his money. However, Navarro added, Jader more than ever feared the long reach of U.S. law enforcement agents. He felt his arrest in Bogotá two months earlier had been "set up" by a U.S. drug agent from Mexico who had "dated the sister of one of his girlfriends."

Marlene also told Robert that one of her clients, whom she didn't name, had owned "most" of the record-setting TAMPA cocaine shipment that had been seized three weeks earlier at the Miami airport. Out of caution she had not acknowledged this fact on the telephone to Robert the day after the seizure.

Marlene said she was nervous because she had "a couple of hundred thousand dollars" in safe deposit boxes at various Miami banks that the government might be able to seize if she were ever arrested. What did Robert think about putting the cash in another form or moving it outside of Florida?

"You are a hundred percent right," Robert said. "Give me all that money. I'll either put it in *my* safe deposit boxes, or I'll keep it outside the country until you give me orders of what to do with it."

As for Luis Fabio Rodriguez's $250,000 certificate of deposit that was coming due, Marlene asked Robert to get her a check for the full amount including interest and she would have it hand-carried to Rodriguez in Lima, Peru. However, she said she expected shortly to receive another $500,000 or $600,000 of Luis's money and would want to purchase another 90-day CD.

"I'm going to give you some very big business very soon, if you keep your commission at one point," Marlene said.

"But you have to stop giving me all these stories," Robert replied with a smile.

"I swear I have not been telling you any stories. Money has been very slow and I have had to send all the cash there for the kidnappers, and there wasn't any way I could use you. But from now on we're going to use Panama, CDs, and cashier's checks a lot more. You are the only one I have, or that I want to have. I have confidence in you."

Robert was pleased. In terms of intelligence, the leisurely breakfast was his most fruitful encounter with Marlene Navarro since their rambling conversation on the afternoon in December when she had identified her boss as Carlos Jader Alvarez.

They talked so long that he was late reporting to Carol Cooper. "It took a long time," he said. "This lady talks like there is no tomorrow. I could feel that she's enthusiastic this time."

"I just hope she starts doing it now, Bob," Cooper said. "It's been a long wait."

"I don't think she'll disappear. I don't think I'll have any problem."

"It's been a long time but we've gained a tremendous amount of intelligence," Carol went on. "As a result we've got the thing on her phone [the pen register], and we'll just keep it going. It doesn't take anything to do the other phone thing [the full wiretap]; all we gotta do is plug the thing into the machine. Then we'll wrap right into her. But this whole thing today sounds very, very good."

"Tom told me not to worry," Darias said. "The operation would run for at least another year. With what I had already accomplished, the operation would have no problems, and I would have no problems."

"I really wish he would have told *us* all those wonderful things," Carol said.

The intrigue inside Operation Swordfish thickened on Saturday when Felipe Calderon and Eddie Hernandez told Darias that Tom Clifford had scheduled a meeting of the Dean International staff at his house on Sunday. Robert mentioned the meeting to Carol, only to learn that she had not been invited. Cooper telephoned Clifford to ask about the meeting. He told her it had been canceled. Then he held the meeting anyway, and instructed Darias and Calderon not to tell Cooper. On Monday, Carol asked Felipe whether the meeting had been held. He said no. That evening Robert told her the truth.

Carol was livid. "He flat-out lied to me. He told me there was not going to be a meeting."

"You have got to protect me when I tell you these things," Robert cautioned.

"Just between us, my gut feeling is that Tom does not want me in the operation for very long. He has to put up with me right now because the bosses put me there. But he's trying to push me out, and I'm not gonna let him do it now. I'm not even gonna say anything to Tom. I'll talk to Billbrough about it. Billbrough wants to talk to me anyway. I want to let him know the games that Tom's playing. I wasn't invited, and I made a special phone call to Tom, and he lied to me about it. Tom's gotta realize I'm not that dumb."

Robert had been right about Carol's secret back-channel to Billbrough.

"You can never let them know that I'm telling you these things or we'll both be in big trouble," Robert stressed. "I am allowing them to believe that I have lost confidence in you. I want them to think that. That way, they will tell me everything."

"So you're infiltrating them now, too?" Carol said with a chuckle. "Jeez, you're incredible."

"Carol, we have to protect ourselves."

"Don't worry. I'll protect you. You're a friend, just like Paul and Frank. They have been very, very good friends to me and they won't let anything happen to me. The same with you. As far as I'm concerned, you're a friend, just as they are. I look at you all the same way."

22

OVER THE THREE WEEKS since the abductions of four university students in Bogotá, their families had reported the disappearances to the authorities as well as to hospitals and the morgue. The word spread to human rights groups in the United States and Europe. In London, Amnesty International issued "Urgent Action" bulletins headed "Legal Concern/Fear of Torture."

"Although several witnesses saw Orlando Garcia being taken away in a military van," Amnesty International said, "his detention has not been acknowledged by either the police or military authorities, and attempts to establish his place of detention have been unsuccessful. Although the precise reasons for [the] abduction are not known, it occurred on the same day that the National University was closed indefinitely by the authorities following clashes between students and the police. Amnesty International is concerned that [the students are] being held in unacknowledged detention without charge or trial, and there are fears that [they] may be ill-treated while in detention. Interrogation under torture of political prisoners in Colombia has frequently been reported in recent years."

Amnesty International had a lot of experience with political kidnappings and had no reason to suspect that the most recent detentions were nonpolitical. Instead of being detained in some dark police interrogation chamber, Orlando Garcia and the other three students were being held secretly in a plush six-bedroom house owned by Carlos Jader Alvarez in north Bogotá not far from his home in El Chico Alto. They were being interrogated solely to see if they knew anything about the kidnapping of the Alvarez children. Though some of them did, they refused to talk, even under torture. Showing remarkable discipline instilled by the M-19, they responded to all questions with the ritual answer: "I am a Colombian citizen."

Within weeks, Carlos Jader Alvarez had them killed.

The guerrilla Bernardo Acosta again grew concerned about the security of his hideout in the mountains above Gachalá. Acosta had received word from Bogotá that someone had kidnapped at least two

National University students who were familiar with the kidnapping of the Alvarez children. How could Acosta be sure that the students under detention did not know where the children had been taken? Even though he had moved the children a month earlier from the original shanty to a more remote location, Acosta decided to move them again several miles higher, into even denser jungle, where he and the guards pitched a new camp at the foot of a huge *yomaquin* tree. There they fashioned a lean-to of branches and plastic sheeting. At about 10,000 feet above sea level, the new camp was colder, wetter, and darker than either of the previous two. Acosta had heard nothing in a long time about ransom negotiations with the children's family.

Tom Clifford and Carol Cooper began fighting over a new issue— when to convert the pen register on Marlene Navarro's telephone to a full wiretap, a "Title Three" in federal agents' lexicon.* Cooper, who had been longing for months to listen to Navarro's conversations, wanted to "go up on the wire" as soon as possible. Clifford preferred to wait; the massive commitment of people and resources that a wiretap required would be better used later, he felt, after Operation Swordfish had accumulated additional evidence against Jader Alvarez and Marlene Navarro through other means.

Avoiding the shouting matches that had marked recent days, Cooper and Clifford waged their new war mainly by bureaucratic maneuvering through Sam Billbrough and Pete Gruden. And they fought it in the context of a larger dispute over timing: How long should Operation Swordfish last? Time was an issue because the federal wiretap law prescribed strict limits on the duration of wiretaps. In addition to getting court approval for the initial installation, an investigative agency had to make a formal application to the court every thirty days if it wanted to extend its tap. And within ninety days of the wiretap's termination the law required that the target of the tap be notified of its existence. The ninety-day period could be extended, but only for limited periods and only with the court's explicit permission.

Once the tapping of Navarro's phones began, therefore, an inexorable countdown toward the tap's termination commenced. The DEA would be forced to end Operation Swordfish and arrest Navarro before she was informed of the tap. Carol Cooper's desire to move promptly reflected the attitude of her new back-channel patrons in the bureaucratic caldron, Billbrough and Gruden, who had grown un-

*"Title Three" refers to the title, or section, of the federal law that governs wiretaps, the Omnibus Crime Control Act of 1968.

comfortable with Operation Swordfish and welcomed its termination, especially in the wake of the St. Patrick's Day Massacre and the vicious infighting it had ignited. But Tom Clifford, who had been promised at the outset that Operation Swordfish would last two or three years, was determined to resist any plan that would force the closing of the operation to meet the legally mandated schedule of a wiretap that would have been started, in his opinion, too early. Even though Clifford on occasion had considered closing Dean International for security reasons, the recent challenge to his authority had steeled his commitment to a fully realized operation.

Despite Clifford's protests, Billbrough instructed Carol Cooper to draft an affidavit for the federal court in support of a wiretap application. When Clifford learned of the order, he told Cooper to "hold off." Billbrough told her privately to proceed anyway. She began making notes for the affidavit at home.

Vice President George Bush toured a captured drug boat in Miami Beach in late March and promised that the federal government would use everything from Treasury Department accountants to army helicopter gunships to stop the drug traffic.

"It's good to be back in a community that one day will be known as America's comeback city," Bush said. "I know that's going to happen and I'm determined to work with all of you to be sure it happens."

The official in charge of the vice president's narcotics task force, which had been created two months earlier to coordinate law enforcement efforts in South Florida, declared victory in the initial phase of the effort to slow drug smuggling. "There's a little bit coming in, but compared to the flow we faced a while back, it's down to a trickle," said Admiral Daniel Murphy, the vice president's chief of staff.

"It's going to be a long haul," Murphy cautioned. "It's not a problem you can solve overnight."

Like so many public officials before him, Murphy was engaging in wishful thinking. The Bush task force, in fact, had had little effect. The various agencies supposedly being coordinated were still going their own ways. Life at the DEA had changed very little.

Marlene Navarro called Robert Darias to her house on Friday morning, April 2, to "pick up some papers." For the first time Special Agent Eddie Hernandez accompanied Darias to Costa del Sol. Marlene's "papers" turned out to be $100,000 in a plastic bag, which she asked Robert to deposit in one of Dean International's local bank accounts until she gave Dean some additional money within a few days.

"Collections are going to start now, and I will be giving them to you," she said. It was her first deposit with Dean International since December. Marlene walked Robert to his car, and he introduced Eddie Hernandez as his bodyguard, a stretch of plausibility since Robert was a powerful six-footer and Hernandez was only five-four.

By accompanying Darias to Navarro's house, Hernandez felt he finally had breached the wall that Carol Cooper had erected around Darias. On Wednesday, April 7, however, Cooper reasserted her proprietary claim to the star spy. For the first time Cooper herself went with Darias to Costa del Sol when Marlene summoned him to pick up a "fairly large quantity of paper." Carol stayed in the car.

Inside the house, Marlene pulled a brown leather traveling bag from a closet and asked Robert to keep the contents—an uncounted amount of cash—for her at the Dean office until she gave him further instructions. As Robert was leaving, Marlene warned him, "Be careful in restaurants, Roberto. Many of the *federales* in town have covers like waiters, waitresses, and bartenders, who can listen to you during a meal."

"You should talk only to people you know," Robert said.

"You and Lester are the only ones who know what I am doing," she said, referring to her lawyer, Lester Rogers.

Navarro did not follow Darias to his car, so Carol Cooper in her role as Carol Collins, Dean's secretary, could not yet claim she had actually met Marlene Navarro.

In anticipation of flying to Toronto for the weekend, Marlene spent the next morning at her hairdresser, the Avant-Garde salon on Ponce de León Boulevard in Coral Gables. She was off to visit her new boyfriend, Scottish engineer Alexander McIntosh, whom she had met over New Year's at a resort in the Dominican Republic.

Marlene telephoned Darias from the Avant-Garde and asked him to meet her at the Brickell Avenue branch of the Bank of Miami at twelve-thirty, and to bring $70,000 in cash with him. When Darias arrived, again accompanied by Carol Cooper, Marlene got out of her Mustang and into the backseat of Darias's Cadillac. She was carrying a plastic bag containing about $20,000. Darias introduced Cooper as "my secretary, Carol." Marlene asked him to drive her to the Seybold Building, one of the older office buildings in the heart of downtown Miami several blocks away. Cooper handed Navarro the leather bag containing $70,000, which Navarro proceeded to count on her lap as they moved through the traffic. Chatting amiably as she consolidated the currency in the leather bag, Marlene said she was going to purchase a $90,000 diamond ring "for my boss in Bogotá" from a jeweler in the Seybold Building.

Darias and Cooper waited for Navarro for nearly an hour, then drove her back to her car. In English, Marlene told Robert and Carol that she was flying to Toronto that evening, would be back in Miami on Monday, and would fly to Bogotá the following weekend. She also said she had just bought a new BMW. In Spanish, Marlene told Robert that her money courier in Los Angeles had been shot in the head and killed the night before and that another courier was bringing $500,000 to Miami. Marlene said she would receive the money Monday or Tuesday and would turn it over to Robert for wiring to Panama.

On their way back to Dean International, Robert translated the Spanish for Carol. Both were pleased with the encounter. Carol and Marlene had hit it off. And Carol had proven to Robert's satisfaction that even though she was a blue-eyed blonde from rural Illinois she was competent to perform her undercover role credibly in the presence of the sophisticated and wary Marlene.

"I wish she lived in a place where we could watch her a little bit, see what she actually is doing," Carol said. "We can't get near her in that Costa del Sol unless she tells the guard to let us in."

Late that afternoon, Tom Clifford summoned Carol Cooper to his office at the DEA and fired her—again—as Robert Darias's control agent. He also relieved her of any further duties onsite at Dean International. The firing, which was phrased as a "reassignment," was civil and quiet. Clifford was polite. Cooper said little; she was stunned, having had no warning through her back-channel to higher management. Clifford told Cooper she was being placed in a new "financial investigations group" under his supervision in the Phoenix Building, where she would be expected to collate intelligence on Marlene Navarro and begin preparing the requisite paperwork for the wiretap on Navarro's telephone (the paperwork he had told her a few days earlier to "hold off on"). Clifford explained that Operation Swordfish was being reorganized into an "all-Latin" enterprise. Eddie Hernandez or Nick Zapata would accompany Robert Darias and Felipe Calderon anywhere that an agent's presence was required and would prepare the requisite written statements documenting their activities. The only non-Latin assigned to the Dean site would be Clifford's assistant, a senior DEA agent new to Operation Swordfish named Dan Hoerner, who was being placed in overall charge of day-to-day activities at Dean. Unlike Frank Chellino, Hoerner would not have an undercover name or any significant role outside the Dean offices. Whenever criminal targets visited the offices, Hoerner would conceal himself in the storage room and operate the video cameras.

Clifford did not delineate for Cooper the real reasons for her reassignment. He did not remind her that he was implementing precisely what he had threatened less than a month earlier—on St. Patrick's Day evening at the Le Sabre Club. Nor did Clifford tell Cooper he felt her continued carping was fouling the atmosphere at Dean International.

Darias, who was at home, groggy from Sinutab, was one of the first people Carol called.

"I'm out of there."

"Out of where?"

"The operation. I'm back in the main office. I report there tomorrow morning."

"What happened?"

"Nothing. They just reassigned me."

"You had an argument or something?"

"Nope. Didn't open my mouth."

"You're back in your old group?"

"No, I'm in Tom's group now."

"Then you're still in the operation."

"Yeah, but I won't be there at all. They're making it an entire Latin operation. And a word of warning for you: They're gonna insist that Eddie or Nick be with you at all times. Don't tell them I told you this."

"And they expect to go out and meet with Marlene and talk with Humberto Garcia and all these people?"

"Yeah."

"They are going to have a very short operation. It doesn't matter if it's Latin or Chinese. They don't have anybody there qualified to meet any of my people."

"Well, do what you gotta do. I didn't even have an argument, Bob, and I got kicked out. Just because I got blonde hair and blue eyes."

"I can still talk to you if I want to, right?"

"Sure. I'll be having to keep somewhat in touch with you anyway because of Marlene's thing. We'll be doing the wiretap. I'll still take you out for a drink once in a while, kid."

True to pattern, Carol called Robert again later with Paul Sennett on an extension. Paul had just learned of Carol's firing.

"Boy, I tell you, I don't know how in the hell this is going to end," Robert said.

"You're going to get an ulcer, I'm gonna get an ulcer, and she's going to get an ulcer," Paul said.

Carol said, "I may take tomorrow off. I don't want to be available to anybody."

Paul said, "I know how they feel about me and Frank and what we had to say. But they seem to think they can put Carol on a back burner someplace and let her do all the goddamned work and get all the aggravation and yet not be able to have her hands in anything that you're doing. I told you before, she's the brains behind all the god-damned operation."

"I don't care if they have Chinese agents in there," Robert said. "The moment they mix these agents in, my targets are not going to talk to anybody. If they don't blow the operation, it is going to come to a standstill. Like today, if Carol had mentioned drugs, Marlene would have jumped right out of the car."

"That never even crossed my mind to bring that up," Carol said.

"I know, and that's why I was at ease. It doesn't make any differ-ence if they are Latins or not. It's a question of knowing—"

"When to close your mouth and when to open your mouth," Paul said.

"Humberto will never allow Nick or Eddie into his office, it's as simple as that. Remember he even said at the beginning he thought *I* was DEA. And I had known him thirty years."

Carol said, "I don't know if Gruden and Billbrough know about this. I don't think they know. I think they would have told me them-selves before I found out from Tom. I think they would have prepared me." Carol was still too stunned to call them.

"I think you should take tomorrow off and try to relax," Robert said.

"We just don't want to put you in a bad situation, Bob. All of us consider you a very close friend, and we want you to be aware of that."

"I do, too. I consider you people my best friends."

"We'll still go to the shooting range and we'll still go drinking," Carol said.

"We will let Paul drink two beers, that's all, and that is *after* the shooting," Darias said with a laugh, recalling Paul's drunken evening just before Christmas.

Carol's laughter was hollow. Her second removal from her under-cover role in Operation Swordfish was one of the worst moments of her life. Within a few weeks she was diagnosed as suffering from hypertension.

On Tuesday morning, Marlene Navarro asked Darias to return an additional $90,000 from the deposits she had made with him the previous week. They met at the Pizza Hut on 36th Street near Red Road. Eddie Hernandez, who accompanied Darias and maintained custody of the cash, stayed in the car. "I should receive the five hundred thousand from California tomorrow or Thursday," Marlene said, referring to the courier replacing the one who had been shot. At Robert's signal, Eddie got out and put the $90,000 in the trunk of her Mustang. Robert again referred to Eddie as his bodyguard.

Despite Carol Cooper's summary removal from the loop of authority, Robert reported to her later.

"Who's handling all this now, Bob?"

"Nobody. Bob Russo had forgotten what bank Marlene's money was in. I had to remind him where it had been deposited."

"That's part of the problem. Nobody knows what's going on."

"It's all right. They are following my orders right and left, because none of them knows what to do."

"You got that right."

"Eddie claims the bosses know you were taken off the thing."

"I don't think they do. I'm gonna talk to Mr. Billbrough tomorrow. There's no way I can work with Tom."

"Eddie feels it was a very bad move to take you out of the office."

"Let me tell you, Bob, Eddie is doing me no favors at all. He did Frank no favors before. I don't believe a thing he says. He tells us he stood up for all of us and he didn't. He named every one of us and claimed we were shutting him out of the operation."

"I don't want to introduce anybody else to Marlene," Robert said. "She's going to wonder what in the hell kind of operation I have. I cannot bring anybody to this office now. It looks like hell." The new occupants of Dean International had stopped cleaning the offices. Stale cigarette butts overflowed the ashtrays. The rest rooms looked and smelled like those in dirty gas stations. Nick Zapata and Eddie Hernandez had occupied Frank Chellino's old office, and Chellino, a neat freak, would have been shocked to find it strewn with old newspapers.

"I'm going to ask Billbrough to let me out of Tom's group," Carol said. "If they refuse to do that, I may do something drastic. I don't want to leave you hanging. The whole thing is very confusing."

"The cases are going to suffer."

"I know."

With Cooper's knowledge and approval, Robert called Tom Clifford at home and asked him to reinstate Cooper as his control agent.

"I gotta say no to that, Bob," Clifford said. "Carol has to be pulled out. And this is between you and I. I don't want you to talk to her about it. She is pulling the same crap. She won't help us. I asked her to take Felipe's statements, and she said, 'I'm too busy. Darias keeps me occupied all day. Bob is mine. I control Bob.' "

"She can be a very difficult person, I realize that."

"We've got to have team members. It's gotten to the point where I just can't take it anymore. I tried and tried and tried. I told her, let's forget the past. But she keeps saying, Bob is mine. I control Bob. *I, I, I. My* case. Bullshit! It's no one's personal case."

"Okay. I understand. I get along with Nick and Eddie."

"I'm sorry, Bob. But I've got to cut the cord."

Robert reported to Carol on his talk with Clifford, and she briefed Robert on her meeting with Billbrough and Gruden.

"They were not aware of any of this. And they were surprised. And keep this between you and I because I want to see what Tom tells you."

"Yes."

"They told me they definitely want that wiretap on her. They told Tom that, too, and granted, I am the most logical person to do it. But they have absolutely no intention of pulling me out of the operation."

"How do they feel about me not having anybody to report to?"

"That was one of the main points. I told them I've got Bob out there running around and he's got nobody to talk to or help him. He's been totally taken away from me. And they were surprised at that. I don't know exactly what is going to happen, but they have no intention of pulling me out forever, so I want to see if Tom gives you the indication that I am gone permanently."

"I think he thinks you are."

Although Robert continued to speak to Carol every few days, neither she nor anyone else documented his activities as she once had. Days passed when no one systematically debriefed him or prepared the detailed "confidential informant statements" that Carol had drafted since Robert had joined the operation ten months earlier. The new agents were still too busy learning the basic rudiments of Operation Swordfish to bother with Robert.

On Thursday afternoon, April 15, Robert had a long conversation with Humberto Garcia at Refricenter of Miami. They talked about Antonio Uribe. They talked about other cocaine dealers whose money Garcia wanted Robert to handle. They talked about Garcia's keeping two sets of books to conceal his growing drug activities within the business structure of Refricenter. Darias preserved the entire talk on his concealed tape recorder. But in the chaos of Dean International, the DEA agents lost the cassette.

23

AS MARLENE NAVARRO had grown to trust Robert Darias over the months, she had begun looking to him for small services ranging beyond banking and finance—things that in a traditional Latin society, and even in many segments of America, a female expects of a male, and that affluent people everywhere enlist other people to do for them. When Marlene's home had been burglarized, Robert had purchased burglar alarms and installed them on her windows and doors. When she had wanted a large flashlight to keep in the nightstand next to her bed, he had selected it. When Jader Alvarez had asked her to find him an attaché case and a bulletproof vest, Robert had located and bought them. Marlene always paid Robert in cash, which he turned over to the DEA together with receipts for the purchases.

Now, on Monday, April 19, Marlene wanted a new television set and a videocassette recorder, and Robert and Felipe Calderon were examining various models at a large discount house on Southwest 8th Street. At about twelve-thirty, Marlene beeped Robert and asked him to meet her as soon as possible at the Bank of Miami on Brickell Avenue. Darias called Dean International and got Tom Clifford.

"I am with Felipe and he's the only person I would introduce her to at this point," Robert said. "I want her to realize that there really is a Colombian working in our office."

Clifford said he would have an agent, probably Nick Zapata, observe the meeting from a discreet distance.

At the bank Darias spotted Marlene's black Mustang in the parking lot and pulled in next to it. Leaving Calderon in the car, Darias entered the bank and after a few minutes emerged with Marlene, who was saying that she had finally convinced Jader Alvarez to allow her to make full use of Dean International.

Opening her trunk, she pointed to a large blue suitcase. "There is a million dollars," she said.

Robert hefted the suitcase into his trunk. Then he copied the deposit instructions from Marlene's notebook—First InterAmericas Bank, Panama City, and an account number. He introduced Marlene to Calderon, who had gotten out and opened her car door for her, and she drove away. As Robert and Felipe were leaving, Felipe said, "That woman looks at you like you were her father or something."

When they arrived at Dean International, Darias and Calderon learned that, contrary to Tom Clifford's instructions, no DEA agent had witnessed the meeting with Navarro. Nick Zapata by mistake had been sent to 1000 Biscayne instead of 1000 Brickell and had not checked the address before leaving. It was another indication that the careful management practices of Carol Cooper and Frank Chellino were no longer governing Operation Swordfish.

Although Nick Zapata said little, he was enraged by the error, which he blamed on Darias. Zapata confided later to Eddie Hernandez that he no longer trusted Robert.

After stacking the huge quantity of currency on the oval table in the conference room, the men of Dean International Investments stared at the cash as if it were a slumbering beast of uncertain disposition. No one present—Russo, Zapata, Calderon, Darias, and the new supervisor of the undercover site, Dan Hoerner—had ever seen so much money. It was the largest deposit of narcotics proceeds yet received at Dean International by a factor of more than two, and again the absence of Chellino and Cooper was evident. No one took charge.

Supervisor Hoerner, a quiet agent known as "Gentleman Dan," had never processed a currency delivery before. Nick Zapata was still new and felt insecure, especially about complicated paperwork, which was not his forte. Bob Russo was reluctant to assert himself since he recently had been reprimanded for taking too much authority. Felipe Calderon was unfamiliar with the Marlene Navarro investigation. That left Robert Darias in de facto control of the money, and the irony amused him. Here was the elite DEA with its corps of highly trained special agents and supervisors, each of them bonded, background-checked, security-checked, credit-checked, and in some cases polygraphed to verify their honesty and pristine reputation. And who did the agency have in charge of counting, packaging, transporting, depositing, and wire-transferring one million dollars of fresh and instantly negotiable U.S. currency? A man who had been prosecuted for felony grand theft and had done time for lying on an income tax return. If Marlene Navarro and Carlos Jader Alvarez ever went to trial and their lawyers learned of this episode, they would charge that it constituted a flagrant breach of security, reflecting a broad breakdown in the control of Operation Swordfish, tainting the entire operation. If a judge agreed, the prosecution could be jeopardized.

Darias first organized the laborious task of counting the money. About a third of it appeared to be hundred-dollar bills, the rest twenties, tens, and fives. There was a small quantity of Canadian currency. The processing was complicated by the presence on the conference table of $85,000 that Navarro had given Darias a few days earlier, and by $66,000 in a grocery bag from Humberto Garcia's client, Antonio Uribe.

Bob Russo could not contain his amusement. "Can you believe the only one who knows what to do with this money is Darias?" Russo said with a sly smile. "When did you pick up this eighty-five thousand, Bob. Was it Friday?"

"It was Saturday," Darias said.

"And where does the money go?"

"To Panama. I have the name and number."

"And how do we transmit it?"

"Well, we deposit it first—"

"Oh, my God!" said Dan Hoerner. "What's going on here? Is *he* the only one who knows what to do?" Everybody laughed, except for Nick Zapata.

At home with Amelia, Darias was exultant over Navarro's million-dollar deposit and its demonstration of his crucial and controlling role in Operation Swordfish.

"Marlene is even bigger than we thought," he said.

"I feel sorry for her," Amelia said. "I feel sorry that a *woman* has to go to jail."

Robert smiled. "You can't compare her to any woman you and I know. She is *unique*. This is a woman who carries millions of dollars in cash all over Miami in the trunk of her car, without a gun. This is a woman who is Latin but who has a Scottish lover who lives in Canada, where she flies on the weekend. This is a woman who never talks about cooking or cleaning house, not only because she has other people clean and cook for her, but because she isn't *interested in* talking about cooking or cleaning house. So you shouldn't feel sorry for her because she is a woman."

"I still feel sorry for her. She seems so nice on the telephone."

"She *is* nice on the telephone. She's nice in person, too. But you shouldn't feel any sorrier for her because she's a woman than you would if she were a man. She can take care of herself better than most men can."

Marlene Navarro's deposit of $1 million with Dean International signaled a sea change in the financial fortunes of the struggling undercover operation. Over the next several days Dean suddenly was swamped with new cash. The Colombian Kids asked Darias to pick up $235,000 in two grocery bags at a guarded apartment complex in southwest Miami. Humberto Garcia had him pick up an additional $265,000 from Antonio Uribe, then another $285,000, and then—in rapid succession—$286,300, $155,000, $687,000, and $400,000.

After five months of tantalizing promises, and a few small deposits, Humberto Garcia and Antonio Uribe had abruptly given Dean International $2.1 million in dirty currency in a few days.

The processing problems which seemed amusing to the Swordfish staff when Marlene Navarro deposited her $1 million turned into a nightmare. The demands of handling and accounting for the new flood of money overwhelmed Dean International and its inexperienced agents. Robert Darias could make sure a deposit went to the correct bank account in Miami, or was wired to the correct account in Panama, via the correct account at the La Salle National in Chicago, or was exchanged for the right amount of pesos in Colombia. But Darias could not take charge of the crucial documentation of money transfers. Only bonded DEA special agents could write the detailed reports, fill out the welter of government forms, and complete the accounting that was required not only to keep track of the money but also to ensure the maintenance of a credible record for purposes of later prosecution of the drug lords in court.

The agents were not up to the task. Eddie Hernandez and Nick Zapata proved especially inept at writing reports. Documentation grew sloppy, some deposits were not properly accounted for, and tensions at Dean International rose, in part because Hernandez and Zapata seemed oblivious to the problem. Managing the onslaught of cash was not their priority. They were intent instead on gaining control of the *source* of the new money, Robert Darias.

Zapata and Hernandez knew what all agents knew—that an extraordinary spy could make his control agent's career. They viewed the Jader Alvarez–Marlene Navarro investigation in the hands of Darias as a "career case," and with Carol Cooper out of the way they were determined to take control. Tom Clifford, after all, had instructed them to. "I'm gonna get my hands on this boy," Zapata told Hernandez. *"This is it!"*

But Darias would have no part of Zapata and Hernandez. He had vowed privately to Carol Cooper that he would never allow them entrée to his relationship with his targets. And by late April Darias was having to face them down.

"You can start introducing Eddie and me to these people and we can take over," Zapata told Darias one day.

"Don't start giving me that bullshit because that's not going to work with me," Darias retorted. "You do that with Felipe if you want, but I handle my people."

"I know, but what if you get sick?" Zapata asked.

"I'm not going to get sick. If I do, we'll handle it. You have been here just a couple of weeks. I have been trying for a year to get Marlene to bring me a million. Nobody is going to jeopardize that."

"But we have to be in with these people, too," Hernandez said. "Otherwise, it's just your word."

Darias got even angrier. "You think my word is meaningless? If the government can use people like Johnny Crump,* I am Mr. Clean compared to those guys. Plus the fact that we have all kinds of evidence against these targets, in addition to my word."

There was intra-ethnic tension, too. Nick Zapata accused Darias of being prejudiced against Mexicans. Robert laughed. "Let me tell you, Nick, I personally don't have anything against Mexicans but apparently other people around here do," Darias said, a reference to strains that were evident between Zapata and Felipe Calderon, and to perjorative comments made about Zapata's Mexican heritage by several Colombian and Cuban clients of Dean International.

Tom Clifford's "Latinization" of Operation Swordfish was, in fact, being undermined within weeks of its implementation by a deep fallacy in Clifford's thinking. He had been wrong to suppose that *just any* Latin could supervise another Latin more effectively than *any* gringo could. The Latins were no more interchangeable than the gringos. And Clifford had failed to consider or even notice the grain of truth in certain broad stereotypes of the Latin nationalities. Colombians (the sons and daughters of "The Athens of the Andes") generally considered themselves superior in breeding, culture, and intellect to Cubans, who in turn considered themselves superior to Puerto Ricans, who were considered by other Latin nationalities to be imitation Latins because their country is a territory of the United States. And Colombians, Cubans, and Puerto Ricans generally felt superior to Mexicans. "Don't do a Mexican on me" was a common Colombian admonition not to "do me wrong."

---

*Johnny Crump (see page 18) had accepted a reduced sentence and entered the Federal Witness Security Program in exchange for telling the DEA what he knew about drug trafficking by officials of the government of Cuba.

Apart from failing to grasp those broad shadings, Clifford also had failed to discern the stark differences and potential conflicts among the particular Latins he had placed in Operation Swordfish. Robert Darias, the dynamic, outgoing, streetwise Cuban; Felipe Calderon, the reserved, aristocratic Colombian banker, a member of Bogotá high society; Eddie Hernandez, the exuberant rookie DEA agent and former shoeshine boy off the streets of San Juan and the Bronx; and Nick Zapata, the blunt, rough-and-tumble ex-CIA close-combat instructor from the hardscrabble Mexican ghetto of San Antonio.

The Spanish language was perhaps the only thing the four had in common. Eddie Hernandez and Nick Zapata would have found it difficult to supervise Robert Darias and Felipe Calderon under the most benign of circumstances. But there was a more compelling reason why Darias, at least, was not about to submit to Hernandez and Zapata. After nearly a year of exacting work, Darias considered his targets *his*. He felt the same pride of ownership in Marlene Navarro as Carol Cooper still felt in him.

Tom Clifford remained oblivious. He was back at the Phoenix Building proclaiming his "all-Latin" plan a success. Under pressure from his superiors, Clifford had been desperate for results, and now he had them. Look at the flood of deposits from Marlene Navarro, Humberto Garcia, and others since the gringos were banished, he was saying, failing to grasp that the money was flowing not because of the new Latins in the operation, but because of the year of patient nurturing of the targets by Robert Darias and those very gringos Clifford had banished.

Carol Cooper and Frank Chellino, though they were pleased for Darias, were devastated and furious at the award of credit to people who were not responsible.

"I owe you a party," Cooper told Darias, when he called to brief her. "Keep it quiet, though. I'm not gonna invite everybody."

The anxiety over security that the DEA had felt since Dean International had received the threatening telegram in January finally was relieved. On Wednesday, April 28, the company that had been known for more than a year as Dean International Investments at the Windmill Gate shopping plaza in Miami Lakes disappeared. It was reconstituted as International Investments about a mile east, near the next exit from the Palmetto Expressway at the Central Bank Plaza, a shopping center on Red Road near the Opa-Locka Airport. Central Bank Plaza was newer than Windmill Gate—there were no trees and little landscaping. But the new suite of offices was larger—seven rooms instead of six. And it had an enclosed garage at the back where clients could unload their wares without being seen by neighbors and casual onlookers. The removal of "Dean" from the company's name was apt. At Tom Clifford's instruction, the name Frank Dean had been expunged from virtually all documents associated with the undercover business.

Early the evening of Friday, April 30, Robert Darias went to Costa del Sol to connect Marlene's new television set and VCR. For the first time he met her new boyfriend, Alexander McIntosh.

"Robert is the only real gentleman I know," she told Alex with a laugh. Alex and Robert shared a bottle of beer. Alex was a husky man in his early thirties with sandy hair, a heavy Scottish accent, and a stream of jokes and quips that Marlene found hilarious.

Crouched among the wires in her bedroom, Robert noticed a few pornographic movies among the films she had rented for the weekend.

Pepe Cabrera and Luis Fabio Rodriguez were trying to help their friend Jader Alvarez negotiate with the kidnappers of his children. The three men were continuing to pool large amounts of U.S. currency from narcotics sales in North America in anticipation of a ransom payment. On Sunday, May 2, Cabrera and Rodriguez flew $1 million cash in a DC-3 to a scheduled rendezvous in La Guajira, the northeasternmost province of Colombia, a desolate peninsula jutting into the Caribbean just west of Curaçao and Aruba. Landing at a supposedly clandestine airstrip, they found no kidnappers. But a police patrol detained them and seized the money. It took a few days and 12 million pesos (about $200,000 U.S.) for their organizations to gain their release.

Gregory English, the legal adviser from Washington who had devoted seven months to Operation Swordfish, and whom the Swordfish agents had last seen when he bought them drinks on St. Patrick's Day, was suddenly reassigned by the Department of Justice to prosecute an organized crime case in Cleveland. The move was unrelated to the chaos at the DEA in Miami. It was the sort of cavalier, wasteful move of which the federal bureaucracy occasionally was capable. Never mind the accumulation of work that English had committed to Operation Swordfish. The Justice Department, in its dubious wisdom, needed him in Cleveland, and English had been a circuit-riding prosecutor long enough to accept the decision with equanimity.

Operation Swordfish now came under the jurisdiction of the United States Attorney in Miami. The U.S. Attorney's office had been transformed in the early months of 1982. The Reagan Justice Department had finally gotten around to replacing a Carter administration holdover with Stanley Marcus, a dynamic, thirty-six-year-old career prosecutor who had just concluded four years as head of the Justice Department's Organized Crime Strike Force in Detroit. A native of New York and a Phi Beta Kappa graduate of the Harvard Law School, Marcus moved aggressively to expand the understaffed federal prosecutor's office in Miami with experienced attorneys from outside Florida, many of them veterans of complex cases in the large cities of the Northeast and Midwest.

Bolstered by new funds from Washington, Marcus seized control of a number of major Miami investigations from a beleaguered Justice Department bureaucracy stretched thin by the burgeoning drug crisis. Operation Swordfish was the largest and most important of the undercover investigations that had been initiated in Miami over the past several months, and to supervise it Marcus appointed Michael Pasano, a thirty-two-year-old honors graduate of the Yale Law School who had just arrived in Miami from four years as a federal prosecutor in Washington, D.C. Pasano was briefed by Tom Clifford and then conferred with Carol Cooper on Wednesday, May 12.

Pasano's first challenge was dealing with the war raging between the two factions of DEA agents. He felt as if he had been put in charge not of one operation but two, with conflicting goals and philosophies, and conflicting bureaucratic power centers, maneuvering to undermine each other. Tom Clifford wanted to delay tapping the telephones of Marlene Navarro. Carol Cooper wanted the wiretap as soon as possible. Clifford wanted an all-Latin operation. Cooper contended that the only criterion should be competence for the task at hand—infiltrating the South American drug mafia. Pasano sensed that the conflict between Cooper and Clifford transcended disputes over policy. Although he didn't learn the full details of their estrangement for some time, it was evident that they hated each other and were rooting for each other to fail. They agreed on only one issue: the key to Operation Swordfish was a spy named Robert Darias. Without him, there would be no operation. With him, they had a shot at infiltrating the organizations of Carlos Jader Alvarez and José Antonio Cabrera, two of the most important of the South American godfathers.

Darias saw less of Carol Cooper, but they still conferred by telephone in the evening. Cooper was at home working on the affidavit supporting the Navarro wiretap. Although Tom Clifford did not like his people to work at home—he believed in the camaraderie of an office—he allowed Cooper to go her own way for the moment because he did not want to be blamed for aggravating her high blood pressure. The investigation of Marlene Navarro was the only thing Cooper had salvaged for herself from Operation Swordfish, and Carol clung to Marlene as her personal crusade. An extremely hard worker and an optimistic person by nature, Carol hurled herself into the task at hand, and Robert could hear the excitement in her voice as she monitored the pen register and analyzed the growing body of intelligence on Navarro.

"There is no doubt in my mind, Bob, that you're ranking very, very high in Marlene's structure right now," Carol told him. "Like when she comes back from these trips, she'll call Jader on the first or second phone call. Then you're either her third or fourth phone call. Every single time you're right up there."

"Keep in mind," Darias said, "that with Marlene I can make her say whatever we need her to say."

"I know that, and I have every intention of telling you when we are on line."

"There are ways that I can steer the conversation into any areas that you want me to."

"If we know something that she's doing, I might be able to give you some insight and you can think about how you might want to steer her one way or another."

Other patterns were emerging from Cooper's analysis of the pen register data. Navarro spoke frequently by phone with several Miami attorneys in addition to her primary lawyer, Lester Rogers. "A whole lot of attorneys—I got attorneys coming out my ears," Cooper told Darias. "Normally we can't tape attorneys. You have to turn the machine off then. It's like a personal relationship, like if she's calling her husband. But I'm flat out gonna tell them, hey, these attorneys are involved in these deals. I don't care if she calls an attorney or not, I'm going to listen to it. Especially Lester. And I definitely got another attorney connected with the Cabrera thing. That attorney was her first phone call the morning you got the million. And in addition to attorneys, we've got all the people she's talking to identified now. I believe they're going to come over that telephone with drug conversations. I must have twenty-five names of people she's actually talking to that I think are involved in it."

"Oh, my God," Darias exclaimed. It was the DEA's hope, of course, to eviscerate the Carlos Jader Alvarez organization by building a case not only against Marlene Navarro and Alvarez but also as many of their associates as possible.

"I know, it's incredible," Carol continued. "We also now have the structure behind Jader Alvarez. We know who the stuff's coming from to get to him."

"From Peru."

"We don't know who in Bolivia and Peru yet, but we know who it goes to in Colombia." The DEA considered the implicating of people in Bolivia and Peru critical to dismantling the entire syndicate.

"She's still calling Peru?"

"Oh, yeah."

"Well, Luis Fabio is there."

"There are major, major people involved in it down in Bolivia and Peru." Cooper was still reluctant to give Darias names he had not yet heard from Navarro.

One of the attorneys "coming out of Cooper's ears" was Sherwin David Jaffe, or S. David Jaffe, as he preferred to be called. A thirty-seven-year-old Chicago native, Jaffe had an office on Biscayne Boulevard and lived in a luxury condominium on the inland waterway in the most exclusive section of North Miami Beach. The Navarro pen register had picked up a number of recent calls to Jaffe's law office. Separately, Jaffe's name had surfaced on the wiretap in Bogotá on the telephone of José Antonio Cabrera, in a veiled conversation about the shipment of 600 kilograms of cocaine from Colombia to the U.S. (Navarro had told Darias that the $1 million she deposited with him for wiring to Panama on April 19 was Cabrera's money.)

In the second week of May, Marlene informed Robert that she was supposed to pick up $2 million from David Jaffe's law offices, but a messenger that she had sent ahead to case the place had told her the office was "full of cops." Mystified, she asked Darias to go and determine what was happening.

"Ask for David J. and tell him 'Chiqui' is asking about his welfare," Marlene said. "Chiqui, that's me, that's the code. Say 'Chiqui wants to know if your health is all right.' "

Jaffe's health was fine. The "cops" had been two police officers guarding a witness that Jaffe had been interviewing. As for the money Marlene was to pick up, Jaffe gestured to two suitcases in a corner of his office. The next day Robert called for Marlene around noon at the Avant-Garde hair salon and they drove to Jaffe's office for the money.

"This is the most trustworthy man I know," she said of Robert in introducing him to Jaffe.

The suitcase Jaffe gave them contained only $300,000. He assured Marlene he would have another $1.5 million for her by the end of the week.

"They are the lawyers in charge of collecting money in Los Angeles and everywhere," Marlene told Robert in the car a few minutes later. "They are also in charge of distributing everything [which Robert took to mean cocaine]. David J. is very intelligent—a Jew, after all."

Marlene agreed to accompany Robert to International Investments so that he could process the cash immediately. In the conference room of the new offices on Red Road, Marlene removed $7,000 from the suitcase and put it in her purse, then turned the suitcase over to Bob Russo and Nick Zapata with instructions to wire the money to the same bank account in Panama City where the $1 million of Cabrera's money had been sent two weeks earlier. After Marlene made a few telephone calls, Darias drove her home. But since the videotape cameras had not yet been installed at the new site, the agents had failed to capture Marlene on tape on her first visit to the undercover offices, the breakthrough visit that Tom Clifford had been demanding for so long.

Darias was forced to continue warding off the advances of Nick Zapata and Eddie Hernandez, and Robert finally complained to the new supervisor, Dan Hoerner.

"I don't have to take all this bullshit from these guys that have no knowledge of how to handle people like this," Darias asserted. "I am in charge of this operation with my people till the end. You blow this operation and each one of you goes to another job. You blow this operation now for *me,* and the government is going to give me a zero. You have come too far with me carrying the ball to get somebody that doesn't even know how to *play* ball to take the ball from me now. This is going to be my way. I know what my legal limitations are and I abide by them and that's all."

Dan Hoerner listened and sympathized. In only a few weeks at the undercover site, he had concluded that Hernandez and Zapata were "inappropriate" for Operation Swordfish. "Eddie is very enthusiastic, but he's so naive," Hoerner told Darias. "And Nick just doesn't fit in with the higher echelon of the drug business. He's a rough-and-tumble individual. What you're trying to do here is over their heads."

Tom Clifford talked Gruden and Billbrough into postponing the wiretap—at least from May until June—for a technical but compelling reason. When a law enforcement agency asks a court to approve a wiretap, the request goes to the rotating "duty judge," the judge designated to rule on such things during the month in which the request is made. Once a judge approves a wiretap, he or she continues to supervise it, so the agency must live with that judge's rulings for the duration of the wiretap. The duty judge for May at the Miami federal court was known for being especially strict, and the DEA had been hoping to put the request before a judge whose attitude toward possible extensions of the wiretap would be flexible. Clifford suggested waiting to see who the DEA would draw at the courthouse in June. Gruden and Billbrough reluctantly agreed.

It was just as well. Darias learned that Marlene Navarro wasn't going to be using her phones for a while. She was leaving for two weeks in Europe with her new Scottish boyfriend.

24

RONALD J. CAFFREY, the senior DEA official overseeing Operation Swordfish from Washington, summoned six special agents—three from Miami, and one each from Bogotá, Los Angeles, and New York—to a "working conference" at headquarters on the burgeoning dimensions of Swordfish.

Caffrey called the meeting to "raise the agents' consciousness" as the operation entered its next, critical phase—the wiretap on Marlene Navarro's telephones. The six agents together held virtually all of the U.S. Government's meager knowledge of the Latin drug mafia's financial networks. Caffrey wanted the agents to share their information about the Swordfish targets, so that reactions to any revelations on the wiretap could be swift.

Carol Cooper flew up from Miami, as did Special Agents Peter Nies and David Wilson, who had arrested the master money mover Isaac Kattan in early 1981. The Kattan investigation and others had made Wilson and Nies familiar with Swordfish targets such as Carlos Jader Alvarez and José Antonio Cabrera, and Wilson was known for his "computerlike" retention of information. From Bogotá came Special Agent Michael Kuhlman, who had been conducting part of the Colombian end of the Jader Alvarez investigation, and had shadowed Robert Darias when he flew to Cali to negotiate with Santiago Ocampo the previous year. From Los Angeles came Special Agent Larry Lyons, who was in the midst of an undercover investigation of California-based elements of the Colombian mafia. From New York came Special Agent Art Anderson, an expert on the vast Colombian drug and money networks there.

For four days in late May, Ron Caffrey and the agents, as well as several headquarters intelligence analysts and computer experts, sat around a table in a closed conference room sharing information, opinions, and analysis of their targets. They were joined for part of the meeting by the U.S. ambassador to Colombia and by the second-in-command of the DEA, John C. Lawn.

The headquarters intelligence analysts presented a specially prepared twenty-eight-page classified memorandum entitled *Major Co-*

caine Violators—United States and South America, which contained
the agency's latest intelligence data on the twenty individuals whom
the DEA considered the most important and powerful godfathers
(and one godmother) of the Latin American drug mafia. In addition
to Carlos Jader Alvarez and José Antonio "Pepe" Cabrera, the memorandum profiled three men with whom Jader Alvarez had been arrested in Bogotá in 1979: Bernardo Londoño Quintero, Juan Mata
Ballesteros, and José Estupinan.

DEA intelligence believed that Londoño Quintero, who was nicknamed *El Diplomático,* had financed eighty percent of the record-
setting 3,906 pounds of cocaine that had been seized two months
earlier at Miami International Airport.

Mata Ballesteros, who had no fewer than thirty-nine aliases and
nicknames, was listed as a "Class I cocaine distributor with a well-
structured organization which has influence and protection by military and government officials in several South American countries."
In addition to being a fugitive from indictments in the United States,
Mata Ballesteros was wanted for murder in Mexico and Honduras,
his native country.

José Estupinan, along with his wife, Cecelia (who was listed separately as one of the DEA's top twenty), had been Carlos Jader Alvarez's principal liaison with Isaac Kattan in Miami and was himself
a major smuggler.

The group of twenty also included Colonel Luis Arce Gomez of
Bolivia, the former interior minister and death-squad commander
who had formed an alliance in Bolivia with Klaus Barbie, the former
Gestapo chief of Lyons, France, to accept bribes in exchange for
protecting drug trafficking between Bolivia and Colombia.

And the roster listed Jaime Murcia, the Jader Alvarez aide who had
jumped bail after being arrested at the Opa-Locka Airport and whose
nephew had been assassinated at the Miami airport in 1980.

A chart fashioned by the DEA analysts grouped Jader Alvarez,
Cabrera, Londono, and Mata Ballesteros as a "consortium" operating at the center of the cocaine industry in Colombia, with José
Estupinan still functioning on their behalf in Miami. The DEA believed that the consortium accounted for a major share—perhaps a
third, perhaps more than half—of all the cocaine imported from
Colombia into the United States.

Carol Cooper was able to inform the Washington group that Marlene Navarro was on the phone regularly to the Bogotá telephones of
two of the four-member consortium, Alvarez and Cabrera, and had
recently been in touch with the Estupinans in Miami, with Jaime

Murcia, and with a large California branch of the Jader Alvarez syndicate.

With Isaac Kattan in prison, it appeared that Navarro was on her way to becoming the U.S.-based chief financial officer for some of the most powerful godfathers of the Latin mafia.

The conferees adjourned invigorated by the knowledge that Operation Swordfish could hardly have set its sights higher.

Having concluded that Robert Darias was the pivotal figure in Operation Swordfish, Michael Pasano, the new prosecutor from the U.S. Attorney's Office, summoned Darias to a get-acquainted meeting the last week of May. Pasano, a compact, energetic, Italianate man with a neat mustache, asked Darias what motivated him to undertake such dangerous work. "You could vanish anytime sitting out there alone at Marlene Navarro's house," Pasano said. Darias replied that in addition to the money he was being paid he wanted "credit and recognition" for having done the work. "Pretty much the same things that motivate you to be a federal prosecutor," Darias told Pasano. Darias made a good impression. Pasano told his associates that Darias was "one of the strongest-minded, most driven people he had ever met— very savvy, very bright, very talented, very productive."

Shortly after she returned from Europe near the end of May, Marlene summoned Robert "urgently" to Costa del Sol to pick up money— $293,130 in plastic bags—which she wanted exchanged for cashier's checks. She asked him to leave immediately because she was expecting other people and she did not want them to see Robert. But they were arriving as he left and he caught one of two names, "Oscar."

Dan Hoerner, whom Robert had alerted after Marlene's call, was waiting in his car on 36th Street two blocks from Costa del Sol, and fell in behind Robert for the drive to International Investments. "It is not possible to conduct surveillance on Navarro's residence due to a security guard at the entrance to her complex requiring a resident to approve all persons entering," Hoerner noted in his report. But with the wiretap approaching, the DEA deemed it important to corroborate Darias's activities with as much surveillance as possible.

After placing Marlene's latest cash in the DEA's non-drug evidence vault overnight, the agents took it to the Federal Reserve, which wired it to the La Salle National Bank in Chicago, which wired it to the International Investments account at the Republic National Bank branch in Hialeah, which issued the cashier's checks. Darias was away for a couple of days, so Felipe Calderon and Eddie Hernandez took the checks to Marlene Navarro. Wearing shorts and a T-shirt, Marlene rode her bicycle the quarter-mile to the Costa del Sol guard gate to meet them. A smiling Eddie Hernandez handed her the envelope containing the checks and remarked that she appeared to have lost a few pounds and looked very attractive. A bit bemused, she made a mental note to tell Darias that his diminutive body guard had made a pass at her.

Carol Cooper returned from Washington ebullient about the imminent wiretap of Marlene Navarro.

"Everybody was very impressed," she told Darias. "They couldn't believe you were getting some of the stuff you were getting. Jader and Cabrera are two of the five major, major people who work together. These principals are super, super big. Luis Fabio is talking to somebody really big in Peru. It's of prime importance that I know as soon as I can if Luis goes back down to Peru. Lima is very, very interested in him because of the people he's talking to down there. They have been trying for years to get these people identified. That may be a major, major link that could go even higher than the five in Colombia. We think we know who it is. All in all it's a massive, massive case, Bob. Everything's resting on this wire to pull in all these people, and Marlene is talking to three of the five."

Marlene and Robert were sipping coffee in her living room on the morning of Friday, June 4, when she quietly asked if he would be interested in purchasing 100 kilograms of cocaine. Before he could answer she went on to explain that it was an excess quantity from a Jader Alvarez shipment that was in Miami and was available immediately. Robert could have it at a reduced price—between $4.5 million and $4.8 million rather than the going wholesale price of $6 million. He could pay a modest amount down—perhaps $500,000—and the rest within a few weeks.

Darias controlled his excitement and wished he had brought his tape recorder. "Of course, I am very interested," he said evenly. "Some of my clients might be interested at such a good price." He asked for further details, and while she spoke he pondered the ramifications of her proposal.

The offer of a multimillion-dollar quantity of cocaine meant that Marlene Navarro was more than Carlos Jader Alvarez's chief financial officer. It was now evident that she also played a controlling role in the sale and distribution of the product itself. Navarro was an even bigger target than the DEA had imagined.

Ordinarily a DEA undercover operative would have leapt at such an offer. Enticing targets into selling drugs, thus facilitating seizures and arrests, was the heart of the DEA's mission. Removing narcotics from circulation was a principal objective, and success led to rewards and promotions for agents and spies faster than any other form of accomplishment. Although there had been a few major seizures of cocaine in recent months, the opportunity to confiscate as much as 100 kilograms was rare.

And yet Robert knew that the main targets of Operation Swordfish were not cocaine shipments, whatever the size, but rather major people and assets. Confiscating a hundred kilograms from the Jader organization at this stage probably would be impossible without disrupting—and indeed ending—Operation Swordfish. The DEA would have to arrest Marlene Navarro at the time of the confiscation, forfeit the wealth of intelligence it believed it was about to obtain from the wiretap, and give up any possibility of arresting and prosecuting Jader Alvarez, Pepe Cabrera, and their high-ranking colleagues. The only alternative to confiscation would be purchasing the cocaine for the asking price to preserve the fiction that Robert Darias and his colleagues were genuine drug financiers. And the U.S. government under no circumstances would agree to part with between $4 million and $5 million in such an effort. Nevertheless, Darias knew there would be controversy over how to respond to Navarro's offer. There would be a reflexive institutional tendency on the part of at least some people in the DEA to want to seize such a large shipment of cocaine, whatever the cost to other objectives.

Darias finished his coffee and told Navarro he would get back to her. He immediately informed his control agents of the offer and found he had guessed correctly. Carol Cooper wanted to reject the cocaine and get on with the wiretap. Tom Clifford wanted to figure out a way to seize the shipment, contending that it would be "unconscionable" to allow 100 kilograms of cocaine onto the streets of the United States if the DEA had an opportunity to seize it. Clifford, who had abandoned a career in psychology because he became too involved personally in his cases, now thought of how many American children might die from Marlene Navarro's hundred kilograms of cocaine. Clifford did not want to end the operation. He suggested it might be possible to concoct a way to seize the cocaine in a manner that would not compromise Darias's undercover role. He suggested they try a "cold hit," wherein the DEA attempts to use intelligence to locate and seize a shipment of drugs either well before, or well after, it is in the possession of the undercover agent. If the agency, for example, could determine that the Navarro shipment would be brought to International Investments in a particular automobile, it might use an unmarked car to cause an accident, let the investigating traffic police discover and seize the drugs, and hope that the drug dealers would not suspect the truth.

That seemed farfetched and foolish to Darias. Siding with Cooper, he persuaded Clifford to hold off. "Tom, another hundred kilograms is going onto the streets whether I take *this* hundred kilograms or not," Darias said during a loud discussion at International Investments. "Every time we launder five million dollars we help them send another *thousand* kilos into this country. I thought your purpose was to get the people and the money, and in *that* way disrupt their ability to bring in the cocaine." Clifford seemed finally to concur but he clearly was troubled by the issue. They agreed that Darias would string Navarro along in hopes of delaying a purchase of cocaine until the end of the operation, when the agents would be ready to arrest the targets in any event.

Darias reported back to Navarro that he was unable to give her an immediate answer. She did not press him because she was about to leave on another jaunt to Europe, this time with her cousin from Bogotá, Carmenza Valenzuela. The two women met at the airport in San Juan, Puerto Rico, settled into the first-class cabin of a Lufthansa 747, and flew to Frankfurt, Germany. Robert was unable to learn the specific reason for the trip. A DEA agent in Germany shadowed Marlene and Carmenza from the moment they arrived on Friday, June 11, and checked into the Inter-Continental Hotel in Frankfurt. They did nothing suspicious. From her room Marlene telephoned Paris, Milan, and Jerusalem. None of the phone numbers showed up in the NADDIS computer. On Sunday, they left for Baden-Baden.

Operation Swordfish had become glamorous. In the cloistered, need-to-know circles of government that were aware of the operation, it gradually had become an object of fancy, of speculation, an enterprise to be watched, envied, and kibitzed. The targets had turned out to be the most significant drug lords of Latin America—rich, violent, ruthless people responsible not only for a major share of the narcotics in the United States but perhaps for a major share of the homicides in South Florida. Having started slowly, the operation now commanded the full attention of the headquarters of the DEA, of intelligence operatives on the Latin American desk at the State Department, and of the American Embassy in Bogotá. The DEA field divisions in Los Angeles and New York, where agents had been tracking leads at the bidding of Miami, were maneuvering for a larger stake so they could claim credit at the end. The drug crime specialists in the FBI, the IRS, and the Customs Service, who had been given minimal liaison briefings to deter inadvertant intrusions from their own investigations, were clamoring for more information.

What those lusting for glory did not know was that internally— inside the offices of International Investments at the Central Bank Plaza, and inside the offices of the DEA Intelligence and Financial Investigations Groups in the Phoenix Building—Operation Swordfish had turned into a monster—huge and belligerent, close to slipping its chains and lurching out of control.

Riven by the plots and counterplots of warring factions, International Investments barely functioned. The offices were in disarray. The new supervisor, Dan Hoerner, seemed unable to gain control. At least one important secret tape recording had been lost. The corporation's principal checkbook had been misplaced for a period of time.

The new agents were making a "fantastic mess" of the recent onslaught of cash deposits, Robert Darias confided to Carol Cooper. Fresh drug currency lay in the safe, sealed in plastic evidence bags but uncounted and unmarked, except for the name "Darias."

Tom Clifford and Dan Hoerner, as well as Darias, were furious at Nick Zapata and Eddie Hernandez for what appeared to be laziness and incompetence. The new agents had become objects of ridicule. Behind their backs they were invariably referred to in tandem: "Nick 'n' Eddie," as if they were a matched set, paired buffoons like Amos 'n' Andy or Cheech 'n' Chong.

For their part, Zapata and Hernandez were mutinous. Having been promised major roles in the operation, they felt they had been relegated to the status of go-fers for Robert Darias and Felipe Calderon, and were furious at Tom Clifford for, as they saw it, welshing on a commitment. Zapata and Hernandez had withdrawn into a sulk, spending hours incommunicado behind the closed door of Frank Chellino's old office.

The new prosecutor, Michael Pasano, who had moved into a large vacant office on the third floor of the Phoenix Building with three other lawyers from the U.S. Attorney's Office, was horrified at the chaos at International Investments. And Pete Gruden and Sam Billbrough, as the responsible DEA executives in Miami, were concerned and fretful, knowing they were not in full control, uncertain how to assert control for fear of further damaging the operation.

Most debilitating of all was the entrenched feud between Tom Clifford and Carol Cooper, which was now taking the form of a vicious struggle over the impending wiretap. Clifford seemed to have lost control of the operation he had founded. He still wanted to postpone the wiretap. What was the hurry? he kept asking anyone who would listen. Once the tap was in, because of the strict legal time limitations on telephone eavesdropping, the life of the operation would be measured in months. The DEA originally had committed itself to a three-year operation, accepting Clifford's contention that it would take time to infiltrate the huge Latin American criminal organizations. Clifford had wanted to induce the traffickers not only to launder their money through Dean International, but to invest it in tangible assets—real estate around South Florida and securities traded on the New York Stock Exchange that the DEA later could seize. That goal seemed to have been lost in the rush to the wiretap.

The tap had distorted the operation, Clifford believed. Although Marlene Navarro was important, having led the DEA to the top of the mafia, she was not the entire operation. Humberto Garcia and his associates in Medellín held the promise of becoming just as significant. And yet Garcia now was being all but ignored (except for occasional contacts by Darias), as were other targets.

And there were additional reasons for waiting. Clifford did not feel that the operation in its current chaotic state could handle the added burden of a wiretap. The tap itself would require the participation—and the importation from other cities—of at least two or three dozen extra DEA agents to monitor telephone conversations around the clock and prepare prompt translations and transcriptions. By Clifford's count, there were already sixty-seven videotapes and about a hundred audiotapes which had accumulated in the first year of Swordfish that had not been translated. Preparations for this huge logistical burden had only begun. And yet his bosses, who had never run a major undercover operation, were pushing him to move quickly. Pete Gruden wanted the wiretap "now." Carol Cooper was pushing even harder. Having been removed from her undercover role, she had lost interest in other facets of the operation. And she had something else in mind as well. Unbeknownst to Clifford, Cooper was maneuvering to wrest control of the wiretap from him.

"Tom doesn't know what I'm doing," Carol told Darias on the phone one night. "I'm doing all sorts of little things behind everyone's back. I'm just manipulating. It's hard for me to tell the front office what Tom's doing because he's my boss, but I can tell you. He does not want the wire in. He has fought me every inch of the way on it."

"But why?"

"I am trying to get it taken away from him."

"Give me one explanation why?"

"Keep all this quiet! I made some major moves yesterday, and I'm probably going to get in a whole lot of trouble for it, but I really don't care. I'm trying to get the wire taken away from Tom! I don't think Tom wants the wire to go in simply because there is going to be a limit on the operation at that point."

"Carol, they haven't touched Humberto's case."

"I'm well aware of that," Carol said.

"They are letting it slip away."

"Tom is all excited about this hundred keys [kilograms]," Carol continued. "And yet you're looking at an entire *organization* here. It's the *organization* I'm after. They could care less if they lose a hundred keys or even six hundred keys. If they lose three million dollars it doesn't phase them. They've had labs seized down in Colombia. Entire labs. Didn't stop them at all. That is the magnitude of this group. I could care less if we get two kilos from this crew at the end. If I get the *people* that's what I want. But if Tom keeps fighting me on this wire I don't know if it's ever going to go. It's absolutely incredible at this point."

"Oh, boy," Robert sighed.

"Tom's the only one who doesn't want this thing to go. Everybody is ready. Headquarters is telling me go. Bogotá is ready to go on line and do their thing. I've got L.A. in a holding pattern. I've got New York in a holding pattern. Everybody is ready to jump. And Tom is asking for it to be postponed again. All he has done is fight me. I'm going to talk to Gruden tomorrow, and I am going to get an answer on this one way or the other. Gruden wants it on today. He wanted it on yesterday. I've got three attorneys from the U.S. Attorney's office in a holding pattern. They're pissed. Tom is fighting it every inch of the way."

"How can Tom go against Gruden?"

"He's doing it behind his back."

"How can he do something behind Gruden's back? Gruden's giving an order."

"Gruden doesn't know what's going on yet. He's going to find out tomorrow morning. If I have to be the one to tell him, I'm going to tell him. Push has come to shove at this point. Like Paul says, 'What is the worst they can do to you, transfer you to Miami?' "

Carol speculated that it was Tom rather than Nick and Eddie who was delaying their written reports so as to delay the wiretap. "I can't update the wiretap affidavit until I get the reports. Tom will not make those guys write the reports. We're two months behind. I have not seen one report since I've left. Not one."

"I know this case is going to be huge," Darias said.

"If I can get it to go," Carol said. "But if Tom keeps fighting me on this wire, I don't know if it's ever going to go. It's absolutely incredible at this point. The attorneys are beginning to wonder who's in control. I think they know *you* are. There was no doubt in their minds after they met you that you were basically running the operation."

"Did you talk to Gruden?" Robert asked Carol the next day.

"Yeah, yeah. Don't let anybody know that. I was specifically instructed not to tell you when it's going on (the wire). Tom doesn't know I went and talked to Gruden. He knows nothing about what I'm doing. Tom has stopped speaking to me. There's all sorts of moves afoot that he doesn't know about. Keep it under your hat, but I think Paul's going to be working on the wire with me."

Actually, Peter Gruden had decreed that day that the wire would begin as soon as possible, in late June, or July at the latest. Clifford had wanted it delayed until at least August.

It was clear to Robert that Carol was feeling her oats. Her secret back-channel to Gruden and Billbrough had born fruit. She had defeated the founder of Operation Swordfish.

On Friday afternoon, June 11, an exhausted Tom Clifford said to no one in particular, "I've totally lost control of this thing."

He decided to keep a promise to his wife and children and depart on a long-planned camping vacation that would take the Cliffords through several states of the East and Midwest over the next three weeks. Leaving for such a long period was an exceptional step for a DEA supervisor in charge of a big undercover operation that was about to launch a wiretap.

But as far as Tom Clifford was concerned, Carol Cooper could have her "Title Three."

2 5

ALTHOUGH GOVERNMENT AGENCIES and big corporations purport
to welcome employees' complaints, bureaucracy in reality hates
a tattler. The annals of bureaucracy bulge with stories of whistle-
blowers crushed. And if the complainant puts his story in writing the
institutional ire grows. The act of creating a paper record of such
things is considered at least as offensive as the complaint itself. A
typed document, even if handled discreetly, forces action that whis-
pers do not.

On Monday evening, June 14, Operation Swordfish was jolted by
a written assault. Eddie Hernandez and Nick Zapata confronted the
DEA's chain of command with a carefully typed litany of their bitter
complaints against the people in charge of the operation. In a three-
page diatribe on official United States Government Memorandum
sheets, Zapata and Hernandez alleged that "operational problems"
and mishandling of funds were jeopardizing Operation Swordfish,
endangering prosecutions, and posing embarrassment to the DEA.

"We are in a dilemma," the memorandum began.

Under the heading of "operational problems," Hernandez and
Zapata assailed Robert Darias (cited by his number, SG1-81-0020,
not his name) for refusing to involve them in negotiations with his
targets and thus failing to establish what they considered adequate
corroboration of his activities. "In our professional experiences, we
have never encountered any situation whereby a confidential informant has not been able to introduce an agent to a violator within a
one and a half year time frame," they asserted. "Most of the evidence
obtained has been gathered by him without corroboration by anyone.
. . . [He] has always stated that 'this is not the right time,' that he has
to 'gain their confidence,' or that we would not be 'accepted and
trusted' by these people. This has been the same excuse he has been
giving us and other agents since the beginning of the operation. . . .
By failing to facilitate corroboration, he may hinder the successful
prosecution of high echelon violators and the seizure of valuable
properties owned by these violators."

Hernandez and Zapata also noted that International Investments was using some of the commissions it had generated in "laundering narco dollars" to defray some of the expenses of the operation such as rent and travel. "It is our understanding that any commission fees received are considered evidence and should not be tampered with in any way, shape, form, or manner. If we are right, this could jeopardize the whole operation. . . . If we are wrong, we would like to have something in writing . . . informing us that this is legal. . . ."

The two agents demanded that the DEA "control and direct the informants to involve us in all phases of undercover meetings and narco dollar transactions. . . . The informants should be made aware that operational decisions should be made by Swordfish agents and not by them."

With Tom Clifford conveniently away for vacation, Hernandez and Zapata presented the memo to Dan Hoerner and left copies at Gruden and Billbrough's offices. The normally mild "Gentleman Dan" erupted in anger, loudly accusing Zapata and Hernandez of making false charges, and also of "cowardice," in avoiding a direct confrontation with Clifford.

"I can't believe you've said all this," Hoerner railed.

Although the memorandum was handled discreetly, the document's general contents hit the Phoenix Building grapevine by the next day. And the grapevine also picked up an explosive rumor not contained in the memo but also attributed to Nick Zapata and Eddie Hernandez.

A great deal of money—perhaps a quarter of a million dollars—was missing from the coffers of Operation Swordfish.

"Eddie follows Nick's leadership," Darias told Cooper and Sennett that evening. Though neither Robert nor the agents had seen the memorandum, they knew its contents from the grapevine. "They made a very big mistake when they let Eddie choose the next guy coming into the office."

"Yeah, they're buddies," Carol said. "They're good friends from way back when."

"Let me tell you, Tom's got a problem on his hands," Robert said. "It's a lot worse than the problems he had with you. Tom cannot go back to Gruden and tell him that he has *another* problem. Because then they are going to fire Tom. He's stuck with these guys."

"I know, he's stuck. There's no way he could change personnel again. There's absolutely no way."

"I don't know who in the hell said that I wanted an all-Latin operation," Robert said, referring to a notion that Clifford had incorrectly attributed to him. "I was very happy the way the operation was."

"That's the excuse Tom's been using."

"If this is the type of Latin they meant, I don't need them. Let me tell you something, Carol, Americans see Latins and they take for granted that they are all the same. Latins have the same problem with English and Americans and Chinese and Japanese. You consider all Latins the same. And yet there's a lot of animosity between Puerto Ricans and Cubans. Not with me, but generally. Puerto Ricans and Cubans. Mexicans and Cubans. Colombians and Mexicans cannot look at each other eye-to-eye, because they hate each other. That's what some people in the front office don't understand."

"Yeah, I know."

"But whatever his nationality, this guy Nick is a total disgrace in the office," Robert continued. "The guy doesn't know how to dress. He doesn't know how to speak English. He doesn't know how to speak Spanish. I don't know where in the hell they found him. He said that he worked for the CIA. I don't know what in the hell he did for the CIA. Nick is the type of guy that cannot keep a conversation or an argument on a gentleman's level. He's all the time talking about how tough he is."

"How much of a problem do you have working with Eddie?"

"Well, the guy is not a bad guy. But he's a big mouth and he tries too hard. When Eddie and Felipe delivered a check to Marlene, and he met her on her bicycle at the guard house, Eddie jumps out of the car, the big Latin lover, the first thing he tells Marlene, hey, you have lost a few pounds, you are looking well. Marlene tells me, that guy is really a Latin lover, he's trying to make a pass at me. You know, I am working with this girl for a year and I have never made a pass at her." Carol and Paul laughed.

"When you people left and I was left alone in there," Robert continued, "I had to create my own little castle and fight everybody from taking over what I had."

"I think they basically resent that," Carol said.

"Beginning with Tom. And Tom was the first one that I took off the walls of my castle. And then they hate my guts because they think that I am just a CI and they are giving me too much leeway."

"That's right," Sennett said. "They do think you're just a CI. But we know exactly what you are and what you do, and we consider you one of us. And no matter what kind of pressure people put on us, and what kind of pressure they put on you, remember to always watch what you do, watch what you say, control yourself. We're all gonna be famous."

"To be honest with you, Bob," Carol said, "I'm gonna try and get you back under my control where I can give you some direction on this thing. I'm trying to do that."

"I hope it happens."

"Keep that up your sleeve, but those moves are in the works right now." Carol added that she also was trying to get Paul back into the operation, and eventually would try to recall Frank Chellino.

Robert said his good-nights. His daughter wanted him to watch Buck Rogers with her on television.

After Dan Hoerner's angry reaction to their memorandum, Hernandez and Zapata demanded an audience with the new prosecutor, Michael Pasano. Although the U.S. Attorney's office had no formal authority over how the DEA managed its affairs, the lawyers did have the power to direct the preparation of cases they would be prosecuting in court. And Pasano knew that if Hernandez and Zapata's allegations were true and ever became known, they could seriously damage the government's case. Attorneys for those indicted could cite the "Nick 'n' Eddie Memo" as an indication that Operation Swordfish had been mismanaged, possibly tainting the evidence gathered and rendering it inadmissable in court.

After hearing the allegations, Pasano called meetings of everyone involved in either handling money at Operation Swordfish or supervising Robert Darias. Those meetings led to more meetings. Efforts to grapple with the "Nick 'n' Eddie Memo" consumed much of the month of June while Clifford was away on vacation, critical weeks when the agents should have been preparing for the wiretap. Pasano took no immediate action on the "missing" $250,000 because Peter Gruden appointed an auditor from the DEA's internal affairs branch to look into the matter. As for the DEA's using commissions that International Investments collected from its targets to defray office expenses, it appeared there was nothing inherently illegal about the practice. Pasano warned Dan Hoerner and Bob Russo, however, that such expenditures must be strictly accounted for, and that cash should not be kept at International Investments for long periods of time.

Michael Pasano was also concerned about the DEA's management of Robert Darias. The allegation that a convicted felon had been running a sensitive undercover operation would look just as bad in front of a jury as the allegation that funds had been mismanaged. Both charges could undermine the credibility of the government's case. Zapata and Hernandez told Pasano flatly that for all practical purposes Operation Swordfish was being run by Darias. However, Dan Hoerner denied that, and assured Pasano that Darias was reporting directly to him in Tom Clifford's absense. Cooper, too, defended Darias's insistence on keeping Hernandez and Zapata away from his targets.

"Bob will do anything to make those the best cases that he can," Cooper told Pasano. "But he will not introduce *those two guys*. It's not that he's trying to be superprotective of his people. He has introduced agents before." Cooper cited instances where Darias had introduced her and Frank Chellino to Marlene Navarro.

After Pasano had conducted his inquiry and issued his warnings, Dan Hoerner found himself relying for advice on the main object of Zapata and Hernandez's scorn—Robert Darias.

"Nick and Eddie don't know anything about business," Darias said. "That is the main problem. Maybe they are very good agents on the street, but they don't realize that this operation cannot be run like a regular drug deal." Robert's remarks echoed comments he'd made several months earlier about Frank Chellino's insufficiently businesslike attitude in the early stages of the operation.

Hoerner agreed. "I cannot work with these guys," he told Darias.

Hoerner tracked Tom Clifford to a campground in the Smoky Mountains of North Carolina and got his reluctant authorization to remove Nick Zapata and Eddie Hernandez from International Investments and put Carol Cooper back in charge of Robert Darias.

Tom Clifford's "all-Latin" concept, along with much of his authority over his operation, lay in ruins.

Marlene Navarro had introduced Robert Darias to three of her aides at her house one day in early June. She had used first names only—Oscar, Ricardo, and Nelson—and indicated obliquely that Oscar would handle the sale of the 100 kilograms of cocaine that she and Robert had discussed.

Oscar called Robert several times while Navarro was in Europe, once at 5:00 A.M., another time at 7:00 A.M. The second time, he told Robert that he had just arrived on the red-eye from Los Angeles and was leaving immediately for New York.

"I wanted to let you know that Lisandro Otero and his Orchestra will be arriving Tuesday, or Wednesday, at the latest," Oscar said.

"Lisandro?"

"Lisandro Otero. And he is bringing his orchestra with him."

"Okay," Darias said. Oscar obviously preferred to speak in code over the phone. Though Robert was unsure what Oscar was referring to, the phrase "Lisandro Otero and his Orchestra are arriving" reminded Carol Cooper of another phrase that Isaac Kattan had used to refer to a coming cocaine delivery. "There's going to be a coronation."

Marlene Navarro flew into Miami from Paris Saturday evening, June 26, after a little more than two weeks in Europe. The DEA had given up tracking her and her cousin Carmenza after they had checked out of the Inter-Continental Hotel in Frankfurt on Saturday, June 12, since Tom Clifford had instructed his people in Europe not to risk being "made," i.e., seen by Navarro under any circumstances.

One of Marlene's first calls on arriving at Costa del Sol was to Darias.

"Have you talked to anyone?" she asked.

"Well, Oscar called me. He said that on Wednesday they are coming with the orchestra, Lisandro Otero and his Orchestra."

"Oh, yes, yes, for the party," Marlene said. Darias inferred she meant a cocaine delivery.

Darias met Navarro and Alexander McIntosh for breakfast at Neighbors on Monday morning. They spoke English for Alex's benefit. Marlene presented Robert with a black and gold S.T. Dupont pen that she had bought for him in Paris. "Everybody uses Cartier here," she said. "The Dupont is not so easily found in Miami."

"Thanks very much," Robert said. "That's beautiful."

"I didn't know what to get you."

"You hit it."

After describing the weather in Europe and the World Cup soccer matches in Barcelona, Marlene said, "Alex, I'm sorry, but I'm going to speak in Spanish."

"Sure."

"So try to learn Spanish, okay?" she said with a laugh.

"I'm just going to eat my eggs."

Even in Spanish Marlene spoke in the codes of the drug trade.

"Are you sure that your friends would be interested in the hundred pairs of shirts monthly?" she asked Robert.

"Sure."

"Because on Friday I'm going to travel over there to the land where my friend is and talk to him, and then you'll talk to him afterward, so that it will be firm," Marlene said. "And your friends would pay me cash."

"Yes, cash," Robert said. "They have a totally responsible person here."

"I am not going to negotiate with them."

"I take responsibility," Robert said.

"It's with you that I'm going to negotiate. You make all the arrangements. The only thing I have to do is that he should pay me. That's generally what I do. I don't see those things—"

"Of course."

From previous conversations Robert knew that a "hundred pairs of shirts" meant a hundred kilograms of cocaine and that her "friend" in "the land where my friend is" meant Jader Alvarez in Colombia. He also caught her allusion to his meeting with Jader ("and then you'll talk to him afterward, so that it will be firm") to conclude their deal. The DEA was eager for Darias to meet Jader Alvarez, preferably in a "neutral" country where it might have an opportunity to arrest him.

Marlene then told Robert that a man in Miami who owed Jader Alvarez over a million dollars had signed over three plots of South Florida real estate as a downpayment on the debt. "The guy called me almost crying," she said. " 'Marlene, I've had a bankruptcy. I don't want to make a bad impression on Carlos. I'm afraid.' " Jader had assigned Navarro to inspect the property and advise him what to do with it. There was a house in Coral Gables, a plot of land in the Falls, and a twenty-six percent interest in a development in Kendall, "The Valleys of Kendall," where forty-two homes were under construction. The Falls and Kendall were communities on the south side of Miami.

Robert agreed to accompany Marlene to look at the property and help her decide how to handle it.

"Everything is under my name, but I put Lester down as a trustee," she said, referring to her lawyer Lester Rogers.

Unnoticed by Marlene, Robert, or Alex McIntosh, DEA Special Agents David Wilson and Peter Nies sipped coffee at a nearby table. Carol Cooper had sent them to the restaurant to see what Marlene looked like. They and other agents would be observing her much more closely in the weeks to come. Physical surveillance was a crucial accompaniment to tapping a telephone, which was only days away.

2 6

A TALL, KOJAK-BALD man with a handlebar mustache and a slender, well-groomed woman with reddish brown hair sipped coffee in a booth at Denny's on Ludlam Road in Miami Lakes and talked of compromising Operation Swordfish.

The man had "real important" information to sell. The woman was buying. The price was very high.

The man was Brooks Muse III, a construction company executive and deep-sea fisherman, who lived in Miami Lakes. The woman was Barbara Mouzin, who also lived in Miami Lakes and was a narcotics dealer and money manager for a California branch of the Colombian drug syndicates. Muse and Mouzin were friends and former lovers. They had met a few years earlier at Le Sabre, the wood-paneled bar on Miami Lakes Drive where the undercover agents of Operation Swordfish frequently drank after hours.

Brooks Muse, a Miami native who spoke in a soft southern accent, was known around the west side of Miami as a "DEA groupie." In the course of his business, Muse had leased a number of buildings to the Miami DEA field office. He had gotten to know a lot of DEA agents. He loved to sit around the bars west of the airport in the vicinity of the Phoenix Building hearing their war stories.

Unbeknownst to most of his DEA friends, Muse also was close to the other side of the drug wars. He enjoyed the netherworld of smugglers, money movers, bail bondsmen, private detectives, airline stewardesses, and low-rent attorneys, who hung around some of the same bars.

In the spring of 1982, Brooks Muse heard rumors about Operation Swordfish. He did not hear the names Swordfish or Dean International Investments. But he did hear rumblings about a "very heavy federal undercover investigation" of high-level narcotics dealing and money-laundering. And he heard that the investigation was centered in Miami Lakes.

To almost anyone, the talk would have made intriguing bar gossip. To Brooks Muse, it was talk which he believed to be true and was in a position to verify. He saw it also as a chance to make a lot of money.

One of Muse's closest DEA drinking buddies was Special Agent Steven Gibbs of Group Four. After eleven years in the DEA, Gibbs was mentally exhausted. In the course of extended undercover work the bearded agent had begun drinking heavily, and was up to a fifth of Scotch a day, most of it consumed in the same bars where Muse hung out. Gibbs had confided to Muse that he was "disillusioned" because "the very people we work against—these rich drug smugglers—are the ones who have everything in life."

Brooks Muse knew that Steve Gibbs had access to the NADDIS computer, the repository of highly classified information on DEA targets worldwide. On occasion Muse had suggested to Gibbs that NADDIS information might bring a high price if sold to the right outsiders. In May 1982, Muse confided that he would pay money to Gibbs "just to check a name occasionally" in the computer. At first Gibbs declined. Then he changed his mind.

In the booth at Denny's on the evening of Thursday, June 17, Brooks Muse asked Barbara Mouzin if she had deposited any drug money with an investment company in Miami Lakes. Mouzin said no, and reminded Muse that while she lived in Miami Lakes and maintained an office across Miami, she conducted her drug business mainly on the West Coast.

"Well, this office in Miami Lakes is part of a major DEA undercover operation—very heavy," Muse drawled. "They're going to arrest a lot of people. I think your name may have come up."

Barbara Mouzin looked stricken.

"I'm working with a buddy in the DEA who is willing to sell inside information," Muse continued. He extended his wrist, showing an expensive watch purchased, he claimed, with the profits of such information.

"Could you see if I have a problem in Los Angeles?" Mouzin asked Muse to "run" her name as well as those of three of her California cohorts.

Barbara Mouzin, a forty-two-year-old native of Vincennes, Indiana, had lived in the Miami area for nearly a decade. Polished and urbane, she had divorced her husband, an Indiana farmer, and moved to Miami with her four children to work in the women's clothing business. By the early 1980s, her business had become a cover for laundering millions of dollars in California narcotics money, which Mouzin routinely deposited in two Los Angeles banks on behalf of the Latin mafia. From the autumn of 1981 until the spring of 1982, Barbara Mouzin had run more than $25 million in drug cash through the banks. She also had begun dealing extensively in cocaine.

In addition to a town house in Miami Lakes, Mouzin rented a luxurious four-bedroom house in the Benedict Canyon section of Beverly Hills for which she paid $8,000 a month. While ranking far below Marlene Navarro in the hierarchy of the mafia (the two women did not know each other well personally), Mouzin and Navarro knew and worked with people in common such as Carlos Alvarado, the Alvarez money courier who was called Tocayo.

In April 1982, Barbara Mouzin had begun hearing rumors in Los Angeles about a federal investigation of drug dealing and money-laundering possibly involving her. While she had been unable to obtain specific information, and had been told not to worry, the rumors had whetted her appetite for Brooks Muse's overture in June.

Mouzin flew to California the day after her conversation with Muse, who promptly slipped the four names to Special Agent Steve Gibbs. Late that morning, Gibbs obtained classified computer printouts from NADDIS revealing that federal authorities in Los Angeles were indeed investigating Barbara Mouzin and the others. To avoid calling attention to the four names, Gibbs ran several other names through the computer as well.

When Muse saw the material, he told Gibbs that "information on how far this investigation has progressed would be worth a considerable amount of money." Over the next few days, Gibbs telephoned two Los Angeles DEA agents—trusting friends who were unaware of Gibbs's true motive—and learned that an indictment was imminent, that two undercover agents posing as drug traffickers were on their way to Miami to meet with Barbara Mouzin, that Mouzin's Beverly Hills phones were tapped, and that the investigators had even given the Mouzin group a name—the Grandma Mafia—because Mouzin and two of the other targets, though only in their early forties, were grandmothers.

In passing classified information through Brooks Muse to the Latin drug syndicates, Special Agent Steve Gibbs was putting the lives of DEA agents working on the California case at significant risk.

Upon returning to Miami on Tuesday, June 22, Mouzin found a message from Brooks Muse asking that she call him "urgently." They met at his Miami Lakes office where he gave her the bare details from four green-and-white NADDIS printouts—one each on her and her three colleagues. Muse told Mouzin that "everyone you're working with is a DEA agent. The case is before the grand jury in Los Angeles. Indictments are coming down maybe this week. You will be arrested."

Barbara Mouzin again looked stricken.

"This information and all the details will cost a hundred fifty thousand dollars," Muse added.

Mouzin said she could get the money, and Muse offered to introduce her to an "old fishing buddy" who was a bail bondsman.

They met again that evening at Le Sabre, where Mouzin asked Muse if he could run two additional California names in the NADDIS computer. "That wouldn't be a good idea at this time," he said, and advised her to avoid her Miami Lakes town house, which might be under surveillance.

Mouzin checked into a Holiday Inn in Hialeah for the night. The next day she took $350,000 cash from her office safe, instructed an associate to destroy her files, and checked into another Holiday Inn near the airport. Brooks Muse arrived at her room late that afternoon with his "old fishing friend," a bail bondsman named Arthur J. "Artie" Balletti.

Artie Balletti, one of Miami's most successful bail bondsmen, had become a legend earlier in his career as a private detective. He had shadowed the estranged wife of Firestone heir Russell A. Firestone, Jr., in Palm Beach. He had shadowed the comedian Dan Rowan in Las Vegas on behalf of the gangster Sam Giancana in an effort to determine whether Rowan was seeing Giancana's girlfriend Phyllis McGuire. Balletti prided himself on his ability to get inside information on imminent criminal indictments. It enabled him to position himself ahead of other bondsmen in offering bail arrangements to the people indicted.

At Muse's request, Steve Gibbs had run Balletti's name through the NADDIS computer a few weeks earlier and found nothing.

Now, Artie Balletti looked on as Brooks Muse opened his briefcase and gave Mouzin the classified NADDIS printouts that Steve Gibbs had provided. Balletti assured Mouzin that, if she were indicted and arrested, he would make her bail arrangements promptly so she would likely spend minimal time in jail prior to trial. She agreed to turn over $1.6 million in cash and jewelry to Balletti as security against what they anticipated would be a multimillion-dollar bail.

Barbara Mouzin and Brooks Muse met again the next evening, Wednesday, June 24, at the bar of the Kings Inn, another of the many hotels in the orbit of Miami International Airport. In a room Muse had rented, Mouzin opened an overnight case and produced $150,000 cash in packeted bills, which she handed to Muse.

Later, Mouzin telephoned an associate in California, another of the grandmothers, and told her, "Everybody we've been dealing with are federal agents and we're going to be indicted."

In fact, a federal grand jury that day in Los Angeles had returned a secret indictment against Mouzin and two dozen other people on twenty-nine counts of racketeering and drug smuggling. The authorities had sealed the indictment because they did not want to tip off the defendants before they could be arrested. DEA agents in Los Angeles assumed they would have several days to locate the defendants before the indictment was made public.

Early the next morning, Friday, June 25, Barbara Mouzin and Arthur Balletti flew separately from Miami to San Francisco, where Mouzin obtained $1.6 million in drug cash and turned it over to Balletti to be used if needed for bail money. Then she drove to Los Angeles and rendezvoused with another of the young grandmothers under investigation, Dorothy Hackett. On Saturday, the two women flew to El Paso, Texas, and slipped across the border into Mexico. With their Los Angeles pursuers none the wiser, they flew to Mexico City and disappeared.

In Miami, Brooks Muse was eager to cash in again. Having sold the classified Los Angeles information for $150,000, he still had the "very heavy federal undercover investigation" in Miami Lakes to sell. Artie Balletti had a possible buyer in mind: Raymond J. Takiff.

Takiff was one of Miami's most flamboyant criminal defense lawyers, with a mellifluous baritone speaking voice, a fustian manner, and a courtroom vocabulary larded with words like "verities" and "multifarious." The bearded son of Russian immigrants, Takiff had pioneered the legal defense of Colombians accused of laundering drug money in the United States beginning in the late 1970s. He was known in legal circles nationwide for representing such people.

Ray Takiff had done a lot of business over the years with bail bondsman Arthur Balletti. Takiff was Balletti's lawyer, and the two men had become close friends. By referring clients to Balletti for bail arrangements, Takiff had helped make Balletti rich. And Balletti was always alert for ways to repay Takiff by referring lucrative legal clients to him.

Shortly after returning from California with $1.6 million of Barbara Mouzin's cash and jewelry, Artie Balletti dropped by Ray Takiff's law offices in Coconut Grove. Balletti handed Takiff a list of names handwritten on a plain sheet of paper.

"Can you use this?," Balletti asked.

"What is it?" Takiff replied, glancing at the list.

"Look at the names," Balletti said. "Recognize any of them?"
Takiff read the names.

> *Carlos Jader Alvarez*
> *Marlene Navarro*
> *José Antonio Cabrera*
> *Lester Rogers*
> *Arthur Karlick*
> *S. David Jaffe*
> *Carlos Alvarado*
> *Barbara Mouzin*
> *Dorothy Hackett*

There were several other names as well.

"I think I may have heard of Lester Rogers," Takiff finally said. "David Jaffe is very wired through the Bahamas. I'm not sure about the others. Who are they?"

"These people are the targets of a federal undercover investigation in Miami Lakes—a *very heavy* investigation of drugs and money-laundering," Balletti confided.

"Where did you get this?" Takiff asked.

"None of your goddamned business," Balletti replied. "Just say thank you."

"Thank you."

"Can you use it?"

"No, I don't think so, and you shouldn't have it," Takiff said.

"Do you know who represents these people?" Balletti asked.

"No. I've never *heard* of most of them."

Takiff kept the list, and locked it in his safe. As Balletti's attorney, he feared it might get the bail bondsman in trouble. It was clear to Takiff that the secrecy surrounding a major U.S. Government undercover operation had been seriously breached.

27

ROBERT DARIAS sat in Marlene Navarro's living room on Thursday afternoon, July 1, sipping Pouilly-Fuissé with her and Alex McIntosh. Marlene again switched to Spanish after a few pleasantries.

"We got this shipment," she said.

"Oh, yes, how much did you bring in?"

"We got six hundred."

"Good," said Robert. Apparently Lisandro Otero and his Orchestra had arrived with 600 kilograms of cocaine. That translated to 1,320 pounds, which would command roughly $30 million wholesale.

"I told them to keep a hundred for you until I tell them what to do."

"Oh, you give them the orders?"

"Well, I can tell them who gets what."

"That's good, then. We have no problem."

"I just want to deal with you. I don't want to deal with anybody else."

"That's the same with my people," Robert said. "They don't want to meet anybody. Everybody in this thing has to be very careful. How about Oscar?"

"Don't worry about Oscar. Oscar works for Jader. Whatever Jader tells him to do, he does. I have already talked to Jader and he has approved you, and whatever you want, you get."

"Well, that's good. At least I have credit with somebody," Robert said with a smile.

"Don't worry if we have to wait a week or ten days. I'll hold it for you as long as necessary. After this delivery, if you are going to be taking a hundred or hundred fifty a month on a regular basis, Jader would like to talk to you. Panama or Curaçao."

"No problem with Panama?"

"No, I don't think so. He will go to Panama."

"Good."

"Luis went to Peru," Marlene said. "He's coming back tomorrow—no, Saturday. He gets the rough stuff for Carlos, the base."

Events were moving too fast for the DEA, which was still debating whether to try to purchase or seize the cocaine shipment without compromising Operation Swordfish. The wiretap was imminent.

"I'm trying to think how we're going to put this off," Carol said. "They're literally handing you this thing. You're going to look like an idiot if you pass it up. Holy Cow, we're going to have to work something out."

Carol's instructions were getting increasingly precise.

"Tuesday, see if you can get her into the restaurant and I'll try and get somebody over there that maybe could sit nearby that also may know Spanish. You will be taping it anyway."

"Now remember that in public she's not going to say 'six hundred kilos of cocaine,'" Robert said. "She's going to say six hundred automobiles, six hundred cars. But then when I ask the questions I am going to make it clearer."

"Well, don't make it so clear that you scare her."

"No, I know how to bring it out. I will handle it."

"How're you going to bring it out?" Cooper asked.

"Don't worry. That's my problem. I will bring it out."

"Well, I want to know what you're going to say before you say it."

"Well, Carol, you cannot plan a conversation three days in advance. As the conversation develops, I am going to make clear what she's talking about."

"Okay, but make sure when she starts talking to let *her talk*. Let her sink herself."

They agreed that he would try to defer the cocaine purchase while still feigning long-term interest.

Robert met Marlene at Tony Roma's in Coral Gables on Tuesday afternoon. His tiny Sony had been outfitted with a new microphone.

"How pretty that is," he said, referring to a topaz on a gold chain that Marlene was wearing. She said it was one of the few pieces of jewelry not taken when her house was burglarized the previous February.

"I think we won't be able to do anything this time," Robert said. "I was with him this morning," referring to his imaginary cocaine client. "The problem is that he can't get out of the commitments he already has. But he told me, 'Look, I am very interested in working with you.'" Robert continued, "I've been handling all his money for three years, and I represent great security to him in everything."

"The next shipment will arrive in three weeks," Marlene said. "What price do you think could be acceptable for him?"

"I think between forty-five and forty-six," Robert said, meaning $45,000 to $46,000 per kilogram. "Now, what possibility is there to reserve a hundred fifty, or at least a hundred, for the next time. You don't have to tell me now. But I don't want to lose him."

"Most of it is coming in three weeks. Since I know you handle their banking interests, I don't think there will be any problem. And we'll find some other way to sell the hundred pairs of shoes that I had said to keep in reserve. I saw Oscar the other night and he said, 'Oh, Marlene, with the hundred that you are going to help move, we'll have everything liquidated.' "

Marlene clearly was disappointed that Robert was not purchasing the cocaine she had set aside.

"But do you think that between forty-five and forty-six there is a possibility of getting the deal?" Robert asked.

"Yes, I think so. I've heard the market is pretty much flooded lately. Of course, there's the quality. I understand that it's a very, very good quality, quite superior. You take that very much into account for price, right? Because it seems there are shoe stores where the quality is very much second class, according to the stitches and all that. But I know that these people take care that their finish is a perfect finish. And the price goes with the quality."

Robert asked Marlene why she had not used him recently to handle deposits of cash. She mentioned the courier in Los Angeles who was to collect a million dollars but had been shot to death. And she informed Darias that $1 million belonging to José Antonio Cabrera had been seized at the Boca Raton airport on May 25. That money and the Los Angeles money both had been destined for Marlene.

"Then Pepe lost the money, not Carlos?" Robert asked.

"Not Carlos, it was the two of them. They work together. Pepe owes Carlos $16 million."

"Everything is loud and clear," Darias told Cooper later. "I put that thing right in front of her mouth."

"It's taken time, and now she's right where you want her," Carol said. "What you're giving us obviously is the basis for the vast majority of what we're doing. The wire's gonna give us solid, concrete evidence against those two guys down there [Jader and Cabrera]. And even if we don't get them out of Colombia now, some day, some time, they are going to venture out of Colombia. They'll go to Spain, they'll go someplace else, they'll go to see the soccer games or whatever. We'll indict them, and because of that wire we're going to have evidence that can be preserved. So twenty years from now, if they set foot out of that country, they're going to get snapped up."

Tom Clifford returned from his camping vacation on Wednesday, July 7, having been away nearly four weeks. It had been the worst vacation of his life. Telephone calls from Miami about Nick Zapata and Eddie Hernandez's allegations had dogged him throughout the trip. Clifford's first move back in his office was to summon Hernandez and Zapata.

"You people are ignorant," Clifford charged. "I use the term very kindly. Ignorance is the absence of knowledge, and in this particular case you have an absence of knowledge about this operation. In writing that memo, and in spreading the rumor that I stole two hundred fifty thousand dollars, you are ignorant."

"Me 'n' Eddie didn't say you stole two hundred fifty thousand dollars," Zapata interjected. "It's whether some money might not be accounted for right."

"Whatever," Clifford continued, "you have defamed my character. You have slandered my name. You're ruining my reputation, and you're going to answer for it. I'm going to sue you."

"We'll see *you* in court," Hernandez said. "We're gonna drag *your* ass into court."

"I'm keepin' a book on you, buddy," Zapata told Clifford. "When you go out for a beer it goes in my book." Zapata waved a small black notebook at Clifford.

Tom Clifford officially banished Hernandez and Zapata from their undercover roles at International Investments (Hoerner having already done so less formally) and assigned them to desks in the Phoenix Building.

For the second time in less than four months, the founder of Operation Swordfish had gutted the operation of its undercover DEA agents.

The man called Oscar shipped 100 kilograms of cocaine, which had originally been designated for Darias, to the Jader Alvarez distribution network in New York. Days passed, and no money was forthcoming. Oscar went to New York but was unable to collect the money—about $5 million. Jader Alvarez grew concerned, but Marlene Navarro assured him the money was in hand.

"IN THE MATTER OF THE APPLICATION OF THE UNITED STATES OF AMERICA FOR AN ORDER AUTHORIZING THE INTERCEPTION OF WIRE COMMUNICATIONS.

"This application seeks authorization to intercept wire communications of Marlene Navarro, Carlos Jader Alvarez Moreno, José Antonio Cabrera Sarmiento, Luis Fabio Rodriguez, Carlos Alvarado, Lester Rogers, S. David Jaffe, Carmenza Valenzuela, and others yet unknown, from the telephone bearing telephone numbers (305) 592-7106 and (305) 592-7180 subscribed to by Marlene Navarro. . . ."

Tom Clifford's resistance having crumbled, Peter Gruden ordered the DEA to proceed with the wiretap.

After briefing the wiretap desk at the Justice Department by telephone, Prosecutor Michael Pasano sent the application by special courier on Friday, July 9, to the Office of Enforcement Operations of the department's Criminal Division in Washington, formally requesting authorization to proceed. The application was accompanied by an "Action Memorandum."

"This investigation is part of a long-term and sensitive undercover operation by the Drug Enforcement Administration and known by the code name 'Operation Swordfish.' Several high level narcotics organizations have been identified and penetrated by 'Swordfish' operatives. The instant investigation focuses upon at least two major and interrelated Colombian-based organizations which have been smuggling large amounts of cocaine into the United States on a regular basis and which have been laundering the multi-million-dollar proceeds of this drug trafficking to locations outside of the United States. . . . Most of the decisions regarding the timing and location of deliveries of cocaine, negotiations for its purchase, and plans for disposition of the proceeds occur via a series of telephone calls to and from the home of Marlene Navarro."

There were several other documents in the sealed package as well:

—A 10-page affidavit sworn to and signed by Michael Pasano delineating the legal rationale for the application.

—A 31-page affidavit sworn to and signed by Carol Cooper describing Operation Swordfish and summarizing the vast amount of intelligence provided by Robert Darias. The Cooper affidavit attested to the reliability of Darias, who was not identified by name, only as a "confidential informant" whose information had been "corroborated by independent investigation by the Drug Enforcement Administration and never has been proven to be false."

—A letter for the assistant attorney general to send to the United States Attorney in Miami authorizing the application;

—The actual court orders to be signed by a U.S. District Judge in Miami instructing the DEA and the Southern Bell Telephone Company to proceed with the wiretap and to take steps to preserve its secrecy.

The Justice Department would take several days to process the application.

Although Tom Clifford had lost the battle for control of the wiretap, his conflict with Carol Cooper resumed shortly after his return from vacation. The point of contention was whether Robert Darias should continue negotiating with Marlene Navarro for the purchase of a large quantity of cocaine, and if so, in what manner and to what end. Cooper and Clifford had reversed their positions since the issue had first arisen. Clifford, having favored the purchase, was now opposed. Despite his desire to remove large amounts of drugs from the streets whenever possible, he couldn't forget his original vision of Operation Swordfish—a gradual, two-or-three year infiltration of high-level drug traffickers and their assets, with the drugs themselves by necessity a lower priority. He still wanted to prolong the operation and was inclined to oppose moves such as confiscating cocaine shipments that would end it quickly. Cooper, for her part, had fallen in step behind Peter Gruden and Sam Billbrough, who wanted to get on with the wiretap but were willing to end it and the operation prematurely if necessary for a large drug seizure. In contrast to the inventive Clifford, Cooper, like Gruden and Billbrough, was ultimately a by-the-book agent, and the book said seize the drugs.

The debate intensified on Saturday morning, July 10, when, over a quiet breakfast with Darias at the Costa del Sol coffee shop, Navarro increased her offer of cocaine from 100 kilograms to between 300 and 600 kilograms. The cocaine was available "now." She referred to the difficulty the syndicate had encountered in collecting $5 million in New York and suggested that Darias would be a more reliable partner.

"It's the whitest I have and it burns over ninety," she said, referring to a purity of over ninety percent. Assuming a price of around $45,000 a kilogram, the total purchase price would be between $13.5 million and $27 million. Navarro agreed to defer any payments for three weeks or more. It was clear to Robert that she had planned on his purchasing a big order and had been surprised and inconvenienced when he put her off a few days earlier. Robert again said he would get back to her.

Without hesitation Tom Clifford instructed Darias to decline the cocaine for the time being.

"Under the circumstances, no," Clifford said. "It would blow the operation too quickly."

Since Navarro was now offering as much as six times what she had last offered, Carol Cooper was angry.

"Tom didn't *ask* me. He *told* me," Cooper told Darias. "I wanted you to take it. I want this thing over. It's getting to be a pain in the neck."

Darias said, "Sometimes I think I am in the middle of an ocean in a big storm and I don't know what in the hell is going on." Robert understood Clifford's reversal but not Cooper's. It seemed to him that the enmity she felt was driving her reflexively to the opposite side of any issue from Clifford's position.

"Tom's gonna look like a blundering idiot," Carol continued. "He's now passed up seven hundred kilos. What if we don't get anything on the wiretap? Then what are we gonna look like? Goddangit! There is no question in my mind that I would have had you take it."

Cooper laid plans to bring the matter to the attention of Gruden and Billbrough. Reluctant to overuse her back-channel, she decided to draft a teletype to Washington headquarters that would mention Clifford's decision to decline 700 kilograms of cocaine. Since Gruden or Billbrough had to sign any outgoing teletype, they would thereby become aware of what Clifford had done.

"People are going to be made aware of what happened today," Carol said. "Tom should not have made that decision on his own. That is way, *way* too much dope. I'm going to create so many waves, he's not gonna know which end's up."

Carol drafted a teletype for headquarters and on Sunday called Robert and had him edit it. "I will send it out first thing in the morning and it's going to get up in the front office because they have to sign off on it. It's gonna come to a screeching halt. I have my little devious ways to do things. I have all sorts of devious little ways."

She instructed Robert to delay telling Marlene that he could not take the 600 kilograms. Instead, he was to clarify how much cocaine she was offering, negotiate a price, and then say that he would have to check with his people before making a final commitment.

Oscar called Robert Sunday evening. "Marlene and I have been calling you all day. I have some things for you. When can we get together?"

"Maybe we can have breakfast tomorrow morning," Robert replied. "I'll speak to Marlene later."

28

THE TEMPERATURE WAS already rising toward ninety and rain had begun to fall when Darias switched on his microrecorder and emerged from his car in front of Navarro's house just before ten o'clock Monday morning. Oscar waited in the living room while Marlene met Robert at the door.

"Hello, Roberto, how are you?"

"Your car is going to get wet inside, Oscar, the windows are open," Robert shouted.

Robert went inside as Oscar, a fat man under six feet tall whom Marlene called "the jolly drunk," hurried out to his car.

"Last night you know what happened?" Marlene said. "I locked myself in the bathroom for almost three hours."

"How?" Robert asked with a laugh.

"The phone rang. I was in the sauna and got out running because I knew it was Jader, but when I reached it he had hung up. When I returned I slammed the door. It stayed locked. I got out at one-thirty."

"How did you finally do it?"

"First I took bobby pins, I took everything, then in the end a fingernail file. That's how I opened it. It took a lot of smarts."

Marlene and Robert were laughing as Oscar returned and settled on one of the Empire chairs between the sofas. "Explain to him what you want," Navarro told Darias.

As Marlene puttered about the kitchen, listening, Robert repeated to Oscar an updated version of the story he had told Marlene the previous week: Because of the delay, his buyers had gone ahead and purchased 150 kilograms of cocaine from another supplier. They were "serious people," however, and wanted to do business with Robert at the next opportunity.

"That's no problem," Oscar said. "I told Marlene as soon as it arrived I would put aside a hundred for you. So I had these put aside that were very good. It is good in percentage, and it shines. But we'll wait. How do you want to do it?"

"My people don't want to meet anybody," Darias said.

"I don't either," Oscar said. "The less people I know the better."

"When I propose something like this, they tell me *you* deliver, since there are so many problems here in Miami."

"Sure."

"So when it arrives, how much can I count on?"

"Three hundred, four hundred," Oscar said, indicating that the total shipment would be 2,000 kilograms. He quoted a tentative price of $46,500 per kilo, and no more than $48,000.

"That's a little high, but let me see," Darias said, noting the size of the full shipment for the first time.

Two thousand kilograms was 4,400 pounds, significantly more than the record-setting TAMPA seizure at the Miami airport in March—the event that had shattered the U.S. Government's illusions about the magnitude of the drug scourge in the America.

"He told me he was flexible with respect to the quality," Robert said.

"Roberto," said Marlene, still moving about the kitchen and living room. "Roberto, a Bally shoe is not the same as a Christian Dior shoe. It all depends on the quality."

"What's arriving, rocks or loose?" Robert asked.

"There is more rock than powder, and it has a shine," Oscar said. "They like rock."

"I'll separate them, the more rocks, the better," Oscar said. "And I would appreciate it if you'd not give me any money," Oscar added. "You settle with her," gesturing toward Marlene.

Carol Cooper's latest tactical maneuver against Tom Clifford worked. Gruden and Billbrough read her teletype reporting Clifford's decision to pass up 700 kilograms of cocaine, and by late afternoon the decision was reversed. The institutional tendency to confiscate large amounts of narcotics, whatever the consequences to other objectives, was still very strong in the DEA. Even a faint possibility of seizing all or part of a shipment of up to 2,000 kilograms, with a wholesale value in Miami of over $90 million, was too great to pass up. The seizure might set a new record and Clifford's bosses felt it would bring glory to the DEA.

Clifford was ordered to take as much of the cocaine as Operation Swordfish could get. Ideally, intelligence would be sufficient to enable the DEA to confiscate the entire shipment before it got to Navarro or Oscar, thus avoiding any compromise of Robert Darias. Failing that, the agency wanted Darias to buy part or all of the shipment from the

Jader Alvarez organization if he could get it for a very modest down payment. The agency was prepared to live with the necessity to arrest Navarro, and close the operation by the time the full payment was due, even if that meant forfeiting the opportunity to prosecute other targets like Jader Alvarez whom the government might be able to lure out of Colombia and arrest if the operation could continue.

Savoring her new victory, Carol Cooper immediately called Darias. "Number one, we're going after the two thousand," she said. "And number two, is there any way that you can find out from them *when* that thing is coming in. The thing is, generally, what I'm looking for is, if we do have an opportunity, we'll hit the whole thing before you even get involved in this."

"You just find out for me how much is the world record so we can break it, okay?" Robert said with a laugh.

"I want to make sure they give you the entire thing. I don't want them to give you two hundred at a time."

"I will really get under Oscar and he will tell me a lot of things," Darias said. "He's fairly open with me. And it's the first time he talked to me. So once I talk to him a couple of times and take him for lunch and a couple of drinks, he will really open up."

"This whole case, Bob, is a credit to you. You're the one that's putting this thing together."

Darias eased Carol off the phone so that he and Amelia could watch Blake Edward's movie *S.O.B.* on television. While he regretted the DEA's decision to risk forfeiting long-range goals by seizing the 2,000 kilograms, the reward the agency likely would pay him would be a consolation. When it had paid him by the case, the rough formula had been one percent of the wholesale value of drugs confiscated. With cocaine currently going for around $50,000 a kilogram, 2,000 kilograms would be worth in the range of $100 million. His bonus would be $1 million.

Darias met with Clifford, Hoerner, and Russo at International Investments on Tuesday afternoon. Clifford said that if Darias could get 500 or 600 kilograms from the next shipment, or even the entire 2,000, the DEA would have to take it and live with the consequences.

Robert said, "I want to work with Paul. I want to have him around me. I trust him, and this is going to be touch and go. I won't feel comfortable if he's not there."

"I don't think that can be arranged," Clifford said.

"Well, it would be good if you could arrange it," Darias replied.

"Well, let me see what I can do."

Paul Sennett was immediately reassigned to Operation Swordfish. The spy was still controlling his control.

The 94th Aero Squadron was a restaurant and cabaret on Red Road. It nestled in a grove of pine trees on a small triangle of land tucked between the Dolphin Expressway and the south perimeter of Miami International Airport. The motif of the place was World War I—cannons, armored vehicles, and insignia of the First Air Pursuit Group. The pine trees covered the restaurant's parking lot with deep shade and a coat of pine needles, providing a feeling of sheltered serenity from the roar of Avianca and Pan Am jets a few hundred yards away.

Summoned by Oscar, Darias drove into the Aero Squadron parking lot just after two o'clock on Wednesday afternoon, July 14, and found Oscar and his associate Ricardo, whom Robert had met briefly at Marlene's, waiting in a tan Chevrolet Caprice at the rear of the restaurant. The temperature was in the nineties, and the parking lot felt like a moist oven. Darias motioned Oscar into his car and kept the engine and air conditioner running; a DEA technician had adjusted the microphone in his microrecorder so that it would pick up voices over the sound of the air unit.

"Sit down for a moment so that we don't take in the heat here," Darias said. He told Oscar that his people were prepared to make a firm commitment to purchase a large quantity of cocaine.

"Could you deliver six hundred to me?" Robert asked.

"I can supply six hundred, eighty-seven, one twenty-seven, one thirty-seven—there's about one forty available now," Oscar said, gesturing to the trunk of the Caprice. "Or two thousand in eight to fifteen days."

"I have three people," Robert said. "They'll wait for me no matter when I tell them—fifteen days, eight days. It can be fifteen days or three weeks. All they want is to have the certainty that I will deliver."

"That's for sure." Oscar suggested that Darias take the 140 kilograms in the Caprice or at least a 10-kilogram sample to show his clients. Darias, following Carol Cooper's warning against a piecemeal arrangement, said he would prefer to wait for the full shipment of 600 kilograms or perhaps even the full 2,000. Darias said his people wanted to pay $46,000 "per unit."

"I'll have to talk to the *compadre*," Oscar said, referring to Carlos Jader Alvarez. "I'll talk to the *compadre* today. Very good, Don Roberto."

Oscar returned to the Caprice, and Darias drove home, having

captured Oscar on tape agreeing to sell 2,000 kilograms of pure cocaine for $92 million in cash wholesale—cocaine that would be diluted
and resold all over North America for roughly $1 billion retail—a
crime for which Oscar, as well as Marlene Navarro and Carlos Jader
Alvarez, could be imprisoned for many years.

As Oscar and Ricardo drove out of the parking lot and headed
south on Red Road, they were followed by Special Agent David
Wilson, who had been parked, unnoticed, about thirty yards away. At
Wilson's command by shortwave radio, three other agents in separate
vehicles also followed. After conferring by radio with Cooper and
Sennett, Wilson then decided to end the surveillance for fear of being
noticed.

Later in the day, the DEA changed its mind again and decided that
Darias should arrange to take the 140 kilograms that Oscar had
offered him. But Robert was unable to reach Oscar, and Marlene was
in Coral Gables having her hair done, a difficult setting in which to
conduct a discreet conversation about a multimillion-dollar drug sale.

As it vacillated on purchasing Jader Alvarez's cocaine, the DEA
proceeded apace with the Navarro wiretap, which was set to begin
over the weekend. The wiretap had taken on a momentum of its own.
Some forty DEA agents, many of them on temporary duty from out
of town, were assembled in Miami to work on the tap. About a dozen
of the agents were native speakers of Spanish. Once the wiretap was
approved by the court and connected, they would sit, two at a time,
at twin banks of three tape recorders each in the Phoenix Building
listening post, monitoring via earphones all incoming and outgoing
telephone conversations on both of Navarro's lines. The Spanish-
speaking agents who were not actually monitoring phone conversations would translate, transcribe, and analyze the conversations once
they were recorded. Most of the other agents would be assigned to
surveillance teams that would attempt surreptitiously to follow
Navarro and her associates wherever they went, observing and establishing links between what they said on the phone and what they did
in response to the phone conversations.

Since Navarro's telephones were to be monitored around the clock
the agents were assigned to eight-hour shifts. They were on call even
when they were off duty, however, and DEA headquarters had authorized 720 hours of overtime to accommodate the demands of the
wiretap.

On the morning of Thursday, July 15, all forty agents were summoned to the listening post, a windowless room, roughly ten feet by

fifteen, in Tom Clifford's suite of offices. Spilling out of the room, standing, or sitting on chairs or desks, the agents listened as chief prosecutor Michael Pasano briefed them on the rigid and strictly enforced procedures that federal law prescribed for the administration of electronic eavesdropping.

"Before your electronic surveillance begins, all monitoring agents should read the authorizing order and supporting affidavits, especially noting the designated crimes and the subjects," Pasano said, referring to a nine-page, single-spaced, typewritten document entitled "Wiretap Instructions."

"Your objective is to execute the order, recording only those conversations which are specifically designated, and minimizing the interception of nonpertinent or privileged communications. The law makes no distinction between 'listening,' 'monitoring,' and 'recording' a conversation. Courts generally regard an electronic listening device like any other search warrant: it authorizes a *limited* 'search,' and *limited* 'seizure' of evidence. Whether a conversation is merely overheard or also recorded makes no difference legally; it has been seized.

"If you seize everything that is said over the telephones the fruits of your investigation are likely to be suppressed," Pasano warned. "We have to establish that we neither *listened to* nor *recorded* conversations we had no right to overhear."

Pasano then recited the names of the people who were "subjects," or targets, of the wiretap and the alleged violations of federal criminal law being investigated.

"Listen to the beginning of each conversation only so long as is necessary to determine the parties and the nature of the conversation. If the parties or the nature of the conversation are not covered by the court order, *turn off the machine. Stop listening.*"

The agents were instructed, however, to "spot monitor" such conversations after the initial determination. "Use your judgment as to when to spot-check conversations because many factors enter into your decision: the parties to the conversation, the precise relationship of the parties, the length of the relationship, the number of conversations between the parties, the present status of the investigation, the past conduct of the parties, etc."

Pasano warned the agents against intercepting conversations covered by various "legal privileges."

"Consider this an absolute rule," Pasano said. *"Never* knowingly listen to or record a conversation between a subject and his attorney where the conversation in *any way, shape, or form* relates to legal advice or representation. To listen to any such conversation could result in the dismissal of the indictment."

But what if an attorney is an active participant in the crimes under investigation and isn't simply acting in an advisory or representative capacity? "A limited degree of spot monitoring may be maintained" to make this determination, Pasano said. "Two of the proposed interceptees, Lester Rogers and S. David Jaffe, are attorneys. Conversations in which these persons are parties, insofar as these conversations relate to offenses set out in the court order, may be monitored and recorded.

"All conversations between a parishioner and his clergyman are to be considered privileged. We could not obtain an eavesdropping warrant to listen to a man confess his sins to a priest in a confessional booth; similarly, we must not listen to a subject discuss his or her personal, financial, or legal problems with his or her priest, minister, rabbi, etc.

"Any conversations a patient has with a doctor relative to diagnosis, symptoms, treatment, or any other aspect of physical, mental, or emotional health is privileged. The instant it is learned that our subject is talking to a doctor about his health (or someone else's health), *turn off the machine. Stop listening. Stop recording.*

"Any conversation between a husband and wife, which relates in any way to the marital relationship, is privileged.

"If they discuss their sex life, *don't listen, don't record.* If they discuss problems their child is having in school, *don't listen, don't record.* If they discuss a fight or argument they had a night or day or week ago, *don't listen, don't record.* However, if it appears that a spouse is involved in a husband or wife's crime, "a limited degree of spot monitoring may be maintained."

With his briefing to the forty agents, Michael Pasano had disseminated the details of Operation Swordfish to a substantially greater number of DEA people than previously had known them. The enlarged group included Special Agent Steve Gibbs, who had been secretly conspiring with construction executive Brooks Muse to solicit bribes in exchange for information on a "very heavy" federal undercover operation in Miami. Gibbs had been assigned as a surveillance agent for the Navarro wiretap.

As Michael Pasano was lecturing the DEA agents at the Phoenix Building, Tocayo, "the chauffeur," was dropping off a briefcase crammed with $220,000 of Jader Alvarez's money, mostly in tens and twenties, with Robert Darias at International Investments. Tocayo wanted $100,000 exchanged for hundred-dollar bills and the rest conveyed to Colombia via a peso exchange.

While Darias counted the money, Tocayo bemoaned Marlene Navarro's apparent lying to Jader Alvarez about the recent problem Oscar had had collecting $5 million in New York for 100 kilograms of cocaine he had smuggled there after Robert Darias had declined the shipment in Miami. Marlene evidently had assured Jader that the money was being collected when in fact it was not. Jader had reprimanded her.

"I think it is a very serious mistake, very serious," Tocayo said.

"I have told her, too, 'Marlene, this is bad, because Jader trusts you completely,'" Darias said.

"This is most serious, most serious!" Tocayo said, more upset than Darias had ever seen him. "Jader called me yesterday. He said, 'You must be doing something to Chiqui. Something's happening to Chiqui.' Jader is already starting to distrust her."

"Yes."

"I told her, 'Look, Marlensita, for your own good, don't cover up for anyone. It's best for you to tell Jader they have not delivered anything and let them settle it among themselves.' These people are not exempt from being shot or killed."

"Something can happen to her," Darias said. "You are absolutely right."

"I am asking you as a favor to speak to Marlene since you have more influence with her," Tocayo said. "I do not want to risk my freedom in order to make money. She is telling lies. There is no reason for her to lie, Roberto."

"No, no, it's not worth it."

"Let them kill each other if that's what they want to do."

"If they have to kill Oscar, let them kill Oscar," Darias said. "Because when they start looking for somebody, they are going to be looking for Marlene, because they are going to think she took the money."

Still frustrated and clearly afraid, Tocayo departed, saying he would return the following day for the hundred-dollar bills.

"How pretty the horse is," Robert said. He had just arrived at Marlene's and was admiring an antique brass horse about a foot high on a stand between the Empire chairs in her living room.

"You haven't seen my horse?"

"No, I had not seen it. It is beautiful."

She described the piece as Chinese, about 600 years old. It stood on a small round wooden nineteenth-century Epoch table of inlaid wood.

"If you notice, the house looks empty," Marlene said. "And now I am telling myself that I have to fill it up. I told my designer to call you and give you the name of the Japanese man who did my flowers."

"Yes, I am interested in going by his store because there are several things that I need."

"Go, because he has a lot of nice things."

"I need a wine rack for my wines."

"I also want one."

"I want something big, that will hold three cases of wine."

"I need one mainly because the red has to be in this position," she said, gesturing.

"Exactly."

"I have to call the designer because he is going to send me the curtain man for my bedroom."

"Did you talk to Oscar?" Darias asked.

In order to avoid being overheard by the maid, Navarro lowered her voice and sat next to Darias on one of the twin white sofas. He eased his wallet purse containing the microrecorder onto the sofa between them.

"He went to pick up two million dollars that will go to Panama."

"He is going to California?"

"Yes."

"The two million will be delivered on Monday and I will tell him, pick everything up and I will go there." In the event of an unusually large cash delivery, Marlene sometimes flew to wherever her people had taken possession of the money and personally saw to its disposition.

"And what he is bringing today is to be sent in cash?" Robert asked, referring to a smaller deposit.

"To be sent in cash. Because it's small, two hundred or so. Oscar told me if *el papi* [Jader Alvarez] calls, tell him 'I delivered two hundred to you,' but I said no. 'I will not make the same mistake of telling him you delivered. I will say that you are *going* to deliver.' "

"Tocayo this morning was telling me he's worried about this problem."

"But that was fixed already." She did not say how.

"He is very nervous," Robert said. "Tocayo is a very nervous person."

Marlene shuddered. "I am afraid of him, Robert. God forbid, if something happens, before they ask Tocayo something, he will be talking." Tocayo was nervous, Marlene said, not because of her but because several other people with whom he did business had just been indicted in California. This was a reference to Barbara Mouzin and her "Grandma Mafia" associates, whose indictment had been previewed for Mouzin by Brooks Muse and DEA Special Agent Steve Gibbs. The authorities and most of the rest of the Latin drug and money networks, including Marlene Navarro, remained unaware of the compromise and of Mouzin's whereabouts.

"Tocayo is afraid," Marlene continued. "But I told him and gave him a lesson: 'Tocayo, the first thing you have to do is *don't talk*. You call Lester, he will post your bond, you don't have to do anything,' I told him it will be worse for you if you talk."

"Yes."

"I asked him as a favor to help me because I covered up for Oscar. They delivered wrong for Oscar. Remember? They tricked him in New York? Now, until I have everything in my hands, I will not cover up even for my mother!"

"No, don't get mixed up with that."

"Because, look, I could have lost Jader's confidence in me."

"Oscar told me that in eight to ten days he would be getting two hundred," Robert said, referring to kilograms of cocaine.

"No, two thousand," Navarro said.

"Two thousand, yes. Then he asked if I didn't want those hundred forty he had with him."

"Yes. He just wanted you to keep them and make that a part of your shipment."

"Oscar has authority so that if he told me this, I can count on it?" Robert asked.

"Oh, yes, yes. He is the one who is in charge of distributing all the shirts and the shoes and everything. There is no problem."

Marlene said she was reluctant to continue receiving large amounts of money at her home.

"Since we are going to have a lot of money coming in, I don't want too many people coming to this house."

"The guy smiled when I came in."

"Oh, yes?"

"The young boy at the gate."

"It makes me laugh. They talk about the number of lovers I have."

"Yes, you have to be careful, because don't think they are so dumb, the type of car, and everything, Marlene, people get suspicious, and you being Colombian and all—"

She agreed to start having her people deliver money to the International Investments offices and said she also was afraid of talking on the phone. "I hope they don't talk about anything because—Roberto, I was told that there were forty-five hundred telephones tapped in Dade County."

"I don't believe that."

"That is what Tocayo told me."

"Talk to your lawyer, and you will see that that is impossible."

"Why is it impossible?" she asked.

Without being specific, he explained the complex procedures that the government had to follow to get a wiretap approved and the number of people required to operate a single wiretap.

"The private phone that was only for Jader is not that exclusive anymore," Marlene said with a laugh, "because Jader gave the number to Oscar, Oscar gave it to Ricardo, Ricardo gave it to Luisito, Luisito gave it to what's-his-name—"

Robert laughed. It was the first time she had explicitly confirmed that the black phone next to her bed was intended for the exclusive use of Carlos Jader Alvarez. It was evident that she was so concerned about security that she did not have the Jader line patched to her phones on the first floor.

It occurred to Robert as he was leaving Costa del Sol that he had gathered more incriminating evidence against Marlene Navarro and learned more about the modus operandi of the Jader Alvarez organization in the past week than he had gleaned in the preceding year of tracking her. He wondered if the DEA fully understood that he was now getting a daily avalanche of evidence *only* because he had devoted a year to laying the requisite groundwork of courting Navarro—not only providing banking services but also dining and drinking with her and her boyfriend, arranging ballet tickets, installing a security system in her home, and purchasing a bulletproof vest for her boss.

Robert and Carol speculated that night about what would happen if Jader Alvarez and Marlene Navarro were actually arrested and prosecuted.

"I'm sure it's gonna hurt them for a good long time if we can get him," Carol said. "That's why he's important to us."

"It has to be a good case, Carol."

"She doesn't have a prayer. She's got dynamite going against her."

"I think they are going to go after her."

"Oh, I know they are."

"They are going to kill her. Even if they believe that she didn't knowingly do what she did, they are going to kill her for being stupid."

"Yeah, well, that's something I gotta think on. I'll start concentra-

ting on how to approach her when she goes down. Because she's
gonna be a major figure. If she does turn around and cooperate with
us, because she's scared half to death, that could be a major turning.
I don't know. We'll have to see what happens. I would love for her to
tell us everything."

Carol Cooper coached Darias closely on how to handle his next
encounter with Tocayo, who was picking up $100,000 in hundred-
dollar bills at International Investments on Friday afternoon and
presumably putting it on a flight to Colombia. On the one hand, Carol
hoped Robert could elicit enough information from Tocayo to enable
the DEA to identify the flight and intercept the money. On the other
hand, she didn't want it to be apparent to Tocayo if the shipment was
intercepted that Darias was responsible.

"The thing I want to be cautious with, I don't want you probing,"
Cooper said. "If he tells you, fine. I'm afraid if you probe too much
and he tells you things and then the plane gets hit. . . . When I hit the
plane I want to be on the tap with her, because it's gonna instigate all
sorts of phone calls. And I want the benefit of those phone calls.
That's definitely gonna link the money into them. And we're gonna
get all their arrangements on what they plan on doing next."

Later, at International Investments, Darias said to Tocayo, "I
spoke to our friend and I was asking her about that problem"—
misleading Jader Alvarez about the $5 million in New York.

"Yes?"

"She told me that, no, no, that she would never do that again, that
she had gone out of her way for Oscar because Oscar was a nice guy."

Tocayo unwrapped the package Darias handed him and began
stuffing packets of hundred-dollar bills (fifty to a packet) into his
boots. He explained that he didn't have his briefcase and didn't like
to carry money in paper bags.

"I feel sorry for her that she may have gotten into really serious
trouble," Tocayo said.

Darias replied, "It would be a pity to lose the possibility of having
good deals with Jader. Oscar and she have guaranteed me a big
delivery. They are guaranteeing me that within the next eight days,
more or less, I will be receiving two thousand kilos."

Tocayo unbuckled his belt and inserted packets of money inside his
trousers and then his shirt.

"You look as if you had eaten too much in a Cuban restaurant,"
Darias said, surveying the ludicrous figure of a slender man with
$100,000 in hundred-dollar bills lining his light summer clothing.

When Tocayo left International Investments, he was followed by a surveillance team of five DEA agents in separate cars. He drove to an engine parts store in nearby Opa-Locka and loaded his station wagon with boxes. He drove to his home in Hialeah and unloaded the boxes. He drove to a warehouse west of the Palmetto Expressway only a few blocks from the DEA headquarters, but the watching agents couldn't see whether he was loading or unloading. He stopped at another warehouse nearby and went inside for a few minutes. Then he drove home. The agents staked out the place and waited.

"They're still with him," Cooper reported to Darias. "He hasn't done much yet." Carol was in touch with the surveillance agents by shortwave radio while she spoke by phone with Robert.

"He still has the money with him?" Darias asked.

"We can't tell. He could have dropped it off a couple of places."

"I'm going to be calling her."

"She's not home right now. She's been gone all afternoon."

After an early dinner with Amelia, Robert called the office and got Tom Clifford.

"We're sitting on his house," Clifford said. "He's there."

Actually, Tocayo was in the house calling Marlene because he was frantic. He had spotted the cars following him. When he finally reached Navarro late in the evening, he was cryptic and nervous.

"I am very, very sick," he said. "My disease may be contagious to you, Chiqui. Be very careful. Please call Doctor Roberto immediately. See if he knows how to cure this illness."

Navarro was weeping when she reached Darias and repeated what Tocayo had said. She did not have to interpret the words. He knew that narcotics smugglers used the lexicon of illness as a code for arrest, surveillance, or perceived jeopardy from the police.

"He says his disease may be contagious to me," Marlene told Robert. "I am staying at Gustavo's tonight. Please help me," she pleaded. Her interior designers, Gustavo Delgado and Dick Lawrence, shared a house on Greenway Drive in Coral Gables. Robert assured her that even if Tocayo was in jeopardy she was insulated since she did not personally transport currency to planes. He suggested that they meet with Tocayo the next morning and clarify his problem.

Marlene agreed. Then she raced into the bathroom and vomited.

"She's staying at Gustavo's tonight," Darias told Cooper. "She doesn't want to go home."

"Oh, no!" Carol gasped, visualizing her wiretap being switched on at Marlene's residence just after Marlene fled.

"I told her I want to meet with her to see what the problem is."

"Meet with her as quick as you can, Bob."

"The problem is that Tocayo noticed that somebody was following him."

"Man, that's exactly why I didn't want to put anybody out there!"

Indeed, there had been a debate about whether to follow Tocayo, and Carol had lost. "They stuck to him like glue," Cooper said later. "And they should have gone out there with the understanding, if you lose him, you lose him. That was out-and-out dumb."

"I want to surface right away," Darias said. "I don't want to run away from them."

"Exactly, as quick as possible."

"I told her, any other problems, call me anytime tonight."

"Does she think there's a problem with you?"

"She doesn't know anything for sure, Carol." Robert was agitated.

"I'm going to have to leave it up to you. Try to soothe it over as much as you can. I want her back at her house, obviously."

"Tocayo will tell me what happened."

"You've gotta convince Marlene that she was not involved in any of that activity today, and how in the world could they ever connect *her*."

"Sure."

"She's nervous enough that she moved out of her house tonight. Goddang it! Of all times! I don't believe it."

"Right."

Carol sighed with frustration. "You've got to convince *her* that there's no problem with *her* because she had absolutely nothing to do with it. There's no way anybody could connect her with it."

"Yes."

"I have to be in court in the morning, Bob."

"Tomorrow? Saturday? What is happening in court?"

"Your thing."

"Which one?"

"Your thing. The thing I'm doing."

"Okay, yeah, I know."

"Since I can't tell you, all I can say is 'your thing.' "

"I know."

The government was prevented from telling anyone without an absolute need to know, even a spy at the center of the case, that it was about to install a court-authorized wiretap.

"Do your best tomorrow," Carol said. "It's critical. I think you know that we're ready to go on this thing. I want her at home using that phone. If she's that nervous she's gonna be less on it. But do your best with it, kid, and definitely tape it. I've got to get her back in her house."

"She will go tomorrow back to her house," Robert said. "The timing is not bad, Carol. This lady is going to need me now more than ever."

"Keep her super-calmed down until she gets home. Shoot! I want her to make those phone calls tomorrow down to Colombia."

"She might make them from somewhere else at this point."

"I know. That's what I'm afraid of. Do your best with it tomorrow. Holy cow!"

"Take it easy. You are more nervous than she is," Robert said with a laugh.

"Well, let me tell you. After what I've been going through, you would be, too. The main thing I want to do is get her back in that *house,* get her using that *phone,* and making sure she doesn't change her phone numbers now!"

After another chat with Marlene, who was still vomiting, Robert reported back to Carol. He had agreed to pick up Marlene at Gustavo's the next morning and the two of them would get together with Tocayo. Carol said she would put Paul Sennett on surveillance.

At the deserted Capitol Bank Plaza on Red Road after midnight, the sound of breaking glass shattered the silence as someone smashed in the front door of International Investments. The burglar alarm did not sound.

part four

THE WIRETAP

"There is no moment between human beings that I cannot record!"

> *—Wiretapper Bernie Moran, played by Allen Garfield, mocking wiretapper Harry Caul, played by Gene Hackman*, The Conversation, *a film by Francis Ford Coppola*

She talked as thirsty men drink.

> —Heart of Darkness

29

AD MARLENE NAVARRO been the only target of Operation Swordfish the DEA could have arrested her based on the range of evidence that Robert Darias had already accumulated, including several recent acknowledgments on tape that she was a ranking executive in a major narcotics organization negotiating a large cocaine sale to Darias. But the DEA still wanted to go all the way to the top—infiltrate and prosecute Carlos Jader Alvarez and Pepe Cabrera, as well as seize as much of their money as possible. In the six months since the pen register had been attached to her telephones, Marlene Navarro had spoken to someone on Jader Alvarez's phones in Bogotá a total of 107 times and on Pepe Cabrera's phones 44 times. Although the DEA had been able to infer some of the contents of those conversations by analyzing Navarro's activities following the calls, inferences alone were not admissible as evidence in a court of law. Now, after months of wrangling between Carol Cooper and Tom Clifford, the DEA was poised to actually listen to Navarro's telephone conversations.

United States District Judge Sidney M. Aronovitz* received Carol Cooper along with the prosecutors, Michael Pasano and his deputy, Mark Schnapp, in his courthouse chambers at eleven o'clock Saturday morning, July 17. Pasano had flown to Washington the previous day and walked the wiretap documents through the required steps of approval at the Department of Justice. The judge reviewed and signed them, and by noon, Pasano, Schnapp, and Cooper were handing the court order to DEA Technical Agent Rick Vasquez. Vasquez, who had installed the pen register in January, entered the listening post and connected wires from the tape recorders to another set of wires from the telephone audio circuit that had been legally off limits until now.

Vasquez had rigged two banks of three cassette tape recorders—an amalgam of Marantz, Sharp, and Superscope equipment, a bank for each of Navarro's phone lines. One recorder in each bank would make

---

*It was Judge Aronovitz who had sentenced Robert Darias to prison in 1978 for filing a false income tax return.

an "original" tape that would be removed, sealed, and placed in an evidence vault immediately upon completion of a recording. The second recorder would make a "master" tape that would be kept in the listening post and used to make copies. The third recorder would make a "work" tape that translators, analysts, and transcribers would remove from the machines and use for immediate analysis.

The recorders would start automatically when they sensed the change in circuit voltage that occurred when a call came into Navarro's phones or her receiver was lifted. Lights and buzzers would alert the DEA monitors in the listening post when recording began. The target would hear nothing unusual.

The monitors were to record all "activations," incoming and outgoing, on both of Navarro's telephones, not only conversations, but busy signals, no-answers, and misdials. They would also note each activation in a specially prepared log—ruled sheets of white paper accommodating three calls each with blanks for the monitor to write the date, time, number of the call, whether it was incoming or outgoing, the telephone number dialed, the speakers intercepted, and the gist of the conversation.

For the time being the tape recorders were still, the logs blank, and the DEA's eager monitors idle because the focus of their attention was not at home using her phones. She was across town in Coral Gables at the eighteen-room home of her friends and interior designers Gustavo Delgado and Dick Lawrence off the sixth fairway of the Grenada Golf Course.

Late Saturday morning Darias picked up Marlene for their meeting with Tocayo. She was still nervous.

"Tocayo called me again a little while ago. He said, 'I'm very sick,' and I told him, 'Yes, but I have to see you because the one who will die of a heart attack will be *me*.' "

"I'm afraid of Tocayo," Darias said. "He is a very nervous guy. If one's nerves are like that, one should be an insurance salesman. You cannot let Tocayo transfer his nervousness over to you."

"From the beginning," Marlene said, "Tocayo will try and save his skin and say that the money 'it's not from drugs' and '*she* gave it to me' to take responsibility off himself. The only way the police could get something on me is for Tocayo to have said my name or if they were following him. But the police never saw me give him anything. Nobody has seen me delivering to him."

"Of course."

"I haven't called Jader yet. I have not told him anything."

"Don't alarm him without being able to tell him exactly what happened," Darias suggested.

The Westland Mall was crowded with Saturday traffic. Their first stop was a pet shop where Marlene had ordered a German shepherd puppy for Carlos Jader Alvarez. She and Darias determined that the dog would be available for her to take to Bogotá early the following week.

They chatted with Tocayo on benches in the center of the mall. Tocayo was still upset. He described four automobiles that he said had followed him on Friday afternoon. Fortunately for the DEA he apparently hadn't noticed the surveillance immediately after he left International Investments. He had seen the cars only *after* he had stopped at his own house and headed for the two warehouses west of the Palmetto. Thus he didn't seem to link the surveillance to International Investments or Robert Darias. Tocayo had never gotten the $100,000 in hundred-dollar bills to his pilot, and now returned the money to Darias together with an additional $90,000 for transmission to Colombia by another means yet to be chosen.

With Paul Sennett observing, Darias drove Navarro back to the house in Coral Gables and again recommended that she stop associating with Tocayo. "If he's hot, we don't want to see him." As an alternative to smuggling cash on planes, Robert suggested that Marlene open a Miami bank account for Carlos Jader Alvarez in the name of International Investments. She asked that he put that proposal in writing so she could show it to Alvarez.

"You look like you need a drink," Gustavo Delgado told Marlene. He served her a glass of white wine. To be sociable Darias accepted a Chivas on the rocks and lingered a while to make sure that Marlene was at ease.

At home later he called Carol Cooper to relay Tocayo's description of the four cars he claimed to have seen on Friday. She acknowledged that at least some of the cars were the DEA's and said she had instructed the surveillance agents to stay back from Tocayo. "That was ridiculous yesterday," she said. "The attorneys were mad about it this morning."

Robert said that from what he could observe Gustavo Delgado and Dick Lawrence appeared not to be involved in Navarro's drug business, although she clearly purchased a great deal of furniture through them, likely with drug cash, some of it for shipment to Jader Alvarez in Bogotá. "They have excellent taste," Darias said. "Fantastic taste."

Carol seemed disappointed to hear that Delgado and Lawrence

weren't involved. Federal agents root for as many people as possible to be implicated in the crimes under investigation.

"Needless to say, at this stage of the game, Bob, we want her back in that house and we want her using that telephone," Cooper said.

"Yeah, she will be there tomorrow," Darias said. "At this point she depends on whatever I say. She is completely helpless now."

"Okay, get her back to her house using that blasted phone. I've got forty-some-odd agents buzzing around wanting to do their thing."

Marlene did not return to Costa del Sol until early Sunday evening. A DEA car followed.

There was great anticipation at the listening post. It had been more than twenty-four hours since the wiretap had been connected, and the only sounds the monitors had heard were four incoming calls—unanswered—on the special line reserved for Carlos Jader Alvarez. The agents had dutifully logged the calls, one at 8:20 Saturday evening, and three more during the noon hour Sunday. By Sunday evening, knowing Navarro was on her way home, the monitors were edgy, like long-distance runners at the starting gate waiting for the gun.

Carol Cooper was especially nervous. Much of the energy behind the wiretap had been hers. All her efforts since the St. Patrick's Day Massacre four months earlier had led to this moment—the surveillance, the investigations, the telephone subscriber information, the pen register, the phone calls, the memos, the teletypes, the affidavits, the paperwork, all had seemed endless. And the infighting, the running battle with Tom Clifford, the back-channel maneuvering with Gruden and Billbrough over when (and even whether) to begin the wiretap, had consumed her. Cooper had won the battle. Now, largely because *she* had convinced the DEA to go forward, the agency had disrupted the lives of dozens of its agents and was spending many thousands of dollars assembling them in Miami for the extremely exacting task of listening to and digesting Marlene Navarro's telephone conversations. If Navarro proved to be as important a criminal as Cooper thought she was, if the phone calls produced hard evidence against Jader Alvarez and Pepe Cabrera, and especially if the tap led to a record drug seizure, then the DEA, the Justice Department, and the U.S. Attorney's office in Miami would be happy and Carol Cooper's career would prosper. If the wiretap did not produce significant evidence, Cooper would be deeply embarrassed and might never be promoted above GS-12.

Navarro arrived home a little after seven and flicked on *60 Minutes*. At 7:35 she called Gustavo Delgado about furnishing her upstairs guest room. In accordance with Michael Pasano's instructions about "minimizing non-pertinent conversations," the monitors began spot-monitoring.

At 7:45 she dialed Alex McIntosh's number in Toronto. There was no answer.

At 7:46 she called Tocayo. "I'll see you tomorrow morning at eleven at the nurse's office to give you the cream," Marlene said, an apparent coded reference to a previously scheduled meeting at the Bank of Miami.

At 7:57 Darias called Navarro. She said she was considering buying Gustavo and Dick's house in Coral Gables.

At 8:00 Alex McIntosh called from Toronto. She put Robert on hold and told Alex she would call him in a few minutes. When she clicked back to Robert, he told her that he felt the house in the Gables would be a good buy. She asked him to bring his written proposal for handling Jader Alvarez's money to the meeting with Tocayo on Monday morning.

At 8:03 Marlene again dialed McIntosh. The line was busy. At 8:04 she got through. Alex said he was eager to see her. Marlene said she was going to Bogotá Tuesday or Wednesday but would see him in Toronto next weekend. She cautioned him against mentioning names over the telephone. After a quarter of an hour, the conversation settled on personal matters, and the monitors began spot-listening until it ended just before 9:00.

At 9:27 an unidentified man called on the special bedroom phone reserved for Carlos Jader Alvarez. On the assumption that the caller was indeed Jader, the monitors listened intently. It was the first time they had heard the voice of *el padrino*, the godfather.

"Hello."

"Hello!" he said.

"Hello. Where have you been?" Marlene asked.

"And where have you been?"

"Because I called you yesterday. I left you a message there. Did they give it to you?"

"Oh, yes, yes, but I arrived very late. I was at the farm. I have tried calling you and you haven't been in."

"Yes, since Friday I have been over at some friends. Here in Miami. What's new, old man?"

"Nothing, nothing, whatever you say."

"Well, let me tell you something. I believe your things will not be delivered to you today or tomorrow but rather on Tuesday."

"Oh, don't tell me. Damn."

"Yes, because the driver had a heart attack." It was Marlene's first allusion to Tocayo's difficulty in shipping the $100,000.

"Shit!"

"They did not want to take the chance of having the other driver take it."

"Yes."

"Actually, it only *seemed* that the driver had a heart attack, because he had a very heavy cold and would have felt ill if he had traveled."

"Yes."

"Exactly. So in order to prevent the others from catching a cold, they decided to send it another way, which they will explain to you in person."

"Yes."

"Thank God, everyone is healthy and the furniture didn't get scratched."

"Yes, yes."

"In reality it was a passing cold, but it was useful because these people now will take care of their health. Right?"

"Yes, naturally."

Having reassured Jader without departing from the sickness metaphor, she went on to tell him about the German shepherd puppy that she expected to deliver to him within a few days.

"Aha!" Jader said.

"What legs! What a dog! You can tell that it's a clever dog."

Navarro arranged to confer with Jader in Bogotá Tuesday or Wednesday.

"I saw *el barrigoncito* [the little pot-bellied one]," she said, an apparent reference to Oscar. "He's going to call you. And if he also tells you about the heart attack it's because I told him, right?"

"Okay."

"*El barrigoncito* told me he has a quantity of records—music records—and he first wanted to talk to you to see what to do." It was unclear to the DEA whether this was a reference to cocaine, money, or something else.

"Whatever you decide, let me know," she said.

"Okay."

There was brief, innocuous talk of two people called "Louisa" and "Dr. Teo." The mafia often disguised real names with nicknames, first names, and gender switches, female derivatives of male names, and vice versa. It appeared likely that "Luisa" was Luis Fabio Rodriguez,

Jader's liaison to coca growers in Peru, and that "Dr. Teo" was Teodoro (alias Baltazar and Ivan) Terselich, the fat Yugoslav who had last surfaced in the DEA computer in August of 1980 when he helped Maria Lilia Rojas load a suitcase containing $1.6 million of Jader's money into a car the day before Rojas was arrested and the money discovered in Monopoly boxes at the airport.

Jader indicated he was confused about a delivery of "240," presumably $240,000. He said Teo had told him he had given it to Oscar. Marlene said she had not received it, and they agreed they would ask Oscar about it.

Jader asked Navarro to dial a number in "the city of lemons," which the area code revealed to be Lima, Peru, and patch him through. He had been unable to connect directly from Bogotá. All Marlene got in repeated attempts, however, was a recorded message about circuit congestion. So she and Jader said good night.

There had been no apparent reference to the problem of collecting $5 million in New York.

At the listening post Carol Cooper and her monitors were pleased. They had missed many of the coded references, but those presumably would become clearer as they listened to more conversations. The importance of this conversation was that they had confirmed that Navarro was in direct contact with Carlos Jader Alvarez—that she hadn't been speaking to maids or butlers in the 107 calls to Jader's phones that the pen register had noted. Her mention of the German shepherd puppy had cinched the identification of Jader; the DEA knew through Robert Darias that Jader had asked Navarro to buy the dog.

At 10:02 Navarro called Oscar's pager and asked that he call her.

Oscar called Marlene at 11:00, and she instructed him to call Jader immediately.

"*El papi* is looking for you," Marlene said. "He asked me if they had brought some records and I said yes but I had no idea of how many."

A man named Nelson phoned Marlene from Los Angeles twice between 2:00 and 3:00 A.M. Eastern time to say he was worried that a delivery of "flowers" had not been made. She told him "everything is okay" and she would check on it in the morning. Robert Darias had reported meeting a Nelson at Marlene's house a few weeks earlier.

With three surveillance agents looking on, Darias and Tocayo waited for Marlene Navarro in the Bank of Miami parking lot on Brickell

Avenue late Monday morning. Robert was complaining that Marlene
expected him to do petty favors for her but was giving him little
profitable business.

"I've reached a limit and I'm going to tell her," Robert said. "Right
now I had to go to Bird Road, in a hurry, because she's leaving
tomorrow and Jader needs some bulbs for some flashlights that I've
sent him. I'm not a damned flashlight salesman."

"The same thing happened to me," Tocayo said. "Blue jeans for
Jader. 'Did you get some blue jeans for Jader?' she asks me."

Darias suggested that they wait in his car with the air conditioner
on.

"I've been working with Marlene over a year," Robert continued.
"I have yet to make ten thousand dollars with her."

Navarro's new gold BMW drew up, and she joined them in
Darias's leased Cadillac. They drove across Brickell Avenue to the
Four Ambassadors Hotel.

After they ordered breakfast, Darias presented Navarro with a
written proposal to open a Miami bank account for Jader Alvarez in
the name of International Investments.

"I'll open an account for him and send him signature cards so he
can sign them, and nobody here at the bank will know who that
person is."

"The signature he always uses?"

"Anything he wants. He doesn't need identification. I'm the one
who has to identify myself."

Marlene agreed and handed Darias an envelope containing $8,500
in hundred-dollar bills with which to open the account. Darias remarked that using a bank account would eliminate the need for secret
cash shipments that attract attention such as the four cars that apparently followed Tocayo on Friday.

"I will never live through that again," Marlene said to Tocayo.
"Because *that* didn't worry me, I swear to God, what worried me was
you. I was vomiting and vomiting all Friday night. I don't want to go
through that again." Tocayo looked sheepish.

"They are focusing precisely on whoever carries the money and the
movement of money," Navarro said. "Jader has lost more than three
million dollars." (His money had been seized at airports on several
occasions.) "And we are talking about a man of intelligence. I would
give him an IQ of one eighty. He's a super genius, tremendous capacity."

They all agreed that Jader was foolish to insist that currency be
flown to Colombia rather than let International Investments handle it.

Darias made another pitch for more of Jader's business. "Marlene, you know that you and I have been in this a year or more. And you know that whenever there's a problem I help you."

"No, I know, Roberto."

"In whatever has to be done."

"And I appreciate it like you have no idea."

"But, Marlene, I have to start making a profit in this business."

"Why don't you get me the blank signature cards for the bank account for me to take to him."

There was no further activity on Navarro's telephones until that evening. She had a lengthy talk with Gustavo Delgado about interior decorating, which the monitors surmised was probably genuine—not a coded discussion of cocaine or money—because she followed it immediately with a call to the china department at Burdine's department store in the Dadeland Mall. She asked Darias to make reservations for her to fly to Bogotá on Tuesday evening or Wednesday morning. (Now he was playing travel agent.) She reprimanded Oscar for failing to stay in touch and make a delivery, possibly the $240,000 that Jader had asked about, but the allusion was cryptic. She had a brief chat with a woman friend who had just arrived in Miami from Paris. She tried unsuccessfully to reach Luis Rodriguez. She spoke with Alex McIntosh in Toronto around eleven o'clock and complained that she had had a busy but fruitless day. Jader called at three minutes past midnight, and Navarro told him she planned to fly to Bogotá on Wednesday.

Robert's call awakened Marlene at 8:51 Tuesday morning.

"Our friend is going to call you," she told him, "regarding those things we were talking about," an apparent reference to Oscar and either money or cocaine.

"You got to speak to him, then?"

"Yes, but I'll tell you those things in person."

Robert had booked her first class on Eastern Airlines flight 7 to Bogotá Wednesday afternoon.

Later in the morning she talked to Gustavo about furniture, crystal, and a trip to New York. She talked to a woman about attending some fashion shows in New York. She made a hair appointment for that afternoon at the Avant-Garde in Coral Gables. She tried to reach her soon-to-be-ex-husband, Henry. She spoke to her banker and her handyman. She called Lester Rogers, who was not in. She called her Brickell Avenue answering service for messages.

Robert met Marlene at the Coral Gables Burger King on Alcazar Avenue, off LeJeune Road, next door to the Avant-Garde just after her hair appointment.

"This is where he has to sign," Robert said, pointing to the bank signature cards he had just obtained for Jader Alvarez.

"What happened to Oscar?" Robert asked.

"He is going to call you. He is always running. He will give you two or three but has not collected it yet. And he said he will be around here Friday to deliver the other thing to you." Robert interpreted "two or three" to mean $200,000 or $300,000 and "the other thing" to be the cocaine they had discussed.

"Oscar leads a very disorganized life," Robert said.

"Yes. He called me last night crying about a kid who worked with him. They killed him to steal his money. I told him to be careful because sometimes they kill people in this business so they don't have to pay."

"Miami is very dangerous," Robert said.

"I am afraid of going around at night. I want to buy a gun. Since they followed Tocayo I've been waking up in the middle of the night."

"You have to be very careful."

"Jader always says not to do anything with people you do not know."

As Darias was arriving at Navarro's early that evening, Luis Fabio Rodriguez was leaving. Darias had not seen Rodriguez since December when Luis had purchased the $250,000 certificate of deposit. Rodriguez was riding a black motorcycle and wore a black jacket and helmet. A tennis racket was slung over his shoulder. After Luis had gone, Marlene told Robert that Rodriguez had delivered 20 kilograms of cocaine and owed Jader $920,000, which he had promised to pay by the following week. Oscar, according to Marlene, "is in the same boat." She also disclosed that the Jader syndicate owed a pilot $1.8 million for flying in the 2,000 kilograms of cocaine that she and Oscar had discussed with Robert. The going bribe for the illegal deliveries was $900 a kilo. They had planned to use part of the missing New York money to cover the pilot's fee, but since that money was still unaccounted for, the pilot was holding the cocaine hostage, presumably somewhere in the Miami area.

Later, Darias and Cooper went over what likely would be a fast-moving effort to deal with the cocaine and money which Marlene had said Oscar would deliver later in the week. The DEA agents were preparing for three contingencies: If they could trace the cocaine to the place where the pilots were holding it, or have the local police intercept Oscar with it before he delivered it to Darias, they might be able to seize it without compromising the operation. If that proved impossible, they would try to acquire the cocaine at International Investments for a token down payment, still avoiding exposure of the operation. If that failed, they likely would seize the cocaine and arrest Oscar and Marlene, ending Operation Swordfish.

"Tom was talking about installing a tape recorder in my car," Robert said. "Tell him to forget about that. I'm not going to have twenty different gadgets in my car that these people are going to be able to find. Carol, these people are already spooked."

"Make sure she totally understands the arrangements when you meet with Oscar," Carol said. "That meeting I definitely want taped."

"Oh yes."

"And I definitely want to know where *you're* at. I want somebody there."

"Yes."

"And see if you can get a telephone number for Oscar. I don't want to follow him, Bob, if I can help it. But I need to know where he's moved. They've had a tremendous amount of countersurveillance out. It's incredible. I'm gonna instruct them to follow very, very loosely." Surveillance agents had noticed targets looking around a lot and thought they had detected countersurveillance cars near the target cars.

That evening on the south side of Los Angeles, DEA agents alerted by Carol Cooper observed several suspected drug traffickers moving two large and obviously heavy suitcases out of a black BMW into a house, and later out of the house into a silver Ford. Cooper and her colleagues believed the suitcases contained the $2 million in narcotics currency which Marlene Navarro had told Darias a few days earlier that Oscar was picking up in California. The agents followed the Ford to Los Angeles International Airport around 11:00. But they lost it in traffic and were unable to locate the car, the passengers, or the suitcases at the Eastern Airlines terminal, where a flight left for Miami at 11:30.

The wiretap monitors had heard Marlene Navarro dial a Los Angeles number twice late that Tuesday evening, apparently failing to get through. At 4:00 A.M. Eastern time, a Los Angeles DEA agent awakened Carol Cooper to let her know the two suitcases might be aboard the Miami-bound flight. Cooper and several other agents converged at Miami International around 7:00 and watched the passengers and luggage come off the L.A. red-eye. They did not see any luggage fitting the description they had been given.

An hour later, when Oscar called Marlene just after eight, Marlene told him she had spoken to Nelson "last night."

"He ran the errand that you told him to run," she said. "But when he went to run the errand, to visit the bride, it looked like there were some cousins of this other guy who also were around."

"Oh!" Oscar gasped.

"So then he got scared, not that he got scared of the cousins, but he didn't want to cause trouble."

"Yeah."

Marlene said that Nelson was due in Miami within a few hours and would contact Oscar.

Oscar said he would make his "delivery to Roberto" today or tomorrow.

In reviewing the monitors' log notes on the conversation as it occurred, and their recording of the conversation itself, the DEA analysts surmised that Marlene's references to Nelson's "running an errand," "visiting the bride," and being surprised and frightened by the "cousins of the other guy," were codes for Nelson's attempting to pick up a large amount of cash at the residence in Los Angeles, noticing what he thought might be police surveillance, and deciding to back off. They also determined that when Marlene had spoken with Nelson late the previous evening, the monitors had failed to identify Nelson or record an accurate and complete gist of the call. By morning, however, the license tag on one of the cars at the Los Angeles residence where the suitcases were exchanged was traced to a man named Fulgencio Nelson Batista of Miami (obviously named for the ex-dictator of Cuba). The agents then remembered that a man named Nelson had called Marlene a night earlier, and that Darias previously had encountered a Nelson at her house. It appeared that Marlene or Oscar had assigned Nelson to pick up the $2 million that Navarro had mentioned to Darias.

Oscar arrived at Costa del Sol at 11:30 that morning and immediately called Nelson Batista's Miami residence, obviously to clarify the status of the California money. It appeared Oscar hoped to use it instead of the New York proceeds to pay the pilot in Miami who was holding hostage nearly $100 million worth of cocaine. Nelson's wife, Violet, suggested that Oscar try Nelson's pager. He apparently had just gotten off a plane from Los Angeles.

"Nelson, call me at Chiqui's, it's urgent. Call me at Chiqui's, Nelson, it's urgent," Oscar said to the pager. Nelson called four minutes later.

"Where are you?" Oscar asked. "You're the only one who can save me."

They agreed to meet at an apartment on 8th Street which apparently they had used previously but whose location was not specified so that the DEA monitors couldn't catch it. Paul Sennett and two other agents had set up surveillance outside Costa del Sol, hoping someone might lead them to the meeting. They saw Marlene's black Mustang leave the compound just after noon but lost it in traffic and were unable to identify the driver because of the car's tinted windows.

Oscar returned to Marlene's about 2:00 and took a call from Darias. They agreed to postpone their meeting until Thursday morning. Oscar was always cryptic on the phone, so it was unclear how much cocaine or money he might deliver. The surveillance agents lost Oscar after he left Marlene's.

A few minutes later Gustavo Delgado picked up Marlene and drove her to the airport for her flight to Bogotá.

When the break-in at International Investments was discovered on Saturday morning, Tom Clifford had asked Washington headquarters to send a security team to Miami to conduct a "TSCM" (technical security countermeasures) survey. The security team swept the premises, electronically and physically, and reported officially on Wednesday that it had found "nothing to indicate the presence of any hostile intelligence collection devices."

That afternoon, Clifford and his agents laid plans for what appeared to be a likely transfer of cocaine and money from Oscar to Robert Darias the next day. Oscar had said he would meet Darias, though it was unclear how much cocaine and cash he would have with him. Oscar had agreed to use Robert's car in case Oscar's car was being watched. The DEA outfitted Robert's car with an electronic transmitting device that would enable agents to track the vehicle without getting close when Oscar took it from Darias.

"You can't imagine where they installed that beeper," Robert told Cooper. "I told them these people are spooked already. We have to be careful. You opened the engine and you could see that thing sticking there."

"If you hear from Tom, give me a call and let me know what's happening," Cooper said. "I probably shouldn't say this, and don't ever tell him I told you this, but I don't necessarily want you talking to Tom about what's going on with this deal. Tell *me* what's happening and then I can manipulate on our end."

"Okay."

Cooper said she still couldn't officially tell Robert that the wiretap had begun and was frustrated because she was prohibited from using him to decipher codes. "As of right now we're fishing around. It's ridiculous. Everything she says is in code."

DEA and Colombian F-2 agents who met Eastern Airlines flight 7 when it arrived in Bogotá did not see Marlene Navarro. She had not checked any luggage, and probably got out of the airport fast, they surmised. Or she might have taken Avianca at the last minute. Surveillance was an art, not a science.

Thursday loomed as a long, tense day. Without telling Carol Cooper, Tom Clifford asked the FBI to put a tracking plane in the air that morning to aid in pursuing Oscar once he took Darias's car. The DEA hypothesized that Oscar would go to a secret stash, perhaps where the pilots were, ransom the 2,000 kilograms of cocaine with the money Nelson apparently had brought from Califonia, and bring the cocaine to International Investments. The plane could follow the radio signals from the beeper that the DEA had installed in Robert's car, eliminating the need for close surveillance on the ground.

But Oscar stood everybody up. He did not call Robert at 9:15 as he had promised, nor did he call later in the day.

The FBI called Carol Cooper at 10:30. "We've got a plane up. It's been up for over an hour. What's going on?"

"Put it down. Who told you to put a plane up?"

"Well, the thing was supposed to go at nine-fifteen."

"We should have had you wait till we knew the thing was going. These Colombians all own expensive watches. They just don't know how to read them."

Cooper called Darias.

"Did you hear from him?"

"No."

"What do you mean? I knew this was gonna happen. I knew it."

"They're all the same."

"I know. They're all the same. Not like Cubans, huh?"

"No, the Cubans are the same as the Colombians."

"I figured this would happen. Tell him to hurry up and call. I've got planes running around and crashing into each other up there."

With Laura Darias spending the day with a friend, Robert and Amelia were home alone—a few rare hours. Frank Sinatra singing "Someone to Watch Over Me" was on the stereo when Carol Cooper's next call interrupted. She was still seething at Oscar's failure to appear as promised.

"Why don't you give your girlfriend a call?"

"I have been thinking about that. Are you sure that's a good idea? I don't want to sound too eager."

"You gotta come across that you were trying to help them out and you made all sorts of arrangements. And you wasted time, and you were ready to do it, and Oscar didn't even have the courtesy to call you. I mean, you heard nothing. That's where I think you have a right to call."

"Well, I'll call her right now. I am going to say that I always come through with my appointments and I like to have people do the same thing."

"Exactly. When we get down the road here, I don't want to be messing around for four days trying to get the shipment. And that's what this guy'll do. So let's teach him a lesson right off the bat. I'm thinking that if you don't call her tonight down there, and, say, she doesn't come back till Saturday, and if you don't lodge your complaint till then, it's gonna lose something."

Robert reached Marlene at her cousin Carmenza's glass-fronted high-rise apartment in North Bogotá.

After asking about the weather and her health, Robert said, "I am accustomed to dealing with you, and when we have a date, we come through. I don't like to tell my lawyer to get the office ready and to have all the papers ready for the closing and then these people don't show up. They didn't even call to let me know that they were not going to show up."

"Roberto, I don't know what happened. He has more interest in talking to you than you have in talking to him. I don't know what happened. I'll try to find out."

After four days of listening to Marlene Navarro's telephone calls, 166 calls in all, the DEA felt it was gaining insight into the functioning of the Carlos Jader Alvarez organization. A few intriguing facts had been established. The organization apparently was having difficulty collecting $5 million from cocaine sales in New York. One or more pilots in the Miami area seemed to be withholding 2,000 kilograms of cocaine because they had not been paid their bribe for flying it in from Colombia—a bribe that was supposed to come out of the $5 million

from New York. Oscar seemed to hope he could ransom the cocaine
with the money that Nelson Batista presumably had brought from
Los Angeles.

The DEA monitors were frustrated by the work, which they found
confusing, maddening, and—for long stretches of time—numbingly
tedious. They did not know the reason for the collection difficulty or
the location of the cocaine. They did not know whether Oscar's failure
to deliver cocaine to Darias was related to the difficulty. They did not
know the fate of $2 million that supposedly had been collected in
California and flown to Miami. The monitors were awash in murky
code words: "things," "books," "catalogs," "photographs," "records," and "papers" seemed to refer to currency; "flowers" and
"gifts" seemed to refer to cocaine. But those were just suppositions,
inadmissible in court.

Other things were clearer, however. Marlene Navarro worked directly for *el padrino,* Carlos Jader Alvarez, with whom she spoke
nearly every evening around midnight. She supervised a network of
operatives on both coasts of the United States—Luis Rodriguez, Nelson Batista, Teodoro Terselich, Ricardo, Oscar, and others. Oscar, it
was clear, was unreliable.

The monitors welcomed the hiatus while Navarro was out of town.
Some of her telephone habits were irritating. She pressed the touch-
tone buttons hard and held them down longer than necessary, particularly the last digit of a number.

For a full year, Operation Swordfish had stymied its crosstown rival
Operation Greenback, which was still chafing to indict Lionel
Paytubi. Greenback Prosecutor Charles Blau had repeatedly deferred
to Tom Clifford's argument that Paytubi was leading DEA undercover agents to the top of the Latin drug mafia. Greenback's team of
IRS and Customs agents, who cared nothing about Operation Swordfish (they called it "Tunafish") and wanted to scoop their rivals at the
DEA, had grown increasingly restive and, indeed, nearly mutinous in
their anger at Charles Blau's delays. In April the DEA in Miami had
staved off Greenback only after an acrimonious meeting in Washington between officials of the Treasury and Justice departments.

In the summer, Operation Greenback gained a new and unwitting
ally. It was announced in Miami that the largest banking chain in
Florida, Barnett Banks, had filed an application with the Federal
Reserve Board to purchase the Great American Bank, Lionel
Paytubi's former employer and the institutional focus of the Green-
back investigation. If Barnett Banks swallowed the Great American

Bank, with all its files and records, the government's criminal investigation of Paytubi and the bank would be severely complicated. Charles Blau was prohibited by law from sharing secret information on his investigation of Great American with the Federal Reserve, or with Barnett, as a means of delaying the merger. Blau told Tom Clifford, therefore, that Operation Greenback had no choice but to proceed with its indictment of Paytubi and the bank within two months, before the Barnett-Great American merger was consummated.

Exhausted by the long interagency struggle, and by the many strains within Operation Swordfish, Clifford and his DEA bosses gave in. They set September 8—seven weeks hence—as the closing date for Operation Swordfish. The wiretap would end. Marlene Navarro and other targets likely would be arrested. The agency would try to confiscate as much money and as many additional assets as possible. It would also attempt to lure Carlos Jader Alvarez and Pepe Cabrera out of Colombia to a country where they could be arrested and brought to the U.S. without extradition proceedings. In the interim the DEA and the prosecutors would continue to build their cases against the targets.

"There's a lot of political problems that you're not aware of," Carol Cooper told Darias. "And they're getting way out of hand. September 8 is the absolute deadline. It *will* go down then. That's it. Final."

3 0

THE THREE-BEDROOM stucco house faced east in a residential neighborhood a few blocks off the Florida Turnpike in southwest Miami—a little more than a mile east of the Miami Zoo.

The young woman who was sleeping there Saturday night did not hear the fat man who stopped his car outside, splashed gasoline along the base of the garage door, and set it afire. The blaze burned itself out after superficial damage to the garage and house, and the woman inside did not discover the remains of the fire until she awakened late Sunday morning. She called the fire department, and to the investigating lieutenant she seemed "suspicious and afraid."

"She somehow knew the house was going to be burned," the officer reported to a Dade County arson investigator, who was unable in his initial interrogation to extract much information from the woman, identified as Tammy Neiss. She claimed the house was owned by her uncle, Jorge Castello, who was in Venezuela on business ("she did not know what type"). Though the uncle had lived in the house for three months, he had no home phone, no business phone, and no business address, according to Neiss. Declaring she was leaving the house "within the hour," she said it had been broken into several days earlier, and she expected it to be burned again.

Unbeknownst to the confused fire investigators, the house was a "safe house" used by the Alvarez syndicate to hide drugs, money, and people. The arsonist was Teo Terselich, the fat Yugoslav money broker who also went by the names Baltazar and Ivan. Terselich set the fire as a warning to Oscar and other collectors for the syndicate who had been using the house and who, Terselich felt, were responsible for the missing $5 million from drug sales in New York.

Though Marlene Navarro had told Robert Darias that the issue of the New York money was "settled," it in fact was not and she had grown increasingly anxious about Oscar's continuing failure to collect it. Before leaving for Bogotá, she had tried to reach the other collectors—two young Colombian brothers named Ricardo and Said (pronounced sah EED) Pavon. Robert Darias had met Ricardo at Costa del Sol and had encountered him again with Oscar in the parking lot of the 94th Aero Squadron when Oscar had tried to get Darias to take 140 kilograms of cocaine. The Pavons were supposed to have arrived at the "safe house" and to have reported to Marlene. Unable to locate them, she had turned for help to Terselich, who was one of the senior members of the Alvarez syndicate. Terselich felt Oscar was incompetent and unreliable. He also disliked and distrusted the Pavon brothers. Terselich had telephoned and driven to several locations around Miami looking for Oscar and the Pavons while Marlene was in Bogotá. He did not find them, and finally set the "safe house" afire, knowing the Pavons and Oscar would go there eventually.

Marlene Navarro returned from Bogotá on Saturday afternoon. Alexander McIntosh had already flown down from Toronto and was waiting for her at the house in Costa del Sol.

"I'm going to wait for her to call me, right?" Robert Darias asked Carol Cooper.

"Yes, just wait. I want her to think you're not anxious."

Cooper and several other agents were out looking for Oscar until 4:00 A.M. Sunday without success.

Navarro's phones were quiet on Sunday until after Alex McIntosh left to fly back to Toronto in the late afternoon. Marlene then tried to reach Nelson Batista but found that he had left for Las Vegas.

When she spoke to Gustavo Delgado early in the evening, the DEA monitors heard something ominous. The conversation concerned "Roberto."

"Roberto doesn't need to know about the business, the products, or anything," Marlene said. "Don't tell him anything because he can get us in trouble."

"Yes," Gustavo said.

"It's hard to talk business when someone you don't trust is in the room."

The only "Roberto" the DEA monitors knew was Robert Darias. Latins usually called him Roberto. Or could it have been a different Roberto?

The monitors phoned Carol Cooper at home, and she was alarmed. Though she trusted Darias, based on a year and a half of working with him, agents were instinctively wary of spies they were running, and always alert for danger signals, especially signs of trouble in the relationship between the spy and his target.

The most popular rumor about Robert Darias and Marlene Navarro was that she was sleeping with him, not that she distrusted him. But Carol had never believed that Robert and Marlene were lovers. If they were, Carol felt, there would have been signs, and there had been none. There also had been no indication that Robert might have been corrupted financially—that he had stolen money from his targets—although Nick Zapata and Eddie Hernandez had told people they had distrusted Darias since the day in April when Zapata had been sent to the wrong address and thus failed to witness Darias's receipt of $1 million cash from Marlene Navarro in the parking lot of the Bank of Miami. Cooper had discounted that suspicion, too, as-cribing it to Zapata and Hernandez's anger at being excluded from Darias's activities.

Cooper decided to do nothing for the moment about the conversa-tion the monitors had overheard. She would have plenty of opportuni-ties to test Robert's relationship with Marlene without revealing her new doubts.

Oscar called Marlene at 9:37 that Sunday evening. "I saw *el papi,*" she said. "Everybody sends you their regards."

"We'll talk in the morning, because this guy's garage—it's burnt," Oscar said. "The house is burnt. I'm worried about Ricardo."

"He's not around," Marlene replied, avoiding the subject of the house.

"But why is he tying me down, then? Leaving me in the middle." Oscar was angry. He had heard from contacts in Bogotá that Ricardo and Said Pavon were blaming him for failing to collect the $5 million in New York.

"Don't stand me up tomorrow," Marlene said. "Bring the books and bring everything."

They agreed to speak first thing Monday morning.

The DEA monitors assumed "books" stood for money but missed the references to the burned house.

Marlene called Darias a few minutes later. *"El papi* liked very much the idea of the transactions that we talked about," she said, referring to Jader Alvarez's new bank account in Miami. "He signed the papers."

She claimed that Oscar hadn't called her, even though she had just gotten off the phone with him, an apparent effort to defer any ques-tions Robert might have about the prospective cocaine delivery, which now seemed in doubt because of the collection problems.

Marlene mentioned that she had brought Robert four bottles of a sinus medicine that supposedly was superior to Sinutab.

She asked him to be available Monday afternoon.

Robert then called Carol.

"If she gets a large amount of money during the day tomorrow, I would think she would call me immediately," Robert said.

"I know she's looking for money, trying to straighten things out," Carol said. She instructed Robert to leave the hidden transmitter on his car.

Carol said nothing about Navarro's comments earlier in the evening about the "Roberto" whom she mistrusted and who could "get us in trouble."

Lester Rogers and Navarro talked just before nine o'clock Monday morning. "So, how did it go in Colombia?" he asked.

"Well, things are going more or less—the kids, you know. Nothing yet."

"Nothing?"

"He [Jader] is a little down and depressed, so it's normal. But business-wise it's not bad." There had been no recent word about the kidnapped children.

Oscar, having promised to call Marlene first thing Monday morning, did not call her until after 1:00 P.M., and she was furious.

"What happened to you?" she snapped.

"The problems I've had!"

"Listen, I don't have a husband or a lover, so you always make me suffer for *you*. When you set an appointment and you can't make it, call me, because I worry about your health since you had that cold! Always report in! I was waiting all morning and now I have to leave. I have to talk to you personally. That's why I wanted to talk to you this morning."

They agreed to meet at nine that evening.

Robert sat in Marlene's living room that afternoon munching an apple and popcorn as she told him that the 600 kilograms of cocaine she had promised him probably would be delayed.

"I don't know about our shoes," she said. "Jader said he doesn't want to get into anything or any commitment until his children show up or until he decides if they don't show up. He said 'I no longer have the energy to work like before. I don't feel like myself anymore. I'm destroyed. I'm not in the mood to fight or to work.' He looks, not tired, but—"

"Depressed?" Robert was familiar with that condition, although he had not experienced it recently.

"Depressed. It shows in his face." Navarro indicated that Robert could still probably get a hundred kilograms of cocaine because Jader had said, 'For that I don't have to work hard.' "

She added that Oscar was having a very difficult time collecting for the last shipment. "The people who should have paid, haven't. He had to go to New York to collect, and he couldn't even contact the people." That problem, she reminded Robert, had held up a payment to the pilots who had flown the next shipment—2,000 kilograms—from Colombia to the U.S. The pilots were holding the cocaine until they were paid. The Alvarez syndicate apparently was not the smoothly running machine that the Latin drug mafia was sometimes portrayed to be. Could it be as faction-riven as the DEA? Darias mused.

"If the pilot doesn't want to deliver, if they don't pay, he's absolutely right," Marlene said. "If I were they I wouldn't either. They should have paid the pilots."

Marlene told Robert that Jader Alvarez wanted to open one or two additional bank accounts in International Investment's name in Miami so that he could avoid depositing huge amounts of money in a single bank. She handed him the signature cards for the initial account, with an illegible signature inscribed by Jader.

While they were talking, Marlene took a call from a woman in Vancouver, British Columbia, regarding a drug transaction. Marlene agreed to call the woman back from a coin telephone at 7:30 Eastern time and asked if Robert could receive currency in British Columbia. He said he could. It occurred to him that while she was on the phone she was being recorded by the DEA in two locations, at the listening post in the Phoenix Building and in her own living room on Robert's tiny Sony.

"She's going to be meeting with your friend, Oscar, tonight," Carol Cooper told Darias in the late afternoon. "And we'll probably be up pretty late trying to follow this character around. He is going to get landed somewhere tonight." "Landing" was agent lingo for tailing a target to the place where he spends the night.

"I'm going to stay home," Darias said. "I didn't want to go out at all today. My sinus is killing me. And Humberto is completely out of his mind. He's drinking again and I had three drinks with him." Operation Swordfish had been neglecting its case against Humberto Garcia.

"Holy Cow. Listen, if you can't get me later it's because we're out on the street literally chasing this guy."

Marlene was on the phone with Nelson Batista when Oscar arrived at 10:00, an hour late, obviously high on something, likely cocaine or Scotch or both. Batista said he was leaving tonight "for another town" and asked Marlene to get a number where he could reach Oscar.

Oscar stayed only a few minutes, and Cooper and Sennett again followed him several miles into southwest Miami. But they were stopped by a traffic policeman for speeding, and by the time they showed their badges and were released, Oscar, who had also been speeding, had disappeared.

Oscar arrived at Costa del Sol at 11:30 the next morning and immediately made a call to Bogotá from Marlene's telephone. To the monitors, he sounded enraged and again high on something. Marlene had referred to him as a "jolly drunk," but he was not jolly now. It seemed that Ricardo and Said Pavon, who still had not turned up at the "safe house," had passed the word directly to Jader Alvarez that Oscar was responsible for the recent problem with deliveries and collections. As Oscar was driving out of the Costa del Sol compound he rammed his car through the barrier at the gate before the guard could lift it. With the rod lying broken in the street behind him, Oscar accelerated, took the first corner on two wheels and sped off.

The gate guard immediately called Marlene and reported the incident. The DEA monitors heard the conversation, learned that Oscar was driving a gold Toyota with tinted windows, and alerted the surveillance agents outside Costa del Sol. They had noticed a Toyota being driven recklessly, but had not identified the car as Oscar's. Prompted by the monitors, the agents followed Oscar to a shopping center in southwest Miami where he spoke briefly on a coin telephone. He then parked in a closed garage nearby, emerged and spoke to a cab driver, went back into the garage and drove out in a blue gray Toyota with two passengers, and headed west on Kendall Drive following the taxi. Reluctant to press their luck, the agents terminated the surveillance.

As the agents were following Oscar, Marlene beeped Darias, who called her right back.

"I saw my friend *el barrigoncito*. He's so sad. He's so worried. Because he feels very hurt from all the nonsense they do to him."

"Yes."

She told Robert that Oscar had crashed through the gate of Costa del Sol. "Roberto, do me a favor, if you talk to him, tell him one has to take it easy. I'm going to tell him not to come back here, Roberto, because one of these times he's going to get into an accident and it'll be blamed on me. Perhaps he'll listen to you more than he would to me."

"Sure."

"And I told him not to take things to heart so much."

"Does he still have those earrings he bought in Mexico?" Robert asked, alluding to the smaller shipment of 100 kilograms of cocaine which Marlene had said was still designated for Robert.

"Yes, I believe so. And he wanted to talk to you. Because it seems that he wanted to change the earrings and he wanted you to see them. He doesn't know much about earrings. He is going to give them to his wife as a gift, and he wants to be sure that he is giving her a good gift."

Oscar was supposed to call Robert by 3:00 P.M. He did not call.

"I'm going crazy because nothing is happening," Robert told Carol that evening after speaking to Navarro. "It gets to your nerves a little bit, and you take it out on the family. I feel unimportant because I'm not doing anything."

"I know, I know. Paul and I know you feel left out right now and we both wish we could do something about it. Paul and I are working like sixteen hours a day. We're getting exhausted. I wish I could bring you in and let you do half of this crap. But I just can't."

Carol, who had developed a bad cough and fever, stressed that Robert must persevere. "The little bits and pieces," she said. "The little dinky things are super important. Every little thing she says at this particular point is critical. It really is. Even though you may not think something is super important, let us know every single thing she says. Because it may tie in another conversation that you're not even aware of."

Robert asked what he should do about the cocaine.

"It depends on how you feel about it, Bob. You might want to start putting a little pressure on her at this particular point."

"I did. You will listen to the tape."

"That's fine, well and good, talking to her, but now she's gotta get off her rear end and start getting on Oscar's case to do it."

"I don't think they have the cocaine," Robert said. "Oscar has some problems."

"There is a problem. I can tell you that. I don't know exactly what the problem is. They're not discussing it. But he does have a major problem." Cooper was inferring the "problem" from Oscar's mood and Marlene's anger rather than specific information.

Carlos Jader Alvarez called Navarro just before midnight.

"I was in the bathroom," she said.

"I always catch you when you are in the bathroom, right? You didn't stay locked in this time."

"No, I don't close the door anymore."

"Have you seen this girl, *la barrigoncita?*" Jader asked, using the gender switch in referring to Oscar.

"He told me this morning that he has many problems, and that he is trying to locate these people who were going to do the medical examinations, to give you the results, and that he has not found anybody—that they don't show up. And I told him, 'Look, although you may not have any good news to give him, call him so that he'll know you are all right,' to call you no matter whether the news was good or bad, but that the important thing is she should call you. Then she said, 'Yes, but I am so down, I don't know what to say,' etc. etc."

"I warned him real good that I need at least fifty shares," Jader said. "The stock exchange is down but one has to resort to any means."

"I think there are plenty of shares, but they weren't paying him," Marlene said. The monitors logged "stock exchange" and "shares," which apparently were references to the difficulty collecting the New York money.

"Oh, I see."

"That is what he told me, because he was quite, quite crestfallen."

"Well, have him call me tomorrow night. In any case, get in touch with Doña Teofila [Teodoro Terselich], because she has instructions." Marlene had not heard from Terselich since he burned the "safe house."

"Okay, I will tell him."

The monitors were noticing that Jader and Navarro often did not bother to maintain the gender-switch codes through an entire conversation.

"And how is everybody doing there?" Marlene asked.

"No, everything is the same, dear."

"There is nothing at all?"

"Nothing at all."

"Oh, gee, I thought that around this time you might have some good news," Marlene said, referring to the children.

"Nothing, nothing, nothing, nothing," Jader said, his voice trailing off.

The Colombian police informed the DEA in Bogotá that a wiretap on the telephones of another godfather, Carlos Lehder Rivas, revealed that Lehder had referred a potential buyer of hundred-kilogram quantities of cocaine to Carlos Jader Alvarez. The list of the "Top 20" godfathers compiled by DEA intelligence listed Carlos Lehder as "the largest supplier of cocaine into the United States." The report from Bogotá said that Lehder had told his client that Jader Alvarez could supply "unlimited quantities of cocaine."

"My sinusitis is a little better—I think the pills are doing me good," Robert told Marlene just before nine Wednesday morning, July 28.

"It's really true—take them every morning," she said. "Listen, Robert, *el papi* called me last night. I want to talk to you regarding Oscar's matter. There's an impasse."

They agreed to talk later in the day.

Robert called Carol immediately. "I guess you know I talked to her."

"Yeah."

"She said there's an impasse with Oscar."

"Yeah, I heard that one."

"I only hope they don't kill Oscar at this point."

"No, they won't."

"This waiting is really getting to me."

"I know. Go for a swim. Cool yourself off."

"I'll be ready in case he calls. She might be calling before noon."

"Okay, get your little tape recorder ready."

Nelson Batista called Marlene from Caesar's Palace in Las Vegas.

"I'm a little worried over our friend here, *el barrigoncito,*" Marlene said of Oscar. "He goes around, he acts strange and he does things he shouldn't have done. And it looks like our friend, the little one [Ricardo Pavon], has played a dirty trick on him." Ricardo not only had failed to meet Oscar at the "safe house" but was in Bogotá blackening Oscar's name.

"I feel responsible at times because I was the one who introduced them to each other," Marlene said.

"Yes."

"Just between you and me, what happened was that the credit cards were delivered to him without the signatures. And it isn't a small credit card but rather quite a few. This one is really going to cost him dearly, because it's about five big ones."

The monitors surmised that this was another reference to Oscar's failure to collect $5 million in New York. "Many things are happening," Navarro continued. "He hasn't reported to *el papi* in a week. *El papi* is beginning to get alarmed and to have doubts, which is quite normal."

"Sure."

"Because we're not talking about a small shirt shop. Yesterday he came in such a nervous wreck that I got scared, and he almost killed himself at the entrance here. All these things make me very fearful. Now don't tell him I'm telling you all these things."

"No."

"We had told him not to deliver the credit cards without getting an advance. He delivered an exorbitant amount."

"Ricardo has done nothing at all?" Nelson asked.

"He's disappeared, which is the worst part."

They agreed that Marlene would have Oscar call Nelson in Las Vegas.

The frustrated DEA monitors were still confused about the collection difficulties. They informed Carol Cooper, who decided to deploy Darias to try to clarify what Marlene was talking about. It was also an opportunity to probe the extent of Marlene's trust in Darias, in light of her comments to Gustavo Sunday evening about the mysterious "Roberto."

"I have an assignment for you," Carol told Robert.

"Yes."

"I want you to meet with her as quick as you can."

"What's going on?"

"She's all excited and I want her to tell you about it."

"She got some money?"

"No, I can't tell you what she's excited about. But she is excited and I want you to get together with her. I think she'll tell you about it."

"I thought she was excited because of a problem that Oscar had."

"Well, that's part of it."

"Okay, let me call her and I call you back."

Robert called Marlene immediately. She sounded worried. He was calm and reassuring.

"I'm not very well, because we're very worried about this friend of ours, *la barrigoncita*," she said.

"Yeah?"

"She had some jewels, the ones we talked about, and they've been stolen."

"Oh, my—"

"At least they don't want to pay her for the jewelry she sold. It was an inheritance from her father. It's about five million dollars."

"Imagine that!"

"This girl is very worried and we're very worried for her, and today we're making the rounds to see if we can help her."

"Yes."

"Because, of course, she feels very bad, because she can't lose that jewelry of her father's."

"No way."

"We're trying to figure out how we can locate those two girls she delivered the jewelry to."

"The earrings you were going to give me in order to have them appraised, you won't be able to?"

"I think those are pending. Tomorrow I can give you some assurance, and we can talk in person about some things."

Robert called Carol back.

"Okay?"

"You're doing a fine job," she said. "I *thought* she'd tell you what was going on. I wanted *her* to tell you. I think we know what's going on."

"She's lost over a hundred kilograms. Five million dollars. It may be the load I turned down . . ."

"Yeah, I think so. I'm glad she told you about it. Looking good, kid."

Carol was relieved. Robert's talk with Marlene provided verification of the syndicate's problems collecting $5 million. While details remained unclear, it appeared that Ricardo and Said Pavon had been at least partly responsible for conveying the cocaine Robert had rejected to New York and for collecting the $5 million. But the Pavons had disappeared, and Oscar, who also bore some responsibility, was unable to locate them.

The conversation also seemed to indicate that Marlene still trusted Robert. Her Sunday night comments about "Roberto" must have referred to someone else.

Oscar showed up at Marlene's half an hour after her talk with Robert with a man the DEA could not immediately identify. Whatever was said in the house frightened Marlene because a few minutes later, with fear evident in her voice, she called Eastern Airlines and booked a reservation on the next flight from Miami to La Guardia Airport in New York.

"What is the last name?" the reservation agent asked.

"One second."

Marlene conferred hastily in Spanish with two male voices in the room.

"Rojas. R-O-J-A-S."

"And when Mr. Rojas gets into New York does he need a car or a hotel?" the flight agent asked.

Robert Darias in 1939 at age five in Camagüey Province, Cuba. The circumstances of Darias's childhood and youth equipped him better than most Americans for the psychic and physical dangers he later faced as a battalion officer at the Bay of Pigs and as the chief spy in Operation Swordfish. Political treachery and purposeful violence were part of the fabric of Darias's early life. His father and uncle were members of the secret society known as ABC Radical, which in the thirties used terror to help rid Cuba of President Gerardo Machado, a dictator of exceptional brutality and corruption. Darias studied at the University of Havana, served in the Cuban government as it crumbled under Batista, and married into two socially elite families, the first before he left Cuba, the second in Miami, where both families took refuge from the Castro regime.

Current photographs of Darias have been omitted to protect his security.

Marlene Navarro: Her friends called her "Hummingbird." The *Miami Herald* called her one of the "world's deadliest criminals." Chief of North American operations for a major Colombian drug syndicate, she marshaled vast sums of drug money and directed a complex network of drug distributors and couriers. Born in rural Colombia and educated in Paris, the multilingual Navarro later earned a degree in economics from the University of Miami. During Operation Swordfish, she grew so afraid of being shot that she began to bleed internally.

SEMINARIO GRUPO CONSOLIDADO
HOTEL TAMANACO CARACAS 28-5-85

Marlene Navarro at a business conference in Caracas, where she lived for over a year under a false name and passport. Active on the diplomatic cocktail circuit, she had an affair with the president of the Supreme Court of Venezuela, elder statesman, diplomat, and intellectual Rene de Sola.

Marlene Navarro in Israel, where she lived for extended periods and converted to Judaism. Similar photographs were on display in her study in Miami alongside Paris gallery posters, international monetary reports, and stacks of *Economist* magazines.

Marlene Navarro's three-bedroom town house in Miami, where she concealed a secret flow of millions of drug dollars and carried on an affair with a Scottish engineer. The DEA tapped both telephones in the house, one of which she reserved solely for conversations with her boss in Bogotá.

Thomas J. Clifford, the DEA's Miami intelligence chief and the founder of Operation Swordfish. Enlightened officials of the Department of Justice called Clifford's ideas for infiltrating the narcotics mafia "revolutionary." But he was not so popular in his own hidebound DEA bureaucracy. His feud with Special Agents Frank Chellino, Carol Cooper, and Paul Sennett disrupted Swordfish and nearly derailed all of their careers.

Carol Cooper's reception desk at Dean International Investments in Miami Lakes. Well into Operation Swordfish, the DEA moved Dean International to another location and changed its name out of fear that its true mission had been compromised.

DEA Special Agents Paul Sennett, Carol Cooper, and Frank Chellino in a rare snapshot together.

Sennett (*left*), who recruited the spy Robert Darias, posed as Dean International Vice President Paul Shafer. Sennett threatened to "beat the shit" out of anyone who interfered with the authority of Carol Cooper, his partner before Operation Swordfish.

Cooper (*center*), posing as Dean International aide Carol Collins, was Robert Darias's primary control. Skilled at bureaucratic infighting, she wrested control of the Navarro investigation from Swordfish founder Tom Clifford.

Chellino (*right*), who played the undercover role of investment counselor Frank Dean, was called "Little Hitler" by his colleagues because of his bossy manner, mustache, and short stature.

José Antonio "Pepe" Cabrera, one of the founders of the drug industry in Colombia and a partner of Carlos Jader Alvarez. Under arrest in the United States, Cabrera posted $1 million in emeralds as bail and fled to Colombia. After the assassination of the Colombian Minister of Justice, which Cabrera knew of in advance, he was arrested again and extradited to the United States, where he later turned state's evidence against General Manuel Noriega.

La Iglesia (the Church): Carlos Jader Alvarez's five-story mansion, purchased from Pepe Cabrera, in one of the most exclusive neighborhoods of Bogotá. Christmas presents for the Alvarez children lay in the house unwrapped as Alvarez and his men searched for the kidnappers.

Carlos Jader Alvarez, "*El Muñeco*" (the Doll), godfather of a vast Colombian narcotics syndicate and Marlene Navarro's boss. When guerrillas kidnapped three of his young children, Alvarez directed Navarro to smuggle millions of dollars in cash from the United States to Bogotá for use as ransom—an event that complicated Operation Swordfish. Alvarez and his fellow drug lords, galvanized by several brazen kidnappings, created and deployed the vigilante force Death to Kidnappers against the guerrillas. Alvarez is shown here flanked by two aides in the Bahamas on the way to Miami to shore up his damaged drug empire.

Four months after abducting Alvarez's children, the kidnappers photographed them to prove that they were alive as of the date of the newspapers they were holding. *From left to right:* Zuleika, seven; Xouix, five; and Yidid, six.

The hamlet of Gachalá at the end of a dirt road deep in the Andes. When the vigilante group Death to Kidnappers began interrogating and killing suspects in Bogotá, the guerrillas who had kidnapped the Alvarez children moved them to a remote hideout near here.

The shack in the mountain meadow above Gachalá, where the kidnappers held the children for several months. The unmapped area is called *Las Brisas* (the Breezes) because of the cold damp winds that blow constantly.

Special Agent Steve Gibbs and construction executive Brooks Muse III. Their criminal conspiracy to compromise an undercover operation endangered the lives of U.S. agents.

Rogue Miami drug lawyer Raymond J. Takiff. The existence and names of the targets of Operation Swordfish were leaked to Takiff when the top-secret operation was at its most sensitive stage, more than three months before it ended. At the time, Takiff did nothing to alert the government. Later, in different circumstances, he became a spy for the government.

Assistant U.S. Attorney Myles H. Malman, the lead prosecutor of Carlos Jader Alvarez and Marlene Navarro and later the co-lead prosecutor of General Manuel Noriega.

Alcee Lamar Hastings, the outspoken federal judge who presided at the trials of Carlos Jader Alvarez and Marlene Navarro. Of Ronald Reagan's "Just Say No" anti-drug campaign, Hastings said, "Give me a break!" After Hastings was prosecuted for and acquitted of bribery, his fellow judges, believing he was guilty, began investigative proceedings against him—proceedings that generated distracting publicity during the Alvarez and Navarro trials. Eventually Hastings was impeached and convicted by the U. S. Congress. Still later he was elected to the same Congress by Florida voters.

"No, I don't think so."

It appeared to the DEA that the Alvarez syndicate might be sending an enforcer to New York—someone with more sway than Oscar, Ricardo, or Said—to take care of the $5 million shortfall.

Later, Marlene dialed Bogotá urgently and repeatedly, and finally got an aide to Jader Alvarez, a man called Hugo.

"I'm here suffering for both of us," she said, "Sometimes instead of starting to cry I break out laughing. I said to myself, since Hugo and I look like the bad guys, we take the rap."

"And what's new?"

"Your friend and partner, this guy Ricardito, disappeared on these people. Remember the machinery they'd delivered to him?" She meant the cocaine that had been sent to New York.

"Oh, yes, he has that," Hugo said. "He's here."

"Well, why doesn't he report it? Because, imagine, they were saying that it was because I'd recommended him so much, it must be that we're plotting something. What do you think?"

"Look, tell them if they want I can speak to *el papi* here."

"No, no, no. Don't even think of that, darling. Don't stick your foot in it." They shouted at each other through a weak connection.

"But the brother is there," said Hugo, a reference to Ricardo's brother Said Pavon being in Miami.

"But they haven't been able to find him. He hasn't turned up. They are on the lookout for him and he's not showing up anywhere."

"He's there."

"Then why doesn't he at least get in touch with me to be sure that everything's going all right."

"Ricardo left his brother there attending to the warehouse."

"But the brother closed down the warehouse, hasn't reported in, didn't pay the taxes, nor has he even called to sign the letters of credit."

"I'll call him in a little while and tell him to call you."

"*El papi* there doesn't know this," Marlene said. "What he knows is that there are some things that are lost, but he knows neither who, how, or when. Try to help me get rid of this worry hanging over my head." Marlene's voice was angry and commanding.

"Calm down, calm down," Hugo said.

"Darling, help me, I didn't sleep last night."

"Don't worry. I'm on top of it."

They agreed to talk again at 9:00 P.M.

A man wearing gold-rimmed glasses, designer jeans, a multicolored T-shirt, and gray loafers, checked in at Eastern Airlines at 6:00 P.M.

and purchased the ticket that Marlene had reserved in the name of H. Rojas. As three agents watched from dispersed positions, he boarded Eastern flight 28 for LaGuardia.

Carol Cooper asked the New York DEA office to set up surveillance on "Rojas" when he arrived. Summing up her analysis to that moment, she stated in a teletype that she expected Rojas "to meet with someone in New York, who received in excess of 100 kg. of cocaine. Rojas is to press the unidentified customer for payment, as the organization needs $1.8 million for payment to pilots in Florida who are holding 2,000 kgs. shipment."

Teo Terselich called Marlene at 9:14 that evening.

"Richie turned up," she said, referring to Ricardo Pavon.

"Richie turned up?"

"Yes."

"Well, I have some news for Richie."

"Yes."

"I sent that house flying," Teo said, referring to the "safe house" he had set afire. "I don't know if he complained to you or not. Is he here?"

Her other line rang. It was Ricardo Pavon calling from Bogotá. She clicked back to Teo, who said, "Don't mention anything to him." Teo said he would be at Marlene's house in an hour.

She clicked to Ricardo.

"Son, I was worried," Marlene said.

"I'm dependable in my things, Marlencita, and it angers me for Oscar to say those things and to alarm people, because you know that I am very dependable, and I've never had any, any, *anything* being said about me doing something to anyone. Forgive me, I'm so upset!" The voice was young, intense, and self-righteous—another high-strung courier. Oscar clearly had launched a counterattack against the Pavons's accusations of incompetence.

"I know it, darling," Marlene said, "and I was suffering a great deal, precisely because you know that I couldn't have given any better references than what I gave. What's happened, darling, is that no-body, nobody, nobody showed up—"

"It's a lie. That is false, because Said has been at the house waiting for two days for the gentlemen to show up. Said will deal with you directly, because there's nothing more to talk about, but for Said to deliver all the catalogs of the machinery to you, because almost all of them are ready."

"All right, and when will Said show up around here?"

"Said is at the house waiting for you."

"Listen, just between you and me, my love, there is confusion. I believe you because I know that—"

"It makes me very angry, Marlencita, because everybody knows me and nobody has to say anything about me. And, and, and they start making judgments, which is very touchy, Marlene."

"I know, imagine, I had recommended you. I said, 'Yes, and I continue to recommend him.'"

"But we cannot play with people's reputations, Marlencita, my love, that's very delicate. That shows a lack of respect, even a lack of friendship, and lack of everything. And so it seems to me that's very childish and very much like a beginner."

"Just between you and me, love, I'm on your side. But you have to understand that he [Oscar] was upset."

"I'm going to talk to Jader today, because it makes me furious."

"No, no, don't talk to him yet. He still doesn't know anything. We've been trying to cover things up. He has no idea. Don't tell him anything, so it won't spoil things for the future. The only thing I want is for you to tell me what to do in order to locate Said, so that they won't do anything to him"—she was thinking of Rojas the enforcer— "because I'm afraid that perhaps—"

"What?" said Ricardo, even more agitated. "I'm flying there right now. So that they shouldn't *do anything to him? Like what?* Explain it to me well, Marlencita, because I mean I'll take off and go there!"

"No, no, don't get like that. I just want to get in contact with him and see to it that everything goes well."

"Let Said deal with you only, please."

"Okay, darling, don't worry."

"And, my love, tell that gentleman that I'm very surprised at his behavior, as well as his manner."

Ricardo gave Marlene a Miami telephone number where she could reach his brother Said.

Agents from the New York field office of the DEA were waiting when Eastern flight 28 landed at LaGuardia at 10:15 that evening. The man called Rojas emerged from the plane with a young woman. Each of them made calls from public telephones, and then were met by a man in a gray Volkswagen, who drove them to an apartment building in Queens. There they exchanged the Volkswagen for another automobile, which was in the NADDIS computer as registered to the sister of a man who had smuggled 200 kilograms of cocaine, $10 million worth, from Bogotá to Miami on or about June 10, less than two months earlier. The surveillance agents then lost track of Rojas, but he was later identified tentatively as a close associate of two major Colombian narcotics lords—colleagues of Carlos Jader Alvarez.

Oscar, Luis Rodriguez, and Teo Terselich all came to Marlene Navarro's house late that evening and did not leave until after midnight. The monitors knew that much by listening to her telephone conversations. But since they could not listen to conversations in the house off the phone, they seemed to have reached a plateau in their efforts to glean what the organization was up to. They had heard at least one reference to a burned house but had not yet grasped its significance. Darias probably could learn more from Navarro, but that would take time.

Marlene's call awakened Alex McIntosh in Toronto at fifteen minutes past midnight.

"Sorry, darling, I didn't mean to disturb you. They left about five minutes ago, and I am a little more relaxed, so I said, okay, I am going to see if McIntosh is *alone! Aha!"*

"Oh, I'm alone, all right. Not only that, I'm by myself."

"Okay, darling, now I am going to let you sleep. I have so many things tomorrow."

"Busy, busy girl."

"I am. Believe it or not, I am. So, go back to sleep, darling. I won't interfere any more with your sleep."

With the Johnny Carson show murmuring across the bedroom, Marlene dialed the number that Ricardo Pavon had given her for his brother Said. She told the woman who answered to have Said "call Chiqui, urgently, early in the morning."

31

FRANK CHELLINO WAS abruptly recalled from four months of exile and reassigned to Operation Swordfish in late July. Tom Clifford summoned Chellino on orders of Gruden and Billbrough, who had been prodded quietly by Carol Cooper. Chellino's return sealed Cooper's victory over Clifford.

On the organization chart, Cooper, Chellino, and Paul Sennett still reported to Clifford, along with the rest of Operation Swordfish. In reality, Cooper reported directly to Gruden and Billbrough, who had lost a good deal of confidence in Clifford's managerial abilities. Whatever the merits of individual conflicts, Clifford's fight with Chellino and the others in March, followed three months later by his fight with their replacements, Nick Zapata and Eddie Hernandez, made it appear to the bosses that Tom Clifford did not have control of his operation, that he might be the problem, not the agents. From Clifford's point of view, Gruden (and Billbrough) had become a "nemesis," who "failed to comprehend" Operation Swordfish.

Carol Cooper had emerged from the controversy as a favorite of Gruden and Billbrough. When she was assigned a new Chevrolet Malibu to drive, Sam Billbrough had helped her put on the license plates. And now she was personally supervising the most important Swordfish cases, including the wiretap of Marlene Navarro. Chellino and the others now worked for her, reversing their positions at the beginning of the operation.

Though he still made brief appearances in the role of Frank Dean, Chellino spent most of his time at a desk alongside Cooper's outside the listening post in the Phoenix Building, helping Cooper manage the burgeoning dimensions of the wiretap and the forty agents working on various aspects of it. Cooper also guided Paul Sennett, who ran the tricky surveillance of Marlene Navarro and her accomplicies as they moved about Miami.

Tom Clifford rarely challenged Cooper's judgment or decisions, and confined himself to supervising the relatively modest efforts still in progress at the offices of International Investments to infiltrate other groups of narcotics smugglers and financiers. Felipe Calderon had gradually learned to control his fear of death at the hands of the drug mafia, and by July his patient cultivation of the Colombian banker Victor Covo was beginning to pay off. Covo made four deposits of narcotics proceeds at International Investments totaling nearly $1.5 million. Covo also entrusted Calderon with the care of two machine guns and a pistol.

The trip to New York by the man called Rojas, together with Marlene Navarro's telephonic lashing of her colleagues in the Jader Alvarez organization, apparently had the desired effect. Someone—the DEA failed to determine who—delivered $750,000 in cash to Marlene's house before noon on Thursday, July 29. While only a down payment on the full amount owed, it was enough to ease the pressure.

The elusive Said Pavon, Ricardo's brother, called Marlene early that afternoon on the special Jader phone on her nightstand.

"What's up, Marlencita?"

"Darling, you are really something? I was afraid, because Oscar was a bit annoyed. Not anymore, because I had a chat with Ricardo last night and explained to him."

"They were looking for Oscar all over the place," Said stated.

"Who's looking for him?"

"Jader. I don't know who."

"No, no, no, precisely. *We* were looking for him," Marlene emphasized, "because he had disappeared, because he was going around looking for *you*. Since you all hadn't reported, poor Oscar didn't know how to present himself. But everything's already taken care of, cleared up. The only thing is that he was a bit annoyed. And if he did some nonsense [a purposely vague and misleading reference to the fire at the "safe house," which had been set by Teo Terselich], I hope you are more calm. Make Ricardo understand."

"But I've been looking for Oscar all over."

"Oscar was annoyed and you know he's quick-tempered. If he did something, Said, if he did some nonsense, don't take it too hard, remember that he was also worried because he didn't know what to tell *el papi*. Understand him. He's a good boy, Said. And he's very fond of you all."

"Yes."

"But he was annoyed for a few days, whether he was right or not, he thought he was right."

"Really! What must he have been thinking! Imagine!"

"He must have been thinking everything possible. I think he went to your house, and since he didn't find you—"

"But the house, the niggers set fire to my house."

"That's what he told me." Marlene was relieved that Said did not suspect Oscar or Teo of burning the house.

"Oh, Marlene, you don't know how relieved I am that I found you."

"Oh, and I am so relieved, Said, because I spoke to Ricardo yesterday. He was in such a mood. He was mad as hell. But I calmed him down."

"Yes."

"I also calmed Oscar down. The important thing is for us to keep working and for this misunderstanding never to happen again."

Marlene's other line rang. It was Oscar. She asked Said to call her back in a few minutes. Oscar was still in a mood to make trouble ("I'm going to tell *el papi* to go to hell"), but Marlene upbraided him like a drill sergeant. "No, *señor*, no, *señor*, listen to something first! You're not going to do that! You're going to remain silent! I'll tell you when!" He muttered off, and she instructed him to be at her house at seven.

Said Pavon called back. Marlene told him, "It was Oscar. He's in a bad mood."

"Yeah?"

"Oh, yeah. Poor thing. I understand him. I tell him, 'Don't do this.' But he doesn't pay attention to anybody."

She gave Said directions to Costa del Sol and asked him to come as soon as possible so she could speak to him in person. Then she called Jader Alvarez in Bogotá.

"I finally have some good news for you," she said. "The situation of *el barrigoncito* got cleared up. The guys who had disappeared finally turned up. Everything's normal."

"Yes?"

"I was in the middle of everything, since I started to look for these guys, I was also a little agitated, but anyway things got solved. And please try to be a little magnanimous with [Oscar], because the guy is quite nervous."

"Right, right."

"He was worried. He had to answer to you, but anyway things got solved, thank God."

"Yes, yes."

"And precisely as a result of these calls, one of the guys showed up today with seven-fifty." It was unclear to the monitors who had brought $750,000.

Jader instructed her to give $500,000 of the $750,000 to a woman called Bertha, whose North Miami Beach phone number he provided, and the rest to the "chauffeur" Tocayo for shipment to Colombia.

Jader Alvarez called Navarro again that evening to go over receipts and disbursements. Working from coded telex printouts, they covered more than $3,200,000 of transactions in recent days involving Teo, Oscar, Luis, Nelson, Ricardo, Said, and others. The DEA monitors were thrilled to intercept the conversation. Although the talk was veiled, it was clear in the context of other conversations that Jader and Navarro were discussing cocaine transactions in the millions of dollars. It would be a dramatic piece of evidence to present to a jury, even though it did not solve all the mysteries still surrounding the $5 million from New York, the $2 million that Nelson Batista supposedly had brought from Los Angeles, the cocaine that Oscar had agreed to sell to Darias, and whether that was part of the 2,000 kilograms the pilots apparently had been holding somewhere in Miami.

Oscar showed up at Costa del Sol at 10:30 with take-out food from a Colombian restaurant in Southwest Miami. Marlene got Jader Alvarez on the phone again and instructed Oscar to speak to him.

"You finally showed up," Jader said, his voice flat and cold.

"What do you mean, 'finally showed up'?"

"I call you at night and nothing, and I'm calling you Saturday and Sunday and nothing."

"I was looking for some friends," Oscar said. "I needed some money that they had to give me. And they just showed up today."

"All right, but one gets desperate . . ."

"I'm not hiding or anything. You commented to Teofila [Teo Terselich] that something was fishy, that I had disappeared. I was not hiding."

"It's not that. It was your safety."

"No, no, no. I was out on the street working. But hiding, no. I contact Marlene every day. But Teofila told some friends, and some friends told me, that you were saying things I didn't like. Pardon me for saying that."

"Understand—it's for your safety."

"But you led Teo to believe that I wanted to disappear together with the merchandise," Oscar said.

"No, no, no. But we have to take care of you. It's for security."

Oscar left, and again the DEA agents outside the compound lost him.

Teo Terselich called Marlene just before midnight angry that Oscar had not contacted him.

"Someday these people have to start doing what they're supposed to be doing and showing up when they are supposed to show up," said Teo.

"Yes, but he had to talk to *el compadre* first."

"Yes, Marlene, but this is happening over and over, and it's always the same, he never shows up. And I am sick and tired of it. I am going to Bogotá."

"Ai, carambola! When can Oscar call you to make arrangements to see you?"

"It's too late. It's too late to make arrangements. I'm going to Bogotá. I don't let people run over me like this."

"I will make sure he calls you immediately."

"If he doesn't call me tomorrow, I'm going to Bogotá."

The woman called Bertha, whom Jader had asked Marlene to summon, drove from North Miami Beach to Costa del Sol, arriving at seven minutes past midnight. Marlene turned over $500,000 that Jader had designated for Bertha, who turned out to be a money manager for Pepe Cabrera.

Since the Costa del Sol coffee shop was closed on Friday mornings, Marlene asked Robert to meet her at Neighbors. They ordered big breakfasts.

The conversation was another Marlene monologue.

"Oscar is really, really depressed," Marlene said. "He's going through a stage where he's considering not working anymore." She said she would be away over the coming weekend and asked Robert to be available to receive money from Oscar.

"There will be a further delay, but no real problem, with your shoes," she said. "You should have it by August 15."

"Okay."

Marlene complained about how she had had to mediate disagreements between Jader and Oscar. Her telephoning on Wednesday and Thursday had led to the release of $750,000, part of the $5 million owed, she said, but it had also required a threat of violence—the trip to New York by the man known as Rojas. The burning of the house had helped also.

"The people Carlos is sending here to do these things are people that use force instead of their heads," she said. Marlene commented that it was unwise to complain if one worked for Jader Alvarez. "I never go complaining to him," she said. "I learned that once already. He tells me, 'Marlene, if someone comes to me complaining, I hear them out but then I get rid of that person. Just like he comes complaining to me, he can go and complain to someone else.' "

She said that 100 kilograms of cocaine had been turned over to the pilots in lieu of money as a guarantee of their fee, and that they had released the 2,000 kilograms they had been holding. The delayed shipment had gone to established wholesale smugglers around the United States who had been waiting ahead of Darias. He mused to himself that the DEA would have to wait longer for a record-setting seizure.

She asked if Robert could handle money in Denver and Las Vegas. He, of course, said yes.

It was clear to the DEA that Marlene trusted Darias more than ever, and confided in him in a way she did not confide in others.

Marlene gave various people various stories of where she would be over that weekend. She told one person she was going to New York. She told another she was going to Washington. She told another she was going to Washington, then New York, then back to Washington. She told Jader Alvarez she was going to Kentucky on Friday (where she occasionally visited Alvarez's first wife Maria Lilia Rojas in the federal penitentiary at Lexington), to New York on Saturday, back to Kentucky on Monday morning, and to Miami Monday afternoon. Only Robert Darias and Gustavo Delgado were told the truth: She was going to Toronto to visit Alex McIntosh. Her travel agent dropped off her airline ticket and boarding pass with the Costa del Sol gate guards. Gustavo took her to the airport, where she was shadowed by a DEA team led by Steve Gibbs, the agent who had secretly sold information on the undercover investigation in California to Brooks Muse and Barbara Mouzin.

There was celebration at the listening post when the surveillance agents confirmed that Marlene's flight had left for Toronto. Her departure meant that the monitors had been given a weekend pass after some long days and nights of intense, exhausting work.

"It's nice that she goes on the little weekend trips for us," Carol told Robert. "She's driving us nuts. Everybody was grinning from ear to ear. Get outa here, lady! Man, she's a pain in the neck."

During a single two-hour period Marlene had made sixty telephone calls.

Frustrated though they were, the monitors had crossed a key threshold: they had begun to identify Marlene's network by their voices and personalities as well as the substance of conversations— Oscar, the fat drunk and coke head who was alternately jolly and enraged; Ricardo and Said Pavon, the whiny and emotional young brothers; Luis Rodriguez, the lothario who called Marlene *"biscocho"* (delectable); Teo (Baltazar) Terselich, the arsonist who spoke Spanish with a Yugoslavian accent; Nelson Batista, who often called from

Caesar's Palace in Las Vegas and the only Cuban detected in the inner circle so far—other than Robert Darias.

"It's just getting incredible," Paul Sennett told Robert that afternoon. "This woman just dials the phone and talks like crazy. She's talking to the whole world. She is talking a mile a minute. I know Washington is just going crazy about it."

Sennett had more than a casual feel for headquarters' thinking. His close friend, Ron Caffrey, with whom he had experienced a deadly shoot-out in 1972, was the primary officer in charge of monitoring Operation Swordfish in Washington. Caffrey had chaired the intelligence review conference that Carol Cooper and other agents had attended in May.

With Operation Swordfish scheduled to end in six weeks, Robert Darias and the DEA began laying plans to move the Darias family out of Miami to ensure their security. Although Darias's name would not appear in the grand jury indictments of the targets of the investigation, the names "Dean International," "International Investments," and other pertinent details of Operation Swordfish would become public. It was inevitable, therefore, that Darias's role in the operation would become apparent to the various criminal groups that he had infiltrated. And experience showed that his life and even that of his family would be in grave danger. Colombian drug criminals were notorious for taking revenge not only upon the spy but also upon his wife, children, and relatives.

The DEA offered the Dariases the option of entering the Federal Witness Security Program, under which the Department of Justice moved spies and witnesses deemed to be in jeopardy to other parts of the country, gave them new identities complete with false credentials and credit histories, and found them employment. Robert and Amelia felt that less drastic measures would suffice and would not force them to sever their ties to the Cuban community of Miami where they had lived for more than two decades and wanted to stay. They wanted Laura to grow up near her Cuban grandparents, uncles, aunts, and cousins.

It was critical, however, that the Dariases leave their home in the Tamiami section where they had lived for three years. Some of Robert's targets knew where he lived. One of them had come after him with a machine pistol there a year and a half earlier. Though that threat had been neutralized, the Dariases surely would be in new danger when the world learned of Operation Swordfish.

Robert and the DEA discussed a move to the Miami exurbs, perhaps somewhere in Broward or Palm Beach counties an hour or so north of Miami. It had been the DEA's experience that while drugs were nearly as widespread in the suburbs as in the city, there were fewer major drug smugglers in the suburbs and considerably less violence. The mafia seemed more comfortable in the heavily Latin quarters of Miami than in the predominantly Anglo communities to the north and west.

By the last weekend in July, the Dariases had decided to look for a house to rent in Coral Springs, an affluent bedroom community north of Fort Lauderdale. Paul Sennett and other DEA agents lived in Coral Springs and had recommended it to Robert as a safe, pleasant community with good schools and little crime. On Sunday, August 1, Robert and Amelia left Laura with her grandparents and spent the day house-hunting in Coral Springs.

Darias again did not hear from Oscar, and Marlene did not return to Miami until Monday evening, August 2.

"When I talk to her I'm going to ask her if Oscar is still the person to talk to," Robert told Carol. "Or who is going to be calling the shots."

"I think you can legitimately ask that, based on what she told you. I want to make sure I'm not putting anything in your mind that she didn't tell you, that you're not supposed to know yet."

"No, I know."

"My gut feeling is that they may be looking for somebody else to control the next shipment, or they've already got the guy picked out, if Oscar doesn't come through. They may have been giving him a chance the last couple days to get that money"—the remainder of the $5 million from New York.

Carol told Robert that the DEA and the prosecutors considered the wiretap a major success. The U.S. Attorney's office had proclaimed it the "most significant wire" the office had ever supervised. And it was the *only* federal wiretap in the jurisdiction at that moment, an ironic fact in view of Marlene's and Tocayo's belief that 4,500 phones in Dade County were tapped.

"I was really concerned about it," Carol said. "They were putting a heck of a lot of people down here to do this, and if it turned out to be a flop, my name was gonna be mud." She chuckled. "I didn't want people getting gung ho and super-excited about this until I knew for sure. Now I know for sure. It's a very, very productive wire. And Gruden and everybody else is very pleased with it. Obviously we're gonna get quite a few people. But keep in mind, whatever you can get on your end, powder-wise, that's gonna be the icing on the cake. That's gonna make a tremendous case."

"Well, my understanding in talking to her, I don't see any problems."

"No, I agree. Bob—let me tell you, we seriously checked it out the last two weeks—she is totally in your hands." Carol chose finally to tell Robert about the conversation which Marlene had had with Gustavo Delgado on Sunday evening of the previous week that had cast doubt on Marlene's trust in Robert. "Don't tell him anything because he can get us in trouble," Marlene had said to Gustavo about the man called "Roberto."

"I purposely had you doing things," Carol said, "just to know if she had a problem with you. Because that one phone call kinda had us all on edge. Because if she was hesitant about telling you what was going on, there could've been a problem.

"Let me tell you, Bob," Carol continued, "that is the *only* phone call, throughout this whole thing, that has been any indication, even the slightest hint, that there might be something wrong with you. And I don't think they were talking about you. I think you're in very, very good standing with her. With this latest seven-fifty, she told you exactly what she was doing. She's not trying to hide anything from you."

"Right."

"It's funny how she's working, but she's not lying to you. She's not telling you everything—that's understandable, that's the way they work. Which is why we have the wire going. We wanta know everything. We're nosy."

"The guy who doesn't completely trust me is Jader. She tells me every time she comes back that he keeps asking her if she's sure that I am not a federal agent. She said the last time, 'If he's a federal agent, then I shoot myself, because I trust him a hundred percent.' She's really going out on a limb."

"She's already out there. She's out on a little twig."

"I feel bad about her. I think we should tell her at the end that she's going to be in real danger, that this is not a game, and see if she wants to cooperate."

"Oh, we will at the end. She's gonna know exactly where she stands."

"Because they are going to kill her. If she thinks that she can get out of there on a bond and stay alive, she's nuts. They are going to kill her two minutes after she walks out of that federal court."

"Yeah, I agree. If she doesn't realize it, it will be told to her."

"I think she knows. Because she did mention what she told Tocayo, if he had any problems and he went to jail, he better keep his mouth shut. But that is not going to save *her*. Keeping her mouth shut doesn't have anything to do with the fact that these people are going to hate her for what she let us do to them."

"Yeah, nothing is gonna save her. Even if she talks to us, nothing is gonna save her."

Robert was chilled by the thought of the mafia's killing Marlene because she had trusted him. "It's one thing to run an operation, find out that somebody is doing something bad, and cause them to go to jail," he said to Amelia after his talk with Carol. "It's quite another if they kill her because of what I'm doing."

Chief Prosecutor Michael Pasano and his deputy Mark Schnapp held a "target conference" with DEA agents and intelligence analysts at the Phoenix Building the next morning, Tuesday, August 3. Pasano told the group that the evidence to support the coming indictments was "a mess—in disarray," in part because Nick Zapata and Eddie Hernandez still had not completed their written reports on drug money transactions now months old. Pasano insisted that the DEA prepare "flow charts" documenting each step in each transfer of money. Large charts had been prepared for the meeting—a who's who of each group under investigation, the Jader Alvarez-Navarro organization, the Cabrera organization, the Humberto Garcia-Medellín group, and others. The agents and lawyers tried to define weak spots, targets where more evidence would be required to support an indictment. They discussed the bankers—whether Lionel Paytubi and Manuel Sanchez should be indicted together with Marlene Navarro and Carlos Jader Alvarez, or with other defendants with whom they might have been more closely affiliated.

The single disappointment was the case against Pepe Cabrera, who was not emerging as the full-fledged member of the Jader syndicate that the DEA had believed him to be. Neither Cabrera nor his people had consistently turned up on Marlene's telephones. The DEA had been misled by Jader's frequent use of phones that were in Cabrera's name.

After more than a year as the pivotal figure in Operation Swordfish, Robert Darias was frustrated. With the wiretap now established as the main source of information on the Alvarez-Navarro organization, Robert found himself sitting at home reacting to intelligence rather than moving around the city initiating intelligence.

"She's getting her hair done," Cooper told Darias on the phone shortly after Navarro had left for an appointment at the Avant-Garde. "You know how she is. She's getting all spiffied up for you."

"I tell you, this waiting is getting to me."

"There's a possibility there might be something tonight, and then I would think she'd give you a call." The monitors had picked up hints that Marlene was expecting a delivery of money.

"Very good. I am happy to have somebody to tell me what is going on. I've been pulling my hair."

"Hang on a second. I'm putting the little guy to work here. He can field some of these phone calls."

Robert laughed. "Tell him that is what he gets for creating problems. Now he's under you and me."

Frank Chellino came on the phone. He and Darias had not spoken since just before the St. Patrick's Day Massacre.

"She went to the hairdressers," Chellino said. "She goes to the hairdressers a lot."

"Well, I guess she got her hair all messed up in Canada this weekend."

"Yeah, some fingers running through it." They both laughed.

"What else can you tell me about Oscar?" Chellino asked. Cooper had assigned him to gather background information on the members of Navarro's network, especially Oscar, whose erratic driving made him difficult to follow.

"Very little. The guy mainly has been working in L.A. He is not happy here and he wants to go back to work there."

"What other information, *any tidbit* of information of where he stays, where he's from, whether he lives here, how does she get in touch with him?"

"Well, he's from Medellín, but that's about all I know about him. He's supposed to be working directly for Carlos Jader. He is supposed to be handling large amounts of dope."

"Jesus, he's tough to come up with. There ain't nothin' I can grab onto."

"He's careful."

"Yeah, he sure is. How old is he?"

"I would think he's about twenty-eight to thirty years old."

"That young?"

"Yeah. He looks older because of the fact that he's fat and the amount of coke he uses, I guess."

"How tall?"

"He's about five-nine, five-ten, maximum."

"How much weight?"

"He's overweight, mainly in the waist."

"What else can you tell me about him?"

"That's all."

"Shit."

"Sometimes it's difficult even for Marlene to get in touch with the guy."

"Yeah, we've noticed in the logs."

"She told me that the guy had some problems collecting from some people."

"All right, if you think of *anything* that can be traced on Oscar, any slightest piece of information, give us a call."

Although he still thought Frank Chellino was obnoxious, Darias found his clipped, curt questions a relief after the unfailingly cordial but meandering, repetitive conversations, often late into the night, often difficult to draw to a close, that he had with Carol Cooper.

Marlene phoned Darias late that Tuesday evening and asked him to call her at eight the next morning.

Robert phoned Carol at home.

"Okay, she called me."

"Yeah."

"How could you know so fast? I just hung up and called you."

"Big Brother is always watching. We listen to everything she says. I was waiting for one particular thing to happen tonight, and when it did, she called you."

"Then she got a delivery somehow. Oscar?"

"That I don't know. But somebody's in there."

Oscar was in there. He had brought $450,000. After a little while he left and came back with another $110,000, bringing the night's total to $560,000.

Robert met Marlene at Neighbors around ten the next morning. It was her last meal before major dental surgery that afternoon—the second in a year.

"It was cold and drizzling rain in Toronto," Marlene said. "Imagine those autumn days in Paris. That is how it was." As often happened when she visited chillier climes, she had returned to sweltering Miami with a cold.

Robert gave her a Republic National Bank checkbook in the name of International Investments for Carlos Jader Alvarez. As for the cocaine shipment, she again put him off, saying "I will personally check into it myself."

He assured her that he could help her purchase a certificate of deposit for the woman narcotics trafficker in Vancouver, British Columbia.

After breakfast they returned to Costa del Sol in their separate cars, and Marlene gave Robert a bag containing what turned out to be $487,430. She asked him to wire the money to Jader's account at the First InterAmericas Bank in Panama City and said she was sending the rest of the new money to Bogotá with Tocayo.

32

SORE FROM WISDOM-TOOTH surgery that required thirty-five stitches, Marlene Navarro awakened Thursday morning to a steamy rain punctuated by thunder. The storm brought little relief from the hottest period of the year—nineteen consecutive days of temperatures over ninety degrees with high humidity. The seven-month summer was not even half over.

The headline on that day's *Miami Herald* read: "Four Shot to Death Execution Style." The story was written by veteran police reporter Edna Buchanan.

"The execution-style mass murder of four Latin men Wednesday in a well-kept and quiet Miami apartment building apparently was drug-related, police said. None of the victims, aged 25 to 35, lived in the fourth-floor apartment where they died. They were bound, gagged, and face down on the chocolate-colored shag carpet when somebody shot each one of them in the head. It is the first quadruple murder that Miami police have investigated this year."

Navarro shuddered, suspecting she would hear more about the murders, and she was right.

Oscar called. "A friend of mine got killed, Alfredito, a friend of *El Loco*'s and mine," Oscar said. "He was going to work with us. I'll go over and see the wife later on." The man called *El Loco* was a high-ranking official of the Jader Alvarez syndicate in Bogotá.

"Be careful," Marlene cautioned, "because remember they must be following all of those who are going to offer their condolences."

Oscar called again and told Marlene that the murder victim's family needed legal advice. Who could sign the papers to have the body removed to Colombia?

"Be careful not to get in trouble by helping somebody," she warned. "Do not show yourself or sign anything yourself."

Nelson Batista called that evening, and Marlene told him of the killings. "The husband of a friend of mine had a little accident and she wants to know how to claim him at the morgue."

"We shouldn't discuss that on the phone," Batista replied. He arrived at Marlene's fifteen minutes later, and urged that she warn

Oscar sternly not to get involved in the homicides. She beeped Oscar and he called her back.

"I want to ask you for a big favor. Don't come close or get near any of those things."

Oscar indicated that he had to take the victim's girlfriend to Orlando. He would be driving all night and return by morning.

"I don't want you even to be seen with her," Marlene said. "Nelson is here and is going to get another person to solve that problem for you."

Batista took the phone and told Oscar to "leave Chiqui the information" tomorrow.

As Nelson Batista left Costa del Sol and passed the Doral Country Club just after eleven o'clock that night, he was followed by five DEA agents in four cars. Paul Sennett and Frank Chellino were together in one vehicle; Carol Cooper drove another.

Not long after heading south on 87th Avenue, Batista noticed one of the pursuing cars, a light BMW driven by Special Agent Gilles Charette. Though he didn't see the other cars, Batista watched the BMW change lanes when he changed lanes, following him south to the Tamiami Trail, west to 107th Avenue in Little Managua, south along the border of Florida International University and Tamiami Park to Bird Road, and west again two blocks to the El Molino Restaurant and Sandwich Shop where Batista bought sandwiches.

When he emerged from the restaurant Batista saw the BMW parked in back. Batista then drove to a nearby 7-Eleven and went in. The BMW pulled up in front. When Batista came out of the 7-Eleven, he stared at the BMW, walked toward it, and very deliberately noted its license number, Florida XEB 556. When he continued on west on Bird Road, the BMW followed him for several blocks and then disappeared.

Satisfied that he had lost the tail, Batista drove to the house where he was staying and called Marlene Navarro. It was 11:55 P.M. and it was obvious that he was frantic.

"Where did you notice you were being followed?" she asked.

"We got out at different places. I got out and bought milk. I bought sandwiches and I bought everything. And he got out and he stopped the car."

"In order for you to see him?"

"Yes."

"That is to say, he wasn't hiding?"

"He wasn't hiding. A blond and fat gentleman."

Marlene said that the BMW following Batista sounded like the car of her next-door neighbor, who also fit the description of the driver.

"Is the gentleman blond and fat?" Nelson asked.

"The gentleman is blond. He's fat."

"Damn!" said Nelson.

Peering through the shades on her bedroom window as she talked, Marlene said that the license number sounded familiar, but that it would be morning before she could check it. She was afraid to go outside at midnight.

"It's strange that he let himself be seen," Marlene said. As she talked to Nelson the black Jader phone rang persistently but she ignored it.

"It wasn't that he *let* himself be seen," Batista said. "He glued himself to us but he didn't know I had caught on."

"It must have been a coincidence."

"No, *señora.*"

Marlene said the man next door was polite but reserved, and she hardly knew him. The gate guards despised him, she said. He was stingy at Christmas. And she had heard scuttlebutt that he had served time in prison for income tax evasion.

Batista asked Marlene to call him immediately after she checked the license number in the morning. "I'm hardly going to be sleeping," he said.

"What I'm going to do," Marlene said, "is what I told you before: to cut down on everybody coming here."

"Everybody?"

"Everybody. Nobody."

Hearing Batista's call to Navarro, the DEA monitors immediately radioed Carol Cooper, who was in her car heading home. Her first call in the door was to Darias, who was asleep.

"Sorry to bother you so late—we have a bit of a problem," Cooper said. "Basically what happened is Nelson, who you have met, went over to her house tonight. About four or five of us were trying to follow him and put him down somewhere. And he apparently made one of the cars. Apparently Nelson called her and told her that he had been followed. I want you to be aware of it. She may bring it up to you and you may be able to help soothe it over."

"Yes."

"Nelson somehow got the tag on the car. He spotted our guy at a 7-Eleven. How he could have spotted him before that, I don't know. But anyway, he started making a few moves so we let him go. Apparently he landed somewhere and called her and told her to be careful because he thinks she's being watched, too."

"But that's a normal reaction, to call her and tell her to be careful."

"Right, it could be anybody, and she immediately told him—just so you know how she's thinking—she immediately told him that it could be her neighbor's car."

"Do you think I should call her?"

"No, it's going to look funny for you to call her this late. It's out of character for you to do that."

"If she mentions it to me, I'm going to tell her that they can just deliver the money to my office."

"That may be a very good idea. To be honest with you, Bob, I don't know how in the world he spotted our guy, I really don't. I was with him the whole time."

"Carol, you have to realize that these people are already expecting that."

"I realize that."

"This is the second time."

"She didn't seem to be too upset."

"But that is the way she is. She calmed Tocayo in the same fashion, but she was *worried* about it when that happened to Tocayo. And she asked me several times if I thought it had anything to do with her."

"I guess the main thing is that if she brings this issue up to you is just to make sure *she*'s calmed down."

"What kind of car was it?"

"A Toyota," Carol said, referring to Nelson's car. "We got Toyotas coming out of our ears. They all have Toyotas and they're all the same color. I think they got a package deal on them."

"I am going to tell her they can come in my office in the back and nobody is going to see what they are delivering."

"If she brings it up to you and really thinks it's a serious problem, go ahead and suggest all that."

"If she does bring it up, I'm going to tell her, Marlene, are these the same people you told me that burned that guy's house and had that problem? Because maybe somebody's trying to kill them. That would put another idea in her head."

"Give me a holler in the morning, as soon as you give her a call, so I know what's going on. I'll give all the orders tomorrow morning, who goes where."

Nelson Batista called Marlene the next morning. "You didn't let me sleep last night," she said.

"What about the number?"

"It is different. It is not the same."

"Yes?"

"But the neighbors have two other Mercedeses that I haven't seen yet," she said, confusing Mercedeses and BMWs.

When Darias arrived at Costa del Sol at half past noon, Marlene confided her anguish to him, and he had to pretend he was hearing about the surveillance of Nelson Batista for the first time.

"Do you think they are following me or him?" she asked.

"Marlene, that is a sixty-four-thousand-dollar question. You have to be careful. But I don't think it's you. You are a lady and you have your friends and you know what you're doing and you know how to get around town. I never see anybody following *me* when I leave here, so they must not be watching you. But you know how these guys are. They get high on dope and they drink and they have two dozen girls, and they talk to too many people. Maybe one of them is hot. And then again it might just be Nelson's imagination."

"Oh, no, it wasn't his imagination. They started following him at 87th Avenue and he stopped at a restaurant and then he stopped somewhere else and then he stopped at a 7-Eleven and then he was able to come around and look at the gentleman."

Robert again urged her to use his office for money deliveries, and stressed that it was in a shopping center with a garage in back that concealed whatever was happening inside.

Marlene told Robert that he could have at least 100 kilograms of cocaine, perhaps 150, by August 15. After a token amount down, full payment would not be expected for a few weeks.

And she confided that Oscar was a friend of one of the men who had died in the quadruple homicide in northeast Miami.

The woman named Bertha arrived at Costa del Sol as Robert and Marlene were talking, and Robert got his first look at her. In her middle thirties, she was dark-haired, elegant, and carried herself well but was a bit heavy. She wore lots of jewelry, including a golden bee with diamonds on it.

Marlene introduced Robert as her banker, and he helped her count $500,000 to give to Bertha, the second half-million dollars Bertha had picked up in recent days.

Marlene told Bertha about Nelson Batista's having been followed the previous night, and warned her to be alert for surveillance. "Look around so nobody can follow you after you pass the Doral Country Club."

After Bertha left, Marlene told Robert that Bertha had "a big problem in Colombia with drugs." Not wanting to appear too curious, Darias did not press for details.

"She is *very* nervous," Robert told Paul Sennett later in the afternoon. "We cannot wait too much longer. I think these people are getting paranoid—if they get too many hints like last night, they are going to fly away. And for these people that's very easy, and then we are not going to get anybody. Marlene told me that Nelson saw the car following him and stopped at a 7-Eleven. And Nelson was able to go around and take a good look at the guy."

"Well," said Paul, "I think they've got problems within their organization with some people. That's probably what they're concerned about. I don't think they're concerned about Marlene."

Nelson called Marlene at around 6:00 P.M. He was very angry, having talked again to Oscar, who was still with the girlfriend of the murder victim.

"I asked him, 'What do you think this is, a game?' He told me, 'No, I'll call you back.' He hasn't called me."

Nelson asked about Marlene's neighbor, but she had concluded he had not followed Nelson.

"I'm positive that car came out of your area," he said. "Because they did not follow me before I got there. I was looking back. I do that all the time. And there was nobody behind me when I got there."

"Yes, but they still could have been following you."

"No, no, I know they didn't because I didn't have anybody behind me. When I left is when I started seeing them, around Neighbors."

"Well, don't be paranoid. There may be a simple explanation."

Nelson said he wanted to come into the Costa del Sol compound and drive around to see if anyone followed him or if he saw the car.

"You know, Nelson, I told some friends I had here to look when they left to see if there was any problem. And they called me later and told me there wasn't. And I have been careful to watch when I go out and *I* didn't see anybody. So apparently it's a coincidence or the problem is with you."

"I'm positive it's not paranoia because the guy followed me the whole time after I left here."

"Keep in mind," Robert urged Carol that evening, "that these people are *very* spooked. I have been able to calm her down considerably, but she's still spooked. These people are completely paranoid right now."

"I don't think they're nervous about you. She may have been jumping at anything today."

"If they get one or two more signals, they might start flying the coop. And we might have to end this thing in two hours' time."

"No, it's not going to get to that point. It won't."

"I have been able to pacify her a little bit. She wants to use the office, she wants to use the telex. She's expecting a couple of million bucks more. She's waiting for two million from the same guys whose house they burned," a reference to the "safe house" used by the Pavon brothers. "But these people are going to start running."

33

N BOGOTÁ ON Saturday, August 7, as soft breezes ruffled flags under azure skies, fifty-nine-year-old Belisario Betancur was sworn in as president of Colombia.

Betancur was the second of twenty-two children born to a peasant family who lived near Medellín in a village so small it had no doctor. Sixteen of his siblings died of disease and malnutrition. An uncle enrolled him in a Roman Catholic seminary but Belisario dropped out and put himself through law school instead. He entered politics in 1951 at the height of *La Violencia,* the protracted civil war in which upward of 200,000 people died.

Instead of holding his inauguration in the Congress Building where his predecessors had, Betancur took his oath outside on the steps of the Supreme Court Building in front of 50,000 cheering Colombians jamming the Plaza Bolívar. Instead of the customary cutaway, the new president wore a business suit. And there were other signs that his administration might be different from those that preceded it. Betancur appointed women to most deputy minister posts. He indicated that Colombia's foreign policy would be less aligned with the United States. And he proposed an amnesty with leftist guerrillas, the M-19 and others. A huge cloud of white pigeons was released as a symbol of the overture of peace.

Vice President George Bush, whose "South Florida Task Force" ostensibly was in the midst of an all-out war on drugs in the United States, conferred privately with Betancur before his swearing-in. Betancur said nothing publicly about the narcotics problem, however. Nor did he mention that he had accepted campaign contributions from the Colombian drug mafia—$800,000 from a group that included Carlos Jader Alvarez.

Alvarez had reason to hope that the search for his children and their kidnappers would get the new president's immediate attention, especially since Alvarez was convinced that the kidnappers were members of the M-19, the guerrilla movement to which Betancur was proposing to grant amnesty.

Betancur did not disappoint. On the weekend of his inauguration, the new president put the Colombian National Police and the Colombian Army at the disposal of Carlos Jader Alvarez. It was as if the president of the United States had put the FBI and the U.S. Army at the disposal of John Gotti. Betancur deputized his brother, Juvenal Betancur, to act for the president in the kidnapping investigation. To make sure their relationship began on the right note, Carlos Jader Alvarez promptly slipped Juvenal Betancur a briefcase containing $10,000 in cash.

Juvenal Betancur in turn summoned the commanding officer of the F-2 branch of the National Police to a secret meeting with Jader Alvarez. This was the same F-2 that in January had arrested Alvarez with 3 kilograms of cocaine in his possession and, in a search of his mansion, discovered a ransom note from the kidnappers of his children. On that occasion, Alvarez had asked the F-2 not to investigate the kidnapping because, he told the agents, he feared an investigation would endanger his children. Privately he also feared it would threaten the security of his narcotics empire. But the passage of time and the ascension of Belisario Betancur to the presidency of Colombia had changed the dynamics fundamentally. Jader Alvarez was now in a position to control an investigation, keeping it away from his business affairs. And after ten fruitless months of searching for the kidnappers himself, he had no assurance that his children were not already dead. He concluded that at this point a bold public gesture involving the highest levels of the National Police might be helpful. Alvarez was not naive about the capacities of the F-2 branch. Generally he held the Colombian police in contempt. In his career as an organized crime boss he had learned that many of them were ineffectual—lazy, corrupt, incompetent, badly trained and equipped, and ill-suited for a sensitive, complicated investigation. Jader Alvarez would be using F-2 agents as errand boys and foot soldiers, but not much else. He would even have to finance the investigation himself. What passed for justice in Colombia was reserved for those who could pay for it.

At the meeting with Juvenal Betancur and the commander of the F-2, Alvarez made clear that he would support the F-2's investigation with money, people, motor vehicles, aircraft, and whatever else might be needed. Alvarez turned over the ransom notes, the recordings of telephone conversations with the kidnappers, and the photographs of the children posing with the newspaper dated in February. He recounted for the F-2 his frustrating contacts with the kidnappers—the wild-goose chases around Bogotá. But he did not confide that in March he and the vigilante group Death to Kidnappers had detained four students from the National University and, after interrogating and torturing them, and learning nothing of value, executed them.

It was decided that the warnings in the ransom notes against making the kidnapping public would henceforth be ignored. The F-2 and Alvarez agreed that he would immediately take large advertisements in the major newspapers and on television displaying photographs of his children and pleading for public help in locating them.

A polite, soft-spoken, matter-of-fact man who identified himself as "a friend of your *compadre*" awakened Marlene Navarro on the Jader phone at 8:22 that Saturday morning. He said his name was Alex. It would be the third "Alex" that the DEA monitors would have to track, not to be confused with Marlene's lover, Alex, who was in bed beside her at that moment, and her son, Alex, in The Netherlands.

"I've been charged with taking an order to you," the new Alex said. He indicated that he probably would call again within a week and asked her to verify his arrival with anyone who called from "over there" asking about him.

"We'll have a cup of coffee and get acquainted," Marlene told him.

It appeared to the monitors that the new Alex was in Miami to coordinate the distribution of a major new shipment of cocaine, perhaps the 2,000-kilogram shipment which the pilots presumably had recently released.

When Robert Darias called Marlene just after nine, she told him she had had a "good call from a friend of our mutual friend" and there would be a "pretty large shipment for the coming week."

On Saturday afternoon Robert and Amelia made offers on three houses that they were considering renting in Coral Springs. Robert offered three months rent in advance, cash, and told the landlords that he was a self-employed investment counselor. The DEA had warned him not to use Paul Sennett or other DEA people who lived in Coral Springs as references because of the risk that he might thereby be linked to the government.

"We're losing all our environment," Robert told Carol later that day. "We're moving into a hundred percent American environment. We don't have any qualms about it; I'm sure we will be meeting people there and all that—*but* we have all of our friends *here,* in Miami, and we are Latin, we are Cuban. And you like to associate with your people. I cannot go to Coral Springs and associate with my people." The Dariases had seen little of their friends in recent months but did spend a good deal of time with their relatives.

"It's not going to be easy for you, I know," Carol said.

"Have you noticed any changes in Marlene's conversations?" Robert asked.

"No, she's acting very normally. Had we not known there was a problem with Nelson, we wouldn't have known. She's talking to a few people about it, but not everybody."

"What I mean is that she's not afraid of the phone."

"No, not at all."

Marlene's cousin Carmenza Valenzuela called at 11:27 Saturday night to report that she had attended President Betancur's swearing-in. "He gave such a fantastic speech, very sentimental," she said. "It was very, very dramatic."

The monitors were beginning to listen more closely to Marlene's talks with Carmenza, whom they had learned was a rich foreign exchange money broker in Bogotá and possibly handled Jader Alvarez's money once it arrived from the United States.

Marlene's eighteen-year-old son Alexander awakened her Sunday morning with a call from The Netherlands.

"Mommy, I've been in an accident."

"What happened, Alex?" she replied, her voice heavy with sleep.

"I was riding my motorcycle and fell off. I scratched my head. They have given me a tetanus shot."

"How did it happen?" she asked, obviously very concerned.

"I fell in the center of the city. Somebody cut in front of me and made me fall."

"How are you feeling now?"

"I've got a fever from the tetanus shot and my joints ache."

"You have to take care of yourself. *Ai,* Alex, if you don't have one problem you have another. Will you have a scar on your forehead?"

"No, I don't think so."

"My *friend* Alex here says to tell you that with a scar on your head and no teeth you'll look like Frankenstein." Her son laughed. He had lost some teeth playing soccer.

"I'll send you your July check by Wednesday," Marlene said. "I left the June check with you when I saw you, didn't I?"

"Yes."

"You must be careful," Marlene said. "Take care and go to the doctor."

"Okay, Mommy."

"I send you kisses."

Carol Cooper and the monitors were confused by a conversation about a "hundred boxes," apparently of furniture, which they had heard just before midnight Saturday between Marlene and a man named Herman.

"It may be legit," Cooper told Darias. "She's gonna make a move on it, and I'm afraid to put surveillance on her if it's legit. She's going to have it. She's going to where the furniture is, quote unquote furniture."

"Carol, take out of your mind that she would go to where the coke is. She would *not* go to where the coke is. I am convinced that she would not be close to that thing."

"They're talking about, like, a hundred boxes."

"They are getting a shipment ready to go. That I know."

"The real furniture?"

"They are not shipping anything *else* to Colombia. They are not shipping coke *back* to Colombia," he said with a smile.

"No, I know that, but see, we don't know what they're doing with it. All we know is that there's a hundred boxes and they've got her initials on them and they're all numbered. Whoever it is is calling her from hotels, moving around from hotel to hotel. And it's not Gustavo."

Robert pointed out that it was difficult for him to help without hearing the tape. Carol was still prohibited from allowing him to listen to it.

"We initially thought it was legitimate," she said. "However, there are certain portions in the conversation that everybody—and I mean everybody—is saying something is wrong here. Gut feeling, something is wrong, and we don't know what it is. The main conversation came in about midnight last night. Now, why would a legitimate company be calling her at midnight on a Saturday night? Something's happening. I don't know what it is, but something is happening."

"When I meet with her again, I'll be able to get a little more from her," Robert said. "If there is any indication that there is a problem, we are ready to round these people up pretty fast, aren't we?"

"Well, as soon as we start getting major information that there is a problem, we can take them pretty quick."

"I would hate for something to happen and let these people go, after so much work."

"If there is a problem and they're gonna scramble and we get an indication of that, yeah, we'll take them immediately. I don't think there's going to be a problem, though, Bob. They're nervous right now but they're not nervous enough to run."

"She feels that nobody sees her delivering the money to anybody, so she's safe."

Carol mentioned that the prosecutors would like to assemble additional evidence that Marlene's lawyer, Lester Rogers, actually knew about her narcotics dealings. For example, did Rogers know that the Miami real estate properties which someone had recently turned over to Carlos Jader Alvarez were in partial settlement of a drug debt?

"The next time I tape her," Darias said, "I'm going to go over it again and I'll get it for you."

"When you do that, Bob, see if you can get some conversation about Lester being totally knowledgeable that it is behind a dope deal. For us to go after an attorney, let me tell you, they're going to come up with every trick in the book. And if we got it solid, then there's no question about it."

"Okay. Don't worry about that."

Robert reminded Carol that Marlene had asked him to accompany her to look at some of the real estate on Monday.

"I'm going to tape her when I pick her up," Robert said. "Since we are going to see the property, it's the proper time to ask about Lester."

"That's a dynamite time."

"How about Jaffe? Do we have a little bit on Jaffe?"

"I think he's going. The attorneys are going to indict him. But obviously it's going to be much better if he comes up over the wire. Or if you can meet with him and tape him or something like that. But the attorneys are willing to go after him."

On Monday afternoon Darias and Navarro drove to South Miami to inspect one of the properties that Jader Alvarez had been given in settlement of a drug debt—a condominium development called the Valleys of Kendall.

Marlene was hung over from drinking with Alex and her decorators, Gustavo and Dick, on Sunday evening. "Everyone is looking for that Oscar," she said. "That Oscar! He lives in his own world. Now they are going to give him the two million, but in Denver. I told him, 'You go to Denver and you call me. When you already have the two million in your hands, *then* you call me, so that I can go there with Roberto. Otherwise, I'm not going. No way am I going to be sitting around in a hotel for three days.' "

She expected that she and Robert would go to Denver within a few days. It was unclear to Darias whether the $2 million was part of the $5 million from New York, much of which remained unaccounted for.

Mindful of the DEA's interest in additional evidence against the lawyers, Robert asked Marlene about David Jaffe. "He mainly handles Pepe's money," she said.

As for Lester Rogers, she said Rogers knew that Carlos Jader Alvarez was the owner of the interest in the Valleys of Kendall. The share was in Marlene's name but Lester was the trustee.

"He was the one who drew up all those papers and he knows that it was a debt?" Robert asked.

"Yes, yes. He knows everything about debts. Lester knows everything, everything, just like he knows what I have, what I don't have, what is in the [safe deposit] boxes, for whom it is. Because since I'm alone, Robert, you have your wife, it's different. I always tell him, 'Lester, today I put it in boxes so and so—' "

"In other words, he is a totally trustworthy person with us?"

"Exactly. In fact, he's the only person I have who is really close. He knows that we were meeting today, you and I. He knows everything."

The Valleys of Kendall ("On the way to your dream!") was a five-acre site just off North Kendall Drive between the Florida Turnpike and the Don Shula Expressway. Some forty-two beige-and-brown town houses, two-, three-, and four-bedroom, were in various stages of construction. The development was convenient to Dadeland and the Miami-Dade Community College South Campus. Marlene and Robert strolled about and chatted briefly with the developer. With Robert's endorsement, Marlene decided to advise Jader Alvarez to hold onto the investment for the time being.

On the way back north to Costa del Sol they stopped for a beer and sandwich at a Steak and Ale on Kendall Drive, and then at the Magnum Gun Shop on Flagler where Marlene bought a Remington 870 twelve-gauge shotgun, also known as a riot gun, for $300 cash.

Later, Robert reported to Cooper. "I made a very good tape. She incriminated the two lawyers up to their necks. Lester knows every penny she has in all the accounts, and she always gives him a rundown on everything whenever she leaves, in case something should happen to her. He knows how to direct the money to Carlos."

"You got all that on tape?"

"Yes."

"Super."

Under surveillance by four DEA agents, including the secretly corrupt Steve Gibbs, Navarro dined that evening with Oscar and Teo at La Carretta on Southwest 8th Street, one of a chain of Cuban restaurants. She was home by nine, having eaten very little. She was having diarrhea, and was frightened to find it was accompanied by considerable intestinal bleeding. Her first thought was of cancer. She called a doctor and several hospital emergency rooms and learned that the soonest she could be examined was early Wednesday morning.

Marlene spent the next two and a half hours dialing Gustavo and Alex McIntosh, but got no answer. She retired early and conducted a full day of business on Tuesday with Oscar, Nelson, Darias, and others. She told none of them of her illness.

The lead story on the eleven o'clock news that Tuesday night was the discovery of the bodies of three women who had been shot to death in a house in a quiet, affluent neighborhood of South Miami, near the border with Coral Gables. Police estimated that the women, who were said to be in their late twenties or early thirties, had been killed several days earlier. The bodies were badly decomposed. Early leads indicated that the killings might have been retribution for the failure of a shipment of cocaine to reach its destination. One of the victims was identified as a member of a cocaine smuggling ring based in Medellín, Colombia. There was no indication that the triple-slaying was linked to the quadruple-homicide in which Oscar's friend had died.

Marlene hardly slept. Now they were killing women.

She had asked the overnight gate guard to give her a wake-up call at 6:00 A.M. By seven she was at Mercy Hospital in South Miami being tested for colon cancer. By late morning she was told she had a benign polyp, aggravated by stress and nerves. She was told she was under too much strain and to go home and relax.

She drove from the hospital to her dentist and had some of her stitches removed. She drove from her dentist to the Avant-Garde and had her hair done.

The DEA in Bogotá reported overnight (3:16 A.M. Wednesday) that a telephone intercept indicated that S. David Jaffe, Pepe Cabrera's lawyer, might be traveling to Bogotá on Wednesday with several hundred thousand dollars in cash in his luggage.

Classified confidential and marked "immediate," the teletype said that Pepe Cabrera had asked Jaffe on the phone if "two or three" would be coming. Jaffe had replied that there probably would be "only two" because of a problem with "quality."

The agents felt that "two or three" might have referred to money— perhaps $200,000 or $300,000, or even $2 million or $3 million.

DEA agents in Miami took up positions at the airport and watched as Jaffe arrived for a flight late Wednesday afternoon. He was accompanied by three young women. They checked eight suitcases. After the luggage had passed along the conveyor belt out of sight, it was opened and searched by DEA and Customs agents. No money was found.

When the flight, Eastern 19, arrived in Bogotá around 8:00 P.M., Special Agent Michael Kuhlman observed as Pepe Cabrera and a driver-bodyguard met the Jaffe party. It became clear that the reference on the telephone to "two or three" had not been to money. It had been to "two or three" young women for Cabrera.

34

AS DAVID JAFFE was flying to Bogotá that evening, a distinguished-looking man in his middle fifties landed in Miami on an Aerotal flight from Bogotá. The man was Juvenal Betancur, the brother of the new president of Colombia, Belisario Betancur, who had been inaugurated on Sunday. Before flying to Miami, Juvenal had conferred with several top police and military officials and had been given grounds for hope that the Alvarez children might be found alive.

Juvenal Betancur had compelling reasons to be in Miami. One of his sons, who had been injured in a traffic accident a month earlier in Colombia, was being treated at Mount Sinai Hospital in Miami Beach. Juvenal went straight to the hospital from the airport.

The most important piece of paper Juvenal carried to Miami was a very private letter of introduction. The letter had been written by Carlos Jader Alvarez, addressed to Marlene Navarro. The previous week Betancur had lost a briefcase full of U.S. currency that Jader Alvarez had given him. He needed more.

"I've been worried about you," Robert told Marlene shortly after she arrived home from the Avant-Garde.

"Oh, Roberto, I was nervous and I couldn't sleep all night. I have been bleeding internally."

"Oh?"

"I went to the doctor early this morning. They made a biopsy and it was not cancer. But until they see the x-rays and make more tests they won't know exactly what it is. But it's not cancer. They gave me some medicine to stop the bleeding."

"Good."

"And then I went to the dentist this afternoon and had ten stitches removed."

"So, you spent the entire day at doctors' offices."

"Yes, and I'm not nervous now that they told me it's not cancer. I made an analysis of my conscience last night, Roberto. To have money is good. To work is good. But to have your health is the best. Roberto, we should dedicate ourselves to our families and the people who love us. We need to dedicate more time to people we love. That is the only thing that counts. What is the point in making all this money if I have to spend it on doctors."

"You're right," Darias replied.

Having listened to Marlene Navarro's telephone conversations for nearly a month, the DEA again was struck by the depth of Robert Darias's penetration of her life. It was clear that he occupied a position of extraordinary intimacy. Virtually alone among Marlene's friends and associates, Darias knew the salient facts about all the major phases of her life, which she generally kept isolated one from another. Although she had a knack for seeming to confide in most people she dealt with, she was in fact a discreet person. Oscar and Nelson and Teo and Ricardo and Said and Luis and her other employees knew about the drugs and the drug money, but nothing about her personal life. While Gustavo Delgado and Dick Lawrence knew a lot about her furniture-buying and decorating interests, and were also social friends familiar with her relationship with Alex McIntosh, they apparently knew little about her narcotics business, which she also kept largely hidden from McIntosh. Her boss Carlos Jader Alvarez knew about her business but little of her personal activities.

Only Robert Darias, it appeared, knew everything, or at least the outlines of everything. He knew the vast extent of her drug trafficking and money-laundering and had met most of her employees. He knew that she spent vast sums of both her own money and Jader Alvarez's money ($300,000 of Jader's money alone in just the past few months) on furniture and art objects, purchased through Gustavo and Dick, whom he had also met. He knew about her two marriages and about her current romance with Alex McIntosh, with whom he had drunk Pouilly-Fuissé. He even knew that Marlene suspected that McIntosh had another girlfriend in Toronto. And now he knew about Marlene's stress-induced intestinal bleeding, which she had told Gustavo and Alex about but seemingly no one else.

Robert had learned all this while rarely pumping Marlene for information, and without becoming her lover. He had simply befriended her and made himself available, an avuncular presence, at all hours of the day and night, over the course of a year. And it had not been onerous work. They enjoyed each other's company. And by the summer of 1982 she had grown to trust him like no one else—no one, with the possible exception of her lawyer Lester Rogers, who remained something of an enigma to Darias and the DEA as they strove to probe even deeper into the Jader Alvarez organization under their tight new deadline, now only a month away.

"Dr. Juvenal will be arriving there, calling you tonight, carrying a note from me," Jader Alvarez told Navarro shortly after six that evening. "Take good care of him. He's the boss's brother here, the brother of the Supreme Chief."

"That's great," Marlene replied.

"Well, he has a son in Mount Sinai Hospital, that hospital for the Jews."

"Yes, I know which one it is."

"Be very nice to him."

"Of course, since he is your friend I will help in everything I can."

"He has an unlimited letter of credit."

"Any amount?"

"Yes, more or less."

Marlene told Jader that his second wife, Marina, had asked her to purchase a porcelain statue of the Baby Jesus, from a limited edition from Prague, made only by Cybis. It would cost several thousand dollars. Marina, the mother of two of the kidnapped children, seven-year-old Yidid and six-year-old Xouix, was a deeply religious person and kept a room in the house called *La Iglesia* exclusively for religious statues and other objects.

"Bring it," Jader said. He sounded nervous and preoccupied, and Marlene resisted the temptation to ask if there was news of the children.

The Jader phone rang at quarter to ten.

"Marlene, good evening. This is Juvenal Betancur."

"Don Juvenal, I have orders to welcome you and take care of you the way that you deserve."

"That's very nice of you."

"He [Jader Alvarez] says you are a gentleman, and he said that whatever you need, he told me, 'Look, make believe, not that he is me, but that he's three times me, so that you'll take care of him for me.' "

Betancur quoted from his letter of introduction from Jader Alvarez: " 'Take care of him for me as though it were me. . . .' He told me if I were in Bogotá, or if I were here, or if I were in New York, to place myself in your hands." Betancur spoke in a formal manner, pure Castilian Spanish, a bit grand and fustian.

"Yes, exactly," she said. "Don Juvenal, I'll tell you something, you have open credit, anything you need."

"You are very kind."

They agreed to meet at Mount Sinai Hospital at 11:30 Thursday morning.

Navarro immediately called Darias and told him about Juvenal Betancur. "I want you to place him in the bank which you think can give him the best service."

"Exactly."

"And everything comes out well for him, because remember whose brother he is, right?"

"Surely."

"And that they should always take care of him for me, and everything."

"Completely."

"Now, I would like it if he could have a bank on Brickell, for example, or something like that, so that he wouldn't have to go far."

"Yes, of course, I'll look for something which will be convenient for him."

"Exactly. Something accessible for you so that you can help him all you can."

"Surely."

"Don't make any commitments for lunch, so that we can take care of the gentleman, and lunch would be a nice gesture on our part—"

"Of course, of course."

"In other words, Roberto, in the morning you can prepare a good account for him, do you understand?"

"Surely."

"Don't say who he is. It's not necessary that a lot of people know. Maybe to the president of the bank or someone like that."

"Yes."

"But neither the employees nor anybody else should know because then things will start about 'Oh, the brother' and like that. Do you understand?"

"Sure. And he is a good friend of *el papi?*"

"Quite. That is, the new president is a closer friend, and this one is like an assistant. But *el papi* is precisely the one who is sending him to me. *El papi* told me 'whatever he needs.' He told me, 'Marlene, take care of him better than you would me.' "

"I know the banker already. The banker will be waiting for us. I'll just say that he's a good friend of mine and that I guarantee the account."

"Exactly, exactly, Roberto. I appreciate that and now I'll let you go to sleep. We won't have breakfast but I'm pretty sure we will be able to have lunch."

As violent thunderstorms drenched West Miami, Darias called Carol Cooper. The DEA monitors, and therefore Cooper, who was home exhausted nursing a fever, hadn't immediately grasped the identity and importance of Juvenal Betancur. It dawned gradually as Carol spoke with Robert.

"Tomorrow I'm going to meet the brother of the president," Robert said. "Can you imagine that?"

"Yeah? Tell me more," said Carol, confused.

"They stole a suitcase full of money from him the other day. And the guy comes recommended by *el papi,* Carlos Jader. He's his best friend. And the president also is a very good friend. I am going to open an account—take him to Manny Sanchez downtown."

"This is the brother, the actual brother, of the president?"

"She didn't say names. I'm going to meet the guy tomorrow."

"Okay. What are you supposed to do?"

"His son is at Mount Sinai. That's where she's going to be with him tomorrow. He wants to open an account. I am going to call Manny first thing in the morning and explain to him what is going on. Okay?"

"Yeah."

"And tell him that this is a dynamite connection for him—to treat the guy right because we should be making a lot of money later with the guy. Of course, she doesn't want Manny to know that he is the brother of the president but I'm going to tell Manny. And I'm going to tell Manny not to say that he knows."

"Is this the current president—the one that just went in?"

"Of course. Belisario Betancur. I asked her, is this guy a very good friend of Carlos, of *papi?* 'Oh, yes, he's very close to him. He told me to do whatever I had to do to help him.' " Robert paused. "You realize that this is getting a little too complicated. Now we are talking about bigger fish."

"Yeah, I know. I told you, Bob, she considers you up on that little pedestal. You're *her person.* You do not run around like all these other idiots she deals with."

Carol and Robert both had afterthoughts, and spoke again an hour later, just before midnight. It was their sixth telephone conversation of the day.

"The only thing I'm thinking of, Bob, if he ever sees that tape recorder, that's gonna be it. And I always have to question, is it worth the chance?"

"Well, if *anybody* sees that tape recorder, that's it."

"Oh, I know. I really don't see any reason to tape it. But if you definitely think you can get this guy to talk business, go ahead and tape it."

"I'm not even going to try. I don't think she would risk even *trying* to talk business the first time."

"Okay, put on your finest tomorrow, kid. What are you going to wear?"

"Oh, I'm going to use one of my suits, I guess. Pierre Cardin or something like that."

"I'm sure you can impress him. I have all the faith in the world in you."

Robert finally got Carol off the phone at 12:15. He was as exhausted as she was.

3 5

"**Y**OU NO GOOD, CONNIVIN'** son of a bitch," Frank Chellino said when he reached Darias Friday morning. "You really are going to topple the government, aren't you?"

Darias laughed.

"Nice move," Chellino continued. "Would it be fair to say you're tight with Marlene?"

Darias was still laughing. He still found Chellino amusing, even early in the morning, and even though he didn't like working for him.

"I am curious to meet this guy," Robert said.

"Nervous?"

"No, no. *Curious.* What in the hell do I have to be nervous about?"

Chellino laughed. "He's just another scum bag in the drug business."

"I don't think he's going to say too much today."

"I don't either."

"I'm just going to try to finagle him a little bit and give him a little bullshit."

"Where're you gonna take him for lunch?"

"I don't know. Do you have any special place you want me to go?"

"Well, the only thing we want to do is send one person out. We want to make sure that person sees you in the restaurant and then he'll disappear. Just to confirm the meeting, okay? Is that all right?"

"Definitely."

"And nobody's going to follow anybody. We're going to leave you all the latitude in the world on this one. Pick the best restaurant in town and use your gold card."

"Well, I will ask him if he wants some Spanish food, some seafood. I'll take him to the Centro Vasco. That's easy for you to send somebody in."

"Okay, you have to go through the restaurant to get to the rest rooms, don't you?"

"Yes."

"So our guy can go take a piss, see you, and leave."

"Okay."

Frank gave the phone to Carol.

"Sounds good," she said. "You're doing a fine job. Just do your little thing. Frank's threatening to pop in on you, to test your reflexes, to see if you react appropriately."

All three laughed uproariously. They had come a long way since the previous October, when Chellino had infuriated Darias by barging in on his luncheon with the Colombian Kids.

Robert picked up Marlene a little past noon. He had decided to tape his conversation with her in the car but not tape Juvenal Betancur.

"Heidi [the maid] is laughing at me," Marlene said. "She tells me that she hasn't seen me dressed up like this in a long time. She says, 'Bye, Marlene, are you going to see your boyfriend?' I told her I don't have time for boyfriends."

Robert laughed.

"I ask you this favor," Marlene said. "He is a fine gentleman. We are not going to talk about the fact that his brother is the president, so don't even mention it. He wants to pass incognito."

"Fine," Robert said. "What have you heard about Oscar?"

"Yesterday he was doing his errands, this morning I saw him. He was to leave for Atlanta because they called him. They have it ready, a million and a half." Wary of picking up money out of town after the recent difficulties, she asked Robert to accompany her to Atlanta. Though she had said previously they were going to Denver, he let the confusion pass and asked about the "delivery of the hundred, hundred fifty" (kilograms of cocaine).

"I'm going to Bogotá on Monday so I can talk with Carlos about that."

"I don't want to be delayed too much longer," Robert said.

Marlene reported that Alex McIntosh planned to move to Miami in the middle of September to live with her. "I'm really happy that he's coming so I won't be alone during this time, Roberto. Every time I see that they kill women, Roberto, I get so I can't sleep. I put my rifle underneath the bed."

"Put it on the side."

"Yes, on the side, not underneath. I sleep like this, Roberto. I close the doors. I put on the alarm. I lock myself in my room, so they would have to take me with machine guns or something."

"You shouldn't open the door for anybody. If you don't have an appointment with somebody, Marlene, and even if you know the person, if you don't have an appointment—"

"I told Oscar, don't ever again go to my house at night."

"Nobody knows what could happen."

"Exactly, because I told him someone could make him come over and have me open up the door." Quiet terror was evident in Marlene's voice.

"That's why I have said that using your house is dangerous," Robert said.

"I have told Oscar, no appointments at my house at night or Sunday, so we can be sure we have a code: if you come by night, or on Sunday, I'll know something is wrong."

It began to rain as they drove over the Julia Tuttle Causeway to Miami Beach, obscuring the voices on the tape. Robert dropped Marlene at the entrance to Mount Sinai Hospital and parked the car as she went upstairs.

Juvenal Betancur was a dignified, handsome man of average height and build with wavy salt-and-pepper hair and green eyes. He wore a tropical suit and brown horn-rimmed glasses.

After they had greeted each other outside his son's room, Betancur told Navarro he was hopeful that the children of Carlos Jader Alvarez would be returned alive by their kidnappers. He personally had galvanized the police and military authorities in Bogotá in recent days, he said, and there were grounds for optimism. The major newspapers, *El Tiempo* and *El Espectador,* were both running prominently displayed photographs of the children, together with pleas from the Alvarez family for their release.

After about half an hour, Marlene brought Betancur to the lobby of the hospital and introduced him to Darias. Juvenal gave Robert his business card: Juvenal Betancur Cuartas, with an address near the Tequendama Hotel in Bogotá, and a phone number. It occurred to Darias as he chatted with Betancur that the debonair Colombian's most noticeable feature was the overpowering scent of too much Aqua Imperiale Cologne.

Betancur wanted to return to his son, so they decided to postpone having lunch and opening a bank account until the next day. However, Marlene handed Juvenal an envelope containing $5,000 in hundred-dollar bills from the accumulated drug cash in her safe.

On the way back to Costa del Sol Marlene told Robert about Betancur's efforts to find the Alvarez children. "Jader gave several hundred thousand dollars to his brother to get elected and that's why they owe him so much," Marlene said. "They have generals going around trying to get the kids back."

At the house she gave Robert $10,500 cash from a bag containing recent cocaine proceeds and told him to put $9,500 in a new bank account for Betancur and $500 each in two new accounts for Jader Alvarez.

"How is *el papi?*" asked Teo Terselich on the phone in the early evening.

"They have very good news," Marlene said. "Between now and Sunday they are supposed to know something about the children."

"I talked to my wife in Bogotá," Terselich said, "and apparently they know who is responsible for the kidnapping."

"Yes, I was told there is a seventy-five percent chance that they are alive."

An hour later, Marlene went with Gustavo Delgado and Dick Lawrence to visit a Hungarian antiques dealer in Gables Estates, the most exclusive section of Coral Gables, to look at statues of Buddha for Carlos Jader Alvarez, who collected them. She examined and priced several statues which the dealer had just imported from Burma. She also purchased some Thai pieces for her own home.

Darias had found Juvenal Betancur to be pompous. "This guy is a crook," he reported to Cooper.

"Obviously it's great if we can get the guy in before we have to shut down," Carol said, rooting for Betancur to show that the drug mafia extended all the way to the presidency of Colombia.

"Just the fact that Marlene deposited ten thousand dollars—gave me ten thousand for him," Darias said. "That puts him in the category of a crook, because to take cash from these people and deposit it—and I am supposed to be a crook, a launderer, and a bad banker. The money is coming from Jader. It doesn't matter for what purpose he is using the money."

"I was just wondering whether we were anticipating any large amounts of money from the brother," Cooper said.

"Apparently the guy is planning on depositing large amounts of money. And where in the hell is he going to be getting money from? It has to be from this business. And the fact that the guy is using me to open accounts in the banks is because he's dirty. And he doesn't want anybody to know that he's the brother of the president because he's doing something dirty and he doesn't want anybody to find out."

"Yeah, if he is that super bad and everything, and if he's going to be using you, obviously the sooner we can get him to start working with you, the better off we're going to be."

Carol said she had told very few DEA people about Juvenal Betancur. "I specifically did not tell people today what you were doing," she said. "They don't know you. Nobody knows who you are. They know you exist as an entity. And they know we have someone inside these people. But they don't know who you are. And I specifically didn't tell them what you were doing today because I didn't want to jack everybody up."

"I know. I was skeptical. When she went upstairs and half an hour went by, I said, oh, this guy doesn't want to meet with me. Then the guy came down and he's a big mouth."

"I went in and I told Tom, and I closed the door because I didn't want the whole office to know. But I wanted to let Tom know because now you're playing with foreign governments and it creates all sorts of new headaches for us. I don't want the world jumping all over me if the guy wasn't who he said he was."

Despite her loathing for Tom Clifford, Cooper had felt compelled to brief him on Juvenal Betancur because Clifford had much more experience with drug trafficking by officials of foreign governments than she did. At his request, she had drafted classified teletypes about Betancur to be sent the next morning to the top officials of the DEA in Washington.

Marlene spoke with Carlos Jader Alvarez just before midnight.

"I am happy," she said, "because Don Juvenal told me to buy *El Tiempo* and *El Espectador* because there is some good news about the kids."

"Well, I don't think so. There's no news. I just saw the *commandante*. I gave him all the details and all the information I have gathered, which they need to proceed. But there's nothing new." He sounded depressed and exhausted.

"Oh, I'm sorry."

"These people want me to do everything for them, to catch them, to turn them in," Jader said, his contempt for the police having reached a new level. "I am very disappointed, to be honest. I was told that I should apprehend them and surrender them to the authorities."

"You must have hope that they are going to be okay," Marlene said. "And, Carlos, if we ever get to see them again, you can count on me to take them anyplace and help them."

"Thank you, dear."

"Whatever it takes. I am not a great believer, but this evening, I don't know, I went to see your Buddhas and the man who has them *is* a great believer, and I was telling him the story, and he gave me a small ivory Buddha as a gift and he told me 'rub his belly and ask.' I rubbed his belly and I don't know, I experienced some hope all of a sudden."

"God willing, yes."

"I am taking good care of Don Juvenal. He is a fantastic person, and feels the utmost friendship and admiration for you. I opened an account with ten. He is going to do whatever is necessary to retrieve those kids."

"He has a blank check. Whatever he wants."

"He really wants to help you regarding the children. He seems to be a very good person, a man of vast culture."

"Yes, his brother is like him."

"You sound like you have a cold," Marlene said.

"Yes, I have a chest cold. I was up all night."

"Take care of yourself, dear. Cheer up! I ordered your Buddhas." She described the statues she had inspected that evening at the antiques dealer's: a sitting Buddha of lacquered wood with gold from the Burmese court in the eighteenth century; another from seventeenth-century Burma crowned with wings, encrusted with gold; another that was stone-lacquered with colors and golden thread; and a standing Buddha with small diamonds and precious stones with wings on the back. The last was five feet tall. They were priced from $9,000 to $22,000.

"I will send the photographs, descriptions, and certificates of authenticity with the chauffeur."

"Okay, love, I'll think about it."

"Well, old man, have faith. I send you big kisses."

Herman the furniture packer called early Friday morning and woke Marlene out of a deep sleep.

"I went to sleep at four A.M. with the TV on," she said. "With all these women they are killing, I am afraid. You know, Herman, they are killing men, but they also are killing women."

"I know, you have to be careful."

"You know, Herman, there is good news about the *muñequitos* [little dolls, a reference to Jader's children]. They are running their pictures in the newspapers, and they think that by Sunday they are going to have some good news."

She asked that he postpone the shipment of furniture to Jader Alvarez until he decided whether to include one or more of the Buddha statues. The monitors had concluded tentatively that Marlene and Herman were, indeed, talking about furniture.

"Three things," Marlene said when Robert called an hour later. "Our appointment with Juvenal is at the hotel, not the hospital."

"Okay."

"Second, we need to send an order to Palmira, extra, extra urgently." Jader had asked her to wire $100,000 to Panama.

"Yes."

"Third, they know who the kidnappers are, but Carlos is very, very discouraged." This was an exaggeration, based on what Jader had told her.

"Oh."

"Also, Juvenal is being honored at a party to be given by a doctor in Miami Beach. They will show a videotape of Belisario's inauguration. He's invited some Cuban personalities and some Colombian personalities to his home to have a drink, play the tape, and discuss the financial situation of the Latin countries."

"Is the lunch still on?"

"No, as a matter of fact, the lunch has been canceled."

Frank Chellino, in the role of Frank Dean, met Darias at Manuel Sanchez's office at the Intercontinental Bank around noon to open the accounts for Juvenal Betancur and Carlos Jader Alvarez.

Darias then drove to Miami Beach to the Beach Palace Hotel on Collins Avenue where he met Navarro and Betancur. They sipped Colombian coffee while perusing the photographs of the Alvarez children in the Bogotá newspapers. Darias had Betancur sign the signature cards for the new bank account and gave him his temporary checks.

Betancur invited Darias to the reception that evening which Marlene had mentioned, where several "political figures" would appear. Robert politely declined.

"I try to avoid getting mixed up with politicians because they are always being investigated and I don't want to get near them," Darias said. (The real reason was that he was preparing to move his family from Miami to Coral Springs that day and wanted to keep his DEA work to a minimum.)

"Well, the doctor has been very nice to me," Betancur said of his host. "He says his house is my house."

"He should have learned a lesson from Fidel Castro," Darias said. "When Castro arrived in Havana, a lot of people put signs outside their houses saying, 'Fidel, this is your house.' He took them all."

Betancur and Navarro laughed, and she and Darias returned to the parking lot, where she gave him a package containing slightly more than $57,000 in cash to put toward the hundred thousand that Jader Alvarez wanted wired to Panama.

He asked her where, precisely, they were going to pick up the money which Oscar supposedly was collecting. In recent days she had said Denver, New York, Atlanta, and Tampa. Now, she said it was Denver for sure.

At Marlene's house that afternoon Robert again reminded her of the "hundred, hundred fifty," referring to the cocaine she had promised him.

"You don't think there is a problem, do you?"

"No, for sure this weekend we will find out. Jaffe is in Bogotá, and Carlos will tell him: when, how much, and where. Jaffe will tell me."

"So, we are waiting for Jaffe."

"Juvenal has a guy with $10 million to launder," Marlene said. "He's going to talk to me tonight about it."

"You ask him how much commission. We can put it in a bank outside the U.S."

"He has to make money now that his brother is president," Marlene said. "He says he has worked all his life and doesn't have a dime."

Having been drawn into the Betancur matter by Carol Cooper the previous day, Tom Clifford continued to monitor it. When he heard about the cocktail reception for Juvenal Betancur he insisted that Darias go.

"I realize that there will probably be absolutely no conversation there, maybe, but there could be," Clifford said.

"I realize that. You want me to see who is there?"

"There could well be things said that could be very important to us," Clifford said, referring to intelligence regarding drug trafficking by officials of Latin American governments such as Colombia and Cuba.

Much to the dismay of Amelia, who was preoccupied with moving to Coral Springs, Robert dressed quickly and drove to Miami Beach. The party was to begin at six.

Almost nobody came. Only Marlene, Juvenal, Robert, and the doctor's wife were there. The doctor arrived late. Robert and Marlene hesitated to ask what had happened to the "Colombian personalities," the "Cuban personalities," and the "political figures" whom Juvenal had mentioned.

Marlene took Robert aside and asked him to make reservations on the first flight the next morning to Denver and the last flight from Denver back to Miami. He called Amelia and asked her to book the reservations, and to reserve a Lincoln town car at the Denver airport. Marlene said they would be picking up a minimum of $1.5 million and perhaps more.

There was no "pertinent" conversation, as the DEA defined incriminating talk, during the party. The videotape of Belisario Betancur's inaugural address was shown. Robert took Marlene to the Forge Restaurant on Arthur Godfrey Road for dinner and then escorted her back to Costa del Sol.

"Tell Tom he owes me one," Robert told Carol when he arrived home exhausted.

"He certainly does. Holy cow! What happened?"

"This is too much. All I accomplished was goodwill from this guy."

"I'm glad you spent umpteen hours getting him to like you. It may pay off, but I don't know whether it was worth all this."

"I think it was a good move. Besides the fact that they had Black Label."

Carol chuckled.

"I had to follow her all the way home."

"Why, was she blitzed?"

"No, but she was afraid, she said."

"Okay."

"This guy Juvenal is the biggest bullshitter I have ever met in my life. He was very nice but he's still a big bullshitter."

Carol laughed again. "Let me know what's going to happen tomorrow out there," she said, referring to Denver.

"Well, the money's waiting. Minimum one and a half million, maybe more. Remember, Carol, these are Colombians. It might be a million, it might be half a million."

"You've got *something* out there. I can tell you that. I don't know how much."

"I want a name and a number," Robert said. "As soon as I leave from that hotel with the money in the trunk of the car, somebody will be following me. I give him the money and I don't want to hear any more about it. I don't know anybody in that town. Tell them whatever they do, at least with her, to try to keep it loose. I don't want to spook her."

"The only thing I can stress, Bob, is the number that I give you, call it as much as you possibly can to let them [the DEA command center in Denver] know what's going on. Because they know nothing as of right now. We'll give them a call yet tonight and let them know. But they don't know you. They don't know anything. Keep that in mind at all times."

"Tell them to understand that in Denver I don't have my 'it' with me." Carol caught Robert's reference to a gun.

"I was sleeping," Alex McIntosh grumbled when Marlene's call awakened him at five past eleven. Marlene's talks with McIntosh were among the very few conversations the bilingual monitors heard in English, although Alex's Scottish brogue was almost as difficult for them to penetrate as Marlene's drug codes.

"We saw the film about the president," Marlene said. "It was so boring, darling, let me tell you the truth, boring. The hostess was a bitch."

"No cartoons and popcorn?"

"No, darling. There was whiskey and *aguardiente.* No champagne, darling. No Perrier Jouet at all. And then Roberto took me to the Forge, the old Club 41. Like always, he was a gentleman. He took me home."

Alex said it was cold in Toronto.

"I love you," Marlene said.

"I love you, too."

"Bye, darling. You know I miss you."

She blew kisses through the phone. "Tell me that you love me."

"I do, I really do, Marlene."

"Are you sure, Alex."

"Yes, Marlene."

Carol called Robert again after midnight to tell him that Special Agent Alfredo Duncan, known as Fred, who had been working as a monitor at the listening post, would be on the flight to Denver.

36

DARIAS AND NAVARRO caught a Continental flight at eight o'clock Saturday morning for Houston where they would connect with another Continental flight to Denver. Anticipating a long, tiring day, they dressed casually: Marlene wore a blue-and-red silk blouse, designer jeans, six-inch lizard pumps, a gold necklace, gold bracelet, and pearl earrings. Robert wore a beige polo shirt and beige slacks. Neither checked luggage, although Darias took a briefcase and a large red-and-blue nylon shoulder bag, both empty. He did not take his tape recorder; it would have been too risky. He had no idea whom he might be encountering or in what circumstances.

Over breakfast in the first-class cabin, Navarro told Darias that he should receive his "hundred-fifty" (150 kilograms of cocaine) from Oscar during the coming week: "The load is expected," she said. On other occasions she had indicated she would need Jader Alvarez's permission to sell the cocaine to Robert. He raised the question.

"If Jader is hesitant about dealing with someone he has not met, I would be willing to travel to Colombia," Darias said. "But I would want to go in a private plane to minimize red tape."

"Perhaps," she replied, having said previously that Jader might like to meet Darias in Panama or Curaçao.

Marlene also commented to Robert about growing strains within the Jader Alvarez organization. "Luis is trying to take business away from Oscar," she said. "Oscar has been in such trouble. He works so hard but never makes any money." Robert had surmised in recent weeks that the younger operatives such as Oscar, Luis Rodriguez, Nelson Batista, and the Pavon brothers competed with each other for the favor of Carlos Jader Alvarez, and engaged in a good deal of back-stabbing. The only consensus seemed to be that Oscar was unreliable.

At the Houston Airport Navarro went to a bank of telephones and dialed the Ramada Renaissance Hotel in Denver. "Room 228," Darias heard her say, and then, "We will be arriving a little early for lunch but we would still like to meet for lunch." Their flight was due in Denver at 11:37 Mountain time. So as not to appear to be eavesdropping, Darias left Navarro and entered a men's room. Special Agent Alfredo Duncan, who had sat two rows behind them on the flight, followed and identified himself to Darias.

Darias joined Navarro again at the telephone just as she was hanging up. "They have it," she said. "They are sitting on it."

At Stapleton International Airport in Denver, Fred Duncan, joined by a Denver-based DEA agent, followed Navarro and Darias to the Budget rental car desk adjacent to the baggage claim area. Two more agents monitored Navarro as she called the hotel again and reported that they would arrive shortly. Darias, on the ruse of calling his banker, checked in with the DEA communications center from another phone. Then he and Navarro took a shuttle bus to the Budget lot and their Lincoln town car.

It was as hot in Denver as in Miami—in the low nineties—but the air was dry. Two unmarked DEA cars followed as Darias and Navarro drove onto I-70, connected three miles east with I-225, exited at Parker Road in the suburban community of Aurora, and gave the car to a valet at the entrance to the contemporary, five-story salmon brick Ramada Renaissance. DEA agent Gloria Woods, who was waiting in the lobby, entered the elevator with them and confirmed that they went to Room 228. In all, ten agents took up positions around the lobby and parking lot and waited.

In the room Navarro introduced Darias to Said Pavon, Ricardo's brother. Said was a balding young man of medium build with glasses, a mustache, and slightly Oriental eyes. His colleagues in the syndicate called him "the Chinaman." Pavon gave Darias a business card with addresses in Bogotá and Milan, Italy. Suave and well-spoken, Pavon said he had $1 million to turn over to them. Navarro and Darias looked at each other; they had been expecting more. Estimates had ranged up to $2 million. Oscar, who presumably had been in charge of collecting the money, was nowhere to be seen.

Pavon made a brief phone call but Darias could not hear much of what was said because the television was blaring, an obvious security gesture by Pavon. However, Darias did hear Pavon tell Navarro that he needed more "merchandise" because he had a new Italian client who wanted 200 kilograms a month. Navarro remarked that Said had sold about 130 kilograms in the Denver area over the past month, worth over $6 million. By the DEA's calculation that would have been roughly one-sixth of Carlos Jader Alvarez's estimated monthly export to the United States.

Pavon at first said the $1 million would be brought to the hotel, but after a while it appeared to Darias that he was stalling. Finally Robert spoke up. "I didn't come here to waste time," he said. "So please call whoever you have to call." Pavon made another call and then announced he was going after the money. He took Darias's empty briefcase and shoulder bag and the three of them went downstairs to the lobby. At the entrance to the hotel Pavon got into a silver-and-blue Volvo driven by a rotund man known to the DEA as Papa Al Levy, a sixty-year-old Denver-area distributor for the Jader Alvarez organization.

"They aren't very well organized," Darias remarked to Navarro as they settled into a booth in the hotel restaurant. "I hope we have not come all this way for nothing."

In the gift shop after lunch they bought toy monkeys—Navarro's for Gustavo Delgado and Darias's for his daughter Laura. Then they returned to the room to find that Said Pavon had already returned with the money.

"It's about eight hundred," Said said. Navarro flipped through the currency quickly and hesitated.

"It appears to be less than that," she said.

"It's correct, love, it's correct," Said insisted.

"Okay, we have to hurry, we'll miss our flight," she said. "I have to sign the receipt."

Darias interjected, "Marlene, if you are going to sign a receipt for money that you haven't counted, you write on there, 'received without counting.' " She complied.

They put the currency back into Darias's briefcase and shoulder bag so that he could take it to his "banker." Claiming to be familiar with Denver from frequent ski trips to Colorado, Robert declined help with directions, went downstairs, and called for his car, which he drove north on Parker Road. After several blocks a trailing DEA car pulled alongside and motioned him into the parking lot of a large shopping mall. The agents, after identifying themselves, emptied the cash into a black garbage bag. Darias also gave them Said Pavon's business card.

"It's supposed to be about eight hundred thousand, but we didn't count it," he said. "That's only about half of what is owed."

When Robert returned to Room 228 Said Pavon said, "That was fast." There was another man in the room, who was introduced as Alex Galeano. Like Pavon, Galeano was calm and well turned out. He asked if Darias could launder between $8 million and $10 million in Switzerland.

"Alejandro, I can do anything that an international bank can do," Darias said, "and a couple of things that banks don't do." Galeano said he would be in Miami later in the week and they could talk further.

Darias took the occasion to lecture Said Pavon on business etiquette. "My people and I don't work the way you do," Robert said. "We are on time all the time. When I say I am going to be someplace at three o'clock, I am there at three o'clock. You told Marlene that you had one and a half million and that you were sitting on it. We get here and you are not sitting on anything and you have only eight hundred. And you attract attention by renting a hotel room and carrying large suitcases in and out."

"Don Roberto is a businessman," Marlene said, with a little laugh. "Don't fool around."

Pavon smiled and said quietly, "Don't worry. Next Friday we are going to have at least one million."

DEA agents photographed Navarro and Darias as they reclaimed their car and returned to the airport. With Fred Duncan and one of the Denver agents following close by, they caught a Delta flight to Atlanta with a connection to Miami.

"David Jaffe is in Bogotá and is setting up everything for the new delivery," Navarro said on the plane. "It is expected this week and there should be big money within two or three weeks. We will make good use of Jader's new bank accounts."

"Good," Darias said.

"It's odd," she added. "I expected to see Oscar in Denver. He was supposed to be there. I wonder what happened."

Exhausted, Marlene fell asleep on Robert's shoulder as dusk fell. It was the first time in a year of knowing each other that either of them had touched the other in an affectionate way. They had come to feel affection, even at times tenderness toward each other. Robert had never felt sexual stirrings, though he had been amused at the provocations—the nude photographs of Marlene in her study, the erotic drawing on her staircase, and the pornographic movies in her bedroom. Now, in the night sky over Florida, instead of thinking about sex with Marlene who was snuggling against his shoulder, he thought about sex with Amelia who he knew was home worrying about his having spent the day alone and unprotected with violent drug traffickers in a strange city.

Robert dropped Marlene off at Costa del Sol and then drove home, arriving around 3:00 A.M. He and Amelia were so excited to see each other that they laughed and jumped up and down as they embraced, and then made the deepest love they had made in a long time.

37

CARLOS JADER ALVAREZ'S widely advertised pleas for public help in finding his children produced a breakthrough in the investigation—the first since the children had been kidnapped ten months earlier. Within a few days after the Bogotá media carried the children's photographs, several residents of the Talavera neighborhood, where the children had been held in October and November, called the F-2 to report "suspicious movements" during that time by the family in town house number six. Two of the callers identified photographs of the children. The F-2 interviewed the owner of the house. It had been rented on September 19, 1981, two and a half weeks prior to the kidnapping of the children, by two National University students named Pedro Pablo Silva and Edgar Helmut Garcia Villamizar. Since Pedro Silva had been underage, the lease had been cosigned by his mother, who told the F-2 that she had signed only after her son had pleaded. She also informed the F-2 that her son had been missing since early March.

For the first time, Carlos Jader Alvarez thought he might be close to solving the case. Pedro Silva had been one of the two students his men had kidnapped near the National University in March. The other's name had been Orlando Garcia Villamizar. Although both had refused to talk and eventually had been executed, it now appeared that Alvarez had been on the right track. Could Orlando Garcia Villamizar have been related to Edgar Garcia Villamizar? It did not take long for Alvarez and the F-2 to determine that they were brothers, and to flesh out their identities. Edgar Garcia was a twenty-year-old sociology major at the National University. He also was a member of the M-19, and two years earlier, along with other students, had occupied the four-hundred-year-old La Tercera Church in downtown Bogotá for seventeen days to protest the policies of the then-president of Colombia, Julio César Turbay.

Jader Alvarez and the F-2 acted immediately on the new information, while withholding it from the public and the media. On Tuesday, August 17, Edgar Garcia got a telephone call summoning him to submit some papers at a branch of the Ministry of Education across from the Colombian Academy of Language in downtown Bogotá. The next morning he set out from his home accompanied by his four-year-old nephew, the son of his missing brother Orlando. En route to the ministry, some men with guns surrounded Edgar and forced him into an unmarked van. They left the child alone on the street crying, "Don't kill him! Don't kill him!" The child was immediately picked up by another vehicle under the command of Major Jorge Vanegas of the F-2 and taken to the female barracks of the Colombian National Police. It was several days before the child was returned to the Garcia family. The family determined that the call summoning Edgar to the education ministry had been a hoax. Having now lost their second son in six months, the Garcia family notified various police agencies of Edgar's disappearance. They also informed the office of the new president of Colombia, Belisario Betancur. Someone in the president's office promised the Garcias that the matter would be investigated.

Exhausted from the trip to Denver, Marlene Navarro called Oscar's pager all day Sunday with rising concern in her voice. He did not call until eight-thirty that evening.

"Why do you always get lost on me like that?" Marlene asked angrily. "I went to look for the order, and you didn't show up."

"Which order, love?"

"The guys' order! Do you remember?"

"You went there?"

"Of course, I have the papers."

"Said already gave them to you?"

"Of course. I was waiting and waiting for you. Listen, are you all having a party or what?" The sound of female voices and laughter could be heard in the background.

"Said already gave it to you?" Oscar asked again.

"Yes, dear, but not everything. Only eight hundred."

With the eleven o'clock news in the background, Marlene dialed Carlos Jader Alvarez in Bogotá.

"Is there anything new about the children?"

"No."

"How come? I thought there was to be good news by the weekend."

"Nothing."

"God willing, soon you will learn something."

"We know the identity of the kidnappers," Jader said. "We know exactly who they are. I delivered the names to the colonel. Now it's up to them."

"So what is the next step?"

"I don't know. It's up to them."

"Okay, old man, yesterday I was in Colorado, and they gave me only eight hundred signed cards."

Jader said he did not have even half the cash he needed and asked Marlene to prepare an accounting of recent collections for Aunt Teodora (Teo Terselich) to bring to Bogotá.

Juvenal Betancur reported to Marlene a few minutes later that he planned to fly to Bogotá early Tuesday to try to accelerate the effort to recover the Alvarez children.

"I'm going to have lunch with the general," Betancur said. "The problem is that they weren't ready to move this fast. They are taking their time. But I am sure he is going to be able to help Carlos."

"If you need any more money just let me know."

"The important thing is to find the children," Betancur said. "That would be payment enough."

Marlene called Oscar the next morning. "I need to make a report of all you have received that is new," she told him. "We have to send an accounting to *el papi* tomorrow with Aunt Teodora, because she's leaving. *El papi* told me that I should send in a report of everything. *El papi* says that there's a shortage, that nothing's been collected. He says that there's still a great deal missing."

She instructed Oscar to come to her house at six that evening.

IN THE MATTER OF THE APPLICATION OF
THE UNITED STATES OF AMERICA FOR AN
EXTENSION OF THE ORDER AUTHORIZING
THE INTERCEPTION OF WIRE COMMUNICATIONS

"Between July 17 and August 10 approximately 700 telephone conversations have been recorded," the prosecutors wrote in their application for an extension of the wiretap. "The interceptions to date provide some evidence. . . . However, the conspirators' use of code words in their conversations has retarded the investigation. . . . Furthermore, the identities of some of the conspirators still need to be ascertained. . . . Lastly, the delivery of a large amount of cocaine to the Operation Swordfish offices is still pending."

The DEA and the U.S. Attorney's office were late getting their application for an extension of the wiretap to Washington and back to Judge Sidney Aronovitz in Miami in time to prevent the original 30-day order from expiring. Thus they were forced to stop intercepting Navarro's phone calls at 10:29 on Monday morning, August 16. To avoid any later accusation of an illegal intercept, Michael Pasano ordered that the tape recorders be unplugged and the listening post locked. It was midafternoon before Carol Cooper took the new documents to the court house and got Judge Aronovitz's signature. The monitoring resumed at 3:43 P.M.

The cash that Said Pavon had turned over to Navarro and Darias in Denver was flown to Miami by two DEA agents and counted on Monday. Instead of the $800,000 Pavon had insisted was there, it came to only $695,000. Darias drove to Costa del Sol to give Navarro the news. She was shocked and immediately paged Oscar, who, for a change, called her back promptly.

"I need for you to locate Said any way at all," she said. "The bank just called me and from the cards we were supposed to have sent for the wedding, we are short precisely 105. Instead of 800,000 they gave me 695. I need for you to make this complaint. After all, we are not playing with silly things. You'll find Said fast?"

"Yes, I'll find him immediately," Oscar said.

Marlene told Robert she was glad she had heeded his advice to write "received without counting" on Said's receipt in the Denver hotel room. She asked Robert to wire $500,000 of the Denver money to Panama and give $195,000 to Tocayo for immediate airborne smuggling to Bogotá.

"What did you talk about regarding the kids today?" Marlene asked Juvenal Betancur when he called just after eight o'clock Monday evening.

"I made an appointment with the general and I'm going directly from the airport to the general police station."

Juvenal said he would return from Bogotá by Friday when he was scheduled to address the Lions Club of Coral Gables. He added that he had lost his credit cards and asked Marlene to enlist Robert Darias's help in obtaining new ones.

Marlene spoke to the Jader aide called *El Loco* in Bogotá at 10:17.

"Everything is okay here," she reported. "They are working and collecting all the birthday cards. Aunt Luchita (Luis Rodriguez) didn't give me anything today but tomorrow she will. The delivery for Palmira [Panama] was done and the chauffeur is going this week."

"Okay."

"What about the kids?"

"They are putting the screws to this guy so that he talks. They are trying to see at least one of the kids before they turn over any money. They are separated now. They told them they would pay but they want to see the kids alive."

"That sounds hopeful."

"Yes."

"Will you be seeing Marina?"

"Yes."

"Tell her that I got everything for her, and that the Jesus from Prague is coming." Marlene had asked Gustavo Delgado to locate the limited edition porcelain statue.

The "guy" that *El Loco* had told Marlene they were "putting the screws to" in Bogotá was Edgar Garcia, one of the students who had rented the house where the Alvarez children had been held. Like his brother Orlando, whom Jader Alvarez had tortured and killed six months earlier, Edgar Garcia was refusing to talk. "I am a Colombian citizen," was the mantra he repeated.

The kidnappers sent a ransom note to Carlos Jader Alvarez for the first time in six months. They were still demanding 25 million pesos, whose dollar value had dropped below $400,000. They assured Alvarez that his children were alive.

Teo called Marlene later that night and they discussed the missing Denver money. She sounded concerned. "I haven't seen these young fellows yet to get the $105,000 we need," she said. "Of course, they cannot refuse because they know they have it. I've had enough. I'm not going to take this from them. Period."

Her concern was further evident when she spoke to Robert.

"You still haven't verified that?" he asked. "I'm sort of worried about that."

"I'm not *sort of* worried," she said. "I am really and truly worried!"

"Those are things which are very delicate," Robert said. "I hope Oscar doesn't get a bad impression about my part in that."

"Oh, no, on the contrary. He's mad at the guys and he said, 'How could they even think of doing that to Don Roberto?' On the contrary!"

When Darias spoke to Cooper, he had begun to worry that the Denver problem might affect the syndicate's inclination to sell him cocaine.

"There's no indication on her end that there is any problem," Carol said.

"She was very nice to me when I talked to her."

"She's been very nice all day. She's not concerned about you. If she was, she would have been on your case early this morning. She's still busy tonight from what I understand."

"She might be expecting some more money."

"She's gathering it today. She's gotten phone calls and told people she'll call them back later. She's busy. She doesn't want to be bothered."

"That means she's counting money."

"That's what we're assuming," Carol said. "You're the only one she tells the truth to."

One by one, Teo, Luis, and Oscar arrived at Marlene's through the evening and brought with them a total of $449,000 in cash. Oscar left, but Teo and Luis stayed to work on the accounting for Jader Alvarez.

Marlene mentioned her incipient dispute with Ricardo and Said Pavon over the missing $105,000 from Denver.

Luis said her concern was well founded. "They'll kill you for five cards," he said.

Fear overcame Marlene after Luis and Teo left. Unlike the dispute that involved $5 million owed by an indistinct group in New York, the controversy over the Denver money, though a smaller amount, involved Navarro directly. She had been to Denver. She had handled the money. She had taken delivery of it. Now she had challenged Said and Ricardo Pavon personally.

She confided her anguish to Gustavo Delgado, to whom she had already mentioned the problem briefly.

"You know these guys with the 105?"

"Yes."

"People say they are stealing from me. They deny it and will try to say that Roberto Darias stole it from me. I am not even going to mention this to Roberto. If he asks me I will just say there was an impasse but everything is solved. You know, Gustavo, I may lose in one day what I made in one year. Because I'm going to tell Carlos I'll just pay for it. And when I find out who it is later, I will settle accounts."

"You should tell Carlos. You know him very well."

"Not now, not now. I will tell him when I see him."

"Damn, that's a lot of money."

"Said claimed 'the money went through my hands, your hands, and the banker's.' When he mentioned Roberto I almost kicked him in the balls. I am definitely not going to tell Roberto. I am afraid that Roberto will withdraw from me if I tell him. *Ai,* Gustavo, I am very nervous about this whole thing."

"Maybe you will learn something from it."

"One thing, Gus, I will not receive five cents from that guy, Said. He is going to be the one who is fucked."

"You have to be very careful because you don't know who you are dealing with."

"That is why I've remained silent. I know that Carlos will straighten this out. But I don't want to get Oscar upset because he might want to solve it in a *bad* way. And if he does that, I might get involved as well." Oscar was known to carry a machine gun in the trunk of his car.

By late evening Marlene was terrified. She beeped Oscar, who called her back just before 11:00.

"I was just with that guy (Said) and he says he gave you everything complete," Oscar said.

"All right, leave it like that," she said quietly.

"No, no, love. We have to clear this up with him."

"No, no. Leave it like it is. It's better for things to be quiet. He's partly right. This happened because of him, me, and Mr. Roberto. Perhaps I made a mistake, but Don Roberto, never!"

"I know, my love. That's why I want to clear this up with this guy already."

"The only thing I think, Oscar, between us two, is that he wouldn't do anything to me, would he?"

"No, I don't believe he will, dear, no. Forget about that."

"He has to know that you're behind me." Marlene was starting to cry. "There are a lot of people behind me. Something can happen to me, but something can happen to him also." She was weeping softly.

"Forget it."

"This is what I want you to help me with—*that nothing should happen to me!*" she sobbed. *"Por favor!"*

"Don't get nervous. Nothing is going to happen to you. Forget it."

Oscar said he would bring Said Pavon to see Marlene in the morning.

She called Gustavo again. Anger was evident in her voice; she had stopped crying.

"What I am afraid of is that I may be in danger from Said. What I have to do is make Said believe that I believe him. That way I am not going to be in danger. You realize that here in Miami they do anything they want to a person for $5,000. You can imagine what they could do for 105. You have to be damned careful here in Miami. So what I'm going to do is declare myself responsible for this money. This way there won't be any more problems. So, Gus, I lost that, but I still have my car, my house, my travel, so you know, you can't have everything in life."

"I know it hurts," Gustavo said.

"I promise, if I can, to fuck him up eventually."

"I know you will, but not now. Later."

"I feel really bad, like I've been hit in the head with a stick. Listen, Gus, I would like to get the Virgin statue, and the Jesus of Prague tomorrow." She was also taking a Virgin Mary to Marina in Bogotá.

"They only made ten of the statues and only twenty of the Jesus," Gustavo said. "It's not that easy to get them because they have to look all over for them."

Marlene reached Alex McIntosh in Toronto before midnight.

"If I tell Robert that I doubt him," she said, "then he's going to tell me, 'Okay, Marlene, I don't want to work with you anymore.' "

"You're dealing in big money, and you should have been a lot more careful," Alex said.

She said she might have to make up the loss from her own funds.

"That's a lot of money for anybody," Alex said. "You worked all year for it."

"It wasn't my living, but my savings."

"You've been working very hard this year. You've already made yourself sick with work. I don't know what to tell you, Marlene. I feel sorry for you in a way, but I warned you so many times. *You're playing with the big boys.*"

"You know who was the one who did that against me? Ricardo and Said."

"You're talking about a hundred thousand dollars here. You don't seem to understand. People kill for *fifty* dollars."

"*Ai*, Alex, don't say that word, please! I am afraid."

"Don't be afraid."

She sighed, crying softly. "Well, I am upset."

"You can't trust people."

"I *did,* Alex. I *did.*"

"This is big money and you can't trust people."

"I know it was my mistake."

"You should have checked."

"It's too late."

"You're going to get an ulcer."

Marlene told Alex she was considering an offer of a diplomatic post in the new government of Colombia. "We'll go someplace else, okay?"

"It doesn't matter where we go."

"They have asked me to become the Colombian Ambassador to UNESCO in Paris."

"Your whole head's all mixed up right now, because you're just so upset. Just take it easy for a little while."

Navarro's anguish prompted the monitors to brief Carol Cooper, who awakened Darias after midnight.

"Apparently she's very, very upset about this money that's missing," Carol said, "and apparently Oscar's wondering if it may be you, and she's totally standing up for you. She's willing to take the loss herself if she has to. But she totally trusts you—she flat out said that. 'It can't be my banker, I trust him with my life.' But apparently she *is* upset. She's calling the world, telling everybody about it."

"How do you read it?"

"How do I read it?"

"Yes, we have a problem of communication," Robert pointed out, "in that I cannot hear the actual words they are using."

Carol again explained that she was prohibited from letting Robert hear the tapes.

"She has not spoken to Said yet," Carol said. "But she's totally backing you, with no problem. She's upset because she's afraid that she herself is going to have to make it up."

"This came at a very bad moment, Carol. If Oscar is against me, Oscar is not going to deliver any of those drugs to me. If he thinks I took that money, how in the hell is he going to give me five million in drugs?"

"But I think a lot of it is in her control, though."

"Yeah, but remember, I've never really had Jader's confidence either. The guy has always been telling her, be careful with Cubans."

"She hasn't told him about this yet. But she's saying 'I totally trust my banker with my life.' She totally trusts you and she doesn't really know these other yo-yos that well. So she's totally backing you."

"Well, then, I don't think I have any problem. *They* are going to have problems. Somebody is going to have problems."

"Keep in mind, too, that Oscar is in a bad light with the guy down south, too," Carol said.

"Good point. Maybe that's why he's afraid. I think this is going to be the end of his career."

"See how she approaches you in the morning. Get a readout. And be careful with what *you* tell *her,* what *she's* told you, and what *I've* told you."

"Yeah, I will only react to what she tells me. But they are going to have a big argument."

"But you're not going to be involved."

Marlene began dialing Bogotá after midnight, the number where she knew Carlos Jader Alvarez would be, the most private number in the big house called *La Iglesia.* After several "busy circuit" messages, she finally got through on the ninth try.

"Hello, dear. What's happening." He had been waiting for her call and sounded exhausted.

"My love, the reason I'm calling is because of three different things. One is, hi, what's going on, did you see Don Juvenal?"

Jader had sent someone to meet Betancur at the airport.

"The other thing is, what good news do you have for me about the kids?"

"No, nothing, Marlene."

"What do you mean, nothing."

He explained again that they "know everything" about the kidnappers except where they are. "The whole organization has been unmasked," he said. He gave no details of the ongoing but thus far fruitless interrogation of Edgar Garcia.

"I don't know why, but I think everything is going to come out all right," Marlene said. "You will see that I am right."

She reported that Teo was leaving Thursday for Bogotá and would bring the accounting that Jader asked for. Jader asked about recent collections, the Denver money in particular.

"The guy there in Colorado made a mistake in the count and instead of eight hundred cards, only a little less than seven hundred were delivered and no more."

"*Ai, carambola!*" Jader said.

"I was afraid that all of a sudden they would send somebody to take care of *me,*" Marlene said. "I wanted to tell you about this 105, so that you can help me recover it real quietly, because Aunt Luchita [Luis Rodriguez] told me that we should be careful because even for five cards, they are, you know . . ."

"Yes."

"Then so you can help me, we will act dumb, because that is what we have to do, act dumb. . . . I gave Aunt Luchita some instructions in case I got sick or something happened to me. I told her to give you all the details of how things were."

"Yeah, yeah."

"Listen, man, I hope to God that you help me, so things won't be like that, you hear?"

"Like what, Marlene?"

"That because these guys, all of a sudden, because they want to keep something, they might want to do something to *me!*"

"Oh, yeah, yeah . . ."

"Please!" Her anguish was audible but she was not crying as she had with Alex and Oscar.

"Sure, don't worry," Jader said.

3 8

SHE WORRIED. She worried about the missing $105,000 for which she was directly responsible. She worried that she would be shot in the course of resolving the problem.

She spoke to Oscar first thing Wednesday morning, August 18.

"It wouldn't surprise me if Said had been deceived, and then had to cover himself," she said. "I need you to tell Said to call me."

"I just spoke to him," Oscar said. "He is giving the same excuse. 'You already signed for it.' Ricardo is easier. I'm better off dealing with him."

"I will not take receipt of anything further from Said, not even five cents. I won't have anything to do with him any longer."

"Leave that up to me, my love," said Oscar. He was to see Ricardo Pavon at three that afternoon.

"We're in no condition now to quibble," Marlene said. "Remember, Osquita, we're in a position where something could happen to us for ten dollars."

"Said is insolent," Oscar said. "I won't put up with him anymore."

Marlene said they needed to send *el papi* as much money as possible by the coming weekend. "It's for the children this time."

"You must steer away from these people for the time being," Luis Rodriguez advised Marlene. "With everything that is happening you are going to lose." It was Luis who had told her the previous evening that Said and Ricardo would "kill her for five cards."

"What has me worried now is Roberto, my banker," Marlene said. "He told me that he definitely wants to talk to these people. Otherwise, he says, everyone is going to think *he* took the money. He has some big guys behind him, Italians, and I'm afraid of what could happen."

"Well, everybody here is big," Luis said. "I think they should talk."

"I sent a message to Said to call me. It was like a bird shooting at a shotgun. They said they had nothing to talk to me about. So I am very worried."

"How is *el papi?*"

"He was kind of low last night. Hopefully, at the end of the week, he'll have some good news."

The high command of the Miami DEA met and postponed the termination of Operation Swordfish from September 8 until September 14–15. The agents and lawyers needed additional time to assimilate evidence from the wiretap. Carol briefed Robert.

"If we hear anything I'll give you a hoot and a holler," Carol said. "You sound tired."

"Yeah, well, I can't even sleep. I am pent-up. I guess until she leaves tomorrow I'm going to be like this. I want to get rid of her." Navarro was scheduled to fly to Bogotá for the weekend.

"Yeah, I know. We're all anxious to get her out of here."

"I hope she doesn't come back until Monday at least."

"You and about forty other people here."

"Biscocho." The suggestive Spanish word for "delectable" was Luis Rodriguez's usual come-on when Marlene answered the phone.

She laughed tolerantly. "I learned a big lesson, Luisito. When things are going to happen they will happen and you have to face them. I sent these guys a message that I wanted to talk to them, and they sent a message back to me that was very specific: since I have signed a receipt I have to live with it."

"Aha."

"El papi told me not to worry, that things would get resolved."

"Any news on the kids?"

"I talked to him last night and he said within a week they think they will know something, because these people—they talked to them last night—made a money demand. Marina asked for proof that they have the kids. We have to trust in God that they are still alive. It doesn't matter what happens as long as they are alive."

"There is an eighty percent chance of finding Don Carlos's children alive," Juvenal Betancur announced to Marlene on the phone Thursday evening.

"Oh, do you really think so?" she exclaimed.

"The army saw them alive," Betancur said. "They have them surrounded. The colonels are at Carlos's disposal. He is to use them for whatever he needs."

"Carlos told me, 'anything for Juvenal, anything for Juvenal,' " Marlene replied. " 'Juvenal is worth his weight in gold.' "

She called Gustavo. "Juvenal told me the army saw them and they are alive."

"Oh, my God!"

"I'm just waiting to talk to Carlos and send him a big kiss."

"Wow!"

"Why don't you put your batteries on and get me that Jesus of Prague tomorrow."

Gustavo said he would try.

She dialed Alex McIntosh in Toronto nine times and got no answer.

At 11:07 she called Jader's number in Bogotá and got *El Loco,* who said, "Everything is turning out fine."

"I'm glad because I just talked with Don Juvenal and he says he is optimistic and he thinks the children are alive."

"Yes."

"I hope to God it's true. That would be the best news we have had this year. I'm not a great believer, old man, but for the first time I'm praying to Him as much as possible that they show up."

Jader Alvarez came on the phone.

"Don Juvenal just called me to say he was very happy, very optimistic, eighty-five percent optimistic that everything would be taken care of soon."

"Everything is okay," Jader said.

"What did you say?" The connection was poor.

"Everything is okay."

"Is that true, really?"

"Well, more or less. They are very optimistic."

"I was supposed to have the Baby Jesus delivered today," Marlene said, "but they did not deliver the Jesus de Praga. Rather it was only the little Virgin."

She told Jader that Oscar was "lost."

"I am worried because the day before yesterday he agreed to get me the brother of this guy with whom I have the problem. So I think that maybe something happened to him."

"Well, let me know."

"Do you want me to give a message to Don Juvenal?" Marlene asked. "Do you want me to tell him anything?"

"No, that I thank him, and everything is fine."

Everything was far from fine. The euphoria in Bogotá over the identification of some of the people apparently involved in the kidnapping had been conveyed to Miami too optimistically, particularly by the fustian Juvenal Betancur. The Colombian Army, eager to please the personal emissary of the new president, had exaggerated. It had actually seen no one alive and had no one surrounded.

The next day the monitors were listening as Marlene called Maria Lilia Rojas in Bogotá, the mother of Zuleika, the oldest of the three missing children. Maria had recently been released from prison in the United States where she had served time for smuggling money in Monopoly boxes.

"Lilia, I have faith in God that now everything will indeed get straightened out for us," Marlene said.

"Well, yes, dear, God willing."

"You'll see that if I take a small Virgin and some little things to you, you'll see that it will. Cheer up and be optimistic because now everything will really come out all right."

Marlene asked Lilia to have someone meet her flight that evening. *"El papi* is absentminded."

FM DEA MIA
TO DEA HQ WASHN
  IMMEDIATE
SUBJ: G1-81-0371 NAVARRO, MARLENE ET AL.
  TITLE III INTERCEPT IN ABOVE REFERENCED INVESTIGATION SCHEDULED TO TERMINATE 9/15/82, CULMINATING IN MULTIPLE ARRESTS AND SEIZURES. POTENTIAL ARRESTS INVOLVE SEVERAL COLOMBIAN NATIONALS, FOR EXAMPLE, CARLOS JADER ALVAREZ, JOSE ANTONIO CABRERA, CARMENZA VALENZUELA, JUVENAL BETANCUR. IT IS REQUESTED THAT HQ AND AMEMBASSY BOGOTA ADVISE MIAMI DIVISION OF STATUS OF RECENT TREATY FOR ARRESTS AND EXTRADITIONS OF COLOMBIAN NATIONALS LOCATED IN COLOMBIA. MIAMI DIVISION WILL ALSO ATTEMPT TO LURE POTENTIAL DEFENDANTS TO INDEPENDENT THIRD COUNTRIES; HOWEVER, LIKELIHOOD IS IMPROBABLE AT PRESENT TIME.
  ANY QUERIES CONCERNING THIS MATTER, PLS CONTACT SPECIAL AGENT CAROL COOPER, GROUP 8, MIAMI.

Though the DEA agents had been preoccupied with Marlene Navarro, they were still intrigued with Humberto Garcia as a businessman prominent in the Miami Cuban community with ties to major drug traffickers in Medellín, Colombia. For months Garcia had been telling Darias about a Cuban cocaine dealer in West Miami known as *el gallero,* "the roosterman." True to his name, the Roosterman raised fighting cocks for commercial exploitation—cock-fighting was a lucrative business in Miami and all over Latin America. But since the Roosterman also dealt in hundred-kilogram multiples of cocaine, Darias conceived the notion—and cleared it with Carol Cooper—of selling the cocaine he was to purchase from the Alvarez organization to the Roosterman, with a generous commission to Humberto Garcia, thus implicating them in the same criminal web. On Thursday, August 19, Humberto finally took Robert to meet the Roosterman, and although Darias had been briefed he still was not fully prepared for what he saw.

The Roosterman, who gave his first name as "Roberto," operated out of a secluded six-acre compound not far from Tamiami Park. The place was patrolled by three guards in golf carts carrying MAC-10 submachine guns. In a small outbuilding toward the back of the property Darias glimpsed several more submachine guns with silencers lying on a table. In a barn was evidence of the man's nickname— hundreds of roosters.

The Roosterman, delighted to find that Darias was a Cuban, broke out a bottle of Black Label and poured generous servings for Robert and Humberto. The Roosterman admired Darias's black nylon jacket, which he had been given only that day at Marlene's house by Luis Rodriguez. In a gesture typical of the Latin gentleman, Darias immediately took the jacket off and gave it to the Roosterman.

They talked about cocaine only in general terms. In the Latin world, one became friendly socially before getting down to business. The Roosterman said that the next time Darias and Garcia visited he would invite a few girls to join them for the afternoon.

"This Roosterman, really, is a fine gentleman," Robert told Carol later. He was still high from the Scotch.

"Did you meet him?"

"Yeah, he has a very fine bottle of Black Label at his house."

"So you had a good time with him, huh?"

"The guy is big and very dangerous," Robert continued. "Very, very dangerous. The guy has three guys in golf carts going around the inside of that compound. He has six acres. And all the houses in the compound belong to him and his family. They all live there. He has three guys in golf carts with MAC-10s going around inside that compound."

"Holy cow!"

"He was at ease with me," Robert said. "I am a convicted felon." They laughed. "But I am only business. When I drink I am only business."

"I don't want to hear any more grief from Amelia that you've been out drinking with Frank."

"I think everything is looking good on every angle," Robert said.

"Yeah, I want you to spend some time with your wife now."

"Tell Frank that I hate the fact that he's going to get credit for this operation, because he hasn't done anything."

Chellino had been listening. "Get off the goddamned phone so we can go have a drink, please."

"Let me tell you, Carol, I would love to get this Roosterman," Robert said.

"We'll see what we can do with him. Let me think about him a little bit more."

"This guy is big, Carol. Big, big, big."

In ninety-two-degree humidity and haze, Robert and Amelia Darias made three round-trips between Miami and Coral Springs in a rented van on Saturday and Sunday, August 21 and 22, moving a number of items to their new home—a three-bedroom ranch house—that they did not want to entrust to the care of the movers, who would come the following week. There were a number of valuable art objects and forty-one cartons of books, including Robert's leather-bound first edition of the writings of José Martí, the poet, patriot, and father of independent Cuba, published in Spain in 1953. Robert frequently read from Martí to eight-year-old Laura.

Juvenal Betancur reached Darias late Sunday afternoon, seeking a meeting on Monday, and Robert called Carol, who was at home plotting the tactics of arrests, seizures, and search warrants with Frank Chellino.

"He just called me," Robert said. "I'm going to tape him. I'm going to be trying to get this guy as much as I can in these few days."

"Exactly."

"At least I'm going to incriminate him a little bit so the government can use that against them in the future if they need to."

"Yeah."

"He said he has some business to discuss with me, whatever that means."

"Do you think, Bob, you're in a position, if he doesn't bring it up himself, to kinda give him a few hints?"

"I'm going to flatly tell him what I do. The guy is too intelligent and too old to play games with me. I want him to understand that Marlene and Carlos Jader are my partners in everything I do. And I want that in the tape. So if he wants to be my partner—the tape will explain that he's doing business with Carlos Jader and also Marlene."

"Okay, make sure you say the name 'Carlos Jader.' No use pussyfooting around with this yo-yo. Call me first after Juvenal. Let me know what happens. That's critical. I gotta stay right up to the minute on that one." The prospect of implicating the brother of the president of a head of state in serious narcotics crimes had drawn the interest of the State Department and the CIA. Cooper was fielding their queries.

Carol and Robert fell into a discussion of the vicissitudes and psychological perils of spying.

"As long as I know you're thinking normally, that you're not thinking you're somebody else," she said. "This does get to you after a period of time."

"I am doing things that somehow work within my personality," Robert said. "I am not a bad guy, but I can *think* like a bad guy, and it comes naturally. It might be a bit difficult to understand, but it's my way of thinking as a Cuban. That's what most people don't understand. Cubans tend to bend the law."

"To justify in their own minds what they're doing?"

"Carol, I used to live in Cuba. The Cubans that are born here get accustomed to your laws and have your frame of reference. When I was in Cuba, my father was big in government. It was a way of life to act and do things with money, to do deals and business with people that were not quite legal. But they *were* legal within the system in Cuba, because in all these Latin countries everybody makes a buck out of everything."

"Sure."

"Where it's totally illegal here, it wasn't there. So that's why my mind can click on the same wavelength with these guys—Marlene and these people. Of course, I wasn't dealing with drugs, but when you're talking about exchanging money it's the same thing. That wouldn't have been illegal in Cuba, and it's not in Colombia."

"The main thing with you," Carol said, "is the fact that you *will* do what we say, within reason. You *should* argue back with us, if you don't think it's going to work. Because we're looking at the legal end and we're looking at all the various and sundry things that we want to do to make a case. Now if you don't feel that they're going to work, you can argue with us. But the main thing is that you're constantly reporting in, which is critical. It gives us an outlook on how you're thinking. If you really believed in what you were doing, from the bad side, I would be able to detect that in you. And that's crucial. I want to be able to tell people, yeah, I've talked to him almost every single day, at length, and there's no problem with anything he was doing."

"Well, I have something else, Carol, that keeps my sanity completely a hundred percent. And it's Amelia and my daughter. I enjoy talking to you, and 'let's do this to these guys and do that to the other guy.' But I look at that more like a spy novel than anything else."

"Amelia and Laura bring you back to reality, no matter what's going on. That's your real life. As long as I know you've got a good family life and you're talking to me normally, I feel very comfortable."

"With the wiretap, you have been able to understand me a little better."

"I never questioned you."

"But still, now you have a real insight into my relationship with Marlene."

"There's no doubt in anybody's mind."

"Well, before there was doubt in some minds, you know that."

"Yeah, I know."

"But now nobody can argue that point. I kept telling everybody that it wasn't true."

"I know, so did I."

"Men are like that. Men think that in order to get along with a woman you have to go to bed with her."

"Ridiculous. There's no question about that now, and the fact is you're doing your job and you're thinking logically, which is what I want you to do. You have not changed at all, basic mental attitude, from the time when you started this thing. Which is commendable, for you to go through it for this period of time, especially now because I know there's a lot of pressure on you."

"Right."

"As long as you keep a perspective on what you're doing, what's real and what's not real. I don't think you've ever had a problem with that."

"No, not at all."

"I'm going to be in court for the next twenty years, thanks to you. Just the wire alone, and keep it under your chin, Frank and I figured it out this weekend, we're looking at twenty-five people, just on the wire, that are solid, *solid* cases."

"My God."

"The wire is an excellent case, obviously. People are elated about it."

"I could have made Humberto's case as big as Marlene's."

"I agree."

"Look how much it developed. If I could have gone after him gung-ho, it would have been—"

"I know. That irritates me. But I think the wire's gone very, very well. Helluva case. Washington is very enthusiastic about it. The director, the CIA, the State Department, and everybody else is involved in it now. It's gone to the highest levels I can get it to. You're a star, kid. The main thing is, we just gotta hold it together for the next three weeks. And I think we can do it. Thank God she left this weekend for your sake and mine. Everybody got some rest. All I can tell you right now, kid, is go after your friend Juvenal tomorrow. Cut out all the b.s. that he's been giving you, and just get down to the nitty-gritty."

"I don't have time to lose now."

"We know that we have three weeks to deal with and we're looking at getting him as solid as we can. We've got three weeks to play with him. If he doesn't come around, well and good, but there's enough on him at this point to make people raise a few eyebrows. I'd love to be able to take him. I'd love to get him good."

3 9

LIKE A VILE summer cold, the "Nick 'n' Eddie" controversy clung to the DEA bureaucracy through June, July, and August. The only thing that Carol Cooper and Tom Clifford agreed on—they still hated each other—was their loathing of Special Agents Nick Zapata and Eddie Hernandez. Clifford had banished them from their undercover assignments at International Investments after their incendiary memorandum, and only the cumbersome federal personnel management rules he was required to follow had kept him from firing them from Operation Swordfish entirely. For the time being they were assigned to desks in Clifford's suite of offices, their presence a daily reminder of the abysmal staffing mistakes the founder of the operation had made.

For hours each day, Zapata and Hernandez paced back and forth, mumbling over their notes as they struggled to reconstruct undercover assignments that had occurred months earlier, and that were supposed to have been recorded in writing within five days of their occurrence. The reports were among the many that Michael Pasano needed for the prosecution.

The errant agents' close proximity to Clifford and Carol Cooper spawned angry outbursts. Hernandez and Zapata loudly maintained that the "operational problems" and "mishandling of funds" that they had alleged in June had not been corrected. Corridor gossip still crackled with the rumor that $250,000 was missing from the coffers of Operation Swordfish, an allegation that had been tentatively but not conclusively denied by auditors. Clifford vowed repeatedly that he would sue Zapata and Hernandez for defamation of character. The two agents consulted a lawyer about suing Clifford and the DEA. "I'm keepin' a book on you, buddy," Zapata said to Clifford more than once.

Even though Michael Pasano had determined that Zapata's and Hernandez's allegations were baseless or that any problems were being corrected, Peter Gruden appointed a new assistant special agent-in-charge, Jack Lloyd, to investigate further and prepare a report. After several lengthy meetings with all concerned, Lloyd con-

cluded that the two agents were inappropriate for Operation Swordfish and reassigned them to other enforcement groups on Monday,
August 23. Angry, bitter, and vowing that Tom Clifford had not heard
the last of them, they departed—with their Swordfish reports still
unfinished.

Carol Cooper was awakened at five o'clock that morning by a
report from Bogotá that wiretaps on various telephones of José Antonio Cabrera indicated that Cabrera intended to smuggle 280 kilograms of cocaine—$13 million worth wholesale—from the Bahamas
into South Florida around September 1. The DEA surmised that the
cocaine that Marlene Navarro had promised Robert Darias, 100 to
150 kilograms, might come from the Cabrera shipment. The agents
had never been able to trace the 2,000 kilograms which presumably
had been ransomed from the pilots and already dispersed through the
United States.

Darias and Juvenal Betancur met for breakfast at the Sharon Hotel
on Miami Beach. Robert took his tape recorder, and a DEA surveillance agent was posted outside the hotel.

Betancur's Aqua Imperiale cologne was so enveloping that Darias
feared it would stick to *his* clothing. The president's brother asked
Robert to help him apply for new American Express and VISA cards.
"I lose things," he said. "I've lost three cards already. I also lose my
glasses." He paused. "I don't lose my jewelry."

"Well, you never take it off," Darias said with a smile.

Betancur asked if Darias ever traveled to Colombia. Robert said
that he preferred not to because Colombian stamps on a passport
tended to attract the attention of investigators in the United States,
which Darias wanted to avoid.

"What I do is simply handle the money of my friends here," Darias
said. "I transfer it to Panama or Switzerland or wherever they want.
Carlos Jader is a client of mine, and Marlene—I talk over everything
with Marlene. She is a very honest person, a hard worker, and very
pleasant."

Betancur agreed, confiding that Marlene had said, "We don't do
anything without Roberto."

"In the world of business, I was never involved," Betancur mused.
"I am an intellectual." Betancur in fact had worked in advertising and
journalism in Colombia.

"With your connections we could do a lot," Darias said, "without
any type of repercussion to you or your brother." He explained that
he moved large quantities of cash for his clients into banks, and
between banks, in the U.S. and abroad. "For example I went with

Marlene last week to Denver to pick up some money that she had
there. I have a bank in Denver, I have a bank in Chicago, I have a
bank in New York, I have a bank in Los Angeles, I have a bank in San
Francisco. I don't physically move cash all over the country. Within
an hour I have that cash secure in a bank. It's much more secure than
carrying it around in suitcases."

Juvenal mentioned a friend of his, a rich Colombian, who wanted
to move $10 million. Darias said he could help, and explained the
advantages of the secrecy cloaking banking activities in Panama and
the Bahamas. For one thing, it enabled clients to evade U.S. taxes.

Juvenal said, "I'm going to make you a list to give to Marlene—
names, telephone numbers. If I have time I will accompany you to see
them. Of course, people are afraid to talk by phone."

Darias agreed. "If someone does not introduce you in person,
people become afraid." He asked about the man who wanted to move
$10 million. Juvenal said he lived in Bal Harbor, around Collins
Avenue and 95th Street, just a few miles up the beach from where they
were sitting.

"He's got the money here?" Darias asked.

"He has it here. He has it in Colombia. He has it in New York."

"I'll send it wherever he wants. We will do it perfectly," Darias
promised.

They agreed to be in touch within the next day or two, and to see
each other again when Marlene returned to Miami.

Reviewing the conversation as he drove back across the causeway,
Robert felt he had made progress toward implicating Betancur. Robert had indicated strongly that his own business activities were illegal.
He had mentioned that he wanted to avoid investigations, that he
dealt in large amounts of cash in suitcases, that he used secret foreign
bank accounts, that he evaded income taxes, that he performed banking services for Carlos Jader Alvarez, who Betancur surely knew was
a godfather of the drug mafia.

Betancur had not seemed puzzled by any of this. He had mentioned
a friend who needed help in moving $10 million and held out the
possibility that Robert would be asked to do it.

After a stop at International Investments, Darias went to lunch
with Humberto Garcia at the Airport Marriott. Cooper and her colleagues remained determined to make the case against Garcia, particularly now that Darias had linked him to the Roosterman.

Robert had grown to dread his lunches with Humberto. They
dragged on for hours, and Robert felt obliged to match Humberto
drink for drink—a debilitating burden for one who rarely drank

before evening. Again today, they started at the bar, Humberto with a Black Label and water, Robert with a gin and tonic. They talked about the Roosterman. "I will deliver to him any amount he wants," Darias said.

"If we can get into this without problems we will be millionaires," Humberto replied.

"My people have no problems," Darias said. "I deliver, collect, and transfer their money anywhere they want."

Darias asked where the Roosterman was from in Cuba.

"Havana," Humberto said. "He is thirty-eight years old. And all those houses belong to him, the uncle's, the father's, and his wife's."

"How about that beautiful girl with the Corvette?"

"No, that's his sweetheart."

"Right there at his home?"

"Oh, yes, he brings a lot of girls in. We will invite you, six or eight girls, and the three of us."

"I can't do that anymore," Darias said. "I have to keep it for home."

They ordered B&Bs after lunch.

"Are you sure you don't want to have lunch one day with Roosterman with a bunch of girls?" Humberto asked. Darias demurred. "I want to keep it strictly business with him."

"The guy has great potential," Humberto said.

They drove to Refricenter, where Humberto gave Robert a briefcase containing what Humberto said was $85,000, but which in fact was $74,976, for a peso exchange in Cartagena.

Humberto then took Robert for another lengthy but inconclusive visit with the Roosterman, this time with Paul Sennett observing from outside the compound.

Marlene flew in from Bogotá that Monday afternoon, August 23, and from four o'clock until eleven she made forty-nine telephone calls, none of them of much consequence to the DEA. She summoned Robert, who arrived at 6:25. She told him his 100 kilograms of cocaine should arrive the first week of September.

"Oh, boy, what a day!" Robert said to Carol, sighing deeply. "I hope we don't have too many left like this."

"I got to get you to slow down!" Carol said.

"Oh, my God," Robert said, with another deep sigh. "Carol, let me tell you, I'm getting to the point—I noticed it today when I was talking to this guy Roosterman—and it is beginning to get hard for me to really listen to these people. They talk to you like they are real nice people. And boy, I tell you, they are doing so much damage, and they try to tell you that they are real nice citizens. And this guy is showing me *eight MAC-10s. Eight MAC-10s.* With silencers."

"Okay."

"This business is really getting to me. I am happy that it is going to end soon because it is getting harder for me to talk to these people."

"Yeah, I know."

"I despise them. It's a question of—you can *lie* and *lie* and *lie* but you reach a point where you really want to get them by the throat."

"Yeah, I know. Paul and I talked about that, Bob, and I think basically you've just got to slow down a little bit. Don't be running around like you did today, going from one thing to another to another. Everybody, on your end and on our end, everybody's got to take everything very, very slow. There's too many people getting way too excited about this whole thing. You're looking at three weeks down the road here. People are getting excited on our end, and I'm going, hey, wait a minute, time-out, guys, we've still got three weeks. Everybody's got to keep a level head and keep this thing at an even pace until the very end."

"I'm just trying to make the cases as good as possible."

"Let me tell you what we need as we go along here, okay? At this particular point, your cases are made. Humberto's down. Paytubi's down. Marlene is down and that whole crew. At this particular point do what you gotta do to service them. The only one to pursue is Juvenal."

"Did they transcribe that tape for you?" Robert asked, referring to his morning talk with Betancur.

"They didn't transcribe the entire thing, but they did listen to it, and we're in very good shape."

"Did they tell you where he says that this guy has ten million dollars to move? That's incriminating, isn't it?"

"Sure. I talked to the attorneys about it and what we need to do is get one delivery down on the money, if we can. Just one transaction is all I need."

"I hope we have time."

"I think we will. The other cases are made. We could take all these people off today. The only ones we can't are Juvenal and Roosterman. There's no need for you to be running around like you are."

"The main thing is that I'm getting sick and tired of listening to these people. It's gone on too long."

"Yeah, I'm sure it's getting to you. I'm surprised it hasn't come sooner with you."

"You are imitating somebody that you're not. You are lying constantly to these people, and that starts getting to you because you don't like them, really, and you're trying to be nice to them. You have to realize that I give a different treatment to each one of these guys. And different stories and different lies."

"I'll give you specific directions at this point, specific things we may need as we go down the road here. I may need to get Marlene to make a certain statement so we can execute a search warrant on somebody. But there's no sense in you running around like a wild man at this point. We want to pursue Juvenal as much as we can. And there may be one or two people down the road here that we may need very minimal statements from."

"Like who?"

"Like Lester Rogers. Just minor statements to make sure he's still in the picture here."

"From her, or directly from him?"

"From her."

"But you have that in several tapes. You have one where she says that he knows everything she does."

"Oh, he is going to be arrested. But we're looking at bank accounts, his entire assets, everything that he owns. And we're looking at search warrants for his office. That's the reason why I might need certain little statements from her."

"Okay, you tell me exactly what you want her to say and I make her say it."

"Time is on our side right now. I just don't want you running yourself ragged for no reason. We're not gaining anything at this point, other than those three areas: Juvenal, Roosterman, the drugs from Oscar. That's it."

Oscar informed Marlene that he had solved the mystery of the $105,-000 missing from the Denver money. Ricardo and Said Pavon had removed the cash to settle a debt to Pepe Cabrera.

"Just between you and me, maybe I'll have to pay for that someday," Marlene said. "But do you know something? *They're* the ones who are going to end up losers, because now this gentleman [Jader Alvarez] will never again give them work."

International Investments was no longer the center of Operation Swordfish. Though Dan Hoerner and Felipe Calderon, together with a small staff of newly assigned agents, continued trying to develop a handful of lesser cases, work on the major investigations had shifted to the listening post. However, Robert Darias still depended on the undercover company for handling his targets' financial transactions, and its efficiency had deteriorated further. It failed to wire Marlene Navarro's latest deposit to Panama on time, and Jader Alvarez's bank bounced a $150,000 check.

"Robert, the shipment to Palmira was delayed," Marlene said on the phone early Wednesday morning. "What's more they have returned a check!"

"Yes?"

"Imagine what a position you have put me in! On Thursday you told me you were going to fix that, remember?"

"Yes, of course."

"I called you on Friday. You told me it was taken care of."

"Well, it was not the fault of—"

"The issue is, Robert, that they've *returned a check!* That's what I don't want happening again in the future."

He explained that Jader's bank was a small bank that depended on wire transfers from larger banks within Panama. There were sometimes delays of a day or more.

"Imagine, a check worth a hundred fifty thousand is returned! I would appreciate it, Robert, if you would settle this thing for me."

"Surely."

The DEA and the prosecutors again postponed the termination of Operation Swordfish, this time until early October. For the second time Michael Pasano assailed the agents and supervisors for failing to prepare evidence on time. Out of 360 tapes only 193 had been transcribed. And there was another reason for the delay: The White House was preparing to have President Ronald Reagan announce a major new initiative against the Latin drug mafia in October, and the Department of Justice had decided that announcing the Swordfish indictments around that time would be good public relations.

The delay angered Darias because of its likely impact on his delicate negotiations with Marlene Navarro for a delivery of cocaine. After prodding her for weeks, he might now have to concoct another excuse to postpone the drug purchase.

"I have been telling her every single day that my people are pressuring me," he complained to Cooper. "She's going to think that I am full of hot air. I lose credibility."

"It's being dictated down, Bob," Carol said, referring to the directives from the U.S. Attorney's Office and the Justice Department. "It's way, way over our heads. We're all screaming. The mandates are coming down to other people, and we're getting them relayed to us and nobody knows who's doing what."

On the spur of the moment, Marlene asked Robert to escort her that evening to a dinner party for Juvenal Betancur at the Omni International Hotel.

"Give me a jingle after this dinner tonight," Carol said. "Remember just keep the business very very general."

"If I can. *If I can.* This is a problem when they have told you to push for something and now they are telling you to hold back."

"Just don't be aggressive at this point. Just lay back. Let them come to you."

Carol called Robert back a few minutes later with Frank Chellino on the line.

"I just got a call from headquarters," she said. "Critical importance that we get these people identified that you're meeting at this dinner tonight."

"Names?"

"Full names if possible and phone numbers. If you can get a business card, that'll help. It really is critical. Do your best with it, kiddo."

Chellino chimed in. "Don't forget your *perfuuuume,*" he sang.

"That is your style, not mine," Darias retorted.

"I need all the help I can get," Chellino said. "I'm not as suave as you."

"You can say that again," Cooper said. "Just make sure your cologne doesn't clash with Juvenal's. People here ask me what the president's brother looks like. I say don't worry about that. You'll know him when you smell him."

For the dinner at the Omni, Darias wore a dark Pierre Cardin suit which he had bought in Europe years earlier when he had money. Marlene wore a white designer dress and a white gold Piaget watch that Robert had not seen before. In Robert's car on the way to the hotel, they discussed how best to initiate business with Juvenal Betancur. Robert questioned Betancur's credibility, but Marlene disagreed.

"He is *not* doing this because I have pretty eyes or a nice laugh," Marlene said. "He wants to make money."

"So he has an exact idea of what we're going to do?"

"That Juvenal doesn't have a dumb hair in his body. I think that he knows what he's doing more than the two of us together."

Marlene consulted Darias on another of her clients.

"Robert, do you know that they are still investigating and freezing the accounts of the people who worked with Isaac Kattan?" A woman

Marlene knew who had been associated with Kattan wanted to transfer money out of Switzerland and was having difficulty. "I was going
to give her your name."

"I will transfer it out, Marlene," Robert said. "She has a good
amount over there?"

"Millions," Marlene said. "What is the benefit of having an account today in Switzerland, Robert? They can give information to the
DEA and everybody."

The party for Juvenal Betancur was held in a roped-off section of
a Chinese restaurant. Darias knew none of the guests. He managed to
get the names of a newspaperman from Colombia, a Cuban lawyer,
a man whose grandfather had been president of Cuba, and several
others, who for the most part turned out to be a well-educated group
of professional men and women. Robert knew the DEA would be
disappointed that none of them appeared to be in the narcotics business.

It was unclear who, if anyone, was the host of the party. Robert got
stiffed with the bar bill of $220. Marlene paid the orchestra, $900 cash,
and wrote a check to cover the dinner, around $500. Juvenal, attired
in a white safari suit, jovially told them not to worry; he would make
sure they were reimbursed the next day. (He never mentioned the
subject again.) Marlene and Robert weren't concerned, though. The
money they had spent all belonged to Carlos Jader Alvarez.

40

"**F**EDERAL DRUG AGENT accused of smuggling," said the banner page-one headline in the *Miami Herald* on Friday morning, August 27.

Jeffrey Scharlatt, forty-one years old, a sixteen-year DEA veteran and a supervisor in Vice President Bush's Florida Task Force, had been indicted by a federal grand jury for smuggling narcotics, accepting bribes to allow another smuggler to import drugs, and suborning perjury before a grand jury and trial jury. He was arrested and pleaded not guilty. Formerly Scharlatt had supervised Miami's Group One and had worked in the DEA's internal security unit, which investigates allegations of criminal behavior by DEA agents.

It was the DEA's worst nightmare—one of its own agents corrupted by the criminals he was sworn to combat. It was the reason that J. Edgar Hoover had kept the FBI out of drug law enforcement for several decades. The extraordinary amounts of easy money in narcotics made corruption a constant possibility.

DEA agents shuddered at the news, especially Jeff Scharlatt's colleagues in the Miami field office. And the agents of Operation Swordfish were particularly uneasy: Swordfish was reaching its most sensitive stage, and breaches of security were an acute concern.

For Robert Darias, the news about Jeff Scharlatt stood as further validation of his decision a year earlier to record his telephone conversations with the DEA agents.

Darias and the agents remained oblivious, however, to Brooks Muse III and Special Agent Steve Gibbs's attempts to sell information about Swordfish to the drug mafia. Nor did they know that Muse's close friend, bail bondsman Arthur Balletti, had given a list of targets of a "very heavy" federal undercover operation in Miami Lakes to defense lawyer Raymond Takiff.

In late August, an indictment surfaced in Los Angeles that prompted Takiff to remove the list from his safe and examine it more closely. Authorities had unsealed the indictment of the Barbara Mouzin group, and Takiff recognized Mouzin's name on the Balletti list.

While Mouzin was in hiding in Mexico, her photograph had been circulated in international police circles. After several weeks on the lam she was detained by two men identifying themselves as agents of the Mexican federal police. They informed her that her life was in danger from Colombian drug dealers who feared that she would talk if arrested. An arrest warrant had been issued, they said, and the two officers asked for money in exchange for reporting her dead. That would end the search for her. She said she had little money left and gave them $3,000. They finally let her go.

Fearing for her life, and lacking experience as a fugitive, Mouzin returned to California, where she surrendered and, in hopes of leniency, offered federal agents information on "misconduct and corruption" by employees of the U.S. Government. She also told the agents about the $1.6 million in cash that she had given to Arthur Balletti to arrange her bail. Federal agents immediately served a subpoena on Balletti in Miami, ordering him to relinquish the money and give information on his contacts with Barbara Mouzin.

Balletti turned to Ray Takiff, who arranged for Balletti to turn over the $1.6 million and tell the authorities what he knew in exchange for immunity from prosecution. The authorities agreed to give Takiff and Balletti a reward of $75,000 for their cooperation.

In custody in Los Angeles, Barbara Mouzin learned that the federal prosecutor in charge of her case had refused to grant leniency in exchange for information on corruption by U.S. agents. She therefore declined to provide details of her contacts with Brooks Muse III and his DEA source. Arthur Balletti did not reveal the existence of his list. Thus, the authorities in Los Angeles had no basis for warning their colleagues in Miami that an undercover operation might be in jeopardy.

Marlene Navarro spoke on the telephone seventeen times before nine o'clock the morning of Friday, August 27. The pen register printer at the listening post backed up like an old-fashioned stock ticker in heavy trading.

She spoke to Marina, the mother of two of the missing children.

"Any news?"

"More or less nothing."

"Aren't they optimistic?" Marlene asked.

"Well, yes, a little bit."

"You have to keep in your head that the news will be good," Marlene said. "You have to be optimistic."

"I know," Marina said. She was crying softly.

Marlene spoke to Jader Alvarez, who told her that the kidnap situation was "stagnating."

She spoke to a courier for the Jader Alvarez organization who had been arrested and tortured by the Colombian F-2 in Bogotá but had refused to divulge any information. Finally he had been released for lack of evidence, and Jader had sent him to Miami for a holiday and rewarded him with $20,000, which Marlene was to give him.

She spoke to the woman called Bertha, the money handler for Pepe Cabrera to whom Marlene had transferred $1 million and was about to give more.

She spoke to Carmenza Valenzuela's husband about Juvenal Betancur's party the previous night, and about shipping Lalique crystal lamps to Bogotá.

She spoke to a friend in New York about Saks Fifth Avenue's fall line.

She spoke to her accountant about her income taxes.

She spoke to Lester Rogers, Alex McIntosh, and others, including Oscar, who soon arrived at her house with two bags containing a total of $735,360.

Marlene asked Darias to pick up the money, hold it overnight, and prepare $500,000 in hundred-dollar bills for Bertha, whom she would bring to International Investments on Saturday morning. Marlene and Bertha drove to the offices in separate cars—Marlene in Teo Terselich's Toyota Cressida, and Bertha in a mint silver-and-blue Cadillac El Dorado with a license tag so new that the number did not yet appear in the computer of the Florida Department of Motor Vehicles.

Paul Sennett and Frank Chellino, who had retrieved $500,000 from the DEA vault earlier that morning and left it with Darias, were watching from a Mobil station across the street. Darias was alone inside the offices, except for Dan Hoerner, who was in the concealed room operating the hidden videotape cameras.

When Robert escorted the women into the conference room, Bertha rubbed her bare arms against the chill of the air-conditioning. Outside, the temperature was headed toward the nineties and huge tropical thunderheads threatened rain.

Although the money had been counted the day before, Darias ran it through the counting machine again to impress the women, while Marlene regaled Bertha with tales of the confusion in Denver two weeks earlier that had led to the $105,000 misunderstanding.

"Carlos, of course Carlos is very fair," Marlene said. "He knows

I wouldn't steal from him. But how are we going to recover that money? Last night, Ricardo, the brother, called me, playing dumb. 'Hello, Marlene, how's it going?' I said, 'Hello, darling, how are you?' And he said, 'I need to see you.' I said, 'Surely, Ricardo, we have a lot to talk about.' He knows, but I didn't mention it. He would vouch for his brother—that his brother had not kept the hundred thousand, that it was either me or the banker that kept it. Imagine going all the way to Denver, Colorado, to steal that money! It would be easier here."

"The most I've ever been short is five or six thousand dollars," Bertha said.

Bertha was impressed with the counting machine. "Every time you deliver money, Roberto, it's perfect," she said. "Not even one bill short."

"That eliminates the problem of counting by hand," Marlene said. "From now on we will do all the transactions like this."

After Bertha left with the $500,000 packed in a beige suitcase, Robert turned to Marlene.

"You told me that you would ask during the weekend about the shipment of the one hundred silk shirts," Robert said.

"The one hundred shirts. I know that a person who will be in charge of their safekeeping has already arrived. I can say, Roberto, that I will have something definite before the thirteenth of September."

"But you think you won't have a problem."

"For one hundred, yes. There's no problem. More, I don't know."

"My client is driving me crazy. He wants to know what quality we're talking about." Although Cooper had cautioned Darias not to push for the cocaine in view of the postponed deadline, he knew it would take weeks to get the delivery in any event.

"Pure silk, one hundred percent, the same kind you know about," she said.

It occurred to Robert that Marlene was inside the offices of International Investments speaking freely into a hidden videocamera for the first time. It had taken him more than a year of patient nurturing to bring her to this point for the DEA investigators. No defense attorney could cross-examine a videotape.

Leaving the office, Robert accompanied Marlene to the Magnum Gun Shop on Flagler, where she purchased an Uzi semiautomatic rifle for $300 in twenty-dollar bills. The gun was for Jader Alvarez's birthday the next week.

When DEA analysts had reviewed the audio tape Darias had made as he was driving Navarro to the party for Juvenal Betancur at the Omni Hotel, they had been struck by a comment Marlene had made about the bank account of a woman in Switzerland who had worked with Isaac Kattan. The account apparently was being frozen by the authorities.

The analysts knew there was such an account, and that it was linked to one of Isaac Kattan's major clients, Juan Mata Ballesteros, who had been arrested in Bogotá with Carlos Jader Alvarez in 1979. Mata Ballesteros was one of the four godfathers who appeared on the DEA's master intelligence chart in the "consortium" at the heart of the cocaine industry, along with Jader Alvarez, Pepe Cabrera, and Bernardo Londoño, the man the DEA believed had financed most of the massive, illusion-shattering TAMPA cocaine shipment that had been seized in March.

"Some of the people in the office got all excited," Cooper told Darias Saturday afternoon after he'd returned home from the Magnum Gun Shop. "This opens up another whole arm of this thing."

"Oh, boy."

"We might be able to force this guy to surface, too, or, if nothing else, she might give us some indication of where he is. And if we could catch him, that'd be good. He's wanted all over the place for murders and this and that. And he owns quite a bit of property. He's an ugly son of a gun."

"What is he, Colombian?"

"He's either Colombian or Honduran. He's a big, big guy."

"Okay."

"I don't want you to do anything until next week. The whole thing's got to be calculated. Meanwhile, I want you to approach Marlene to firm up some other areas, the brother routine, Juvenal, different angles that we might be able to get him to start doing something. I want her pushing the guy, too. All the social activities with him are over. He's done. I've had enough of it, and I'm getting mad at him and I haven't even met the man."

"Oh, he's incredible."

"There's too many people—way, way high up—that are getting antsy about this thing. So we'll just put the pressure on him, and see what he does. Once that's done I'll get some of these yo-yos off my back. Everybody is very, very hot on this particular subject. That's why I'd like to at least get a money deal done as quick as we can. That'll prove to them flat out that this guy, he's *wrong*. It's just getting him before we have to end this thing. He's out-and-out wrong. I think you believe it, and you don't know half the stuff that we're hearing."

F-2 agents in Bogotá had told the DEA they believed Juvenal Betancur was actually dealing in cocaine.

"He's a crook," Robert said.

"Yeah. So, I just want to get him. I'm dealing with ambassadors, the State Department, and everybody else. All I'm doing right now is taking care of the brother problem, and I don't like spending that much time on one stupid person."

The DEA's investigation of the brother of the president of Colombia was the subject of a meeting at 4:00 P.M. Tuesday, August 31, in Room 272 of the Executive Office Building of the White House. Admiral Daniel Murphy, Vice President Bush's chief of staff, convened the session to ensure that the State Department was fully informed on the investigation and its possible outcome. Two officials from the DEA's Washington headquarters attended, along with three State Department officers, and two lawyers from the U.S. Attorney's office in Miami.

The lawyers informed the group that though Betancur had become a target of Operation Swordfish, "no case" had been made against him "at this point" and no indictment would be returned "without notice to State."

Cooper informed Darias that the government would begin presenting evidence from Operation Swordfish to a federal grand jury on Thursday, September 2.

"That's not in open court, is it?" Robert asked.

"No, no, no, no, no. Totally secured. Secret grand jury. And even when the indictments come down, they'll be sealed. Nobody'll know about them until we're ready to arrest the people."

Although the investigations were incomplete, the government needed to allow plenty of time for the grand jury proceedings, which would lead to indictments in early October.

"You can't go in there and blow these guys' minds," Cooper said. "They're just normal ordinary citizens. They don't know diddly-squat. And they ask a lot of questions. So it's going to take time. We don't want to give them any more than we have to."

"Carol, isn't there the possibility that somebody might say something and somebody might get wind of what's going on?"

"We're very concerned about that. It's another chance we got to take. We have no choice."

"That's a helluva chance."

"I know. It's a calculated risk. But you always have that little risk the minute you let it outside your agency. But I think it's a small risk in this situation. We're not going to let these people run, after all this work."

"I would hate to see them go."

Cooper also mentioned that the wiretap would end on Monday, September 6, Labor Day. "It's a dynamite tool for us, but it is creating a tremendous amount of work. And we're not gaining anything at this point. You wouldn't believe the work it's generated. You've basically got the entire office working on this right now. And we can't keep up with it. It's driving us nuts. So Monday at midnight it will come off?"

"So I don't have to ask any more tricky questions?"

"Yeah, right. Just talk normally. It looks good for us, the government, that we're pulling it ahead of time. They can't say we're abusing it." (The government could have continued the wiretap until mid-September under the extension authorized by the court in the middle of August. And presumably it could have gotten further extensions.)

"The Christ child, thank God, exactly the Christ child that Marina wanted has arrived," Marlene told Jader Alvarez late the evening of Wednesday, September 1. "It was blessed by the Pope. And there are only ten in the world. You tell that to Marina, because she has as much faith as I do that if this baby appears, the other babies also will appear. So she can begin to pray as of now."

Marlene said she would bring the statue to Bogotá within a week.

41

GRAND JURIES work differently from trial juries. While a trial jury of twelve people meets in a public courtroom and hears a single case on consecutive days for as long as required, delivers a verdict, and then is excused, a grand jury of twenty-three people meets in secret on a regular protracted schedule—typically one day a week for eighteen months—and hears evidence in a variety of cases. While a trial jury establishes the guilt or innocence of a single defendant or group of defendants, a grand jury considers a number of targets in unrelated cases, and decides, under the guidance of a prosecuting attorney, whether to return indictments against those targets.

Grand Jury 82-8 was still fresh, having been gathering on Thursdays for only a few months of its tour. Michael Pasano had impaneled it himself and considered it a bright and competent group, qualified to fathom the complexities of Operation Swordfish.

Guided by Pasano's questions behind the locked and guarded doors of the drab grand jury room in the federal court house, Carol Cooper outlined the various facets of the Marlene Navarro–Carlos Jader Alvarez investigation since the summer of 1981. Although Cooper described the elaborate role of Robert Darias, she did not refer to him by name, only as a "confidential informant," or "CI."

While Cooper was testifying in secret downtown, Marlene Navarro, still being overheard by the DEA monitors, was at home in Costa del Sol conducting her usual round of morning conversations with her maid Heidi about extra work in the house, with her handyman Mike about leaks in her ceiling, with Gustavo Delgado about her furniture, and with Lester Rogers about insurance, real estate, and her pending divorce from her second husband, Henry Kourany, a Miami man from whom she had been separated for some time.

"About the kids, things look much better," she told Rogers. "It seems they are going to have the kids any minute. At least we know that they are alive—"

"Great."

"—which is the important thing."

"Right."

At the listening post the weary monitors were losing interest. The DEA believed it had more than enough evidence to indict and convict Navarro, Carlos Jader Alvarez, and the other principal members of his syndicate, if they could be arrested. Now, with the wiretap set to end at the conclusion of the Labor Day weekend just ahead, the monitors were listening for references to three specific subjects which the agents and analysts had defined for them: the arrival of a new cocaine shipment, the inclinations of Juvenal Betancur, and the status of the Swiss bank account that might provide a clue to the whereabouts of Jader Alvarez's fugitive colleague, the drug lord and murderer Juan Mata Ballesteros.

Though Nelson Batista still believed he was being followed, Marlene continued to doubt that any surveillance was directed at her. She told Robert that Batista had been followed previously by people trying to steal drugs and money.

"Obviously they're not following *us,*" she said. "It's *him.* They are trying to take his money."

To Batista on the phone she said, "I have these two friends who came to see me and nobody saw anything, and I have been taking care also, and I haven't seen anybody."

"Yes, I know," he replied. "The problem isn't with you. I don't think it's with me either. But it might be with some of the people who go to your place. I'm going to talk to Roberto, and see if we can figure it out."

"Yes, talk to him because he's very intelligent, and I'm sure that the two of you will figure out what is going on. I think it's a coincidence."

Batista asked Darias to meet him in the parking lot of the International House of Pancakes at Coral Way and 87th. Nelson was in his gold Buick Regal, and Robert saw five other men in two separate cars who obviously were with Nelson as bodyguards and lookouts. Batista told Darias that although he had been followed in the past by people after his money and drugs, the recent surveillance, he was convinced, originated with someone who was following Robert and Marlene. Robert said he and Marlene had been careful and had not detected anyone.

Nelson tried to give Darias a bag of cash to deposit but Robert refused it, saying, "I will not receive money in parking lots. It's too dangerous. You'll have to bring it to my office." Nelson got angry. Robert, knowing Nelson was suspicious of him, left and called Navarro immediately. "This is not the type of person we should be meeting," he said. "This guy is dealing in small amounts of coke and he's going to really heat us up. We have enough of a problem the way we are. I don't want to see him again."

Marlene agreed henceforth to have Nelson deliver to Oscar instead of to her.

Carol Cooper found Batista's concern amusing.

"For some ungodly reason, and I don't know why, he is super paranoid. Because we honestly have not had anybody out there."

"He thinks that they are following Marlene or me," Robert said. "Today he was trying to see if they were following me, or if I had somebody with me."

"He's concerned about it but I don't think she is," Carol said.

"Well, I'm not going to pick up money in any parking lots, that's for sure. This guy has too many people around him and I don't want to risk a shoot-out somewhere."

"He is not of any major importance anyway. He's dead anyway. We've got him. What's funny about this thing, and even the attorneys have said it, is that Nelson is the only one that's smart, and nobody's listening to him."

"Let me tell you, this guy wasn't very happy today. He doesn't really trust me for some reason. Maybe he thinks I'm too slick or something."

"Why does he think the heat is on you and Marlene? I can understand him maybe thinking the heat's on Marlene, but why you."

"I don't know. He doesn't know exactly what type of relationship I have with Marlene. Maybe he even thinks that I am shacking with her. You never know what these people think."

"The whole thing's ridiculous. I don't know what this guy's doing."

"I tell her, and she keeps telling me, that this guy is paranoid. He's seeing ghosts. Apparently she doesn't believe him too much."

In Girardot, Colombia, southwest of Bogotá, on Sunday, September 5, the telephone rang in the home of the Garcia Villamizar family. It was Edgar Helmut, who had disappeared two weeks earlier. Sounding frightened, Edgar told his parents that "they" would release his brother, Orlando, the following week, and let Edgar go later. The conversation was brief. Edgar did not identify "they," nor say where he was calling from.

Since Alvarez's men and the F-2 had kidnapped him, Edgar had been held prisoner in a warehouse owned by Alvarez in north Bogotá. Neither he nor his parents knew that his brother Orlando, missing since March, was dead—tortured and executed months earlier by MAS and the Alvarez syndicate.

Alex McIntosh flew to Miami that weekend to begin a new life with Marlene Navarro. He had resigned from his engineering job in Toronto, planning to look for new work in Miami and live for the time being at Costa del Sol. Gustavo drove Marlene to the airport to meet Alex and they spent much of the weekend in the Keys.

At the DEA listening post, the monitors' log dwindled to long lists of no-answers, until Labor Day evening when Robert called Marlene.

"I spent the weekend going around with Alex like a tourist," she said.

"What is happening with Juvenal?"

"He's in Colombia."

"He's there making contacts for us?"

"Yes, he's making the contacts, so when he comes back we will have them. Could you call me in the morning? I'm going to need you."

"Sure."

"I'm expecting a call from Nelson."

"What about *el barrigoncito?* I need to talk to him."

"I'm waiting for his call. He should have arrived last night or maybe today. I need to talk to him, too."

"Yeah, I want to know what is new about the things that he has to give me."

"Yes, that's another thing I want to ask him about."

"If you talk to him, please ask him about my shirts."

"Make sure you call me tomorrow at nine."

It seemed appropriate that the last recorded call of the wiretap was the spy checking in with his prime target.

Just before midnight, Carol Cooper, witnessed by two other agents, disconnected the tape recorders and wrote in the log: "TITLE III wire intercept terminated at approximately 11:58 P.M., end of Shift III." Cooper and the others left the room and locked the door.

From 11:00 A.M. on Saturday, July 17, until two minutes before midnight on Monday, September 6, the DEA had recorded 2,833 "activations" on Marlene Navarro's two telephones. Out of the total activations, there were 2,017 completed calls in which two or more persons spoke to each other, an average of 41.2 calls per day. She spoke to Carlos Jader Alvarez 21 times, Oscar 100 times, Robert Darias 121 times, Alex McIntosh 82 times, Tocayo 25, Nelson Batista

38, Lester Rogers 46, Teo Terselich 44, Luis Rodriguez 15, Carmenza Valenzuela 34, and Juvenal Betancur 15.

The monitors were exhausted. They were sick of the sound of Marlene Navarro's voice. They had listened to each conversation and each activation, and all the buzzes, beeps, hisses, clicks, squawks, static, and tones that went with them. They had recorded everything on 311 Maxell UDS-I 90-minute tape cassettes (not counting work copies), which filled nine cardboard cartons. And they had documented everything in a log of 1,164 pages.

The monitors' work was finished. But for Carol Cooper and her agents a great deal of labor lay ahead before they could dismantle the massive, rich, violent narcotics and money syndicate of Carlos Jader Alvarez and Marlene Navarro.

The Dariases hated Coral Springs. They felt lonely and isolated. The community was populated largely by transient Americans, employees of big corporations "on their way from Chicago to Phoenix," as Amelia had remarked to Robert. There were none of the multicultural flavors of Miami. Eight-year-old Laura was the only Cuban in her class at school, and was miserable. She missed her grandparents and her aunts, uncles, and cousins in Miami.

But at least the Dariases did not feel the fear in Coral Springs that had gripped them in Miami as Operation Swordfish moved toward its climax. Robert tried to put the best face on the move when speaking to the DEA agents.

"How's everything at home?" Paul Sennett asked when he called on Tuesday morning. Always Robert's favorite among the agents, Paul had been especially attentive since the Dariases had moved to Coral Springs where Paul also lived.

"Pretty good," Robert said. "Everybody has calmed down. Laura is very happy with school. It's very quiet."

"It's different to get used to—I dunno," Paul said.

"I like it. It's a lot quieter than Miami. I think it will be very nice to stay here for a while."

"Do you think you'll ever go back down below?" Paul often referred to Miami as if it were hell.

"Eventually. Remember that our whole life is down there. And we will be going down pretty often."

"I've got to listen to this all the time because my wife wants to move back to New York."

"For us it is even stronger. Everybody here is American, which is very good for the time being, for a while, till things cool off."

"What you need is a vacation. Probably Amelia needs a vacation."

"Oh, yeah."

"Because it's a strain. On her more than it is on you."

"Well, I am feeling a lot better now because I have had a few days of calm. But there was a moment that I told Carol, I can*not* talk to these people anymore. It's making me sick."

"I know."

"You get to the point, Paul, where some people from the outside might think that it's very nice and very interesting to be an 007, but let me tell you, you start talking to people you don't like and try to start selling them ideas that are not your own and there's a breaking point in your character where you cannot take any more."

"It's a very difficult thing. You're going to have to take two or three weeks someplace and just get away when this thing is over. You have to, and not even talk to anybody. Just forget about it. And it's hard to do because it takes, like, a week before you actually start winding down and stop thinking about this stupid going to work and everything."

"I *dream* about this whole program—"

"That's no good. That's no good."

"—about what I'm going to tell them, how I'm going to convince them, how can I bring them to do this, to do that."

"You probably have a lot more pressure on you than myself or Carol does. It's a different kind of pressure. You got pressure from them. You got pressure from us. You got pressure from your family. You got all sorts of pressure. You're going to have to get away from it. Otherwise, it's going to affect you."

"That is a big problem for me now. I'm getting sick and tired of talking to them. I want to talk to normal people."

"Of course you do."

"People that I don't have to be listening to what they're saying so I can *get* them, you know what I mean?"

"Of course."

Darias hadn't "gotten" Marlene Navarro yet. On Tuesday, he took her and Alex McIntosh to lunch at the Mutiny—a notorious haunt of on-the-make Miamians on both sides of the law—in Coconut Grove, and then reported to Cooper.

"She was telling me today that Nelson said he believed that either her phone or my phone was tapped, and that's why they were able to follow him every time he talked to her."

"But does *she* believe that?"

"I don't know. I feel that he's transmitting to her a little bit of the paranoia, that's why she doesn't want to receive anybody in her house if she can avoid it."

"Which is okay."

"I don't want to look too brazen either, because if she thinks that I am not afraid of *anything* she might consider the idea that there is something wrong. I am playing it down but I am still concerned. I keep telling her that I am pretty sure that *he* is the one that is hot. I don't see anybody around me. I told her, even today, 'I came here and picked you up. Did you see anybody following us? I didn't see anybody following us.' "

"She hasn't seen anyone, right?"

"No, she feels there is something of truth and something of exaggeration. She *does* believe that they were following *him*. That is why I don't want to get too far away. And now that we don't hear her phone I think I have to be a little more aware of what is going on. I don't have the information you used to give me all day long."

"There's really nothing you have to do out of the ordinary. The drugs are the only thing I want to pursue at this point. If we can get the brother, we'll go ahead and get him. Those two items still remain top priority, the drugs being the most. Everybody would like the drugs."

"Yeah."

"She's basically using you right now, and that's fine. We'll be using *her* in about a month. She's going to be in a little bit different situation. I haven't talked to anybody at all about this, but do you think it would be better if she doesn't know about any connection to Dean International at first, when she's taken off? Would it be better if we just had somebody go and arrest her, period, without Frank, Paul, myself, you, or any of us there. And just let her wonder what the heck is going on?"

"But what are you going to gain by that?"

"She may talk a little bit more, not knowing, or be a little more afraid."

"She might talk more. She might talk less."

"If she isn't talking, then one by one all of us go in, and let her know she's down solid."

"She's not going to open her mouth if she doesn't know that she's completely dead."

"You don't think so?"

"No, I am sure. The way I see her is when she gets arrested, she's going to play the game that, as soon as they set a bond, Jader is going to bond her out and she's going to leave. But if the bond is big enough she's going to realize that this guy is not going to pull her out."

"Okay."

"You've got to keep in mind what I told you. They are going to kill her and they are going to kill her son."

"I know."

"For sure she's going to get killed because of what she let me get into."

"I know. Everybody's aware of that. We're prepared to offer her protection for her son and all that kind of stuff."

"She's going to think about that. Really."

"Yeah. We'll play with her mind a little bit."

"And she knows these people. She knows that they can do it."

"If she doesn't cooperate and she wants to make a phone call, do you think she's going to call Lester to bail her out of the attorney situation?" Carol asked.

"If she doesn't know that Lester is involved, yes, sure."

"She's not going to know."

"That will be her first call."

"We'll arrest *him* right then, right after she makes the phone call."

"I see."

"We're not going to arrest him before that. And if she's cooperating I don't want him to know about it. But if she isn't, our gut feeling is she'll call him, not knowing who else to call at that particular point."

"Right."

"And if push comes to shove and we're at that point of the game, we'll arrest him right away and we'll let her know he's just been arrested, too. Let her think every single person she's going to call now is going to go down the tubes, too. And *then* see what she says." Carol laughed, but Robert felt uncomfortable. He found the talk of "playing with her mind" distasteful.

"I wonder if she'll call you," Carol asked.

"I don't want to create a personal thing with her, like I'm laughing at her, you know? After all I did to her, I'm making fun of what I did."

"I understand."

"I want her to believe that it was a job and that I'm not really happy or unhappy about whatever happened. I did what I had to do and that was it."

"We really want to get her to cooperate so we'll use every angle we can on her legitimately to convince her it's the best way for her to go. Especially if we can get the other two guys down south, Carlos and Pepe. If they're gone and we could tell her, I hate to tell you, Marlene, but your two buddies down there are now in custody, behind a U.S. deal—not a Colombian deal, a U.S. deal—and they cannot buy their way out now—if we could tell her that, I think she may realize she's in serious, serious trouble."

"Right."

"But all we're doing right now is buying time till everything else is ready. The two items are to get the load, that's the icing on the cake, and if we can get the brother, one deal with the brother, that's it. I can't ask for anything more. Dynamite case."

"Right."

"But other than that, Bob, just sit back and relax now. Maintain the credibility. You don't have to push at all. As I talk to the attorneys there might be a few loose ends where we might have to have you get a little statement from them right towards the very end. But as of now everything looks very, very good. We're sitting fine. Holy Cow. You did another good job. If anything can bail you out of the IRS problem, this can. If that problem is to get resolved, this is your best opportunity to do it."

It had become clear long ago that the DEA's possible intercession with the IRS on Robert's behalf was a *quid pro quo*. If he performed up to the DEA's hopes and expectations, it would at the very least put in a good word for him. If he did not, it would not.

Having conjectured to Navarro on Tuesday that either her phone or Darias's was tapped, Nelson Batista placed several calls to Darias on Wednesday afternoon at International Investments. Darias, who was in his car driving during most of the afternoon and evening, did not learn of Batista's calls until late that evening from Cooper.

"It doesn't make sense for him to be calling me," Darias said.

"Not unless he was looking for you or Marlene," Cooper said.

"I know, but what for?"

"I don't know. Maybe he thought Marlene was with you."

"Maybe he has some money." Batista had not called Darias at home or beeped him.

"Don't be surprised if you see him tomorrow. She might tell him to bring it straight to you."

"She's leaving Friday, so we're going to have a few days of calm. She's taking the porcelain Jesus statue to Bogotá."

"Thank God. Just stumble through the next few days and we're in good shape. We're planning to arrest these people the first week of October."

The Swordfish grand jury was scheduled for its second weekly session the following day, Thursday, September 9.

42

A MAN WITH A LATIN accent telephoned Lester Rogers's office on Thursday morning, September 9, and refused to identify himself.

"I'm a friend of Marlene Navarro," he told the secretary. She put the call through to Rogers.

"Hello."

"Mr. Rogers?"

"Yes, who is this?"

"I am a friend of Marlene Navarro and I thought you would be interested to know that the company she has been dealing with called Dean International Investments, or International Investments, is a federal undercover operation, that Roberto Darias is working undercover for the DEA, that Lionel Paytubi is an informant for the FBI, and that Marlene, Paytubi, you, and Arthur Karlick are going to be indicted."

"Who is this?" Lester Rogers demanded.

"You should also know that Marlene's telephone has been tapped for a year and half, since she first met Roberto Darias, around the time she moved to Costa del Sol."

"Who is this?" Rogers insisted.

The caller hung up.

In a panic, Lester Rogers hurried down the street one block to the law office of his cousin, Harvey Rogers, who had more experience in criminal law than Lester.

"Harvey, I just received the craziest call you ever heard," Lester said. "I received an anonymous call that Marlene Navarro is going to be indicted and that Roberto and Paytubi are government informants. What should I do?"

Harvey Rogers telephoned Navarro and told her to come to his office immediately. Then he sent an aide to the federal courthouse to see if he could learn anything about indictments or grand jury proceedings.

Two hours later—at around noon—the phone rang at Robert and Amelia Darias's new rented home in Coral Springs. Amelia, who was alone in the house, answered.

"Mrs. Darias?"

"Yes."

"We know that your husband is a federal agent. We are going to kill him, and we are going to kill you, and we are going to kill your daughter."

"Who is this?" Amelia gasped. The caller, a man speaking unaccented Spanish, hung up.

Crazed with fear, Amelia dialed Carol Cooper's number at the DEA. Cooper was preparing to leave for the court house to testify again before the Thursday grand jury. Amelia was so hysterical that Carol did not at first recognize her voice, and then had difficulty understanding her.

"A man said they are going to kill us all! They said they know who Robert is, that he works for you, and they are going to kill him, and me, and Laura!"

"Oh, God!" Cooper said. "This is what we've always been afraid of. Did he say anything else?"

"No, he just hung up! Where is Robert?"

"He's out and about. I'll get in touch with him. But you stay there and lock the place up. If the phone rings, don't answer it. You'll be okay. We're on our way."

Robert Darias's pager sounded as he drove west on 36th Street along the north border of Miami International Airport. He had just left Humberto Garcia's office and was headed for International Investments. The call-back number on his pager screen was unfamiliar, but he stopped at a coin telephone and returned the call.

"Mr. Darias," the caller said. It was a man speaking unaccented Spanish.

"Yes."

"We know who you are, and that all of the people in your office are federal agents, and that is why we are going to kill you and all of your family."

"Who is this?" Darias snapped.

The man hung up.

Within seconds Robert's pager sounded again and the screen displayed Carol Cooper's number at the DEA.

Darias dialed Cooper. An agent in the office told him that Carol and Frank Chellino had already left for Coral Springs, and that Robert should come straight to the DEA, taking care that no one was following him. His wife would be protected, the agent said. Robert hung up and headed straight for Coral Springs instead, his Smith & Wesson on the seat beside him.

After speaking to Cooper, Amelia Darias got out her Colt .38 special and confirmed it was loaded. She scurried through the house locking doors and windows and closing blinds. She briefly considered fetching Laura from school but decided the child probably was safer there.

Calmer now, she paced, and peered through the blinds at the tranquil suburban street, deserted in the sweltering sunlight. She was reminded of the day the previous year in Miami when a man had gone after Robert with a submachine gun. She also thought of her childhood in Havana in the fifties when her grandfather's chauffeur on occasion would arrive at school to whisk her home because of terrorist violence. She had been afraid then. She was terrified now.

With their unmarked car's hidden siren blaring and the flashing blue light placed atop the dashboard, Chellino and Cooper raced north up the Palmetto, around the Big Bend, and onto the Florida Turnpike. Averaging over ninety miles per hour, they took less than thirty minutes to reach Coral Springs, a drive that normally took an hour. They found Amelia still very upset, but there was no sign of surveillance or other ominous activity in the neighborhood. Robert, too, arrived within a few minutes and, after comforting Amelia, he and the agents began brainstorming the origin of the two calls.

Nelson Batista was the prime suspect. Of all Darias's targets, Batista was the only one who had become openly suspicious. Having concluded several weeks earlier that someone was following him, Batista had grown more exercised, and had strongly hinted when they had met on Friday that he did not trust Darias. And just the day before Batista had left several messages for Darias at International Investments.

Threatening to kill a man and his family, however, implied a state of mind beyond suspicion. Had Batista learned something new in the past twenty-four hours? Had he been in touch with Marlene? Was she involved in the threats? She had said nothing unusual to Robert when they had talked early that morning.

Perhaps Batista in his paranoia had just been probing, looking for a reaction. Whatever the case, there was little for the moment that the DEA could do. It could not arrest Batista without compromising the operation. And suppose the agents were wrong, and someone else had made the calls?

Darias, Chellino, and Cooper were still weighing their options when Marlene Navarro beeped Robert. He called her back at Lester Rogers's office, and Darias and the agents were alarmed to learn that the threatening calls to him and Amelia were not the only anonymous calls of the day. Navarro calmly described the call Rogers had received that morning claiming that Darias and Paytubi were federal agents.

"He said that you two were from the fuzz," Marlene said.

"Yes?"

"And that I was under indictment. And when Lester said, 'Who is it?' they hung up on him."

"Yes."

"What they want to do is scare you, do you understand me, because the only people who know the connection between me and Lionel Paytubi is Lester, you, and I."

"Yes."

"Nobody else knows it. Nelson doesn't know it. Nobody does."

"Sure."

Marlene suspected that Lionel Paytubi was behind the call to Rogers. "We were always scared—do you remember?" she said, recalling that she and Darias at one time had speculated that Paytubi might become disgruntled if he learned they had cut him out of their ongoing business. "They mentioned Paytubi's name, and that's when Lester put his thinking cap on, because he told me it has to be somebody who is very close to you and me. It wasn't me."

"Marlene, this is the problem that *I* have," Darias said, telling her of the threatening calls to him and his wife. "They have placed a call, one of the calls came through the new beeper. It has to be somebody real close."

(When the Dariases had moved to Coral Springs the DEA had arranged for them to retain the same unlisted undercover phone number they had in Miami, so that no one would suspect they had moved. Robert did get a new pager, however, explaining to his targets that it had better fidelity and a bigger range.)

"You gave the beeper number to Alex and me and nobody else," Marlene said.

"Nelson knows it, too."

"It's not Nelson, it's not Nelson," Marlene insisted. "Because Nelson would not know about Paytubi."

"Sure." Darias did not point out that the person who had called him and Amelia had not mentioned Paytubi.

"That's why Lester is scared, because if it's not you, it's Paytubi. You can imagine, Robert, I have been vomiting, having diarrhea and everything, you understand."

"Yes."

"What can we do so we can see each other?"

"Okay, Marlene, let me take a good look at how things are, and I'll get in touch with you." The agents had instructed Robert to stall.

Marlene said she wasn't going home. After she got her hair done, she would be staying at Gustavo Delgado's.

Could the call to Rogers and the calls to the Dariases be related? Darias and the agents asked themselves. Could one person have made them? Were two people more likely? What if someone had called Lester Rogers, and then after Rogers had warned Navarro, she had alerted Nelson Batista, knowing he had been suspicious of Darias? Could Batista then have made the calls to Robert and Amelia? Or could Marlene have had someone else make the calls, just to test Robert's reaction? Either sequence seemed plausible.

The agents also considered a range of other possibilities, even remote ones. "Who has an incentive to fuck the operation?" Chellino asked.

Could there have been a leak from the grand jury? That was always a concern, once sensitive information was given to twenty-three strangers, despite their oaths of secrecy. What about court house employees familiar with the grand jury proceedings? What about the disgruntled agents of Operation Greenback, who knew the salient facts of Operation Swordfish, most notably the name of Lionel Paytubi, and deeply resented the DEA's role in delaying Greenback's indictment of Paytubi and the Great American Bank?

And what about Nick Zapata and Eddie Hernandez, who had been expelled from Operation Swordfish and remained furious—convinced their careers had been ruined? Could they be seeking vengeance?

The agents remained unaware of efforts by their colleague Special Agent Steve Gibbs and his partner Brooks Muse III to compromise Operation Swordfish for money. They knew nothing of Artie Balletti's visit to lawyer Raymond Takiff with a list of people under "heavy federal scrutiny" in Miami Lakes.

But the agents were most urgently concerned about trying to divine the state of mind of Marlene Navarro. How seriously did she take the call to her lawyer? Did she now genuinely suspect that Robert Darias was a federal agent? Was she really as calm as she had seemed on the phone? Was she toying with Darias, trying to smoke him out? Set him up for a hit?

For Operation Swordfish, a secret enterprise which had been plagued by a sequence of crises from a threatening telegram to internal turmoil to burned surveillances, this was the biggest crisis yet.

The DEA stationed an armed guard at the Dariases' home overnight. Robert and Amelia did not fall asleep until very late, and Carol

Cooper's call awakened them early Friday morning. "We probably are going to have you try to push for a meeting with her today at a neutral location," Carol said.

"She's pushing for a meeting at Gustavo's house," Robert said.

"That's not where it's going to go down. You absolutely under no uncertain terms are going to go over there. If that's the only place she'll meet you, then she's not going to meet you. We're going to get you into a public place, a restaurant or something.' "

Though they hadn't told Darias, the DEA agents had come to suspect that Gustavo Delgado was part of Navarro's organization. He was a target of the grand jury.

"I just wanted to touch base and make sure you're okay and have you stand by your phone," Cooper continued. "We'll call you. If you do leave the house take Amelia with you, just in case. I don't want her there with any other phone calls."

"The more I think about it the more I think it was maybe Nelson," Robert said. "She might have told him about the call that Paytubi and I are federal agents. And the guy started doing things."

"I still think it's him, Bob. We don't really know, and I don't know if we ever will know."

Having stayed the night at Delgado's, Navarro called Darias again from Lester Rogers's office. She and Rogers were pondering whether anyone other than the two of them, together with Paytubi and Darias, could have known about Paytubi's dealings with Navarro the previous summer when Rogers and his office mate Arthur Karlick had introduced them.

"The day you came over for the first time, you came with someone," Navarro said. "Do you remember who it was? Someone who speaks very good English."

"And it wouldn't be Paytubi himself?"

"No, no, no."

"Then it could only be Frank."

"Which Frank?"

"Frank Dean."

"Well, I know him, no?"

"Yes."

"Lester says he's an American."

"Well, ask him if he was more or less like Frank, short, with grayish hair."

"He says he looks more or less your age."

"Marlene, you're talking about the day I met you?"

"Lester says it was the first time you came here."

"Wasn't it the day I gave him the receipt?"

"Yes, it was that day."

"I'm almost sure it was Paytubi who was with me that day."

Marlene asked how many people now had Darias's new pager number. "You didn't give cards to Nelson or anyone, did you?"

"Yes, I gave Nelson a card with the new beeper number on it the last time I saw him."

"Well, I saw him last night. He was calm. For the first time I saw him very calm last night. It's not Nelson. It's someone who knows us very well."

"Yes." Did Marlene seem a little too insistent that Nelson was not involved?

"Lester is telling me that the person who talked to him yesterday was talking in not too good English, like if he had learned it here, learned it from working, not like an educated person. He didn't have my vocabulary."

"Marlene, I'm going someplace to meet someone I totally trust."

"We know they wouldn't do anything to your daughter." Marlene had never before mentioned Robert's daughter.

"Well, what worries me is that the calls to my house were another kind of call."

"What kind?"

"Well, threats."

"Against your life."

"Exactly, another kind of call, another kind of problem."

"The *federales* couldn't have made those calls."

"Well, no, the one I got, for sure, it wasn't."

"And the call I received here? Do you think they could have?"

"I don't know, but at least they didn't call and say they are going to kill you or anything like that."

Marlene said she planned to fly to Bogotá on Saturday morning to deliver the Jesus statue to Yidid and Xouix's mother, Marina Alvarez.

Lionel Paytubi called Darias to arrange for him to meet the principal figure in a Quaalude deal that Paytubi had been promoting all summer. Darias put him off until the next week. It was evident to Robert that Paytubi had not yet been informed that an anonymous caller to Lester Rogers's office had mentioned his name as a federal undercover informant.

Prompted by the agents, Robert called Marlene at Gustavo's again that evening to try to further probe her state of mind.

"The man, the fat man, the one we've been talking about," Robert said.

"Yes."

"Paytubi."

"Yes."

"You know that he's had a big case against him for a long time." Robert referred to Operation Greenback.

"Yes, yes."

"And it's always appeared strange to me that he has never had any problems." Robert was suggesting to Marlene that Paytubi might indeed be working undercover for the government, though Robert knew through the DEA that Paytubi was not.

"And Lester is mistaken," Robert continued. "The person who went with me to turn over the receipt to Lester *is* Paytubi. This morning I got confused because you insisted that it had to be another person."

"Lester insisted that it was another person."

"Paytubi told me about a lot of things from that office at the beginning—that you handled a lot of money."

"Yes, ah, no, Lester did know that. Robert, I'm trying to tell you—nobody knows except you, Lester, the other attorney, and me, and Paytubi [about the original dealings the previous year]. Nobody else. It's somebody that knows you real well. It's somebody who is real close and knew everything and also knows that Lester is my trusted person."

"Sure."

"And nobody else knows that he is my person."

"Marlene, I have sent someone that I trust to investigate this. It may take several days because they have to go personally, and they have to talk with some people. To see if there have been any questions at the banks or anything."

"Oh, yes."

"But, Marlene, my problem is totally different from yours. I don't see you involved in my problem."

"The threats, you know, it's not like the *federales* to make threats," Marlene said.

"Sure, but I believe the threats were to scare me more than anything else."

"Talking with the lawyers, we feel they did it to see what move you'd make."

"Yes, well, *all* the calls were made to see what would happen."

"To scare me, and also to leave you without any business. They know they can scare me like they scared Lester."

"I have found no indication that this is a problem with the *federales*. Because that's what would worry me."

"If they were the *federales*, they would have come directly to us."

"Sure. But they wouldn't have any solid proof."

"Then, Robert, since we don't have anything to fear, life goes on." Marlene seemed tired and less concerned than she had earlier. "We're going to have to meet and have a cup of coffee next week, or as soon as possible. You can come over to the house and have a drink with me."

"Yes. Sure."

"So don't be worried."

"You live your life normally, and I'll do the same," Robert said. "Neither you nor I have any problems nor have done anything illegal."

"Exactly."

"We don't have anything to get worried about, nothing except a crazy man out there in the street."

"You know, Robert, it's not impossible that somebody you're in business with thinks you have taken his commission away from him or something."

"Yes."

"Look and see who it could be. Look and see what reason Paytubi might have to do that."

"That could be."

"Think also who might have put ideas in Frank's head."

"Sure."

"On Monday or Tuesday we'll have a cup of coffee at the house. I want to demonstrate to you that I can now play the organ." Marlene had just purchased a small electronic keyboard for her home.

Robert laughed. "Sure. That's good."

"Don't worry. My house is always your house, I don't care what anyone says."

"Thank you very much, Marlene."

"Oh, Robert, another thing that this person said: he said that my phone had been tapped for a year and a half, ever since we've known each other."

"Yes?"

"He said it had been tapped since around the time that I moved to Costa del Sol."

"Really. That's precise, precise information."

"Robert, it's somebody who knows you real well, and knows me very well through you. When we met, I had just finished moving, remember? So think about that. It's another clue."

"It's a shame that Lester was unable to record the call."

"Lester thinks the person is inside your organization, that he knows you real well. From now on we are going to have to be very careful, Robert."

"Exactly."

"Call me at home to talk to me as always about orders and everything, understand?"

"Sure."

"If that stops, there will be suspicion."

"Sure."

"You keep on calling me and we'll talk about anything."

"Fine."

"So, Robert, be calm."

Robert was relieved. Whatever Lester Rogers's state of mind, Marlene seemed sanguine, very much wanting to believe that while a disgruntled Lionel Paytubi, or perhaps a jealous partner of Robert, might have had something to do with the anonymous call to Rogers's office, Robert himself was innocent of both the call, and of being a federal agent.

"How's everything with Marlene?" Paul Sennett asked when he called a few minutes later.

"I am flabbergasted, totally flabbergasted," Robert said. "Somehow I have convinced her that the people making these calls are bad guys."

"They don't know. I don't think they know."

"They know *something*," Robert said.

"We have to be very careful."

"She's being very sweet. Her house is my house as always. I have to go there and have a couple of drinks with her and Alex."

"Well, you've got to be very careful. Just take it easy this weekend."

"She wants me to call once in a while just to let her know that I am all right. She sounded like she's really worried about me."

"I'm sure she is."

"I don't see any problem for me to take her all the way to October 7th."

"I'm going to try to find out where this leak is coming from," Tom Clifford told Darias, "somewhere down at the courthouse. I guess

Lester's going around destroying all those records. Did Lester think
he was being indicted?"

"That she didn't say, and I didn't want to imply that because I am
not supposed to know anything."

"Right, right."

"If we are going to believe what she's saying, I have to face her,"
Robert said. "I have to talk to her. I will have to meet with her."

"Yeah, we got to do a planned meeting and we got to do that
right," Clifford said. "Mike Pasano just told me in a public place but
I said, no, not around here in a public place. It has to be some kind
of secret meeting. You can't go to her house. I think the most secure
place is the International Investments office because we can control
it."

"She will not go there," Robert said. "No, she's telling me the
problem is in my end. How the hell is she going to go there? But I have
to face her, because if I don't, then we have to blow the operation next
week. I have to prove to her that I am willing to talk to her."

"We'll talk about it tomorrow. I've got too many things on my
mind."

"You can imagine what I had on *my* mind when they called my
wife and threatened her and my kid. I blew my top."

Clifford sympathized, and Robert continued, "She told Nelson
maybe about this whole conversation with the lawyer, about me being
a federal agent. And maybe Nelson, being a Cuban, jumped his gun
and started calling me and my family and threatening my life, and
calling me a federal agent."

Robert finally reached Chellino and Cooper to report on his latest
telephone talk with Navarro.

"She talked about twenty minutes," Robert said.

"Twenty minutes!" Chellino exclaimed. "How'd it go?"

"She's trying to tell me that these are bad guys making these calls,
not federal agents. And she's afraid something will happen to me
because of some crazy guy. And to find out about Frank, and to find
out about Paytubi, find out if somebody is mad at me. And maybe
somebody wants to separate her from me, so she doesn't give me any
more business."

"They're playing games, Bob," Carol said, still uncertain of
Navarro's state of mind.

"Well, I can play games with them until October 7th. She's afraid
of some crazy guy going after me."

"Yes."

"I still am not very pleased with the phone calls here," Darias continued. "I mean, one thing is talking to her and another thing is somebody threatening my life. That's two different things." Robert reported that Amelia had answered the phone twice that day and that the callers had hung up.

"We had a meeting tonight, Bob, with the bosses, the SAC and the ASACs," Chellino said. "They just want us to low-key it. Let these people come to us. Let them tell *us* what's going on. We're not going to shut the business down, so if anybody wants to call there and find out, they'll see the business is still operating. The bosses want everything taped. They want to be advised immediately if anything happens to you over the weekend. They're pretty concerned, but they think these people are playing games."

"I do, too," Darias said.

"And they think we should give them a little rope, just lay back."

"This is a very good tape."

"Punch the holes out of the back," Chellino said. "Is the tape out of the machine?"

"Yeah, but you know what? I was playing some music and I think I have some music on top of it."

Frank and Carol laughed giddily.

"You and Richard Nixon both," Chellino said. "Punch the holes out, you son of a bitch. I've been over here all night worrying about you, you bastard. Don't give me any shit."

Robert laughed, and went on to say that he had asked Marlene if "Lester could tell if the guy had a Cuban accent, a Colombian accent, a Mexican accent, or a Puerto Rican accent." Carol and Frank exploded in laughter, catching the allusion to Nick Zapata and Eddie Hernandez.

Chellino told Darias to "lie low" until the middle of the following week. "We have to do a few things ourselves and give us some time."

"If somebody called her and said I was a federal agent, she must have some doubts," Robert said.

"She has some doubts, but I don't think they're that prevalent," Carol said. And Chellino asserted: "Bob, don't forget what's happened over the past few days here. You're definitely going to see some changes in her behavior and you have to adapt accordingly to them. But believe me, if she suspected you in any way, shape, or form, she would not be continuing to call you."

"I think she's trying to defend you," Carol added. "She wants to believe you. She's trying very very hard. She's trying to convince herself. Give her a little time and I think she will."

As Marlene tried to reassure herself, Lester and Harvey Rogers were in touch late that Friday with Arthur Karlick, the lawyer with whom Lester Rogers shared office space and who had first put Lionel Paytubi together with Rogers when Marlene Navarro was seeking "banking" services a little over a year earlier. It was now suggested that Karlick contact Paytubi and see if he knew anything about the anonymous call to Rogers.

Arthur Karlick called Paytubi at home that evening and said he needed to talk, but in person—not over the phone. They arranged to meet near a gas station at the intersection of Okeechobee Road and 12th Avenue in Hialeah at ten o'clock.

Karlick told Paytubi that the anonymous caller had told Lester Rogers that Dean International Investments was a government undercover operation, that Lionel Paytubi was an FBI informant, that Robert Darias was a DEA spy, and that several people had been or soon would be indicted, including Marlene Navarro, Paytubi, and others, perhaps including Rogers and Karlick.

"Lester is very worried and upset," Karlick told Paytubi, and it was clear to Paytubi that Karlick, too, was very concerned. "We've been friends for a long time and I don't want to see you hurt," Karlick said. "I just want to make sure you know who you're dealing with."

Paytubi said he had had nothing to do with the anonymous call—there must have been a misunderstanding. Karlick asked Paytubi to come to the law offices on Saturday and discuss the matter with Lester Rogers.

Between midnight Saturday and dawn Sunday the telephone rang twice at the Dariases' house in Coral Springs. Both times the caller paused momentarily, and then hung up without a word.

With the $30,000 porcelain Jesus packed carefully in her carry-on luggage, Marlene Navarro flew to Bogotá on Saturday with Alex McIntosh, whose birthday was Sunday. They stayed in a small hotel in north Bogotá, and Carmenza drove them around the spectacular countryside in her brown four-door Mercedes. That evening they had dinner at Tramonti, an intimate Italian restaurant with a fireplace and a panoramic view in the mountains above the city.

Marlene delivered the Jesus statue to Marina Alvarez and was exhilarated by recent hopeful developments in the kidnapping investigation. The events of the week in Miami did not mar her enjoyment of the weekend.

part five

THE FOREST PRIMEVAL

"Pueblo pequeño, infierno grande"
"Small town, big hell"
—Colombian proverb

43

AFTER NEARLY A YEAR marked by shrill ransom notes, threatening phone calls, wild-goose chases, and excruciating periods of waiting, Carlos Jader Alvarez sensed that he was close to penetrating the mystery that surrounded the kidnapping of his children.

On Saturday afternoon, September 11, a burgundy Mercedes and a yellow Ford van stopped outside an auto body shop on busy Avenida 68 in industrial west Bogotá. Four men with guns emerged from the vehicles and forced the owner of the body shop, Hernando Ospina Rincon, to accompany them. The Mercedes belonged to the family of Carlos Jader Alvarez. The van was owned by the F-2.

The next day, a young man named Guillermo Prado, whose car had been at Hernando Ospina's body shop awaiting repair, was detained outside his home in the Polo Club neighborhood by several armed men and forced into the same burgundy Mercedes that had been used the previous day in the abduction of the body shop owner. Prado, a law student at the National University, was a friend of Edgar Helmut Garcia, who had been abducted three weeks earlier, and of Orlando Garcia and Pedro Silva, who had been abducted in March. The four students had often played chess together at the University Club. After Edgar had "disappeared" in August, Guillermo Prado had gone to the police and asked questions. He had learned nothing about Edgar but had attracted attention to himself. Now, as his mother and sister looked on, the men with guns beat Guillermo in the back seat of the burgundy Mercedes as it sped away.

The next morning, another National University student, a mechanical engineering major named Edilbrando Joya, left his home for the university where he was scheduled to take an examination. He did not show up. He also failed to appear for a scheduled meeting with his brother that afternoon. A neighbor later reported seeing two armed men forcing Edilbrando into a red pickup truck.

One by one, as they were abducted, Ospina, Prado, and Joya were taken to one of the several residences that Carlos Jader Alvarez owned—a six-bedroom house with a Jacuzzi and indoor pool on

Carrera 14 in north Bogotá, a couple of miles below *La Iglesia* in El Chico Alto.

Alvarez idled as several of his men and some F-2 agents interrogated the three most recent arrivals. Neither Guillermo Prado nor Edilbrando Joya were enduring the torture as well as Edgar Helmut Garcia had. And now that his friends Prado and Joya were beginning to talk, Edgar Garcia too was losing his will to resist.

Eleven months after the kidnapping, Jader Alvarez was finally learning how his children had been targeted. According to the reluctant admissions of the students in the house on Carrera 14, the plot had been an inside job, of sorts. It apparently had begun with a young man named Alberto Trujillo, an economics student at the National University and a member of the M-19. Alberto Trujillo was a distant relative of Carlos Jader Alvarez—so distant that Alvarez had barely heard of him. Alvarez's second wife, Marina, had a niece named Neisla. Neisla's husband was named Alfredo Trujillo. Alberto Trujillo was Alfredo's cousin. Neisla and Alfredo had lived for a time in a house owned by Jader Alvarez across the street from the house where Guillermo Prado and Edgar Garcia were now being interrogated. It seemed that Alberto Trujillo used to visit Alfredo and Neisla at the house. A shy, quiet, bookish young man, Alberto would stay for hours. He would study there. He once borrowed a typewriter from Neisla.

During one of Alberto's visits, the Alvarez family chauffeur left two of Jader's children—Yidid and Xouix—at the house for an hour or so. After they left, Alberto asked his cousin Alfredo where the Alvarez family lived, whether they were rich, whether he could visit their home. Alfredo, who gave vague answers, had found it odd that Alberto would ask such questions.

Alberto Trujillo had been friendly with Orlando and Edgar Garcia as well as other members of the guerrilla movement at the National University. The students said they could not be positive that Alberto had conceived the kidnap plot. Edgar, who had signed the lease on the town house in Talavera, claimed he had been involved only in maintaining custody of the children, not in the kidnapping itself. And there was no way now to verify the role of Alberto Trujillo. In December 1981, two months after the kidnapping, Alberto had been killed while holding up a bank on the university campus. But his connection seemed plausible to the students, and Carlos Jader Alvarez agreed. Late that night he told Marina that her niece's husband's cousin, Alberto Trujillo, had been behind the kidnapping.

It had taken considerable torture to extract the name of Alberto Trujillo from Edgar Garcia. It took more torture to extract information on where the children might have been taken from Bogotá. Edgar Garcia and Guillermo Prado finally disclosed that the guerrillas apparently had taken them to a small town called Gachalá, which many people in Bogotá had never heard of.

So far as Garcia and Prado knew, the children were still alive.

Frightened and befuddled by Arthur Karlick's warning, Lionel Paytubi did not call Robert Darias until Monday.

"Have you talked with our female friend?" Paytubi asked.

"Yes, I've talked with her numerous times," Darias replied.

"Did she tell you about the problem?"

"Yes, she told me something about that. What did she tell you?"

"The first one who called me was my associate, to say that *his* associate had received some calls. And they mentioned several problems that I don't want to mention here. Because I'm calling from my home."

"Why don't you leave and call me from outside."

Darias told Paytubi to call his pager number from a pay phone, dial the number into the pager, and wait for Robert to call back. Robert claimed he was changing phones, too, so that they could have total security.

While Darias was waiting for Paytubi, Carol Cooper called.

"We've listened to the tape very, very carefully," she said, referring to his twenty-minute conversation with Navarro on Friday.

"I know. She's playing games," Robert said.

"She's playing some games, but we all feel very comfortable that she honestly wants to believe you, Bob."

"I know, but she's not telling me exactly what is going on, you can tell."

"Right. The guys can tell, too. There's something there that she's holding back. But she's trying honestly to believe in you. We want to keep close tabs on the situation. I don't want to lose it."

"Maybe we did already."

"If she does not surface this week, then I'm going to get nervous. I'd like to wait and see, when she comes back, what kind of reaction we get."

"You're really expecting her to come back, eh?" Robert asked.

"Yeah, I really am. I honestly think she'll be back."

"Gustavo told me she took the Madonna with her. [He meant the

Jesus statue.] That's a thirty-thousand-dollar item that you're not going to be carrying around unless you are going to take it directly to where it has to go."

"I think she's coming back," Carol said with a frustrated sniff. "If we have to throw her an excuse, we may at that point, as far as your end, if she's still very, very nervous. If she's not, I don't know. I think everything'll go according to plan. *She wants to believe you.* She may be able to rationalize the whole thing out in her own mind, and we won't have to do diddly-squat."

"But that's what I don't believe. I don't really believe she's trusting me that much."

"I want to know who's making these phone calls. 'Cause if there's a problem on *our* end with a leak somewhere—"

"That is where we have to be careful, Carol."

"Yeah, I know."

"Lester's telling her to be careful with everybody, including me. You know there might not have *been* a phone call to Lester."

"I think there was a phone call. Gut feeling is there was a phone call. It could be from bad guys making up a bunch of garbage. And they happen to be hitting key things. Lester, in the position he's in, should flat out know that there is no way in God's creation you can keep a wire going for a year and a half. But I think there was a phone call. The information may have been very skimpy. Their imaginations are running amok right now. They do not know what is going on. They are fishing. She is totally convinced it's not the feds. I want to see what her reaction is going to be when she comes back. I also want to see what Paytubi's going to be saying."

"What happened is as follows," Paytubi said when he and Darias resumed their conversation a few minutes later. "Friday night Karlick called me at home from the street, Karlick the attorney. 'I need to talk to you but I don't want to talk over the telephone.' Understand? So I went out and met with him. He told me that Lester had received a telephone call from a man with a Latin accent, and that the man mentioned my name, Marlene's, and yours. And that an indictment was going to be coming out against us three. That Dean International was working for the other side, for the Feds, and that I was an informant. That you were on the side of the Feds, and that I was an informant for the FBI! Imagine that! And that Marlene was in tremendous trouble, and that she was going to get hit with a huge indictment."

"Yes."

"This smells fishy to me because let me tell you something: the only one that knows about the association of Lester Rogers and Marlene is you, I, Karlick, Lester, and Marlene, but no one else. Then I said, damn! I have to investigate this or talk to Robert because there's something here that's not right. Because nobody makes a call like that if it's not to incriminate someone or without some purpose behind it."

"Sure."

"Damn! This has me sick now!"

"What's your idea? Why do you think this happened?"

Paytubi claimed that Lester and Marlene used to have a personal relationship. "Lester broke up with her and now he has another broad who is Cuban. It might be the *broad* who is screwing around and wants to start a hassle and get us in trouble. Anyway, Karlick said 'Why don't you talk with Lester?' "

Paytubi said that he'd gone to see Lester in the office on Saturday morning. "I don't like the man, you know? I don't like the man because I've been told numerous things about him. And he has defended two or three guys like these in various cases," a reference to drug clients.

Robert said, "Do you remember when we took that receipt and he said that he knew Carlos [Jader Alvarez], and had managed for him, and that he had the office full of money, and this and that? He made a big deal about it."

"Yes, I remember."

"That's when we went and took him the receipts."

"Well, I'm openly at your disposal as to what you tell me, because this has me messed up. It has me messed up."

Paytubi said he was now afraid to proceed with the Quaalude deal they had been planning. "There can't be any mistakes, because they will take all of us to hell! I don't want you to have any doubt about me."

"No, no, no—"

"Why she wants to start the hassle with us I don't understand, because I haven't done anything to that lady, nothing. *I'm* the one who should be pissed at *her*, because she's fucked me. Because she continued doing business with you after I was cut out of the thing."

"Sure."

"Now I'll tell you what Karlick told me—that the man [Rogers] had a new girlfriend, that she was Cuban. If he opened his mouth to this new girlfriend, then she wants to pressure him for money? You know women are capable of anything."

"Sure."

Paytubi maintained that he was not a target of Operation Greenback. "I'm not a target for shit. The target there is Marvin Warner.[1] My attorney said 'I've been told that you aren't the target of any investigation, so don't worry about it any more because they are after Marvin Warner.'"

"This is just a bunch of crap created by these people," Darias said.

"Look, Robert, it jeopardizes us. It's got me pissed. It's got me real pissed."

Darias suggested that Lester Rogers might have concocted the episode in order to ease himself out of his business relationship with Marlene Navarro so that he could join something more lucrative. "That's the only thing I can imagine, but you don't know, and neither do I."

Paytubi said, "I will have to go and see a Babalao [African rites priest] for good luck. I don't know, this really has me pissed off. Pissed off! I don't know, I check my telephone every month. I'm careful that I'm not being followed. I know what type of cars they use and everything."

"Sure."

They agreed to meet within the next few days. "Be careful of this broad now, because I'm suspicious of everything," Paytubi said.

A tall Latin man rang the doorbell at the house recently vacated by Robert and Amelia Darias in the Tamiami section of Miami. Speaking accented English, the man told the landlord, who was inside the house painting, that he needed to reach Robert Darias urgently. He declined to identify himself or give a reason for the visit. But he demanded a forwarding address. The landlord, who had neither the address nor a phone number, was noncommittal. The man returned two or three times on Saturday, September 11, and again Sunday and Monday. He would park for a while, look around, come to the front door, look around, leave, and return later.

Darias learned of the visits by chance on Tuesday morning when he called the landlord to arrange for a refund of his security deposit. The landlord said someone had been looking for him very insistently.

Robert immediately called Carol Cooper. "We have a big problem," he said, describing the visits by the stranger. "At this point, I'm

---

[1]Marvin Warner, who was the chairman of the Great American Bank's parent company, had been the United States ambassador to Switzerland and was a major fund-raiser for the Democratic Party. The Reagan Justice Department, through Operation Greenback and its lawyer Charles Blau, yearned to implicate him in the Great American Bank scandal.

not going to meet anybody, I'm not going anywhere, I'm not going to—I don't know what the hell is going on."

"Yeah," Carol agreed. "Stay home until we figure it out. Let me toss it around a little bit with Frank and Paul. Stay at home, kid."

Sennett drove past the house in Tamiami a few times that day but was unable to spot the stranger looking for Darias. The agents were reluctant to interrogate the landlord, whom neither Darias nor the DEA knew anything about, for fear of compromising Darias's under-cover position and risking that such information might be passed to the stranger.

That evening, without further reference to the visits by the stran-ger, Carol asked Robert to call Gustavo Delgado to see if he had heard from Marlene. But Robert had been thinking all day about the stranger's visits to the house in Tamiami—the house where a man with a machine gun had once accosted Robert. And he had been mulling over his last conversations with Marlene, picking up threatening nu-ances. Amelia was terrified. And Robert found himself more afraid than he had been at any other time since beginning work for the DEA. He felt his fear was well grounded, healthy.

"I am not calling anybody," he told Cooper. "I am not going to keep playing games, Carol. I am not very happy with the way that everybody is handling this thing. I feel that I am being put on the line, Carol. I think you have enough tapes and enough things that explain to you what is going on. I don't want to talk to anybody else until we find out what in the hell is going on. We have killers after me now. I feel that I am putting my whole family on the line now, and that is a different story."

"We understand how you feel."

"When people can find out where I used to live, that is pretty bad news for me. How in the hell did these people know where I lived? They followed me apparently. When these people *find* me, that's it!"

"We know that. We talked about that tonight. We're not playing with kids. But my gut reaction is that they don't have any idea where you are right now."

"These people must have *some means* of finding out things when they were able to go by my house, Carol. And that's what's *really* worrying me to death today. This morning I wasn't too excited be-cause I just said, let's find out—maybe it's somebody that I know. But I have called *every single person* that I know who has in any way been connected with me and could have gone by that house. *Nobody. Nobody, but nobody.* Very few people, *very* few people, *very very very* few people know where I used to live."

"Yeah, I know. It bothers us, too. It really does. It's a very serious thing that we're looking at. I want to give it a day if I can, and see what we can come up with. Paul's gonna go down and sit there all day tomorrow and see if we can find out who it is. But we're not leaving you out in the cold. We're very concerned about this thing. Headquarters called me and said if we've got to move you again, let us know right away and we'll get the money and we'll move you. They're not playing games either. We're walking a tightrope now, I know it. It's not easy for any of us either. I hate to ask you to do things. But I don't know how else to resolve it because we don't have other agents in there that can do it."

"I am not going anywhere. I'm going to stay with Amelia and I am not going to let her out of my sight until we resolve this and we have these people under control."

"We're not going to leave you out in the cold, kid. We're playing games, I admit it. They're games that we're almost forced to play to try and save everything else and also try and make sure that nobody gets hurt."

"I am the rusty nail in their skin. That's why they are trying to take me out. Marlene keeps telling me, 'I want you to be careful because I don't want anything to happen to you.' I don't know whether to take that as a threat or as real concern."

"We're definitely not going to do anything to get you or your family hurt. It's frustrating to us 'cause we don't want to just go out there and grab these people and that's it. And it might be even more involved than we thought it was. But anyway, be assured, we are *not* gonna leave you out there in the cold. We're all going through the same thing you are."

"Well, but they're looking for *me.*"

Having calmed down a bit, Robert relented and called Gustavo Delgado, who was cryptic and cold, obviously cognizant of the anonymous call to Marlene's lawyer. Delgado confirmed that Marlene was out of town but said he was afraid his own phone might be tapped and did not want to get involved in her affairs.

Marlene and Alex flew back to Miami from Bogotá on Tuesday, and Marlene began trying to reach Darias. She called his home number and was shocked to get a "disconnect" signal; in the wake of the threatening calls, the DEA had for the weekend disconnected Robert's undercover line, the number Marlene had always known as his home number, and inadvertently failed to reconnect it. She called

International Investments and was told he was out of town. She called his pager, which he had turned off.

Robert's fear of meetings had passed, but he did not get a message that Marlene had returned and was trying to reach him until two days later, Thursday. He called her immediately.

"Oh, Robert, you sure do get lost," Marlene said.

"How are you? It's been days since we talked."

"You're a bad friend. As soon as there's a problem, instead of contacting your friends, you get lost."

"I've been afraid with those telephone calls, and those problems, Marlene."

"Yes, Robert, but why should you be afraid? You know that friends are for when we have problems."

"That's true. I have been unreliable."

"Your phone is disconnected."

"My telephone has been malfunctioning, and also I haven't been home."

Juvenal Betancur also had called International Investments looking for Darias.

"I told him that you were having problems and they were threatening you," Marlene said. "It looks like poor Juvenal got frightened. It's not advantageous to him. He is the president's brother and doesn't want to be involved in any problem."

"Surely."

"Tell me, Robert, when are we going to see each other?"

"Well, let's see if we can meet soon, I guess tomorrow, or if not, Monday."

She invited him to join her at Gustavo Delgado's cabana on Key Biscayne over the weekend.

"Ah, perfect," Robert said.

"Gustavo says that he, too, is frightened."

"But you don't have any problems, Marlene, because you haven't done anything by yourself."

"Yes, nor you."

"Clearly."

"Gustavo used to call me five or ten times a day, and now no more than two. Alex is concerned, too. He says, 'What's Robert's problem, he doesn't call, he doesn't come by.' "

"Marlene, it's that my family has been very nervous. You know how those things are."

"I told him about your telephone calls."

"Because they called my wife and they threatened her. And that was very bad. Whoever did that? *Whoever did that,* it was very bad."

"Robert, be very careful. Because if they are criminals, *there* is where we have to be careful."

"Sure."

"If it was the *federales,* they wouldn't be doing a thing like this. There is no problem with threats. They arrest you and take you to jail."

"Sure."

"But the *other* people you have to be afraid of, Robert."

"Yes."

"Robert, I'm asking you a favor, if you could please give me a little time tomorrow or Saturday."

"Why not."

"To meet or something, I'll be grateful, and don't get lost, because I'll think that something has happened to you, you have been killed or something."

"No, I'll call you."

"Because there is danger for you and your family."

"Exactly."

"Remember that you have a little girl—remember that—who you have to take care of. Remember that, hear?"

"Sure."

"Then, Robert, we'll have a coffee, here in the club, or come to this house, this is your house."

"Okay, Marlene, say hello to Alex."

"Okay, Robert."

"I talked to your friend," Robert reported to Cooper. "She's playing games. She was very nice. She invited me to go and see her Saturday at the beach." Robert urged Carol to allow him to meet with Marlene in Key Biscayne that weekend.

"Well, let's listen to the tape and see what we think," Carol said.

"That place is totally open," Robert said. "There's no way anybody can hide or do anything there. Too many people. Right on the beach."

"Let us look at the location and see what we're looking at."

After dispatching Paul Sennett to pick up the tape of Darias's latest talk with Navarro, Cooper drove downtown to the federal court house and resumed her secret testimony before the grand jury. The jury's session the previous Thursday had been canceled because of the threatening calls to Robert and Amelia Darias, although the jurors were not told the reason for the delay. Now Michael Pasano took Cooper through the highlights of the last three weeks of the wiretap, Navarro's trip to Denver with Darias (who was still unnamed), the discovery of the hundred-thousand-dollar shortage, and the entrée of Juvenal Betancur into the activities of Marlene Navarro and Carlos Jader Alvarez.

After Cooper's testimony, Frank Chellino began presenting the government's case against Humberto Garcia and his associates in Medellín and elsewhere.

Cooper and Chellino then returned to the Phoenix Building and were given a précis of Darias's conversation that morning with Navarro. Chellino called Darias.

"We think we're dead with you," Chellino said. "We essentially agree that she's playing games with you. And we think it's a dead issue with you. We're just trying to figure out how we can fuck with her now. I don't know, Bob. We're in the middle of it and we're left with no options. What do you think?"

"She wants me to believe she's my friend and everything is all right, but you realize that she keeps threatening me," Robert said.

"Yeah, I know. I got the subtle hints today."

"Well, let me explain exactly how she said it. She said, you know, these are bad guys, and I am afraid for you and your family, and you have to be careful because you have a little girl, a little daughter that you have to take care of. And be very careful with her."

"I know. I know. Enough said. What was your gut feeling at the end of the conversation?"

"That she's just gaining time for whatever she's doing. I feel that she is going to fly away someday. In the meantime, if there are no more developments that touch her, I think she is going to stay put, she'll be here on October 7, but she is going to be fooling around."

"Our decision is either leave it alone or to fuck with her a little bit," Chellino said. "And if we fuck with her, the risk we run, as you say, is that she's going to leave. This just drives me up a wall, Bob, having to sit back on this. It just drives me bananas to have to sit still on this thing." Chellino sighed deeply. "I don't know. *We* don't know and we're not going to make any moves until next week. You can take what she says either way. Either she is really legitimately concerned about you and/or your family—"

"I don't think so."

"Or she is giving you a subtle hint."

"She's telling me to lay off, or something is going to happen to me and to my family and to my little girl. She knows that every time she mentions my little girl, I hit the ceiling. *That* she knows. She's using that. She never mentioned my little girl before in any conversation until just the other day after those phone calls. I don't know if you realize that."

"No, I'm sure. *It just pisses me off to no fucking end that she can get away with this.* But you are *not* meeting with her at all—period. That's off. Tom said it, I said it, Carol said it: You are *not* meeting her at all unless it's under our control."

Darias still tried to convince Chellino to allow him to meet Navarro on Key Biscayne that weekend. "I'll go there. I'll go there alone. I won't go there with my family."

"You ain't going nowhere," Chellino said.

"I'm not afraid of the beach. I already landed on a beach one day."

"Oh, no, no. You ain't goin' to no beach."

Chellino paused. "Where do you think we stand with Humberto and Paytubi?" he asked.

"Oh, with Humberto we're in good shape. And Paytubi wants to go tomorrow and meet this guy with the Quaaludes. I think I should go. I cannot postpone that anymore. I don't have any qualms about that."

"Well, I do."

"I mean, if we are going to start getting pussyfoot now, I might as well disappear totally and forget about the whole operation."

"I don't know that that's not in order."

"No, it's not," Darias asserted. "I'm not going to let Humberto off the hook, when I have been dealing with him and bringing him around to get this guy, Roosterman, with a quarter of a million bucks in cash, down payment in the office, to get delivery of a hundred kilograms of coke. And I am not going to let Paytubi go either if this guy really has five million Quaaludes."

"Let's go to the potential—and I'm leveling with you at this point—let's go to the theory that Paytubi is in cahoots with Marlene," Chellino said.

"I don't know. I don't read Paytubi that bad. That's why I am eager to meet with him and see what he plans. I don't want to be left out."

"You don't feel uncomfortable with Paytubi?"

"No, he's not lying to me. He just needs the money desperately. And the deal is so good—people are very greedy— and he feels that he's going to make about fifty thousand to sixty thousand in one shot."

"What about Humberto?"

"Humberto is no problem at all."

"Humberto's a helluva case. That is a *helluva* case." Chellino was taken with the notion of penetrating the Medellín syndicate through Humberto Garcia. "The lawyers complimented you today. What an outstanding job! I said, I'll never tell him that. It'll go right to his fucking head."

Darias laughed. "I'll tell you, at this point, nothing can go to my head. That queasy feeling about my family really is difficult to take."

"Hey, I know, man. I would feel the same way."

"I really want to do Paytubi. I want to go and meet this guy."

"Let us kick it around. I don't know, Bob."

"I also want to get this other guy, Roosterman. He's a big shot and nobody knows him. The guy has eight MAC-10 submachine guns."

"From this point until the end, I want total and absolute coverage on you."

44

BY AIR AND LAND, the "secret guys," as they came to be called, descended upon Gachalá without warning just before noon on Tuesday, September 14. Three helicopters—two Bell 206s and a Huey—circled the town briefly and then landed on the soccer field next to the school. About a dozen armed men disembarked and moved out toward the main square of town two blocks away. At the same time, a caravan of four Jeeps pulled into town from the twisting mountain road and stopped in the square in front of the small police station–city hall. Another dozen armed men emerged from the Jeeps, and rendezvoused with their colleagues from the helicopters. The visitors wore civilian clothes—heavy sweaters and trousers.

The people of Gachalá, whose only sidearms were machetes and small pistols, had never seen so many big and powerful weapons—assault rifles, machine guns, and a variety of handguns. The armed men moved quickly to establish their authority. Their leader identified the group to the lone uniformed constable at the police station as agents of the F-2 branch of the Colombian National Police from Bogotá. In fact, the men comprised an irregular mixture of F-2 agents and henchmen of Carlos Jader Alvarez, who was in ultimate command of the operation. He had rented all three helicopters and owned most of the Jeeps.

The agents had brought two prisoners with them—Edgar Helmut Garcia and Guillermo Prado. Both showed signs of a long night of brutal interrogation. Their faces were bloody, their noses broken. Several agents commandeered a small hotel, where they chained Edgar Garcia to a bed and resumed beating him. Other agents walked Guillermo Prado around the streets. They were searching for a man whom both the students knew, the chairman of the Guavio Victims Committee, the guerrilla Bernardo Acosta. The students had reluctantly identified Acosta as the man who could lead them to the Alvarez children.

The agents soon found Acosta on one side of the square. They moved to detain him, but he pulled a gun, fired into the air, and began running. Under orders to take Acosta alive, the agents subdued him a block away, along with his brother, Mario Acosta, who had come to his aid.

As townspeople gathered, the agents hustled the Acosta brothers off to the soccer field where the helicopters waited. There, they separated and blindfolded them, and began interrogation. Where were the Alvarez children? The Acosta brothers denied knowing anything about the children. The agents produced Edgar Garcia and Guillermo Prado. The Acosta brothers maintained their denials. The agents beat them.

After a few hours, the agents extracted the name of Guillermo Alvarado, the *campesino* who had transported supplies to the hideout in the mountains where the children had been kept. Several of the agents, with the prisoners in tow, climbed aboard two of the helicopters. With a local man to guide them, they lifted off and flew seven miles east to the Alvarado home where they landed on a stretch of pasture in front of the two-room adobe house.

The unsuspecting Alvarados were at that time on the streets of Gachalá, wondering what the commotion was about. When they arrived home in the afternoon, the place was a mess. The agents had ransacked the house, ripping apart containers, poking holes in the ceiling, and destroying one of the speakers on a battery-operated tape player.

The leader of the agents, tall and brash, greeted them.

"Well, it's 'Bolívar,' " he said, using a nickname applied to Alvarado by several people in Gachalá.

"My name is not Bolívar—it is Guillermo Alvarado. What are you doing here?"

"Are you Bolívar's wife?" the tall agent asked Ana Elvira Alvarado.

"My husband's name is Guillermo Alvarado."

The agents kicked Alvarado and frisked him. He said he did not own a gun. They asked if he had seen three children who had been kidnapped. He denied knowing of a kidnapping but acknowledged that he had encountered three children in the area several months earlier.

"If you don't tell the truth, we'll take you to jail," the tall agent said.

Alvarado recounted the trips he had made up the Medina trail with supplies for what Bernardo Acosta had told him was a new branch of the Guavio Victims Committee. Alvarado acknowledged having seen three children on the trail.

The agents dragged Edgar Helmut Garcia from one of the helicopters and brought him forward. He was blindfolded and his legs were bound with heavy tape. They removed his blindfold. "Here is your friend," they said to Alvarado. *"Caballo."*

"I have never seen this person," Alvarado said. "He is not my friend."

Then, on looking more closely at the young student with the bloody face and broken nose, Alvarado admitted that he had encountered him once before—as the man who had claimed to be the father of the three children in the dead of night on the Medina trail the previous November.

As they questioned Guillermo Alvarado, the agents continued their rough interrogation of Edgar Garcia. Among other things, Garcia admitted that he had participated in a robbery of the bank on the campus of the National University. But, aside from making a vague gesture up the Medina trail into the mountains, he denied any knowledge of where the Alvarez children were.

As night fell, the agents turned their attention to Bernardo Acosta, who lay on the ground under a plastic sheet, his eyes covered with a red rag, his legs bound with rope and encased in a gunny sack. Acosta denied any knowledge of the Alvarez children. Far into the night, the agents tortured him. He screamed. The agents played loud music through the Alvarados' one remaining battery-operated speaker to try to drown out Acosta's screams. The Alvarados' terrified young daughter wanted to give water to Acosta, but the agents refused permission.

Late that night, Carlos Jader Alvarez appeared at the Alvarado house. With a few of his men, he had been searching up and down the Medina trail for clues to the whereabouts of his children. He had found nothing. Dressed in Bogotá street clothes, he was soaking wet and covered with mud from the treacherous trail. While Jader Alvarez sat on the Alvarados' bed sipping coffee and soup, Ana Elvira washed his socks and dried them in front of the wood fire. The *padrino* offered the Alvarados money to help him find his children. They said they had told the agents everything they knew.

After screaming from torture most of the night, Bernardo Acosta finally lost consciousness. He had told his interrogators nothing of value.

Carlos Jader Alvarez's helicopters lifted off the next morning, bearing the agents, the prisoners, and Alvarez himself. In Bogotá, Bernardo Acosta was logged in at the headquarters of the F-2 and locked in a cell. Early the following day he was questioned by an F-2 lieutenant in the Office of General Investigations. The questioning was brief, and much gentler than the brutal interrogation in the mountains. Acosta provided no additional information bearing on the Alvarez children.

Bernardo Acosta was not logged out of the F-2. Along with his brother, Mario, he was removed secretly, under guard, without paperwork, and taken to the private jail of Carlos Jader Alvarez in the six-bedroom house with the indoor pool and Jacuzzi in north Bogotá. Several of the National University students, including Edgar Helmut Garcia, Guillermo Prado, and Edilbrando Joya, were already in the house.

Since torture and more conventional police interrogation hadn't worked on Bernardo Acosta, Jader Alvarez took a different tack. He tried to soothe Acosta, telling the guerrilla he meant him no harm. He allowed Acosta to rest his battered body and made sure he was given good, restorative food. Then Alvarez offered Acosta a deal: If Acosta would disclose where the children were, Alvarez would give him a lot of money, hide him from the police and the M-19, and guarantee him safe passage out of Colombia with false documents.

"You don't have to worry about the police anymore," Jader Alvarez said. "You are in my custody now. Neither the police nor the M-19 will know where you are if I send you out of the country."

Still exhausted and ill from the torture in the mountains, Acosta said nothing. Hours passed, and the frustrated Alvarez turned Acosta back over to his interrogators, who resumed the torture. They tied Acosta up. They beat him. They used an electric cattle prod on his genitals and other parts of his body. They put a bag over his head and nearly suffocated him. They beat him again.

Acosta still refused to talk, and his interrogators developed a grudging admiration for the husky guerrilla's courage.

Then, from another part of the house, Carlos Jader Alvarez produced Acosta's brother, Mario, who also had been tortured and had given no useful information.

"If you don't give us the information we know you have," Jader Alvarez told Bernardo Acosta, "we will kill your brother and your entire family!"

For the first time, Bernardo Acosta looked at Jader Alvarez with undiluted terror in his eyes.

"Where are my children?" Alvarez demanded.

"I can show you."

"Are they alive?"

Acosta shook his head. "I don't think so. I think not."

It was dawn on Saturday, September 18. Jader Alvarez quickly

notified the high command of the F-2 that the children might be dead
and that Acosta would lead the police to the place in the mountains
above Gachalá where they last had been seen. Alvarez held out hope
for a miracle—that the children were somehow still alive.

The F-2 commander ordered the police Special Operation Group,
known by the Spanish initials GOES, an elite squad of commandos
who specialized in search, rescue, and assault missions, to take over
the search for the children. A GOES team went immediately to the
house on Carrera 14 where Bernardo Acosta was being held and took
him to the heliport on the city's western outskirts.

Carlos Jader Alvarez drove to *La Iglesia* to give Marina the news
and to comfort her. She prayed over the statue of Jesus that Marlene
Navarro had brought from Miami.

45

ROBERT DARIAS SENSED correctly that Marlene Navarro no longer trusted him.

Indeed, she was panicking.

Despite her calm voice on the telephone that morning, her inability to reach Darias earlier in the week—the no-answers and then the disconnect message on his phone—had fed her suspicion that the anonymous phone call to Lester Rogers might have contained grains of truth.

Why would someone make such a call to Rogers if the information was *entirely* false, she asked herself. And even though Robert had been cordial and reassuring on the phone when he had finally called, she reluctantly concluded that her trust might have been misplaced.

She kept thinking of the extremely limited number of people who knew about the dealings in August 1981 among Lester Rogers, Arthur Karlick, Lionel Paytubi, herself, and Robert Darias. Arthur Karlick had conferred with Paytubi on Friday night and had gotten the impression that Paytubi knew nothing of the anonymous telephone call or the information it contained. Paytubi could have been lying, but if he wasn't, that left Darias as the likely, or at least possible, focus of whatever truth the call might have contained. (Other possibilities never occurred to her.)

She mulled not only the anonymous call but the events of the summer that had preceded it—events that continued to haunt her.

She decided it had been naive of her to believe that the apparent surveillance of the chauffeur Tocayo in July, and of Nelson Batista in August (it appeared that Nelson had been followed at least twice, once in Miami and once in Los Angeles), had been unrelated to her. She could not be sure, but she felt she could no longer take the risk.

And Marlene's gnawing doubts about Darias were cast against other terrifying recent events—the execution of Oscar's friend as part of a quadruple homicide, the drug-related slaughter of three women in South Miami, the threatened violence over the delayed payment for Jader Alvarez's cocaine in New York, the ugly dispute over the missing $105,000 from Denver—with overtones of threat and violence.

The tension and fear in Marlene had accumulated gradually, leading to a bleeding intestine and a cancer scare.

Now the anonymous telephone call to Lester Rogers had made her ill again.

Ironically, it had taken the perspective of a relaxing weekend in Bogotá with Alex, and the hopeful news about the Alvarez children, to reveal to Marlene the depth of her terror.

The final blow had come that very morning, when she arrived back at Costa del Sol. A lawyer friend had *advised her to flee Miami.*

After a session at the Avant-Garde late in the afternoon, during which her hairdresser told her that she *looked* terrified, Marlene drove home and told Alex McIntosh that she was leaving the United States. Having moved to Miami to live with Marlene less than two weeks earlier, McIntosh was nonplussed.

But Marlene was determined, and was moving fast. She removed $10,000 in cash from the safe in her broom closet and asked McIntosh to drive her to the airport just after dusk. Pretending to be on a short outing, in case she was being watched, she carried only a large purse containing the cash and a few toiletries, and wore very casual clothes—black Calvin Klein jeans, a striped blouse, a light leather-trimmed jacket, and flat shoes, which, because of her short stature, she rarely wore outside her home. She avoided Miami International, thinking it more likely to be under surveillance, and directed McIntosh up I-95 to the Fort Lauderdale airport instead.

Shortly after eight o'clock she boarded an Eastern flight to La Guardia in New York, paying cash for her ticket, and flying coach, thinking she would be less conspicuous than in first class. As a striking woman, she was accustomed to men's stares and the occasional come-on. Now, however, she was in full panic, and each look, even from a flight attendant, chilled her. At La Guardia she took a taxi to the Plaza Hotel, where she had stayed many times, and checked in. It was midnight. Calmer now, she called a friend, a personal shopper for Saks Fifth Avenue, and spoke briefly, revealing nothing of her panic.

After a fitful sleep, she checked out of the hotel early Friday morning, took a cab back to La Guardia, and located the Air Canada terminal. A uniformed pilot struck up a conversation with her and asked if she was returning to New York soon. She declined his request for her phone number. Again feigning an intention to return promptly to the United States, she bought a round-trip ticket to Montreal and charged it on her American Express card. Aboard the plane she glimpsed a three-day-old headline that Princess Grace of Monaco had died after an automobile accident in France. It occurred to Marlene that she had not read a newspaper all week, unusual for her.

In Montreal she purchased a ticket on to Toronto, a city she had grown to like in the months she had been seeing Alex McIntosh. During the short hop she fell into a deep sleep and had to be awakened by a flight attendant after the plane arrived. She took a taxi to the Four Seasons Hotel downtown, and checked in, again showing American Express. Ensconced in her room, she called McIntosh in Miami and instructed him to pack some of her clothes. She ticked off detailed lists of garments in her closets, assuring him that the maid Heidi would help him. Then she asked McIntosh to take the approximately $50,000 that remained in her safe, load everything in her BMW, and drive it to Toronto as rapidly as possible. The confused McIntosh dutifully set about his tasks.

He left Miami Saturday morning and drove Navarro's BMW straight up I-95. He drove all night, and by late Sunday morning was on I-81 near Binghamton, New York, when a New York State trooper pulled him over for speeding. He had been doing over 100. The officer gave him a ticket but did not search the car. The $50,000 was secure. McIntosh crossed the border and arrived in Toronto late that afternoon.

Marlene was still in a panic. She had called Bogotá and briefed Carmenza but had insisted that Carmenza not tell Jader Alvarez about her predicament. Marlene did not know *for sure* that Robert Darias was a federal agent. And if he was, she was afraid of what Alvarez might do. Marlene knew the savage code of the Colombian drug mafia. When Maria Lilia Rojas had been arrested and jailed, Marlene twice had warned her never to talk. When she had sensed weakness in the chauffeur Tocayo, she had warned him never to talk.

Now she had to consider her own predicament if Robert Darias proved to be what she suspected. He knew everything about her. He knew her employees. He knew how she moved money and where. He knew she could command shipments of millions of dollars' worth of narcotics. He knew her relationships with Carlos Jader Alvarez, whose Miami bank accounts he controlled, as well as with José Antonio Cabrera, Juan Mata Ballesteros, Isaac Kattan, and Juvenal Betancur.

Darias could destroy her. He could destroy Jader Alvarez. He could embarrass the president of Colombia.

But was Robert Darias working for the U.S. Government?

She was afraid to tell Jader until she was sure. But by then it might be too late.

For Carlos Jader Alvarez might have her killed, and her family as well.

Sitting in the Four Seasons Hotel in Toronto, with $60,000 of drug cash, four large suitcases of designer clothes, and a thoroughly confused lover, Marlene Navarro was consumed by terror.

4 6

THOUGH BERNARDO ACOSTA had told Carlos Jader Alvarez he "thought" the children were dead, the *padrino* had refused to believe him.

Bernardo Acosta had been telling the truth. He had seen the children die.

In the chill of the sodden jungle several miles above the meadow called *Las Brisas,* the guerrillas had ordered the Alvarez children out of the hut at the foot of the giant *yomaquin* tree and hustled them farther up the mountain. The sun had been up for hours, but it had been dark in the dense, misty forest. The treacherous climb through the tangled wilderness had been easier for the children than for the adults on the rocky, mossy, viny incline. About a hundred yards higher, the group had come to another huge tree, a *chuguacá.*

The guerrillas had blindfolded the three children.

The five-year-old boy Xouix had been moved several yards from the group and ordered to stand still. Another guerrilla had raised his rifle and shot Xouix in the back of the head, splattering blood and brain tissue, killing the child instantly. A silencer on the rifle had kept the sound from reverberating through the mountains.

The younger of the two girls, six-year-old Yidid, had been brought forward and executed in the same manner.

It hadn't been so simple with seven-year-old Zuleika. She had clasped her hands to her face, and her body had tensed and flinched, as a rifle bullet slammed into her right temple. Still alive, she had writhed on the ground. The guerrillas had waited, reluctant to leave evidence that any of the children had not died instantly. Zuleika had continued to writhe. After more than half an hour, with the child still moving, they had shot her again, this time above her left eye. Terror had contorted her face as she died.

The guerrillas had stuffed the children's bodies into loosely woven gunny sacks called *costalles,* which they then wrapped in plastic sheets and buried at the base of the *chuguacá* tree.

Two of Carlos Jader Alvarez's rented helicopters, carrying ten GOES commandos and Bernardo Acosta, lifted off from Bogotá and headed east. The copters had to maneuver around low clouds shrouding the mountains, finally finding an opening directly above the Montserrate Church overlooking the Old City. It took only half an hour to reach the skies over Gachalá, where the pilots found the weather clear.

Acosta guided the copter pilots to the mountain meadow called *Las Brisas* southeast of Gachalá. The copters could not land where Acosta said the children were. The mountain was too steep, the jungle too dense. After circling for a few minutes, the pilots decided they could not even get close. They put down on a shoulder of meadow several miles below.

The GOES commandos, with Acosta in tow, immediately started up the mountain, staying in radio contact with the pilots, who were wary about being left alone with two expensive helicopters in what was reputed to be an isolated and dangerous spot—guerrilla territory. After about a mile, the hikers came upon the wooden shanty where the Alvarez children had been taken in the dead of night on the last Sunday in November. There were no signs of recent life. The mountains above loomed steep and dark as the midday clouds enveloped their peaks.

Acosta was now insisting that the children were dead and had been dead for some time. The commander of the GOES team, however, was unwilling to take his word, and ordered the group to move as fast as it could. Acosta led the group up and to the left through meadow and into the jungle. The ground was rough underfoot and the upward slope averaged forty-five degrees. Assuming the helicopters could land at their destination, the commandos had not dressed for a long, difficult trek through jungle and mountains. Their shoes and socks already were drenched and muddy.

Thrashing through the jungle along a streambed, Acosta located the remains of the even cruder hut where the children had been kept for a time. Again, there were no signs of recent life. Acosta headed on up through the jungle and then to the right, back into open country, a rocky, muddy meadow, ever more treacherous underfoot. On the mountainside above the meadow, the mist-shrouded jungle loomed like a forest primeval, darkening as they moved higher. The GOES commandos had been in difficult terrain all over Colombia, but none more daunting than these mountains, the Rocky Cliffs of Medina, covered by an equatorial rain forest at 10,000 feet above sea level. It was terrain duplicated in few areas of the world. The jungle would have been difficult enough to penetrate if it had been level, but on this slope it seemed impossible at times. The searchers slipped on the mud and moss. They tripped over wirelike vines. They edged around house-sized rocks, and climbed over large trees leveled by landslides and erosion. The air grew colder and damper as the afternoon clouds thickened. The only comfort was the absence of the deadly *talla equis* snakes, which could not live at such high altitudes and low temperatures.

Six hours after leaving the helicopters, the exhausted, sweat-drenched commandos and their prisoner arrived at the remains of a hut made of a few tree branches and plastic sheeting at the foot of the huge *yomaquin* tree. Here, they found a few signs of life—a sardine can, a sausage can, three toothbrushes, a pair of children's shoes, and a child's red stocking.

Bernardo Acosta balked. If the children were dead, the commandos demanded to know, then where were their bodies? The weary guerrilla claimed he could not remember where the children were buried. The commandos were furious at his stalling.

"You will die right here if you don't tell us where they are," the commanding officer declared. "Tell us right now! If you don't tell us *right now,* we are going to kill you *right here!"* They punched and kicked Acosta, who was already in pain from torture at the hands of Carlos Alvarez's men. He finally relented, leading the commandos on up the jungled mountain, which was steeper, slipperier, and denser than ever. Each step was perilous. Handholds were as crucial as footholds. About a hundred yards up, the group came to another huge tree—the *chuguacá.* Bernardo Acosta gestured to the foot of the tree and its tangled, moss-coated root system, a small jungle in itself.

Grappling with the roots, the commandos began digging. About a yard beneath the surface of the wet earth, they came upon plastic sheeting. The muddy plastic enclosed two gunny sacks. One sack contained the bodies of two young children. The other sack contained the body of a slightly older child. The bodies were quite well preserved by the cold temperatures. It was unclear how long they had been buried. The oldest child, a girl, was lying on her right side. The younger children in the other bag were jammed together, facing each other.

The commandos rewrapped the bodies, secured them with rope as best they could, and groped back down the mountain to the remnants of the hut at the foot of the *yomaquin* tree. It was dusk. The commandos radioed the helicopter pilots, who refused to stay in the area past sundown. Unable to go farther in the dark, the commandos had to face the night in the jungle, without food or water.

The helicopters lifted off, hovered overhead, and attempted to drop a container of coffee to the commandos. It smashed against the side of the mountain.

The commandos handcuffed Bernardo Acosta and tied him to a tree. After dark, it rained heavily, and the temperature dropped nearly to freezing. The men tried to use their socks and handkerchiefs to kindle a fire, but they were too wet. They took turns through the night huddling in what remained of the plastic hut. No one slept.

At dawn, ten hours later, the group made its way tortuously, carrying the children's bodies reeking in the humidity, back down the mountain. The helicopters picked them up late that morning and returned them to Bogotá, where all ten commandos and Bernardo Acosta were treated at a hospital for exposure.

Carlos Jader Alvarez and his chauffeur, together with police medical examiners, formally identified the bodies as Zuleika, Yidid, and Xouix. Zuleika would have turned eight years old just ten days earlier, on Friday, September 10.

Alvarez and the F-2 branch were shocked finally to learn from a broken Bernardo Acosta that the children had not been killed recently. They had been dead for months, perhaps since April. They had been executed as punishment for what the kidnappers considered Jader Alvarez's niggardly failure to pay any ransom to recover his children, and as revenge against the killings of more than forty young members of the M-19 by the combined forces of the Jader Alvarez organization and the drug lords' vigilante group, MAS. Sometime in April, several weeks after the disappearance of the four National University students, the kidnappers in Bogotá had dispatched the order to Bernardo Acosta to execute the children. As Acosta reconstructed the story, he had complied because he wanted to maintain his new relationship with the M-19 and the possibility that it would lead to financing for his own guerrilla movement in the mountains.

After the executions, the kidnappers had concocted the fiction that the children were still alive in order to prolong the possibility of extracting ransom, and to avoid angering the new president of Colombia, Belisario Betancur, who had proposed granting amnesty to the M-19 guerrillas.

The discovery that the children of Carlos Jader Alvarez had been summarily slaughtered, after several weeks of hopeful expectation that they would be found alive, was front-page news in Bogotá, stunning and enraging the city and the highest levels of the government of

Colombia. The Minister of Justice vowed to bring the full force of law
to bear on the kidnappers. "We have to apprehend these criminals no
matter what, and we have to take them to a court of law so they can
be tried and condemned to the maximum penalty the law provides
for," the minister declared. The president of the Supreme Court,
César Ayerbe Chaux, said that the "assassination of the children
should be condemned by society as well as by the executive, judicial
and legislative branches of the Colombian Government. It is pitiful
that these barbarians exist." The leadership of the M-19 movement
issued a statement denying any connection to the kidnapping. "Nobody should try to shield themselves in the banner of popular rebel-
lion to justify these barbaric acts. Nobody should try to use this
painful case for the Colombian nation and for the Alvarez family as
a personal opportunity or as a political one, because crimes against
humanity will never have a place in the universe of politics." Even the
drug lords' group MAS made a public statement denying any involvement in the disappearance of the missing National University students.

The discovery of the children's bodies shocked the town of Gachalá
more profoundly than it did the city of Bogotá. The residents of the
town and the surrounding mountains were stunned that people from
their midst had imprisoned three young children in exceptionally
crude circumstances in remote mountains for several months, and
then murdered them in cold blood and buried them in gunny sacks.
After generations of living in isolated simplicity—in what seemed a
state of grace and innocence at the end of a dirt road in the Andes, the
campesinos felt soiled, even cursed. The news from the jungled mountain above *Las Brisas* meadow heightened their old fears and supersti-
tions about the *Farallones de Medina,* the Rocky Cliffs of Medina,
where the ghosts of hostile Indians were believed still to be guarding
a lake of gold.

One of the *campesinos,* a man who eked out a living handling teams
of mules in the mountains, found himself composing a mournful song
in the weeks after the children were found:

> *I'm going to tell you the story*
> *Of what happened in Gachalá,*
> *The story of three children they killed out there*
> *They started on the road,*
> *The road that would not come back from the heart of the jungle.*
> *One child rode on a man's back, the other two were on a mule.*
> *The jungle is silent.*

Up there in the mountains, the mountains of the brutal crime,
When they killed the children, their coffin was a gunny sack
The F-2 in action, helicopters flying,
They did not find ammunition, only a little pair of shoes.
The children's souls must be getting to heaven now.
Their poor father is mourning them.

The Alvarez family held the funeral at the Church of Christo Rey, an angular, contemporary *parroquia* known for lavish weddings and funerals. White stucco with a red tile roof, the church was situated on Calle 100 in north Bogotá. The children's bodies were laid out in wood-and-*faux marbré* coffins on a blue-gray carpeted altar beneath a gold six-foot statue of Christ and another of the Virgin Mary. More than a thousand people, including members of the Alvarez family, the children's teachers, and hundreds of friends, jammed the church and overflowed the sidewalks and parking lot outside. A priest from the Abraham Lincoln School, which two of the children had attended, was among the clergy presiding.

"Only divine justice can fall with all its weight upon these assassins," said the priest. "We feel deeply affected by this catastrophe and we reject this horrible crime." A string ensemble played "Ave Maria," "Serenade for the Angels," and "Close to Thee."

The funeral procession then moved west for three blocks and took the *autopista del norte* several miles north, past the site where the children had been kidnapped, to the *Jardines del Recuerdo,* the Gardens of Remembrance. With the flags of Colombia and Bogotá flying overhead, mourners lined both sides of the road into the cemetery and threw flowers at the hearse as it eased past. The Alvarez children's tomb was in the most prominent part of the cemetery, Sector B-3, a circle of hedges, flowers, and trees centering on a looming forty-foot statue of Christ in yellow and white stone. The statue's arms were outstretched, its hands beckoning and enfolding. The children were buried at its feet.

"It is preferable that our lips become mute and that from the deepest part of our soul we reject those actions that make our spirit tremble," intoned the presiding priest of the Church of Cristo Rey. "Toward such actions the Church always pursues brotherhood. But if justice really has power, then that justice must make itself present here."

A hubbub of weeping welled up as the priest said, "Zuleika. Yidid. Xoiux. We will not say 'good-bye.' We will say 'until we meet again.'

Because with every hour, every minute, every second that passes, we are getting closer to you. And soon we shall meet again in the House of the Lord."

As the tomb was closing, someone shouted, "These are things that not even heaven forgives."

47

FEARFUL OF BEING DETECTED, the DEA had discontinued its surveillance of Marlene Navarro weeks earlier, and therefore was oblivious to her sudden flight to Canada. Carol Cooper and the other agents believed she was spending the weekend at Gustavo Delgado's cabana on Key Biscayne where she had invited Robert Darias to meet her.

"I was thinking, Carol, do you think it might be a good idea to send someone to see what in the hell is going on there," Darias suggested on Saturday morning, September 18.

"Nah, they're not doing anything but laying on the beach, probably. They're not waiting for you."

"But they might be receiving some other people there."

"They may be," Cooper said, "but there's no plot or anything. They don't know if you're gonna be there or not. It was left up in the air. Marlene's just having a nice relaxing weekend. All I know is that in three weeks, *my* weekends are gonna be nice and *hers* can be ruined. I have every intention of ruining her life for a while."

Darias did not press Cooper to let him go to Key Biscayne. Amelia was vehemently opposed. Rather than ease stress, the security precautions the Dariases had been employing since the threatening calls seemed to exacerbate it. They drove circuitous routes into and out of Coral Springs to make sure they were not being followed. They drove past Laura's school two or three times a day to check for strange people or cars lurking about. Robert wore a baseball cap and sunglasses everywhere he went. And he had fortified their house with extra locks.

"We just got word this afternoon that the three kids were found, and they're all dead," Cooper reported to Darias on Tuesday.

"Oh, my God!" Darias exclaimed.

"Yeah. I guess they found them last night."

"They had been killed recently, or what?"

"The word is they were all shot in the head, and they may have been killed as of April."

"Oh, boy," Darias said, with a sigh.

"So we're looking at that situation now," Cooper continued. "I'm sure she's gonna take off and go down there." Carol was perplexed. "Not because she's fleeing or anything, but just to be with him. The question is how long."

"Of course."

"That could create all sorts of havoc, too. You are a minor problem on her mind right now."

Cooper and Chellino testified again before the grand jury on Thursday, September 23. The jurors were shown videotapes of Lionel Paytubi, Marlene Navarro, Luis Rodriguez, and Nelson Batista laundering drug money at Dean International Investments. Chellino and deputy prosecutor Mark Schnapp presented testimony about Humberto Garcia and his Medellín associates, and the Colombian Kids. The grand jury proceedings were abbreviated because the air-conditioning failed and the rain and heat outside made the court house sweltering.

"My gut feeling is—and I don't know for sure—my gut feeling is that she's in Colombia and Alex is probably back in Canada," Carol told Robert that evening. "Our people in Bogotá are trying to locate her."

"Paul told me that her car wasn't at her house."

"That's correct."

"But did you check Gustavo's house?"

"Yeah, it's not there, either. Every other time, Bob, that she has left, she has either had Gustavo pick her up and take her to the airport and left her car at home, or taken it over to Gustavo's house."

"But this time it isn't there."

"This time God only knows where it is. Alex may still be here running around with it. There's no doubt in my mind that she's in Colombia, in light of what happened with the kids. I think she'll be back either Tuesday or Wednesday. I think she'll stay down for the weekend, but I don't think she'll stay much longer than that. Keep this very, very quiet because Tom doesn't even know about this yet. *This operation will not be terminated unless she is in town.* She has to be here before it goes down."

Robert was relieved. "I thought I had the possibility of ending the thing and not taking her. That is what I have been mad about all these days. Because I was losing her. That's exactly why I was mad. It's my case and I hate to see it just dissolve into nothing."

"They will not take it down without the major player here," Cooper said.

The major player had no intention of being there. After a few days of brooding at the Four Seasons in Toronto, Marlene Navarro had boarded an Air Jamaica flight for Curaçao, via Kingston, with an open ticket on to Bogotá, intentionally avoiding U.S. air carriers and U.S. Customs checkpoints. Alex McIntosh drove her BMW to a relative's house south of Toronto, left the car under a tarpaulin, returned to Toronto, and flew back to Miami, which he still hoped to make his new home.

When Marlene arrived in Curaçao she checked into the Curaçao Hilton and heard for the first time, from Carmenza's business partner in Bogotá, that the Alvarez children's bodies had been discovered. She left immediately for Bogotá, and by the time she had to face Jader Alvarez she had concocted an elaborate explanation for her flight from Miami. She told Jader and others in Bogotá that Robert Darias had called her on the morning of September 16 and told her to go to a pay phone and call him back. "When I called, he told me that *he* was under investigation by federal authorities for laundering drug money and that he didn't want anything to happen to me, so I should leave the United States as soon as possible. I left that evening." Although Jader was concerned about the fate of his U.S. network, the explanation seemed to absolve Marlene of the responsibility that would have befallen her if it had appeared that she had been duped by an American spy. Jader could hardly blame her for having done business with other criminals in Miami in the course of managing his tainted money. And he had no way of knowing that her story was a lie, and entirely implausible.

With Operation Swordfish scheduled to end in two weeks, Darias and the agents turned their attention back to Lionel Paytubi. He was one of their original targets, important in his own right as a deposed officer of a major Miami bank, and the man who had led them to Marlene Navarro and Carlos Jader Alvarez. The DEA furthermore was determined to indict Paytubi before Operation Greenback could.

It was clear that the anonymous phone call to Lester Rogers's office had not deterred Paytubi from proceeding with the pending narcotics transaction he had discussed with Darias.

"Did you talk to your friends, the lawyers?" Darias asked, referring to Lester Rogers and Arthur Karlick.

"No, and I'm not telling them anything about our other things," Paytubi replied, referring to the Quaalude deal. "They might be even more scared."

"That's good," Darias replied. "I don't want anybody in this town to know what I am doing. Things are too hot."

They made plans to meet soon with Paytubi's contact for the Quaaludes.

If Operation Swordfish hadn't already been irreparably compromised, the security of the operation suffered another blow from a leak of unknown origin to the *Miami Herald.* On Saturday morning, September 25, the *Herald* appeared with a banner page-one headline:

"U.S. Planning over 200 Miami Drug Busts."

The article listed four secret DEA investigations by name, including Operation Swordfish, which it characterized as a "massive undercover investigation into cocaine smuggling."

"Arrests are expected to total more than 100 (in the Swordfish cases), but details are closely held secrets," the article said. "Rather than go-fers and employees, the bulk of those that will be arrested in all of these cases will be high-level businessmen, lawyers that are directing this on both sides of the Caribbean, doctors, and bank officials."

Sam Billbrough of the DEA was quoted as saying: "You're going to see us go: Bam! Bam! Bam!" Incredibly, Billbrough had spoken to the *Herald* in the belief that the article would be held until after the indictments and arrests in the various operations. From that day forward, the embarrassed administrator was known as "Bam Bam" Sam.

Even though it mentioned the name "Operation Swordfish," a coded designation which had never been used outside the DEA, the article fortunately gave few details of the operation and did not name the undercover businesses, Dean International and International Investments. Nor did it disclose the location of the business, or give the names of any agents or targets. Thus, it afforded deniability to Swordfish operatives in the event of inquiries by their targets. Still, the article devastated the Swordfish agents.

"There's a major leak somewhere," Cooper told Darias that morning. "I'd wager a safe bet that if we went down to the airport today we could wave good-bye to everyone. They very well may shut down the business."

"They caught us way off guard," she continued. "My gut feeling is that [the targets are] probably gone. Or they're packing their bags now and getting ready to go. The general gut feeling is going to be that that article very seriously damaged this whole operation. We're just going to have to play it by ear and see what happens."

"Goddammit," Darias bristled, "a year and a half we have been trying to get these people and then for some stupid reason they are able to fly away. Because I had her right in my pocket to the last minute."

They agreed that Robert would call Lionel Paytubi, Humberto Garcia, and Manuel Sanchez to assure them that the enterprise called Operation Swordfish which they might have read about in the *Miami Herald* had nothing to do with Dean International or International Investments.

In conversations over the next few days, Darias was surprised, relieved, and a bit bemused to find that none of the three was uneasy.

The DEA decided to make one more pass at the enigmatic Juvenal Betancur, who had not yet firmly implicated himself in the crimes of the Jader Alvarez syndicate. Betancur called Robert Darias on Monday, September 27, and asked to meet. He seemed to have missed the *Herald* article, and it appeared that any uneasiness he might have felt over Marlene Navarro's report of the anonymous call to Lester Rogers had ebbed.

Two teams of undercover DEA agents observed as Darias and Betancur met for breakfast at a small cafeteria near the Sharon Hotel on Miami Beach.

Examining and smelling various plates of food, the ever-fragrant Juvenal piled his tray with eggs, sausage, bread, fruit, coffee, and juice, and then managed to maneuver Darias into picking up both checks.

"Have you talked to Marlene?" Darias asked.

"I saw her," he said. "I respect that girl a lot. She went to Bogotá to be with Jader in his hour of need and supported him. The whole country was living that tragedy and was moved by that tragedy."

"How many people were involved in the kidnapping?" Darias asked.

"Oh, it was a group, a subversive group."

"I hope Jader didn't pay."

"No, he never paid. But he was ready to pay. I was the one who took Jader to the officials of the government who helped him find the children."

Darias changed the subject and spoke quietly. "I don't know whether Marlene has ever adequately explained to you what my business is. I launder millions of dollars for people like Jader who are sending drugs here. That's where I make all my money and that's where Marlene also makes her money. I guess you know that?"

"Yes, I know that."

"Well, that's my main business. I asked Marlene if you had any friends who might need laundering services."

"Things in Colombia are very slow economically," Betancur said.

"But that doesn't affect my business," Darias said. "My business is with the drug money here in the U.S. and that has nothing to do with the economic situation in Colombia. Very little of that money goes back to Colombia. That money stays here, in Nassau, in Switzerland, and other places."

"The funeral was very sad," Betancur said. "Marlene was very sad. She is very close to Jader. I saw her at the funeral. It was a very, very sad funeral."

It was an odd conversation. Aside from confirming that he knew that Navarro and Darias earned money from laundering drug cash, Betancur parried each overture by Darias with a deflection on to another subject.

The brother of the president of Colombia seemed to have no compelling interest in involving himself in the narcotics business with Robert Darias and Marlene Navarro. It was unclear to Darias and the agents why he had wanted to meet.

The Department of Justice ordered the DEA and the Miami U.S. Attorney's Office to postpone the indictments ending Operation Swordfish for another week—until Friday, October 15—so they would coincide with an announcement from the White House of a major U.S. initiative against the Latin drug mafia. Washington deemed the pairing of the two events sufficiently compelling public theater to merit going ahead whether or not Marlene Navarro had returned to the United States.

48

THE LOGBOOKS at F-2 headquarters in Bogotá indicated that Bernardo Acosta had been returned to custody there after guiding the GOES commandos to the children's grave. In fact, Acosta had been secretly turned back over to Carlos Jader Alvarez, who again imprisoned him in the house on Carrera 14. Also being held in the house were Edgar Helmut Garcia, Guillermo Prado, and several other National University students and others whom Alvarez believed had been involved in the kidnappings.

Exhausted by the year-long ordeal of searching for his children, Alvarez was more sad than angry, and felt relief in the days after the bodies were recovered. At least he had a sense of closure. In contrast to the previous week, he treated his prisoners well, allowing them rest and nourishment. He even brought in a doctor to minister to Bernardo Acosta's torture wounds.

But Alvarez had conceived a unique fate for his prisoners—actually two fates, one for Bernardo Acosta, the *campesino* who had softened and led the commandos to the children, and another for the National University students, the young intellectuals who had reverted to sullen silence.

On Thursday, October 7—the day after the first anniversary of the kidnapping—Alvarez summoned the same team of GOES commandos who had recovered the children's bodies. Late that night, two carloads of commandos took Bernardo Acosta to a deserted stretch of the *Autopista Medellín,* a two-lane highway on the western outskirts of Bogotá, a few miles beyond the private airport where Alvarez had rented his fleet of helicopters. Earlier that evening the commandos had stolen a blue Renault off the streets for the occasion. They put Acosta in the driver's seat of the Renault and fastened the seatbelt. On the back seat, they placed a wig, a ski mask, a cap, a wallet containing personal papers, and a gray-and-white briefcase bearing the symbol of the International Amateur Basketball Federation and the insignia "Basketball '82." Inside the briefcase they put a loaded .38 revolver and six rounds of ammunition. In the front seat they placed a Walther 7.65, which they had just fired several times. The commandos then blindfolded Bernardo Acosta. Without warning, they stepped back and opened fire on Acosta from both sides and the front of the Renault with their German MP-5 semiautomatics. He died quickly of more than a dozen bullet wounds. The commandos then removed the blindfold and rigged the scene to appear as if Acosta had died in a shoot-out which he had started. Then they called the police.

The rigged shoot-out became part of the official version of Bernardo Acosta's demise, the version the Bogotá press carried the next day: He had escaped from the custody of the F-2; he had been spotted in west Bogotá in a blue Renault; F-2 agents had run him to ground on an exit from the Medellín Highway and shot him only after he had opened fire.

Carlos Jader Alvarez had not intended that Bernardo Acosta suffer unduly at the end. The guerrilla had suffered a great deal already. And in certain quarters of heavily Roman Catholic Colombia, sudden execution of people like Bernardo Acosta was the ultimate torture because it gave them no time to repent their sins and thus doomed them for eternity to the worst corner of hell.

Jader Alvarez, however, had something extra in store for the National University students—for Edgar Helmut Garcia, "El Caballo," "the Horse," who the police concluded had rented the house in Talavera where the children were taken on the morning of the kidnapping, and then pretended to be the father of the children in the mountains; for Guilleado, "El Flaco," "the skinny one," who allegedly had disguised himself as a traffic policeman and stopped the Alvarez station wagon on the morning of the kidnapping, and who later helped hold the children prisoner in the mountains for several months; and for the other students, for whom Alvarez had developed the deepest loathing.

Having quietly informed a high police official of his intentions, Alvarez flew the students to his ranch in the llanos, the jungled plains east of Bogotá beyond the eastern range of the Andes. At the ranch, Alvarez and his men took the students deep into the jungle. This was sea-level, tropical jungle—the real thing, quite different from the high jungle in the Andes which had little wildlife. Alvarez's men stripped the students naked, tied them securely to trees, and left them—not just alive, but healthy, rested, well-fed, and fully conscious—for the wild animals to discover and devour.

A few days later, Alvarez's men returned and took color photographs of the remains of the students—legs, feet, a head—after pumas, panthers, snakes, and insects had finished with them.

Though their arrests now seemed problematic, Carlos Jader Alvarez and Marlene Navarro remained the most important targets of Operation Swordfish. In prosecuting them, Michael Pasano and his colleagues on the staff of the U.S. Attorney in Miami intended to use a major new weapon—the "continuing criminal enterprise" statute, or CCE, which had been enacted in 1970 along with the Bank Secrecy Act and the Racketeer Influenced and Corrupt Organization Act (RICO), but whose novelty and complexity had limited widespread use until the early 1980s.

The CCE law defined its target as someone who not only committed a federal narcotics felony but did so as part of a continuing series of violations; who not only participated in the crime but supervised five or more other people; and who derived not just modest proceeds from the crime but "substantial income or resources." Those convicted under the CCE law could receive up to life in prison, be fined up to $100,000, and have their assets seized and forfeited.

Because of the complexity of the law and the severity of the penalties, federal prosecutors were required to get the approval of the Department of Justice before obtaining indictments from grand juries. Thus on Friday, October 8, the U.S. Attorney in Miami, Stanley Marcus, and Swordfish prosecutor Michael Pasano forwarded, by special courier, a fourteen-page single-spaced "prosecution memorandum" to Edward S. G. Dennis, Jr., chief of the narcotics section of the Justice Department's criminal division in Washington. The classified memorandum was drafted as a candid, lawyer-to-lawyer, strictly internal assessment of the strengths and weaknesses of the Swordfish cases.

The memorandum detailed the crucial role of Robert Darias in Operation Swordfish and, for the first time outside of extremely limited circles within the DEA, set forth his name in writing. The document also highlighted the criticality of Darias's role with a candor that was unusual for a bureaucracy acutely sensitive about its use of spies.

"Robert Darias, a paid special employee of the DEA, is the central witness in the case. He was present at virtually every key meeting and involved in every transaction. He will testify about these transactions and about his conversations with Navarro and others. . . . The DEA special agents involved in this case performed basically back-up functions."

Under a formatted heading "possible weaknesses or problems," the memorandum said, "Darias will be subject to bias impeachment [by defense lawyers during cross-examination] by virtue of his status as a paid special employee. He also has a tax conviction which can be used against him. In addition, given the flow of huge sums of money through Darias, the defense will likely accuse Darias of some kind of misapplication of funds."

As to the status of Navarro and Jader Alvarez, the memorandum reported that "the defendants are both presently in Colombia, although Marlene Navarro is expected to return shortly. Extradition could be difficult in light of the fact that Carlos Jader is well connected politically in that country."

Edward Dennis, who received the memorandum in Washington late that Friday, did not take long to give his approval to the continuing criminal enterprise prosecution. He was very familiar with Operation Swordfish, having refereed several disputes between it and Operation Greenback.

At the crowded bar of the Chez Vendome restaurant in the David Williams Hotel in Coral Gables, the spy—the government's "central witness"—was still on the job, his hidden microrecorder rolling. Darias greeted Lionel Paytubi and Paytubi's source for the half-million Quaaludes, Adolfo San Pelayo.

"If not for the shirt we would have looked like twins," Darias said as he was introduced to San Pelayo. They both wore navy blazers and light slacks.

"We are in the same orchestra," San Pelayo said.

"And what do you want to drink?" Darias asked.

"A whiskey sour—I am a homosexual drinker," the dapper Cuban replied.

After the bartender had filled the order, San Pelayo said, "Roberto, we are ready. You bring the van; they will come in a car, and then the person who drives the van delivers the keys to them. You say the password and deliver the keys, and two hours later you pick up the van in the same place. Whatever password you determine."

"Galiano and San Rafael," Darias said with a shrug.

"Galiano and San Rafael," San Pelayo repeated. Galiano and San Rafael were intersecting arterial streets in Old Havana, as familiar to Cubans as Hollywood and Vine were to Americans.

"He can give you references on me," Darias said, referring to Paytubi. "I don't like to meet anybody."

"Nobody likes that."

"He has his reasons," Paytubi said, referring to San Pelayo.

"I was fourteen years in the CIA," San Pelayo confided. "I know all the tricks that you can know. I have very good contacts."

San Pelayo excused himself to go to the men's room.

"I didn't like what he said about he used to be CIA," Darias remarked. "I thought his name rang a bell."

When San Pelayo rejoined them, Darias said, "I will rent the van, a vehicle that has no problems and if it gets caught nobody knows."

"It has been a pleasure," San Pelayo said. "I have gained a friend."

The deal would be consummated on the morning of Friday, October 15.

The grand jury met an extra day that week to accommodate the large number of indictments leading to the arrests on Friday. The indictments would be sealed by the court until after the arrests.

At the Phoenix Building, plans were laid for the sweep of arrests across Miami. It was the policy of the DEA and FBI to use at least three agents in the arrest of each target in case the individual was armed or became violent. Since about three dozen arrests were planned, requiring well over a hundred agents, every DEA agent in Miami would be deployed, not just those who worked on Operation Swordfish. And agents from other federal bodies would be assigned to help, including thirty-five FBI agents.

ALL SUBJECTS ARE TO BE CONSIDERED ARMED AND DANGEROUS AND ARE NOT BE BE GIVEN ANY OPPORTUNITY TO COMMUNICATE WITH OTHERS, an instruction bulletin said.

Carol Cooper and Robert Darias went over a long list of details— possible variations, potential glitches—covering the planned arrest of Lionel Paytubi and his Quaalude cohorts.

"Paytubi feels his Greenback case was dropped," Darias said.

"Yeah, well, fine, let him keep thinking that. He'll find out Friday."

"Are we going to take people like Manny Sanchez also on Friday?"

"Everything goes on Friday," Carol said. "Marlene's case is in very good shape. I just need *her.* That's my only problem."

"President Expands Drug War," proclaimed the headline on the front page of the *Miami Herald* on the morning of Thursday, October 14. "President Gives Plan to Combat Drug Networks," said the *New York Times* page-one headline. Newspapers across the country featured the story, which detailed a $150 million White House plan to expand the government's fight against "high-level organized criminals who deal in drugs" in the nation's major cities.

The effort would be patterned after the government's "concentrated drive" in South Florida "where indictments of dozens of alleged drug traffickers are expected later this month," the *Herald* article reported.

The story did not say that the Florida indictments had been delayed to coincide with President Ronald Reagan's unveiling of the new program.

49

THE ATTORNEY GENERAL of the United States, William French
Smith, spoke with a group of reporters over breakfast in Washington very early Friday morning, October 15. Smith had been briefed on
the climax of Operation Swordfish and proudly recounted how a team
of DEA agents had succeeded in infiltrating the high command of one
of the largest mafia syndicates in South America. The operation,
Smith said, was a dramatic symbol of the Reagan administration's
new effort against the drug mafia which had been publicized the
previous day.

So far as Smith knew, the Swordfish arrests had already occurred.
He had been dangerously misinformed.

In Miami the day dawned gray and muggy. Low clouds were spitting
intermittent rain as Robert Darias, in the DEA's leased gray Cadillac,
picked up Lionel Paytubi at the rear of the Westland Mall at eight
o'clock sharp. They headed down the Palmetto Expressway through
the rush-hour traffic to the Midway Mall, the largest shopping center
in the orbit of the Miami International Airport. A team of undercover
DEA agents followed.

Paytubi was jovial—confident that he was about to make more
money than he had seen since being fired from the Great American
Bank after it was raided by Operation Greenback.

Darias made his way to an expanse of the mall parking lot between
Jefferson's department store and a Kelly tire center. Most of the stores
in the mall wouldn't open for more than an hour, and the parking lot
was nearly deserted. Darias spotted Paul Sennett in a white Econoline
van the DEA had rented for the occasion. Inviting Sennett to join
them in the Cadillac, Darias introduced him to Paytubi as "my buyer,
Paul from New York." As they were waiting, Paytubi noticed a blue
van across the parking lot. "Look at the antennas on that thing," he
said. "That looks like one of those vans the police use."

"Yeah, Lionel, and that car over there is a submarine," Darias said
with a laugh.

Darias's pager sounded, and Adolfo San Pelayo's voice could be heard saying his people were running a little late. After a few minutes, Paytubi, Sennett, and Darias were approached by a man who identified himself as José Martinez and gave the prearranged code words, "Galiano and San Rafael." Sennett gave Martinez the keys to the Econoline and he drove it away. Several DEA agents followed Martinez south on the Palmetto. Darias, Paytubi, and Sennett headed back north and went to breakfast at Denny's on 36th Street. Half an hour later Paytubi called Adolfo San Pelayo, who told him that the van was on its way back to the Midway Mall.

As Darias, Sennett, and Paytubi again drove down the Palmetto, they were startled by a newscast on the car radio.

"In Washington this morning," the reporter said, "Attorney General William French Smith announced that a major undercover drug investigation in Miami has ended with the indictment and arrest of more than fifty alleged narcotics smugglers and money launderers. Known as Operation Swordfish, the investigation identified a number of bankers, lawyers, and other professionals who allegedly conspired to hide millions of dollars of drug dealers' cash."

It was obvious to Sennett and Darias that the Department of Justice had broken the story prematurely, thinking the Swordfish arrests had already been made.

Lionel Paytubi winced. "That scares me," he said. "That sounds big. Those poor suckers."

"Don't worry, Lionel, we're in good shape," Darias said. "That might be the thing that was in the newspaper a couple of weeks ago."

The report gave no names or other details. Paytubi was mollified.

José Martinez, who was waiting in the Econoline at the Midway Mall, summoned Sennett to the back of the van to inspect the cartons of Quaaludes. Sennett opened one of the cartons, pulled out a plastic container, and examined a handful of the white pills, each bearing the insignia Lemon 714. Satisfied that they were genuine, Sennett stepped back and removed his cap, which was the silent arrest signal to the DEA agents deployed around the area, several of them in the blue van with the antennas that Paytubi had noticed when they first arrived at the mall. His adrenaline pumping, Sennett turned toward Paytubi, drew his concealed Walther PPK, produced a badge, and said, "Mr. Paytubi, I am a DEA agent and you are under arrest." Paytubi started to bolt, but Darias shouted, "Don't move, Lionel, they'll shoot us."

Upon the command of other DEA agents who had appeared as if from nowhere, Darias put his hands on the side of the van. Paytubi, now submissive, followed suit. The agents also arrested José Martinez, who was found to be carrying a loaded .25 caliber Beretta automatic pistol. The prisoners, in handcuffs, were driven in separate cars up the Palmetto to the Phoenix Building for processing. Except for Robert Darias, who was discreetly set free.

Robert Darias's work as a spy had ended. The first drug arrests Darias had fostered for the DEA had occurred twenty-one months earlier, in January 1981, in this same parking lot, just a few dozen yards from where he was standing now, alone, on this somber October morning. That case, too, had involved the quiet tension of a Quaalude purchase shattered by the brandished guns of a multiple arrest.

Feeling numb and a bit dazed, Robert got in his car and headed home to Coral Springs. As his adrenaline rush receded, exhaustion replaced it, and then frustration at having ended his days as a DEA spy with the arrest of Lionel Paytubi. Paytubi, who had loomed so large upon his arrival at Dean International, had ebbed in importance as Operation Swordfish had grown. Long since deposed as the principal banker to Isaac Kattan, Paytubi had emerged as nothing more than a greedy go-between for a group of pill smugglers. Arresting him seemed anticlimactic.

The truly important people—the mafia kingpins to whom Paytubi had led Robert Darias, and in whom Robert had invested over a year of exacting, dangerous work—would not be arrested today. Marlene Navarro and Carlos Jader Alvarez apparently were safe in Bogotá, out of reach of the U.S. Government.

Robert felt deflated, unfulfilled, unfinished.

The Phoenix Building bristled with armament, tension, and anticipation as Paytubi and his confederates were brought in, fingerprinted, and photographed. The Paytubi arrest was the first of the day, a signal for more than a hundred armed DEA and FBI agents to fan out across Miami, in small, carefully briefed teams, to arrest as many of the other targets of Operation Swordfish as could be found.

Word of Attorney General Smith's premature disclosure of the operation early that morning had flashed through the building, making the impatient agents even edgier than usual. It would be one of the largest arrest sweeps ever in Miami. The grand jury over the previous two days had indicted a total of seventy-seven people for various crimes growing out of Operation Swordfish. Some sixteen separate indictments had been fashioned to cover the activities of distinct groups of defendants, including targets as far away as Bogotá, Los Angeles, and Madrid.

Carlos Jader Alvarez, Marlene Navarro, and eighteen of their associates were charged in the bulkiest of the indictments. Also named for participating in the Alvarez syndicate's smuggling and money-laundering activities were Luis Rodriguez, Carlos Alvarado (the real name of Tocayo the chauffeur), Oscar Garcia, Teo Terselich, Nelson Batista, and Ricardo and Said Pavon; the lawyers S. David Jaffe, Lester Rogers, and Arthur Karlick; Navarro's cousin Carmenza Valenzuela and Valenzuela's business partner; and Pepe Cabrera's money mover Bertha, whose full name was Bertha Yolanda Paez.

Lionel Paytubi was charged in two indictments, one with his co-horts in the Quaalude deal, the other with the banker Manuel Sanchez for criminal conspiracy dating back to their first contacts with Dean International Investments the previous year. (Operation Greenback had yet to move against Paytubi.)

Humberto Garcia was indicted along with his accountant and several Colombians from Medellín, including Antonio Uribe.

Felipe Calderon's former banking associate in Colombia, Victor Covo, was named in three indictments, together with a host of Covo's accomplices.

By late in the day nearly three dozen people had been arrested, just under half of those charged. The DEA considered it miraculous that none of those arrested seemed to have heard of Attorney General Smith's public breach of security that morning.

As the arrests were proceeding, agents were serving seizure notices on banks and real estate companies. Carlos Jader Alvarez's and Juvenal Betancur's bank accounts were seized, as well as the real estate that Jader Alvarez had received in settlement of a drug debt. Bertha Paez's Cadillac El Dorado was confiscated, as was Luis Rodriguez's BMW. The DEA searched and seized the laboratory where Lionel Paytubi's Quaaludes were being manufactured.

Marlene Navarro's house could not be taken for the time being because it was not registered in her name but in that of the lawyer Harvey Rogers, Lester's cousin, who had not been named in the Swordfish indictment. DEA agents stopped Harvey Rogers as he was leaving Navarro's house that afternoon with a number of items. He declined to show them what he had taken.

Operation Swordfish was a major story on the national television network newscasts that evening and commanded banner page-one headlines in Miami and elsewhere. Although Juvenal Betancur had not been indicted, the DEA made sure that his involvement with Jader Alvarez and Marlene Navarro was made known to the press.

At his office in Coconut Grove, defense lawyer Raymond Takiff again removed from his safe the list of names that bail bondsman

Arthur Balletti had given him three and a half months earlier—the names of people "under heavy federal scrutiny in Miami Lakes." It was now clear to Takiff that most of the people on the list had been targets of Operation Swordfish.

Takiff resolved to seek legal advice on any criminal culpability he might face from having accepted the list and not reported it to federal authorities.

The agents who had run Swordfish—Cooper, Chellino, Sennett, Clifford, and the others—were numb and exhausted that evening. Their initial elation at the exceptionally large number of arrests ebbed as they took broader account: they had not achieved what had become the primary objective of the operation—arresting Carlos Jader Alvarez, Marlene Navarro, and the other principal operatives of the Jader Alvarez syndicate.

Nor had the DEA agents found the huge load of cocaine—$100 million worth wholesale, $1 billion retail—which they believed the syndicate had shipped to Miami in recent weeks. The money and other assets they had seized constituted only a tiny fraction of the huge holdings of the drug organizations under investigation.

Judged by the original objectives that Tom Clifford had established in planning Operation Swordfish—dismantling major mafia groups, arresting their leaders, and seizing their money—the weary agents had to face the dismaying fact that after the most difficult, most exacting, most dangerous year of their lives, they had failed.

What if Operation Greenback had not forced the premature closing of Operation Swordfish? What if there had been no conflict between Chellino and Clifford, splitting the operation into warring factions? What if the anonymous calls and bungled surveillances had not frightened Marlene Navarro into fleeing? Could Darias and the agents, with more time and better security, have lured Carlos Jader Alvarez to Panama or Curaçao, arrested him and brought him to Miami? What about the other godfathers, Pepe Cabrera and the murderer Juan Mata Ballesteros, whom Operation Swordfish had seemed close to snaring?

There was little time for reflection that Friday evening. The sudden influx of three dozen prisoners into the federal criminal justice apparatus during the day produced chaos at the court house downtown. No one was prepared for bond hearings, not the government, the defendants, or the court. In a foul mood, a U.S. magistrate gaveled the hearing to order at 6:30 P.M. in an atmosphere of frantic hubbub in the packed courtroom. Defense lawyers hurriedly consulted their sullen clients. Prosecutors debriefed exhausted DEA agents. For the next eight hours—until 2:30 A.M.—the magistrate conducted the hearings "in a thoroughly abusive tone and arbitrary manner toward the Government," as a federal prosecutor would later state in a memorandum to the United States Attorney.

The magistrate set bonds drastically lower than the government requested. Many of the defendants made bail easily and over the next several days fled to Colombia.

The exodus underscored the DEA agents' sense of futility and loss.

part six

PURSUIT

These are the days when birds come back,
A very few, a bird or two,
To take a parting look.

—Emily Dickinson

50

ARLENE NAVARRO listened to the news of her indictment on television and radio in Bogotá. Operation Swordfish was front-page news in Colombia not only because its primary target, Carlos Jader Alvarez, was a notorious *padrino* of the international drug mafia, but because his children's horrible deaths at the hands of kidnappers were still fresh in the minds of the press and public.

Since arriving in Bogotá in late September, Marlene had been staying at Carmenza's apartment in El Chico Alto. But when the Swordfish indictments were made known, with Carmenza implicated along with the others, her husband blamed Marlene and evicted her from their home. She moved in with a succession of other friends.

Neither she, Jader Alvarez, nor the others were in much danger of arrest in Bogotá. Although President Belisario Betancur announced that his government would arrest and extradite fugitives from the Swordfish indictments, the statement was considered a public relations gesture for consumption in the United States, not a genuine threat to Colombians. Betancur was continuing to pursue a foreign policy more independent of the U.S. than that of his predecessors, and extradition was considered a symbol of acquiescence to the *yanquis,* whatever the merits of specific cases.

Still, Navarro stayed out of sight, unable to rule out retribution by Jader Alvarez and his mafia colleagues.

Alex McIntosh, who had moved back to Toronto, spent a quiet Christmas and New Year's with Marlene in Bogotá, a visit that ended abruptly when they received word that Pepe Cabrera was looking to kill both Marlene and Alex because Cabrera held Marlene responsible for the prosecution of his Miami lawyer, David Jaffe.

McIntosh hurried back to the U.S., and Marlene stayed indoors. She dyed her hair black and set about obtaining false identity papers in hopes of fleeing the country.

Early one morning, a friend named Rafael was driving Navarro to a health club in north Bogotá. When they were a block from the club, two cars forced them off the road, and several men with machine guns appeared, claiming to be police officers.

"You are Marlene Navarro," one of them said.

"No, I'm not," she said.

"No, she's not," Rafael said.

The men took Rafael's gun and demanded that Marlene go with them. She refused. They began kicking Rafael. Marlene then agreed to go, and the men forced both her and Rafael into one of the cars.

The men—it now seemed evident they were kidnappers—left Rafael in a deserted spot a few miles outside of Bogotá with the warning that they had been following his family, and would kill his children if he reported the episode to the police.

They headed northeast from Bogotá along the same road that the M-19 guerrillas had taken when they moved the Alvarez children from Bogotá to Gachalá. This group, however, stopped at a small house near the community of Sopo in the heart of dairy country about thirty miles from Bogotá. Though Navarro was blindfolded and gagged, she was aware of being put in a small room with a dirt floor and given a blanket. She was offered food but declined because the kidnappers wouldn't remove her blindfold so she could see what she was eating.

She did not sleep much that night, and heard birds and cattle as dawn approached. The kidnappers, joined now by others, loaded Marlene into the back of a covered pickup truck and covered her with potato sacks, leaves, and dirt. They drove for what seemed about three hours. Then, deep in the mountains, they stopped, removed her from the truck, outfitted her with a pair of rubber boots, and forced her— still blindfolded—to strike out with them on a trail through the jungle. The boots were too large and she soon developed painful, bleeding blisters.

After a day of arduous hiking through the forested mountains across several streams, the party spent the second night in the forest. Marlene was placed in a tent. She was leery of snakes and was conscious of a waterfall nearby.

On the third day the kidnappers forced Marlene to write a ransom note to her friend, Rafael. They demanded $5 million for her return. A protracted period of negotiation ensued. In Bogotá, Rafael approached Carlos Jader Alvarez, who refused to put up any money.

"It's not that I don't want her alive," he said, "but they're going to do the same thing they did with the kids—kill her anyway."

As the negotiations dragged, Marlene's treatment at the hands of her abductors grew more brutal. Desperately hungry and thirsty, and still blindfolded, she begged for something to eat or drink. The kidnappers placed before her what the odor revealed to be urine and feces.

The men laughed. "Do you miss your champagne and oysters?" they asked.

They raped her several times.

In Miami, the prosecution of the few targets of Operation Swordfish who had not been able to flee to Colombia had done little to assuage the DEA agents' feelings of failure.

Having been indicted twice by Swordfish, Lionel Paytubi finally was indicted by Operation Greenback. He pleaded not guilty to all allegations and stood trial first on one of the Swordfish cases. He was convicted and sentenced to eight years in prison.

Banker Manuel Sanchez was convicted on one count, acquitted on another, and received four years.

Humberto Garcia pleaded guilty, as did Victor Covo, who had been Felipe Calderon's banking colleague in Colombia, and David Jaffe, the Miami lawyer who had worked for Pepe Cabrera. Garcia got only six months, Covo received four years, and Jaffe was placed on probation and disbarred.

The prosecutors failed to convict a minor Swordfish target, a Miami physician with alleged connections to the drug world whom Paytubi had introduced to Dean International as a prospective money-laundering client. The case against the doctor was weak, and the jury acquitted him.

Although the agents of Operation Swordfish had gone on to other assignments within the DEA, they still were haunted by the breach of security which had enabled Marlene Navarro to flee the United States before she could be arrested. Long after the operation ended they had not a single clue to who was behind the leak. But then two unexpected revelations in 1983 offered hope for a solution to the mystery.

In Los Angeles, Barbara Mouzin had pleaded not guilty to the drug and money-laundering charges brought against her in the Grandma Mafia case. She was convicted by a jury after a one-month trial and sentenced to twenty-five years in prison. Her strategy of maintaining innocence having failed, she found herself with only one remaining chance for winning a reduced sentence—by finally telling the government something it did not already know about her last few months as a cocaine dealer and money mover. It was in that setting that Mouzin confided to federal authorities that she had bribed her former lover, Brooks Muse III, to obtain classified information from a corrupt source within the DEA—information that had enabled her to flee to Mexico before she could be arrested. Mouzin had dangled the same story in front of the prosecutor before her trial without result, but now she had nothing more to lose.

The DEA and the Department of Justice immediately began investigations of Brooks Muse III for having compromised the Mouzin investigation. Those inquiries soon led to Special Agent Steve Gibbs and raised the possibility that Operation Swordfish had been compromised as well.

Another unexpected clue to the Swordfish breach emerged in the person of Miami defense lawyer Raymond Takiff, who had been given a list of what turned out to be the Swordfish and Grandma Mafia targets by bail bondsman Artie Balletti while both undercover operations were still secret. Takiff had always been concerned about his possible culpability for failing to report what was an obvious breach of government security. He had kept the list in his safe for several months. Then Takiff was retained by money courier Carlos Alvarado, the man known as Tocayo, to defend him against the Swordfish indictment. Alvarado was to go to trial with Marlene Navarro's lawyer, Lester Rogers.

Takiff suspected that the security breach would become an issue at the trial. The government would attempt to show that Lester Rogers, as the recipient of an anonymous telephone call on September 9, 1982, had acted in subsequent days to preserve the criminal conspiracy of which he was accused of being a part. Rogers would try to show that his actions after the call hadn't constituted criminal conduct. The clash likely would lead to an airing of possible explanations for the call and other breaches of secrecy.

Takiff decided he had to make at least a limited disclosure of his role in the matter. He sealed the Balletti list in an envelope and turned it over to federal prosecutor Michael Pasano. Takiff declined to say who had given him the list or describe the circumstances. He said only that he had kept the list locked in a safe and had not disclosed its contents to anyone.

When their names were mentioned during the Rogers-Alvarado trial, Brooks Muse III and Steve Gibbs made known through their lawyers that they denied any role in the Swordfish leak, and the trial did not produce evidence to implicate them.

The jury found Lester Rogers not guilty beyond a reasonable doubt of three counts of drug trafficking and could not agree on a fourth count of conspiracy. A mistrial was declared on that count and the frustrated prosecutors declared they would retry Rogers. Rogers's cousin, the lawyer Harvey Rogers, who represented the Jader aide Jaime Murcia and later had held Marlene Navarro's house in his name, made known that he would invoke the Fifth Amendment and refuse to testify if called as a witness against Lester. The charges against Lester Rogers's office-mate, Arthur Karlick, were dismissed for lack of evidence.

Tocayo the chauffeur was convicted of one count of conspiracy but acquitted on two others. He was sentenced to four years in prison.

The government's checkered record through the initial trials strained its relationship with Robert Darias, who had been the star witness. There was a subtle tendency to blame Darias for the uneven results.

Although Darias testified effectively on issues of the defendants' culpability, the prosecutors prepared Robert poorly for the defense lawyers' inevitable attacks on his own character, a tactic that courts permit when a witness's truthfulness is at issue. The lawyers, who included some of Miami's most renowned and expensive criminal defense specialists, sought to portray Darias in cross-examination as a habitual liar—a man who had been prosecuted by the IRS for lying on an income tax return, a man who had been prosecuted by the State of Florida for misrepresenting the terms of a real estate deal, and therefore a man whose testimony about the targets of Operation Swordfish could not be trusted.

Instead of making sure to keep his answers on the tax and fraud matters short and nonconfrontational, the prosecutors permitted Darias, a combative man by nature, to engage in debate with the defense attorneys about extenuating circumstances in the two matters, which had been present, to be sure, but which tended to prolong and confuse discussion of those issues, and keep attention focused on Darias, when it should have been focused on the defendants, who were on trial for their own crimes, not his.

It was impossible to gauge the effect of such *ad hominem* attacks on the juries' view of Darias's credibility. Clearly they believed the crux of his testimony, as well as that of other witnesses: they convicted Lionel Paytubi, Manuel Sanchez, and Tocayo the chauffeur. But when the government falls short of a unanimous verdict resulting in a mistrial, as occurred with Lester Rogers, it always looks for someone to blame.

After the failure to convict Lester Rogers (the remaining charge against him was eventually dismissed), the DEA broke a promise that it would maintain Robert Darias's financial security for the duration of the trials. The government in fact engaged in a series of cynical financial maneuvers that left Robert and Amelia Darias destitute and bitter.

First, the DEA summarily halved Robert's monthly pay in the apparent belief that testifying was less important than spying.

Second, Carol Cooper chose to withhold the bonus which Darias was due at the end of Operation Swordfish—$100,000—until after the trials, on the questionable theory that the bonus would not "look good" if juries learned of it during the trials. Cooper seemed oddly embarrassed to acknowledge to the juries that spies work for money just like DEA agents, lawyers, and everybody else, and, like other professionals, are frequently rewarded with bonuses for exceptional achievement. The U.S. Government routinely pays large bonuses to its effective spies, and over the years had paid other spies far more for doing far less than Darias had. Tom Clifford had paid Felipe Calderón *his* bonus promptly, and it had not detracted from the juries' view of Calderón's testimony. Still, Carol Cooper withheld Darias's bonus unilaterally, without consulting Robert or Clifford, even after Clifford had authorized her to pay it.

The third ill-advised government maneuver was that after discouraging Robert Darias from filing income tax returns for security reasons during Operation Swordfish, the DEA hurriedly insisted that he contact the IRS and file returns midway through the trials—an empty gesture since he had little money to pay toward his back taxes. Carol Cooper, however, felt it would "look bad" if the defense could show that Darias had not filed returns. The issue had no discernible effect on the juries' view of Darias. His sudden filing of returns, however, served to call the IRS's attention to Darias and his large back-tax bill, and prompted the tax agency to place a lien on his DEA salary, forcing the agency to cut off his pay entirely for the time being.

Robert and Amelia had to give up their rented home and move in with relatives in Miami, where they were in much more danger. Robert could not look for work to support his family because of continued death threats emanating from both Miami and Bogotá. Miami Cubans in touch with the drug mafia passed word to Darias's father and brother that Robert was in danger. An IRS agent feared he would be in danger if he met with Darias.

As devastating as the DEA's financial maneuvers were, they were only one source of Robert Darias's estrangement from his former DEA colleagues. The DEA made itself a party to a ludicrous challenge to Darias's integrity in the midst of the trials—not the generalized pro forma challenges from the defense lawyers, which the DEA was also mishandling, but a specific allegation from Lionel Paytubi that Robert Darias had stolen money during Operation Swordfish.

Having been convicted and sentenced to eight years in federal prison, Lionel Paytubi also faced a host of charges in two other indictments stemming from Operation Swordfish and Operation Greenback. Confronted by two more lengthy trials, huge legal fees, and much additional prison time, Paytubi made a deal with the government under which he agreed to plead guilty to the main charge in each of the two remaining cases, and testify against other defendants. Prosecutor Michael Pasano felt that Paytubi would be an effective witness against Lester Rogers, as well as against Marlene Navarro, if she were ever arrested. In exchange for Paytubi's cooperation, the government agreed to dismiss the rest of the charges against him, and recommend to the court that all but five years of his additional prison sentences run concurrently with the first sentence. The effect of the plea bargain was to assure him a maximum of thirteen years in prison, far less than he could have gotten.

In entering the plea agreement with Paytubi, however, the government got something it had not counted on. In the course of recounting the history of his relationship with Dean International Investments, Paytubi claimed that Robert Darias had solicited a kickback when Paytubi had arranged Marlene Navarro's first deposit of drug currency at Dean in August 1981. According to Paytubi, Darias had asked him for one percent of the approximately $480,000 which Navarro delivered to Darias and Paytubi in the parking lot of Lester Rogers's office. Paytubi claimed he had removed the one percent, $4,800, and given it to Darias the next evening outside a Winn Dixie store in Hialeah.

Darias flatly denied the story, and pointed out its inherent implausibility: If he had been inclined to solicit kickbacks from Lionel Paytubi or anyone else during Operation Swordfish, he surely would have done it repeatedly, since he had had many opportunities, and could have made much more than $4,800, over the course of the long operation.

It was common for convicted felons such as Paytubi to concoct such tales about people they had grudges against. Prosecutor Michael Pasano had predicted to the Department of Justice that Darias would be accused of misapplying funds.

The DEA agents, however, were devastated when they heard the kickback tale, and Darias's denial did not assuage their fears. The truth or falsity of the story made little difference. There was no conclusive proof either way. It was Darias's word against Paytubi's. As with other issues bearing on Darias's credibility, the agents were concerned mainly about how the story would play to juries in subsequent Swordfish trials. How would it affect the juries' opinion of Darias, who already was under attack from defense lawyers for his tax conviction and the real estate case? But those cases were old. If a jury believed that Darias had stolen money during the very investigation that had spawned the trial at hand, his testimony would be rendered worthless, the DEA agents feared.

Although it was impossible to evaluate how the juries would view the kickback story—impossible to isolate its impact from that of other testimony by Paytubi, Darias, Chellino, Cooper, or other witnesses, the DEA agents panicked. They demanded that Robert Darias take a lie detector test on the Paytubi allegation.

Darias refused. He knew that polygraphs were scientifically unreliable. He knew they were inadmissible as evidence in any court. And he was deeply offended that after more than two years of demonstrably honest work for the DEA, work that had been extremely arduous and stressful, and had involved repeated risks of his life, the agents would turn on him and lend themselves to an attack on his integrity, an attack which was based solely on the word of a thrice-convicted drug felon with a clear grudge against the man who had been instrumental in putting him away.

The agents persisted, however. Carol Cooper tried to convince Darias to take the polygraph. He still refused. So Cooper asked Frank Chellino to call him.

Darias and Chellino had not spoken in some time. Their conversation resonated with all the old strains in the two men's relationship, and indeed with the traumas of Operation Swordfish itself—the power struggles, the cover-ups, the personality clashes—going back years to the beginning of the operation. Even the mode of communication was familiar, since much of Operation Swordfish had unfolded over the telephone.

"How you doing?" Chellino opened.

"Okay."

"I understand we got a problem." Chellino laughed. "What else is new?"

"You have a problem?" Robert said with a smile. "I don't have a problem."

"Well, Robert, we're at a crossroads again."

"Yeah."

"I don't know what to do."

"Well, I know what to do, so you are at a disadvantage apparently."

"Yeah, we are. It's gonna be a problem, Robert. I hope you realize that."

"Well, this is a problem that I didn't look for."

"No, it's a problem that none of us looked for, you're right. And it's a problem we're not surprised has been raised. We expected a lot of shots to be taken—at all of us, you, me, and everybody else."

"Well, up to now I have been taking all the shots."

"Oh, no. You have seen some of them, but you haven't seen or heard of a lot of the shots that we have been taking. But you've been taking your fair share, I admit."

"Well, if we had not had the problems in the office, and I had not had to do what I had to do, taking over the operation until somebody else took over, many things would have not happened."

"I won't argue that."

"And the fact that I have been standing the way I have been standing, that's why all the trials have not been lost. Because if they had found out that I had taken over that whole operation for almost three months, the whole thing would have gone down."

"Lemme tell you somethin'," Chellino snarled. "The fact that you did that for that three months has nothing to do, as far as the prosecution of the case is concerned thus far."

"It has nothing to do with it because they don't *know* about it," Darias said.

"We did have an internal problem, I will admit that to you."

"That's why Mike Pasano has instructed me all the time never to go into those areas."

"Because there's no reason to, that's why. It's personnel problems. It has nothing to do with—it has no bearing on—the facts against the defendants. What it was was internal problems. There's just no reason to open that other unnecessary door. If it comes up, we would have to explain it. But there is no reason to raise it. That isn't the issue. I don't even want to talk about that. That might very well still come up with the remaining trials. If it comes out—we had personnel problems. I left, new people came in, there continued to be personnel problems, and *those* people left."

"Right."

"And that's it, is it not?"

"Right."

"In a nutshell. That's what happened. There *were problems.* And those people came in and they left, and you stayed during the duration of it. What went on and didn't go on may or may not affect the

Marlene case. But that's really not the issue. Unfortunately this thing is coming up with Paytubi and he's not backing down. *I hope you understand our position*—that he particularly has no reason to lie."

Darias restrained himself from laughing out loud. Of course Paytubi had a reason to hurt Darias. He hated Darias. Darias had been the instrument of Paytubi's fall.

"We believe what *you're* saying," Chellino continued, "and we only know that it's gonna really be made an issue of next time, *more* so. So what options do we have? We ask you about it, number one, which Carol and Paul did. They tell me that you deny it. Fine. But there are other more substantive options that we can take, if you didn't take the money, and I don't believe you did. The next trial, I'm tellin' you, it's gonna come up: Well, did the government attempt to give Mr. Darias a lie detector test? And it looks like *shit* for us to say, no, Mr. Darias didn't take a lie detector test. Because the jury will say, well, what does he have to hide? And it looks terrible, Bob."

"Right."

"It really does."

"I don't care," Darias said. "I'm being singled out to clarify doubts about the operation. I feel that I have been thrashed through the mud already enough. And I am not going to take any polygraph test. That's it. I've thought about it, and I've consulted with several people. And I have my lawyers, and they say no, definitely, that there is nothing that I have to prove to anybody."

"Well, I don't know what your lawyers are advising you. But you've got to understand that if Paytubi made those allegations against me, or against Carol, that we would have been required to take it."

"But you are in a different position than I am. And there are many, many other doubts in my mind now. I am getting to the point that I feel that I have been very much mistreated by different people in the operation. I feel that I have taken enough flack already. I am not going to cooperate any more unless a number of things happen."

"Do you realize that quite possibly we'll have to dismiss these cases? That is a very strong likelihood."

"Well, that is completely out of my hands at this point. If we are going to start singling out and putting doubts on people, I want *everybody* to take a polygraph test. I'm not saying that I don't want to take a polygraph test. I want everybody to take a polygraph test."

"He's not *accusing* everybody!"

"I *am* accusing everybody."

"Oh, Robert," Chellino said with a sigh.

"Wait a minute," Darias continued. "If we are going to believe a guy that is already serving thirteen years in jail—just because of what that guy says, people are asking me to take a polygraph test. I want the four guys from Denver to take a polygraph test about the $100,-000. When I take my test, I am going to answer those questions, too. Not only about the $4,800 from Paytubi. I want *everybody* to take polygraph tests about the $250,000 that Eddie Hernandez says is missing. You know that Bob Russo has never been able to square the accounts. You know that, as a fact."

"I know, I know."

"And those are things that I have in my mind. Before, I was very much at ease because I felt that everybody had confidence in everybody. But now I feel that I am just another informant, another criminal, that is going to testify. And I cannot honestly, under oath, say anything that is going to defend the government or DEA. So in order to do that, I would like to see everybody also pass a polygraph test, where everybody's going to come out clean. And I will do the same. I will answer all those questions, too."

"The unfortunate bottom line of this," Chellino said, "is that you *are* an informant for the agency. And that is the bottom line. And you cannot—and you will not—dictate to the agency who is gonna take tests. We didn't cause this problem. Nobody here in this office caused this problem."

"Yeah, but Paytubi is dictating to the agency what you are going to do."

"No, what I think you're doing, Bob, what I really feel you're doing, is that you're taking it much too personally. And I want to clear up another point: When we're talking about a lie detector test, the only question, the *only* question, that is going to be asked of you is whether or not, during the month of August of 1981, you took a $4,800 kickback from Lionel Paytubi. There is not going to be any broad spectrum of questions. That is going to be the *only* question that's gonna be asked of you. I'm telling you."

"What you are saying is even insulting me more," Robert said. "Because what you're trying to tell me is that maybe in the back of your mind you think that I am not taking the polygraph test because if they ask me some other questions something else might come out. Frank, if I would take the test, I would not mind all the questions in the whole world about the whole operation. And that's exactly what I'm trying to tell you. That I would like *everybody,* the people that were involved, Eddie and Nick—"

"Bob—"

"All those things I would like to clear up, and I would love to do the same. I would love to answer about the $100,000 from Denver, the $250,000 . . ."

"Bob, I personally really feel that you're taking this much too personally. You're *not* gonna dictate to the agency who does and does not take lie detector tests."

"I'm not trying to dictate to anybody."

"Well, unfortunately we all got pushed into this. Bob, I do not personally think you did it, nor do Carol and Paul think you did it. And the unfortunate thing about it is that the whole thing could be cleared up in a half hour, if you were willing to not take it so personally, or be insulted. But you obviously have made your mind up about it. It's unfortunate. And it's gonna affect your relationship with the agency."

"I realize that."

"It's going to stop the money." The DEA was paying Robert small amounts as expenses, despite the IRS lien, but had not yet told him that it did not intend to pay him his bonus until after the trials were concluded.

"I realize that."

"I know, and it's a big decision for you."

"Well, I strongly believe you are not saying that as a threat."

"No, I'm not, Bob, I'm telling you as a matter of fact. I'm not gonna let you sit and wonder and wonder and wonder."

"But is that information you have, or just your opinion?"

"Let me put it this way: This whole thing has to go up to management. But I'm sure that management is gonna come back and say, that's it, we're not gonna give you any more money. But no, it's not official yet."

"Then there are several avenues open to me to try to collect monies for work that I already did."

"That's totally up to you."

"I want you to know that I never took a polygraph test before."

"Neither have I." Chellino paused. "Hold on, I've got another call."

Chellino kept Darias on hold for the better part of a minute, and then came back on the line.

"I want you to know that I was *not* threatening you with that, nor would I ever do that to you. I think you know me better than that. But I am saying, as a practical matter, that I suspect that's what gonna happen."

"That's totally their option."

"I know. And I know how they think, and I know what they're gonna say. The unfortunate part of this whole thing, Bob, is that you probably didn't do it, and I *believe* you, and we're gonna cause all kinds of shit over this. That truly is the unfortunate part of it. It *truly, truly is.* Remember I said that."

"Right."

"I believe you. I don't think you did it. Carol doesn't. Paul doesn't. And unfortunately I think this is gonna be irreparable damage. It's truly unfortunate."

"Okay."

"I've got two other calls."

"Okay."

"I gotta run."

51

THE DEA ALLOWED Chellino's threats to linger over Darias for a period of time, but he was steadfast in his refusal to undergo a polygraph. The agents finally were forced to back down, and eventually were compelled by a dramatic event in Colombia to seek a rapprochement with Darias.

On Tuesday, April 30, 1984, a few weeks after Marlene Navarro was kidnapped, two men on a Yamaha motorcycle pulled up behind a four-door Mercedes-Benz in downtown Bogotá. The passenger on the motorcycle opened fire into the rear window of the Mercedes with a MAC-10 submachine gun. Killed instantly, the back of his head blown away, was the Minister of Justice of Colombia, Rodrigo Lara Bonilla.

Despite Colombia's extraordinary, centuries-long history of violence, the killing was the nation's first assassination of a sitting cabinet minister. Lara Bonilla was a sworn enemy of the narcotics mafia, which made no secret that he had been assassinated out of revenge for recent government actions against the traffickers. The episode that sparked the assassination was the seizure and destruction of a huge Amazon cocaine-processing complex known as Tranquilandia. Though Colombian authorities carried out the seizure, Tranquilandia was located through an intricate undercover operation orchestrated in part out of Miami by Special Agent Carol Cooper of the DEA.

The mafia godfathers knew in advance of the assassination plot against Justice Minister Lara. Carlos Jader Alvarez knew all about it. Pepe Cabrera knew all about it.

At Lara's funeral, President Belisario Betancur declared "all-out war" on the mafia and imposed a state of siege throughout Colombia. Betancur also announced that, in a reversal of his policy up to that time, Colombian drug traffickers who had been indicted in the United States would be extradited if they could be arrested.

Armed with the state-of-siege authority, Colombian police and soldiers saturated the country, patrolling roads and highways, stopping and searching vehicles. Several hundred people were detained, among them two of the thirteen Colombian fugitives from the Operation Swordfish indictments, the brothers Ricardo and Said Pavon.

American officials declared that the most crucial test of the Colombian government's new policy would be whether the Pavons and others were actually extradicted—sent to the United States to face prosecution and trial. The extradition process usually took many months. It was the one sanction which the drug mafia had always feared the most and fought the hardest.

In the face of the vastly increased police pressure all over Colombia, Marlene Navarro's kidnappers promptly agreed to accept a ransom offer of $300,000 from Navarro's family and friends. The kidnappers left her bound, gagged, and blindfolded in an abandoned house an hour outside of Bogotá. Tipped by the kidnappers, her friend Rafael found her. Weighing only eighty-four pounds, Marlene spent two weeks in a private clinic recovering from malnutrition, and from infection that had spread through her body from the untended cuts and scratches she had suffered during weeks in the wilderness.

No one knew the identity of her kidnappers.

Not long after leaving the clinic, recovered from her ordeal at least physically, Marlene Navarro disappeared.

In September 1984, a few months after President Betancur had declared "all-out war" on the drug mafia and revived the long dormant policy of extraditing fugitives to the U.S., the police in Bogotá arrested Carlos Jader Alvarez.

Acting on a tip from the syndicate of an envious competitor, possibly the godfather Carlos Lehder Rivas, security agents apprehended Alvarez on a street corner in north Bogotá. He was unarmed, although his bodyguard carried a sidearm. They offered no resistance. Alvarez, however, claimed they had the wrong man, and produced identity papers in another name. But the police identified him positively.

Despite President Betancur's extradition pledge, it took nearly a year for the Colombian government to turn Carlos Jader Alvarez over to American authorities. Under heavy guard, he was hustled aboard a military jet to Miami, where he was taken to the Metropolitan Correctional Center, a federal prison southwest of the city near the Miami zoo. He was placed in solitary confinement.

Jader Alvarez was scheduled to go on trial in late 1985 with the Pavon brothers, Ricardo and Said, who had been extradited with him. The other indicted members of the syndicate—Luis Rodriguez, Oscar

Garcia, Teo Terselich, Bertha Yolanda Paez, and the rest, not to mention Marlene Navarro—were still fugitives.

The DEA and the Justice Department lusted for the trial of Carlos Jader Alvarez. He had been their principal target since the early days of Operation Swordfish, and would be the first South American *padrino* to go on trial in the United States. The trial would test the validity of the entire theoretical underpinning of the operation—whether the United States Government could successfully infiltrate the top godfathers of the South American mafia, secretly build evidence against them, and bring them to justice in the United States.

To proceed, however, the government needed its star spy and witness, Robert Darias. And Darias was balking. By 1985 the DEA had systematically alienated Darias by its devastating manipulation of the monies due him, and by its equivocation and betrayal when Lionel Paytubi had attacked his integrity. Robert and Amelia had waged a campaign of well-reasoned protest letters to top DEA officials as well as to senators and congressmen.

As the trial of Carlos Jader Alvarez approached, the government's relationship with Robert Darias came down to a clear, steel-edged *quid pro quo*. Either the DEA would intercede with the Internal Revenue Service to enable the promised payments to Darias to resume, or he would not testify voluntarily at the trial of Jader Alvarez.

Since Frank Chellino had botched the last negotiation with Darias, Carol Cooper was deployed to try to rekindle her old relationship with Robert: the warmth and good humor that had infused hundreds of late night dialogues at the height of Operation Swordfish.

Robert could not bring himself to refuse a call from Carol. Despite everything, he still liked her. Despite the mistakes she had made, he did not believe any of them had been malicious. Despite the pain she had caused him, he believed she had done what she had felt was right under the circumstances, however misguided.

Like his talk with Chellino, Darias's conversation with Cooper evoked memories of an intense time in both their lives—the Cuban accent and the Midwestern twang, together again across the wires. As usual, Carol's tactic was to be optimistic—hopeful that their current impasse could be resolved.

Perhaps the DEA could appeal to the IRS to allow some money to be released, she suggested. "If I were you," Carol said, "and we get the authorization from IRS to give you any money, and we can give it to you in a lump sum, I would take it and run." She tried to position herself on Robert's side—the two of them against the hated IRS.

"Maybe the Internal Revenue will tell you that until this bonus is resolved, you can pay me expenses," Robert said.

"Yeah."

"And that will solve my problem for the time being."

"We'll work out some agreement and pay you the expenses," Carol said. She cautioned, however, that the DEA might reduce his eventual bonus by the amount of any new expense payments. And that rekindled Robert's anger at Carol for having deferred payment of the bonus in the first place, until after the IRS lien prevented payment.

"Look, Carol," said Robert, "somebody is not being just with me, because I am still hanging around, and Felipe got his money at the very beginning, and is laughing with his $100,000 somewhere—"

"Bob, I totally agree with you. It's *not* fair. Number one, he should never have been paid his money yet, and that was Tom's fault. And Tom also told me that I could pay *you* the money. I'll admit it to you. I knew I couldn't pay it to you yet. All I wanted to do was get through that one last trial, and you were going to get the money."

It was the Lester Rogers trial, at which neither spy's testimony had a discernible impact on the result.

"Well, you should have taken Tom's word," Robert said. "He was your superior."

"Yeah, but I also had to use some integrity of my own. If Tom told me to jump off a bridge, would I do it?"

After three years, Carol Cooper still hated Tom Clifford.

"And because I followed instructions a hundred percent," Robert said—filing tax returns at the DEA's insistence—"and I did exactly what I was told to—"

"Well, it's great being a Monday afternoon quarterback, and I easily could have passed the buck, and said my supervisor told me to do it," Carol said. "I didn't do it. And I somewhat regret it now, because you're going through hell and high water. At the time we made the decision [to withhold the bonus] you weren't even talking to the IRS. They knew nothing about you."

"No, they found out from the papers I was told to file," Robert declared, his anger flaring.

"Yep. And I'll clue you, that's the last time we ever asked anybody to do that, too," Carol said, finally admitting she had erred. "We're all concerned about it. You're not wrong in what you're asking for, and you're not wrong in what you're doing."

Carol said she was hesitant to start preparing for the trial of Jader Alvarez: If Robert was not going to testify, there would be no trial.

"They're jumping all over me," Carol said, "because they want me to do all this work on this case, and I haven't been doing it. And I don't want to spend all that time doing it if you're not going to be around. 'Cause I'm wasting my time."

"What is Frank doing?" Robert asked.

"Frank finally got his supervisor job."

"Yeah? What group does he have?"

"He's got the intelligence group."

"Wasn't that Tom's?" Robert asked. Now they were reminiscing.

"Yeah."

"Where is Tom?"

"Oh, Tom went to Washington. He hates it. He didn't want to go. Nor did he get promoted. It was just a simple lateral transfer for him, and he hates every minute of it."

"Yeah?"

"But Frank's been wanting to be a supervisor for a long, long time. And he's very good. He likes to direct people."

"Yeah, I know that," Robert said. "So what is new." They both laughed.

"You know who works for him?" Carol asked.

"Who?"

"Remember Bob Russo?"

"Bob Russo?" Darias laughed again. Russo had despised Chellino since the early days of Operation Swordfish when Chellino had begun attacking Russo's close friend Clifford. "That is something," Darias said. "Life is something else."

"We all laughed."

They also reminisced about Paul Sennett, who had been transferred to Vienna, Austria, a sensitive DEA intelligence post.

"Washington keeps calling me," Carol said, getting back to the subject at hand. "We got these people now, that were extradited. And Washington does not want to lose this case. It's going to cause *major* problems if we lose any of them."

The U.S. Government believed that if it failed to convict a defendant whom the Colombian government had gone to the trouble of extraditing, there would no more extraditions.

"Well, that's exactly what you have to point out to them, Carol, that you have a person here who is being left to the wolves, and I have to get some money somehow."

"Have you sold everything?" Carol asked. "Have you sold all your furniture and stuff?"

"I am living in a rented place. It has furniture." He didn't want to acknowledge that he was living with his in-laws.

"You sold all your stuff?"

"Yeah."

"Ah, Bob."

"I am not kidding you, Carol. I don't like to cry or to tell people about how bad a position I have, but people should realize that it has been almost a year since I got the last $2,000 for expenses."

"As soon as they started extraditing these Colombians, headquarters keeps calling me, and they want to know the status on the trial, and they want to know how the trial looks. And I flat out told them, you don't have a case at all if you don't have Bob Darias."

"Yeah."

"Now, what I don't want to happen is to get to the point where the government has to *subpoena* you to testify at the trial, without the problem being resolved. You're not going to be happy about that and I'm not either."

"Well, you realize that without being *prepared* for the trial, I'm not going to be of any use anyway," Robert said. "It's going to be a mess."

"I don't know what more I can do, Bob. I can rattle the cages downstairs, and I can give the people in Washington a call and rattle their cages, but above and beyond that I can't push too much. I'd like to get it resolved, because there's no sense in me spending the next three months getting ready for this trial, if there isn't going to be a trial. Even though they can subpoena you, it's not going to be good."

"Well, I'll let you know where in Spain I am going to be so they can subpoena me."

Cooper didn't get Darias's lame little joke, but she got his message. After conferring with her colleagues, she informed Darias the next day that the DEA was making progress on solving his IRS problem and implored him to be patient and cooperative. He was mollified. But the bureaucratic shuffle continued. Weeks passed. The trial date approached.

"Carol, I have been thinking about this whole thing," Darias said finally. "You know how disappointed I am. Because I haven't been able to get any money at all, not even for expenses."

"Yeah, I don't understand either, Bob. I can't tell you any answers."

Darias was convinced that Cooper had done her best. "I am thinking that no matter what happens, I'm going to keep going and cooperate and get to the end of this trial."

"You are?"

"Yeah."

"Okay, I figured you would." Her relief was palpable.

"As soon as you need me, Carol, just give me a call and I will be at your disposal. Whatever you want me to do I'll do."

"You're too good a person," Carol said.

"What I have done in the past," Robert said, "I haven't done for *them* [the DEA and IRS bureaucrats]. I have done because I felt that I should do it. So whatever you need me for, I am the same as always. No matter what happens I am going to be there. Okay?"

"Yeah, I can't believe you're doing that, but knowing you, it doesn't surprise me."

Robert had been telling the truth. He wasn't doing it just for *them*. He was doing it for himself. Money and possible sway with the IRS had not been his only motives in working for the DEA. From the beginning, his journey had also been a search for redemption from the shame his prison sentence had brought to him and his family.

The trial of Carlos Jader Alvarez and the Pavon brothers was postponed from September 1985 until February 1986. Delays were not unusual in a case of such magnitude.

The prosecutor at the initial Swordfish trials, Michael Pasano, had left the government to go into private practice. And his former assistant, Mark Schnapp, had been promoted to head the criminal division in the U.S. Attorney's office. It fell to Schnapp, therefore, to appoint a new prosecutor to conduct the trial of Carlos Jader Alvarez and the Pavon brothers. Schnapp named a new federal attorney, Myles Malman, who had recently come to Miami after a successful decade as an assistant district attorney in Manhattan, where he had specialized in murder cases.

An intense, good-humored native of the Bronx and the U.S. Army, Myles Malman seemed to prefer the company of homicide detectives to that of pinstriped lawyers. He brought a somewhat more elemental, down-to-earth outlook to the cases of Operation Swordfish than had Michael Pasano and Mark Schnapp, and Gregory English before them.

Carol Cooper, who was to be the DEA's principal agent at the trial, didn't like Malman. "We fight all the time," she told Darias. "He's a New York Jewish guy, and he's nasty, he is really nasty. I'm not saying he's not a good attorney, but he's terrible to work with."

Darias and Malman got along famously. Robert had always sensed a faint air of condescension when he dealt with Michael Pasano and Mark Schnapp. But he and Malman hit it off. They were both men of impulse and instinct, men of the street—qualities that would come in handy as they prepared for the biggest Swordfish trial of all.

And there was no more empty talk—by anybody anywhere in the government—of dismissing the case because Robert Darias had refused to take a lie detector test.

5 2

THE NEW VENEZUELAN passport identified the woman as Nora Estrela Ramirez, but most people in Caracas knew her by another name, a Hebrew name, Mihal Kourany. She had turned up in Caracas in late 1984, and moved into a small apartment in Altamira, an affluent neighborhood at the foot of the mountains a few blocks above the American Embassy. She had begun working as a foreign exchange money broker, doing business with a number of major banks, while preparing to open a commercial insurance business. She had clients and friends in Brazil and planned to move to São Paulo eventually, so she enrolled in Portuguese classes at the Brazilian Institute, which was not far from her apartment. It was clear to her teachers that she had a flair for languages, having already mastered French, and English, and gained some fluency in Italian and Hebrew.

A twice-divorced woman who appeared to be around forty, Mihal Kourany enjoyed life in Caracas. She drove around town in a sporty little pink Fiat. Continuing a lifelong practice of staying fit, she took kung fu classes. She dated a number of men in government, business, and diplomatic circles, frequented diplomatic cocktail parties, dined in the smart restaurants in Los Mercedes, the restaurant row of Caracas, and attended European movies at the Cinemateque.

At a United Nations human rights conference in Caracas in 1985, Mihal Kourany met Rene de Sola, a justice of the Supreme Court of Venezuela and soon to become the court's president. A distinguished-looking man in his sixties, Rene de Sola was a genuine elder statesman of Venezuela; he had held many top government positions over several decades, including minister of foreign affairs, minister of justice, president of the Venezuelan delegation to the United Nations, and diplomatic posts in Europe. De Sola was also an intellectual—the author of many scholarly articles on law and government, and a translator of French poetry and plays into Spanish. He had a wife, four children, and several grandchildren.

Rene de Sola and Mihal Kourany became friends. They spoke on the telephone several times a week, always in French, and discussed politics, literature (he gave her a book of Molière he had translated), food (he was a gourmet cook), and a range of other things. They found that they shared a deep knowledge and love of Paris. He had lived there as the Venezuelan ambassador to UNESCO. She had lived there as a teenager and young adult and had attended the Sorbonne.

A few weeks after they met, Mihal and Rene began an affair. He spent every Wednesday afternoon at her apartment. She kept his photograph on her nightstand. They dined together frequently in various secluded restaurants around the city. Two of their favorites were El Gazebo, an intimate spot in Los Mercedes, and the Brasserie at the Caracas Hilton. On her birthday in 1985, De Sola, who traveled a lot, wired her flowers from Europe.

"I am going to take you to Paris," De Sola told her when he returned from one trip. "It's going to be wonderful. You are going to show me Paris differently from the way I have always known it."

"I can't go to Paris," Mihal said. "I can't leave here."

"But why? You seem so lonely." Although Mihal Kourany was a vivacious person, there was a remoteness about her that friends had difficulty penetrating.

"I want to tell you something about my life," she said.

"No, I don't want to hear it," Rene replied. "I'm interested in you *now*. I don't care what happened to you in the past."

During the first part of February 1986, the DEA in Miami was told by a CIA asset that a woman in Caracas, whose passport identified her as Nora Estrela Ramirez, and who went by the name Mihal Kourany, might in fact be Marlene Navarro.

The DEA had received a number of such reports in the three and a half years since Navarro had disappeared. She was said to be in Bogotá but was never located. She was said to be in Rome, in Madrid, in Rio de Janiero. The most promising lead had been a report that she had been arrested in Germany. Frank Chellino and Carol Cooper had been summoned urgently and asked to listen to the detainee's speaking voice over the telephone from Frankfurt. Still familiar with Marlene Navarro's vivacious lilt and cadence after intercepting over two thousand telephone conversations, Chellino and Cooper were disappointed when the voice proved unmistakably to be someone else's.

When he received the report from the CIA, Frank Chellino telephoned Special Agent Robert Candelaria, the DEA's attaché in Venezuela, and sent Candelaria a packet of photographs and other material that might aid in identifying Marlene Navarro. The photographs included a shot of Navarro nude that the DEA had found in her home in Costa del Sol in October 1982.

"The source says she lives somewhere close to the American Embassy," Chellino told Candelaria. "That's all we know. It's probably another wild-goose chase. It wouldn't be our first."

"Well, we can at least have a look," said Candelaria. An urbane Mexican with a twinkle in his eye and a speaking voice faintly reminiscent of Peter Lorre, Robert Candelaria had been stationed in Caracas for two years, after a long tour with the DEA in Mexico. Since Navarro was one of the DEA's most wanted international fugitives, he decided to handle the matter personally, rather than assign it to one of the agents under his command.

After reviewing the material from Chellino, Candelaria called the Venezuelan minister of justice, José Manzo Gonzalez, and asked to see him. A stalwart of the democracy movement in Venezuela, Minister Manzo had spent years in exile and prison during the military dictatorship of the 1950s. As minister of justice, he was the DEA's closest friend in the current government. Robert Candelaria had cultivated the relationship. When the minister's life had been threatened in Miami, Candelaria had arranged for a DEA plane to fly him back to Caracas. When Manzo had found himself alone in a Washington hotel room away from his family on a Father's Day weekend, it had been Candelaria who had taken him a bottle of Chivas Regal.

Within hours, Candelaria had a private audience with Manzo in the offices of the Ministry of Justice on the twenty-fifth floor of the north tower of the Simón Bolívar Center, adjacent to downtown Caracas. Candelaria and Manzo recognized an immediate problem with the matter of the CIA report about the fugitive: Even if the woman in question could be located, and turned out to be Marlene Navarro, there was a complex extradition treaty between the U.S. and Venezuela governing the transfer of international fugitives. Complying with the treaty would take a lot of time and the proceeding likely would become public. It could open Minister Manzo and the government to charges from opposition politicians that they were too friendly with the Americans, always a sensitive issue.

The issue of extradition was academic, however, unless they located the woman in question. At Candelaria's urging, the minister decided to proceed in utmost secrecy. He assigned the investigation to the narcotics branch of the Policia Tecnica Judicial, or PTJ, the Venezuelan counterpart of the DEA and FBI. The director of the PTJ, in turn, detailed six agents to the case. The agents immediately launched a two-track inquiry. One team began a search of immigration and motor vehicle records for the names Mihal Kourany and Nora Estrela Ramirez. (Telephone and utility companies had no record of her.)

Another team, armed with Marlene Navarro's photographs from Miami, began discreet inquiries among apartment-building doormen in the chic neighborhoods around the U.S. Embassy, where the CIA report to the DEA had indicated Navarro might live.

As the PTJ was beginning its investigation, Minister Manzo briefed the president of Venezuela. Robert Candelaria briefed his in-country boss, the acting American ambassador, Deputy Chief of Mission Ludlow "Kim" Flower. (The embassy was without an ambassador for the time being.)

It took a few days, but both of the PTJ's lines of inquiry produced results. Immigration records showed that a Colombian woman named Nora Estrela Ramirez had been granted a Venezuelan passport two years earlier; she apparently held dual citizenship in Colombia and Venezuela. And the doormen at the building in Altamira where the Ramirez woman lived in Apartment 611 identified her as the woman in the photographs, of Marlene Navarro. The doormen could not be positive, however.

A PTJ surveillance team began watching the building and secretly photographing the woman as she came and went. They made a startling discovery: the woman under surveillance, whatever her real name, was keeping company with an eminent figure of the Venezuelan government, a household name and face in Caracas, Supreme Court Justice Rene de Sola.

"We've got to talk," the director of the PTJ told Robert Candelaria on the telephone. They met with Minister of Justice Manzo at Manzo's residence. "This is bigger than we thought," the PTJ director said. "She's dating Rene de Sola. We don't know the extent of the relationship, but this girl obviously has a lot of connections—friends in high places."

Candelaria said he would have the DEA run De Sola's name through its computers on the off chance that he might be linked to Marlene Navarro's drug-trafficking and money-laundering activities. That inquiry, conducted in Miami and Washington, came back negative. It appeared that the relationship was strictly personal.

Nevertheless, Robert Candelaria would not have been surprised if Minister Manzo had terminated the investigation at that point. Some elements of the PTJ were nervous. "Rene de Sola might use his influence with the president, or go to the newspapers and say, 'Look what a foreign government is trying to do in our country,'" a PTJ agent said. "He takes over as president of the court next month."

The minister, however, instructed the PTJ to proceed as quickly as possible. "If we don't do this, the DEA will look unfavorably upon

Venezuela, and drug traffickers will think Venezuela is a haven for them," Manzo said.

The ministry and the PTJ devised a plan to detain the woman on a ruse that would not arouse her suspicion. If the DEA could then positively identify her as Marlene Navarro, the status of her Venezuelan citizenship and passport would be reviewed, and there might be a way to expel her secretly from Venezuela as an "undesirable person" under a procedure that would avoid the time-consuming complexities of the extradition treaty.

On Friday afternoon, February 21, the woman in Apartment 611 of the luxury high-rise building in Altamira was preparing to leave for her kung fu class across town. She deposited a bag of trash in the sixth-floor trash chamber and was returning to lock her door when a tall, dark-complexioned man accosted her in the hallway, showed credentials of the PTJ, and insisted that she go back into her apartment.

She was terrified. "What is this?" she demanded to know.

"There is nothing to fear," the agent said. He told her that the PTJ needed her help in identifying the body of a man who had been a well-known hairdresser in Caracas and apparently had been murdered. The agent claimed that a slip of paper bearing Mihal Kourany's name, address, and phone number had been found on the body. She began to cry, and asked that she be given time to change out of her kung fu costume. Nodding his assent, the PTJ agent moved to a window and signaled someone in the street below. A second agent promptly arrived at the apartment, and they asked to see the woman's passport.

"I don't know where it is," she said, now in jeans and a black tank top, putting on a jacket. The agents searched the apartment and found two passports, Colombian and Venezuelan, both in the name of Nora Estrela Ramirez. They also examined some photographs on her nightstand, including a picture of Rene de Sola, and some letters and papers bearing De Sola's name.

Suspicious now of the agents' true mission, but feeling she had no choice, the woman accompanied them to the PTJ headquarters, a shabby eight-story converted parking garage on the fringe of downtown Caracas. She was escorted into a windowless office whose walls bore photographs of the minister of justice and the president.

The agents told her that they had been asked to check her teeth.

"Absolutely not, that's ridiculous," she said. She started to resist, but one of the agents held her arms while the other forced her mouth open and examined her teeth one by one, checking for evidence of the extensive dental surgery that Marlene Navarro had undergone in 1981 and 1982, on which the DEA had briefed the PTJ.

The agents then asked her to remove her clothing so they could compare her body to a photograph which appeared to have been taken of her posing nude on a beach.

Again she tried to refuse. "I would rather be killed than raped," she declared. Denying any intent to rape her, the agents began forcibly to disrobe her when a PTJ *comisario* entered the room and ordered them to desist.

"What are you doing to me?" the woman demanded of the *comisario*. "What about the hairdresser you want me to identify?"

"Yes, you must fly with us to Maracaibo," he said, referring to Venezuela's second largest city. "That is where he was killed."

The telephone rang. One of the agents answered it, paused for a moment, looked at the woman, and then said into the phone, "Yes, it's her."

The woman asked permission to make a phone call. The agents declined, and locked her in a holding cell. She refused offers of food or drink.

That same Friday afternoon Carol Cooper and Frank Chellino, who had stayed in touch with Robert Candelaria by phone, caught a Pan Am flight from Miami to Caracas, arriving just after dark. Neither agent had traveled much outside the United States. Candelaria and his driver met them at the airport half an hour north of Caracas on the ocean, and drove them across coastal mountains to the central part of the city and the Caracas Hilton.

The next morning, Candalaria took Cooper and Chellino to PTJ headquarters. Escorted to the narcotics section, they were introduced to the PTJ *comisario,* who ushered them into an office and showed them the woman believed to be Marlene Navarro through a one-way mirrored soundproof window. Cooper and Chellino stared. Frank Chellino had not seen Marlene Navarro in person since he and Robert Darias had lunched with her and Luis Rodriguez at the Costa del Sol country club in December 1981. Carol Cooper had only met Navarro once—when Carol and Darias had accompanied Navarro to purchase a $90,000 diamond at the Seybold Building in April 1982. But the agents had been obsessed with tracking her ever since she had disappeared from Miami just before Operation Swordfish ended.

Barely controlling his excitement, Frank Chellino asked the PTJ agents if they could get the woman to smile, without revealing to her that she was being observed. The *comisario* left, and then could be seen wandering casually into the room where the woman was being displayed. He said something that was inaudible to the DEA agents through the glass. It worked. She smiled. And that clinched it. The short, voluptuous woman in the black tank top and jeans on the opposite side of the one-way glass was unquestionably Marlene Navarro.

Chellino and Cooper were driven back to the Hilton, and over the course of the day their euphoria gradually turned to frustration, as they waited in their rooms staring at television with no indication of what would happen next, or when. The impatient Chellino talked occasionally by phone with Associate Special-Agent-in-Charge Sam Billbrough, who was monitoring the operation from his office in Miami. Since the operation was compartmentalized, the agents were not immediately privy to the activities of Robert Candelaria, who was closeted with the minister of justice and an American Embassy legal expert, negotiating the conditions under which the government might turn Marlene Navarro over to the Americans. Although the extradition treaty had been deemed inapplicable to the case at hand, there was general language about extradition in a separate mutual narcotics agreement between the United States and Venezuela, a document that obligated both countries to work together in curbing illegal narcotics activity. But that, too, was subject to legal interpretation and challenge, and would take time.

The group focused instead on Marlene Navarro's status as a Venezuelan citizen holding a Venezuelan passport. There was an inclination to believe that her credentials might be invalid, that she might have obtained the passport under questionable circumstances on the Colombian border, where it was not difficult for a Colombian to get a Venezuelan passport for a certain financial consideration. But resolving such issues with certainty would take a lot of time and might become public.

"If this goes public, we'll have to use *legal* channels," someone asserted.

In the end it was decided to cut legal corners. On the assumption that Marlene Navarro's papers were probably phony, her Venezuelan passport was secretly destroyed, and all indications that she had ever been a Venezuelan citizen were expunged from the government's records. That presumably left the government free to expel her from the country forthwith as an "undesirable person," who had been residing in Venezuela under false pretenses.

The meeting at the ministry of justice did not break up until Saturday evening. Meanwhile, the minister had given informal clearance to allow an unmarked DEA aircraft from Miami to land at the Caracas airport and park in the sector used by private planes. There was no acknowledgement to Venezuelan customs and immigration that the plane was a United States Government aircraft on official business. The pilots, who were from the DEA's air wing in Texas, were picked up by Candelaria's driver and brought to Caracas where they joined Chellino and Cooper at the Hilton late Saturday night.

The authorities had considered having Navarro flown out of the country in the middle of the night, but concluded that such a maneuver might attract more attention at the airport than a daylight departure. Instead, the word was passed quietly to Venezuelan customs and immigration that if "something strange" occurred at the airport on Sunday, they should ignore it.

At the private section of the airport Sunday morning, Cooper, Chellino, and the DEA pilots were checked through immigration. They were identified as private U.S. citizens, not as DEA agents. The pilots filed a flight plan for Miami.

At PTJ headquarters, Marlene Navarro's guards told her that she was going to the airport to be flown to Maracaibo in connection with the murder of the hairdresser, a story she now was convinced was false. She had realized she was snared in a DEA operation when she caught a glimpse of the nude photograph which the PTJ agents displayed on Friday afternoon. She had recognized it as one that she had kept in her house in Miami. The PTJ could only have obtained it from the DEA, which had seized the house and its contents.

Navarro was taken to a van at the entrance to the PTJ building. To conceal her arrival at the airport, the PTJ agents gagged her and forced her to lie under a blanket in the rear of the van. She was not released until the van had come to a stop next to the DEA plane.

With her knowledge of aircraft, Navarro recognized the plane as a Beech Aerocommander registered in the U.S.

"Now I know I am not going to Maracaibo," Navarro told the PTJ *comisario*. "I am going to the United States."

"How do you know?"

"Look at the tail number of the plane. See the 'N'? That means it is registered in America."

The *comisario* said nothing, as Robert Candelaria, whom Navarro took to be another PTJ agent, quickly took her aboard the plane and strapped her in.

A few minutes later Frank Chellino and Carol Cooper, who had been waiting in a private room in the immigration office, climbed aboard the plane. They were both armed.

"Hello, Miss Navarro, welcome to Miami," Chellino said with a smile. He and Cooper flashed their DEA credentials.

Navarro, confused and nonplussed but fearing the worst, recognized Chellino as the man she had known as Frank Dean, Robert Darias's partner at Dean International Investments, which she had since learned was a DEA undercover operation. She did not recognize Carol Cooper.

"I know you are going to kill me," Navarro said, starting to cry.

"We aren't going to kill you," Chellino said. "C'mon, Marlene, if we were going to kill you, we wouldn't have gone to all this trouble. We wouldn't have flown a DEA plane all the way down here."

At Chellino's signal the pilot started to taxi the plane toward the runway.

"Why did you give that photograph to the PTJ?" Marlene asked. "You know which one."

"We just wanted them to be able to see if Mother Nature had been treating you well," Chellino said.

The plane reached the head of the runway, and then suddenly stopped. The pilot turned to Chellino and shouted over the noise of the engines. "We've got a problem. They're denying us takeoff."

"What!" Chellino said, enraged.

"The tower is denying us takeoff, Frank. They won't let us go. We've got to turn around."

"Shit! Can't we just go?"

"We can't go. They'll scramble the air force."

"This can't be happening! Somebody fucked up! Somebody has been paid off! Shit!"

Back at the terminal the plane was surrounded by immigration police, who ordered everybody off.

"Nobody is getting off this plane until you tell me what the problem is," Chellino declared.

"They want everybody off, Frank," said Robert Candelaria, who had seen the plane returning and rushed to the flight apron. "They claim we didn't declare everybody. They see the pilots plus *three* passengers instead of two."

"No. Nobody's leaving," Chellino insisted, his hand on his gun.

"No, no, Frank," Candelaria said. "Calm down. We'll get it straightened out."

"This can't be happening," Chellino said, as the immigration police took him and Cooper off the plane. The PTJ agents, who had remained at the airport to make sure the flight left, put Marlene Navarro back in their van and drove away. Candelaria, who had never met Chellino before that weekend and was surprised at his volatility, implored him to be calm. "If you make a scene, you'll get us all arrested by the immigration police. It could hit the papers, and you can *forget* taking Marlene to Miami. *Forget it!*"

With Chellino and Cooper in the custody of the immigration police, Candelaria raced back to Caracas to find the minister of justice and attempt to resolve the matter.

Chellino and Cooper were taken into the immigration office and forced to sit in a corner under the eye of an armed, uniformed officer. Their passports were seized. They were given nothing to eat and were not allowed to call anyone. Anytime they moved the officer would nudge them back into the corner. Carol Cooper nearly lost her temper. Chellino was demoralized. They were detained for six hours.

At eight that evening, the immigration supervisor reappeared and released Chellino and Cooper with profuse apologies. He returned their passports, and allowed a DEA driver to return them to Caracas. It turned out that the immigration supervisor had not gotten the word from the ministry of justice about the possibility that "something strange" might happen at the airport on Sunday. As the plane was leaving, someone had pointed out that there were five people aboard, when the plane's manifest indicated only four. The supervisor, a young man recently promoted, had ordered the plane to return and those aboard detained.

By evening, the minister of justice had hastily and quietly conferred with other officials of the government, and assured Candelaria that the plane would be allowed to leave the next morning. The Hilton was full, so Cooper and Chellino checked into another hotel and retired, exhausted.

Marlene Navarro was kept in the same holding cell overnight. On Monday morning, the PTJ agents appeared with a large cage bearing the label "U.S. Training Dogs." They forced Navarro inside, locked it and wheeled it to the van, and returned to the airport, where a different immigration supervisor logged the passengers on the DEA plane as four persons and a shipment of dogs.

There would be no record of Marlene Navarro's having been expelled from Venezuela, or ever having been in Venezuela, much less a citizen with a passport. The ministry had made sure everybody had gotten the word. Several high-ranking military and police officials were standing around smiling and apologizing profusely for the hitch the previous afternoon.

In the plane, Chellino said to the pilot, "Get this thing going."

"We've got a small oil leak," the pilot said.

"Shit, I've got an oil leak in my *car,*" Chellino said. "How bad is this one."

"Not that bad. We can make it."

"Fine, get this thing going!"

When they were airborne and over international waters, Carol Cooper formally placed Marlene Navarro under arrest. Formalities out of the way, they relaxed somewhat for the four-hour flight.

"So, Marlene, how are you?" Chellino asked.

"I've been better."

"You look good. You haven't changed. We were told you had had plastic surgery."

"Hey, how is Roberto, Mr. Darias?" she asked.

"Oh, he's good," Cooper said. "He'll be at the court house tomorrow."

"I've never understood why he did what he did."

"Your friend Jader Alvarez is with us, too."

"I know."

"He's going to cooperate."

"What's he got to cooperate with?" Navarro asked.

"We know a lot about him."

"Tell me, do you think that because you have Jader and me you are going to stop drugs in America?"

"Our job is simply to arrest you and bring you back to face an indictment," Chellino said. "You are going to be charged with laundering five million dollars of drug money."

"Where is my commission?" Navarro asked. They all laughed.

"You will face two hundred years in prison if you don't cooperate," Chellino said.

"My fate will be decided by the U.S. justice system, not by you," Navarro said.

"You're right about that."

"I hope I am not going to have to face the press at the airport."

"That is not under our control."

Eight DEA agents and four cars were waiting at Hangar One at the Opa-Locka Airport. Navarro was signed through Customs and taken to the Phoenix Building, where she was booked, photographed, fingerprinted, and allowed to make a single phone call.

She dialed a private number at the headquarters of the Supreme Court of Venezuela. It was after 7:00 P.M. in Caracas, an hour later than Miami. There was no answer.

From the DEA, Navarro was driven to the women's annex of the Dade County Jail near the Orange Bowl, stripped of all her clothing, and placed alone and naked in a cell marked "Suicidal" that was alive with large cockroaches.

Chellino and Cooper drove to the Chellino home in Pembroke Pines. It was Frank's younger daughter's birthday, and they were late for the party.

53

AFTER THREE DAYS, Marlene Navarro convinced her jailers that she was not suicidal, and was moved to the women's section of the North Dade Detention Center, a compact jail on a snake-infested, pine-shaded pond half a mile west of I-95 in scruffy North Miami. Navarro was denied bail, and began interviewing various lawyers who wanted to represent her. She had always made it her business to know an array of lawyers; in her purse when she had fled the United States were the business cards of more than a dozen Miami attorneys.

The government could not try Navarro and Carlos Jader Alvarez together because his trial had already begun when she was arrested. She rebuffed government overtures about pleading guilty and testifying against Jader Alvarez. She would go to trial with the only other Swordfish defendant then in pretrial custody, Bertha Paez (known only as Bertha during the operation), the money manager for José Antonio Cabrera. Paez, a rich, well-educated certified public accountant from Bogotá, had been extradited to the U.S. with Pepe Cabrera, (who was later tried separately and convicted of racketeering and drug smuggling).

Navarro asked an acquaintance for subscriptions to the *Economist,* the *Miami Herald,* and the *New York Times,* subscriptions which caused her name to wind up on the mailing list of Senator Robert Dole of Kansas.

"Dear Friend," Dole's computer wrote in soliciting contributions for Republican campaigns, "I need your immediate help."

"Talk about needing immediate help," Navarro remarked with a laugh. She wrote letters asking help from associates of Carlos Jader Alvarez. One request, which she dispatched by Federal Express, went to Juan Raman Mata Ballesteros, the drug lord and murderer who was in prison in Honduras. Mata did not reply.

Navarro also sent for a book of Emily Dickinson poems, a volume that contained "Indian Summer."

> *These are the days when birds come back,*
> *A very few, a bird or two,*
> *To take a parting look.*

These are the days when skies put on
The old, old sophistries of June—
A blue and gold mistake.

Friends briefed Navarro daily via a coin telephone in the jail on the progress of her boss's trial, which was being conducted by one of the most controversial judges in America, Alcee Lamar Hastings. Alcee Hastings, a frisky fifty-one years old, was less famous for his judicial work, which was average, than for his activity off the bench, which was unusual. As the only black person ever to serve as a federal judge in Florida, Hastings was an important voice in the civil rights movement. He was also one of the few federal judges in the history of the United States to have been prosecuted by the Department of Justice for criminal conduct while in office. Although a jury had acquitted Hastings of bribery charges in 1983, some of his fellow judges, believing that the charges were true and that Hastings had perjured himself, had begun proceedings to try to have him impeached. He had remained on the bench, while his legal problems, together with his provocative personality, kept his name in the headlines, a phenomenon that did not abate during the trial of Carlos Jader Alvarez.

"Hastings sees legalization of drugs by the year 2000," the *Miami Herald* headlined on the third Monday of the Alvarez trial. "I don't advocate the legalization of drugs," Hastings told a reporter, "but that's what's going to happen before the turn of the century. And, quite frankly, I don't give a damn." Hastings predicted that the flow of drugs into the United States would "dry up" if drugs were legalized. The judge had warned the Alvarez jury against reading the newspapers during the trial, and there was no indication that they had seen the article. Still, it seemed an odd interview for Hastings to give during a trial in his courtroom of people accused of drug crimes.

Unusual tension gripped the Alvarez trial. There was extra security in and around the court house because of the Colombian mafia's reputation for bold attempts to escape U.S. custody. There was extra pressure on both the prosecution and defense to win the case because of the prominence of Carlos Jader Alvarez. And there was spontaneous tension as well; friction developed early in the trial between Judge Hastings and the government's principal witness, Robert Darias. It became clear that there was a visceral, cut-of-the-gib animus between Hastings and Darias—a proud, smart, streetwise black and a proud, smart, streetwise Cuban, meeting on a public stage against a background of a quarter-century of tension between blacks and Latins in

Miami. Cubans generally had surpassed blacks economically, and blacks had said in a survey that there were too many Cubans in Miami. But Alcee Hastings and Robert Darias were both too independent to be controlled by ethnic stereotypes. They found specific issues in the courtroom to feud about.

Hastings decided that Darias as a witness tended to give unnecessarily expansive answers to the lawyers' questions. Jader Alvarez's lawyer asked Darias on cross-examination *when* a particular event had occurred. Since Darias did not recall the date, he tried to establish "when" by referring to other events whose dates were known. The lawyer objected. And the judge, after dispatching the jury to the jury room, admonished Darias.

"Mr. Darias, the answer you gave didn't answer the question 'when'?" Hastings said.

"Yes, sir, but when he asked that to me, I couldn't remember the date. So I was trying to pinpoint when. I understand what you are saying, and I'm going to try—"

"No," the judge interrupted, "you are not going to *try*. You're going to *do* what I'm asking you to do."

"Yes, sir."

"Now when you do that again, I'm going to get nasty."

Darias did not show anger, though he was furious. He had been putting his life on the line for the United States Government for five years at great cost. Now, this judge was acting as if *Darias* were on trial instead of Carlos Jader Alvarez.

The next day, Hastings reprimanded Darias again. *"When* does not require a soliloquy," Hastings snapped. "It requires a date. And if you don't know the date, then you can simply say that. But these soliloquies are not going to be tolerated."

"Yes, sir," replied Darias, who had not given a "soliliquy." He seethed but again showed little emotion.

None of the four federal judges who had presided over previous Swordfish trials—trials at which Darias had given much the same testimony as he was giving at the Alvarez trial—had seen fit to admonish him as Alcee Hastings did. Observers speculated that Hastings loathed all government spies; the FBI had used a spy against him in its bribery investigation.

The Alvarez jury, however, seemed to have no difficulty determining not only that Robert Darias was telling the truth but also that the evidence presented by Prosecutor Myles Malman and his deputy, Assistant U.S. Attorney Susan Tarbe, was peruasive. Although the trial took fourteen weeks, the jury took only an hour and a half to convict Carlos Jader Alvarez on Friday, May 9, 1986. Since the main count against him was operating a "continuing criminal enterprise," carrying a possible life term, Judge Hastings sentenced him to forty-five years in prison.

As arduous as the Alvarez trial had been for all concerned, the participants sensed that it had been only a warm-up for the trial of Marlene Navarro. The atmosphere of the Navarro trial, which promised to be the last of the major criminal trials spawned by Operation Swordfish, evoked the finals of an international athletic competition, with Robert Darias, his DEA controllers, and Prosecutors Malman and Tarbe as the reigning champions, and Marlene Navarro and her lawyers the latest challengers determined to defeat them.

For Darias, the Navarro trial was the true climax of his work in Operation Swordfish. Though he had infiltrated and then testified against several important targets, Darias had never had the personal relationship with them that he had formed with Navarro. His courtroom confrontation with her—they would be sitting only a few feet apart when he was on the witness stand—promised to be emotional and dramatic.

The lawyers for Navarro and Bertha Paez were primed to destroy Darias as a witness. They had studied other lawyers' cross-examination of him like game films, and had been coached by those other lawyers—some of the most prominent defense specialists in Miami—on how to question him. Bertha Paez's lawyer was a familiar face—Raymond Takiff, who had been given a list of the targets of the Swordfish and Grandma Mafia investigations by the bail bondsman Arthur Balletti while they were still secret. Takiff had cross-examined Darias at length once before when he represented Carlos Alvarado, the money courier called Tocayo. As Takiff put it to associates, he had not "eviscerated" Darias on that occasion and relished a second opportunity.

The Navarro trial also placed Darias again in potential conflict with Judge Alcee Hastings.

"Let's go on the record. United States of America versus Marlene Navarro."

Judge Hastings convened the trial and began selecting jurors on a steamy Monday morning, September 15, 1986, seven months after Navarro's detention in Caracas. Just the previous evening, the President of the United States and the First Lady, Ronald and Nancy Reagan, had made a rare joint television address to the nation about the deepening drug crisis in America.

"Drugs are menacing our society, threatening our values, under-cutting our institutions and killing our children," the President had asserted.

Reports of the speech appeared on the front pages of the *Miami Herald* and other newspapers nationwide on Monday morning. In the courtroom, Marlene Navarro's lawyer, Michael Brodsky, asked Judge Hastings to determine whether the speech had tainted the objectivity of any of the prospective jurors. Hastings scoffed.

"What about it?" he said of the speech. "I wasn't impressed; were you?"

"I wasn't impressed either," Brodsky said. "But there may be a lot of jurors—"

"But what is Reagan going to do about drugs?" the judge asked. "We're going to 'Just Say No.' Give me a break!"

The judge agreed, however, to mention the speech to the pool of potential jurors.

"Last night, the President and the First Lady of this country spoke on television regarding one of the biggest problems that exists in our country," Hastings began. "And that problem has to do with drugs. . . . Do any of you feel, because these defendants are charged with drug law violations, do you know of any reason, sympathy, prejudice, religious views, or any reason which would make it difficult or impossible for you to sit as an impartial juror in this case?"

Those assembled shook their heads no, and Hastings went on to choose fourteen jurors and alternates—ten women and four men—six whites, five blacks, and three Latins.

Frank Chellino was the government's first witness against Marlene Navarro. Chellino's prominence as a witness—the undercover president of Dean International, now sworn to tell the truth about dozens of complex events five years after the fact—was privately amusing to some people because Chellino was notorious for having a bad memory. It had been a running joke between Carol Cooper and Robert Darias during Operation Swordfish. But Chellino was a smooth, assured witness, and pre-trial cramming seemed to surmount any memory lapses at the Navarro trial. And since the defense lawyers were unaware of the issue, they were unable to exploit it. Testifying at his sixth Swordfish trial, Chellino described the origin of Operation Swordfish and the Miami Lakes company known as Dean International Investments. As the first of the secretly recorded videotapes began rolling—the one picturing Lionel Paytubi and Manuel Sanchez on their first visit to Dean International on July 15, 1981—Marlene Navarro suddenly was overcome by nausea, and dashed into the anteroom off the courtroom. Judge Hastings sent the jury out.

"Seeing those tapes made me go into the bathroom," Navarro told the judge a few minutes later. "I hope God is going to help me through these things."

Robert Darias took the witness stand in a dark Pierre Cardin suit looking as usual like a Castilian gentleman. Darias was always a bit tense at the beginning of a trial because of his less-than-perfect English and because of slight difficulty in hearing, a legacy of the Bay of Pigs. He knew the defense lawyers would take every advantage of his handicaps, and he was wary of Judge Hastings as well. After only a few questions and answers from prosecutor Myles Malman, the judge sensed that the jurors were having difficulty understanding Darias's Cuban accent. Asking him to speak up, the judge told the jury, "Ladies and gentlemen, it's going to be difficult for you following his rhythm, but *believe me,* about a month from now, you will understand him very well—no question." The jury failed to grasp Hastings's sarcasm, but it wasn't lost on Darias, Malman, or the defense lawyers.

As Malman was taking Darias through the events of August 1981, when Marlene Navarro first delivered tainted cash to Dean International, Darias explained how he had first met Navarro's attorney and friend Lester Rogers. From her seat at the defense table Navarro suddenly shouted: "Lester never met Roberto! Roberto never met— that is not true, Your Honor!"

Judge Hastings quickly dispatched the jury to the jury room.

"That's not true!" Navarro shouted, her brown eyes flashing. "He never met Roberto, he never did!"

Hastings sent Darias from the courtroom.

"Bastard! Dirty bastard!" Navarro screamed as Darias passed in front of the defense table. "Somebody as clean as Mr. Lester Rogers. He's an honest man. You're a rat, that's what you are! A rat!"

Robert found himself shaken by Marlene's outburst as he took a seat in the foyer. It had been the most emotional moment yet in all of the Swordfish trials. Robert still felt too much affection for Marlene to enjoy watching her suffer.

In the courtroom, Judge Hastings was trying to soothe Navarro.

"If you feel like you see an outburst coming on," the judge said, "just ask me, and I'll recess, and then you can talk with your lawyer and go back in the anteroom there and scream and holler all you want."

To the lawyers, Hastings said: "I can remove her butt from this court, under the law."

After the jurors had returned, Judge Hastings instructed them to ignore the outburst. "Ms. Navarro is not a person trained in courtroom experiences," Hastings said. "The fact of the matter is that sometimes people don't understand the process in other cultures and other countries."

Since Raymond Takiff had experience cross-examining Darias, it was agreed that he would lead the defense questioning. In effect Takiff represented not only his client but also the other Miami defense lawyers who had been embarrassed by their failure over the course of five trials in five years to destroy Darias. They were egging Takiff on.

In view of the overwhelming evidence against Marlene Navarro and Bertha Paez, the defense lawyers' only chance of winning their acquittal was destroying the credibility of Darias's testimony *about* the evidence and sullying the jury's view of his character. Toward that goal, Takiff tried to nurture doubts in the jurors' minds about Darias's use of deception in spying on Navarro and her associates.

"Mr. Darias, during the course of your employment with the Drug Enforcement Administration, is it not a fact that it was necessary for you to convince various people of various things that were untrue?" Takiff began.

"Yes."

"And in doing that, naturally, it was necessary for you to lie, correct?"

"No."

"Did you speak truthfully at all times?"

"It was a cover. I wouldn't call it a lie."

"A cover?"

"A cover. It was the story that I was told to use by the government and they were things that didn't exist. But it was not, in my concept, used as a lie. It was used as a cover for the operation."

"It's true, Mr. Darias, that you lied and you lied repeatedly, correct?"

"That's not a fact, sir."

With Judge Hastings's permission, Takiff read to the jury from his own cross-examination of Darias at the trial of Lester Rogers and Carlos Alvarado.

"Mr. Darias, while working for the Drug Enforcement Administration, it has been necessary for you to convince people of things that were not true, isn't that a fact?"

"Yes."

"And in convincing people of things that were not true, you lied, correct?"

"Yes."

"And not only did you lie, you were indeed a convincing liar, isn't that a fact?"

"I wouldn't call it a lie. I would call it a cover."

"You were a convincing liar, were you not, sir?"

"I was acting under orders."

"And in acting under orders you were able to fool and trick people by lying to them?"

"I was able to convince people."

"And you did that by lying, correct?"

"By using my cover, yes."

"Did you speak the truth, Mr. Darias, yes or no?"

"No."

"So when you don't speak the truth, you lie, correct?"

"No."

"Your definition of not speaking the truth does not include a lie, is that your testimony?"

"Not when it is in the course of this type of investigation. I call it a cover."

"And you convinced people of things that were not the truth, correct?"

"Yes."

"And you have gotten that down to a science, convincing people of things that were not the truth?"

"I did my job."

"And you did it well, correct?"

"Yes, sir."

"And in truth and in fact your job was to go around and lie and deceive people, correct?"

"No."

It was not surprising that Darias had difficulty answering Takiff's question with perfect candor and consistency. Takiff had struck at the heart of the spy's dilemma. Darias had vented his frustration to the DEA agents more than once during Operation Swordfish. "It is getting harder for me to talk to these people," he had told Carol Cooper late one night. "You can *lie* and *lie* and *lie*. . . . You are imitating somebody that you're not." Cooper had once laughingly called Darias's spiel to his targets a "big line of garbage." To Paul Sennett he had said, "You start talking to people you don't like and start selling them ideas that are not your own and there's a breaking point in your character where you cannot take any more."

It was unclear how the jury was receiving the testimony.

Judge Hastings, while occasionally faulting Darias's testimony as he had at the Alvarez trial, grew impatient with Ray Takiff's cross-examination and began admonishing him for raising questions such as the "lying spy" sequence that were irrelevant to the guilt or innocence of the defendants.

"If Darias was a scumbag to the twentieth degree, raised to the thirtieth power, how does that detract from the [evidence against your clients]?" the judge wondered, out of the jury's presence.

Takiff nevertheless continued to pummel Darias. Had Darias lied on an application for a notary public license or on applications to purchase firearms? No, Darias replied, he had misinterpreted questions on both forms about his criminal record. Had Darias taken a kickback from Lionel Paytubi? Darias denied he had, and Takiff did not pursue the discredited Paytubi allegation (which had not figured prominently in the Alvarez trial either).

The defense tried to serve a subpoena on Amelia Darias and one of her relatives, and on a small corporation they owned, alleging that Robert Darias had illegally concealed assets through the corporation—a charge without foundation. Takiff's questioning revealed that the defense had learned through a private detective the address of the house where Darias and his family had been living in the Miami area. As soon as court adjourned for that day, Robert rushed to a private telephone and ordered Amelia and Laura to move to an out-of-the-way motel in Miami Beach. Then he telephoned Carol Cooper.

"I have the family secured," Darias said.

Darias and Cooper had not spoken on the telephone much during the trial. She was not permitted to prompt him on testimony or other court proceedings that occurred while he was not there.

"Let me ask you a question between you, me, and the lamp post, Bob? Did you derive any income from that corporation of your relatives' that you didn't report to IRS?"

"No."

"Anything else like this, Bob, that's going to come up, any other stuff?"

"No."

"How d'you feel?"

He sighed.

"Drained?" she asked.

"Shocked. This is really a shock to me."

"I want you to get some rest and relax, as much as you can. We *will* take care of your family. You know that. We *will* do it."

Knowing Raymond Takiff would ask Darias on the witness stand about any out-of-court conversations, Carol quickly reviewed the gist of their conversation. "We did not talk about anything of any substance, other than they tried to subpoena your family," she said. "We can talk about that, and I simply advised you to move out of that location."

"Right, I called you to ask if you could give me protection until after the trial. That's it."

Robert managed only about two hours of sleep that night, and his fatigue was evident in court the next morning.

Like a fighter smelling blood, Takiff stepped up his attack.

"Mr. Darias, since you testified yesterday, have you discussed with anyone those things that you have testified to in court?"

"No, sir."

Takiff went on to probe the irrelevant financial details of Robert's relatives' corporation, and the judge, after sending the jury out, again admonished Takiff.

"There are a lot of ways to unduly prejudice a jury," Hastings said. "You've consumed a lot of time on nitpicking nothing. You have not dealt specifically with anything having to do with the charged offenses against [the defendants]."

The judge announced to the jury that a scene for *Miami Vice* would be shot in the courtroom the following Thursday.

Alcee Hastings's propensity for landing on the front page of the *Miami Herald* intruded on the Navarro trial.

"Did Hastings Lie at His Bribery Trial?" bannered the *Herald* on a Sunday in December. "14 judges say yes, embattled jurist says no." The article, the first of a series, set forth the findings of a "judicial council" of judges conducting the latest investigation of Hastings. The article spanned two full pages inside the newspaper, each page headed: "The Case Against Judge Hastings."

In court, Navarro's lawyer Michael Brodsky questioned the effect the articles might have on the Navarro jurors.

"This article tends to imply that you may have committed the crime for which you were charged," Brodsky argued to the judge. "If the jurors read that—have that feeling because of the implications in the paper—I think my client has certainly not an unreasonable thought of why should she sit in a trial where a juror thinks that a judge has committed a crime which he had not committed."

"Quite frankly, I don't care what they think," Hastings retorted. "I don't care what you think; I don't care what your client thinks; I don't care what the Judicial Council thinks; I don't give a damn what the Congress thinks. A jury has spoken and ultimately Congress will. However, I do think you're entitled to your questions concerning whether or not there is anyone on this jury who doubts or questions my presiding in *this* case."

Hastings called in the jury and asked whether they had seen the *Herald* article. Four jurors acknowledged having "seen" the article together with photographs of Hastings but assured the judge that they had not read the article.

"Please note that it had nothing to do with this trial," the judge cautioned.

Darias and Cooper conferred frequently by phone over the Christmas holidays.

"What bothers me is how can Takiff tell the judge that something is mine when it is my relatives'," Darias said, referring to their corporation. "That's what really makes me mad. It's totally untrue. Takiff is lying through his teeth."

"I thought Takiff looked like an idiot, screaming and hollering," Cooper said.

"I am mad and I am discouraged because of the way the judge has let Takiff get off the track of the trial itself."

"I don't want Takiff harassing your family."

"He has to confuse the jury somehow because he doesn't have anything else."

In early January, Robert Darias testified that Marlene Navarro had occasionally talked explicitly of smuggling cocaine when they were alone together. At the defense table, Navarro began muttering angrily. The judge sent the jury out.

"Now what's the problem?" the judge asked.

"We need a composition break for Ms. Navarro," Brodsky said. "She needs to compose herself."

"A 'composition break,' that's good language," replied Prosecutor Malman. "In my very limited knowledge of Spanish, what I heard emanating from her mouth was the word, quote, unquote, 'F-U-C-K-I-N-G N-I-G-G-E-R,' something or another. And then I heard an expletive in Spanish I haven't heard since my days as a prosecutor in the ghettoes of New York. And I'm not attributing any ill will to the ghettoes of New York, but I'm saying it's street language and it's inappropriate in a U.S. District Court House." (Navarro's second comment translated to: "Your mother is a whore.")

Navarro erupted again three weeks later, calling Darias "maricón," the Spanish word for "faggot."

Though Darias showed little emotion at these outbursts, they saddened him. He knew they reflected the pain and anguish which he had helped the government bring to Marlene or, as the agents would say, helped her bring on herself. He found himself thinking back to the pleasant moments between them—the Christmas perfume he had given her, the wine and laughs he had shared with her and Alex McIntosh, the quiet talk on the plane returning from Denver when she fell asleep on his shoulder. Sometimes it was difficult to remember that Marlene Navarro was a rapacious drug profiteer, destroying lives in the pursuit of money.

On Friday, January 30, 1987, Darias completed his thirty-fifth and last day on the witness stand since October 31. It was his longest court appearance by far in the Swordfish trials. Though Frank Chellino and other DEA agents had assured the jury of Darias's honesty and effectiveness during Operation Swordfish, the defense lawyers' prolonged assault on his integrity had been excruciating. He still felt he had done the right thing in helping the government prosecute Marlene Navarro. But the testimony, particularly the cross-examination, had exhausted and depressed him.

"Testifying against these people is much harder than infiltrating them," Robert told Amelia in their Miami Beach hideaway that evening.

"It wasn't worth it," she replied. "None of it was worth being driven from our home." Amelia had been under a doctor's care and taking antidepressants and tranquilizers since the subpoena in December had forced the family into hiding.

After several weeks, Judge Hastings finally quashed the baseless subpoena.

As the Navarro trial dragged on in Hastings's courtroom on the fifth floor of the court house, a shorter trial was held on the ninth floor before Judge William Hoeveler. Brooks Muse III and Special Agent Steve Gibbs had been indicted for "corruption, fraud, dishonesty, trickery and deceit" in compromising the Grandma Mafia investigation and allowing Barbara Mouzin to flee the United States. The indictment did not mention the compromise of Operation Swordfish. Muse and Gibbs had pleaded not guilty. Barbara Mouzin, who was still trying to win a reduction of her twenty-five-year sentence, was the star witness against them. Muse and Gibbs were convicted by the jury and both sentenced to three years in prison—a term the government considered too lenient.

"Brutal Cocaine Bosses Terrorize Colombia."

The banner headline in the *Miami Herald* on Sunday, February 8, appeared over the first of a four-part series of articles entitled "The World's Deadliest Criminals." Beginning on page one, the first article spread across two full pages inside the newspaper. A rogue's gallery of more than two dozen photographs included pictures of Carlos Jader Alvarez and Marlene Navarro.

In the courtroom, before bringing in the jury, Judge Hastings pronounced the publication of Navarro's photograph during her trial a "dastardly deed." But when the judge asked the jurors whether they had read or heard anything about the trial or anyone involved in it, they said no.

The jury's interest had ebbed noticeably during the defense's prolonged battering of Robert Darias. Now it quickened as Prosecutor Myles Malman called a parade of government witnesses who testified about secret stashes of drug cash and the secret surveillance of airplanes at the Opa-Locka Airport in the dead of night. As Marlene Navarro listened, she faced away from the jury and wept softly.

On February 12, Carol Cooper, who was ill and wobbly from a car accident, began her presentation of about 300 telephone conversations out of the more than 2,000 recorded during the wiretap on Navarro's telephones. The jury was riveted as it heard Navarro deploying the couriers of Carlos Jader Alvarez across the United States—upbraiding the hapless Oscar, cheering the distraught godfather, weeping at the danger of being shot for $105,000. Sitting at the defense table, Navarro evidently had fired her last salvo of overt anger; she was stoic through the playing of the telephone tapes and several videotapes, which ended in the middle of March. By that time, the Navarro trial had become the longest federal trial in the history of the southern judicial district of Florida.

"Hit team targeted Prosecutor: U.S. Attorney under Guard against Colombian Drug Traffickers."

The six-column page-one headline in the *Miami Herald* on March

17 referred to Leon Kellner, the United States Attorney in Miami and the boss of Swordfish prosecutor Myles Malman.

"Kellner and his family were put under 24-hour armed guard after federal drug enforcement officials learned that a Colombian hit team was being sent to assassinate him," the *Herald* reported. The threat had been conveyed to U.S. authorities by a "very sensitive source in Colombia," the story said. In speculating about possible sources of the plot, the *Herald* mentioned that the alleged narcotics traffickers who had been extradited to stand trial in the U.S. included Marlene Navarro, who was currently on trial. Judge Hastings again warned the jury against reading the newspapers.

Marlene Navarro spent a month on the witness stand in her own defense. Looking surprisingly vibrant after more than a year in jail, she was dressed and coiffed conservatively, and seemed far less threatening than she had appeared in her photograph as one of the "world's deadliest criminals" in the *Miami Herald*.

Since the beginning of the trial, Navarro had become a figure of myth and mystery to the habitués of the courtroom. Most of those present (except for the jury) knew that she had been an international fugitive and had been spirited under questionable circumstances out of Caracas, Venezuela, where she had been living under an assumed name. The spectators had heard testimony *about* Marlene Navarro every day. They had eyed her at the defense table, her silent repose broken occasionally by angry outbursts. They had listened to her recorded voice in 300 telephone conversations and on a number of videotapes. Now, they savored the prospect of her testimony.

Navarro had decided to testify in English. She did not want to relinquish control of the nuances of language to court-employed interpreters. She could switch from fluent English to broken English as it suited her.

Michael Brodsky asked Navarro how she developed a relationship of trust with Robert Darias.

"Roberto was, for me, since the beginning, a very special person," Navarro testified. "He knew how to treat me. Hey, I thought, this is the first time somebody take care of me. So I start depend on him for everything. I also looked for protection in men, that was what I did. And Roberto did everything that my grandfather did. He talk very soft to me. He was very attentive. And, unfortunately, he got a certain physical features that my grandfather has as the color of his eyes, and maybe his nose. So for me, Roberto was the best thing that I thought could happen in my life. Nobody can understand that, only me, because I know what I felt for him."

Brodsky asked Navarro if she had ever slept with Darias.

"Never, Michael, never. As a matter of fact, he was a married man. He was a father. He was a good husband. He portrayed to me as my grandfather was. For me, he was the most honest, the most good father. A fantastic husband. He got whatever I expected in a man. So, no, sir, never. I never was attracted to him sexually. It was a special kind of relationship, as I had with my grandfather."

Though she told the truth about her relationship with Darias, Navarro used most of her testimony to weave an elaborate web of lies about her role as the chief North American operative for Carlos Jader Alvarez.

She denied knowing that Alvarez and José Antonio Cabrera were godfathers of the narcotics mafia. She claimed that Alvarez was a legitimate businessman, and that her many references to "Pepe" were not to Pepe Cabrera but to a bullfighter named Pepe who did business with Carlos Jader Alvarez.

She claimed that the millions of dollars in cash that she had marshalled for Jader Alvarez were the revenues of cattle transactions, real estate transactions, diamond and emerald transactions, and farm equipment transactions.

She denied ever having discussed cocaine shipments with Robert Darias.

She denied that Luis Rodriguez supplied the cocaine paste—the "rough stuff"—to the Alvarez syndicate from Peru.

She denied knowing and having worked with Isaac Kattan, her predecessor as one of the main North American financial managers for the Latin drug mafia.

Judge Hastings had to adjourn the trial for a few days during Navarro's testimony when she was taken ill. The initial diagnosis was a colon infection, but eventually doctors found two uterine cysts. Her lawyer reported to Judge Hastings that apparently Navarro not only had to endure pain but the indignity of being assaulted by other female prisoners awaiting gynecological treatment in the lock-up at Jackson Memorial Hospital. "They kicked Marlene, they poured milk down her throat," Brodsky explained to the judge. "When she complained, they said, 'Are you pregnant? Your baby needs milk.' "

Brodsky, however, agreed with Hastings's observation that Navarro's ability to testify had not been affected.

Like a seasoned long-distance runner, prosecutor Myles Malman began his cross-examination gently.

"Tell us what degrees you have," he asked Navarro.

"Well, my first degree was in France, the baccalaureate. Then I got a fine arts degree. Then I have a course in European politics from the College of Economics and Politics in France. Then I came to this country and I went to the Miami-Dade College here. I did my two years of college."

"What did you study?"

"I took the requirement in order to be a subject of the University of Miami."

"In what course?"

"Many. Especially was language, humanities, computers, accounting, all the requirements. They are sixty credits, but I think I made more because I always liked to study."

"And eventually you achieved a degree at the University of Miami, didn't you?"

"Yes, I did. Not only one, I did many, I was in several."

"Well, let's talk about the first one, your Bachelor of Arts. What was that degree in, ma'am?"

"It was major in economics, minor in art."

"And you went on to the MBA, the Master of Business Administration program at the University of Miami, didn't you?"

"Yes."

Malman handed Navarro a copy of her subpoenaed transcript from the university and began referring to it.

"And you studied, among other things, the legal system, didn't you?"

"Yes, it was the course I didn't pay attention to."

"Did you study International Economics?"

"Yes, that was my major."

"Did you study economic theory?"

"Yes."

"After you achieved your degree in economics, what type of courses did you continue to take at the University of Miami?"

"I continued having several. It was one in Law and Real Estate, the other was in International Business. And I continued, I think, with one language, that at this particular time wasn't very fluent, which was Italian. Maybe I continued having, oh, Hebrew, too, and some of them that I don't recall anymore."

Having established Navarro's impeccable educational credentials, particularly her expertise and sophistication in international financial matters, Malman then questioned her about her money management business, culminating in her handling of money for Carlos Jader Alvarez.

"How much money do you say that you caused, either personally or through other folks, to be delivered to Robert Darias? What is the round, ballpark figure? Not down to the penny."

"That he stole, too? The money that he stole?" Navarro asked, referring to her empty contention that Darias had embezzled money from her.

"The money that *you delivered to him.* So if he stole, you say he stole money, it would include that."

"I don't recall, sir. The truth is I don't have paper. My only recollection are my soul, my despair. That is my recollection, sir. I don't have figures in my mind. I have my anguish, that is what I have. No figures."

"From whatever you have, Ms. Navarro. Approximately how much—in cash?"

"I don't recall, sir."

"More than a million?"

"I think so, sir."

"Was it more than two million dollars?"

"Yes."

"Was it more than three million dollars?"

"That I cannot tell you, sir. I don't recall."

"Would your best recollection be that it's somewhere between two and three million dollars?"

"Yes. To the best of my recollection, yes."

The actual figure was well in excess of five million dollars, which excluded many millions more that Navarro had sent to Colombia by other means.

Malman accelerated, piling up Navarro's lies, providing the government an opportunity to prosecute her later for perjury if it chose to do so.

"Of course, you had no contact with anyone that was in the cocaine business at all, correct?"

"Correct, sir."

In a last effort to elicit juror sympathy for Navarro, Michael Brodsky invoked the kidnapping of the Alvarez children.

"In September of 1982 did you still believe the money you had sent to Colombia was for use of the ransom to pay the kidnappers?"

"Yes, sir."

"Why did you believe that?"

"Because the kids *had been kidnapped*. I was a witness of that. I mean, everyone knew. It was in the newspapers. It was on television. The President, himself, led the funeral procession. The President, himself, was on television giving condolences to the family. The people of Colombia, most of Bogotá, people went in front of the President, asked for punishment for the kidnappers. Everybody knew, sir, and I knew, that the money was for the kidnapping."

Bertha Paez also took the stand in her defense against the charges that she had aided the Jader Alvarez organization in its movement of drug money. The jury seemed tired and restless.

"Marlene Navarro has claimed that she was basically a legitimate businesswoman," Myles Malman asserted in his closing argument to the jury, "handling some money, handling all these different businesses, helping Mr. Carlos Jader Alvarez. And that she was misguided, misled, led around by Robert Darias. *Relied* on Robert Darias. And Robert Darias is the one who basically led her astray. Well, if you go back and believe the Miami Airport incident in August of 1980, with Maria Lilia Rojas and the Monopoly boxes and Pepe Cabrera, you go back to Lionel Paytubi and Isaac Kattan, you know that the connection to Jader Alvarez started before she met Darias. And I submit to you that Marlene Navarro was *handling this organization* for Carlos Jader Alvarez. Do you really think that a man like Carlos Jader Alvarez, a man so powerful—power that reaches to the top of the Colombian government—do you think that a man so intertwined in this business, this cocaine business, and a guy like Pepe Cabrera—do you think people like that would trust some *fluff brain* to handle millions and millions of dollars in cash? Do you really think that?"

The jury took three days to sift nine and a half months of evidence and return a verdict of guilty against both Navarro and Paez.

Marlene Navarro appeared for her sentencing on the last Thursday in July 1987, in a blue two-piece suit, a white blouse, and six-inch heels. The courtroom was full. A number of DEA agents were present, including Carol Cooper, who was now based in Washington, and Frank Chellino, who still held Tom Clifford's old job in Miami, chief of intelligence.

"Ms. Navarro, is there anything you wish to say?" asked Judge Hastings, chewing on a coffee stirrer.

A defiant Marlene Navarro strode to the podium.

"I say, Your Honor, that Ms. Cooper and Mr. Chellino came to my funeral, and that is nice of them. But I don't intend to bury myself today, Your Honor. I will fight as I have been since five years ago. My tears are not tears of defeat. They are tears of anger." She alluded to her Jewish faith, and accused Frank Chellino of anti-Semitism.

"When I was kidnapped in Venezuela, Your Honor, the undercover police knew that I couldn't let another person go down with me. That person was ready to be the chief of the Supreme Court in Venezuela. The undercover police told me that if I don't go in the dog cage, they will bring that matter to the public, and he will be accused of being the lover of the biggest drug dealer in the world. I couldn't let an old person finish his days in the shame that my situation will bring him." Navarro was referring to her love affair with the president of the Venezuelan Supreme Court, Rene de Sola.

"I don't blame you, Your Honor," Navarro continued. "I know that they chose the hardest time of your life to be in the middle of my trial. I wish you the best. I wish you to have better conditions than I do."

Hastings was taken aback. Navarro was addressing him as if *he* were on the verge of going to prison.

"I did love those children, Your Honor," she went on. "Mr. Darias has money, freedom, and his family. Ms. Cooper is in Washington. Mr. Chellino is the chief of intelligence. Mr. Bush is still the vice president of the United States. And the kids? They are dead. So what is the result of this?"

Michael Brodsky asked Hastings to impose the minimum sentence the law allowed—ten years in prison. "Any sentence above the minimum would only further destroy her," Brodsky pleaded. "It would be like breaking a wild horse."

Myles Malman took the podium and attacked Navarro without the subtlety that had characterized his cross-examination.

"In all my years in law enforcement, I can number Frank Chellino and Carol Cooper among the finest law enforcement professionals that I have ever encountered, and to say that Frank Chellino is anti-Semitic is a lie of the most outrageous proportions," Malman declared.

"Ms. Navarro is educated. She is cultured. She is manipulative. She is cajoling. She, in reality, has great disdain for this country. Her testimony was filled with lies, and the jury so found. She is unwilling to face the reality of her acts. She's very, very educated. She is very bright. She is extremely articulate, and then she comes before this court and says that it was all for the children. She comes into this court asking for compassion and mercy, and crying.

"When Ms. Navarro cries before you and asks you for mercy and forgiveness, I know that the Court will also think of the tears of the mothers in this country who cry tears because their children, their husbands, their fathers, their sons are destroyed by this poison, by this cocaine, and Ms. Navarro stands before you, Judge, and says it wasn't cocaine. It was just money.

"Judge, the money is why this business is accomplished; and the most pernicious thing that I can conceive of is hiding behind children who are kidnapped, children who were murdered, and saying that this case is about kidnapping. It is not about kidnapping. It is about drugs and the money that is generated from drugs, and it is about the way that this drug money corrupts and pollutes the moral fiber of people, and Ms. Navarro must be held accountable, and I think the focus should be on the damage that the organization of Carlos Jader Alvarez brought to this country. The organization could never have flourished, could never have achieved one single result, could never have made one single penny, if it was not for the conduct of Marlene Navarro."

It was time for Alcee Hastings to have his say.

"Ms. Navarro, concerning your personal reference to me about it being the most difficult time of my life: Wrong. It was not the most difficult time of my life. The most difficult time of my life is yet to come, and that is the day that I die. By and large, I live my life to the fullest. Even though I am going through some personal travail, it has no bearing on any of my rulings in this case whatsoever, and I am sure that your lawyer, as well as the government, if anything, were surprised that I could do the work that I did during that period of time.

"I listened very carefully to all of the things you said," Hastings continued. "I didn't hear a single moment of contrition."

"I don't know how to say the word," Navarro said.

"You don't know how to say, 'I am guilty.' You don't know how to look, as all of us did in this courtroom, at the videotapes with piles of money. It would not have mattered had it been Carol Cooper and Frank Chellino, or Mickey Mouse and Donald Duck, that was sitting there. Nobody—*nobody*—takes piles—suitcases—of money to a storefront operation to do *legitimate business*. Your mouth ran off all over those tapes, and all that was talk about laundering money, and *those profits came from drugs*. Make no mistake about it.

"And so for that reason, you see, if you stood there and told me,

'Say, hey, Judge, you know, these people used me, and this jury found me guilty, and I was involved,' then I would tell you I would be thinking entirely differently about your sentence. But, no, you do not do that. Still you accuse. You accuse the government. You accuse the functionaries of the government. And then you accuse some arbitrary something out there."

"Your Honor—"

"Let me tell you," Hastings snapped, "what is in your best interest right now is not to interrupt me. You are going to have to live with this particular sentence. And so as we don't have any misunderstanding, I think you were guilty, and I think that the jury was correct in their assessment."

Hastings toted up Navarro's sentence on the various counts, including operating a "continuing criminal enterprise."

"You are committed to the custody of the Attorney General of the United States or his authorized representative for imprisonment for a term of thirty-two years."

ROBERT DARIAS stared at the ocean from the balcony of a small apartment near a weedy beach north of Miami. He and Amelia had rented the place under an assumed name. Sparsely furnished, it had few comfortable chairs and no carpets. The rent was paid by relatives.

The same United States Government that had abandoned Darias and his comrades at the Bay of Pigs a quarter century earlier appeared to have abandoned him again. He had not heard from the DEA agents or the Justice Department lawyers after the conviction and sentencing of Marlene Navarro. Nothing had been said, not even a phone call, about his crucial role in the trial.

The agents and lawyers toasted each other after the Navarro verdict at a celebratory dinner to which Darias was not invited. Nor had he been included previously when the Department of Justice and the DEA showered the agents and supervisors of Operation Swordfish with promotions, salary raises, awards, plaques, and certificates of commendation.

Carol Cooper and Frank Chellino had been promoted to GS-13.

Paul Sennett, Robert Russo, and Dan Hoerner, who already were GS-13s, had been given raises in salary.

Tom Clifford, despite his problems during the operation, had been transferred to Washington, promoted, and given the Attorney General's Award, one of the Justice Department's highest awards. (The honor to Clifford angered Frank Chellino and Carol Cooper, who felt it was not merited.)

The DEA had given commemorative plaques to a number of people outside the agency like Angel Santiago, the banker who had coached Tom Clifford in the procedures of starting an investment company, and Robert Force, the assistant vice president of the La Salle National Bank in Chicago, who had helped provide cover for Dean International's financial transactions. In all, some ninety people inside and outside the U.S. Government had received recognition of their role in the operation.

In another wave of approbation, around the end of the Navarro trial, the United States Attorney in Miami, Leon Kellner, sent an extraordinary letter of commendation about Special Agent Carol Cooper to Vice President George Bush at the White House.

The letter—four pages, single-spaced—described Cooper's "extraordinary efforts and outstanding achievements" in "some of the most significant narcotics cases in the country," including Operation Swordfish. "Throughout all these investigations and prosecutions, Agent Cooper has worked tenaciously, unselfishly and with the highest tenet of professionalism. Everyone in this office who has worked with Agent Cooper unequivocally respects and admires her unique dedication to serve her country. Agent Cooper is considered the best at what she does. . . . We feel strongly that she should receive the proper recognition which she deserves."

The entire top echelon of the U.S. Attorney's Office signed the letter, including Swordfish prosecutor Myles Malman. The letter did not mention a more candid and highly confidential analysis of the relative importance of Carol Cooper and Robert Darias, which the same U.S. Attorney's Office had sent to the Department of Justice near the end of Operation Swordfish:

"Robert Darias, a paid special employee of the DEA, is the central witness in the case. He was present at virtually every key meeting and involved in every transaction. . . . The DEA special agents involved in this case performed basically back-up functions."

Darias knew nothing of either letter, but it wasn't the lack of a letter, plaque, or dinner invitation that concerned him the most. It was that nothing had been said about the $100,000 the DEA owed him. And nothing had been said about the DEA's promise to intercede with the Internal Revenue Service on his behalf.

Through desultory days and fretful nights, Darias kept recalling the encouraging words of the DEA agents during Operation Swordfish. He even reviewed his tape recordings of a few conversations with Carol Cooper and Paul Sennett:

"You're basically the operation—I think you know that."

"You are really one of us."

"You're the primary guy."

"You're the hub of the operation."

"All of us consider you a very close friend, and we want you to be aware of that."

"What you're giving us is obviously the basis for the vast majority of what we're doing."

"We swear by you—as far as we're concerned, you're a gold mine."

On the specific question of interceding on Darias's behalf with the IRS, the DEA agents had been equally comforting:

"It will be taken care of—there's no problem."

"We will get it resolved."

"We'll go through this thing together—we will get it resolved."

"Things are rolling. Hang tight. I don't play around."

"Paul and I—I think you know—we're gonna do our best to take care of you at the end. We're gonna be backing you up. Don't worry about that. We're not gonna leave you out there hanging."

What seemed to Darias the most cynical comment of all had come from Carol Cooper at the height of her bureaucratic war with Tom Clifford for control of Operation Swordfish—the pivotal months when Darias himself effectively was running the operation while Cooper, Sennett, and Chellino were in exile—their careers in jeopardy, and when they were rooting for Darias to intercede with their DEA bosses on their behalf.

"Hopefully, at the end, we can take care of your tax problem, number one. Number two, you should get enough [money] at the end that—I can't give you a figure, but you're gonna be able to live very, very comfortably. And number three, we'll take care of you through the trials. I don't see any problem with any of that."

The DEA as an institution, whatever ineffectual attempts Cooper and the others had made, had in effect reneged on all three promises. It had halved his salary midway through the trials, and then stopped it entirely before the Alvarez and Navarro trials. It had used part of his bonus to pay expenses during the trials, thus reducing the bonus from $100,000 to about $73,000. And it had not paid him the balance of the bonus.

As callous as the DEA seemed to Darias, the Internal Revenue Service was worse. He had spoken to a string of IRS bureaucrats who had given new meaning to the words "Kafkaesque" and "Orwellian."

"I think we can come to some understanding on this matter," said a polite, condescending lawyer in the IRS's Southeast District Office in Jacksonville. "I'm desirous of wrapping this thing up. But I think it's important for you to understand, Mr. Darias, that it will require *good faith—a child-like good faith*—on your part. You have to say, 'I will tell you everything. I have nothing to hide. I am going to pay to the Government everything I can pay, recognizing that of course you have to have clothes on your back. But not anything like 'I must retain this' or 'I must retain that' or 'I have to have luxuries.' It's not a bargaining type process. We're not here to bargain."

"A child-like good faith." Robert smiled ruefully to himself. It seemed to him that he had invested a "child-like good faith" in the United States Government on repeated occasions from the Bay of Pigs to Operation Swordfish. And what had it gotten him?

"What I have to do," the IRS man droned on, "is ultimately take to the [IRS] District Director's office an offer from you. I cannot guarantee anything but I believe I understand what they're looking for. In some sense, what I'm doing is acting as your attorney to a degree. I'm going to tell you what I think is an acceptable offer."

Darias smiled again at the notion of an IRS lawyer acting as *his attorney* in a dispute with the IRS.

"We can come to an understanding," the lawyer assured him.

In subsequent months, the IRS lawyer in Jacksonville seemed to have disappeared—at least he had stopped taking Darias's calls—and Robert had found himself on the telephone listening to the sweet, girlish voice of a woman who apparently had been assigned the Darias case in the Fort Lauderdale office of the IRS.

"There are a lot of factors to be considered, okay?" the woman said. "I don't have the final say. I just review it, and then I make a report of what I feel should happen." She acknowledged that she hadn't yet read Darias's file.

After the Navarro trial, in the summer of 1987, Robert and Amelia had the worst fight of their marriage over the IRS impasse. She harangued him for not "acting more decisively." He shouted that he was "doing all I can!"

"The only thing you did by making this great sacrifice was to have a group of agents promoted!" she screamed, adding that if he ever testified again she would leave him. She stormed out of the house, and he spent the rest of that day with a friend experimenting with new computer programs.

Amelia drafted two letters for Robert's signature, one to Myles Malman at the U.S. Attorney's office, the other to Carol Cooper and Frank Chellino at the DEA (Paul Sennett had been transferred to Europe). There were no threats or accusations, just cries for help.

"Amelia and I both feel so let down, so totally used, abused and discarded that there is no future as long as my tax problems exist. . . . ," he wrote to Cooper and Chellino. "It is not just or humane that the Government of the United States is doing this to someone who has cooperated and put his life on the line for them. . . . I can remember all those telephone conversations when you asked for my help. You both know that whenever you called, I jumped and I was there. You are both fair people. You know that what I am saying is true. . . . I am slowly dying and nobody gives a damn. Please help me. I want to live."

To Myles Malman, Darias said, "My life is in shambles. My wife is ill and we are experiencing very serious personal conflicts caused entirely by my cooperation with the DEA. . . . I feel totally isolated as well as discarded because of my cooperation with the Government. . . . My tax case is lost in the endless maze of cruelty that is the IRS for me."

It was Myles Malman in the end who broke the impasse, which he viewed as mainly a clash over bureaucratic turf. He had always felt that Darias's trouble lay not so much at the IRS as at the DEA, with the stubborn Carol Cooper and the cautious Frank Chellino.

"The problem is with the DEA, not the Internal Revenue Service," Malman told Darias on the phone. The IRS was refusing to settle with Darias until the DEA paid him his now-reduced bonus. The DEA was refusing to pay the $73,000 until Darias had settled with the IRS.

Malman found himself dealing with a personable IRS lawyer based in Fort Lauderdale, who came originally from working-class Boston, a background with a certain similarity to Malman's home ground in the Bronx and Manhattan. Like Malman, the IRS man had served as an army enlisted man in Vietnam. They had experienced a lot of the same places in Southeast Asia in the sixties. Malman found he could talk to the man in a way that he could not to the priggish bureaucrat in Jacksonville who had insisted that Robert Darias show "child-like good faith," or to the functionary in Fort Lauderdale who ended declarative sentences with question marks.

Malman appealed to the Boston man's common sense, a quality rare in the IRS. "If you don't want your agency to wind up on *60 Minutes* looking like a bunch of idiots, you'd better deal with this matter," Malman said.

It took two more years. The IRS demanded all of Darias's bonus in settlement of his tax obligation, which had begun in the early 1970s at around $30,000 but which interest had now inflated—as the bureaucrats had dawdled—to over $300,000, an amount which Darias easily could have contested if he had had the wherewithal. On April 17, 1989, six and a half years after Operation Swordfish ended, a meeting was held at the Miami field headquarters of the DEA. It was attended by Robert Darias, Paul Sennett (now reassigned to Miami), and an IRS representative. Sennett presented Darias with a DEA cashier's check for approximately $73,000. Darias endorsed the check over to the IRS as full settlement of his tax debt. It represented an "out of court" settlement, comparable to those that the IRS makes with corporations and individuals every day.

Since he had testified in open court so many times, Darias was no longer useful as an undercover agent. The DEA again offered to put him, Amelia, and Laura into the Witness Security Program. Often the witness never sees his relatives and friends again. The Dariases declined; they wanted to maintain their ties to the Cuban community of South Florida.

But those crucial personal relationships were severely strained by Operation Swordfish and its aftermath. Very few people knew the truth about what Darias had done for the U.S. Government, and he did not feel free to discuss it with anyone except his most intimate relatives. A number of people in Miami's Cuban circles chose to believe rumors that Robert had been caught trafficking in drugs and become an informer.

The Dariases were in limbo. Amelia Darias was distraught and undergoing psychiatric care. Laura Darias, now a teenager and fully aware of the crisis in her family, was bitterly unhappy attending a mediocre public school where she was afraid to form close friendships. She missed her regular visits with her grandparents, cousins, aunts, and uncles.

It was difficult for Robert to look for work. The family had to live under the threat that Carlos Jader Alvarez, Marlene Navarro, and the rest of the Colombian mafia would take any opportunity for revenge. The drug mafia had assassinated spies far less important than Robert Darias, and they often slaughtered the spies' families as well. The Dariases had no choice but to continue to lie low. They sank into a life of isolation and dread.

In a nightstand next to their bed, Robert and Amelia kept an Uzi submachine gun, a Remington 870 shotgun with a pistol grip, three

.357 Magnum revolvers, a Smith & Wesson 9mm pistol, and a Colt .38 police special revolver. All were loaded.

The only door into their apartment was triple-locked and was wired with an alarm that was activated by touching the outside knob without first unlocking the door with keys. When it was time for Laura to leave for school, Robert and Amelia together took her to the front door of the building. Amelia and Laura waited inside the locked lobby while Robert, fully armed, went for the car, checked it for explosives and then brought it around. When Robert went to the nearby beach, either alone or with the family, he took a concealed stainless steel .357 Magnum and a cordless telephone with which to summon help if necessary.

The telephone in the Dariases' apartment seldom rang. And when it did ring, it startled—resonating through the carpetless surfaces like a burglar alarm, sending chills down the spine.

Robert Darias had achieved the inner redemption he sought. But it was a lonely redemption. He was in from the cold and out in the cold at the same time.

EPILOGUE

ROBERT, AMELIA, AND Laura Darias continue to live in semiseclusion, as does Felipe Calderon.

Carol Cooper, Frank Chellino, Paul Sennett, Tom Clifford, Robert Russo, Eddie Hernandez, Nick Zapata, and the other DEA agents, supervisors, and analysts who participated in Operation Swordfish have gone on to other assignments around the United States and the world.

Marlene Navarro was granted a new trial in 1992, after more than six years in prison, when U.S. District Judge William M. Hoeveler determined that faulty work by court stenographers during Navarro's trial made it impossible to produce a full and accurate transcript of the trial, and therefore impossible for Navarro and her lawyers to prepare an appeal of the verdict. As this book went to press, Judge Hoeveler was weighing a motion by the government to reconsider his ruling. No new trial had been scheduled and Navarro remained incarcerated at the women's annex of the Dade County Jail, after lengthy stretches at federal prisons in California, Kentucky, and Florida.

The conviction of Carlos Jader Alvarez was affirmed by the U.S. Court of Appeals for the Eleventh Circuit in line with legal arguments mounted by Assistant United States Attorney Susan Tarbe. Alvarez remained at a federal prison south of Miami until it was heavily damaged by Hurricane Andrew in 1992. He was then moved to another prison in Wisconsin.

The Eleventh Circuit also affirmed the convictions of Carlos Alvarado, Manuel Sanchez, and Ricardo and Said Pavon.

Oscar Garcia and Nelson Batista pleaded guilty. Carmenza Valenzuela, Teodoro Terselich, Luis Rodriguez, and Antonio Uribe remained fugitives.

José Antonio "Pepe" Cabrera, who had been sentenced to four concurrent thirty-year prison terms, was placed in protective custody in 1991 after agreeing to testify against General Manuel Antonio Noriega. Noriega was brought to Miami to stand trial on drug and racketeering charges following the U.S. invasion of Panama.

Myles Malman, after convicting Carlos Jader Alvarez and Marlene

Navarro, served as co-lead prosecutor of Noriega, who was convicted in April 1992 of racketeering, conspiracy, and drug trafficking. Noriega was sentenced to forty years in prison. In December 1992 the Department of Justice bestowed one of its highest honors, the Attorney General's Award for Distinguished Service, on Malman and two other Noriega prosecutors.

Susan Tarbe, who helped Malman prosecute Carlos Alvarez and drafted the government's appeal brief, which formed the basis for the Eleventh Circuit's affirmation of Alvarez's conviction, went on to convict several other important criminals, including the arms dealer Sarkis Soghanalian.

Raymond Takiff, who represented Swordfish defendants Carlos Alvarado and Bertha Paez, had been retained to represent Manuel Noriega. However, Takiff withdrew after the U.S. Government accused him of income tax evasion. As part of a plea agreement with the government, Takiff acted as an undercover informant against four Florida state judges who were indicted for bribery and extortion. The government of Florida paid Takiff $4,500 per month for spying and testifying, $500 more than the maximum salary it paid Robert Darias for much more dangerous and difficult work.

Frank Rubino, who represented the Alvarez money courier Said Pavon, replaced Takiff as Manuel Noriega's lawyer.

Roy Black, who represented Lionel Paytubi and Lester Rogers, later represented William Kennedy Smith, who was acquitted of rape in Palm Beach, Florida, in 1991.

Mark Schnapp, who prosecuted banker Manuel Sanchez, later served as Black's co-counsel in the William Kennedy Smith case.

Alcee Hastings, the U.S. District Judge who presided at the trials of Alvarez and Navarro in 1986 and 1987 following his own acquittal of bribery charges, was impeached by the U.S. House of Representatives and convicted by the U.S. Senate in 1989 when they determined that he in fact had been guilty of bribery and had committed perjury defending himself. Despite his impeachment and conviction, Hastings was not disbarred. Impeachment and conviction by the United States Congress are not grounds for disbarment in Florida, as conviction in court would have been. Hastings was able therefore to practice law and came to represent one of the judges whom Ray Takiff implicated in bribery. Thus Hastings found himself, as a former bribery defendant, in the position of cross-examining the bribery witness Takiff, whom he had chastised for the manner of his cross-examination of Robert Darias in the Navarro trial.

In September 1992 a federal district court in Washington, D.C., overturned the Senate's conviction of Alcee Hastings on the ground that its procedures had been unfair and violated his constitutional rights. The Senate said it would appeal the ruling to the Supreme Court. Hastings made known that he had no further interest in being a judge; in November 1992 the voters in a South Florida Congressional district elected him to the U.S. House of Representatives, the same body that had impeached him. Relishing the irony, Hastings commented that if the Supreme Court were to uphold the overturning of his Senate conviction, and the House again began impeachment proceedings, "it's distinctly possible that I could vote on my own impeachment."

Under pressure from the drug mafia, the government of Colombia stopped extraditing drug fugitives who had been indicted in the United States. However, Colombian authorities did move against the kidnappers and killers of the Alvarez children. A court in Bogotá convicted the students Edgar Helmut Garcia Villamizar and Pedro Pablo Silva Bejarano, the Gachalá restaurant owner Victor Manuel Reyes Pena, and two of his associates, Hugo Eduardo Parra and Armando Martinez Ruiz, for their roles in the kidnappings and murders. Reyes, Parra, and Martinez, the only ones present for their trials, were sentenced to prison; the others remained missing.

As acute as the kidnapping epidemic in Colombia was in 1982, it grew much worse by 1992. There developed a "secondary market" in kidnap victims, as kidnappers who were impatient to get paid sold their victims to other kidnappers who were more patient. The families of victims formed a lobby to support tough new legislation that would double the prison terms for convicted kidnappers to twenty-five years and freeze assets belonging to families of victims in order to make the payment of ransom more difficult.

The smuggling of drugs from Colombia to the United States, as well as to Europe, Japan, and Africa, rose dramatically in the same decade. And the drug lords began cultivating and shipping heroin as well as cocaine.

Though *Swordfish* is not primarily a book about drug control policy, its writing and publication during a great international debate about how best to combat the scourge of drugs prompts me to attempt briefly to assess the significance of the "experimental" Operation Swordfish in the context of the so-called drug war.

Swordfish became a model for progressively more ambitious and complex undercover efforts to penetrate the top echelon of the Latin American drug mafia and its serpentine banking and financial networks as they expanded in the United States, Europe, and Asia.

The DEA's Tom Clifford, despite his many troubles during Operation Swordfish, initiated another such venture within a year after Swordfish ended. Known as Operation Pisces, the next Clifford operation, which lasted from 1984 to 1987, employed seven undercover investment businesses (similar to Dean International) in Miami, Los Angeles, New York, and San Francisco to infiltrate and dismantle two major smuggling groups associated with the Medellín Cartel. Undercover DEA agents laundered $124 million, eventually seizing $58 million in cash and 24 airplanes. Some 421 people were arrested, none at the exalted level of Carlos Jader Alvarez.

Clifford surfaced again in late 1992 with Operation Green Ice, the first undercover venture in which the DEA and its foreign counterparts definitively established the link between the Colombian cartels and the Sicilian mafia. Climaxing a three-year probe, agents simultaneously arrested more than 200 people (again, none at the highest levels) in the United States, Italy, Colombia, Spain, Canada, and Costa Rica. Millions of dollars were seized from accounts in an array of international banks. The genesis of the operation was a bogus investment consulting firm called Trans Americas Ventures Associates, which Clifford started in San Diego in 1989.

What is the impact of such efforts on the flow of narcotics? The question is difficult to answer simply. Critics of these undercover investigations, and of government efforts to combat the supply of drugs in general, argue that the operations are futile because they have had no discernible effect on the drug flow, which has increased since these investigations began in the late 1970s.

I strongly disagree. To me, that argument is akin to arguing that efforts to investigate and curb international terrorism should be stopped because they have had no discernible effect on terrorism, whose incidence continued to rise for a number of years in the face of intense efforts to stop it.

It is often difficult to measure the effect of efforts to combat crime. However, we as a society do not enact and enforce laws against what we define as crime solely to reduce crime. While that is an important aim, we also enact and enforce these laws because they affirm and protect our values as a civilized people. That, it seems to me, is our only moral course, whether the laws reduce crime or not.

In the case of drugs, the difficulty of measuring the impact of law enforcement is often marshaled as part of a broader argument in favor of "legalization" or "decriminalization" of drugs. Some people don't consider drug smuggling and drug selling to be genuine "crimes." They contend that government has no proper role in prohibiting citizens from using drugs, or that drugs are a medical and public health problem which should be addressed through treatment and education, not law enforcement. Proponents of legalization typically supplement that argument with the assertion that efforts to prevent drugs from reaching the United States don't work anyway, so they should be stopped.

This is not the place for a full airing of that debate. For a well-rounded discussion of the legalization issue, I recommend an article by Professor James Q. Wilson, "Against the Legalization of Drugs," published in *Commentary* in February 1990, and the letters in reply in the issues of May and June 1990. For this brief note, suffice it to say that I believe the smuggling of heroin, cocaine, and other such lethal substances into the United States, and their sale to our citizens, particularly our children, is as heinous an activity as international terrorism and should be treated accordingly by the criminal law. These drugs are of a significantly greater order of lethal and toxic magnitude than alcohol and tobacco. Lumping crack with vodka is specious. And the difficulty of measuring the impact of tough law enforcement on drug trafficking, and the impact of equally important education and treatment programs on drug use, is irrelevant to the basic moral validity of both kinds of effort to fight drugs.

But the difficulty of measuring impact does not mean it is impossible to judge the efficacy of efforts like Operation Swordfish. One of the leading experts on federal drug policy, along with James Wilson of UCLA, is Professor Mark Moore of Harvard, who asserts that "the difficulty of [drug traffickers'] executing transactions is the principal factor constraining the supply of drugs [for any given price] over the long run. . . . It is the drug investigations that put pressure on transactions and make it possible to disrupt and immobilize trafficking networks that become expert in completing the transactions. . . . Each slowed transaction reduces the overall capacity of the system to supply drugs, and each trafficking network that is taken out results not only in the loss of current inventories but also of the future capacity of supply."

There can be no doubt that Operation Swordfish "disrupted and immobilized" the trafficking networks of Carlos Jader Alvarez and Marlene Navarro and "reduced the overall capacity of the system to supply drugs," however temporarily. That is more than ample justification for vigorously pursuing such international investigative efforts.

I believe that those who risk their lives in these dangerous ventures should be numbered among our heroes. Robert Darias has the distinction of being a citizen hero—albeit unsung—of two nations, Cuba and the United States. The greatest injustice of Operation Swordfish—and the greatest scandal—is the U.S. Government's failure to fulfill its commitments to Darias and to resume using him, even if only in an advisory capacity, in espionage against international organized crime. The least the government can do now is give him a presidential pardon for his tax conviction so that he again can exercise his full rights of citizenship.

SOURCES AND METHODS

I WROTE *SWORDFISH* for a variety of reasons. It was an opportunity to tell the story of a group of intriguing people living through a crisis. It was an opportunity to study, from the inside, an agency of the United States Government under siege from a great international menace. It was an opportunity to write about one of the most intractable social and moral issues of the late twentieth century—the drug plague.

And equally important to me as a writer, *Swordfish* presented an opportunity to explore new ground in an important realm of nonfiction writing—the use of dialogue. The direct quotation of conversations between individuals portrayed in nonfiction books has become common in the last decade. When I wrote *Indecent Exposure*, first published in 1982, it was less common, having evolved little beyond the pioneering work of Truman Capote, Tom Wolfe, and Gay Talese. Traditional methods of journalism still called for the use of paraphrase when a writer was not actually present at a conversation being reported. I felt, however, that readers had a right to expect more from book authors, who work for years on a single project, than from newspaper journalists with less time. That meant going beyond paraphrase where possible to convey not only the substance of conversations but the spirit and tone of those conversations and the personalities and speech patterns of the speakers. And that meant reconstructing dialogue, a process I undertook by interviewing separately the participants in particular conversations or meetings, and asking them to try, with the help of written records, to recall precisely what was said by each participant and how it was said. I spent a great deal of time with most interviewees and was able to evaluate their reliability. In explanation of that method, the source appendix to *Indecent Exposure* contained the following:

> Dialogue was reconstructed from many sources and the reader should not assume that the speaker of a line of dialogue is the author's only source, or even among the sources, of that line of dialogue. While the sources often include the speaker, they also

often include other participants in the conversation, and in a few instances they include people who did not participate in the conversation but were reliably informed on it.

The author does not claim that the dialogue represents the exact words used by the characters at the time of the events described. He does assert, however, that the dialogue represents the best recollection of the most accurate interviewees, that it captures the essence and spirit of the conversations that are reconstructed, as well as the personalities and styles of the characters, and that it does so *more* accurately than paraphrase would. Human beings do not speak in paraphrase.

There was relatively little criticism of the dialogue in *Indecent Exposure*, mainly, I suppose, because a number of the characters remarked publicly when the book was published that the dialogue was accurate. However, reviewers have criticized dialogue in other books, and it is fair to say that most of us who try to write books responsibly are attuned to the danger of "taking liberties" with dialogue, and are always searching for ways to refine our methods.

I was especially drawn to Operation Swordfish as a book topic because it afforded the possibility of deriving dialogue from unique sources rarely available to authors. I was intrigued to find that nearly all of the conversations that were crucial to an understanding of the characters and events of Operation Swordfish had been tape-recorded, in some cases without the knowledge of the parties to the conversations, and in other cases with the knowledge of only one party. That meant I would not have to depend on witnesses' recollections of those conversations. I could draw from the conversations themselves, preserved in their entirety in an unimpeachable form. I could listen to—and in some cases view—hundreds of hours of the variety and richness of the actual speech of the characters, examining not only the substance of the conversations but the multitude of ways in which speech patterns reveal character and personality.

Apart from dialogue, it was clear the tapes also would provide a firmer grounding in the details and nuances of the undercover operation than I could glean if I were limited to the memory of the participants years after the events.

As enticing as the tapes were, they also were daunting. Transcripts of the raw conversations run to thousands of pages, and, like virtually all spontaneous conversations, are littered with digressions, irrelevancies, interruptions, false starts, free associations, "er's," "uh's," and countless other tics of speech. Such transcripts are difficult and tedious to read. I knew I would have to edit the key conversations carefully for length and sense—paraphrasing parts of them—while not sacrificing authenticity and flavor. All that loomed as an unusual challenge, different from interviewing, though the book would require a lot of that as well.

While writing *Swordfish*, I tried to bear in mind an admonition of the distinguished literary critic Elizabeth Hardwick, published in the *New York Review of Books* in May 1985, the same month I began interviewing Robert Darias. "Tape recording without an interpretive intelligence is a primitive technology for history," Hardwick wrote, in assailing authors who rely too heavily on recorded talk.

My interviews with Robert Darias, together with the materials he provided, were the heart of my early research. The secret recordings he had made of his conversations with DEA agents and others were of great help in refreshing his memory of the operation. He also used personal notes, photographs, tapes, and transcripts of his conversations with targets such as Marlene Navarro and Humberto Garcia, and his own daily reports of espionage activity ("confidential informant statements," or CIS's). Darias had dictated the CIS's to a DEA agent, usually Carol Cooper, shortly after the events described. The agent then had typed the statements, and Darias had corrected and signed them. Each statement ended with the following affirmation: "I HAVE READ THE FOREGOING STATEMENT AND HAVE INITIALED ALL CORRECTIONS. THIS STATEMENT IS TRUE AND CORRECT TO THE BEST OF MY KNOWLEDGE AND BELIEF. I GIVE THIS STATEMENT FREELY AND VOLUNTARILY, WITHOUT THREATS, COERCION, OR PROMISES." That wasn't a guarantee of truth, but it was more reliable than years-old memory, as were the taped conversations.

The value of the tapes as a source of facts and insight in addition to dialogue was demonstrated when I was researching the fear that agents and spies feel during an undercover operation. In Chapter 19, I write that Felipe Calderon was "petrified" at possible mafia retribution against him and his family. Though Calderon minimized his fear in an interview with me on March 28, 1990, eight years after the event, his fear is portrayed accurately in the book because of tape recordings of Carol Cooper discussing the manifestations of Calderon's fear in detail with Robert Darias on March 9, 16, and 22, 1982, a few days after Calderon communicated it to her, Tom Clifford, and Bob Russo. Whatever his qualms about acknowledging fear to me for publication, Calderon had no motive to repeatedly mislead the agents in the privacy of Dean International, and Cooper had compelling reasons to level with Darias. Their ability to control fear depended on candor with each other.

I interviewed Darias in an apartment I had rented in a secure building in Miami Beach. We kept our relationship secret. Darias's life had been threatened repeatedly by the Latin mafia and he and his family were living in hiding. The major targets of Operation Swordfish were still at large or had recently been arrested and extradited to stand trial, and surely would have tried to kill Darias, the principal witness against them, if they had known where to find him. Nor did Darias and I want the U.S. Government to know we were in contact. The most important Swordfish trials were still to come, and government agents and lawyers never allow a sensitive witness to discuss a case with an outsider before a trial is concluded. They fear, correctly, that defense lawyers will try to exploit any possible conflict between the witness's statements inside and outside the courtroom.

However, as an independent author, I did not need the DEA's permission to interview Darias. Nor was I willing to allow the DEA to dictate my research and writing schedule. I could not have begun my interviews with Darias until years later if I had waited until after the last Swordfish trial. Thus, he and I decided to proceed in secret— confident that if targets, fugitives, defense attorneys, and government agents and lawyers all were kept unaware, our meetings would cause no harm to anyone or any legal proceeding.

Darias would arrive at my building each morning, give an assumed name to the security guard, and I would admit him. The interviews moved slowly; we had to transfer his original recordings of conversations with control agents and targets from his tapes to mine. When I asked questions and he commented, we would stop his tape and record the questions and comments on my tape between the raw conversations. At the end I had a master taped chronology of Operation Swordfish consisting of about 375 hours of Darias's conversations with his targets and control agents interspersed with my interviews with him. I also talked with Darias and his family at considerable length off tape.

While assimilating that material, I approached other important sources without telling them I was in touch with Darias. After Marlene Navarro was detained in Caracas in February 1986, and brought to Miami to stand trial, I began visiting her at the North Dade Detention Center. From April until September, when her trial began, I interviewed her there frequently. Though her lawyer instructed her to answer no questions about the specific charges against her, there was still plenty to talk about, and she seemed to welcome the diversion my attention provided. I have seen her far less often since then, but we still speak by phone.

I conducted extensive research in Colombia, where I gradually gained access to the complete court files on the Alvarez kidnappings. Aided by depositions, maps, and photographs, I visited all the locations in Bogotá and the remote mountains where the kidnapping and subsequent events occurred and interviewed individuals familiar with those aspects of the story. On two occasions, along with a Bogotá journalist and two former members of the Colombian National Police, I rented a team of mules and, with the help of police intelligence maps and local guides, retraced the route of the kidnappers into the mountains. We camped overnight at the shack in *Las Brisas* which had served as the kidnappers' initial hideout after leaving Bogotá. The next day we hiked up the mountain into the jungle to the site of the final hideout and the climactic events of the kidnapping.

I interviewed a large number of special agents, intelligence analysts, supervisors, executives, and other staff members of the DEA in Miami, Washington, Europe, and Latin America. All DEA interviews were conducted on "background," i.e., I could use the information provided but couldn't attribute it to a named source. In most instances, I was able to corroborate the information with documents, including classified internal DEA investigative files. Many of the files are the agency's formal "Reports of Investigation" (DEA ROI), which are classified "DEA Sensitive," the agency says, to designate material whose public disclosure might compromise an ongoing operation. Following an operation, however, defendants' lawyers may have access to the ROIs, and they are used by both sides at trials.

The secrecy of my relationship with Robert Darias was breached partially during the trial of Marlene Navarro, when a private detective hired by the defense to investigate Darias's background turned up two checks I had written to Mrs. Robert Darias under an agreement whereby I was compensating the Dariases for the huge amount of time spent with me. (I paid Marlene Navarro as well.) Mrs. Darias had deposited the checks in a corporate bank account of a member of her family. It had not occurred to the Dariases or to me that anyone would go so far as to subpoena her family's accounts. Upon revelation of the relationship in court, I was served with a defense subpoena "commanding" me to turn over all records of my interviews with Robert Darias. I immediately moved the files to a secure location in New York. Thanks to the legal arguments mounted by my lawyers, Robert Sack and Dan Paul, the judge quashed the subpoena because it showed no need for the files that was sufficiently compelling to overcome the protection afforded journalists' "work-product" by the First Amendment to the U.S. Constitution. That avoided my having to formally defy the subpoena to protect the confidentiality of my files, including the most sensitive tape recordings, whose existence remained secret.

My sources—defendants, DEA agents and lawyers for both sides—were shocked to learn that I knew and had been interviewing Robert Darias. Most of them were sophisticated enough to grasp that I had imposed secrecy to protect my independence and Darias's and my security. A few felt I had betrayed them.

I supplemented my research with the files of the following cases in the archives of the United States District Court (USDC) for the Southern District of Florida (SDF) in Miami.

U.S. v. Marlene Navarro and José Jader Alvarez Moreno, a/k/a Carlos Jader Alvarez, 82-575-Cr.

U.S. v. Lionel Paytubi et al., 82-561-Cr.

U.S. v. Lionel Paytubi, Manuel Sanchez et al., 82-574-Cr.

U.S. v. The Great American Bank, Lionel Paytubi et al., 82-720-Cr.

U.S. v. Manuel Sanchez, 82-574-Cr.

U.S. v. Humberto Garcia-Rivero, Humberto Garcia, Jr. et al., 82-573-Cr.

U.S. v. Antonio José Uribe-Calle et al., 82-572-Cr.

U.S. v. Victor Manuel Covo Torres and Pedro Fajardo, 82-558-Cr.

U.S. v. Victor Manuel Covo Torres, Lucas Gomez Van Grieken, Juan Gomez, and Alfonso Ibarra, 82-557-Cr.

U.S. v. Victor Manuel Covo Torres and Alvaro Barcenas, 82-559-Cr.

U.S. v. Francisco Arevalo et al., 82-571-Cr.

U.S. v. Rodolfo Vergara Sierra et al., 82-564-Cr.

U.S. v. Adolfo Ibarra Bustamente, Gladys Hernandez de Ibarra, and Alberto Silva Martinez, 82-560-Cr.

U.S. v. John Doe, a/k/a 'Fernando,' et al., 82-562-Cr.

U.S. v. Armando de Jesus Velez-Gomez et al., 82-563-Cr.

U.S. v. Jorge Garcia et al., 82-565-Cr.

U.S. v. Luis José Arbalaez et al., 82-595-Cr.

U.S. v. Emiro Mejias et al., 82-576-Cr.

U.S. v. Francisco Navia et al., 81-22-Cr.

U.S. v. Bertram Mark Schwartz, Juan Lozano Crump-Perez et al., 81-62-Cr.

U.S. v. Eric Arias et al., 81-27-Cr.

U.S. v. Steven T. Gibbs and Brooks Muse, 86-268-Cr.

U.S. v. José Jader Alvarez Moreno, Jaime Murcia Duarte, Eddie Joel Perez Jaimes, and Leon Manuel Arenas Parra, 80-545-Cr.

U.S. v. Maria Lilia Rojas, 80-350-Cr.

U.S. v. José Medardo Alvero-Cruz, 80-36-Cr and 80-2018-Cr.

U.S. v. José Antonio Cabrera Sarmiento, 80-317, 80-1274, 80-1262, 80-87, 80-413.

U.S. v. Manuel Antonio Noriega et al., 88-79-Cr.

Also, *U.S. v. Barbara Mouzin et al.,* USDC, Central District of California, Los Angeles, CR 82-518(B).

In most cases the court files include the transcripts of trials and exhibits introduced at the trials. The exhibits include many conversations between Darias and his targets which were secretly recorded on videotape or audiotape. The files of *Navarro* and *Alvarez* also include a court-authorized wiretap—recordings of conversations, transcripts, monitors' logs, prosecutors' reports, and affidavits in support of the motion for the wiretap. (Darias's recordings of his conversations with the DEA agents never became part of any court proceeding; parties to the cases did not know they existed.)

I was present for most of the Navarro and Alvarez trials, which were conducted in Courtroom 5 of the Miami federal court house by U.S. District Judge Alcee Hastings.

The following chapter notes are comprehensive but not exhaustive. References to telephone or other conversations include the speakers' initials, the date, and the number of the call on that date. For example, Robert Darias's third conversation with Carol Cooper on February 2, 1982, is CC-RD (3) Feb. 2, 1982.

NOTES

xiii Main epigraph: "I have never heard": *Sanchez*, July 5, 1984, p. 356.

Part One. The Spy

1 Part One epigraph: *Red and black*: anonymous.

CHAPTER 1

3 The Robert Darias in this book is not the Robert Darias listed in the Miami, Florida, telephone directory.

3 "A WHITE HAZE: All references to climate and weather are taken from *Local Climatological Data* (LCD), National Oceanic and Atmospheric Administration, United States Department of Commerce. These monthly reports give comprehensive weather and climate conditions at three-hour intervals for each day of the month in all major cities. In addition to consulting the LCDs, I have matched them to my observations of weather patterns in Miami over several years of living and visiting there. When I refer to "a white haze that muted the green," etc., it means that the LCD for Monday, December 22, 1980, reported haze in the late morning. From driving Darias's route many times in December, I know how the haze looks at that time of year.

3 Tax case: *U.S. v. Robert Darias*, USDC, SDF, 78-115-Cr-SMA, Indictment, Apr. 12, 1978; Judgment and Probation/Commitment Order, Sept. 14, 1978; Motion to reduce sentence under Rule 35, 1978.

3 Grand theft case: *State of Florida v. Robert Darias et al.*, Circuit Court of the Eleventh Judicial District of Florida, in and for Dade County, 78-18459, Information, Nov. 28, 1978; Adjudication withheld, Apr. 16, 1979; Plea hearing, May 16, 1979. Probation terminated Feb. 24, 1981. Case expunged from the record Oct. 17, 1983.

4 TAMIAMI TRAIL: Named by Juvenile Court Judge William Stewart Hill. *Miami Herald* (hereafter *MH*), Aug. 16, 1987, p. 1G; I have visited all Miami locales mentioned, in most cases repeatedly.

4 The truck episode: Author's interviews with Darias; also mentioned in Haynes Johnson, *The Bay of Pigs: The Leaders' Story of Brigade 2506* (New York: Dell Publishing Co., 1964), pp. 180–82; in Peter Wyden,

Bay of Pigs: The Untold Story (New York: Touchstone/Simon & Schuster, 1980), p. 303; and in Hugh Thomas, *Cuba: The Pursuit of Freedom* (New York: Harper & Row, 1971), p. 1370.

6 Florida is flattest place in North America: Darias's impression confirmed by Joel Garreau, *The Nine Nations of North America* (New York: Avon Books, 1981), p. 189.

6 Narcotics spy: The terms "narcotics" and "drugs" are used interchangeably in this book, as in common parlance, to refer to substances such as heroin and cocaine whose smuggling and sale are felony crimes under the laws of the United States. By strict scientific definition, *narcotics* actually comprise only opium and opium derivatives such as heroin within the larger spectrum of illegal *drugs.*

CHAPTER 2

7 GROUP THREE WAS ONE OF SEVEN: Organization chart of the DEA's Miami Field Division, 1981.

8 José Carvajal: Darias's handwritten list submitted to Sennett. Carvajal is sixth name; Darias testimony re Carvajal: *Sanchez*, July 5, 1984, pp. 423–35; *Navarro*, Jan. 5, 1987, pp. 87–90; Jan. 21, 1987, p. 47.

9 Daughter's drug problem: Author's interviews with Darias; Darias testimony in *Rogers*, Dec. 7, 1983, pp. 1147–48; Darias conversation with IRS agent (secretly recorded) Oct. 18, 1983.

9 Sennett records details of Darias's background: *Personal History Report*, DEA Form 202, prepared Jan. 13, 1981, by Sennett.

10 "shot at without result": Winston Churchill, *The Malakand Field Force* (1898).

10 Sennett shooting incident: The dead agent was Frank Tummillo. Wounded was Thomas J. Devine. Sennett's colleague was Ron Caffrey. Joseph P. Fried, "U.S. Agent and Two Slain in Drug Raid in Midtown Motel," *New York Times* (hereafter *NYT*), Oct. 13, 1972, p. 1; John L. Hess, "Colleagues Still Mourn Slain Agent and Wonder: What Went Wrong?" *NYT*, Oct. 27, 1972, p. 43.

10 Group Three: Author's interviews; Carl Hiaasen, " 'Tedium, terror' haunt undercover agents," *MH*, Oct. 13, 1981, p. 1A; "DEA's Frank White: A 'wizard'—or a reckless, deadly agent?" Oct. 16, 1981, p. 18A.

10 Assault on Cooper: Interviews.

CHAPTER 3

14 Navia case: Author's interviews; DEA ROIs; *Navia*, Indictment, January, 1981; "Pill seizure is world record," *MH*, Jan. 15, 1981.

16 Darias is paid $15,000: *Informant Payment Record*, Jan. 16, 21, 27, 1981.

16 Tax status of payments: The CIA consistently told Darias that he did not have to pay taxes on the money it gave him: RD-CC May 13, 1982.

16 Darias pays balance in real estate case: Receipt no. 13646, Clerk of the

Circuit and County Courts of Dade County, Jan. 23, 1981. Probation terminated: Court order signed Feb. 24, 1981.

17 Ocampo background: DEA internal files; Nathan M. Adams, "Inside the Cocaine Wars," *Reader's Digest*, March 1983, p. 91.

18 Darias and Carew's escape was recalled in 1985 when DEA Special Agent Enrique Camarena was tortured and murdered in Mexico.

18 DEA astounded: CC-RD June 1, 1982, recounting conversation with Special Agent Michael Kuhlman, who shadowed Darias in Cali; CC-RD June 14, 1982.

18 Bert Schwartz and Johnny Crump: DEA ROIs; *Schwartz et al.*, Indictment, Feb. 19, 1981.

18 Encounter with Schwartz: Author's interviews and inspection of site; DEA ROI Mar. 3, 1981; Motion for Revocation of Bond, *Schwartz*, Mar. 4, 1981; *In camera* bond hearing tape recording and transcript, *U.S. v. Schwartz*, 81-1PRP, Mar. 5, 1981; Hearing, Mar. 25, 1981. Motion granted, Mar. 30, 1981. Motion for Reconsideration, 81-62-Cr-EBD, Apr. 21, 1981, and Exhibit A, results of privately administered polygraph examination wherein Schwartz gave a different version of the Mar. 3 incident. Motion denied. Mentioned in *U.S. v. Navarro et al.*, Dec. 11, 1986, p. 5.

18 Eric Arias: DEA ROIs. *Arias et al.*

19 Darias accomplishments: Affidavit of Special Agent Carol Cooper with wiretap application, *Navarro*, July, 1982, p. 5.

19 Darias is paid: *Informant Payment Record*, January–April 1981.

19 ABC Radical and Friends of the ABC: Author's interviews; Victor Hugo, *Les Misérables*, translated from the French by Charles E. Wilbour, (New York: Modern Library, Random House), p. 547; Hugh Thomas, *Cuba: The Pursuit of Freedom* (New York: Harper & Row, 1971) pp. 663, 681, 784.

19 Incursions into Cuba: RD-CC July 8, 1982, and other statements by Darias to the DEA agents; author's interviews with Darias; Some of the incursions, by groups known as "grey teams," are described in Felix I. Rodriguez and John Weisman, *Shadow Warrior: The CIA Hero of a Hundred Unknown Battles* (New York: Simon & Schuster, 1989), pp. 59–60.

20 If one was a Cuban: For a vivid and accurate portrait of Cuban Miami and the psychology of the emigrés, see Joan Didion, *Miami* (New York: Simon & Schuster, 1987).

Part Two. The Target

21 Part Two epigraph: "Ambition must": Alexander Hamilton or James Madison, "The Federalist No. 51: The Structure of the Government

Must Furnish the Proper Checks and Balances Between the Different Departments," *The Federalist: A Commentary on the Constitution of the United States*, "Being a Collection of Essays written in Support of the Constitution agreed upon September 17, 1787, by the Federal Convention"; introduction by Edward Mead Earle, professor of history, Institute for Advanced Study, Princeton, N.J. (New York: The Modern Library, Random House, 1937), p. 337. "Federalist No. 51" is cited by James Q. Wilson in his definitive study, *Bureaucracy: What Government Agencies Do and Why They Do It* (New York: Basic Books, 1989), p. 28. Professor Wilson, the James Collins Professor of Management at UCLA, writes near the beginning of his book, "Readers who want to get immediately to the 'bottom line' can spare themselves the hundreds of pages that follow and turn immediately to Federalist Paper number 51, written two centuries ago by James Madison."

CHAPTER 4

23 FIRST DRUG EPIDEMIC: David F. Musto, M.D., *The American Disease*, (New York: Oxford University Press), expanded ed. 1987.

23 Drug indicia 1960–80: James Lieber, "Coping With Cocaine," *The Atlantic* 257, no. 1 (January 1986), p. 39; Robert Lindsey, "Upper-Income Users Spur Cocaine Dealing," *NYT,* Sept. 5, 1979, p. A17.

24 Drug law enforcement history: Edward Jay Epstein, *Agency of Fear* (New York: G. P. Putnam's Sons, 1977), pp. 104–105; "The Early Years," *Drug Enforcement* 7, no. 2 (December 1980), U.S. Department of Justice, Drug Enforcement Administration (DEA); Mark H. Moore, "Reorganization Plan No. 2 Reviewed: Problems in Implementing a Strategy to Reduce the Supply of Drugs to Illicit Markets in the United States," *Public Policy* 26, no. 2 (Spring 1978); Patricia Rachal, *Federal Narcotics Enforcement: Reorganization and Reform* (Boston: Auburn House, 1982).

25 DEA–FBI contrasts: James Q. Wilson, *The Investigators: Managing FBI and Narcotics Agents* (New York: Basic Books, 1978). The FBI later grew more adept at undercover work.

25 DEA agents overseas: Ethan A. Nadelmann, *Cops Across Borders: Transnational Crime and International Law Enforcement*, Ph.D. diss., Department of Government, Harvard University, 1987, Chapter 6, pp. 229–96.

26 "We didn't know": Author's interviews with Charles Blau, July 13–14, 1987.

26 Florida: Garreau, *The Nine Nations of North America*, pp. 167–206; Frank J. Chellino, *Briefing Book on Miami Field Division*, U.S. Department of Justice, DEA, Miami, Jan. 21, 1986 (internal DEA document); James Kelly with Bernard Diederich and William McWhirter, "Trouble in Paradise: South Florida is hit by a hurricane of crime, drugs and refugees," *Time* (cover story), Nov. 23, 1981, p. 22.

27 Federal Reserve figures: President's Commission on Organized Crime, Interim Report to the President and the Attorney General, *The Cash Connection: Organized Crime, Financial Institutions and Money Laundering*, U.S. Government Printing Office, 1984, no. 524-157, p. 26; Thomas E. Ricks, "Inside Dope: The Cocaine Business: Big Risks and Profits, High Labor Turnover," *Wall Street Journal*, June 30, 1986, p. 1.

28 Cash deposits in Miami: Larry Birger and Bud Newman, "Proxmire: Smugglers' cash threatens banks' soundness," *Miami News* (hereafter *MN*), June 6, 1980, p. 1.

28 "The drug money": Garreau, p. 195.

28 Crime in Florida: Gregory Jaynes, "Florida Seeks Explanations And Cures as Crime Mounts," *NYT*, Oct. 18, 1981, p. 28; Wendell Rawls, Jr., "Crime Termed 'Berserk' in Miami; Refugees and Drugs Blamed in Part," *NYT*, Dec. 3, 1980, p. 1; Kelly, "Trouble in Paradise," pp. 22–32.

29 The best account of the "Dadeland massacre" is in Guy Gugliotta and Jeff Leen, *Kings of Cocaine: Inside the Medellín Cartel—An Astonishing True Story of Murder, Money, and International Corruption* (New York: Simon & Schuster, 1989), pp. 9–17.

Chapter 5

32 Changes in laws governing drug trafficking and racketeering: Thomas J. Clifford, introduction to unfinished and unpublished doctoral dissertation on U.S. Government attempts to investigate the financial aspects of narcotics trafficking, pp. 1–15. The partial dissertation is based on Clifford's experience as a high-ranking DEA official in Miami and Washington during the late 1970s and 1980s, supplemented by his academic and legal research. The dissertation was informally critiqued at Clifford's request by Charles W. Blau, supervisor of Operation Greenback and later deputy associate attorney general and chief of the narcotics and dangerous drugs section of the criminal division of the Department of Justice.

Staff, Strike Force 18, Organized Crime and Racketeering Section, Criminal Division, U.S. Department of Justice, *An Explanation of the Racketeer Influenced and Corrupt Organization Statute*, 4th ed., 69-page internal monograph, 1978.

David B. Smith and Edward C. Weiner, *Criminal Forfeitures Under the RICO and Continuing Criminal Enterprise Statutes*, Criminal Division, U.S. Department of Justice, internal document, Nov. 1980.

Harry F. Myers and Joseph P. Brzostowski, "Dealers, Dollars and Drugs," *Drug Enforcement*, Summer 1982.

Charles W. Blau, Amy G. Rudnick, G. Roger Markley, Juan Marrero, John A. Jarvey, Helene Greenwald, *Investigation and Prosecution of Illegal Money Laundering: A Guide to the Bank Secrecy Act*, Criminal

Division, U.S. Department of Justice, internal monograph, October 1983.

33 Mission of Operation Banco: Kenneth A. Miley, acting regional director, Miami Regional Office, DEA, "Operation Banco—Objectives," internal memorandum to DEA Headquarters, Washington, Dec. 22, 1977.

33 Jonathan Stockstill: Author's interview, Apr. 18, 1988.

33 Operation Banco a failure: Clifford diss., p. 7–9; Andy Rosenblatt, "Diminishing Returns? Critics Say $1 Million Drug-Cash Probe Gets Two-Bit Results," *MH*, June 3, 1980, p. 1B; Jim McGee, "Trouble at top frustrates fight against dopers," *MH*, Oct. 12, 1981, p. 1.

34 Charles Blau: Author's interviews with Blau.

34 OPERATION GREENBACK: Ibid.; Clifford diss., pp. 11–12; *The Cash Connection*, pp. 26–27; Internal undated DEA documents.

36 Concern at the Justice Department: Philip B. Heymann, assistant attorney general, Criminal Division, *Proposed Staffing from Criminal Division of 'Operation Greenback,' a Treasury initiated financial flow investigation in Florida*, internal memorandum to Charles B. Renfrew, deputy attorney general, Mar. 31, 1980.

Part Three. Operation Swordfish

CHAPTER 6

39 Clifford background: Author's interviews.

39 JAGUAR CASE: Arnold H. Lubasch, "$2.75-Million Bail Set in Heroin Case," *NYT*, Sept. 21, 1971.

40n Latin crime groups call themselves "mafia": Tina Rosenberg, "The Kingdom of Cocaine," *The New Republic*, Nov. 27, 1989, p. 27.

40 CONTEMPORARIES ENVIED: Author's interviews.

40 DEA conceives its own plan: Clifford diss., pp. 9–10.

40 NEW TOOL: Smith and Weiner, *Criminal Forfeitures*, pp. 3–4.

40 THE CULTURES OF LATIN: Carlos Fuentes, *The Buried Mirror: Reflections on Spain and the New World* (Boston: Houghton Mifflin, 1992), pp. 129–30, 133–34, 139, 240, 282, 285.

40 THE MODERN LATIN MAFIA: Gugliotta and Leen, *Kings of Cocaine*, pp. 22–23.

41 Clifford consults Angel Santiago: Author's interviews.

43 "proprietary": Webster's Ninth New Collegiate Dictionary, no. 3 definition: "a business secretly owned by and run as a cover for an intelligence organization."

44 Tension between special agents and intelligence analysts: Author's interviews; Moore, "Reorganization Plan #2," p. 255; Wilson, *The Investigators*, p. 155.

45 Chellino background: Author's interviews. "Little Hitler" was used as a nickname, e.g., in CC-RD July 30, 1985.

46 La Salle bank: Author's interviews; Robert Force testimony, *Rogers and Alvarado*, Dec. 20, 1983, pp. 164–80, and Dec. 21, 1983, pp. 18–62.

48 Miami Lakes: Tina Montalvo, "Going Crackers Over Graham's Town," *MH*, June 26, 1986, Neighbors Northwest, p. 8; Beatrice E. Garcia, "From Milk Barn to Main Street," *MH*, June 22, 1992, Monday Business, p. 22.

51 DEA implements Operation Swordfish: I have examined all relevant documents.

52 Agents' social lives limited: CC-RD Nov. 23, 1982.

CHAPTER 7

54 Carvajal: *Sanchez*, vol. 3, pp. 423–35.

55 Carvajal becomes a DEA informant: CC-RD (3) Dec. 16, 1981.

55 Before dispatching Darias, the agents refreshed his understanding of the law of entrapment. The government legally could prosecute only people who were predisposed to committing crimes. If a suspect under arrest could show in court that he hadn't been predisposed to committing the crime he'd been charged with, but had done so only after a government spy had "entrapped," or induced him, the charge could be dismissed.

55 Sanchez's activities are documented in the Sanchez, Paytubi, Navarro, and Alvarez trial records.

55 Kattan: Anders Gyllenhaal, "Drug funds and S. Florida's 'Al Capone,' " *MH*, May 24, 1981; Melinda Beck with Elaine Shannon, "A New Attack on Drugs," *Newsweek*, July 20, 1981, p. 30.

56 Paytubi and Kattan: *Great American Bank, Paytubi et al.*, 82-720. Paytubi's activities are documented in the records of the three cases against him listed above, as well as in the Navarro and Alvarez trial records, and in the Sanchez and Alvarez appellate briefs and decisions. Additional sources are cited below.

56 Sanchez lunch: Chellino testimony, *Sanchez*, vol. 7–9; CIS July 20, 1981.

57 Sanchez-Paytubi relationship: Paytubi testimony, *Sanchez*, pp. 747–1083.

58 Sanchez-Paytubi meeting at Dean: videotape and transcript, July 15, 1981, pp. 1–29.

59 Darias lunch with Sanchez and Paytubi: CIS July 20, 1981.

60 Paytubi at Dean: videotape and transcript, July 21, 1981, pp. 1–36.

62 Warner was never implicated in the illegal acts of the GAB.

62 Meetings with Blau were documented in an undated DEA memorandum.

63 Operation Bancoshares ends: Andy Rosenblatt, "Cash-laundering net snares 28 suspects," *MH*, Aug. 5, 1981, p. 1.

63 Darias's first meeting with Navarro: CIS Aug. 10, 1981. Navarro's activities are fully documented in the *Navarro* and *Alvarez* trial records and in the Alvarez appellate briefs and decision affirming Alvarez's conviction.

64 Navarro first deposits cash with Dean: DEA ROI Aug. 21, 1981, pp. 1–6; videotape and transcript Aug. 14, 1981, pp. 1–10.

66 Darias-Rogers meeting Aug. 20: The meeting is described in "Finding of Facts," *U.S. v. Alvarez*, U.S. Court of Appeals, Eleventh Circuit, 86-5517, June 7, 1989; Affidavit of Carol Cooper, *In the Matter of the Application of the United States of America for an Order Authorizing the Interception of Wire Communications*, USDC, SDF, July 1982, p. 7, 8, 30; CIS Aug. 24, 1981, p. 2, marked as government exhibit 26-B, *U.S. v. Rogers*. At the Swordfish trials Darias testified from his CIS's, using them as notes and memory aids, as the prosecution and defense followed in their copies. The CIS's were marked as exhibits but not shown to the juries. Darias's testimony regarding the Aug. 20 meeting with Rogers begins on p. 65, Nov. 28, 1983. Rogers, who denied ever meeting Darias, rebutted the testimony when he took the stand on Jan. 11, 1984.

66 Darias-Navarro meeting Aug. 24: CIS Aug. 31, 1981, and author's interviews.

67 "powder people": CIS Aug. 31, 1981, Darias testimony, and Eleventh Circuit ruling.

CHAPTER 8

69 HUMBERTO GARCIA: Details of Garcia's activities are set forth in Garcia and Uribe-Calle indictments, and in Darias CIS's. Darias occasionally referred to Garcia in testimony against other people. See *Rogers*, vol. 11, Dec. 13, 1983, p. 1935: "He [Garcia] imported marijuana and cocaine into this country in large amounts." Darias comments on Garcia's background in Cuba in RD-CC June 15, 1982. Refricenter of Miami was not involved in Humberto Garcia's criminal activities.

71 DROVE DIRECTLY FROM THE AIRPORT: RD-CC Sept. 7, 1981.

71 "You pretty well know": RD-CC Sept. 24, 1981.

71 Navarro delays: MN-RD Sept. 19, 1981; CIS Sept. 21, 1981.

72 Garcia client in cocaine business: CIS Sept. 21, 1981.

73 DARIAS AND CLIFFORD DISCUSSION: RD-CC Sept. 30, 1981.

73 Darias-Chellino argument: RD-CC Sept. 30, 1981, and Oct. 20, 1981; RD-PS Oct. 28, 1981.

74 IT FELL TO CAROL: RD-CC Sept. 30, 1981.

75 THE DEA'S WELSHING ON ITS ORIGINAL COMMITMENTS and Darias's decision to record conversations with the agents: Author's interviews with Darias.

75 THE MONEY DROUGHT ENDED: CIS's Oct. 5, 13, 1981.

76 "This is going to get to the point": RD-CC Oct. 7, 1981.

77 Robert advised Carol on grooming: Author's interviews with Darias.
77 Cooper had little social life: CC-RD Nov. 23, 1982.
78 Air-conditioning off to save: CC-RD (4) Aug. 12, 1982; ironing at home: CC-RD Aug. 19, 1982.

CHAPTER 9

79 Alvarez background: DEA, *Personal History Reports* (DEA Form 202), Jan. 10, 1975, Sept. 22, 1980, revised 1982–83.
79 Alvarez kidnapping: Details are contained in five volumes of court documents numbering more than 1,000 pages filed in Superior Court No. 10, Bogotá, Colombia, Case no. 4765 (referenced below by volume and page numbers). All files are in Spanish and were translated for me by Miguel Marcial Castro of *El Tiempo*, the largest daily newspaper in Colombia. Marcial holds dual Colombian–United States citizenship and is fluent in both Spanish and English. The files contain depositions, police investigative reports, maps, photographs, and other material, as well as judicial findings and rulings. One of the most informative documents is Colombian National Police, DIPEC Branch, F-2, *Résumé of Activities Undertaken by Personnel of the DIPEC, F-2, National Police, Concerning the Kidnapping of Zuleika, Yidid, and Xouix Alvarez*, Special District, September 27, 1982 (hereafter CNP Report). Another report, compiled independently of the government by the human rights law firm of José Alvear Restrepo for private clients, is *The Road Through the Fog: The Forced and Unsolved Disappearances in Colombia*, 1988 (hereafter Alvear Restrepo report). The section entitled "The Origin of the Collective Disappearances of 1982," pp. 79–155, covers the Alvarez kidnapping case and related events in detail. In addition to examining these and other documents, I have visited all the sites described and interviewed many eyewitnesses and other people, including Colombian and U.S. law enforcement and intelligence sources who are known to be reliable and whose veracity is periodically checked by polygraph.
79 Deposition of Carlos Humberto Najaro Lopez, court vol. 2, pp. 157–61.
82 Town house: Judicial inspection of the house in Talavera, Dec. 11, 1982, court vol. 2, pp. 346–56; author's visit.
83 Details on Bogotá and Colombia: John Teppler Marlin, Immanuel Ness, and Stephen T. Collins, *Book of World City Rankings* (New York: The Free Press/Macmillan, 1986), pp. 527–38.
83 García Márquez: Gene H. Bell-Villada, *García Márquez: The Man and His Work* (Chapel Hill: University of North Carolina Press), 1990, p. 151.
83 Athens of Andes: Bell-Villada, p. 33; Stephen Minta, *García Márquez: Writer of Colombia* (New York: Harper & Row, 1987), p. 5; R. B. Cunninghame Graham, *The Conquest of New Granada: Being the Life of Gonzalo Jiménez de Quesada* (New York: Cooper Square Publishers, republished 1967), p. 157; Albert E. Carter, *The Battle of South America*

(Indianapolis: Bobbs-Merrill, 1941), p. 51; in *Illustrated South America*, published in 1912 by Rand McNally, W. D. Boyce reported that Bogotá also was known as "the Boston of South America," p. 630.

83 Ruben Dario: Quoted by Minta, p. 5.

83 MORE POETS THAN SOLDIERS: Two poet-presidents were Rafael Núñez (1823–94) and Miguel Antonio Caro (1843–1909), according to German Arciniegas, *Latin America: A Cultural History*, translated from the Spanish by Joan MacLean (New York: Alfred A. Knopf, 1967), pp. 391–93.

84 Cervantes may have used Jiménez de Quesada as model for Don Quixote: Arciniegas, p. 86. Arciniegas is one of the most respected historians in Colombia.

84 ACADEMY OF LANGUAGE: Bell-Villada, p. 33, and author's visit.

84 CHILDREN: Marlin, p. 532.

84 Violence unique: Rosenberg, "The Kingdom of Cocaine," p. 30.

84 Homicide leading cause of death: E. J. Hobsbaum, "Murderous Colombia," *New York Review of Books*, Nov. 20, 1986, p. 26.

84 "violentology": Author's interview with the leading violentologist, Professor Gonzalo Sanchez of the Institute of Political Studies, National University, Bogotá, Oct. 24, 1992; Charles Bergquist, Ricardo Penaranda, Gonzalo Sanchez, editors, *Violence in Colombia: The Contemporary Crisis in Historical Perspective* (Wilmington, Del.: SR Books, Scholarly Resources, Inc., 1992); Juan E. Mendez, *The Killings in Colombia*, An Americas Watch Report, April 1989, p. 3n. Americas Watch is a unit of Human Rights Watch, 485 Fifth Avenue, New York, N.Y. 10017. Despite the diversity and complexity of their theories, the violentologists often are criticized for misinterpreting or oversimplifying the roots of the violence. The critics point out, among other things, that certain limited regions of Colombia such as the Caribbean coast have experienced relatively little violence. The intricacies of that debate are beyond the scope of this book.

84 GOVERNMENT SEEMED UNABLE TO APPREHEND: Jamie Fellner, *The Central-Americanization of Colombia? Human Rights and the Peace Process*, An Americas Watch Report, January 1986, pp. 94–95; *Colombia: A Country Study*, Federal Research Division, Library of Congress, 1990, p. 310.

85 RAZOR BLADES: Author's interview with Penny Lernoux, Bogotá, Feb. 15, 1989. The late Ms. Lernoux, who lived in Bogotá for three decades, wrote frequently about Colombia, mainly in *The Nation*.

85 "social undesirables": Juan E. Mendez, *The "Drug War" in Colombia: The Neglected Tragedy of Political Violence*, An Americas Watch Report, October 1990, p. 11.

85 M-19: Fellner, pp. 20–21; *Colombia: A Country Study*, pp. 304–5.

85 "private justice": Fellner, pp. 94–95; Tova Maria Solo, "The Privatization of Justice in Colombia," *Wall Street Journal*, Jan. 8, 1988, p. 19.

86 *sicarios*: Rosenberg, "The Kingdom of Cocaine," p. 28.

86 NEARLY 400 PRIVATE SECURITY COMPANIES: Lernoux, "Colombia's Dirty War," *The Nation*, Nov. 7, 1987, p. 512; author's interview with Lernoux, Feb. 15, 1989.

86 40,000 AND 200,000 ARMED GUARDS: Fellner, pp. 94-95; Lernoux.

86 "infrastructure of death": quoted by Mary Williams Walsh, "In Colombia, Killings Just Go On and On," *Wall Street Journal*, Nov. 17, 1987, p. 34.

86 Kidnappings: Author's interview with Lernoux; Americas Watch, *Human Rights in the Two Colombias: Functioning Democracy, Militarized Society*, October 1982; *The "MAS Case" in Colombia: Taking on the Death Squads*, July 1983; *Human Rights in Colombia as President Barco Begins*, September 1986; *The Killings in Colombia*, April 1989; *The "Drug War" in Colombia: The Neglected Tragedy of Political Violence*, October 1990. Americas Watch reports on Colombia are respected for their accuracy and objectivity by independent experts in Colombia.

86 First ransom note: court vol. 2, pp. 162-69; deposition of Marina Murillo Moreno de Alvarez, court vol. 2, p. 252.

88 Navarro relationship with the Alvarez children: Author's interviews with Navarro; Navarro testimony, *Navarro*, Apr. 6, 1987, p. 11.

88 "It is an emergency": Darias CIS Oct. 13, 1981, and author's interviews with Darias.

CHAPTER 10

89 José Alvero-Cruz: Kelly, "Trouble in Paradise," *Time*, p. 29.

89 Personal details: Verne Williams, "Agents say drug trading explains one man's fortune," *Miami News*, Apr. 25, 1979.

89 DEA WAS OBSESSED: Jim McGee, Andy Rosenblatt, and Patrick Riordan, "DEA's big cases blend triumph, debacle" (fifth of an eight-part series), "U.S. Drug Enforcement: The Billion-Dollar Bust," *MH*, Oct. 15, 1981, p. 17A.

89 WITNESS REFUSED TO TESTIFY: Author's interview with Jerome Sanford, the prosecutor who witnessed the episode; other instances of intimidation by Alvero-Cruz reported in Nathan M. Adams, "Havana's Drug-Smuggling Connection," *Reader's Digest*, July 1982, p. 102.

89 Alvero links to Cuba: David Asman, "Man in the Middle of Drug Trafficking," *Wall Street Journal*, Sept. 25, 1989, p. A14; Adams, p. 102.

89 Tax case in 1980: *Alvero-Cruz*, Indictments, Jan. 25 and July 30, 1980; trial, Feb. 19-26, 1981; verdict guilty; conviction affirmed on appeal, Feb. 22, 1983.

89 Angie background: Author's interviews.

90 Darias's feelings about brigade veterans: Author's interviews; Background on veterans of brigade and related ventures: Helga Silva and Guy Gugliotta, " 'La Causa' Binds exile community" and "The Battle of Their Lives," *The Cubans: A People Divided, MH (Special Report)*, Dec. 11, 1983, pp. 14M-16M.

91 Navarro phone calls: DEA ROI (Clifford) Oct. 15, 1981.

91 Puppy ad: court vol. 1, pp. 161–69.

92 *MH* series: Jim McGee, Carl Hiaasen, Guy Gugliotta, Andy Rosenblatt, Patrick Riordan, William Long, Richard Morin, and James Savage. Oct. 11–18, 1981. Editorial, Oct. 20, 1981.

92 DEA breaks promise: Author's interviews.

92 "Right now we're just playing": CC-RD Oct. 13, 1981.

93 "Couldn't Frank go": CC-RD Oct. 17, 1981.

94 "You certainly are": Cooper told Darias of her conversation with Chellino in CC-RD Oct. 19, 1981.

94 Lunch with the Kids: DEA ROI (Chellino) Oct. 30, 1981; CIS Oct. 26, 1981; RD-CC (1) Dec. 7, 1981.

95 "What was the point": CC-RD Oct. 19, 1981.

CHAPTER 11

96 "She's been calling": CC-RD Oct. 19, 1981.

96 TELEPHONE RECORDS: DEA teletype Oct. 20, 1981.

96 "As soon as I saw": CC-RD Oct. 20, 1981.

96 Alvero-Cruz wants to deposit: DEA teletype Nov. 6, 1981.

97 GREG ENGLISH: English visited Miami the week of Oct. 19, 1981. Cooper reported to Darias in CC-RD Oct. 20, 1981.

98 Darias-Chellino relationship: Author's interviews.

98 Chellino-Hinojosa relationship: Author's interviews.

98 Chellino-Clifford rift: Author's interviews.

99 Drinking habits: Author's interviews and personal observations.

100 "Are you getting": CC-RD Oct. 20, 1981.

100 Meeting with Navarro, Oct. 21: DEA ROI (Chellino) Oct. 30, 1981; CIS Oct. 26, 1981.

100 Darias admired Chellino: RD-CC-PS June 15, 1982, and author's interviews with Darias.

101 Kidnappers call: Deposition of Marina Murillo Moreno, Dec. 7, 1982, court vol. 2, p. 249.

102 Alvarez attitude: Confidential sources in Bogotá.

102 "We've been trying to keep the FBI out": CC-RD Oct. 23, 1981.

102 Greg English memo: Dated Nov. 16, 1981, and marked: "Attention: The contents of this should not be disclosed to people outside the Criminal Division."

103 Calderon-Covo encounter: Author's interviews with Darias; RD-CC Oct. 26, 1981.

104 Cooper-Chellino clash: CC-RD (3) Oct. 27, 1981.

105 "That's okay, they changed": RD-CC (1) Oct. 28, 1981.

105 "Frank is playing games": RD-PS Oct. 28, 1981.

106 "How bad is your problem": RD-PS Oct. 28, 1981.

107 "It's gonna get straightened out": RD-CC Oct. 29, 1981.

107 PAUL SENNETT WAS LESS CONCERNED: RD-PS Oct. 31, 1981.

107 "Normally," Carol told: CC-RD (2) Oct. 29, 1981.
107 THAT EVENING IN BOGOTÁ: court vol. 2, pp. 161–69.

CHAPTER 12

109 "act more like bad guys": RD-PS Oct. 28, 1981; RD-PS Dec. 7, 1981.
109 Banks back in business: RD-CC (3) Nov. 4, 1981.
109 DEA pressing for "results": RD-PS Oct. 28, 1981.
109 "Your gut feeling": RD-CC (3) Nov. 4, 1981.
110 Carol yearning: RD-CC (3) Nov. 4, 1981.
110 MARLENE CALLED ROBERT: MN-RD Nov. 5, 1981.
110 "There's no way we can put it off": CC-RD (3) Nov. 5, 1981.
110 Frank away: CC-RD (3) Nov. 5, 1981.
110 Navarro deposits $270,000: DEA ROI's (Sennett, Cooper) Nov. 11, 1981; CIS Nov. 9, 1981.
111 "Is Tom happy?": CC-RD Nov. 6, 1981.
111 Dean's financial condition: Author's interviews with Darias and various taped conversations with Cooper.
111 Amelia's anger: Author's interviews with the Dariases.
111 Sennett joins Swordfish: Author's interviews and many recorded telephone references.
111 Sennett-Darias lunch: Darias recorded the conversation, much of which reiterated RD-PS Oct. 28, 1981.
113 FBI bogus CD for Angie, and Angie frantic: Teletype from DEA Miami to DEA Washington, Dec. 8, 1981.
113 Marlene flew back: Darias CIS Dec. 7, 1981.
113 Kidnapping details: RD-CC (4) Dec. 1, 1981.
114 Marta Ochoa kidnapping: RD CIS Dec. 7, 1981.
114 "I heard that name": RD-CC (4) Dec. 1, 1981.
114 "Is there a deadline": Ibid.
114 Meeting in Cali to form MAS: Author's interviews; Gugliotta and Leen, *Kings of Cocaine,* pp. 91–93.
114 Navarro and her boss at MAS meeting: Author's interviews; Brian Freemantle, *The Fix: The Inside Story of the World Drugs Trade* (London: Michael Joseph Ltd., 1985), p. 189.
115 AT THE TOWN HOUSE: Judicial inspection of the house in Talavera, Dec. 11, 1982, court vol. 2, pp. 346–56.
115 Taxi: Ibid., pp. 346–56.
115 "You little motherfuckers": Depositions of Felix Soto Sarmiento and Ernestina Mora de Ovalle, Judicial inspection, pp. 346–56.
115 Kidnappers move children: CNP Report.

CHAPTER 13

116 THE ROAD NORTHEAST FROM BOGOTÁ: I have driven this route four times.
116 *El páramo*: The extraordinary climatic conditions and dramatic topog-

raphy of *el páramos* in the Andes have inspired a number of references in the history and literature of Latin America, e.g., Cunninghame Graham, *The Conquest of New Granada*, pp. 140–41; Arciniegas, *Latin America: A Cultural History*, pp. 481, 504; and Victor W. von Hagen, *The Golden Man: A Quest for El Dorado* (London: Book Club Associates, by arrangement with Saxon House D. C. Heath Ltd., 1974), p. 105. Von Hagen, reporting on the journey of the explorer Nicolaus Federmann, writes, "Federmann, who thought he had been through every form of climate and condition that nature could devise, was unable to find the proper words to describe the desolation of the *páramo* and the deathbite of its winds."

116 CHILDREN, NOW IN HANDS OF A DIFFERENT M-19 CELL: Confidential sources in Bogotá.

117 Gachala is mining country: Author's interviews.

117 "we spend our lives": Author's interviews.

117 Emeralds shipped out and *campesinos* resent: Author's interviews.

117 Hydroelectric project: Author's interviews; deposition of Fernando Alfredo Torres Cuellar, a manager for the Electrical Energy Company of Bogotá, court vol. 2, pp. 108–44.

117 Activities of Victims Committee: Minutes of Guavio Victims Committee, 1978–81, court vol. 2, pp. 108–44; deposition of Fausto Fidel Gonzales, court vol. 2, pp. 398–404.

117 Bernardo Acosta background and activities, and subsequent narration in this chapter: Author's interviews with Guillermo Alvarado Contreres and Ana Elvira Zarate de Alvarado (Guillermo's wife), Gachala, Jan. 11–12, 1992; and the following depositions taken by the Counterintelligence Group, DIPEC, Colombian National Police, Bogotá: Guillermo Alvarado Contreras, Sept. 20, 1982, court vol. 1, pp. 39–41, and Oct. 18, 1982, court vol. 2, pp. 1–21; Ana Elvira Zarate de Alvarado, Sept. 19, 1982, court vol. 1, pp. 37–38, and Dec. 18, 1982, court vol. 2, pp. 492–95; Victor Manuel Reyes Pena, Sept. 20, 1982, court vol. 1, pp. 37–46; Victor Manuel Reyes Pena and Armando Martinez together, court vol. 2, pp. 408–15; Bernardo Heli Acosta, Sept. 17, 1982.

119 Legend of 100 bags of gold: Author's interviews with *campesinos* around Gachala; a similar version of the legend appears in Cunninghame Graham, *The Conquest*, p. 109.

119 THE MEDINA TRAIL: Escorted by *campesinos*, I have twice ridden mules over this trail and the environs described in this chapter.

120 Boots and snakes: Author's interviews.

CHAPTER 14

122 Chellino talks to Paytubi: FC-LP Nov. 16, 17, and 18, 1981.

122 PAYTUBI SAID: Ibid. and CC-RD Nov. 17 and 18, 1991.

122 GANGSTER ANGIE REPORTED: Teletype DEA Miami to DEA Washington, Dec. 8, 1981.

122 MARLENE NAVARRO CALLED: MN-RD Dec. 14, 1981; Darias CIS Dec. 21.

122 "Marlene wants us to wire": RD-FC (2) Dec. 14, 1981.

123 MARLENE CALLED ROBERT AGAIN: CIS Dec. 21, 1981.

123 Intercontinental Bank was not involved in Manuel Sanchez's criminal activities.

123 "Okay, I've made my calls": RD-CC-FC (2) Dec. 15, 1981.

123 Lunch with Marlene: DEA ROI (Chellino) Dec. 18, 1981; CIS's Dec. 21, 1981.

124 "In less than six months": CC-RD (6) Dec. 16, 1981.

124 CHELLINO SHOT A HOSTILE LOOK: PS-RD (1) Dec. 17, 1981.

124 DARIAS AND SENNETT DROVE: DEA ROI (Sennett) Jan. 11, 1982.

124 ON THURSDAY AFTERNOON: CIS Dec. 21, 1981; Darias testimony, *Navarro*, Oct. 28, 1986.

124 Darias purchases perfume: CIS Dec. 21, 1981; Author's interviews with Darias and Navarro.

124 Navarro talks of Carlos, Murcia, etc.: CIS Dec. 21, 1981; Darias testimony, *Navarro*, Oct. 28, 1986.

125 "Dean International": CC-RD (2) Dec. 17, 1981.

126 Significance of Alvarez: See Chapter 15 and notes.

CHAPTER 15

127 Alvarez background: Author's interviews; DEA intelligence summaries; DEA personal history reports (DEA Form 202) 1975, 1980, 1982–83 (compiled by Special Agent Michael Kuhlman in Bogotá).

127 Emerald industry violence: Author's interviews, Bogotá, Feb. 10–15, 1989; Twig Mowatt, "Turning Bogotá into the Emerald City," *NYT*, June 22, 1992, p. D1.

127 NETWORK OF "ENORMOUS PROPORTIONS": Department of the Treasury, United States Customs Service, *Reports of Investigation: Maria Lilia Rojas et al. and José Jader Alvarez Moreno et al.*, both written by Special Agent Michael J. Mulcahy and approved by Group Supervisor William R. Logan, MI02BR040033, Oct. 10, 1980, 20 pages (Customs ROI 1980) and May 8, 1981, 27 pages (Customs ROI 1981); Department of Justice, DEA, *Major Cocaine Violators* (hereafter *Violators*), internal DEA intelligence summary, 27 pages, 1982.

127 Alvarez aliases: *Violators*, p. 2.

127 Insurance policies: Policy applications list names and dates of birth of wives and children.

128 Alvarez arrested in 1974: Personal history, 1980, p. 2.

128 Alvarez phone taps: Customs ROI 1980, p. 1.

128 Arrest and seizure in 1979: Personal history, 1980, p. 2; Customs ROI 1980, p. 12.

128 Seizure of 138 kilograms: Customs ROI 1981, p. 3.

128 Murcia to Miami: Ibid., p. 4.
128 Murcia at Four Ambassadors: Customs ROI 1981, p. 5.
128 Down payment on plane: Ibid., p. 20.
128 Orejuela in charge of shipping: Ibid., p. 3.
128 Orejuela rich landowner: Ibid., p. 6.
128 DEA observes Orejuela: Ibid., p. 4.
128 Carlos Murcia homicide: Ibid., p. 5; files of Metro Dade County police, homicide case 146353-A; Edna Buchanan, "Colombian Killed in Airport Ambush," *MH*, May 9, 1980.
129 Orejuela detained: Metro Dade police file.
129 DEA following Orejuela at airport: Ibid. and author's interviews.
129 Orejuela arrested in Bogotá: Customs ROI 1981, p. 5.
129 DEA believed Alvarez shipped several hundred: *Violators*, p. 3.
129 Alvarez intensifies trouble-shooting, enlists Cabrera: Customs ROI 1981, p. 6.
129 Cabrera background: Ibid.; *Violators*, pp. 6–7; *Cabrera Sarmiento*, 80-317, 80-1274, 80-1262, 80-87, 80-413; Author's interviews, Bogotá, March 1990.
129 Associated with Sicilian Mafia: Customs ROI 1980, p. 15.
129 Alvarez buys Cabrera house: Registrar of Public Documents, Deed Transfer, issued to the American Embassy, Bogotá, Feb. 19, 1986.
129 Wiretaps reveal Cabrera coming to U.S.: Customs ROI 1980, p. 1.
129 Alvarez sends Rojas to Miami: Ibid.
129 Rojas appearance: Ibid., p. 5.
130 Estupinan, Alvarez, Kattan: Ibid., pp. 7–8.
130 "Teo" Terselich: Ibid., p. 12.
130 Rojas at airport: Ibid., pp. 2–5.
130 Navarro background: Author's interviews with Navarro and others; Navarro's testimony in *Navarro*.
131 Records of the University of Miami indicate that Navarro received a certificate of proficiency in international business from the School of Business Administration on July 28, 1976, and a bachelor of arts degree from the university with a major in economics and a minor in art on May 7, 1978.
131 Navarro reduces age: DEA ROI (Kuhlman) Apr. 28, 1983. Kuhlman's investigation of citizenship and identification records in Bogotá determined that Navarro had been born Nov. 9, 1943, instead of the same date in 1948.
131 Nicknames: Author's interviews with Navarro and others.
131 Office with Lester Rogers: Navarro testimony, *Navarro*, Apr. 21, 1987, pp. 17–20.
131 Navarro visits Rojas and offers $300,000: RD-CC July 6, 1982; RD-DEA Supervisor Dan Hoerner July 6, 1982; CIS Aug. 1982, p. 2; author's interviews with Navarro; MN-RD July 6, 1982; statement of Assistant U.S. Attorney Myles Malman, *Navarro*, June 2, 1987, p. 40.

131 Arrest of Cabrera: North Miami Beach Police Sgt. Rolando I. Baldomero, "Offense—Incident Report," Public Safety Department, Dade County, Florida, Case 18582-P, Aug. 28, 1980, 1:20 A.M.

132 Cabrera forfeits emeralds: CC-RD June 14, 1982; Carl Hiaasen and Peter Slevin, "Drug Fugitives Skip Skyrocketing Bond," *MH*, Jan. 17, 1983, p. 1A.

132 Alvarez comes to U.S. and sequence of events at Opa-Locka airport: Customs ROI 1981, pp. 7–27; indictments (original and superseding) and hearings, *Alvarez Moreno, Murcia Duarte, Perez Jaimes, and Arenas Parra*, 80-545-Cr-EPS, Dec. 1, 1980, and Feb. 9, 1981.

133 NAVARRO MADE THE FINAL PAYMENT: Customs ROI 1981, p. 20.

133 Navarro took flying lessons: Author's interviews with Navarro; RD-MN, Aug. 28, 1981; RD-CC, Aug. 28, 1981.

133 Navarro rides on plane to Bahamas: Author's interviews with Navarro; Customs ROI 1981, p. 21.

133 Hired lawyers for Murcia and pilots: Author's interviews; Navarro testimony, *Navarro*, Apr. 23, 1987, pp. 92–94. Harvey Rogers represented Murcia and Lester Rogers represented one of the pilots, Leon Arenas Parra, also a member of the Alvarez organization, during various court proceedings in late 1980.

134 Helps Murcia escape: Author's interviews with Navarro.

134 Visits Rojas in Kentucky: Author's interviews with Navarro.

134 Arrest of Kattan: See Chapter 7 and notes.

134 Navarro wires $400,000 to Panama for Kattan: Prosecution testimony of Bank of Miami employee Joanne Brown and documentary exhibits, *Navarro*, May 26, 1987, pp. 51–52; statement of Myles Malman, *Navarro*, June 2, 1987, p. 42; CC-RD (3) Jan. 22, 1982.

134 Navarro goes to Switzerland: Ibid.

134 Navarro avoided detection: CC-RD (4) Dec. 17, 1981.

135 Chellino and Darias purchase CD: CIS Jan. 11, 1982; DEA ROI (Chellino) Jan. 11, 1982.

135 Sennett gets drunk: CC-RD (2) Dec. 22, 1981; CC-RD (3) Dec. 23, 1981; RD-MD-PS Dec. 23, 1981.

135 Garcia Wednesday and Thursday: CIS Jan. 11, 1982.

135 Rodriguez to deposit millions: Ibid.

135 Dariases to England: Author's interviews with Dariases.

135 Children: Author's interviews with Alvarados and their depositions; Yidid's birthday taken from insurance policy application; presents unopened: Testimony of S. David Jaffe, *Navarro*, May 27, 1987, p. 81.

CHAPTER 16

136 Budget approved for three months: CC-RD Jan. 4, 1982.

136 Teletype to field offices: CC-RD (4) Jan. 13, 1982. The teletype, which had been sent Dec. 28, 1981, did not disclose details or cover names of the operation or the agents.

136 "We can get anything": CC-RD Jan. 6, 1982.
137 Alvero-Cruz retainer and meeting on Aruba: Teletype, DEA Miami to DEA Washington, Jan. 5, 1982.
137 Darias offers to help: RD-CC Jan. 6, 1982.
137 "He's talking up": CC-RD Jan. 6, 1982.
137 Anonymous telegram and DEA reaction: Author's interviews.
138 "We have to sit tight": RD-CC (1) Jan. 7, 1982.
139 "Nothing that this guy": PS-RD Jan. 7, 1982.
139 "He's a strange guy": CC-RD (2) Jan. 7, 1982.
139 Cooper asks Darias to bring gun: CC-RD Jan. 8, 1982.
139 Navarro phoned Darias: MN-RD Jan. 11, 1982; CIS Jan. 18, 1982.
139 Navarro meets McIntosh: Author's interviews; Navarro testimony, *Navarro*, Apr. 7, 1987, p. 23; Apr. 15, 1987, p. 85.
140 Luis Rodriguez socially inferior: MN-RD Dec. 17, 1981. Author's interviews with Darias.
140 SUGGESTIVE REMARKS: MN-RD Dec. 17 and 18, 1981; author's interviews in Bogotá.
140 BAD MANNERS: RD-CC (1) Jan. 8, 1992.
140 Eddie Hernandez background: Author's interviews; CC-RD (4) Jan. 13, 1982.
140 Hernandez worked for CIA: Hernandez testimony, *Navarro*, Feb. 10, 1987, p. 39.
140 "Until we decide who's who": CC-RD (4) Jan. 13, 1982.
141 Angie agreed to the polygraph: Author's interviews; CC-RD (2) Jan. 11, 1982.
141 COOPER KEPT DARIAS INFORMED: CC-RD (2) Jan. 11, 1982.
142 GANGSTER ANGIE INFORMED: CC-RD (4) Jan. 13, 1982.
142 DEA reaction to Angie: Author's interviews.
142 Clifford considers closing the operation: Author's interviews.
143 Agents' reaction to Clifford: Author's interviews.
143 "What do you mean": CC-RD (4) Jan. 13, 1982.
144 "Marlene will give me": Ibid.
145 DESPITE ROBERT'S SOOTHING WORDS: Author's interviews with the Dariases.
146 Growing animus between Clifford and Chellino: Author's interviews.
146 Gruden and Billbrough: Author's interviews; Jeff Leen, "Drug war chief trades battle zone for command post," *MH*, July 31, 1986; Kurt Luedtke, "Sheriff Loses 3 Top Men," *MH*, Feb. 24, 1965.
146 Billbrough's meeting with the agents: PS-RD Jan. 14, 1982; CC-RD (2) Jan. 14, 1982.
147 "The bosses want to break": Ibid.

CHAPTER 17

148 Alvarez grows pessimistic: MN-RD Jan. 13, 1982; RD-CC (4) Jan. 13, 1982; author's interviews in Bogotá.

148 MAS offensive: Gugliotta and Leen, *Kings of Cocaine*, pp. 93–94.

148 Release one child for $1.8 million: RD-MN Jan. 16, 1982; RD-CC Jan. 16, 1982; Darias CIS Jan. 18, 1982.

148 Aguirre in Bogotá: Author's interviews in Bogotá; DEA ROI Jan. 20, 1982 (Aguirre); testimony of Aguirre and Lt. Col. Ernesto Condia Garzon, Colombian National Police, *Alvarez*, Feb. 25, 1986.

151 Cabrera takes over kidnap negotiations: CNP report.

151 An unmarked van: CC-RD (1) Jan. 20, 1982; CC-RD (3) Jan. 21, 1982; author's interviews.

151 Affidavit (2 pages) signed by Carol Cooper; Application (3 pages) signed by Assistant U.S. Attorney Caroline Heck; Order (3 pages) signed by U.S. Magistrate Herbert Shapiro, Jan. 21, 1982; DEA ROI February 1982.

152 THE WHITE HOUSE ANNOUNCED: Robert D. Shaw, Jr., and Fredric Tasker, "U.S. Tackles South Florida Crime," *MH*, Jan. 29, 1982; FBI role in drug war: Jim McGee, "FBI Assumes Leading Role In Drug War," *MH*, Jan. 22, 1982, p. 1A; author's interviews.

153 "It's not worth your while": CC-RD Jan. 25, 1982.

153 Navarro reaction to Alvarez arrest: MN-RD Jan. 20, 1982; CIS Jan. 25, 1982.

153 Alvarez's son kills self: MN-RD Jan. 25, 1982; CIS Feb. 1, 1982.

154 THE DEA IN MIAMI LEARNED: RD-CC Jan. 25, 1982.

154 THE GUARD AT THE GATE: Author's interviews; testimony of Richard Thomas Vasquez, *Rogers*, 1, Nov. 18, 1983, pp. 20–27; DEA ROI Feb. 1982.

155 "We definitely want": CC-RD (5) Jan. 26, 1982.

155 Greenback cancels meetings: CC-RD (2) Jan. 28, 1982.

155 Darias breakfasts with Paytubi: Darias CIS Feb. 1, 1982.

156 Party at the Dariases': RD-CC (6) Jan. 26, 1982; CC-RD (1) Jan. 31, 1982; author's interviews.

CHAPTER 18

158 The Alvarez children: CNP report; depositions of Carlos Jader Alvarez and Marina Murillo Alvarez.

158 Army intelligence search: CNP report; Alvarez deposition.

159 Acosta moves the camp: Author's interviews in and around Gachalá and inspection of the site; CNP report; Reyes deposition; Alvarado depositions and author's interviews with the Alvarados.

159 "She's been calling the world": CC-RD (3) Feb. 2, 1982.

160 Navarro calls and meets Darias: Darias CIS Feb. 8, 1982.

160 Carlos Alvarado background: Various CIS's; trial record of *Rogers and Alvarado*.

160 After breakfast, Darias sees furniture: CIS Feb. 8, 1982; photographs of furnishings and interior of house; author's interviews with Darias and Navarro.

161 IMF report in Navarro's study: Stanley Penn, "Colombia's Syndicates Prove to Be Tough Foe for U.S. Drug Agents," *Wall Street Journal*, Apr. 5, 1983, p. 1.

161 Nude photos taken in Israel: Navarro statement, *Navarro*, July 30, 1987, p. 25.

162 Bancoshares acquittals: Alice Klement, "Jurors convict 4 of 14," *MH*, Feb. 5, 1982.

162 DEA reaction: Cooper to write memo: CC-RD (2) Feb. 4, 1982.

162 Burglary at Navarro's: Metro Dade County Police Burglary Report, 3751 Estipona Avenue, 10:48 P.M., Feb. 4, 1982; CIS Feb. 8, 1982; RD-CC (1) Feb. 5, 1982.

163 Clearest prints on nude photo: RD-CC (3) Feb. 5, 1982.

163 DARIAS RETURNED THAT AFTERNOON: RD-CC (1) Feb. 5, 1982.

164 $500,000 check: Darias CIS Feb. 8, 1982.

164 Darias and Navarro feelings toward each other: Author's interviews with both; Navarro testimony in *Navarro*, Mar. 27, 1987, p. 6, and Apr. 21, 1987, p. 34.

164 PONDERING WAYS HE MIGHT INDUCE: RD-CC (3) Feb. 5, 1982.

164 "The only thing holding me back": CC-RD Feb. 6, 1982.

165 Alvero-Cruz controversy—revoke bail: CC-RD (2) Feb. 16, 1982; CC-RD (1) Feb. 17, 1982.

166 "Fine, if you're going": CC-RD (2) Feb. 17, 1982.

166 COOPER SIGNALED GREG ENGLISH: Ibid.

166 "Between you and I, and I definitely": Ibid.

167 LIVES WOULD BE IN DANGER: Ibid.

167 COOPER AGAIN ADMONISHED: CC-RD (1) Feb. 18, 1982.

167 "The thing with her": CC-RD (2) Feb. 17, 1982.

167 Darias's name removed from computer: CC-RD (1) Feb. 19, 1982; CC-RD Apr. 15, 1982; CC-RD June 14, 1982.

167 Darias's birthday and illness: RD-CC Feb. 11, 1982; RD-CC (1) Feb. 16, 1982; RD-CC (1) Feb. 17, 1982.

CHAPTER 19

168 Plane crash near Bogotá: CIS Mar. 1, 1982; RD-CC (6) Feb. 22, 1982; RD-PS (1 and 2) Feb. 23, 1982; "Missing Plane," *El Tiempo*, Bogotá, Feb. 21, 1982; "Bodies Recovered from El Tablazo Hill," *El Tiempo*, Feb. 23, 1982.

168 NAVARRO TOLD DARIAS OF THE CRASH: Darias CIS Mar. 1, 1982.

168 "The main problem": Ibid.

169 THE SPRAWLING NATIONAL UNIVERSITY: Author's interviews in Bogotá and visits to the university.

169 Bank robbery and kidnapping: Author's interviews in Bogotá; Alvear Restrepo report, pp. 90–91 (see notes Chapter 9). The names of some of those kidnapped and the atmosphere in which the kidnapping occurred

are reported in *Human Rights in the Two Colombias: Functioning De-mocracy, Militarized Society*, An Americas Watch Report, October 1982, pp. 17–18 (hereafter Americas Watch 1982).

169 Marta Ochoa released: MN-RD Feb. 18, 1982; Gugliotta and Leen, *Kings of Cocaine*, p. 94.

169 ENCOURAGED BY THE RELEASE: Author's interviews in Colombia.

170 Splinter group: Deposition of Marina Murrillo Alvarez, court vol. 2, p. 252.

170 THE INVESTIGATION BY ALVAREZ AND MAS: Ibid.

170 ON SUNDAY, MARCH 7: Alvear Restrepo report, pp. 92–94; Americas Watch 1982, p. 18.

171 Cooper's party: Author's interviews.

172 New deposits at Dean: CIS's Mar. 8, 15, 1982; Garcia mentions Uribe: CIS Jan. 11, 1982; Garcia informed Darias: CIS Jan. 18, 1982; Garcia-Uribe: CIS Feb. 16, 1982;

172 Paytubi brings money: Videotape and transcript, Mar. 5, 1982.

174 Covo deposit: DEA ROIs (Chellino) Mar. 5, 1982, (Hernandez) Mar. 19, 1982.

174 Calderon's fear: RD-CC (1) Mar. 9, 1982; CC-RD Mar. 22, 1982; CC-RD June 14, 1982.

174 VIOLENT EPISODE: DEA-FBI statistics.

175 TAMPA seizure: Gugliotta and Leen, *Kings of Cocaine*, pp. 71–73; author's interviews.

175 Navarro reaction: DEA ROI (Cooper) Mar. 15, 1982.

176 "She was talking like crazy": CC-RD Mar. 10, 1982.

176 "I taped Marlene and Tocayo": RD-FC (1) Mar. 10, 1982.

177 Clifford hangovers: CC-RD (1) Mar. 9, 1982.

177 "Don't you ever tell": Author's interviews.

177 Hernandez attitude: Author's interviews.

178 "Eddie is very interested": RD-CC (3) Mar. 16, 1982.

178 Hernandez confides in Clifford: Author's interviews.

CHAPTER 20

179 Eddie got up to dance: RD-CC Mar. 18, 1982.

179 "You're not handling Eddie" and the remainder of the scene at Le Sabre: Author's interviews and frequent subsequent references in Darias's conversations with Cooper, e.g., RD-CC June 24, 1982; Though Darias did not witness the scene, he learned details quickly and later described the scene to Chief Prosecutor Michael S. Pasano, in RD-MP May 8, 1984.

180 "Bob controls *you*": Author's interviews with Darias; CC-RD Mar. 18, 1982.

181 *"Bob is mine"*: RR-RD Mar. 19, 1982; TC-RD Apr. 13, 1982.

181 "You're not really doing this": Author's interviews.

182 "We had an altercation": Author's interviews.
182 Clifford meeting with Congressmen: Author's interviews.
182 "Go sit on it": Author's Interviews.
182 "You have five minutes": CC-RD Mar. 20, 1982.
183 "Tom, please, don't even open": PS-RD Mar. 19, 1982.
183 "I would be sorry": RD-CC Mar. 18, 1982.
184 Clifford hearing only some: Ibid.
184 Cooper-Sennett mood: CC-PS-RD Mar. 18, 1982.
184 "Got a question for you": Ibid.
185 "take Bob with us": RR-RD Mar. 19, 1982.
185 Darias mood: Author's interviews with Darias.
185 Teletype re Greenback: Sent Mar. 18, 1982, 5:02 P.M.
186 Darias loosely supervised: RD-CC (4) Aug. 17, 1982.
186 Darias-Garcia meeting: RD-HG Mar. 19, 1982, audiotape and transcript; CIS Mar. 22, 1982; RD-CC May 13, 1982.
186 "They're crucifying me": CC-RD Mar. 20, 1982.
186 "Tom threatened me": Ibid.
187 *"You can run that operation"*: PS-RD Mar. 20, 1982.
187 Monday meeting: Darias secretly recorded it.
187 Nick Zapata details: Author's interviews.
189 Darias in charge: Author's interviews.

CHAPTER 21

190 Billbrough meetings, times, details: CC-RD Mar. 22, 1982.
190 FOUR BASIC CHARGES: Ibid.
191 ARREST LIONEL PAYTUBI: Ibid.
192 "Unless you tell them differently": Ibid.
193 "They would *crucify* me": Ibid.
193 Billbrough-Darias meeting: RD-CC Mar. 23, 1982; author's interviews with Darias and others.
195 Billbrough-Russo meeting: Author's interviews.
195 Darias-Clifford meeting: Author's interviews; RD-CC Mar. 23, 1982.
196 "There's no way you will stay": Ibid.
196 *"He lies to me"*: Ibid.
196 Darias-Garcia lunch: CIS Mar. 29, 1982.
197 Billbrough resolves crisis: CC-RD Mar. 24, 1982.
198 "Oh, God, what a day": Ibid.
199 "It's been solved": PS-RD (1) Mar. 24, 1982.
199 *"She's in charge"*: Ibid.
201 "Until they tell me": CC-RD Mar. 27, 1982.
201 "I have other avenues": Ibid.
201 "We cannot let anybody": Ibid.
201 Darias-Navarro meeting: RD-CC (2) Mar. 28, 1982; CIS Mar. 29, 1982.

203 Clifford's meeting: RD-Calderón Mar. 27, 1982; RD-CC (1) Mar. 28, 1982; RD-CC (1) Mar. 29, 1982.

203 "He flat-out lied": CC-RD (1) Mar. 29, 1982.

CHAPTER 22

205 Amnesty International bulletins: Issued by the International Secretariat, 10 Southampton Street, London WC2E 7HF, England, AMR 23/13/82, Apr. 2, 1982, and AMR 23/14/82, May 10, 1982.

205 MAS/Alvarez hold students in his house and has them killed: Confidential sources in Bogotá. Brian Freemantle reports that six guerrillas were murdered in revenge for the Alvarez kidnappings. Freemantle, *The Fix*, p. 190.

205 Acosta concerned for security: Confidential sources in Colombia; CNP report; author's visit to site.

206 Cooper-Clifford clash over wiretap: Author's interviews; William M. Beaney, "Electronic Surveillance," *The Guide to American Law* 4 (Saint Paul: West Publishing, 1984), p. 271.

207 Management tells Cooper to draft affidavit: CC-RD (3) Mar. 28, 1982; CC-RD (1) Mar. 29, 1982.

207 Bush tours boat: Fredric Tasker, "Bush Commits New Resources to Drug War," *MH*, Mar. 17, 1982, p. 1A.

207 Murphy comments: George Stein, "Drug smuggling at standstill, U.S. official says," *MH*, Apr. 8, 1982.

207 Navarro summons Darias, Apr. 2: CIS Apr. 5, 1982; DEA ROI (Cooper) Apr. 5, 1982, p. 2C.

208 Cooper goes with Darias: CIS Apr. 12, 1982; DEA ROI (Cooper) Apr. 13, 1982.

208 "You and Lester are the only": CIS Apr. 12, 1982.

208 Navarro telephones Darias from Avant-Garde: CIS Apr. 12, 1982; DEA ROI (Cooper) Apr. 13, 1982.

209 "I wish she lived": Repeated in CC-RD (2) Apr. 5, 1982.

209 Clifford fires Cooper again: Author's interviews.

210 "I'm out of there": CC-RD (3) Apr. 12, 1982.

210 "Boy, I tell you": RD-PS-CC Apr. 12, 1982.

211 Cooper hypertension: Author's interviews; FC-RD Feb. 23, 1983; CC-RD Mar. 14, 1983; PS-RD June 24, 1983; CC-RD July 18, 1983; CC-RD July 10, 1985.

212 Darias returns $90,000 to Navarro: DEA ROI (Hernandez) May 17, 1982.

212 "Who's handling all this": CC-RD (1) Apr. 13, 1982.

212 Office a mess: Ibid., and RD-CC (1) Apr. 24, 1982.

213 "I gotta say no": TC-RD Apr. 13, 1982.

213 "They were not aware": CC-RD Apr. 14, 1982.

213 Darias-Garcia meeting: HG-RD Apr. 15, 1982.
214 AGENTS LOST THE CASSETTE: RD-CC (4) Aug. 17, 1982; author's interviews with Darias and others.

CHAPTER 23

215 Darias buys bulletproof vest and attaché case: Kevlar "jacket" $375; Case $150. Purchased Mar. 31, 1982.
215 "There is a million dollars": RD-CC Apr. 19, 1982; CIS Apr. 20, 1982; DEA ROI (Hoerner) May 28, 1982; receipt from Federal Reserve Bank for $970,020.00 to wire transfer to LaSalle National Bank, Chicago, Apr. 20, 1982.
216 "That woman looks at you": RD-CC Apr. 19, 1982.
216 Zapata angry at wrong address: Ibid., and author's interviews.
217 Darias supervises counting: Ibid.; author's interviews.
217 Robert-Amelia talk: Author's interviews with Dariases.
218 Kids deliver $235,000: DEA ROI (Hernandez) June 4, 1982.
218 Garcia-Uribe deposit $2.1 million: CIS Apr. 22, 26, Dec. 2, 1982.
218 Processing problems: Author's interviews and study of DEA ROIs, which reflect the problems; CC-RD Aug. 30, wherein Cooper refers to a "four-month period (roughly mid-March to mid-July), when everything was so lax and out of control"; CC-RD Aug. 31, 1982, wherein Cooper refers to unprocessed tapes and the difficulty of processing them because "I was missing the four months. . . . There's always that four-month gap"; CC-RD (2) Sept. 1, 1982, wherein Darias and Cooper discuss "confusion for a couple of weeks" in July over processing $220,000 that Navarro deposited with International Investments; CC-RD Oct. 5, 1982, wherein Cooper says, regarding the $1 million delivery on Apr. 19, 1982, "they commingled that million dollars with a whole mess of other money that day . . .": The DEA Manual requires agents to write ROIs within five days after the events they document: CC-RD (2) Sept. 27, 1982.
218 Hernandez and Zapata try to take control: RD-CC-PS June 15, 1982; author's interviews.
218 Darias reaction: RD-CC (1) Apr. 19, 1982; RD-CC (1) May 1, 1982; author's interviews with Darias.
219 Failure of Latinization, intra-ethnic tension: RD-CC (1) Apr. 24, 1982; RD-CC (1) May 3, 1982; RD-CC (1) May 11, 1982; RD-CC-PS June 15, 1982; author's interviews.
220 "I owe you a party": CC-RD Apr. 19, 1982.
220 Office moves: RD-CC Apr. 20, 1982; author's interviews.
221 Frank Dean name expunged: RD-CC (1) Aug. 29, 1982.
221 Darias meets McIntosh, shares beer: RD-CC (1) May 1, 1982; RD-CC (1) May 2, 1982.
221 Pornographic movies: Ibid.
221 Cabrera and Rodriguez arrested: RD-CC May 5, 1982; RD-CC May 16, 1982; confidential sources in Colombia.

221 English reassigned: Author's interviews.
222 Marcus background: Joe Starita, "U.S. Attorney makes tough boss," *MH*, Mar. 29, 1982, p. 1.
222 Marcus moves: Author's interviews.
222 Pasano background: Author's interviews; "Associate Biographies," brochure of the law firm of Zuckerman Spaeder Goldstein Taylor & Kolker, Miami office.
222 Pasano's impressions: Author's interviews.
222 Clifford doesn't like agents to work at home: CC-RD (1) Apr. 26, 1982; author's interviews.
223 "There is no doubt": CC-RD Apr. 19, 1982; repeats RD-CC May 13, 1982.
223 "A whole lot of attorneys": CC-RD (1) May 2, 1982.
223 Navarro calls attorneys: CC-RD (1) Apr. 20, 1982.
224 STRUCTURE BEHIND JADER: CC-RD (1) May 2, 1982.
224 David Jaffe: MN-RD May 13, 1982; CIS's May 17, 1982; DEA ROI (Hoerner) May 28, 1982; Jaffe testimony, *Navarro*, Apr. 8, 1987.
224 $1 million is Cabrera's: CC-RD Apr. 24, 1982.
224 Navarro comes to office: CIS May 17, 1982.
225 Darias wards off Zapata and Hernandez: RD-CC May 13, 1982.
225 Wiretap postponed for more lenient judge: CC-RD Apr. 19, 1982; CC-RD (1) Apr. 24, 1982; RD-CC (1) May 1, 1982.

CHAPTER 24

227 The description of the Washington conference is based on the author's interviews, the two-page agenda with the names of attendees, the 28-page intelligence summary, *Major Cocaine Violators*, the mafia organization chart, and Cooper's comments to Darias before the meeting, e.g., CC-RD May 16, 1982: "The reason I'm going to Washington is because it's such a big case. They're pulling in people from all over so everybody is aware that this wire is going on and all the various points that are going to be touched by it.... We're trying to convince Washington that this is the biggest group since sliced bread...."

The DEA estimated that Colombians smuggled roughly 30 tons of cocaine into the United States each year, that Carlos Jader Alvarez and his colleagues accounted for well over a third of that, and that the only individual smuggler responsible for more than Alvarez was Carlos Lehder Rivas. Jorge Ochoa, the brother of Marta Ochoa, who had been kidnapped and then released by the M-19, was estimated to smuggle considerably less than Alvarez. This was before the DEA and the media began to distinguish between mafia "cartels" in Colombia, e.g., the Medellín and Cali cartels.

Estimate of amounts of cocaine smuggled annually out of Colombia and into the U.S. circa 1981–1982: DEA, *Drug Enforcement* 9, no. 2

(Fall 1982), pp. 8–9; Guy Gugliotta, "DEA feebly attempts to slay 'drug dragon' in Colombia," *MH*, Oct. 14, 1981, p. 1A.

By the middle 1980s, these estimates had evolved considerably as both the demand and supply soared.

229 Darias-Pasano meeting: RD-CC June 11, 1982; RD-CC June 16, 1982; author's interviews.

229 Navarro summons Darias: CIS May 26, 1982; DEA ROI (Hoerner) May 25, 1982.

229 Hernandez delivery: Ibid.; CIS (Calderon) May 28, 1982.

230 Hernandez makes pass at Navarro: RD-CC June 15, 1982; RD-PS June 26, 1982; Hernandez denied he made a pass.

230 "Everybody was very impressed": CC-RD June 1, 1982.

230 Marlene offers 100 kg of cocaine: CIS June 4, 1982.

232 "Tom, another hundred kilograms": RD-CC June 8, 1982.

232 Navarro to Europe: Navarro's American Express receipts; CIS June 8, 1982 (handwritten and typed); teletype (confidential) from DEA Frankfurt to DEA Washington and Miami, June 15, 1982, 12:13 P.M. Greenwich mean time.

232 Other agencies want to be briefed: For example, letter from William Rosenblatt, regional director (investigations), U.S. Customs Service, to Peter Gruden, June 2, 1982, and Gruden's instructions to Tom Clifford, "Do not discuss targets, defendants, undercover site, etc. As a sensitive undercover operation, we can't be briefing everyone who doesn't have an actual need to know."

233 Crisis within the operation: Author's interviews.

233 Tape missing, checkbook misplaced: RD-CC June 16, 1982; RD-CC (4) Aug. 17, 1982; author's interviews with Darias and others.

233 "fantastic mess": RD-CC June 9, 1982.

233 Fury between factions: Author's interviews.

234 "Tom doesn't know what I'm doing": CC-RD June 1, 1982; repeated CC-RD June 9, 1982.

235 DEA neglecting Humberto Garcia case: Ibid.; CC-RD June 16, 1982, and later references.

235 "How can Tom go against Gruden?": Ibid.

235 Delayed reports: Ibid.

236 Cooper confirms Darias in control: Ibid.; CC-RD June 18, 1982; CC-RD (1) July 6, 1982, "You've had more freedom than anybody else I know"; CC-RD Aug. 30, 1982, Cooper refers to a "four-month period when everything was so lax and out of control."

236 "I was specifically instructed not to tell you": CC-RD June 11, 1982.

236 "I've totally lost control": CC-RD June 14, 1982.

CHAPTER 25

237 Nick and Eddie memorandum: Zapata signed above Hernandez on page 3; Jack L. Lloyd, assistant special-agent-in-charge, Miami Field Divi-

sion, DEA, "Swordfish Commissions and Operational Problems Reported by Special Agents N. Zapata and E. Hernandez," six-page single-spaced memorandum to Peter Gruden dated Feb. 28, 1983 (Lloyd memorandum). The Lloyd memorandum is the most authoritative account of the internal investigation of the allegations and is the source of most future references to the controversy in the narrative.

238 Rumor that $250,000 missing: CC-RD June 14, 1982; RD-CC (4) Aug. 17, 1982.

238 Hoerner's anger: CC-RD June 25, 1982, and author's interviews.

238 "Eddie follows Nick's leadership": Ibid.

239 "Americans see Latins": RD-CC-PS June 15, 1982.

239 Eddie makes a pass at Marlene: Ibid.; RD-PS June 26, 1982.

240 "Keep that up your sleeve": Ibid.

240 Pasano calls meetings: Michael S. Pasano, two memoranda to file, July 7, 1982.

240 Possible damage to prosecutions: Darias and Cooper discussed this possibility at length on Mar. 16, 1983, during an internal DEA investigation of the problems during Operation Swordfish. Describing an interview with a DEA investigator, Darias said: ". . . if the defense attorneys had gotten wind of, maybe we would have had trouble with some of the trials, accusing some of these people. Because there were some mistakes, not done on purpose, but there were big mistakes made in there during that period of time. And, in my opinion, were very, very bad for the operation. I told him I had to take charge of the operation, otherwise it would have gone to pieces."

241 "Bob will do anything": CC-RD June 16, 1982.

241 "I cannot work with these guys": RD-CC June 25, 1982.

241 Hoerner tracks Clifford: CC-RD June 18, 1982.

241 Oscar calls Darias: Ibid.; CIS June 19, 1982.

242 Navarro returns from Europe: Teletype, DEA Miami to DEA Washington. RD-MN June 26, 1982.

242 DARIAS MET NAVARRO: Audiotape and transcript June 28, 1982 (38 pages); CIS June 28, 1982; Valleys of Kendall property in Lester Rogers's name: Navarro testimony, *Navarro*, Apr. 8, 1987, pp. 58–59; Lester Rogers testimony, *Rogers and Alvarado*, Jan. 11, 1984, p. 123, and Jan. 12, 1984, p. 49.

243 Wilson and Nies surveil: DEA ROI June 28, 1982.

CHAPTER 26

244 The most succinct account of Barbara Mouzin's version of events is contained in a nine-page DEA ROI written by Paul A. Higdon, Senior Inspector, Office of Professional Responsibility, DEA Headquarters, Aug. 12, 1983, file G1-G1-83-0039, DEA SENSITIVE (hereafter Higdon ROI).

244 Muse-Mouzin meeting: Testimony of Barbara Mouzin, *Muse and Gibbs*, Jan. 7, 1987, p. 86.

244 FORMER LOVERS: Testimony of Dorothy Hackett, *Muse*, Jan. 13, 1987, p. 22; Hackett statement to the DEA, Mar. 16, 1983, p. 6; statement of Muse's lawyer Alan E. Weinstein in bench conference, *Muse*, Jan. 8, 1987, p. 203. Mouzin denied sleeping with Muse.

244 Muse liked to hear DEA war stories: Statement of Special Agent Krusco, recounted in internal memorandum of DEA Intelligence Analyst Charles Bonneville, DEA Headquarters, Washington, D.C., Apr. 17, 1985.

245 Gibbs's state of mind, drinking, etc.: Gibbs letter to Judge William M. Hoeveler, USDC, Miami, undated.

246 Mouzin relationship to Navarro in mafia structure: DEA intelligence chart undated.

246 Gibbs runs names: Testimony of John Scott Baker III, DEA computer specialist, *Muse*, Jan. 9, 1987, p. 86.

246 Gibbs conversations with Los Angeles colleagues: Testimony of Special Agents John Marcello and Paul Beaulieu, *Muse*, pp. 24–29, 32–39.

246 UPON RETURNING TO MIAMI: Higdon ROI; Mouzin testimony.

247 Meetings at Le Sabre and two Holiday Inns: Ibid.

247 Arthur Balletti: Ibid.; Wendy Rogers, "Blonde Takes Stand in Firestones' Trial," *MH*, Feb. 10, 1967; John Brecher, "CIA, Mafia and Castro Linked With Spying on Comedian Rowan," *MH*, Apr. 19, 1975.

247 BAIL ARRANGEMENTS: Higdon ROI; Mouzin testimony.

247 Muse-Mouzin meeting at Kings Inn: Ibid.

248 Mouzin and Balletti fly to California: Ibid.

248 Mouzin flees U.S.: Ibid.

248 Takiff background: Characterization based on my daily observation from September 1986 to February 1987 at the *Navarro* trial, and transcript of *Rogers and Alvarado*. The *Miami Herald* has referred to Takiff in news columns as a "loud, obnoxious, self-obsessed drug lawyer" and "bold, brazen, and overbearing."

248 Balletti approached Takiff, and rest of narrative in this chapter: confidential sources.

CHAPTER 27

250 Pouilly-Fuissé: RD-CC (2) July 1, 1982.

250 Cocaine shipment arrives: RD-CC (3) July 1, 1982; CIS August 1982. The meticulous maintenance of Darias's CIS's deteriorated after Tom Clifford fired Carol Cooper as Darias's control. The length, frequency, and neatness of the vital documents declined in the hands of Dan Hoerner, as did the preparation of DEA ROIs, reflecting the DEA agents' diminished control of the operation. By late June, very few CIS's

and ROIs were being compiled, and there was little daily record of Darias's activities, aside from his own handwritten notes and his secret recordings of his conversations with the agents, which he did not share with them. In late August, Carol Cooper compiled a single CIS of 12 pages covering Darias's activities from June 29 through August 20.

251 Carol's instructions precise: CC-RD (3) July 1, 1982.

251 "How pretty that is": Audiotape and transcript, July 6, 1982 (31 pages); new microphone: Author's interviews with Darias.

252 "Everything is loud and clear": RD-CC July 6, 1982.

252 Clifford returns and threatens to sue Zapata and Hernandez, CC-RD (2) Aug. 17, 1982; RD-CC Aug. 30, 1982; author's interviews.

253 Zapata and Hernandez reassigned: Lloyd memo; CC-RD June 25, 1982.

253 Oscar shipped 100 kilograms to New York: RD-Tocayo tape and transcript July 15, 1982; RD-MN tape and transcript July 15, 1982; CIS August 1982, p. 7; wiretap call NNN-131 July 21, 1982; RD-MN tape and transcript (36 pages), July 26, 1982; teletype, DEA JFK Airport to DEA Washington and DEA Miami, Aug. 10, 1982, 11:17 A.M.

254 Wiretap papers by special courier: CC-RD July 6, 1982 ("It's being hand-carried up there," Cooper told Darias. "Don't let anybody know I told you").

255 Cooper-Clifford battle resumes: CC-RD July 7, 1982, and author's interviews; CC-RD July 9, 1982.

255 Navarro increases offer to 600 kg: CIS August 1982, p. 3.

256 "Tom didn't *ask* me": CC-RD July 10, 1982.

256 Teletype: CC-RD July 11, 1982.

256 "I have all sorts of devious little ways": Ibid.

256 Oscar called: CIS August 1982, p. 3.

CHAPTER 28

257 Darias talk with Oscar and Navarro: Audiotape and transcript (13 pages) July 12, 1982; CIS August 1982, p. 4.

259 SAVORING HER NEW VICTORY: CC-RD (4) July 12, 1982.

259 "I want to work with Paul": RD-CC July 13, 1982.

260 The 94th Aero Squadron: RD-Oscar audiotape and transcript (5 pages) July 14, 1982; CIS August 1982, p. 4; DEA ROI (Wilson) Aug. 5, 1982.

261 Cocaine resold for $1 billion retail: The retail price is derived from a very rough formula used in the early 1980s. See "Cocaine Prices at Successive Stages of Trafficking," *Drug Enforcement* 9, no. 1 (Summer 1982), p. 22.

261 DEA CHANGED ITS MIND: Author's interviews with Darias; CC-RD (3) July 14, 1982.

261 Navarro at hairdresser: Ibid.

262 Pasano briefing: "Intercept of wire communications over telephone numbers (305) 592-7106 and (305) 592-7180, subscribed to by Marlene

Navarro at 3751 Estepona Avenue, Building 19, Townhouse B-2, Miami, Florida."

263 Tocayo drops off $220,000: RD-Tocayo tape and transcript July 15, 1982 (12 pages); DEA ROI (Fernandez) Sept. 16, 1982.

264 "How pretty the horse": RD-MN tape and transcript (30 pages) July 15, 1982; CIS August 1982, p. 4.

267 ROBERT AND CAROL SPECULATED: RD-CC (3) July 15, 1982.

268 CAROL COOPER COACHED: Ibid.

268 LATER, AT INTERNATIONAL: RD-Tocayo tape and transcript (15 pages) July 16, 1982; CIS August, 1982, p. 5; DEA ROI (Delgado) Sept. 13, 1982.

268 WHEN TOCAYO LEFT: DEA ROI (Charette) July 17, 1982.

269 "They're still with him": CC-RD (1) July 16, 1982.

269 "We're sitting on his house": RD-TC July 16, 1982.

269 "I am very, very sick": RD-CC (3) July 16, 1982.

269 Navarro was weeping and vomiting: MN-RD July 16, 1982; MN-RD tape and transcript (41 pages) July 19, 1982.

269 "She's staying at Gustavo's": Ibid.

270 "Since I can't tell you": Ibid.

271 AT THE DESERTED CAPITOL: DEA ROI (Hoerner) July 21, 1982; CC-RD July 17, 1982; James W. Huber, "Technical Security Countermeasures Survey," Aug. 18, 1982 (Huber TSC Survey).

CHAPTER 29

276 HAD MARLENE NAVARRO: Author's interviews.

276 Judge received: Author's interviews.

276 VASQUEZ HAD RIGGED: Author's interviews.

276 "Tocayo called me": RD-MN tape and transcript (32 pages), July 17, 1982; CIS August 1982, p. 5.

277 WITH PAUL SENNETT OBSERVING: DEA ROI (Sennett) July 19, 1982.

277 AT HOME LATER HE CALLED CAROL: RD-CC July 17, 1982.

278 Navarro flicked on *60 Minutes*: Mentioned in NNN-2. All conversations intercepted from Navarro's primary line are designated NNN and a number. Calls intercepted from the special Jader phone are designated 000 and a number.

278 Gustavo: NNN-2.

279 McIntosh: NNN-4.

279 Tocayo: NNN-5.

279 Darias: NNN-6.

279 McIntosh: NNN-7, NNN-9.

279 Alvarez: OOO-6.

281 Oscar: NNN-18.

281 Nelson: OOO-14, OOO-15.

281 Darias and Tocayo meeting with Navarro: Tape and transcript (41

pages) July 19, 1982; CIS August 1982, p. 6; DEA ROI (Beaver) July 19, 1982.

283 Gustavo: NNN-47.

283 Burdine's: NNN-51, NNN-53.

283 Darias: NNN-59.

283 Oscar: NNN-56.

283 WOMAN FRIEND: NNN-64.

283 McIntosh: NNN-66.

283 Jader Alvarez: OOO-17.

283 Darias: NNN-69.

283 Gustavo: NNN-74.

283 Fashion New York: NNN-72.

283 Henry: NNN-77.

283 Banker and handyman: NNN-75.

283 HAIR APPOINTMENT: NNN-76.

283 Lester Rogers: NNN-78.

283 Answering service: NNN-79.

284 Robert and Marlene at Burger King: RD-MN July 20, 1982; CIS August 1982, p. 6–7.

284 Luis Rodriguez: Ibid.

285 There was a sense of anticipation: RD-CC (2 and 3) July 20, 1982.

285 That evening in Los Angeles: DEA ROI July 29, 1982, written by Special Agent Larry Lyons, who had attended the working conference in Washington in May. Los Angeles surveillance referred to by Cooper in CC-RD (2) July 21, 1982.

286 Oscar: NNN-114.

286 Reviewing notes: Wiretap Log A, p. 49.

287 Oscar-Nelson: NNN-131; DEA ROI (Gonzales) July 22, 1982.

287 Oscar-Darias: NNN-142.

287 Gustavo picks up Marlene: DEA ROI (Gonzales) July 22, 1982.

287 Burglary: Huber TSC Survey.

287 "You can't imagine where": RD-CC (2) July 21, 1982.

287 "Don't ever tell him": Ibid.

288 DEA AND COLOMBIAN F-2: Teletype, DEA Bogotá to DEA Miami and Washington, July 22, 1982, 4:18 A.M.

288 FBI plane: CC-RD (1 and 3) July 22, 1982.

289 Robert and Amelia alone: RD-CC (2) July 22, 1982 (Sinatra recording audible).

289 ROBERT REACHED MARLENE: RD-CC (3) July 22, 1982.

289 AFTER FOUR DAYS: Prosecutors' "Five Day Report" to Judge Sidney M. Aronovitz on the results of the wiretap, July 22, 1982, seven pages.

290 Greenback-Barnett: Teletype, DEA Miami to DEA Washington, July 22, 1982; "Barnett Banks Takes Step Aimed at Buying Great American Banks," WSJ, June 29, 1982.

291 "There's a lot of political problems": CC-RD (2) July 21, 1982.

CHAPTER 30

292 Arson at the "safe house": Metropolitan Dade County Fire Safety Bureau, *Investigation Report*, Case 257546-C, File 6646, July 25, 1982.
292 Arsonist was Terselich: TT-MN, NNN-427, July 28, 1982.
293 Navarro returned: DEA ROI (McCracken) July 24, 1982.
293 Alex waiting: NNN-171. McIntosh calls Eastern Airlines from Navarro's house for flight information.
293 "I'm going to wait": RD-CC July 25, 1982.
293 Cooper and others out until 4 A.M.: Ibid.
293 Nelson to Las Vegas: NNN-196.
293 Marlene to Gustavo about Roberto: NNN-201.
293 Monitors phone Cooper: CC-RD (3) Aug. 2, 1982.
294 Oscar: NNN-206.
294 Darias: NNN-208.
295 "I know she's looking": CC-RD (2) July 25, 1982.
295 Lester Rogers: NNN-210.
295 Oscar: NNN-233.
295 "I don't know about our shoes": RD-MN tape and transcript (36 pages), July 26, 1982.
296 Call from Vancouver: CIS August 1982, p. 7.
296 "She's going to be meeting": CC-RD July 26, 1982.
296 Nelson: NNN-270.
297 Cooper and Sennett stopped for speeding: CC-RD July 27, 1982, and author's interview with Darias.
297 Wiretaps on Alvarez's phones: Teletype DEA Bogotá to DEA Miami, July 29, 4:24 A.M.
297 Oscar's reckless driving: NNN-308; CC-RD (2) July 27, 1982.
297 Surveillance of Oscar: DEA ROI (Marin) July 27, 1982.
297 Navarro-Darias: NNN-307.
298 "I'm going crazy": RD-CC (2) July 27, 1982.
298 Alvarez: OOO-35.
299 Carlos Lehder refers buyer to Alvarez: Teletype DEA Bogotá to DEA Miami, July 28, 1982, 12:21 P.M.
300 Darias sinus: NNN-349.
300 "I guess you know": RD-CC (1) July 28, 1982.
300 Nelson from Caesar's Palace: NNN-386.
301 "I have an assignment": CC-RD (4) July 28, 1982.
301 "I'm not very well": NNN-387.
302 "You're doing a fine job": CC-RD (5) July 28, 1982.
302 Marlene calls Eastern Airlines: NNN-393.
303 Hugo: NNN-409.
304 Surveillance of Rojas: Teletype, DEA JFK Airport to DEA Washington and DEA Miami, Aug. 10, 1982, 11:17 A.M. (JFK teletype).
304 "Richie turned up": NNN-427.

304 "Son, I was worried": NNN-428.
305 Surveillance of Rojas: JFK teletype.
306 "Sorry, darling": NNN-439.
306 "call Chiqui": NNN-440.

CHAPTER 31

307 Chellino: Cooper confided his return to Darias in advance in CC-RD July 27, 1982 ("Keep that under your shirt") and confirmed it in CC-RD July 30, 1982 ("We got the little guy back, Frank"); power dynamics discussed in CC-RD (4) Aug. 12, 1982, and CC-RD (4) Aug. 17, 1982.
307 Billbrough helps with license plates: CC-RD July 9, 1982.
308 Covo deposits: DEA ROIs (Hoerner) Aug. 14, 1982, and (Marin) Sept. 3, 1982.
308 Delivery of $750,000: OOO-54.
308 Said Pavon: OOO-52, OOO-53.
309 Oscar: NNN-472.
309 Alvarez: OOO-54.
309 Alvarez receipts and disbursements: OOO-64 (16 pages).
310 Take-out food: NNN-472.
310 Alvarez and Oscar: OOO-68.
310 Teo complains: NNN-531.
311 Bertha arrives: Gate guard calls Navarro in NNN-533. Bertha had called for directions in OOO-65 at 9:00 P.M.
311 Bertha, a money manager for Cabrera: RD-CC (3) Aug. 27, 1982; RD-CC (3) Aug. 29, 1982.
311 Marlene and Robert breakfast: Tape and transcript (17 pages) July 30, 1982.
312 To New York: NNN-464.
312 To Washington: NNN-465.
312 To Washington, New York, Washington: NNN-566.
312 To Kentucky, New York, Kentucky: OOO-62, OOO-69.
312 Gibbs surveillance: DEA ROI (Gibbs) July 30, 1982.
312 Celebration at listening post: CC-RD (3) Aug. 2, 1982.
313 "It's just getting incredible": PS-RD July 30, 1982.
313 Darias to move: Author's interviews.
314 "When I talk to her": RD-CC (3) Aug. 2, 1982.
314 Wiretap a success: Ibid.; CC-RD Aug. 8, 1982.
315 "we seriously checked": Ibid.
316 "It's one thing": Author's interviews with Dariases.
316 Target conference: Pasano notes.
317 "She's getting her hair done": CC-FC-RD (2) Aug. 3, 1982.
318 "Okay, she called": RD-CC (3) Aug. 3, 1982.
318 Oscar's deliveries: NNN-651.

318 Robert and Marlene breakfast: Tape and transcript (8 pages) Aug. 4, 1982; CIS August 1982, p. 7–8.

319 Delivery of $487,430: Ibid.; DEA ROI (Handoga) Sept. 21, 1982; RD-CC (3) Aug. 4, 1982.

CHAPTER 32

320 Sore from surgery: NNN-57.

320 Weather reference: NNN-57.

320 Oscar re homicides: NNN-752.

320 Nelson: NNN-772.

321 Oscar: NNN-778.

321 Surveillance of Nelson: DEA ROI (Charette) Aug. 6, 1982; MN-NB NNN-783; CC-RD (3) Aug. 5, 1982.

321 Nelson: NNN-798.

324 "Do you think they are": CIS August 1982, p. 8; RD-PS Aug. 6, 1982; RD-CC (3) Aug. 6, 1982.

325 "She is *very* nervous": Ibid.

325 Nelson: NNN-841.

325 "Keep in mind": RD-CC (2) Aug. 6, 1982.

CHAPTER 33

327 Betancur inauguration: "Betancur Assumes Office in Colombia" (Associated Press dispatch), *NYT*, Aug. 8, 1982; Warren Hoge, "Colombian President Governs with Maverick Touch," *NYT*, Dec. 4, 1982.

327 Campaign contributions: Alvarez testimony, *Alvarez*, vol. 29, May 7, 1986, pp. 77–78; memorandum from Michael S. Pasano, Assistant U.S. Attorney, to Stanley Marcus, U.S. Attorney, entitled "Juvenal Betancur—Operation Swordfish," Sept. 20, 1982, in which Pasano states: "It appears that Alvarez is a major political contributor and supporter of President Betancur."

328 Betancur puts police at Alvarez's disposal: Alvear Restrepo report.

328 Alvarez gave or "loaned" Juvenal $10,000: Deposition of Juvenal Betancur Cuartas, *U.S. v. $10,126.73*, USDC, SDF, 83-0768, June 15, 1983, p. 5. Betancur testified that no paperwork documented the "loan," which was to help pay his son's medical expenses in Miami Beach. Many of Betancur's activities are also detailed in other documents associated with that case, including transcript of hearing, April, 1984 (62 pages); and finding of fact and conclusions of law, and final judgment of forfeiture, Apr. 17, 1984. Additional details appear in a sworn affidavit of DEA Special Agent John N. Lawler and seizure warrant, *U. S. v. All Monies Contained Within Account Number(s): 1505006801, at Intercontinental Bank, 10 S. E. 1st Avenue, Miami, Florida, As Well As All Monies Belonging To the Following Named Individual(s) In Said Bank: Juvenal Betancur-Cuartas*, USDC, SDF, 82-2293-HSS, Oct. 15, 1982. In

addition to writing the memorandum to Marcus cited above, Michael
Pasano outlined the chronology of Betancur's activities in a memoran-
dum to Kevin R. March, Chief, Fraud and Public Corruption Section,
Office of the U. S. Attorney, Sept. 23, 1982.

328 F-2 commander met with Alvarez: CNP and Alvear Restrepo reports.
329 Advertisements: CNP report.
329 "friend of your compadre": OOO-92.
329 Darias: NNN-854.
329 Darias offers on houses: RD-CC Aug. 7, 1982, and RD-CC (2) Aug. 8, 1982.
329 "We're losing all our environment": RD-CC Aug. 8, 1982.
330 Carmenza: NNN-873 (translated by RD).
330 Alex, the son: NNN-874 (translated by RD).
331 "hundred boxes" conversation: OOO-94; CC-RD (1) Aug. 8, 1982.
332 Need additional evidence against Rogers: Ibid., and CC-RD (2) Aug. 8, 1982.
332 Valleys of Kendall: RD-MN tape and transcript (24 pages) Aug. 9, 1982;
     color brochure; CIS August 1982, p. 8.
333 "I made a very good tape": RD-CC (1) Aug. 9, 1982.
333 Gibbs surveillance at La Carretta: DEA ROI (Cox) Aug. 9, 1982.
333 Diarrhea: NNN-940, NNN-941.
334 Paytubi: RD-LP tape and transcript (13 pages) Aug. 10, 1982.
334 Homicides: George Stein, "Slayings May Signal Renewal of Drug
     Wars," *MH*, Aug. 12, 1982, p. 1A.
334 David Jaffe to Bogotá: Teletype DEA Bogotá to DEA Miami and
     Washington, Aug. 11, 1982, 3:16 A.M.; teletype DEA Miami to DEA
     Bogotá, Aug. 13, 1982, 1:40 P.M.; DEA ROI (Kuhlman) Aug. 16, 1982;
     CC-RD (4) Aug. 11, 1982.

CHAPTER 34

336 Juvenal Betancur: NNN-1082
336 "I've been worried about you": NNN-1080.
337 McIntosh's other woman in Toronto: RD-CC (4) Aug. 11, 1982.
338 "Dr. Juvenal will be arriving": NNN-1082.
338 room for religious statues: Author's interviews with Navarro.
338 "Marlene, good evening. This is Juvenal Betancur." OOO-77.
339 "I want you to place him": NNN-1104.
340 "Tomorrow I'm going to meet": RD-CC (5) Aug. 11, 1982.
340 "The only thing I'm thinking": CC-RD (6) Aug. 11, 1982.

CHAPTER 35

342 "You no good, connivin' ": FC-RD-CC Aug. 12, 1982.
343 "Heidi [the maid] is laughing": MN-RD tape and transcript (25 pages)
     Aug. 12, 1982; CIS August 1982, p. 8.

344 Description of Juvenal Betancur: Ibid.; passport photograph and information.

344 Juvenal's cologne: Author's interviews with Darias.

344 "Jader gave several hundred thousand": RD-CC (2) Aug. 12, 1982.

344 At the house she gave: CIS August 1982, p. 8.

345 "How is *el papi*?": NNN-1181; log summary supplemented by Darias translation.

345 "Obviously it's great": CC-RD (2) Aug. 12, 1982.

346 Cooper to send classified teletypes: Ibid.

346 "I am happy . . . because Don Juvenal": OOO-138.

347 "I went to sleep at four": OOO-139.

347 "Three things": NNN-1205.

348 Chellino met Darias: DEA ROI (Chellino) Aug. 13, 1982, plus signature cards and starter deposit tickets.

348 Darias and Betancur at Beach Palace: RD-JB tape and transcript (4 pages) Aug. 13, 1982, supplemented by Darias translation for author; DEA ROI (Trouville) Aug. 13, 1982; CIS August 1982, p. 9.

348 Marlene gives Robert $57,000: Ibid.; DEA ROI (Charette) Aug. 13, 1982.

349 "You don't think": Darias translation for author; CIS August 1982, p. 9.

349 Clifford orders Darias to the party: TC-RD Aug. 13, 1982; CIS August 1982, p. 9.

350 "Tell Tom he owes": RD-CC (4) Aug. 13, 1982.

351 "I was sleeping": NNN-1256.

351 Duncan to be on flight: CC-RD (5) Aug. 13, 1982 (numbered as if before midnight).

CHAPTER 36

352 Denver trip: CIS August 1982, p. 10; DEA ROI (Duncan) Aug. 17, 1982; DEA ROI (Moody) Aug. 16, 1982.

352 Description of Navarro and Darias and sequence of surveillance: Testimony of Special Agents Angelo Saladino, Gloria Woods, and Darryl McClary, *Alvarez*, May 5, 1986, pp. 105–31.

352 "The load is expected": CIS August 1982, p. 10.

352 "If Jader is hesitant": RD-CC Aug. 15, 1982.

352 "Luis is trying to take": Ibid.

352 Houston airport, arrival in Denver, drive to hotel, encounter with Said Pavon: Ibid.; CIS August 1982, p. 10.

354 Receipt of money: Ibid.

354 " 'received without counting' ": RD-CC (4) Aug. 17, 1982.

354 Alex Galeano: Ibid.

354 "Alejandro, I can do": RD-CC Aug. 15, 1982.

355 Darias lectures Said Pavon: Ibid.

355 "David Jaffe is in Bogotá": Ibid.
355 Navarro falls asleep and subsequent: Author's interviews with Dariases; nude photo, erotic drawing, pornographic movies: RD-CC Nov. 2, 1982.

CHAPTER 37

356 Talavera residents call F-2: CNP report; Judicial inspection of the house, court vol. 2, pp. 346–56; judge's finding regarding Maria Priscilla Bejarano de Silva, court vol. 2, pp. 456–61; deposition of Ana Esteher Puentes de Montanez, court vol. 2, pp. 421–24; deposition of Ligia Alvarez Torres, court vol. 2, pp. 430–32.
356 Kidnapping of Edgar Helmut Garcia: Alvear Restrepo report, pp. 103–105.
357 Navarro calls Oscar: NNN-1279, NNN-1305.
357 "Why do you always get lost": NNN-1308.
357 Navarro-Alvarez: OOO-188.
358 Navarro-Betancur: OOO-189, OOO-192.
358 "I need to make a report": NNN-1333.
359 Denver cash shortage: CIS August 1982, p. 10.
359 "I need for you to locate": NNN-1364.
359 "What did you talk about": OOO-196.
359 "Everything is okay here": OOO-201.
360 "I haven't seen these young": NNN-1438.
360 Darias: NNN-1441.
360 "There's no indication": CC-RD (4) Aug. 17, 1982.
361 Teo, Luis, and Oscar arrive: NNN-1446, NNN-1452, NNN-1458 (Costa del Sol gate guard announcing their arrival).
361 "They'll kill you for five cards": OOO-213.
361 "You know these guys": NNN-1462.
362 Oscar carries machine gun: RD-CC (2) Aug. 18, 1982.
362 Oscar: NN–1465.
362 Gustavo: NNN-1467.
363 McIntosh: NNN-1469.
364 "Apparently she's very, very upset": CC-RD (5) Aug. 17, 1982.
365 "Hello, dear. What's happening": OOO-213.

CHAPTER 38

367 Oscar: NNN-1472.
367 Luis: OOO-214.
368 Termination postponed: CC-RD (2) Aug. 18, 1982.
368 "I hope she doesn't come back": RD-CC (1) Aug. 18, 1982.
368 *"Biscocho"*: OOO-216.
368 "There is an eighty percent chance": NNN-1665.

369 "Juvenal told me": NNN-1668.
369 "Everything is turning out fine": OOO-219.
370 "Lilia, I have faith": NNN-1711.
371 Roosterman: RD-CC-FC (2) Aug. 20, 1982; CIS August 1982, p. 12.
372 Moving to Coral Springs: RD-CC (2) Aug. 22, 1982.
372 Juvenal Betancur: Darias translation Aug. 22, 1982.
372 "He just called me": RD-CC (2) Aug. 22, 1982.
373 "As long as I know": Ibid.

CHAPTER 39

377 Hernandez and Zapata depart: Lloyd memorandum.
377 Cabrera to smuggle 280 kg: Teletype, DEA Bogotá to DEA Miami Aug. 24, 1982, 3:45 A.M.
377 Darias and Betancur: Tape and transcript Aug. 23, 1982 (8 pages); CIS undated, p. 1; DEA ROI (McCracken) Aug. 23, 1982.
378 Darias and Garcia: Tape and transcript Aug. 23, 1982 (7 pages, plus supplementary translation by Darias); CIS undated, p. 1.
379 Marlene makes forty-nine calls: Wiretap log, pp. 681–97.
379 100 kilograms to arrive: CIS undated p. 1.
379 "Oh boy, what a day": RD-CC (2) Aug. 23, 1982.
381 Oscar: NNN-1830.
381 Debt to Cabrera: RD-MN tape and transcript Aug. 25, 1982 (20 pages).
382 Delay termination: CC-RD (2) Aug. 25, 1982.
382 "I have been telling her": RD-CC (2) Aug. 25, 1982.
383 "Give me a jingle": CC-RD (2) Aug. 25, 1982.
383 "I just got a call": RD-CC (3) Aug. 25, 1982.
383 "He is *not* doing this": MN-RD tape and transcript Aug. 25, 1982 (20 pages).
383 Party at Omni: Author's interviews.

CHAPTER 40

385 *MH* story was by Carl Hiaasen; also Roy Ishoy, "U.S. Magistrate sets strict bail terms for accused drug agent," *MH*, Aug. 28, 1982.
386 Mouzin's return from Mexico and aftermath: "Declaration submitted *in camera* (under seal)" by Barbara Mouzin, filed with *Muse and Gibbs* and *Mouzin et al.*; Mouzin testimony in *Muse*.
386 Balletti turned to Takiff: Confidential sources.
386 Navarro spoke seventeen times: Wiretap Log A, pp. 768–71; Log B, pp. 187–89.
386 Marina: OOO-272.
387 Alvarez: OOO-274.
387 Courier: OOO-268, OOO-273; reward for torture: NNN-2031.
387 Bertha: NNN-2045.

387 Carmenza's husband: NNN-2026.

387 Friend in New York: NNN-2031.

387 Accountant: NNN-2044.

387 Lester Rogers: NNN-2039.

387 Alex McIntosh: NNN-2022.

387 Oscar: NNN-2043.

387 Oscar brings $735,360: CIS re Navarro undated, p. 2; DEA ROI (Sennett) Aug. 30, 1982.

387 Marlene and Bertha at the office and surveillance: CIS re Navarro undated, p. 2; DEA ROI (Chellino) Aug. 30, 1982; MN-BP-RD videotape and transcript Aug. 28, 1982 (16 pages).

388 Navarro buys Uzi: CIS re Navarro undated, p. 2.

389 Swiss bank account: RD-MN tape and transcript Aug. 25, 1982, pp. 15–19.

389 "Some of the people": CC-RD (2) Aug. 28, 1982.

390 White House meeting re Betancur: Handwritten notes, one legal-size page, unsigned.

390 "That's not in open court": RD-CC (1) Aug. 30, 1982.

391 "The Christ child": OOO-300, 000-307, 000-314.

CHAPTER 41

392 GRAND JURIES: Procedures and regulations.

392 Cooper testimony: "Testimony of Carol Cooper," *In the matter of Marlene Navarro*, Federal Grand Jury 82-8, Federal Court House, Miami, Florida, Sept. 2, 1982, pp. 1–86.

392 Maid: NNN-2326.

392 Gustavo: NNN-2366, NNN-2367, NNN-2369, NNN-2383.

392 Lester Rogers: NNN-2371, NNN-2377.

392 Optimism re Alvarez children: RD-CC Aug. 31, 1982.

393 Mood at listening post: Author's interviews.

393 Nelson believes he's being followed: NNN-2412; NNN-2441.

393 "I have these two friends": NNN-2453.

393 Nelson in parking lot: CIS re Navarro undated, p. 4; RD-CC Sept. 2, 1982.

394 "For some ungodly reason": RD-CC Sept. 3, 1982.

394 IN GIRARDOT ON SUNDAY: Alvear Restrepo report, p. 104.

394 Edgar held in warehouse: Confidential sources in Bogotá; author's visit to warehouse.

395 McIntosh to Miami; he and Navarro to Keys for weekend: NNN-2424, NNN-2425; NNN-2464.

395 "I spent the weekend": NNN-2509; RD-CC Sept. 6, 1982.

396 "How's everything at home": PS-RD Sept. 7, 1982.

397 "She was telling me": RD-CC Sept. 7, 1982; CIS re Navarro undated, p. 4.

400 Nelson calling Darias: CC-RD Sept. 8, 1982; CIS undated re Navarro and Paytubi cases, p. 1.

CHAPTER 42

402 A MAN WITH A LATIN ACCENT: Lionel Paytubi testimony (quoting Arthur Karlick), *Rogers and Alvarado*, Dec. 14, 1983, pp. 160–61, 169; Lester Rogers testimony, *Rogers and Alvarado*, Jan. 11, 1984, pp. 141–43, in which Rogers confirmed the gist of the phone call but denied the caller had said lawyers would be indicted; MN-RD, tape and transcript, Sept. 9, 1982 (4 pages).

402 HARVEY ROGERS TELEPHONED NAVARRO: Lester Rogers testimony, *Rogers and Alvarado*, Jan. 12, 1984, pp. 198–99.

402 Harvey Rogers sent an aide: Lester Rogers testimony, *Rogers and Alvarado*, Jan. 11, 1984, p. 148.

402 Call to Amelia: CIS undated re Navarro and Paytubi cases, p. 1; author's interviews with Amelia Darias and others.

403 Amelia's call to Cooper: Ibid.

403 Darias conversation with anonymous caller: CIS undated re Navarro and Paytubi cases, p. 1; author's interviews with Robert Darias and others.

403 Darias call to Cooper: Ibid.

404 Amelia in the house: Author's interviews with Amelia Darias.

404 CHELLINO AND COOPER RACED NORTH: Author's interviews.

404 Robert and the agents brainstorm: Author's interviews with Darias and others.

404 Robert and Marlene talked early: CIS undated re Navarro and Paytubi cases, p. 1.

405 "He said that you two were from the fuzz": MN-RD, tape and transcript, Sept. 9, 1982 (4 pages).

406 More brainstorming: Author's interviews with Darias and others.

406 An internal investigation at Operation Greenback revealed no evidence that its agents had leaked Swordfish information. Eddie Hernandez and Nick Zapata denied they had leaked.

406 Ray Takiff concluded later that Gibbs "had something to do with" the Swordfish leak. See Takiff statements on the record in *Rogers and Alvarado*, Dec. 6, 1983, p. 832, and Jan. 10, 1984, p. 3; Gibbs's lawyer, Daniel Forman, denied any Gibbs role, Jan. 11, 1984, p. 3.

407 "We probably are going": CC-RD (1) Sept. 10, 1982.

407 Gustavo Delgado a target of the grand jury: Testimony of Carol Cooper, *In the matter of Marlene Navarro*, Federal Grand Jury 82–8, Sept. 2, 1982, pp. 5, 45; Stanley Marcus, United States Attorney, SDF, "Action Memorandum," *Request for Authorization to Apply for Extension of Interception Order Under Title 18, United States Code, Section 2518*, pp. 1, 3, 8; Hearing on change of plea, *U.S. v. Gustavo Delgado*,

82-575-Cr-Atkins, USDC, SDF, Sept. 6, 1983, in which Delgado pleaded guilty to a misdemeanor charge of aiding and abetting the possession of cocaine; Defendant's Motion to Reduce Sentence, Ibid., Feb. 8, 1984; Order Withholding Adjudication, Ibid., May 1, 1984.

407 "The day you came over": MN-RD (1) tape and transcript Sept. 10, 1982 (10 pages).

408 Marlene to deliver Jesus statue: CIS undated re Navarro and Paytubi case, p. 1; RD-CC (2) Sept. 10, 1982.

408 Paytubi called Darias: CIS undated re Navarro and Paytubi cases, p. 1.

409 "The man, the fat man": RD-MN (2) tape and transcript Sept. 10, 1982 (25 pages).

411 "How's everything with Marlene": PS-RD Sept. 10, 1982.

411 "I'm going to try to find out": TC-RD Sept. 10, 1982.

412 "She took about twenty minutes": RD-CC (3) plus FC Sept. 10, 1982.

414 Karlick called and met Paytubi: Paytubi testimony, *Rogers and Alvarado*, Dec. 14, 1983, pp. 148–75.

414 Phone calls in the middle of the night: RD-CC (1) Sept. 12, 1982.

414 Statue worth $30,000: RD-CC (1) Sept. 13, 1982; the Coral Gables jewelry store where Navarro purchased the statue listed its "current replacement value" as $10,500.

414 Navarro takes porcelain Jesus to Bogotá: RD-CC (3) Sept. 12, 1982; author's interviews with Navarro and others.

CHAPTER 43

417 Kidnapping of Ospina Rincon: Alvear Restrepo report, p. 97.

417 Kidnapping of Guillermo Prado: Ibid., p. 99.

417 Kidnapping of Edilbrando Joya: Ibid., p. 106.

418 Students tortured at Alvarez house: Confidential sources in Bogotá; author's inspection of house.

418 Role of Alberto Trujillo: Alvarez deposition, court vol. 2, p. 298.

418 Alberto's activities and conduct: Depositions of Antonio Trujillo Trujillo, court vol. 2, p. 89, and Luz Neisla Murillo de Trujillo, p. 102.

418 Alberto's curiosity: Antonio deposition, p. 102–103.

418 Alberto's death: Deposition of Marina Murillo Moreno de Alvarez, p. 251.

418 Alvarez tells his wife that Alberto was responsible for the kidnapping: Ibid., p. 252.

419 More torture: Confidential sources in Bogotá.

419 Paytubi calls Darias: LP-RD (1) tape and transcript Sept. 13, 1982 (4 pages).

419 "We've listened to the tape": CC-RD (1) Sept. 12, 1982.

420 "What happened is as follows": LP-RD (4) tape and transcript Sept. 13, 1982 (21 pages); the tapes and transcripts of the Darias-Paytubi conversations on Sept. 13, 1982, were Government Exhibits 104, 104-A, 105,

and 105-A in *Rogers and Alvarado* and 68 and 68-A in *Navarro*. Speculation about a "personal" or "social" relationship between Lester Rogers and Marlene Navarro was mentioned in an on-the-record bench conference in *Rogers and Alvarado*, Vol. 16, Dec. 21, 1983, p. 65. Paytubi's speculation about the possibility of such a relationship, and about the possibility that Rogers had a "new girlfriend," are reported here not as evidence of the truth of such relationships, but as an indication of Paytubi's thinking about possible motives for the anonymous phone call to Lester Rogers.

422 Though Warner was not charged in the Great American Bank case, he later went to prison for securities law violations in the collapse of the Home State Savings Bank in Ohio.

422 A TALL LATIN MAN RANG THE DOORBELL: RD-CC (1) Sept. 14, 1982.

422 "We have a big problem": RD-CC (2) Sept. 14, 1982.

423 "I am not calling anybody": RD-CC (4) Sept. 14, 1982.

424 Darias calls Delgado: RD-CC (5) Sept. 14, 1982; CIS undated re Navarro and Paytubi cases, p. 2.

425 "Oh, Robert, you sure do get lost": MN-RD tape and transcript Sept. 16, 1982 (7 pages).

426 "I talked to your friend": RD-CC Sept. 16, 1982; CIS undated re Navarro and Paytubi case, p. 2.

426 Cooper resumes grand jury testimony: Testimony of Carol Cooper, Federal Grand Jury 82-8, Sept. 16, 1982, pp. 1–42.

427 Chellino testifies about Humberto Garcia: Testimony of Frank Chellino, *In the Matter of Humberto Garcia*, Federal Grand Jury 82-8, Sept. 16, 1982.

427 "We think we're dead with you": FC-RD Sept. 16, 1982.

CHAPTER 44

430 BY AIR AND LAND, THE "SECRET GUYS": Alvear Restrepo report, p. 109, supplemented by CNP report; author's interviews in Gachalá.

430 Students identified Acosta: Confidential sources in Bogotá.

430 Acosta pulled a gun and fired: Acosta deposition, court vol. 3, pp. 227–28; Alvear Restrepo report, p. 109.

431 The Alvarados arrive home: Author's interviews with Alvarados, Jan. 18–19, 1992.

431 "If you don't tell the truth": Author's interviews; Alvarado deposition, court vol. 2, Oct. 18, 1982, p. 6.

432 "Here is your friend": Ibid.

432 ALVARADO ADMITTED: Ibid.

432 FAR INTO THE NIGHT: Author's interviews.

432 Alvarez appears at the Alvarados': Ibid.

432 Acosta interrogated at F-2: Acosta deposition, court vol. 3, pp. 227–28.

433 Acosta taken to Alvarez house: Confidential sources in Bogotá.

433 "You don't have to worry about the police": Ibid.

433 Torture of Acosta: Ibid.

434 GOES unit ordered to search: Ibid.; CNP report; author's visit to heliport.

CHAPTER 45

435 Navarro panics: Author's interviews with Navarro.

436 Navarro flees: Ibid.

436 Navarro charges New York–Montreal–New York ticket on American
Express: ticket no. 007 4208850883, Sept. 17, 1982.

436 Princess Grace died: "Automobile wreck kills Princess Grace," *NYT*,
Sept. 10, 1982.

437 Navarro stayed at Four Seasons in Toronto: She charged a bill of
$2,081.21 Canadian, which converted to $1,700.74 U.S., on American
Express.

437 Navarro's instructions to McIntosh: Author's interviews with Navarro
and others.

437 McIntosh traffic citation: NY State Police Uniform Traffic Ticket no. L
681006, Sept. 19, 1982, 10:50 A.M.

437 Navarro state of mind: Author's interviews with Navarro and others.

CHAPTER 46

439 The account of the execution of the Alvarez children is based on confidential sources in Bogotá in whom an eyewitness to the killings confided. I have visited the site and examined police photographs of the
bodies and the medical examiner's reports, e.g., ballistics report on the
death of Zuleika Alvarez, court vol. 2, p. 54, and death certificates, pp.
282–84. In addition, Zuleika's execution was described to Marlene
Navarro, who related it to me.

440 GOES search: Confidential sources in Bogotá, who visited the sites with
me.

442 Alvarez and chauffeur identify bodies: CNP report.

442 Children dead since April: Death certificates.

442 Motives for killing the children: Confidential sources in Bogotá familiar
with Acosta's explanation.

442 Front-page news: The editions of *El Tiempo* for Sept. 21, 1982, contained five articles on the kidnapping and related subjects.

443 Minister of Justice vowed: "Minister of Justice Vows to Apply the Full
Force of the Law on Assassins," *El Tiempo*, Sept. 22, 1982.

443 Supreme Court president: "Jader Alvarez Accuses Three Subversive
Movements of Kidnapping," *El Tiempo*, Sept. 21, 1982.

443 M-19 statement: "M-19 Condemns Assassination of Alvarez Children,"
El Espectador, Oct. 4, 1982.

443 MAS statement: "Suspect Commits Suicide," *El Tiempo*, Sept. 23, 24, 1982.

443 Impact on Gachalá: Author's interviews in and around Gachalá.

443 Song: Author's interview with composer and tape-recording his singing song.

444 Funeral: Author's interviews in Bogotá and visit to church and cemetery; "The Funeral," *El Tiempo*, Sept. 21, 1982.

CHAPTER 47

446 "I was thinking, Carol": RD-CC Sept. 18, 1982.

446 Security measures: RD-CC (1) Sept. 23, 1982; author's interviews with Dariases.

446 "We just got word": CC-RD (2) Sept. 20, 1982.

447 Cooper and Chellino in grand jury: Testimony of Carol Cooper, *In the Matter of Marlene Navarro*, pp. 1–41; testimony of Frank Chellino, *In the Matter of Humberto Garcia*, pp. 1–25; Federal Grand Jury no. 82–8, USDC, SDF, Sept. 23, 1982.

447 Air-conditioning fails: Ibid., pp. 22–24.

447 "My gut feeling is": CC-RD (1) Sept. 23, 1982.

448 Navarro travels to Curaçao: Air ticket costing $892.50 Canadian, $735.92 U.S., charged to American Express on Sept. 23, 1982; Curaçao Hilton bill of 824.82 Curaçao guilders, $464.40 U.S., charged to American Express on Sept. 25, 1982.

448 McIntosh drives the BMW: Author's interviews with Navarro and others.

448 Navarro's explanation for flight: Ibid.

448 "Did you talk to your friends": RD-LP Sept. 23, 1982; CIS undated re Navarro and Paytubi cases, p. 2; RD-CC (2) Sept. 23, 1982.

449 *MH* article by George Stein.

449 "There's a major leak": CC-RD Sept. 25, 1982.

450 Betancur called Darias: CIS undated re Paytubi and Betancur cases p. 1.

450 Betancur and Darias meet: Ibid.; RD-JB tape and transcript Sept. 28, 1982.

451 Postpone end to Oct. 15: TC-RD Sept. 29, 1982.

CHAPTER 48

452 Acosta returned to Alvarez: Confidential sources in Bogotá.

452 Alvarez state of mind: Ibid.

452 Acosta execution: Ibid.; Acosta scene-of-crime report, court vol. 2, pp. 280–81; "Mastermind of Alvarez Kidnapping Dies in Encounter with F-2," *El Tiempo* and *El Espectador*, Oct. 8, 1982; "In a Spectacular

Shoot-out, F-2 Kills Assassin of Alvarez Children," *El Bogotáno*, Oct. 8, 1982.

453 Colombian Catholic interpretation of execution: Author's interviews in Bogotá.

453 Execution of students: Confidential sources in Bogotá, including a person who saw the photographs of the remains.

454 CCE "prosecution memorandum": 14 pages, single-spaced, on official Department of Justice Memorandum paper.

455 "If not for the shirt": RD-LP-ASP tape and transcript (8 pages) Oct. 8, 1982; CIS undated re Lionel Paytubi case, pp. 1–2; RD-CC Oct. 8, 1982.

456 Grand jury meets extra day: Testimony of Frank Chellino, *In the Matter of Lionel Paytubi and Adolfo San Pelayo* (pp. 1–9), *John Doe* (pp. 1–8), *Lionel Paytubi, Manuel Sanchez, et al.* (pp. 1–20), *Francisco Arevalo et al.* (pp. 1–10), *Humberto Garcia, Antonio Uribe-Calle et al.* (pp. 1–24), *Emiro Mejias et al.* (pp. 1–9); testimony of Carol Cooper, *In the Matter of Marlene Navarro et al.* (pp. 1–22), Oct. 13 and 14, 1982.

456 Instruction bulletin for FBI agents posted Oct. 14, 1982.

456 "Paytubi feels his Greenback": RD-CC Oct. 12, 1982.

456 *NYT* article by Leslie Maitland; text of Reagan address, p. A22; *MH* article take from the Los Angeles Times News Service.

CHAPTER 49

458 Weather description amplified by testimony of Special Agent Patrick O'Connor, *Paytubi et al.*, Dec. 15, 1982, p. 213 (two months after the event).

459 Arrest of Paytubi: CIS undated re Paytubi, p. 1; DEA ROIs (Cifuni and Sennett) Oct. 15, 1982; author's interviews with Darias and others.

460 Darias state of mind: Author's interviews with Darias.

460 Phoenix Building atmosphere: Author's interviews.

461 "DEA Arrests 36 in Dragnet," *MH*, Oct. 16, 1982, p. 1, by Carl Hiaasen.

462 Takiff reaction: Confidential sources.

462 Agents' state of mind: Author's interviews.

462 Bond hearings: The 21-page double-spaced memorandum on official Department of Justice memo sheets was written by Prosecutors Mark P. Schnapp and Michael B. Cohen.

CHAPTER 50

467 Navarro listened to news: Author's interviews with Navarro.

467 McIntosh holiday visit: Ibid.

467 Kidnapping of Navarro: Ibid.; Navarro statement, *Navarro*, July 30, 1987, p. 25.

469 Disposition of defendants: Lionel Paytubi: set forth in Paytubi testi-

mony, *Rogers and Alvarado*, Dec. 14, 1983, p. 96; Manuel Sanchez: *U.S. v. Sanchez*, U.S. Court of Appeals, Eleventh Circuit, 84-5914, June 11, 1986, conviction affirmed; Humberto Garcia: pleaded guilty to one count of indictment; sentenced to six months in prison, 60 months probation, and fined $5,000; S. David Jaffe: pleaded guilty to one count of the indictment; sentenced to five years probation and 1,500 hours of community service; fined $10,000; license to practice law revoked.

470 Takiff reaction: Confidential sources.

470 Prosecution-defense colloquy over significance of anonymous calls: e.g., *Rogers and Alvarado*, Dec. 5, 1983, pp. 760–71.

470 Takiff turns over information: Statement of Michael Pasano, *Rogers and Alvarado*, Dec. 5, 1983, p. 802.

470 Gibbs denial: *Rogers and Alvarado*, Jan. 11, 1984, p. 3.

470 Navarro's house in Harvey Rogers's name: Harvey Rogers letter to Navarro dated Dec. 8, 1981; Navarro testimony, *Navarro*, Apr. 29, 1987, p. 13.

471 Harvey Rogers invokes Fifth Amendment: Statements of Michael Pasano, *Rogers*, Dec. 29, 1983, pp. 23 and 31; Jan. 10, 1984, pp. 162–63.

471 Darias was poorly prepared, debated with defense lawyers: e.g., Darias testimony, *Paytubi*, 82-561-Cr-SMA, Dec. 16, 1982, pp. 577–641, and Dec. 17, 1982, pp. 643–73. In addition to preparing Darias inadequately, Michael Pasano tended to undermine Darias's credibility at one trial, calling him a "snitch" in front of the jury: Pasano opening statement, *U.S. v. Suarez-Menendez*, 82-574-Cr-WMH, Aug. 23, 1983, p. 1–14. Cooper told Darias she felt the prosecutors had prepared him poorly: CC-RD July 30, 1985.

471 Charge against Lester Rogers dismissed: The government continued to refer to Rogers on the record as a named unindicted co-conspirator in the case against Navarro: statements of Myles Malman, *Navarro*, Nov. 13, 1986, p. 59, and Mar. 26, 1987, p. 73.

471 Government broke promise, halved monthly pay: Darias letters to Peter Gruden Apr. 23 and May 8, 1984; RD-Felipe Calderon Mar. 11, 1983; RD-Michael Pasano May 8, 1984.

472 Cooper withheld bonus: Ibid. and letters to Gruden; CC-RD June 3, 1985.

472 IRS lien: RD-CC Apr. 23, 1984; RD-CC May 6, 1984.

472 Dariases forced to move: RD-CC-PS Sept. 5, 1984; RD-CC (2) Sept. 11, 1984.

472 Death threats: RD-CC Oct. 31, 1982; RD-CC Jan. 24, 1983; RD-CC Sept. 27, 1983; RD-CC Dec. 4, 1984.

472 IRS agent feared danger: Ibid.

473 Paytubi plea bargain: Paytubi testimony, *Rogers and Alvarado*, Dec. 14, 1983, pp. 95–97.

473 Paytubi kickback allegation: CC-RD Aug. 18, 1983; CC-RD (2) Sept. 7,

1983; Paytubi testimony, *Rogers and Alvarado*, Dec. 14, 1983, pp. 126, 187–94.

473 Pasano predicted accusation: Marcus and Pasano, "Prosecution Memorandum," Oct. 8, 1982, p. 12.

473 Paytubi's credibility: Testimony of Peter Ledon, close acquaintance of Paytubi, that Paytubi was "willing to say anything to get out of the predicament he was in," *Rogers and Alvarado*, Jan. 11, 1984, pp. 74–75; statement of Roy Black, attorney for Lester Rogers, *Rogers and Alvarado*, Dec. 15, 1983, p. 23: "I want to show that he (Paytubi) is the kind of guy that shoots his mouth off and he is a liar." Roy Black had experience with Paytubi's credibility, having represented the disgraced banker at his trial the previous year.

474 Agents demanded that Darias take polygraph: CC-RD Sept. 9, 1983.

474 Cooper tried to convince: Ibid.

474 Chellino pressured Darias: FC-RD Sept. 9, 1983.

CHAPTER 51

480 Assassination of Lara Bonilla: Guy Gugliotta, "Cabinet minister's murder galvanizes Colombian outrage," *MH*, May 6, 1984, p. 29A; Alan Riding, "Colombia Starts Major Crackdown on Drug Trade," *NYT*, May 12, 1984, p. 1.

480 Tranquilandia seizure: Associated Press, "Cocaine Valued at $1.2 Billion Reported Seized in Colombia," *NYT*, Mar. 21, 1984, p. 1; Guy Gugliotta, "Colombian drug dealers retaliate for crackdown," *MH*, Dec. 10, 1984, p. 2A.

480 Cooper orchestrated Tranquilandia seizure: Letter from Leon B. Kellner, U.S. Attorney in Miami, to Vice President George Bush, May 15, 1987, p. 2.

480 Godfathers knew of assassination plot in advance: Testimony of José Antonio Cabrera, *Noriega*, vol. 27, pp. 4719–29, vol. 28, p. 4860.

480 Betancur declares war: Penny Lernoux, "Colombian declares state of siege," *MH*, May 2, 1984, p. 17A.

481 Pavons arrested: Riding, May 12, 1984, p. 1; Gugliotta, "Colombia arrests drug suspects, raids 2nd jungle cocaine plant," *MH*, May 12, 1984, p. 10A.

481 Navarro released: Author's interviews with Navarro.

481 Alvarez arrested: Mentioned in teletype, DEA Bogotá to DEA Miami, May 13, 1985, received 9:23 A.M.

481 Alvarez extradited: Ibid.; CC-RD Mar. 7, 1985; CC-RD May 9, 1985; "5th Colombian extradited to U.S.," *MH*, May 8, 1985.

481 Alvarez in solitary: CC-RD July 30, 1985.

482 Government lusted for trial: CC-RD May 9, 1985; CC-RD June 3, 1985.

482 Darias letters to DEA: Sent to Peter Gruden, Apr. 23 and May 8, 1984.

482 "If I were you": CC-RD June 3, 1985.

485 DEA making progress: CC-RD June 6, 1985.
485 "Carol, I have been thinking": RD-CC July 30, 1985.
486 Cooper comments re Malman: Ibid.

CHAPTER 52

488 Venezuelan papers in name of Nora Estrela Ramirez: H 82 no. 05956864 and H 83 no. 11105954. Spelling of name varies among documents. The spelling used in the text is taken from "Sworn Motion for Evidentiary Hearing and To Dismiss Prosecution," sworn to by Navarro on June 30, 1986, *Navarro*.
488 Mihal Kourany life in Caracas: Author's interviews with Navarro.
488 Description of apartment and Caracas environs: Ibid.; author's visit to Caracas, Mar. 23–27, 1990.
488 René de Sola background: Personal data sheet in Spanish signed by René de Sola on file in library of Time Inc., New York; *Current World Leaders*, vol 29, no. 2 (March 1986), p. 235; Tad Szulc, "Venezuela Ruled by 7-Man Junta; Holdouts Yield," *NYT*, Jan. 24, 1958; "Venezuela Names Exiles to Cabinet," *NYT*, May 29, 1958; "Venezuela: Signs of Ambition," *Time*, June 9, 1958; "The Americas: Construction, Not Criticism," *Time*, Oct. 6, 1958.
488 Mihal and René friendship and affair: Author's interviews with Navarro; statement of Marlene Navarro, *Navarro*, July 30, 1987, p. 17, wherein she referred to having been the lover of a person in Caracas who was "ready to be the chief of the Supreme Court of Venezuela."
489 Agents listen to voice from Germany: CC-RD Mar. 11, 14, 1983.
489 Chellino refers case to Candelaria: Confidential sources in Miami and Caracas.
490 Manzo and the PTJ investigation: Ibid.
491 Surveillance agents identify René de Sola: Ibid.
492 PTJ detains the woman: Ibid.; "Sworn Motion," p. 2. Among the papers the PTJ agents found in the apartment was Rene de Sola's calling card from his tenure as the Venezuelan ambassador to UNESCO in Paris.
493 Cooper and Chellino fly to Caracas: Confidential sources in Miami and Caracas; DEA ROI (Cooper) Mar. 4, 1986.
494 Navarro's documents destroyed: Confidential sources in Miami and Caracas.
496 Aborted departure: Ibid.; author's interviews with Navarro; "Sworn Motion," p. 4.
498 Return to Miami: Author's interviews with Navarro and others; confidential sources in Miami and Caracas; "Sworn Motion," p. 5.
498 Women's annex: Ibid.

CHAPTER 53

500 Navarro at North Dade Detention: Author's first visit was Apr. 1, 1986.

500 Lawyers' business cards: Navarro testimony, *Navarro*, Apr. 29, 1987, p. 14.

500 Paez background: Paez testimony, *Navarro*, May 4–8, 1987.

500 Cabrera tried separately: Randy Loftis, "Cabrera sentenced to 30-year term," *MH*, Dec. 25, 1986, p. 4C.

501 Hastings background: Associated Press, "State NAACP taps Hastings for top award," *MH*, June 13, 1982; 100th Cong., 2d sess., *House Resolution 499: Impeaching Alcee L. Hastings, Judge of the United States District Court for the Southern District of Florida, for high crimes and misdemeanors*, in the House of Representatives, June 14, 1988; Marjorie Williams, "The Perplexing Case of Judge Alcee Hastings," *The Washington Post*, July 7, 1988, p. C1; Philip Shenon, "Judge Acquitted in '83 Says Panel Seeks Impeachment," *NYT*, Aug. 27, 1986, p. 9; Stuart Taylor, Jr., "Top Panel Urges Congress to Weigh Ousting of Judge," *NYT*, Mar. 18, 1987, p. 1.

501 *MH* article Feb. 24, 1986, was by Patrick May, who interviewed Hastings after his views appeared the previous day in an article by David Graham in *The Tennessean* of Nashville.

501 I attended every session of the Alvarez trial.

502 Survey of Cuban and black attitudes: Richard Morin, "A Survey of Miami's attitudes," *The Cubans: A People Changed, A Miami Herald Special Report, MH*, Dec. 18, 1983, Section M, p. 2.

502 "Mr. Darias, the answer you gave": *Alvarez*, Mar. 11, 1986, pp. 47–51.

502 "*When* does not require": Ibid., Mar. 12, 1986, pp. 66–67.

502 FBI used spy against Hastings: Bill Rose, "Judge's dinner: Signal for Bribe?" *MH*, Mar. 25, 1982, p. 1A; Peter Slevin, "Did Hastings lie at his bribery trial?" *MH*, Dec. 14, 1986, p. 1A.

503 I attended much of the Navarro trial.

503 Takiff cross-examined Darias before: *Rogers and Alvarado*, Dec. 7–9, 12–13, 1983, pp. 1147–2010.

503 "Let's go on the record": *Navarro*, Sept. 12, 1986, p. 2.

504 Reagans' speech: David Hess, "Reagans: Let's All Fight Drugs, Indifference Not An Option," *MH*, Sept. 15, 1986, p. 1A.

504 "What about it?" *Navarro*, Sept. 15, 1986, p. 38.

504 "Last night, the President": Ibid. p. 86.

504 Chellino testimony: Ibid., Sept. 26, 1986, p. 2.

504 Chellino's bad memory: CC-RD Oct. 20, 1981: Cooper said of Chellino, "Things go in one ear and out the other"; CC-RD Feb. 12, 1982: Cooper said of Chellino, "He is really bad with names"; CC-RD (2) Mar. 2, 1982: Chellino forgot who Carlos Alvarado was; CC-RD June 26, 1982: Cooper quoted Chellino's wife as saying, "For the umpteen years you've been an agent, I've never heard you identify anybody in your life. You

can't remember faces worth a darn"; CC-RD (1) July 6, 1982: Cooper said, "I know Frank's got a bad memory"; CC-RD Oct. 20, 1982: Cooper said, "[Frank] forgets everything. You know how he is." On only one occasion did Cooper qualify her remarks. "He sits down and pays attention when it gets to be super important." CC-RD Oct. 20, 1981.

505 "Seeing those tapes": *Navarro*, Sept. 29, 1986, p. 35.

505 "Ladies and gentlemen, it's going to be difficult": Ibid., Oct. 16, 1986, p. 42.

505 "Lester never met": Ibid., Oct. 21, 1986, p. 54.

505 Darias feelings: Author's interviews with Darias.

505 "If you feel like you": *Navarro*, Oct. 21, 1986, p. 57.

506 "I can remove her butt": Ibid., p. 58.

506 "Ms. Navarro is not a person": Ibid., p. 68.

506 "Mr. Darias, during the course": Ibid., Dec. 4, 1986, p. 12.

507 "It is getting harder": RD-CC (2) Aug. 23, 1982.

508 "a big line of garbage": CC-RD (3) July 15, 1982.

508 "You start talking to people": RD-PS Sept. 7, 1982.

508 "If Darias was a scumbag": *Navarro*, Dec. 11, 1986, p. 15: The quote is taken from my notes. The court reporter's transcript reads: ". . . if Darias was scumbagged on 20th degree, moved by some power on top of that . . . " The court reporter was terminated from her job later in the trial, according to Hastings, Apr. 22, 1987, p. 71.

508 notary and firearms forms: Defense exhibits 13-A, 18, and 20.

508 Defense tries to subpoena: Ibid., Dec. 11, 1986, p. 162.

508 "I have the family secured": RD-CC Dec. 11, 1986.

509 "Mr. Darias, since you testified": *Navarro*, Dec. 12, 1986, p. 10.

509 "There are a lot of ways": Ibid., p. 111.

509 *Miami Vice*: Ibid., p. 46.

509 "This article tends": Ibid., Jan. 5, 1987, p. 8.

510 "Quite frankly, I don't care": Ibid., p. 9.

510 Hastings asked the jury: Ibid., pp. 12–13.

510 Darias and Cooper confer: RD-CC Dec. 20, 1986; Dec. 27, 1986; Jan. 1, 1987; Jan. 4, 1987.

510 "Now what's the problem": Ibid., Jan. 8, 1987, p. 60.

511 "Your mother is": Ibid., July 30, 1987, p. 31.

511 "maricón": Ibid., Jan. 29, 1987, p. 59.

511 Darias reaction: Author's interviews with Darias.

511 "Testifying against": Author's interviews with the Dariases.

511 Judge quashed subpoena: *Navarro*, Feb. 11, 1987, p. 186.

511 Muse-Gibbs: See notes for Chapter 26.

512 *MH* series: The newspaper withheld bylines to protect the reporters' security.

512 "dastardly deed": *Navarro*, Feb. 9, 1987, p. 4.

512 Navarro wept: Ibid., Feb. 11, 1987 (my notes).

512 Cooper ill and wobbly: Malman statement, Ibid., Feb. 12, 1987, pp. 32–33.
512 "Hit team targeted": By Jeff Leen.
513 Navarro on stand a month: Mar. 26 to Apr. 29.
513 "Roberto was, for me": *Navarro*, Mar. 27, 1987, p. 5.
514 WEB OF LIES: Author's opinion, based on knowledge of the case; Malman statement: ". . . her testimony, it was filled with lies . . . ," Ibid., July 30, 1987, p. 30.
514 Navarro ill with uterine cysts: *Navarro*, Apr. 13, 1987, pp. 16–17.
515 "Tell us what degrees": Ibid., Apr. 16, 1987, p. 81.
516 "In September of 1982": Ibid., Apr. 29, 1987, p. 99.
517 Paez testimony began May 4, 1987.
517 "Marlene Navarro has claimed": Ibid., June 2, 1987, p. 67.
517 Sentencing July 30, 1987.
518 "I say, Your Honor": Ibid., p. 14.
518 "Any sentence above minimum": Ibid., p. 27.
518 "In all my years": Ibid., p. 28.
519 "Ms. Navarro, concerning your": Ibid., p. 36.
520 "You are committed": Ibid., p. 41.

CHAPTER 54

521 ROBERT DARIAS STARED: Author's visit.
521 The agents and lawyers toasted: Dinner at Christy's, 3101 Ponce de León Boulevard, Coral Gables, Florida, July 1987.
521 Cooper and Chellino promoted: Memorandum from Tom Clifford to Peter Gruden, Feb. 15, 1983, p. 2.
521 Sennett, Russo raises: Ibid.
521 Tom Clifford award: The Great Hall, Department of Justice, Washington, D.C., Dec. 12, 1983.
521 Santiago, Force plaques: Clifford memo, p. 4.
521 Ninety people recognized: Ibid., p. 1.
522 Letter to Bush re Cooper: May 15, 1987.
522 "Robert Darias, a paid": Memorandum from Stanley Marcus, U.S. Attorney for the Southern District of Florida, and Michael S. Pasano, Assistant U.S. Attorney, to Edward S. G. Dennis, Jr., Chief, Narcotics and Dangerous Drug Section, Criminal Division, Department of Justice, Oct. 8, 1982, pp. 12–13.
522 "You're basically": CC-RD (2) Feb. 17, 1982.
522 "You are really": CC-RD (1) Jan. 31, 1982.
522 "You're the primary": CC-RD Mar. 22, 1982.
522 "You're the hub": CC-RD (1) Mar. 23, 1982.
522 "All of us consider": CC-PS-RD (CC speaking) Apr. 12, 1982.
523 "What you're giving us": CC-RD July 6, 1982.
523 "We swear by you": CC-RD July 9, 1982.

523 "It will be taken care": PS-RD Oct. 31, 1981.

523 "We will get it": CC-RD Nov. 17, 1981.

523 "We'll go through": CC-RD Dec. 4, 1984.

523 "Things are rolling": CC-RD June 6, 1985.

523 "Paul and I—I think you know": CC-RD July 10, 1982.

523 "Hopefully, at the end": CC-RD (1) Mar. 29, 1982.

524 "I think we can come": RD-IRS employee, June 18, 1986.

524 "There are a lot of factors": RD-IRS employee, Feb. 5, 1987.

524 Robert-Amelia fight: Author's interviews with Dariases.

525 Amelia drafted: Letters dated June 17, 1987.

525 Malman negotiations with IRS: Author's interviews.

525 "The problem is with the DEA": MM-RD June 10, 1986.

526 Meeting at DEA: Check no. 032911 drawn on AmeriFirst Bank, Miami, Florida, endorsed over to the IRS on Apr. 17, 1989. IRS simultaneously released a levy on Darias's property, using Form 668-D, also dated Apr. 17, 1989.

526 In a nightstand, guns, etc.: Author's visit.

Epilogue

529 Navarro granted new trial: David Lyons, "Convicted money-launderer wins bid for a new trial," *MH*, Feb. 19, 1992, p. 3B.

529 Navarro at various prisons: Navarro often has telephoned me from these prisons. With the help of newspapers and friends who accept and relay collect calls, she stays well informed not only on her case but on related matters. For example, Navarro was the first to inform me in October 1991 that José Antonio Cabrera would testify against Manuel Noriega. Navarro still reads the *Wall Street Journal* and the *Miami Herald* every day.

529 Alvarez conviction upheld: *U.S. v. Alvarez Moreno*, 86-5517, U.S. Court of Appeals, Eleventh Circuit, June 7, 1989; Assistant U.S. Attorney Susan Tarbe, "Brief for the United States," May 31, 1988, 57 pages and oral argument.

529 Alvarez moved to Wisconsin after Hurricane Andrew: Author's interview with Navarro, Nov. 9, 1992.

529 Alvarado, Sanchez, and Pavon convictions upheld: "Brief for the United States," pp. 2–3, n1.

529 Garcia, Batista plead guilty; Valenzuela, Terselich, Rodriguez, and Uribe fugitives: Ibid.; DEA ROIs undated.

529 Cabrera sentenced: Randy Loftis, "Cabrera sentenced to thirty-year term," *MH*, Dec. 25, 1986, p. 4C.

529 Cabrera testifies against Noriega: *Noriega,* Oct. 17, 1991, pp. 4538–93; Oct. 23, 1991, pp. 4685–4774; Oct. 24, 1991, pp. 4775–4951.

530 Takiff plea agreement: Office of the U.S. Attorney, SDF, "Notice of Disclosure," *Noriega,* June 8, 1991; "Joint Statement of Dexter W.

Lehtinen, U.S. Attorney, and Janet Reno, Dade State Attorney," June 8, 1991.

530 Florida pays Takiff: Don Van Natta, Jr., "State paying Court Broom informant $4,500 a month," *MH*, June 4, 1992, p. 4B.

530 Hastings impeached: H. Res. 499, 100th Cong., 2d Sess., June 14, 1988.

531 Hastings conviction overturned: Neil A. Lewis, "Senate Conviction of U.S. Judge Is Set Aside as Unfairly Reached," *NYT*, Sept. 18, 1992, p. 1.

531 "it's distinctly possible": "Impeached Judge Feels Vindicated," *NYT*, Sept. 19, 1992.

531 Colombia stops extraditions: Joseph B. Treaster, "Colombians, Weary of the Strain, Are Losing Heart in the Drug War," *NYT*, Oct. 2, 1989, p. 1; Reuters, "Bogotá Says It Will Not Extradite Drug Traffickers Who Surrender," *NYT*, Sept. 8, 1990; Cecilia Rodriguez, "Colombians Forced to Bargain With the Devil," *WSJ*, Feb. 1, 1991, p. A11.

531 Prosecution of kidnappers: "Judge's Conclusions and Rulings," Case No. 4765, Superior Court No. 10, Bogotá, Colombia, April 1988; "Appellate Rulings," Superior Tribunal Court, Bogotá, Colombia, Sept. 21, 1988.

531 Families form lobby: author's interview with Professor Gonzalo Sanchez, Bogotá, Colombia, Oct. 24, 1992; James Brooke, "Kidnap Victims in Colombia Organize Lobby," *NYT*, Aug. 16, 1992, p. 10.

531 Smuggling rose: Joseph B. Treaster, "Smuggling and Use of Illicit Drugs Are Growing, U.N. Survey Finds," *NYT*, Jan. 13, 1992.

531 Heroin shipped: Juan Daniel Jaramillo Ortiz, "Heroin: The Next Act in the Colombian Drug Drama," *WSJ*, Dec. 27, 1991, p. A11; Joseph B. Treaster, "Colombia's Drug Lords Add New Product: Heroin for U.S.," *NYT*, Jan. 14, 1992, p. 1.

532 Operation Pisces: Jeff Leen and Justin Gillis, "Money-laundering probes lead to cartel," *MH* (Reprint—Special Report: *Dirty Dollars*), Mar. 10, 1990, p. 6.

532 Operation Green Ice: Robert Pear, "3 Nations Stage Anti-Drug Sweep," *NYT*, Sept. 29, 1992, p. 1; Sharon LaFraniere, "150 Arrested in 6-Nation Drug Sting," *Washington Post*, Sept. 29, 1992, p. A3. Tom Clifford, whom the DEA designated to speak for the agency, was quoted in both articles.

533 Heroin and cocaine of greater magnitude than alcohol and tobacco: Wilson, p. 26.

533 "the difficulty of executing transactions": Mark H. Moore, "Supply Reduction and Drug Law Enforcement," *Drugs and Crime*, ed. by Michael Tonry and James Q. Wilson (Chicago: The University of Chicago Press, 1990), pp. 144–48.

ACKNOWLEDGMENTS

THOUGH I HAVE WORKED with some excellent editors in both book and newspaper publishing over the years, the professional fulfillment I have felt in collaboration with Linda Healey, the editor of *Swordfish*, stands alone. Linda got to the heart, and to every other vital organ, of a long manuscript with virtuosity and verve. I am deeply indebted to her.

Thanks also to Marjorie Anderson, Lauri Del Commune, Susan DiSesa, Archie Ferguson, Janice GoldKlang, Kathy Grasso, Altie Karper, Grace McVeigh, Anne Messitte, Jennifer Trone, and their colleagues at Pantheon Books, and to Nancy Gilbert for an outstanding job of copy-editing.

Numerous people at the Federal Drug Enforcement Administration, the Department of Justice, and the Office of the United States Attorney in Miami were helpful to me. I cannot name them here because I conducted most of my interviews under rules barring attribution to particular sources. However, I would like to acknowledge the assistance of the following people at DEA Public Affairs: William Ruzzamenti, William Alden, Illa Brown, John Dowd, Cornelius Dougherty, Frank Shults, and Robert Feldkamp.

Patricia Neering, Christopher Boyd, and Carlos Harrison conducted research of high quality in New York and Miami.

A consistent source of enlightenment on Colombia is the *Wall Street Journal*'s "Americas" column. Its editor, David Asman, has been helpful to me.

Miguel Marcial Castro of *El Tiempo* in Bogotá was an indefatigable researcher, adviser, expediter, interpreter, translator, and driver during my six trips to Colombia. Several Colombians who cannot be named provided essential counsel and assistance. They have my gratitude.

Robin Hertlein was among the first to know the secrets and voices of *Swordfish*. Her work in facilitating, organizing, and assembling my initial research was exceptional.

Bruce Stark solved my computer problems with craft and humor.

I could not have stayed functional without the help of Kenneth I.

Starr. He is a valued adviser, as are his colleagues Michael Canter and Alan Ginsberg and his former colleague Lorri Morris.

Dan Melnick and Lucy Fisher have provided crucial support and have done so with great patience.

Robert D. Sack has been my principal legal adviser on publishing matters since we were both young and green. I hope he remains so until we are both old and grayer. Dan Paul, the dean of First Amendment lawyers in Miami, was especially helpful in navigating treacherous legal waters there. Martin Garbus, Michael Frankfurt, and Maura Wogan provided crucial legal skill at an important juncture. Victor Kovner and Elise Solomon played key roles in the legal vetting of the book.

The *Miami Herald*'s Jeff Leen, an eminent investigative reporter, is the ranking expert on the nexus of drugs and money in Miami. His insights have been valuable to me.

James Q. Wilson, Julie Salamon, and Jonathan Schwartz read *Swordfish* in manuscript and offered useful suggestions.

I am especially grateful for the counsel and friendship of Bill Abrams, Tom Alberg, Peter Bienstock, Marie Brenner, Prudence Crowther, Peter Derow, Tom and Lisa Fryman, Barry Kramer, James Landis, Gene and Anne Marie Marans, Wenda Wardell Morrone, Norman Pearlstine, Andrew Tobias, Jane McArthur Tuttle, and John L. Warden.

Kathy Robbins has been a cherished friend to *Swordfish* and, more importantly, to me for many years.

My friendship with Robert, Amelia, and Laura Darias transcends our work together on this book.

Wayne Kabak's counsel has been wide and wise.

I am very fortunate that Amanda Urban is my literary agent. Her talents—and the exceptional range of those talents—have been critical in bringing *Swordfish* to publication.

Dean and Dorothy McClintick, my parents, have been staunch and true, as ever.

Judith Ludlam McClintick, my wife, and Joanna Katherine McClintick, my daughter, are my partners in this and the other important adventures of life. I am eternally thankful to and for them.

D. M.
December 1, 1992
New York City

INDEX